BLACK & DECKER®

PORTABLE

WORKSHOP

**Basic Wood Projects
with Portable Power Tools**

Wood Accents
for the Home

COWLES
Creative Publishing, Inc.

Minnetonka, Minnesota, USA

Credits

Group Executive Editor: Paul Currie
Project Director: Mark Johanson
Associate Creative Director: Tim Himsel
Project Manager: Ron Bygness
Lead Project Designer: Jim Huntley
Editors: Mark Biscan, Steve Meyer
Editor & Technical Artist: Jon Simpson
Lead Art Director: Gina Seeling
Contributing Art Directors:
 John Hermansen, Geoffrey Kinsey
Technical Production Editor: Greg Pluth
Project Designer: Steve Meyer
Project Manager Assistant: Andrew Sweet

Vice President of Development Planning &
 Production: Jim Bindas
Copy Editors: Janice Cauley, Ron Bygness
Shop Supervisor: Phil Juntti
Lead Builder: Rob Johnstone
Builders: Jon Hegge, Troy Johnson,
 John Nadeau
Production Staff: Helen Choralic, Laura
 Hokkanen, Tom Hoops, Jeanette Moss,
 Andrew Mowery, Michelle Peterson,
 Mike Schauer, Kay Wethern

Director of Photography: Mike Parker
Creative Photo Coordinator:
 Cathleen Shannon
Studio Manager: Marcia Chambers
Lead Photographer: Alex Bachnick
Photographer: Rebecca Schmitt
Production Manager: Stasia Dorn
Printed on American paper by:
 Inland Press
 00 99 98 97 / 5 4 3 2 1

COWLES
Creative Publishing, Inc.

Minnetonka, Minnesota, USA

President: Iain Macfarlane
Executive V.P.: William B. Jones
Group Director, Book Development:
 Zoe Graul

Created by: The editors of Cowles
Creative Publishing, in cooperation
with Black & Decker. ●BLACK&DECKER is a
trademark of the Black & Decker
Corporation and is used under license.

Library of Congress
Cataloging-in-Publication Data

Wood accents for the home
        p. cm.—(Portable Workshop)
  ISBN   0-86573-695-2 (hardcover)

1. Woodwork. 2. House furnishings.
I. Cy DeCosse Incorporated.
II. Series.
TT185.W653   1996
684.1' 04—dc20   95-49811

Contents

Introduction

Today's homes seem to look more and more alike all the time. Mass production and other economies of scale are making it ever harder for most homeowners to find ways to step past the clutter of conventional home furnishing products and create a unique home environment. *Wood Accents for the Home* offers a solution to that dilemma. In this book, you will find complete plans and instructions for unique home furnishings you can build yourself using the same simple tools and techniques you employ while maintaining your home on any weekend.

A distinctive wine rack with contemporary appeal; an elegant room divider made from a few dollars' worth of wood; a mirrored coat rack with all the charm of a genuine antique; these projects and many more can be built by almost anyone—even if you don't have much woodworking experience or own a state-of-the art woodshop. And because you build the projects yourself, you can finish them any way you want to create just the right accent for your home.

You don't need a lot of experience working with hand tools and portable power tools, like a circular saw or jig saw, to make the projects in this book. But if you haven't used any of the tools before, it is a good idea to practice using them on scraps of wood before you tackle the actual projects.

This is a book of plans. For each of the 20 projects that follow, you will find a complete cutting list, a lumber-shopping list, a detailed construction drawing, full-color photographs of major steps, and clear, easy-to-follow directions that guide you through every step of the project.

The Black & Decker® *Portable Workshop™* series gives weekend do-it-yourselfers the power to build beautiful wood projects. Ask your local bookseller for information on other volumes in this innovative new series.

Organizing Your Worksite

Portable power tools and hand tools offer a level of convenience that is a great advantage over stationary power tools. But using them safely and conveniently requires some basic housekeeping. Whether you are working in a garage, a basement or outdoors, it is important that you establish a flat, dry holding area where you can store tools. Set aside a piece of plywood on sawhorses, or dedicate an area of your workbench for tool storage, and be sure to return tools to that area once you are finished with them. It is also important that all waste, including lumber scraps and sawdust, be disposed of in a timely fashion. Check with your local waste disposal department before throwing away any large scraps of building materials or any finishing-material containers.

Much of the success of these projects will depend on the quality of the finish. For best results, find a dust-free, well-lit, fully ventilated area to paint, stain and topcoat your work.

Safety Tips
•Always wear eye and hearing protection when operating power tools and performing any other dangerous activities.
•Choose a well-ventilated work area when cutting or shaping wood and when using finishing products.

Tools & Materials

At the start of each project, you will find a set of symbols that show which power tools are used to complete the project as it is shown (see below). In some cases, optional power tools, like a compound miter saw, may be suggested for speedier work. You will also need a set of basic hand tools: a hammer, screwdrivers, tape measure, a level, a combination square, C-clamps, and pipe or bar clamps. Where required, specialty hand tools may be suggested within each article. You also will find a shopping list of all the construction materials you will need. Miscellaneous materials and hardware are listed at the bottom of the cutting list that accompanies the construction drawing. When buying lumber, keep in mind that the "nominal" size of the lumber is usually larger than the "actual size." For example, a 2 × 4 is actually 1½" × 3½".

Power Tools You Will Use

Circular saw *to make straight cuts. For long cuts and rip-cuts, use a straight-edge guide. Install a carbide-tipped combination blade for most projects.*

Drills: *use a cordless drill for drilling pilot holes and counterbores and to drive screws; use an electric drill for sanding and grinding tasks.*

Jig saw *for making contoured cuts and internal cuts. Use a combination wood blade for most projects where you will cut pine, cedar or plywood.*

Power sander *to prepare wood for a finish and to smooth out sharp edges. Owning several power sanders (⅓-sheet, ¼-sheet, and belt) is helpful.*

Router *to cut decorative edges and roundovers in wood. As you gain more experience, use routers for cutting grooves (like dadoes) to form joints.*

Guide to Building Materials Used in this Book

•Sheet goods:
AB PLYWOOD: *A cabinet-grade plywood, usually made from pine or fir. The better side is sanded and free from knots and other defects that require filling. Relatively inexpensive.*
BIRCH PLYWOOD: *A highly workable, readily available alternative to standard pine or fir plywood. Has a very smooth surface that is excellent for painting or staining, and generally has fewer voids in the laminate that require filling. Moderately priced.*
LAUAN PLYWOOD: *Mahogany-based, commonly used as floor underlay. Sold ¼" to ⅜" in thickness. Inexpensive.*
HARDBOARD: *Dense particleboard used for backing. Inexpensive.*

•Dimension lumber:
SELECT PINE: *Finish-quality pine that is mostly free from knots and other imperfections. Relatively inexpensive.*
#2-OR-BETTER PINE: *A grade lower than select, can have minor knots or defects. Because of higher availability, however, selection is better, and you may actually find higher-quality wood in this bin than in the "Select" area. Inexpensive.*
CEDAR: *Naturally moisture-resistant, mostly knot-free, smooth on both faces. Moderately expensive.*
RED OAK: *The most inexpensive and easy-to-find hardwood. Durable and moderately easy to work. Moderately expensive.*

•Miscellaneous wood products:
VENEER TAPE: *Self-adhesive tape used to cover plywood edges.*
WOOD PLUGS: *Flat, ¼"-thick wood discs, usually ⅜" dia., inserted into counterbores to conceal screw heads. Pine, oak, beech.*
MUSHROOM-STYLE WOOD PLUGS: *Same as above, but with a cap.*

Guide to Fasteners & Adhesives Used in this Book

•Fasteners & hardware:
DECK SCREWS: *Sold in a wide range of lengths. Self-tapping. Excellent for use with a power driver. Similar to drywall screws.*
WOOD SCREWS: *Used for finer work, usually with a thicker shank than deck screws.*
NAILS & BRADS: *For finish work, sold in lengths from ½" to 1¾".*
TACK-ON GLIDES/FEET: *Round plastic or rubber discs with a pointed metal stem used as feet or drawer slides.*

•Adhesives:
WOOD GLUE: *Yellow glue is common and fine for most projects. White wood glue has a longer drying time (good for beginners).*

Finishing Your Project

Before applying finishing materials, fill nail holes and blemishes with wood putty or filler. Also, fill all voids in the edges of any exposed plywood with wood putty. Insert wood plugs into counterbore holes, then sand until the plug is level with the wood. Sand wood surfaces with medium sandpaper (100 or 120-grit), then finish-sand with fine sandpaper (150 or 180-grit). Wipe off residue with a rag dipped in mineral spirits. Use good-quality enamel paint if painting. Apply two or three thin coats of a hard, protective topcoat, like polyurethane, over painted or stained wood.

Step Stool

Exceptionally stable and designed to be just the right height to help your toddler reach the countertop or sink, this step stool also features a ladder-style back with rungs for drying dish rags.

PROJECT
POWER TOOLS

Whether you're trying to clean the back of a cupboard or changing a light bulb, our step stool is handy and reliable. You'll reach for this step stool when it comes time to do the household chores. It's small enough to fit in a corner of your kitchen, or even in a nearby closet, so it will always be there when you need it. With a sturdy step stool around the house, you won't have to use a chair to reach that next level. Although it's a practical home accent, our step stool is an attractive addition to any kitchen or pantry. Cover all the countersunk screw heads with contrasting plugs to give it an interesting finished appearance.

Assembling our step stool is an easy process. The entire project is built around a four-piece frame beneath the slats. Once this frame is built, just attach the posts, legs, slats and rungs—and the step stool is ready for action.

CONSTRUCTION MATERIALS

Quantity	Lumber
1	1 × 4" × 6' pine
2	1 × 3" × 8' pine
2	⅜" × 3' dowel

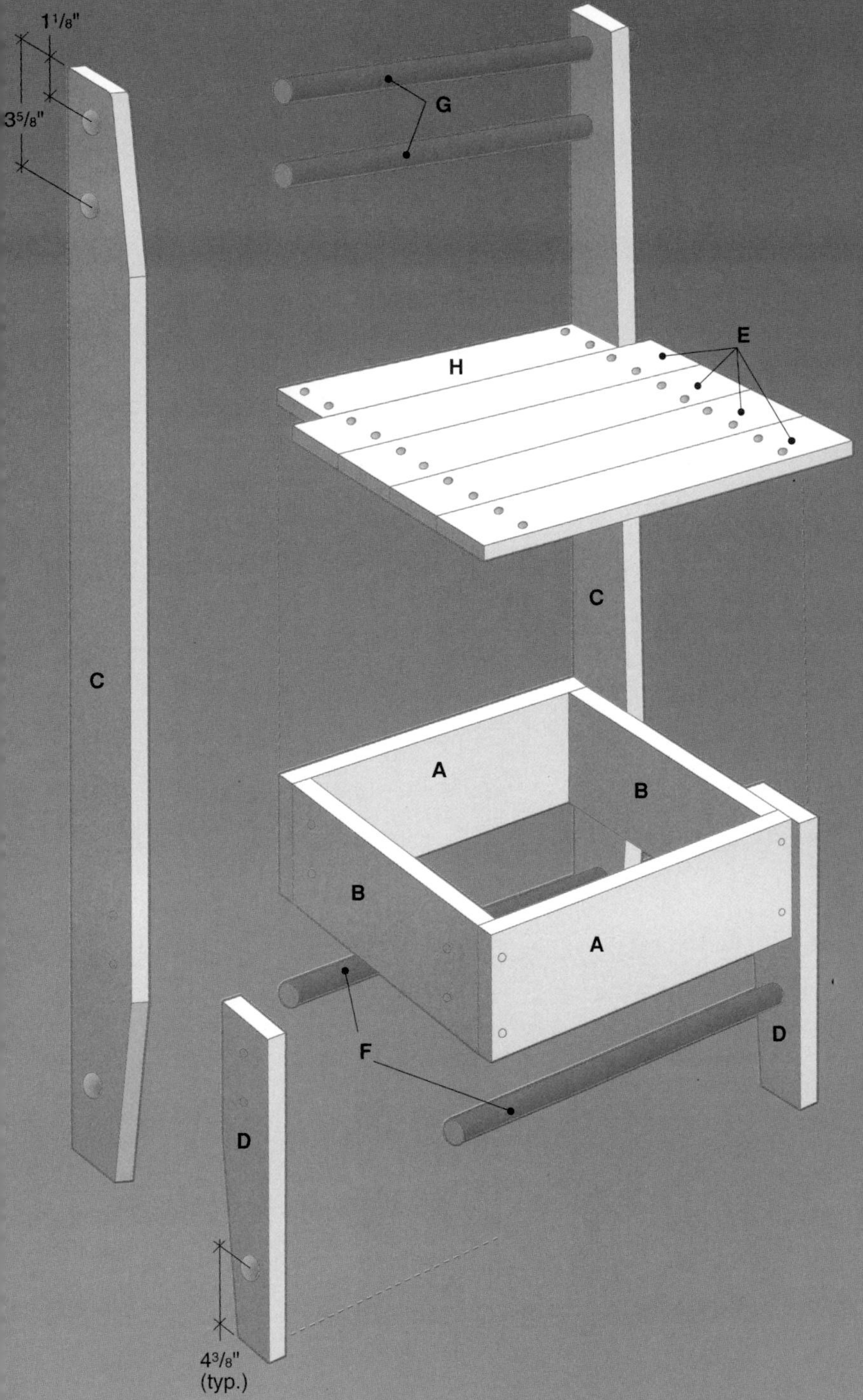

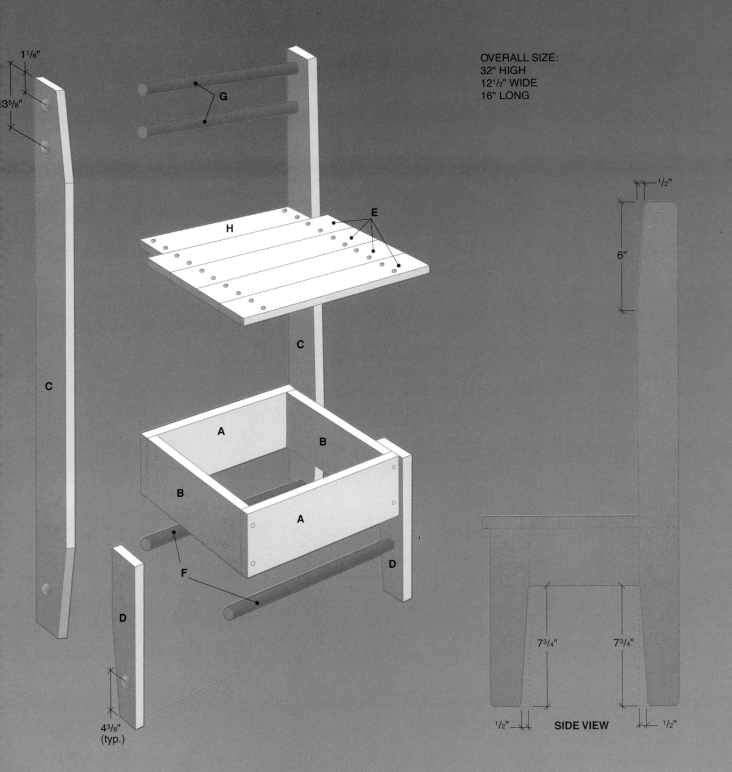

1 1/8"
3 5/8"
G
OVERALL SIZE:
32" HIGH
12 1/2" WIDE
16" LONG
E
H
C
C
A
B
B
A
F
D
D
4 3/8"
(typ.)

1/2"
6"
7 3/4"
7 3/4"
1/2"
SIDE VIEW
1/2"

Cutting List

Key	Part	Dimension	Pcs.	Material
A	Side	¾ × 3½ × 12"	2	Pine
B	End	¾ × 3½ × 9¾"	2	Pine
C	Post	¾ × 2½ × 32"	2	Pine
D	Leg	¾ × 2½ × 11¼"	2	Pine

Cutting List

Key	Part	Dimension	Pcs.	Material
E	Slat	1½ × 2½ × 16"	4	Pine
F	Rung	⅞ × 13½"	2	Dowel
G	Rail	⅞ × 16"	2	Dowel
H	Short slat	1½ × 2½ × 12"	1	Pine

Materials: Wood glue, wood screws (1¼", 2"), 4d finish nails, finishing materials.

Note: Measurements reflect the actual size of dimensional lumber.

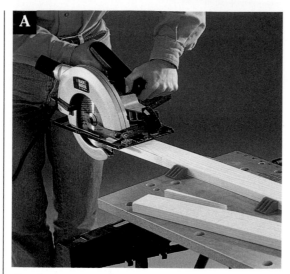

Cut the tapers on the posts and legs with a circular saw.

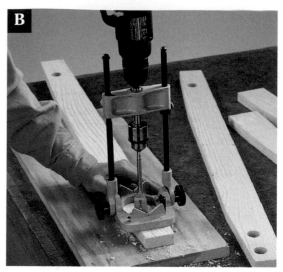

Use a portable drill guide to make straight holes for the rungs and rails.

Attach the posts to the frame so that their back edges are flush with the back edges of the frame.

Directions: Step Stool

BUILD THE FRAME. The step stool is built around a supporting frame. This frame consists of four pieces: two ends and two sides. Start by cutting the ends (A) and sides (B) to size.

Fasten the pieces by driving #6 × 2" wood screws through the sides into the end edges. Make sure all the corners are square and the edges are flush, then sand the pieces with 150-grit sandpaper until they are completely smooth.

MAKE THE LEGS & POSTS. Cut the posts (C) and legs (D) to size. Each leg has a slight taper cut from the back bottom edge. The posts have tapers cut from the front edges on their tops

and bottoms (see *Diagram*, page 9). To draw the taper guidelines, measure and mark points as follows: 7¾" from the bottom leg and post edges, 6" from the top post edges and ½" along the ends. Draw a line connecting the points to form a taper shape. Use a circular saw to make the taper cuts, forming the finished shapes of the legs and posts **(photo A).**

DRILL HOLES IN LEGS & POSTS. The legs and posts must be prepared to hold the dowel rungs (F) and rails (G). The rungs and rails provide stability to the step stool and help give the project a decorative touch. Though they are attached at the very end of the project's construction, you should drill the holes in the legs and posts now, before you attach them to the frame. For the rungs on the legs and posts, measure and mark centered points 4⅜" from the bottom edges on the pieces. For the rails on the upper posts, measure and mark centered points 1⅛" and 3⅝" from the top post edges. Use a

TIP

Our step stool can do more than give you a lift when you're working around the house. The rails on the posts provide a perfect drying rack for wet kitchen towels or rags.

D

Use ¾" spacers under the frame to create a recess when attaching the legs.

drill with a portable drill guide to bore a ¾"-dia. hole through each marked point on the posts and legs. Set a piece of scrap wood beneath the pieces when drilling the holes **(photo B).**

ATTACH THE LEGS & POSTS TO THE FRAME. Before attaching the legs and posts, sand them to finished smoothness, breaking the sharp edges and corners. It's easier to sand the pieces before they are attached to the frame. When the pieces are smooth to the touch, attach them to the step stool frame with glue and counterbored #6 × 1¼" wood screws. Center the screws 8½" and 10½" from the bottom of the legs and posts. When attached correctly, the back edges of the posts should be flush with the back of frame **(photo C),** and the front edges of the legs should over-

lap the front of the frame by ¾" **(photo D).** The bottom edges of the frame should be 7¾" from the bottoms of the posts.

ATTACH THE SLATS, RAILS & RUNGS. Cut the stool slats (E) and short slat (H) to size. Cut the rungs (F) and rails (G) from the ⅞" dowel rod. The rear slat is 4" shorter than the other slats to allow it to fit in between the posts. Attach the slats to the frame with wood screws, starting with the short slat that fits between the posts. The short slat should be flush with the back of the frame. Simply bore two evenly-spaced counterbored holes on each end of the slats for the screw holes **(photo E).** Drill the counterbored holes 2⅜" from each edge. The counterbored holes on the short slats should be ⅜" from the side edges. Apply glue to the sides of the rung and rail holes, and install the rungs and rails. The rails should extend 1¼" beyond

the posts on each side. Fix the rungs and rails in place by driving a 4d finish nail through the legs and posts into each dowel piece.

APPLY THE FINISHING TOUCHES. Make sure all the surfaces are sanded smooth, and fill all the exposed screw holes with glued matching or contrasting plugs. You can make or purchase the plugs to match the stool, or decorate the project with contrasting pieces. We applied a clear tung-oil finish to the step stool.

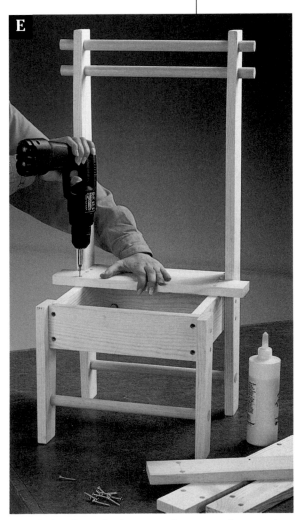

E

Attach the short slat between the posts, then work your way forward with the other slats.

Mirrored Coat Rack

*Nothing welcomes visitors to your home like an elegant,
finely crafted mirrored coat rack.*

CONSTRUCTION MATERIALS

Quantity	Lumber
1	1 × 2" × 3' oak
1	1 × 3" × 4' oak
1	1 × 4" × 3' oak
1	1 × 6" × 3' oak
1	½ × ¾" × 4' molding
1	¼" × 2 × 4' plywood

An entryway or foyer seems naked without a coat rack and a mirror, and this simple oak project gives you both features in one striking package. The egg-and-dart beading at the top and the decorative porcelain and brass coat hooks provide just enough design interest to make the project elegant without overwhelming the essential simplicity of the look.

We used inexpensive red oak to build our mirrored coat rack, but if you are willing to invest a little more money, use quartersawn white oak to create an item with the look of a true antique. For a special touch, have the edges of the mirror beveled at the glass store.

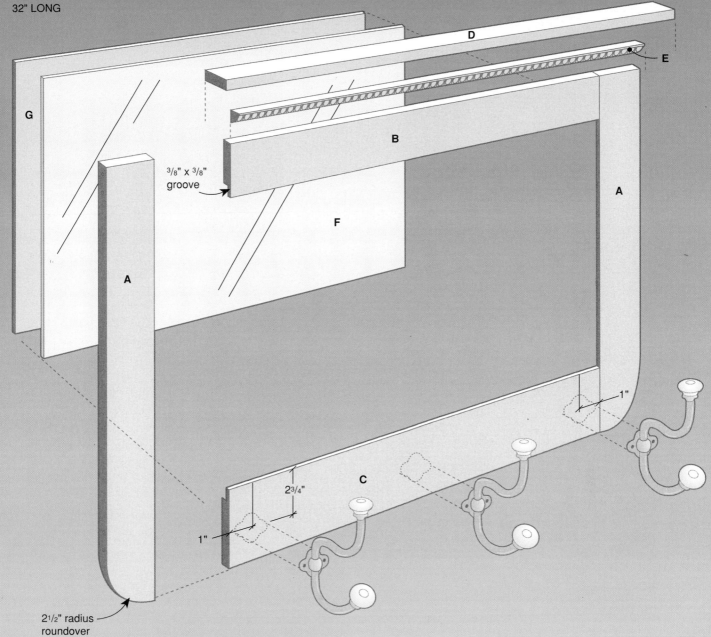

OVERALL SIZE:
22³/₄" HIGH
1¹/₂" WIDE
32" LONG

G

D

E

B

A

³/₈" x ³/₈"
groove

F

A

1"

C

2³/₄"

1"

2¹/₂" radius
roundover

Cutting List

Key	Part	Dimension	Pcs.	Material
A	Stile	¾ × 2½ × 22"	2	Oak
B	Top rail	¾ × 3½ × 24"	1	Oak
C	Bottom rail	¾ × 5½ × 24"	1	Oak
D	Cap	¾ × 1½ × 32"	1	Oak
E	Molding	½ × ¾ × 29"	1	Oak
F	Mirror	⅛ × 12¾ × 24¾"	1	Mirror
G	Mirror back	¼ × 12¾ × 24¾"	1	Plywood

Materials: ¼ × 36" oak dowel, 1½" wood screws, (3) coat hooks w/ screws, 1" wire brads.

Note: Measurements reflect the actual size of dimensional lumber.

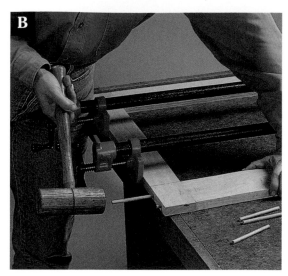

Clamp the frame components together, then drill 3½"-deep guide holes for the through-dowel joints.

Drive glued 4"-long oak dowels into the guide holes to make the dowel joints.

Mount a belt sander to your worksurface, and use it as a grinder to smooth out the roundover cuts on the frame.

Directions: Mirrored Coat Rack

MAKE THE MIRROR FRAME. Start by cutting the frame components to size. The vertical members of a frame are called stiles: cut the stiles (A) to length from 1 × 3 oak. The horizontal members of a frame are called rails: cut the top rail (B) from 1 × 4 oak and cut the bottom rail (C) from 1 × 6 oak. Sand the stiles and rails with medium sandpaper (100- or 120-grit) to smooth out rough spots, then finish-sand with fine sandpaper (150- or 180-grit). We used through-dowel joints to hold the frame parts together. Lay the rails between the stiles on your worksurface to form a frame. Square the frame, then use a pipe or bar clamp to hold the frame together. Drill two evenly spaced ¼"-dia. × 3½"-deep guide holes at each joint, drilling through the stiles and into the rails **(photo A).** Now, cut eight ¼"-dia. × 4"-long oak dowels. Unclamp the frame assembly, squirt a little glue into each guide hole, then drive a dowel into each guide hole, using a wood mallet so you don't break the dowels **(photo B).** When all the joints are made, clamp the frame assembly together. Once the glue has dried, remove the clamps, trim off the ends of the dowels with a backsaw, sand them level with the wood surface, and scrape off excess glue.

ROUND OVER THE FRAME ENDS. On the bottom end of each stile, lay out an arc with a 2½" radius to mark the decorative roundovers (or use a 5"-dia. coffee can as a tracing guide). Cut along the arc line using a jig saw, and smooth out the cut with a belt sander mounted to your worksurface **(photo C).**

DRILL MOUNTING HOLES & CUT THE MIRROR RECESS. Before you attach the decorative top cap, drill counterbored screw

Use a router with a ⅜" piloted rabbeting bit to cut a recess for the mirror in the frame back.

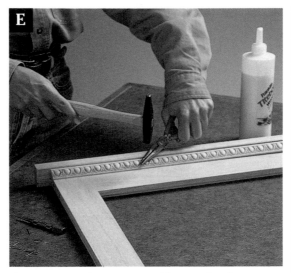

Center egg-and-dart trim molding under the cap, and attach with glue and 2d finish nails.

Install the mirror and mirror back, then secure them to the frame with wire brads, driven with a brad pusher.

oak egg-and-dart style trim (E), or any other trim style you prefer, to length. Sand a slight, decorative bevel at each end. Attach the molding flush against the underside of the rail, centered side to side, using glue and 2d finish nails driven with a tack hammer **(photo E).** Set the nail heads. Sand all sharp edges on the frame.

INSTALL THE MIRROR. Have a piece of ⅛"-thick mirrored glass cut to size at a glass store. Set the glass into the recess in the frame. Cut ¼"-thick plywood to make the mirror back (G), and set it over the back of the mirror. Secure the mirror and mirror back with 1" wire brads driven into the edges of the frame with a brad pusher.

APPLY FINISHING TOUCHES. Fill all counterbores with oak plugs and sand flush with the wood surface. Apply satin and topcoat as desired. When dry, install the coat hooks (see *Diagram*, page 13). Hang the coat rack (see *Tip*, above).

TIP

Try to hit a wall stud with at least one mounting screw when hanging heavier objects on a wall. Use 3"-long screws into wall studs and use toggle bolts to mount where no studs are present.

holes through the fronts of the frame rails, 6" down from the top, so you can attach the mirrored coat rack to a wall. Drill ⅜"-dia. × ¼"-deep counterbores so you can use oak plugs to cover the screw heads after you hang the coat rack. Next, cut a groove around the back edge of the inside frame to make a recess for the mirror and back. The easiest way to cut this kind of groove (called a rabbet) is with a router and ⅜"-dia. piloted rabbet bit. Set the cutting depth of the router

to ⅜", then trim around the back, inside edges of the frame so the pilot at the tip of the router bit follows the inside edge of the frame **(photo D).** Square off the grooves at the corners with a wood chisel.

INSTALL THE CAP & MOLDING. Cut the cap (D) to length from 1 × 2 oak and attach it to the top of the top rail, flush with the back edge, using glue and counterbored wood screws. Make sure the cap overhangs the stiles evenly on the ends (1½" per end). Cut a piece of

PROJECT
POWER TOOLS

Knickknack Shelf

Add some country charm to your home with this rustic pine knickknack shelf.

CONSTRUCTION MATERIALS

Quantity	Lumber
1	1 × 4" × 8' pine
2	1 × 8" × 8' pine
1	1 × 10" × 4' pine
9	¼ × 3½" × 3' beaded pine paneling
1	¾ × ¾" × 6' cove molding

Country style furniture is becoming increasingly popular throughout the world because of its honest appearance and back-to-basics preference for function over ornate styling. In fancy interior design catalogs, you may find many country shelving projects that are similar to this one in design and function. But our knickknack shelf can be built for a tiny fraction of the prices charged for its catalog cousins.

From the beaded pine paneling at the back to the matching arcs on the top and bottom rails, this knickknack shelf is well-designed throughout. The shelf shown above has a natural wood finish, but it is a perfect vehicle for decorative painting techniques, like milk-wash or farmhouse finishes.

OVERALL SIZE:
34" HIGH
9" WIDE
34½" LONG

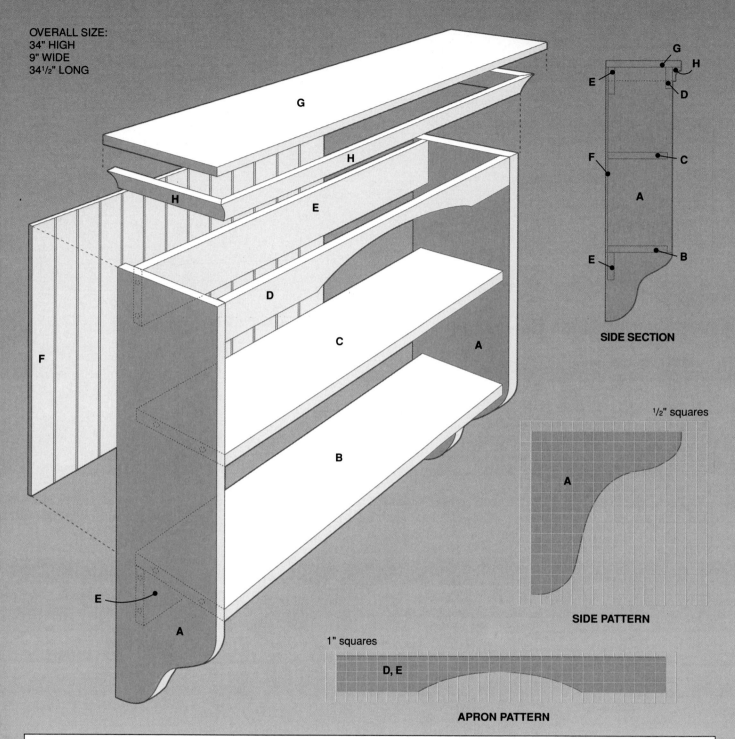

SIDE SECTION

½" squares

SIDE PATTERN

1" squares

APRON PATTERN

Cutting List				
Key	**Part**	**Dimension**	**Pcs.**	**Material**
A	Shelf side	¾ × 7¼ × 33¼"	2	Pine
B	Bottom shelf	¾ × 6¾ × 30½"	1	Pine
C	Middle shelf	¾ × 6¾ × 30½"	1	Pine
D	Apron	¾ × 3½ × 32"	1	Pine

Cutting List				
Key	**Part**	**Dimension**	**Pcs.**	**Material**
E	Ledger	¾ × 3½ × 30½"	2	Pine
F	Back panel	¼ × 3½ × 28"	9	Pine
G	Cap	¾ × 8¼ × 34"	1	Pine
H	Cove trim	¾ × ¾ × *	3	Pine

* Cut to fit.

Materials: Wood glue, #8 × 1½" wood screws, 3d and 6d finish nails, button screw plugs, finishing materials.

Note: Measurements reflect the actual size of dimensional lumber.

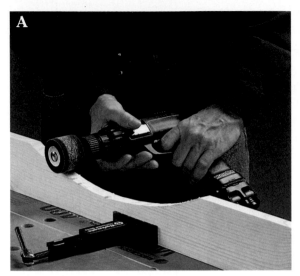

A

Smooth out the jig saw cuts on the apron and ledger with a drill and drum sander.

B

Clamp the sides and ledgers in position, then fasten with glue and screws.

Directions: Knickknack Shelf

MAKE THE FRAME COMPONENTS. Start by cutting the sides (A) to length from 1 × 8 pine. Use the *Side Pattern* on page 17 to lay out the profile of the cutout shape for the sides: draw a grid pattern with ½" squares onto one of the sides, then draw the profile shown in the pattern, using the grid as a point of reference. Cut out the shape and smooth the cut with a drum sander attached to your drill. Trace the finished profile onto the other sides, and make the cutout. Cut the apron (D) and the ledgers (E) to length from 1 × 4 pine. Use the same technique to draw and cut out the *Apron Pattern* (page 17) onto the apron and one of the ledgers. Smooth out any irregularities with a drum sander or belt sander **(photo A).**

ASSEMBLE THE FRAME. Lay the sides on their back edges and place

C

Fasten the tongue-and-groove beaded pine panel pieces to the ledgers with glue and 3d finish nails.

the upper ledger (without the arc) facedown between the sides, with the ledger's top edge flush with the tops of the sides. Clamp the sides and ledger together with a pipe or bar clamp. Fasten the apron across the top front of the sides with wood glue and 6d finish nails. Be sure to keep the top edge of the apron flush with the tops of the sides. Unclamp the sides and insert the lower ledger with its top edge 6¾" up

from the bottoms of the side. Place a ¼" spacer under the ledgers to create a recess for the back panel (F). Clamp the sides to the ledgers, positioning the clamps so you will have room to perform drilling operations. Mark the ledger locations on the sides. Drill two counterbored pilot holes through the sides into the ends of the ledgers—the counterbores should be sized to allow room for mushroom-style button plugs. Unclamp the components, and apply glue to the ledger and apron ends. Position the components according to the marks on the sides, and reclamp the assembly. Secure the ledger in place with #8 × 1½" wood screws **(photo B)**.

INSTALL THE BACK PANEL. To make the back panel (F), we used tongue-and-groove pieces of pine wainscoting paneling, joined together to create a 30½ × 28" panel. Attach the back panel to the back faces of the ledgers, using 3d finish nails, but no glue **(photo C)**. The top of the back panel should be flush with the tops of the sides.

BUILD & INSTALL THE SHELVES. Cut the bottom shelves (B) and middle shelf (C) to size from 1 × 8 pine. Using a router with a ⅜" piloted roundover bit, round over the top and bottom edges on the fronts of the shelves **(photo D)**. Clamp the bottom shelf in place on top of the lower ledger, keeping the back edge flush with the back of the ledger. Drill two evenly spaced holes through each shelf side into each end of the bottom shelf. Remove the bottom shelf,

apply glue to the ends, then fasten in place with counterbored wood screws. Install the middle shelf using the same procedure **(photo E)**.

ATTACH THE CAP & COVE. Cut the cap (G) to size from 1 × 10 pine. Using a router with a ⅜" roundover bit, shape the two ends and front edge of the cap from the top and bottom. Place a bead of glue along the top edges of the shelf sides, apron and ledgers. Position the cap on top of the shelf assembly, overlapping 1" on each end and at the front. Nail the cap in place with 6d finish nails. Cut pieces of ¾ × ¾" pine cove trim (G) to the appropriate lengths to build a 3-sided frame with mitered corners just below the bottom of the cap (see *Diagram,* page 17). Fasten in place with glue and 3d finish nails **(photo F)**.

APPLY FINISHING TOUCHES. Decide where to hang the knickknack shelf, and drill counterbored pilot holes in the upper ledger for driving screws at two wall-stud locations. Scrape off any glue left on the surface areas, then finish-sand the surfaces with fine (150- or 180-grit) sandpaper. Install mushroom-style button plugs in all counterbores, then apply the finish. We chose to finish our knickknack shelf with light oak stain and a satin-gloss polyurethane topcoat.

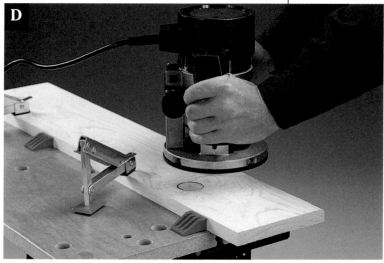

Use a router with a ⅜" piloted roundover bit to shape the front edges of the shelves.

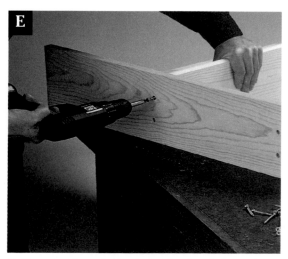

Drill counterbored pilot holes for the shelves, then attach with 1½" wood screws.

Attach the cove molding with glue and 3d finish nails. Hold the nails with needlenose pliers when nailing in hard-to-reach areas.

Cedar Chest

This compact cedar chest has the potential to become a cherished family heirloom.

CONSTRUCTION MATERIALS	
Quantity	**Lumber**
2	1 × 2" × 8' cedar
1	1 × 3" × 10' cedar
1	1 × 6" × 8' cedar
3	1 × 8" × 8' cedar
1	2 × 2" × 8' cedar
1	¾" × 2 × 4' plywood

The cedar chest has a long tradition as a much-appreciated graduation gift, and the appreciation will be even greater for a cedar chest you built yourself. And short of a packing crate, you won't find a simpler chest to build anywhere.

Despite its simplicity, this cedar chest has all the features of a commercially produced chest costing hundreds of dollars. The framed lid is hinged in back, and can be locked open with an optional locking lid support. A removable tray fits inside the top of the chest for storing delicate items. The main compartment is fitted with aromatic cedar panels to keep sweaters and your favorite linen treasures safe from moth damage.

OVERALL SIZE:
19³⁄₈" HIGH
16" WIDE
30" LONG

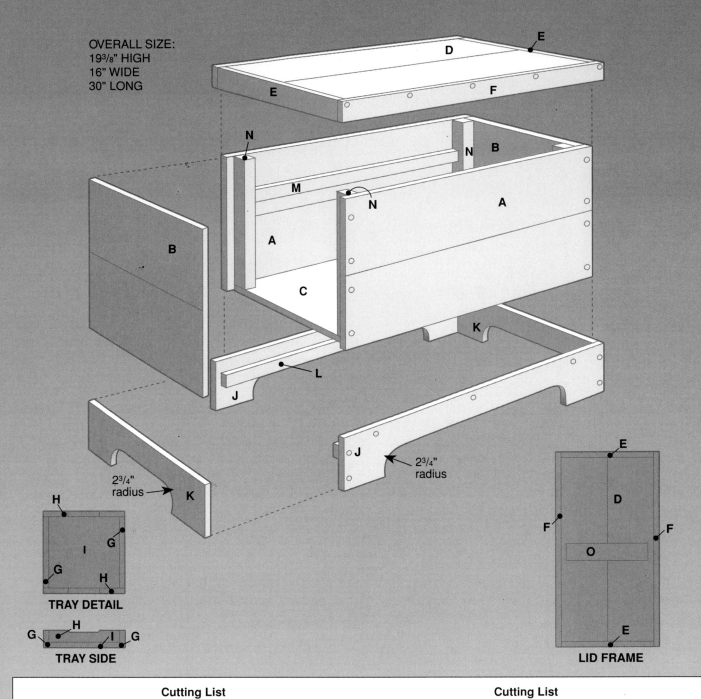

2³⁄₄"
radius

2³⁄₄"
radius

2³⁄₄"
radius

TRAY DETAIL

TRAY SIDE

LID FRAME

Key	Part	Dimension	Pcs.	Material
A	Side	⅞ × 7¼ × 28"	4	Cedar
B	End	⅞ × 7¼ × 12½"	4	Cedar
C	Bottom	¾ × 12½ × 26½"	1	Plywood
D	Top	⅞ × 7¼ × 28½"	2	Cedar
E	End lip	⅞ × 1½ × 14½"	2	Cedar
F	Side lip	⅞ × 1½ × 30"	2	Cedar
G	Tray side	⅞ × 2½ × 12¾"	2	Cedar
H	Tray end	⅞ × 2½ × 12"	2	Cedar

Key	Part	Dimension	Pcs.	Material
I	Tray bottom	⅞ × 2½ × 12¾"	4	Cedar
J	Side plate	⅞ × 5½ × 29½"	2	Cedar
K	End plate	⅞ × 5½ × 14"	2	Cedar
L	Base cleat	⅞ × 1½ × 28"	2	Cedar
M	Chest cleat	⅞ × 1½ × 23½"	2	Cedar
N	Corner post	1½ × 1½ × 13¾"	4	Cedar
O	Top cleat	⅞ × 2½ × 12"	1	Cedar

Cutting List

Cutting List

Materials: Wood glue, wood screws (1¼", 2"), 2d finish nails, cedar plugs, aromatic cedar panels, panel adhesive, (2) 2 × 1½" brass butt hinges, lid support, optional hardware accessories, finishing materials.

Note: Measurements reflect the actual size of dimensional lumber.

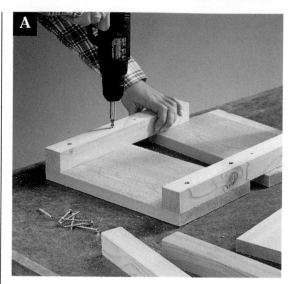

Drive screws through the posts into the ends.

Install the bottom onto the corner posts and fasten it to the sides and ends of the chest.

Directions: Cedar Chest

BUILD THE BOX FRAME. Start by cutting the chest sides (A) and chest ends (B) to size from 1 × 8 cedar. Cut the corner posts (N) to length from 2 × 2 cedar. Sand the chest ends, chest sides and corner posts with medium (100- or 120-grit) sandpaper to smooth out rough areas, then finish-sand with fine (150- or 180-grit) sandpaper. Use glue and counterbored #6 × 2" wood screws to fasten two chest ends to each pair of corner posts, with their tops and side edges flush **(photo A).** When using cedar that is rough on one side, which is fairly typi-

Attach the top cleat to undersides of the tops, making sure it is centered 13" from both edges.

cal unless you are using select, clear cedar, be sure that exposed surfaces are consistent in texture. For this project, make sure all the rough sides are facing inside. Once the chest ends and corner posts are attached, apply glue to the outside edges of the corner posts and fasten the chest sides to the chest ends by driving wood screws through the chest sides into the edges of the

chest ends. Make sure the top and side edges are flush. If the box frame is assembled correctly, there will be a ¾"-wide space between the bottom of the corner posts and the box frame's bottom edges. Cut the bottom (C) to size from ¾"-thick plywood. Turn the box frame upside down and fasten the bottom to the corner posts, ends and sides with glue and wood screws **(photo B).** Seal the inside surfaces

Smooth out the jig saw cuts on the radius cutouts using a drum sander attachment and drill.

Butt the tray ends together and layout the tray handles on both tray ends. Cut with a jig saw and smooth with a drum sander and drill.

with an oil finish or sealer to prevent warping and splitting.

BUILD THE TOP ASSEMBLY. Begin by cutting the tops (D) to size from 1 × 8 cedar. Then cut the end lips (E) and side lips (F) to length from 1 × 2 cedar. Cut the top cleat (O) to length from 1 × 3 cedar. Make sure these parts are ½" longer than the assembled box frame dimensions. Finish-sand the pieces. Apply bar clamps to

hold the tops together, with their ends flush. Use a combination square to measure and mark the top cleat position on the inside faces of the tops. Make sure the top cleat is centered, with its side edges 13" from the outside ends of the tops and with its ends centered between the edges of the tops. Attach the cleat to the tops with glue and #6 × 1¼" wood screws **(photo C).** Attach the

side lips and end lips to the edges of the tops with glue and counterbored #6 × 2" wood screws. Make sure the top edges of the lips and tops are flush.

BUILD THE BASE. Start by cutting the side plates (J) and end plates (K) to size from 1 × 6 cedar. Use a compass to lay out a curved cut with a 2¾" radius on each side plate and end plate. Start the cuts 4" from each side plate end and 3" from each end plate end. Measure and mark carefully, then make the cuts with a jig saw. Finish-sand the side plates and end plates. Use a drill and drum sander attachment to smooth out the radius jig saw cuts **(photo D).** Fasten the side plates to the end plates with glue and counterbored wood screws driven through the front faces of the side plates into the ends of the end plates. Cut the two base cleats (L) to length from 1 × 2 cedar, and fasten them to the inside faces of the side plates, 2¾" from the bottom edges, flush with the top of the cutout.

ATTACH THE BOX FRAME & BASE. Test-fit the box frame into the assembled base, and trim as necessary. Glue the joints, then attach the base to the box

---

TIP

When constructing pieces with intermediate steps that fit within other constructions (as the chest inside the base and top), build the inside portion first. The outer portions can be cut larger or smaller as necessary to fit the assembled intermediate construction.

Tape the tray ends together, then draw a slot across the joint to mark even handle cutouts.

Attach the tray ends to the tray bottom and tray sides with glue and counterbored wood screws.

frame by driving evenly spaced, countersunk wood screws through the end plates and side plates into the box frame **(photo E).** Sand all the surfaces until they are smooth to the touch. Smooth out all sharp edges with a sander.

MAKE THE TRAY. Cut the tray sides (G), tray ends (H) and tray bottom (I) to length from 1 × 3 cedar. Lay out the tray handles by placing the tray ends side by side, with the ends flush. Mark a 1½"-wide × 5"-long slot with 1½"-radius curves centered on each end of the cut where the two pieces meet **(photo F).** Make the cut with a jig saw, then finish-sand the pieces. Use a drum sander attachment on a drill to smooth out the radius cuts. Attach the tray sides to the tray ends with glue and wood screws. Finally, fasten the tray bottoms between the tray sides and ends with glue and screws **(photo G).** Finish-sand the en-

tire tray, and smooth out any sharp edges.

INSTALL AROMATIC CEDAR PANELS. Start by cutting aromatic cedar liner panels to fit the inside of the chest. Attach the liner panels to the sides, ends, and bottom with panel

adhesive and 2d finish nails **(photo H).**

MAKE & INSTALL THE CHEST CLEATS. Cut the chest cleats (M) to size from 1 × 2 cedar, and finish-sand the cleats. Install the chest cleats so their top edges are 3½" from the top of the chest sides. They should fit snugly between the corner posts.

INSTALL THE TOP ASSEMBLY. Place the top assembly over the chest and use masking tape to mark where the lower edge of the lip contacts the back side. Install two 2 × 1½" brass butt hinges on the chest box, spaced 6" in from each end of the chest box. Mount the hinges so the barrels fall below the contact line. Next, place the chest and top assembly on a flat worksurface and prop the chest box against the top so the unfastened sides of the hinges rest on the inside of the lip of the top assembly. Insert spacers (ordinary wood shims work well for this) equal to the thickness of the barrel, between the chest and lip. Fasten the hinges on the lip using the screws provided with the hinge hardware **(photo I).** Test the lid assembly and hinges for proper operation and fit. Install a locking lid support between the lid assem-

Install aromatic cedar lining panels to the sides, ends and bottom, using panel adhesive and 2d finish nails.

bly and the chest box to hold the lid in an open position during use. For just a little more money, you can purchase hardware accessories called soft-down supports, which let the lid close gently instead of slamming down. Install chest handles and brass corner protectors if desired.

APPLY FINISHING TOUCHES. Fill all exposed counterbore holes with cedar plugs. Apply glue to the edges of the plugs and tap in place with a hammer. Sand the plugs smooth until they are level with the wood surface. Finish-sand all outside surfaces lightly. Sand all exposed edges and surfaces of the tray. Set the tray on the chest cleats and slide it back and forth to test the fit. Adjust the fit if necessary with a belt sander or palm sander and coarse (60-grit) sandpaper, then go through the previous sanding steps to remove any sanding scratches and roughness. There are various finishing options you have with the cedar chest. We chose a traditional clear finish to provide a rustic, natural appearance. To apply the finish, we first brushed on a coat of sanding sealer to even out the absorption (a good idea with soft wood like cedar). Then we applied two light coats of tung-oil finish and buffed the surface to a medium gloss with a buffing pad. We also applied a coat of tung oil to the tray and exposed inside surfaces. If one side of a board is left uncoated, the sides will absorb moisture at different rates, and warping is a likely result. After the finish is applied, dried and buffed, you may want to stencil a design or monograms onto the chest—especially if you are building the chest as a gift. If you choose to monogram the chest, look for plain stencils that are 1" to 2" tall, to keep in scale with the size of the chest. Very ornate type styles are hard to stencil, and are generally not in tune with the rustic look of a cedar chest (see *Tip*, above). If you are interested in stenciling a design or emblem onto the chest, also look for a simple pattern. Almost any nature motif (like pinecones) is a good fit.

Install brass butt hinges on the chest box and lid assembly. Use a wood shim as a spacer to help align the hinges.

Firewood Caddy

Make handling firewood easy and clean with our caddy. Just grab a bundle and carry it inside with the leather carrier, and store the wood in the cedar box.

CONSTRUCTION MATERIALS

Quantity	Lumber
1	2 × 4" × 4' cedar
1	2 × 2" × 12' cedar
1	1 × 8" × 12' cedar
1	1 × 3" × 6' cedar
3	1 × 2" × 8' cedar
3	1"-dia. × 3' oak dowel

A fireplace becomes a convenient, clean household feature with our firewood caddy. Our caddy is equipped with a leather carrier that slips easily in and out of the frame. Throw the wood onto the carrier, pick it up with the dowel handles, and carry it indoors without a mess. The carrier slides into the frame, and you don't have to remove the wood until the time comes to build a fire. The contoured base of the storage box makes it easy to clean up bark and wood chips. The firewood caddy is a sturdy, attractive addition to any home.

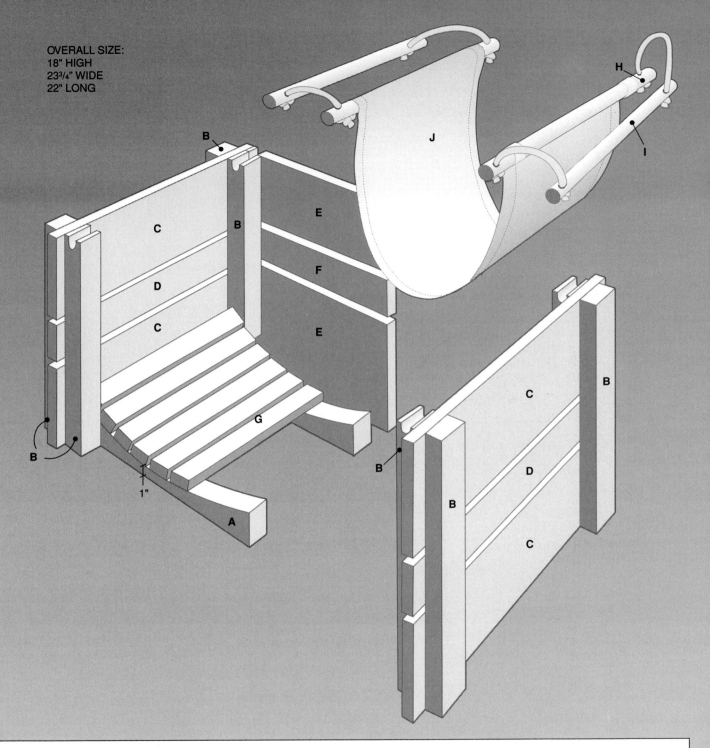

OVERALL SIZE:
18" HIGH
23¾" WIDE
22" LONG

Cutting List				
Key	**Part**	**Dimension**	**Pcs.**	**Material**
A	Base rail	1½ × 3½ × 19¼"	2	Cedar
B	Post	1½ × 1½ × 18"	8	Cedar
C	Wide rail	¾ × 7¼ × 22"	4	Cedar
D	Narrow rail	¾ × 2½ × 22"	2	Cedar
E	Back rail	¾ × 7¼ × 19¼"	2	Cedar

Cutting List				
Key	**Part**	**Dimension**	**Pcs.**	**Material**
F	Middle rail	¾ × 2½ × 16"	1	Cedar
G	Slat	¾ × 1½ × 19"	13	Cedar
H	Dowel	1 × 22"	2	Hardwood
I	Handle	1 × 18"	2	Hardwood
J	Carrier	16 × 48"	1	Leather

Materials: Brass upholstery tacks, moisture-resistant glue, deck screws (1⅝", 2½"), 4d finish nails, ¼"-dia. rope, finishing materials.

Note: Measurements reflect the actual size of dimensional lumber.

Use a flexible tracing guide to draw the arcs.

(above) Drill a 1"-dia. hole centered on the cutting line between two posts.

(left) Cut through the 1"-dia. holes in the 2 × 2's to create four posts with ½"-deep grooves at the ends.

Directions:
Firewood Caddy

MAKE THE BASE RAILS. A base rail is located at the front and rear of the firewood caddy. Each base rail has an arc, which determines the lay of the slats. Start by cutting the base rails (A) to length. Draw the arc by using a thin, flexible piece of metal, plastic or wood as a template, or tracing guide. Tack a casing nail into the center of one base rail, 1" from the top edge. Hook the flexible guide over the nail, then flex each end to the corners. Tack a casing nail at each corner to hold the guide in place as you trace along the strip to draw the arc **(photo A).** Remove the nails, then cut the arc with a jig saw. The arcs should be 1" deep at the center. Sand the arc smooth, then use it as a template for laying out the arc on the second rail.

CONSTRUCT THE FRAME. The frame is made to withstand the inevitable knocks and bumps that will come from loading wood. The posts (B) support the rails on the firewood caddy. They are made from four pieces of 36⅛"-long cedar. Drill a 1"-dia. hole through the center of two of the pieces **(photo B),** and crosscut the four pieces directly through their centers to form eight posts **(photo C).** When you cut the posts to length, you will cut through the centers of the 1"-dia. holes, forming ½"-deep notches on the top edges of the inside posts. Cut the wide rails (C), narrow rails (D), back rails (E) and middle rail (F) to size. Attach the wide and narrow rails to the posts with moisture-resistant glue and 1⅝" deck screws, making sure the inside posts have the notches on the top edges **(photo D).** When the frame is assembled, the wide and narrow rails should extend ¾" beyond the posts' front and back edges. The top and bottom edges of the wide rails should be flush with the top and bottom edges of the posts (see *Diagram*, page 27). There should be a ⅜" gap between

Attach the wide rails flush with the top and bottom post edges.

Place the slats in position to make sure they fit correctly along the arcs on the base rails.

the wide and narrow rails. Finally, attach the back rails and middle rail to the posts with glue and deck screws, forming the U-shaped firewood caddy frame. Use a power drill to continue the notches on the inside posts through the top edge of the back rails. This groove allows the dowels to sit snugly on the frame.

ATTACH THE SLATS. The bottom assembly is made from a series of slats attached to the arcs on the base rails. Begin by attaching the base rails to the inside edges of the posts with deck screws and moisture-resistant glue. Cut the slats (G) to size. Test-fit the slats by laying them across both rails **(photo E).** If their combined width is too wide, plane down the outer slats with a hand plane. Fasten all the slats to the base rails with 4d finish nails.

MAKE THE CARRIER. The carrier section is made from a piece of leather attached to a rope and dowel handle assembly. We chose suede for its pliability and strength. Unlike canvas, suede does not need hemming after it is cut. The

materials in this section can be purchased at most fabric stores. Start by cutting the oak dowels (H) and handles (I) to length. Once the dowels and handles are cut, drill ¼"-dia. holes 3" from the ends of the dowels and 1" from the ends of the handles. These holes are for the ropes and should go all the way through the pieces. Coat the dowel rods with linseed oil before moving on. Cut the carrier material to size, and fasten it to the dowels with brass upholstery tacks **(photo F).** Tape the carrier material in place to make sure it is centered

on the dowels before you drive the upholstery tacks. Because the carrier is expected to carry a fairly heavy load, you should fasten it to the dowel with at least two rows of pins. Finish the handles with linseed oil, and connect them to the dowels with ¼"-dia. × 8"-long ropes, knotted at each end.

APPLY THE FINISHING TOUCHES. Sand out the rough edges with medium-grit sandpaper, and finish the firewood caddy with *twp* clear wood sealer.

Tape the leather to the dowels, and tape the dowels to the worksurface to make attaching the upholstery tacks easy.

PROJECT
POWER TOOLS

Quilt Stand

The creative cactus shapes put the "fun" back in functional in this clever twist on a traditional home furnishing.

CONSTRUCTION MATERIALS	
Quantity	**Lumber**
1	¾" × 2 × 4' birch plywood
2	1 × 2" × 6' pine
1	1 × 3" × 10' pine

Many quilt and blanket designs are based on the distinctive, geometric designs of the American Southwest. So we thought it would be appropriate to pay tribute to that heritage with a Southwest-inspired quilt or blanket stand—and nothing says "Southwest" like a cactus.

But this quilt stand isn't just fun and creative, it is also highly functional. The quilt bars rest in the slots in the end panels, so they can simply be lifted out. This greatly simplifies the task of loading a heavy blanket or quilt onto the stand. And with five quilt bars, you can display multiple quilts at one time.

OVERALL SIZE:
32" HIGH
12" WIDE
36" LONG

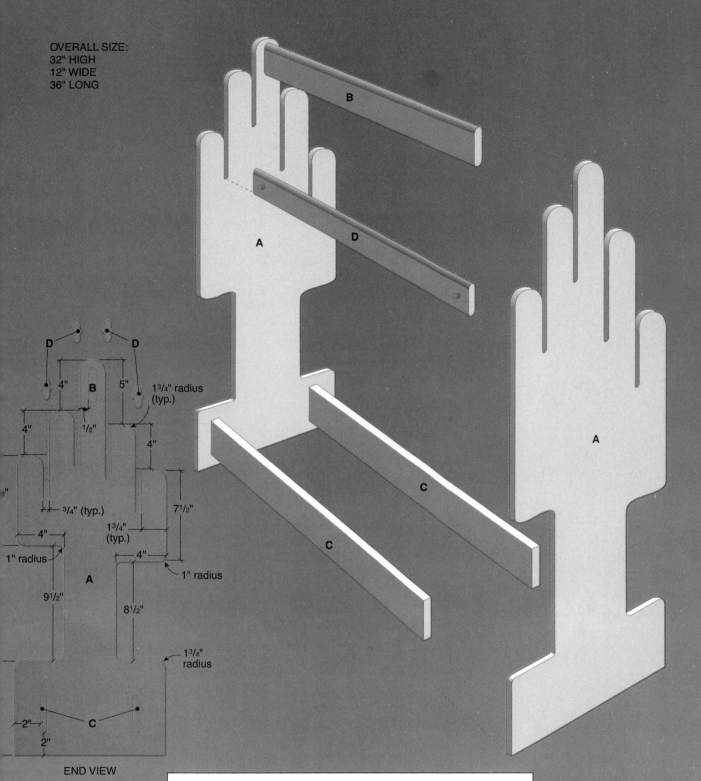

END VIEW

Cutting List				
Key	**Part**	**Dimension**	**Pcs.**	**Material**
A	End panel	¾ × 12 × 32"	2	Plywood
B	Top stretcher	¾ × 2½ × 33½"	1	Pine
C	Bottom stretcher	¾ × 2½ × 33½"	2	Pine
D	Quilt bar	¾ × 1½ × 36"	4	Pine

Materials: ¼ × 24" pine dowel, #8 × 1½" wood screws, finishing materials.

Note: Measurements reflect the actual size of dimensional lumber.

Directions: Quilt Stand

MAKE THE END PANELS. Cut the end panels (A) to size from ¾"-thick plywood stock (we used birch plywood for its workability and smooth, sanded finish). Following the measurements in the *Diagram*, page 31, lay out the design for the cactus-shaped panels on the inside face of one end panel **(photo A).** Also mark and drill pilot holes for the top stretcher on both end panels, according to the *Diagram*. Counterbore the pilot holes on the outside (better) face of each end panel to accept screw plugs. Next, lay the end panels with the layout markings on top of the other end panel and clamp the panels together for gang-cutting. Drill ¾"-dia. starter holes at the bottoms of all the internal cutouts, then cut out the cactus shape on both panels at once, using a jig saw with a combination blade that is at least 2½" long **(photo B).** Cut slowly, being careful to keep the saw fully upright. Once the cutouts are finished, unclamp the end panels and sand all the cut edges smooth. Use a drill and drum-sander attachment for the curved cuts. Using a router with a ¼" roundover bit or a power sander, round over all the edges of each end panel. Sand the edges and surfaces of the end panels smooth with medium (100- or 120-grit) sandpaper, then finish-sand with fine (150- or 180-grit) sandpaper.

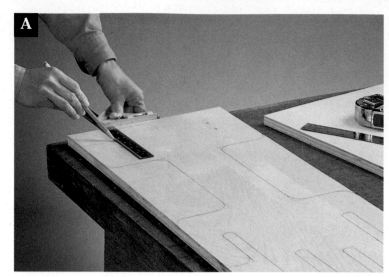

Lay out the cactus design on one end panel, following the Diagram on page 31.

Gang-cut both end panels, using a jig saw, to ensure uniform design.

TIP

Measure the blankets and quilts you intend to display on the quilt rack and adjust the end panel layout if necessary. When cutting out the quilt bar slots on the end panels, you may want to make them a little wider to simplify inserting and removing the quilt bars.

MAKE & INSTALL THE STRETCHERS. Cut the top stretcher (B) and bottom stretchers (C) to length from 1 × 3 pine. Round over the edges with sandpaper or a palm sander, then sand the faces of the stretchers. Apply glue to one end of a bottom stretcher. Stand an end panel on a flat surface, on its bottom edge. Place the glued end of the bottom stretcher on its corresponding mark on the end panel and secure with counter-bored #8 × 1½" wood screws **(photo C).** Apply glue to the opposite end of the stretcher, position it on the appropriate mark on the other end panel, and fasten with screws. Using the same procedure, fasten the remaining bottom stretcher and the top stretcher to the end panels.

BUILD THE QUILT BARS. Cut four quilt bars (D) to length from 1 × 2 pine. Using a router with a ⅜" roundover bit or a power sander, smooth out all the sharp edges of the quilt

With the end panel upright on the worksurface, hold the stretcher in position and secure with glue and wood screws.

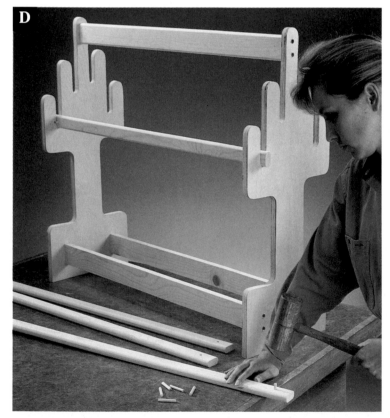

With the quilt rack assembly completed, drive dowel stops through the guide holes at the ends of quilt bars, using a wood mallet.

mer or mallet **(photo D).** Leave ⅜" of the dowel protruding from each side of the quilt bar. There is no need to glue the dowels in place.

APPLY THE FINISHING TOUCHES. Fill all voids in the plywood edges with a quality wood filler or wood putty, then sand smooth after it dries. Fill all counterbore holes with pine plugs the same diameter as the counterbores (⅜" is common) by applying glue and using a hammer or mallet to set the plugs in place. Sand the plugs smooth. Or, if you plan to paint the end panels, you can simply fill the counterbores with wood putty. Finish-sand the entire quilt rack assembly, including the quilt bars, and apply your selected finish. We chose to paint the end panels of our quilt rack with a desert green paint to maintain the Southwestern motif inspired by the cactus shapes, and we left the quilt bars unpainted. We also applied two light coats of satin-gloss poly-urethane over all surfaces for protection. Once the finish dries, your new quilt stand is ready to be put on display.

TIP

If you prefer to have a natural wood finish on projects that are built with plywood, you can substitute wide edge-glued panels for plywood. Made from scraps of hardwood or solid pine that are glued side by side to create wide panels, edge-glued boards (sometimes called Ponderosa Panels) can be finished using any fine finishing techniques normally used on hardwoods.

bars. Next, drill a ⁷⁄₃₂"-dia. hole centered 1½" in from each end of the quilt bars. Cut 1½"-long pieces of ¼"-dia. doweling to make kotter-pin style stops for the ends of the quilt bars (these prevent the bars from slipping past the edges of the end panels). Insert the dowels into ⁷⁄₃₂"-dia. holes in the quilt bars by laying the quilt bar on a flat surface and driving the dowels into the quilt bar with a ham-

Room Divider

Make a decorative barrier to organize your living space with our room dividers, which were crafted from cedar and lauan plywood.

CONSTRUCTION MATERIALS	
Quantity	**Lumber***
3	1 × 4" × 8' cedar
3	¾ × ¾" × 8' cove molding
1	¼" × 4 × 4' lauan plywood

*Materials for a single room divider section.

Strips of lauan plywood are woven between rustic cedar frames to make this room divider. Held together with brass hinges, the room divider panels can be used as a partition to make a romantic dining nook in a large living area. You can position the room divider near a sunny window to establish a tranquil garden retreat without adding permanent walls. There are many other creative uses for this versatile room divider.

The instructions for building the room divider show you how to make one panel. Add as many additional panels as your space needs require.

OVERALL SIZE:
72" HIGH
3½" WIDE
24" LONG

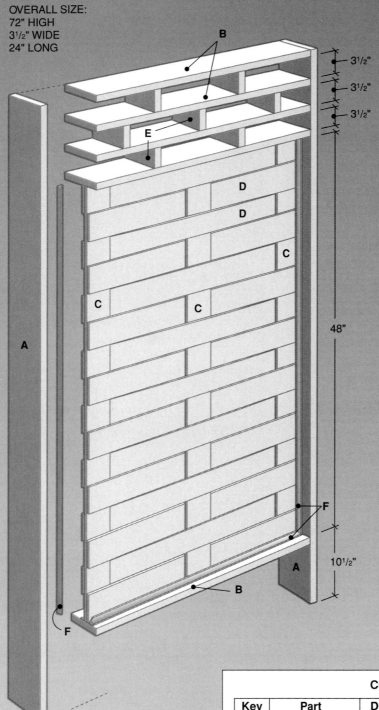

3½"
3½"
3½"

48"

10½"

Cutting List

Key	Part	Dimension	Pcs.	Material
A	Leg	¾ × 3½ × 72"	2	Cedar
B	Stretcher	¾ × 3½ × 22½"	5	Cedar
C	Vertical slat	¼ × 3 × 48"	3	Lauan ply.
D	Horizontal slat	¼ × 3 × 22½"	16	Lauan ply.
E	Divider	¾ × 3½ × 3½"	7	Cedar
F	Retainer strip	¾ × ¾"*	8	Cove molding

Materials: Wood glue, 2" wood screws, 4d finish nails, 2" butt hinges, finishing materials.

*Molding parts cut to fit the panel.

Note: Measurements reflect the actual size of dimensional lumber.

Directions: Room Divider

MAKE THE FRAME. Each frame consists of two legs and five stretchers. Four of these stretchers are positioned along the upper section of the frame. Start by cutting the legs (A) and stretchers (B) to size. Once these pieces are cut, measure and mark the positions for the stretchers on the inside faces of the legs. To make sure the measurements are exactly the same on both legs, tape the pieces together, edge to edge. Make sure the top and bottom edges are flush. Measure and mark a line 10½" from the bottom ends of both legs. These lines mark the top edge of the bottom stretcher. Next, measure and mark lines 48" up the legs from the bottom stretcher's top edge **(photo A).** These lines mark the bottom edge of the next stretcher. The top stretcher should be positioned between the legs, flush with the top ends. Mark the remaining stretcher positions as desired. We positioned them equally between the top and middle stretchers, approximately 3½" apart. To fasten the stretchers, drill holes for two counterbored #6 × 2" wood screws through the legs at each stretcher center position. Once the holes have been completed, glue the joints and fasten the stretchers to the legs, completing the room divider frame.

TIP

Achieving perfectly square corners is critical to the success of any project that uses frames. An easy way to ensure square corners is to measure the diagonal distance between opposite corners. Adjust the frame until the diagonals match, then fasten the corners securely.

Tape the legs together with their edges flush, and gang-mark the stretcher positions on the inside faces.

Weave the 16 horizontal slats through the three vertical slats to make the divider panel.

MAKE THE DIVIDER PANEL. The divider panel is made from 19 strips of ¼"-thick lauan plywood, woven together without any fasteners or glue. This step is easy to complete if you work on a flat, even surface. Begin by cutting the vertical slats (C) and horizontal slats (D) to size. Sand the edges with 120-grit sandpaper until they are completely smooth. Lay the vertical slats on the worksurface. Weave the horizontal slats between the vertical slats in an alternating pattern to form the panel **(photo B).**

INSERT THE DIVIDER PANEL. The divider panel is held in the frame by retaining strips (F), which are fastened along the inside faces of the legs and stretchers. Use a power miter

Attach the retaining strips with 4d finish nails.

Join the divider panels and frames with butt hinges.

TIP

There is significant color variation in lauan plywood, ranging from soft yellow to deep purple, sometimes within the same face of a panel. Keep this in mind when you are selecting your lumber.

screw holes on the outside edges of the legs, and sand all the leg surfaces until they are completely smooth.

APPLY THE FINISHING TOUCHES. Inserting the dividers is the final construction step for the divider panels. These small pieces of cedar are purely decorative and can be spaced apart in any pattern. Since they fit snugly in between the top stretchers, you don't need to fasten them. Friction holds them in place and gives you the option of repositioning them when you see fit. Begin by measuring the distance between the top stretchers, and cut the dividers (E) to size. Sand the dividers until they are completely smooth. Just push them between the stretchers and position them as desired. Once you have made two or three room divider panels, brace the pieces with C-clamps for stability, then attach them with evenly-spaced 2" butt hinges **(photo D).** When clamping the frames, use a cardboard pad to prevent the clamps from damaging the relatively soft wood. Cedar lumber, mahogany trim and lauan plywood do not require a protective finish, so we left them unfinished. If you prefer a glossier, more formal look, apply a coat of tung oil to the parts before assembly.

box or gang-cut the retaining strips to size from ¾"-thick mahogany cove molding. Attach the retaining strips on both sides of the panel to hold it in the frame, between the stretchers and legs. Use a power miter box to miter-cut the retaining strips to fit the inside of the frame. Measure and mark 1⅜"

from one side edge for the first line of retaining strips. Attach the retaining strips to one side of the frame with 4d finish nails **(photo C),** and set the nails with a nail set. Place the woven panel against the retaining strip frame, and secure the panel in the frame by attaching retaining strips on the opposite face of the panel. Fill all the visible

Corner TV Center

This sleek TV center fits snugly into a corner, but with its beautiful birch tones and open design you may be tempted to put it on display in the middle of your living room.

PROJECT
POWER TOOLS

I f finding a decent spot to house your television set is like trying to put a square peg in a round hole, we've got just the solution for you. This trim TV center tucks neatly into a corner, keeping it out of the traffic flow and conserving pre-cious wall and floor space. And as an added benefit, it automat-ically orients the TV screen so it can be seen from anywhere in the room.

Beyond its admirable effi-ciency, however, this special home furnishing is downright beautiful. Rich wood tones come to life in the all-birch ply-wood construction. The subtle veneer tape along the exposed edges makes even close view-ers believe this TV center is made from expensive hard-wood. And the wide-open design has an unassuming ele-gance that won't overwhelm other furnishings in the room.

Ample storage on adjustable shelves adds another useful component to this versatile pro-ject. The shelves are supported by simple shelf pins so they can be moved up and down in ac-cordance with your storage de-mands. And believe it or not, all the parts for this TV center are cut from a single sheet of plywood.

CONSTRUCTION MATERIALS

Quantity	Lumber
1	¾" × 4 × 8' birch plywood

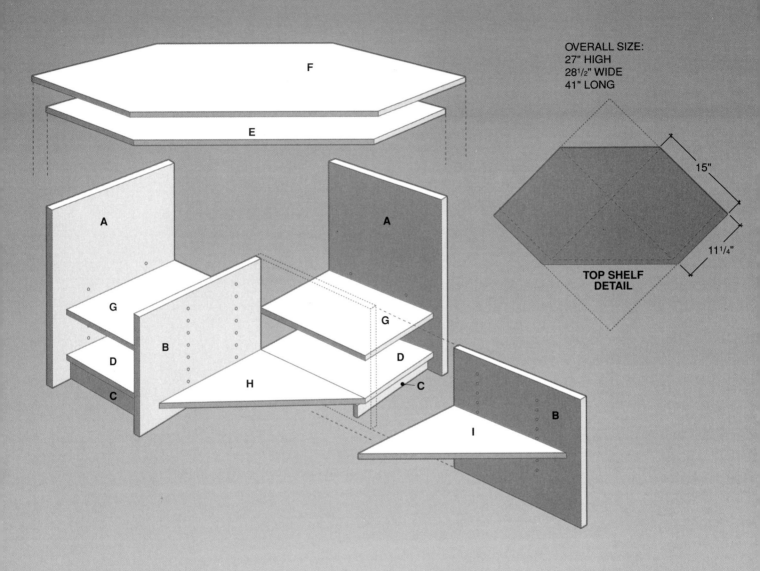

OVERALL SIZE:
27" HIGH
28½" WIDE
41" LONG

TOP SHELF DETAIL

15"

11¼"

Key	Part	Dimension	Pcs.	Material
	Cutting List			
A	Side panel	¾ × 15 × 26¼"	2	Birch plywood
B	Center partition	¾ × 15 × 17¼"	2	Birch plywood
C	Kick plate	¾ × 2½ × 10½"	4	Birch plywood
D	Bottom shelf	¾ × 13½ × 10½"	2	Birch plywood
E	Middle shelf	¾ × 25¾ × 25¾"	1	Birch plywood

Key	Part	Dimension	Pcs.	Material
	Cutting List			
F	Top shelf	¾ × 28½ × 28½"	1	Birch plywood
G	Adjustable shelf	¾ × 13¼ × 10½"	2	Birch plywood
H	Fixed ledge	¾ × 14 × 14"	1	Birch plywood
I	Adjustable ledge	¾ × 14 × 14"	1	Birch plywood

Materials: Wood glue, ¾"-wide self-adhesive veneer tape, 1½" wood screws, finish nails (4d, 6d), ⅜"-dia. birch plugs, shelf pins, tack-on glides, finishing materials.

Note: Measurements reflect the actual size of dimensional lumber.

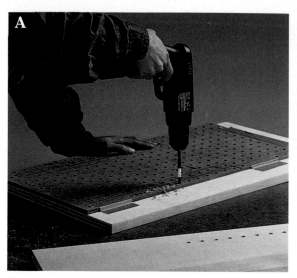

A

Use a piece of pegboard as a template for drilling shelf-pin holes in the side panels and center partitions.

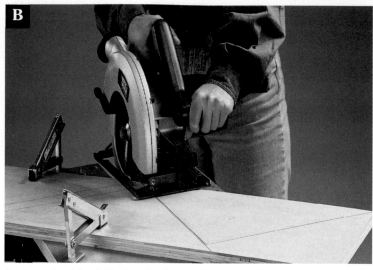

B

Lay out the 14 x 14" triangle-shaped fixed ledge on a piece of plywood and cut out the ledge using a circular saw.

Directions:
Corner TV Center

MAKE THE SIDE PANELS & CENTER PARTITIONS. Start by cutting the side panels (A) to size from birch plywood using a circular saw and straightedge. Measure up from the bottom of each panel 3¼" and down from the top 12", and draw lines across the panels. Lay the end panels flat on the worksurface, marked sides up, then place a 12 × 24" piece of pegboard onto one panel. This will be used as a drilling template for the shelf pin holes. Line the pegboard up with the bottom edge and a side edge of the panel. Use duct tape to hold the pegboard in place. Drill ¼"-dia × ⅜"-deep holes for the shelf pins along two columns in the pegboard **(photo A).** One column should be approximately 3" in from the flush side of the pegboard and panel and the other column should follow the opposite side of the pegboard. Use a piece of masking

C

Fasten the kick plates to the center partitions, with the front plate 3" back from the front edge of the partition, and the rear plate flush.

tape wrapped around the drill bit to mark the ⅜" depth. Drill only the template holes that are between the marks on the panel. Repeat the process for the other side panel. Next, cut the center partitions (B) from birch plywood using a circular saw and straightedge. Lay the partitions flat on a worksurface and measure up from the bottom 3¼" and down from the top 3" and draw lines across the partitions. Use the same piece of pegboard as earlier and lay it on top of a partition, flush

with the bottom edge and a side edge. Let the pegboard hang over the top edge of the partition. Use duct tape to hold the pegboard in place. Drill out two columns of holes between the marks on the partitions as you did previously on the side panels. Repeat the process for the other partition, then turn the partitions over and repeat the drilling procedure. Drill only to the ⅜" depth stop (the masking tape on the drill bit) to

Position the center partition corners together snugly, and fasten the partitions to the fixed ledge with glue and screws.

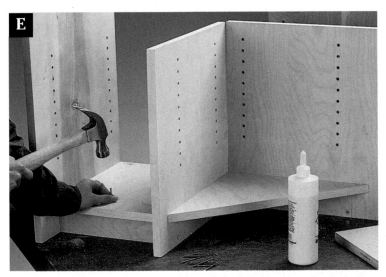

Fasten the bottom shelf to the kick plates, between the side panels, using glue and 4d finish nails.

of the side panels with medium (100-or 120-grit) sandpaper, then finish-sand with fine (150- or 180-grit) sandpaper. Use care with power sanders so you don't sand through the veneer tape.

BUILD THE FRAME. Lay out the fixed ledge (H) dimensions on a piece of plywood by marking a line 14" along one side and another 14" across, then connecting the end points. Cut along the line with a circular saw **(photo B).** Apply veneer tape to the diagonal edge of the fixed ledge, then sand and smooth as necessary. Cut the kick plates (C) from birch plywood using a circular saw. Sand the fixed ledge and kick plates. Attach the kick plates to the center partitions, positioning the front plate 3" back from the front edge and flush with the bottom of the partition, and positioning the back plate flush with the back edge of the partition **(photo C).** Measure up from the bottom of the partitions on the drilled side 2½" and mark a line, then lay one center partition assembly on its side, resting on the flush-mounted kick plate. Place the fixed ledge on-edge on the worksurface and butt the other edge up to the center partition, positioning the fixed ledge on the layout line. Attach the fixed ledge to the center partition

avoid drilling through the other sides of the partitions. When all side panels and center partitions have been drilled for shelf pins, stand the panels on their back edges, one at a time, and apply adhesive-backed wood veneer tape to the front edges. Use a heat gun or a household iron to heat the tape, activating the adhesive. Apply pressure to the veneer tape with the iron (see *photo F*), a putty knife, or a wood block to bond it to the plywood edge. You may find it helpful to use a small J-roller to press the wood tape onto the panel edge after heating and pressing with the iron. Trim the wood tape edges with a utility knife, then hand-sand with 100-grit sandpaper to smooth out the seams and edges. Don't use a power sander for this, it may be too aggressive for the veneer tape. Apply veneer tape to the back edges of the panels, then to both edges of the remaining panels. Sand the faces

TIP

There is an easy way to make a pair of matching triangle-shaped pieces with 45° diagonals in one simple cutting procedure. Cut your material into a square with dimensions equal to the length of the 90° sides of the triangle. Then cut the square diagonally to create matching triangular pieces.

with glue and counterbored #6 × 1½" wood screws. Stand the center partition upright on the worksurface and place two 2½" spacer blocks under the fixed ledge to support it at the proper elevation. Position the other center partition assembly against the fixed ledge, with the corner of the partition tight to the corner of the adjacent center partition. Secure the center partition assembly to the fixed ledge with glue and screws **(photo D).** Place a mark on the bottom of the side panels, 3" from the front edge. Position the side panels against the kick plates, lining up the front plates with the marks at the bottoms of the panels, so the rear plates are flush with the back edges of the side panels. Secure the side panels to the kick plates with glue and screws.

BUILD & INSTALL THE SHELVES. Start by cutting the bottom shelves (D) to size from ¾"-thick birch plywood, using a circular saw and straightedge.

Apply birch veneer tape to both ends of the shelves, then trim and sand the tape. Fasten the bottom shelves to the side panels and kick plates with glue and 4d finish nails **(photo E).** Next, lay out the middle shelf (E), following the *Diagram* on page 39, on a 25¾ × 25¾" piece of ¾" plywood. Start in one corner, measure over 15" along the edge and place a mark. Then, from the same corner, measure up 11¼" along the adjacent edge and place a mark. In the

Diagram on page 39

Apply self-adhesive veneer tape veneer to the shelf edges, using a household iron to press the tape in place, while activating the glue.

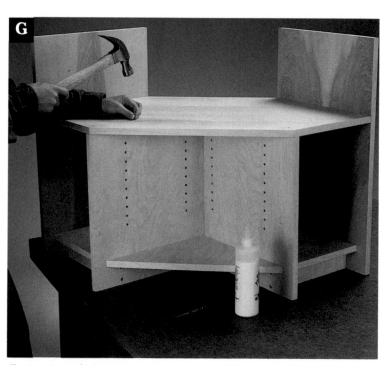

Fasten the middle shelf to the center partitions and side panels, using glue and 6d finish nails.

opposite corner, measure over 11¼" along the edge. Then, measure up 15" along the adjacent edge. Now, connect the 11¼" marks to each other and connect the 15" marks to each other. Cut along the lines using a circular saw and straightedge.

Apply veneer tape to the cut edges **(photo F),** since these will be the exposed front and back edges after installation If the edges are not perfectly smooth, sand them smooth using a power sander. Place the

H

Secure the top shelf to the side panels with glue and screws.

unit. Drill counterbored pilot holes through the top and into the side panels. Counterbore so there is enough room for wood plugs (⅜"-dia. × ¼"-thick is common). Fasten the shelf to the side panels using glue and screws, then glue wood plugs into the counterbores. Sand the wood plugs until level with the wood surface.

APPLY THE FINISHING TOUCHES. Start by making the adjustable components. Cut the adjustable shelves (G) and adjustable ledge (I) from ¾"-thick plywood. Apply veneer tape to the ends of the adjustable shelves and to the diagonal edge on the adjustable ledge. Trim the veneer tape with a utility knife, then sand the edges and surfaces. Finish-sand the entire TV center lightly. Fill any open nail holes, defects or voids with a quality wood filler tinted to match the color of the wood stain (if any) you plan to apply. Sand filler or putty level with the wood. Wipe away sanding residue with a rag dipped in mineral spirits or a tack cloth. Apply a sanding sealer product to the TV center and to the adjustable shelves if applying a darker stain (sealer helps the wood accept the stain evenly, minimizing blotches). Apply the stain (if any), then topcoat the wood after the stain has dried. We brushed on two thin layers of satin-gloss polyurethane. When dry, install tack-on glides at the bottoms of the partitions and side panels, then insert the shelf pins for the adjustable shelves and ledge. Rest the shelves and ledge on the pins, adjusting them as needed to fit your TV components.

middle shelf on the center partitions and fasten with glue and 6d finish nails **(photo G).** Drive finish nails through the side panels and into the shelf edge to secure it in place. Next, lay out the top shelf (F), following the *Diagram* on page 39, on a 28½ × 28½" piece of ¾" plywood. Starting in one corner, measure over 16½" along one edge and place a mark. Then, from the same corner, measure up 14" along the adjacent edge and place a mark. On the opposite corner, measure over 14" along the edge (this should be the same side as the previously marked 14" side). Then, from the same corner, measure up 16½" along the adjacent edge and place a mark. Now,

connect the 14" marks to each other and connect the 16½" marks to each other. Cut along the lines using a circular saw and straightedge. Smooth any rough saw cuts with a power sander. Apply veneer tape to the edges of the top shelf (all edges will be exposed, so they all need to be covered with tape). Trim the veneer tape flush with the top and bottom of the plywood, using a utility knife, then sand the edges. Finish-sand the surfaces of the top shelf. Lay the top shelf on the side panels and line it up so there is a 1" overhang at the side panels and the front of the

Wine Rack

*Build this contemporary-style wine rack and showcase
your wine collection with pride.*

Perfect for a kitchen countertop or a living room corner, our wine rack can accommodate ten bottles of wine, yet it's small enough to fit almost anywhere in the house. There is a classical quality about wine racks that goes beyond most household storage items. Even though it is clearly a practical storage unit, a fully stocked wine rack is a beautiful decorative item that adds a touch of class to almost any room. Our wine rack is easy to make and has a stylish, contemporary appeal. The sides form a simple V-shape, and rows of diamond-shaped cubbyholes create the individual storage areas. For the finishing touches, we used a paint that simulates the classic look of polished granite. You can purchase paints that simulate a variety of materials, or you can simply finish the wine rack to match your room's decor. Either way, the simple wine rack design will stand on its own, complementing your room and providing years of steady service.

We tacked small rubber bumpers under the front edge of the wine rack to keep the bottles tilted backward slightly, maintaining correct wine storage standards.

CONSTRUCTION MATERIALS

Quantity	Lumber
2	1 × 10" × 8' pine
3	½ × ½" × 8' ¼-round molding

OVERALL SIZE:
14" HIGH
9¼" WIDE
27" LONG

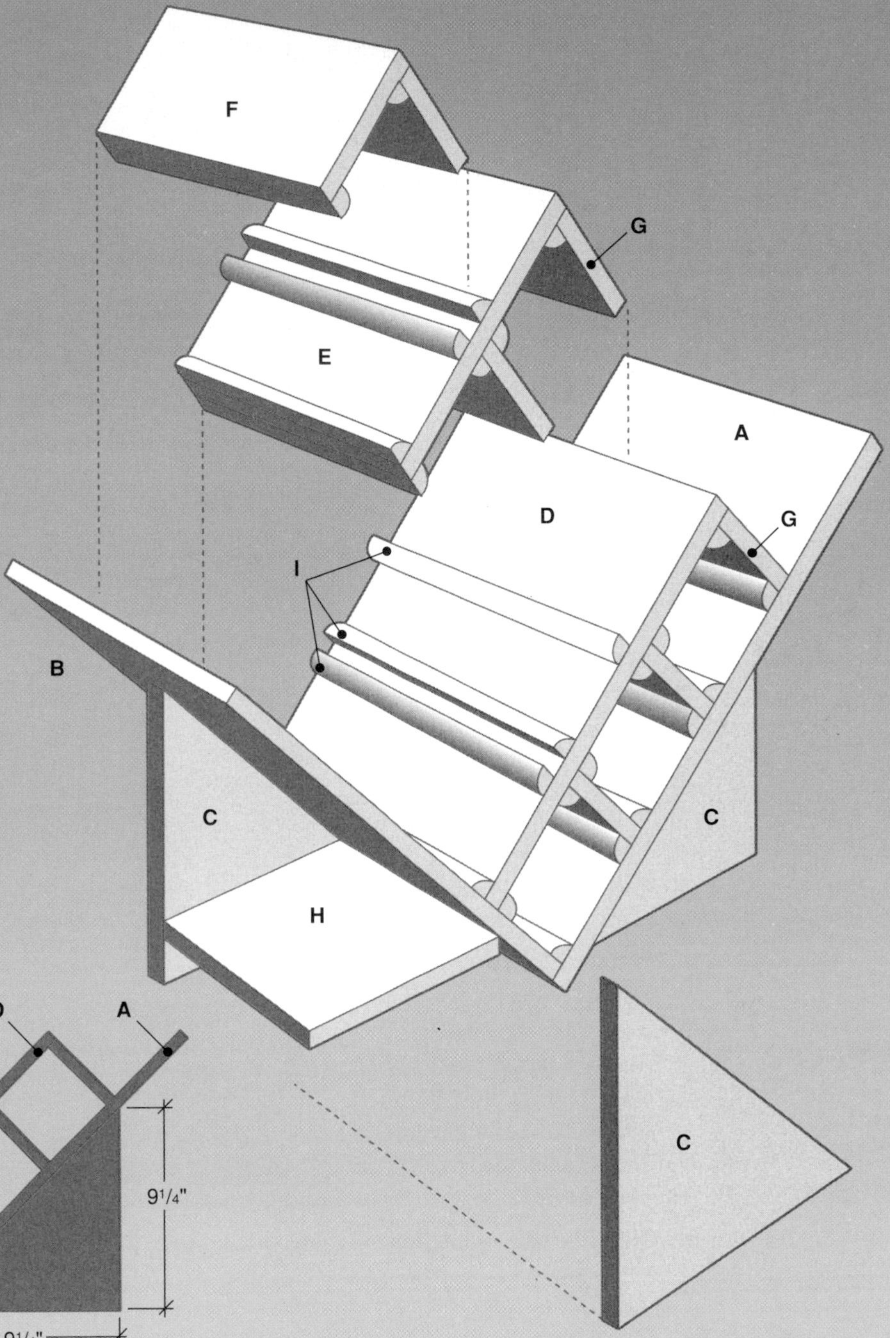

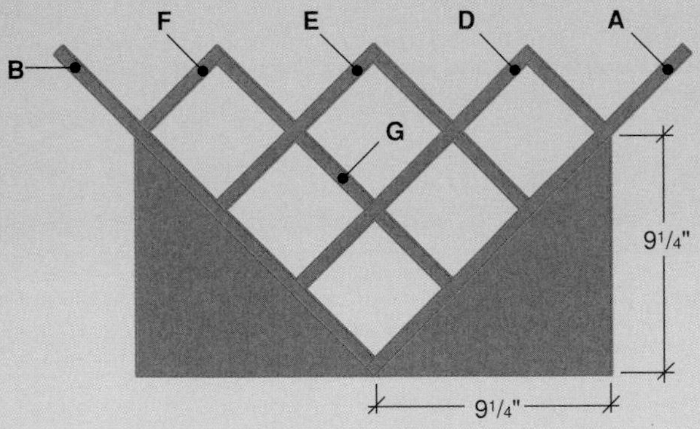

SIDE VIEW

Cutting List

Key	Part	Dimension	Pcs.	Material
A	Long side	¾ × 9¼ × 19¾"	1	Pine
B	Short side	¾ × 9¼ × 19"	1	Pine
C	Pedestal	¾ × 9¼ × 9¼"	4	Pine
D	Long divider	¾ × 9¼ × 14¼"	1	Pine
E	Middle divider	¾ × 9¼ × 9½"	1	Pine

Cutting List

Key	Part	Dimension	Pcs.	Material
F	Short divider	¾ × 9¼ × 4¾"	1	Pine
G	Spacer	¾ × 9¼ × 4"	6	Pine
H	Shelf	¾ × 6 × 7½"	2	Pine
I	Cleat	½ × ½ × 9½"	24	¼-round

Materials: Wood glue, #6 × 2" wood screws, ¾" brads, rubber bumpers, finishing materials.

Note: Measurements reflect the actual size of dimensional lumber.

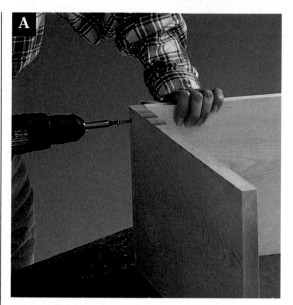

Fasten the short side edge flush against the long side to make a right angle that has 19"-long sides.

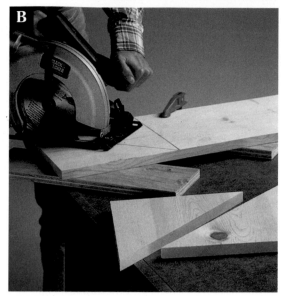

Cut the triangular pedestals from 1 × 10 pine.

Directions: Wine Rack

ATTACH THE SIDES. The side assembly is made from two pieces (the long and short sides) of 1 × 10 pine, fastened together at their bottom edges to form a right-angle V-shape. The side assembly is held in place by the pedestals and shelves, which are attached underneath. When building the side assembly, fasten the short side edge against the long side face (see *Diagram*, page 45); both sides are equal in length. Start by cutting the long side (A) and short side (B) to length. Position the short side so that its bottom edge is flush with the long side's bottom edge. Glue the joint, then drive evenly spaced #6 × 2" wood screws through the long side and into the short side end to fasten the pieces securely

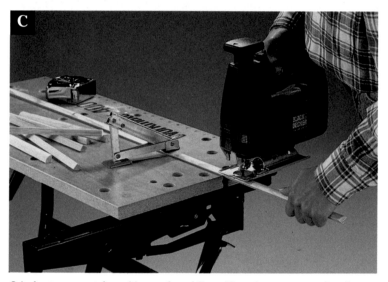

24 cleats are cut from ¼-round molding. The cleats are used to fasten the spacers to the sides and dividers.

(photo A). The resulting assembly forms a right angle with 19¾"-long legs.

MAKE THE PEDESTALS & SHELVES. Use a circular saw to cut the pedestals (C) (photo B) and shelves (H) to size from 1 × 10 pine. The pedestals are simple right-angle triangles with 9¼"-wide × 9¼"-high dimensions. Once the parts are cut, measure and mark guidelines ¾" up from the bottom edges on the pedestals. Attach the

shelves between the pedestals so their bottom edges are positioned along the guidelines. Make sure the outside edges are flush. Finally, glue the joints, and attach the pedestals to the sides by driving wood screws through the sides into the support edges, completing the side assembly. It will be difficult to reach the entire surface area once the wine rack is

Attach the cleats to the long side with glue and brads. Apply glue to the spacer/side joints, and push brads through the cleats into the spacers to secure the pieces.

Attach the short divider to complete the rack assembly. Notice that the spacers are all aligned with each other and separated by an equal distance on all three rack levels.

assembled, so sand the side assembly to 150-grit smoothness at this time.

BUILD THE RACK ASSEMBLY. The rack assembly is a stacked collection of dividers and spacers with room for ten bottles of wine. The spacers are positioned at equal distances on each divider, and ¼-round molding is used along the corners to strengthen the entire assembly. You can attach the cleats to the sides and dividers with glue and ¾" brads. Begin by cutting the long divider (D),

middle divider (E), short divider (F), spacers (G) and cleats (I) to size **(photo C).** Use glue and deck screws to attach three spacers to the long divider with the top edge of each spacer positioned every 4¾". Fit this assembly in place on the long side, and draw guideline marks along the spacer sides to mark their positions. Attach the cleats along the markings on the long side with glue and wire brads **(photo D),** then fasten the long divider between the spacers with glue and brads. Continue this procedure on the other rack levels until the short divider has been attached along the top of the assembly **(photo E).** Remember to affix the ¼-round molding cleats to the upper corners of the rack assembly for added strength and stability. Because of the space restraints, it will be difficult to tap some brads through the molding with a hammer, but you should be able to force them through with a brad pusher.

APPLY THE FINISHING TOUCHES. Sand any unsanded surfaces with 150, then 220-grit sandpaper. Apply the primer, and paint as desired. Finally, install ¼"-thick bumpers under the front pedestals, tilting the wine rack backward for correct wine storage.

TIP

Wine should always be stored in a cool spot out of direct sunlight. If any bottles are stored on the rack for longer than a few months, spin them periodically.

Coffee Table

If you have ever built a picture frame, you already have most of the skills needed to make this clean and simple coffee table.

CONSTRUCTION MATERIALS

Quantity	Lumber
2	1 × 2" × 8' pine
1	1 × 2" × 10' pine
1	¾ × ¾" × 4' pine
2	¾" × 2 × 4' birch plywood
2	½ × 2¼" × 8' beaded pine casing

Some coffee tables are so ornate and expensive that you would never dare come near them with a hot beverage. This coffee table has a beauty all its own, but it is meant to be used—and used and used and used again. Made from birch plywood and topcoated with polyurethane, the tabletop will stand up to just about any abuse you care

to inflict upon it. Even the plain pine structure, painted with white enamel, resists the effects of spilled drinks and heavy shoes.

But the best feature of this sturdy little table is that it is uncompromisingly easy to build. The table base, made from dimensional pine, requires only straight cuts and butt joints that are screwed and glued.

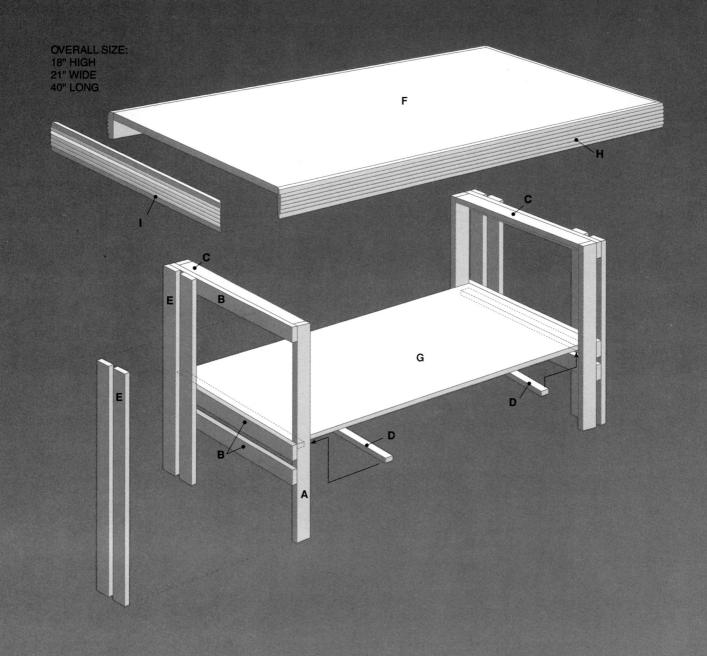

OVERALL SIZE:
18" HIGH
21" WIDE
40" LONG

Key	Part	Dimension	Pcs.	Material
A	Post	¾ × 1½ × 17¼"	4	Pine
B	Rail	¾ × 1½ × 15"	6	Pine
C	Top cleat	¾ × 1½ × 13½"	2	Pine
D	Shelf cleat	¾ × ¾ × 13"	2	Pine
E	Slat	¾ × 1½ × 17¼"	8	Pine

Cutting List

Key	Part	Dimension	Pcs.	Material
F	Top	¾ × 20 × 39"	1	Birch plywood
G	Shelf	¾ × 13½ × 30½"	1	Birch plywood
H	Side apron	½ × 2¼ × 40"	2	Beaded pine casing
I	End apron	½ × 2¼ × 21"	2	Beaded pine casing

Cutting List

Materials: Glue, #8 × 1¼" wood screws, finish nails (2d, 4d), ¾"-wide birch veneer tape, tack-on glides, finishing materials.

Note: Measurements reflect the actual size of dimensional lumber.

Mount the top rail flush with the post ends and the bottom and middle rails on the layout marks.

Fasten the slats to the rails with glue and by driving screws through the inside face of the rails into the slats.

Directions: Coffee Table

BUILD THE FRAME. Start by cutting the posts (A) to length from 1 × 2 pine. Sand the faces and edges of the posts and round over the corners with 80-grit sandpaper. Measure up from the bottom of each post 3" and 6", and place marks on the edges of the posts for the rail positions. Next, cut the rails (B) to length from 1 × 2 pine. Sand the faces and edges of the rails and round over the corners with 80-grit sandpaper. Lay two posts on edge on a flat surface. Position a rail flush with the top ends of the posts and flush with the outside edges of the posts. Fasten the rail to the posts with glue and #8 × 1¼" wood screws. Position two more rails at the previously marked locations on the posts and attach the rails to the posts with glue and wood screws **(photo A).** Drive

Attach the cleats by screwing through the cleat into the rail. The bottom of the cleat should be flush with the bottom edge of the rail.

the screws through the rails into the posts. Use two screws at each end of each rail. When the first rail-and-post assembly is constructed, use the same steps to build the other rail-and-post assembly. Next, cut the slats (E) to length from 1 × 2 pine. Sand the faces and edges of the rails and round over the corners with 80-grit sandpaper. Lay four slats facedown on a flat surface. Place the rail and post assemblies on top of the

slats, with the rails resting on the slat faces. Position one slat even with the ends of the rails, so the top end is flush with the top edge of the top rail, and fasten with glue and screws. Drive the screws through the inside face of the rails and into the slats to conceal the screw heads. Position another slat ¾" away from the first slat, keeping the top end flush with the top rail, and secure with glue and screws **(photo B).** Now, on the opposite end of the rail-and-post assembly, position a slat flush with the outside end of the rails and flush with the top edge of the top rail. Fasten the slat in place, then position another slat ¾" away from the first slat, keeping the top flush with the top rail, and secure the slat with glue and screws. Be sure to drive the screws through the rails and into the slats in order to keep the screw heads concealed.

MAKE & ATTACH THE CLEATS. Cut the top cleats (C) to length from 1 × 2 pine lumber and the shelf cleats (D) to length from ¾ × ¾" pine molding. On the insides of the rail-and-post assemblies, mark a line ¾" down from the top edge of the middle rail. This will allow the shelf to sit on the cleats and be flush with the top of the middle rails. Position the cleats on the layout lines, and fasten with glue and screws **(photo C).** The bottoms of the cleats should be flush with the bottoms of the middle rails. Then attach the top cleats to the top rail and the posts.

MAKE THE TOP. Start by cutting the top (F) from birch plywood, using a circular saw and straightedge **(photo D).** When cutting plywood sheets, it is helpful to set the plywood on scrap lumber, usually 2 × 4s, to give the saw blade clearance between the plywood and the top of the worksurface. With this technique, you can clamp the plywood to the worksurface and have a stable surface for cutting without fear of the cutout piece falling on the floor and getting damaged. Use a power sander to smooth the edges of the top so the apron pieces will have a flat, square edge to be attached to.

MAKE & ATTACH THE APRONS TO THE TOP. Start by cutting a 45° miter on one end of the apron molding material with a power miter box **(photo E)** or with a miter box and backsaw. Cut the miter so the angle goes away from the inside surface of the molding. Lay the top on a flat surface with the top facedown. Position the apron molding against a long edge of the top, holding the heel of the miter tight to the corner of the top. With the

TIP

A straightedge is a useful tool for making accurate, straight cuts. Store-bought straightedges are highly accurate and very durable, since they are usually fashioned from metal. But for many cutting jobs, a long, straight piece of scrap lumber (2 × 4s are a good choice) clamped to your workpiece makes a perfectly serviceable straightedge.

molding held tightly in place, mark the other corner position along the edge and onto the back side of the apron molding. Cut a 45° miter at this

Use scrap pieces of 2 x 4 lumber to elevate the plywood off of the worksurface top and to keep from cutting into the top with the saw.

Use a power miter box to cut 45° miters on the ends of the apron molding. Keep the molding tight to the fence to ensure clean cuts.

Measure the inset for the frame assemblies, then secure to the top with glue and screws driven through the top rail into the tabletop.

mark, so the heel of the miter lines up with the mark and the toe (the pointy part) of the miter goes away from the mark. Using glue and 4d finish nails, fasten the side apron (H) that you just cut to length to the edge of the top, keeping the top surface flush with the top edge of the apron. Now, cut another 45° miter on the end of the apron molding. Place the

molding against the edge of the short end of the top, tight to the miter on the attached side apron. Mark the location of the edge corner on the back side of the apron molding and cut a 45° miter at the mark. Fasten the end apron (I) that you just cut to length to the edge of the top, using glue and 4d finish nails. Keep the top edge of the apron flush with the top surface of the top. Cut another 45° miter on the end of the apron molding. Place the molding against the edge of the long side of the top, tight to the miter on the attached end apron. Mark the location of the edge corner on the back side of the apron molding and cut a 45° miter at the back side of the apron molding, at the mark. Fasten the side apron to the edge of the top using glue and

4d finish nails. Keep the top edge of the apron flush with the top surface of the top. Cut a 45° miter on the end of the apron molding. Place the molding on the bottom edges of the side aprons, with one end fitted into the miter and the other resting on the edge of the side apron so it lines up with the edge of the top and the miter. It can be a little tricky getting a piece that is mitered at both ends to fit perfectly between two mitered pieces. You'll be better off to mark and cut the last end apron a little long, then test-fit it in the frame and trim it down a little if needed. When it fits properly, fasten the end apron to the edge of the top with glue and nails. At each mitered corner, lock-nail the apron miters with 2d finish nails to keep them from separating due to humidity changes (see *Tip*, left).

ATTACH THE TOP TO THE FRAME. Start by cutting the shelf (G) to size from birch plywood, using a circular saw and straightedge. With the tabletop upside down on the worksurface, position the frame assemblies upside down on the bottom side of the top. Place the shelf, on the top cleats, between the frame assemblies to provide proper spacing for the layout. Measure and mark the inset for the frame assembly on the bottom side of the top. Measure in from the inside of the end aprons 2¾", and 2½" in from the inside of the side aprons, and place marks **(photo F).** Position the frame assemblies on the marks. Fasten the frame assemblies to the top using #6 × 1¼" screws through the top cleats into the table top.

through the top cleats into the table top.

APPLY VENEER TAPE TO THE SHELF. Smooth all four edges of the shelf using a power sander. The edges need to be smooth and square for the veneer tape to adhere properly. Clamp the shelf on edge on your worksurface. Cut strips of ¾" birch veneer tape to fit the shelf edges, then set them in place and iron them onto the edges with a household iron **(photo G).** The heat from the iron activates the adhesive backing, and the downward pressure helps create a firm bond. Follow the iron with a flat wooden block to smooth and set the tape. When the adhesive has cooled, trim the veneer tape, if needed, so it is flush with the surfaces of the plywood. Then, sand the edges and corners with medium (100- or 120-grit) sandpaper. Be careful not to oversand or you may wear through the veneer tape.

INSTALL THE SHELF. Turn the tabletop and frame assemblies right-side up and apply glue to the top edge of the cleats and the inside of the middle rail. Position the shelf into place on the cleats between the posts and rails. Secure the shelf in position by driving 4d finish nails through the posts and middle rails, and into the shelf edges **(photo H).** Countersink the nail heads with a nail set and hammer. Be careful when pounding in the nails so you don't mar the posts and rails.

APPLY THE FINISHING TOUCHES. When the coffee table is completely assembled, fill all exposed nail holes with a quality wood filler. Sand the dried putty level with the wood sur-

Apply self-adhesive veneer tape to the shelf edges, using a household iron to heat up the tape and press it in position.

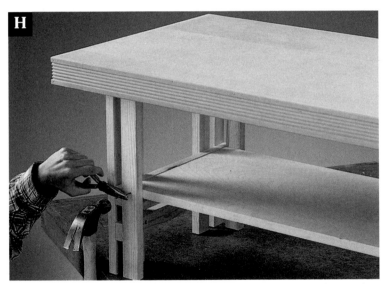

Fasten the coffee table shelf to the frame assemblies with glue and 4d finish nails.

face, then sand out any rough spots, especially on the tabletop, with medium (100- or 120-grit) sandpaper. Finish-sand the entire coffee table with fine (150- or 180-grit) sandpaper. Finish the coffee table as desired. We chose a combination of finishes for our coffee table. First, we applied three light coats of semi-gloss polyurethane to the tabletop, leaving the natural color of the birch essentially unchanged.

Then, we painted the rest of the coffee table with enamel paint to create contrast with the tabletop. After finishing, fasten tack-on glides to the bottoms of the posts.

TIP

Just about any table design can be resized for a different purpose. By reducing the length of a coffee table design to about 24", you can build a matching end table. But be careful to double-check your measurements when altering a tested design.

Overjohn

Convert wasted space above your toilet into usable storage with this compact "overjohn" shelving unit.

It wasn't long ago that few people had ever heard the term "overjohn," but that is changing quickly. An overjohn is a storage unit that fits against the wall above a toilet—a space that is seldom put to good use even in the tiniest bathrooms. Many overjohn cabinets being installed today provide useful storage, but they are heavy and bulky, and they cause the bathroom to look smaller than it actually is. Because the design featured here is open-sided, it has a lightweight, airy appearance that melts into the background virtually unnoticed. Yet our overjohn is spacious enough to accommodate enough towels and linens for an entire family.

This overjohn shelving unit will function as a freestanding unit under normal conditions. But if you plan to store heavier items in it, or have an unusually large volume of traffic through the bathroom, add a cleat to the back of the unit and attach it to the wall.

CONSTRUCTION MATERIALS

Quantity	Lumber
5	1 × 2" × 6' pine
1	1 × 4" × 4' pine
1	1 × 6" × 4' pine
1	1 × 10" × 8' pine

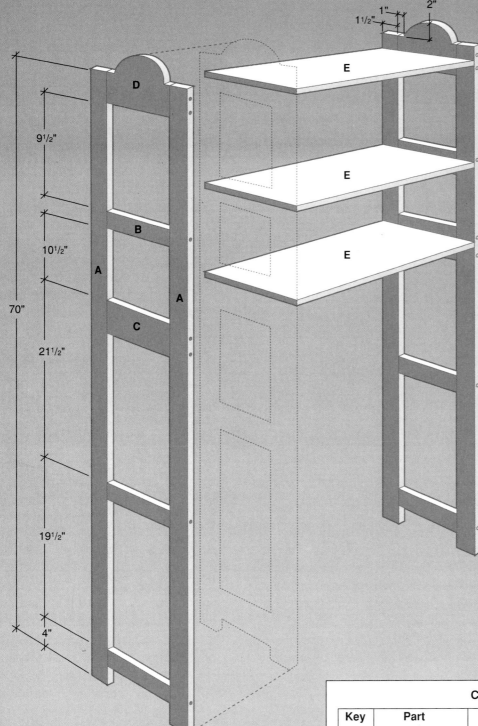

OVERALL SIZE:
72" HIGH
10" WIDE
23½" LONG

1½" 1" 2"

D

9½"

A

B

10½"

C

A

21½"

70"

19½"

4"

E

E

E

Cutting List

Key	Part	Dimension	Pcs.	Material
A	Post	¾ × 1½ × 70"	4	Pine
B	Stretcher	¾ × 1½ × 7"	6	Pine
C	Middle stretcher	¾ × 3½ × 7"	2	Pine
D	Cap stretcher	¾ × 5½ × 7"	2	Pine
E	Shelf	¾ × 9¼ × 22"	3	Pine

Materials: Wood glue, wood plugs, wood screws (#8 × 1½", #8 × 2½").

Note: Measurements reflect the actual size of dimensional lumber.

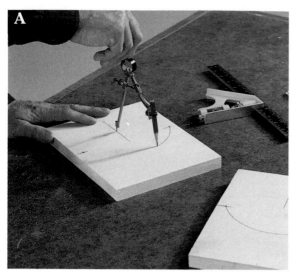

Using a compass, lay out a curved cutting line with a 2½" radius at the top of each cap stretcher.

Mark the stretcher positions, according to the detail diagram, on the posts using a combination square.

Directions: Overjohn

MAKE THE FRAME COMPONENTS. Start by cutting all of the frame components to size. Cut the posts (A) and the stretchers (B) to length from 1 × 2 pine. Cut the middle stretchers (C) to length from 1 × 4 pine and cut the cap stretchers (D) to length from 1 × 6 pine. Following the dimensions in the *Diagram*, page 55, use a compass to lay out a curved cutting line with a 2½" radius at the top of each cap stretcher **(photo A).** Cut out the curved contours with a jig saw.

ASSEMBLE THE FRAME. Lay the posts on edge on a flat worksurface and clamp them together. Following the *Diagram*, lay out the stretcher positions on the posts and, using a combination square, scribe reference lines across all of the posts **(photo B).** While the posts are still clamped together, drill pilot holes through the posts for the screws. Position the holes according to the Dia-

Drill pilot holes through the posts at the stretcher locations.

gram **(photo C).** Unclamp the posts, turn them over and drill counterbore holes for pine plugs. Now, lay the posts flat on the worksurface with the stretcher layout lines facing each other. Be sure to keep the bottoms of the posts at the same end to keep the stretcher positions lined up. Apply glue to the ends of the stretchers, then place the stretchers in their appropriate locations and fasten to the sides with #8 × 2½" wood screws. When both frames are assembled, insert

pine plugs into the counterbore holes using wood glue and a hammer. Sand the plugs so they are level with the wood surface. Using a router with a ⅜" piloted roundover bit, shape the edges and top end on each frame assembly, rounding over from both sides **(photo D).** Sand the frames with medium (100- or 120-grit) sandpaper to smooth out rough spots, then finish-sand with fine (150- or 180-grit) sandpaper.

TIP

Make sure that any overjohn storage unit you build or purchase doesn't restrict access to the tank and plumbing of your toilet. Measure your toilet to make sure that the overjohn allows at least 12" of clearance above the tank top, and 3" of free space at each side.

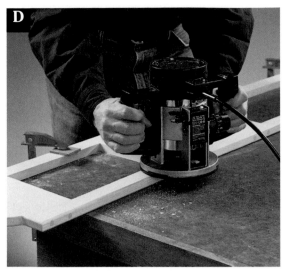

Round over the edges of the frame assembly using a router and ⅜" piloted roundover bit.

Use ¼"-thick wood spacers to create a recess for the shelves at the front of the overjohn.

BUILD & INSTALL THE SHELVES. Cut the shelves (E) to size from 1 × 10 pine. Using a router with a ⅜" piloted roundover bit, shape both edges of each shelf, rounding over from both sides. Lay the frame assemblies on a flat surface and lay out the inside of both frame assemblies for the shelf positions, according to the dimensions on the *Diagram* on page 55. Then, drill three pilot holes at each shelf location. Turn the frame assemblies over and drill counterbores at the pilot hole locations, for mushroom-style button plugs. With the shelf positions marked and drilled, apply glue to the ends of a shelf, place the frame assemblies on their back edge, and position the first shelf. It doesn't matter which shelf you install first. Place two ¼"-thick strips of wood between the worksurface and the shelf edge to provide the proper spacing for the front shelf recess. Clamp the shelf and frame assemblies together **(photo E),** being careful not to overtighten the clamps, which could squeeze the glue right

out of the joint. Screw the frame assemblies to the shelf with #8 × 1½" screws, then remove the clamps. Repeat the steps for the remaining shelves.

APPLY FINISHING TOUCHES. Scrape away any excess glue with a chisel or scraper, then finish-sand the entire overjohn unit with fine sandpaper. Apply the finish as desired. We painted the overjohn, then applied two coats of satin-gloss polyurethane over the paint for extra moisture protection. You may prefer to use stain and a water-resistant topcoat instead. When the finish is dry, fill all

open counterbore holes by gluing mushroom-style button plugs in place **(photo F).** Wipe up any excess glue with a wet cloth. If you want to fasten the overjohn to a wall, simply install a 1 × 4 wall cleat between the side assemblies under the bottom shelf and drill counterbored pilot holes. Finish the cleat to match the overjohn, and fasten it to the wall with screws driven through the cleat and into wall framing member locations. If there are no wall framing members in the area behind the toilet, use toggle bolts to attach the cleat.

Fill all open counterbore holes with mushroom-style button plugs. Apply glue and install with a hammer.

Plant Stand

Our plant stand is a great way to display your favorite potted foliage. Build it for a corner in your sunniest room.

PROJECT
POWER TOOLS

This plant stand is a perfect platform on which to set your favorite indoor plants. The simple lines and ceramic tile surfaces help to focus the attention on the plants themselves, rather than on their stand. Make no mistake, however, our plant stand is a sleek project that fits in with almost any environment or decor. Once you paint it, you can position it almost anywhere to showcase your plants. It's lightweight, so you will be able to move it easily from place to place, but it's strong enough to support heavy pots without fear of a shattering experience.

The leg assemblies provide a sturdy base, while ceramic tile inserts on the shelf and top give our plant stand some weight and stability. It's perfect for a corner nook in a sun room or a kitchen, and the tile pieces make spillover cleanup an easy task. What's more, the ceramic tile will not fall apart or rot with moisture and age, so you are sure to enjoy many years at home with this original and practical plant stand.

CONSTRUCTION MATERIALS

Quantity	Lumber
1	1 × 8" × 4' pine
2	1 × 3" × 10' pine
2	½ × ¾" × 8' pine stop
1	½ × 20 × 20" plywood

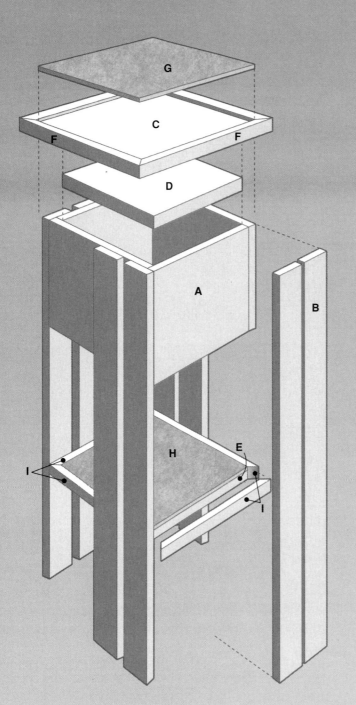

OVERALL SIZE:
30" HIGH
13" WIDE
13" LONG

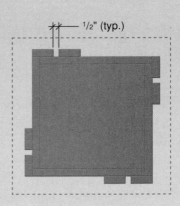

LEG LAYOUT DETAIL

¹/₂" (typ.)

Cutting List				
Key	Part	Dimension	Pcs.	Material
A	Box side	¾ × 7¼ × 8¼"	4	Pine
B	Leg	¾ × 2½ × 29½"	8	Pine
C	Top tile base	½ × 12 × 12"	1	Plywood
D	Box Top	¾ × 7¼ × 7¼"	1	Pine
E	Shelf	½ × 8 × 8"	1	Plywood

Cutting List				
Key	Part	Dimension	Pcs.	Material
F	Top frame	½ × ¾ × 13"	4	Molding
G	Top tile	12 × 12"	1	Ceramic
H	Shelf tile	8 × 8"	1	Ceramic
I	Shelf frame	½ × ¾ × 9"	4	Molding

Materials: Wood glue, tile adhesive, 2" wood screws, deck screws (1", 1¼"), 4d finish nails, ⅜" brads, finishing materials.

Note: Measurements reflect the actual size of dimensional lumber.

Assemble the box using simple butt joints.

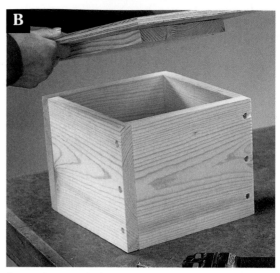
Insert the top tile base and box top into the upper box and fasten with screws.

Attach the leg pairs with glue and wood screws, obscuring the visible joints on the box.

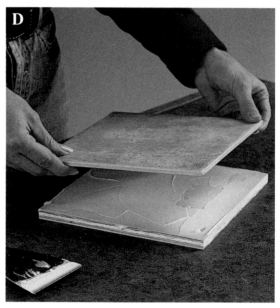
Attach the tile once the shelf is cut to exactly the same size as the upper box assembly.

Directions: Plant Stand

BUILD THE BOX. The box supports and frames a 12 × 12" piece of tile. Tile size varies slightly from piece to piece, so measure it before cutting the top tile base (C). Remember, there should be a ⅛"-wide expansion gap between the tile piece and the top frame. Start by cutting the box sides (A), top tile base (C) and box top (D) to size. Sand the parts with 150-grit sandpaper. The sides are fastened with simple butt joints. These joints ensure an equal length on each box side. When the plant stand is complete, the butt joints on the box are obscured by the legs (see Diagram, page 59). Use glue and #6 × 2" wood screws to fasten the sides together, forming a box (photo A). Make sure the edges are flush. Carefully center the box top on the bottom face of the top tile base. Fasten the pieces together by driving 1"-long deck screws through the top tile base into the box top. Place the top tile base and box top into the box

TIP

Ceramic tile is sold in both floor and wall styles. Floor tile is generally stronger and more scratch resistant.

(photo B). Drive counterbored deck screws through the box sides into the box top to secure the pieces to the sides. Fill all the screw holes with wood putty. Sand out rough edges with medium-grit (100 or 120) sandpaper, then finish-sand with fine-grit (150 or 180) sandpaper.

ATTACH THE LEGS. Each box side has a pair of legs fastened along one edge. Start by cutting the legs (B) to length. Fasten the legs to the box sides with counterbored wood screws. Make sure each outside leg is flush with the side edges **(photo C).** Maintain a ¼"-wide space between each half of the leg pair.

ATTACH THE SHELF. Measure your 8 × 8" piece of tile before cutting the shelf (E) to size. Use a power miter box to miter-cut the shelf frame (I) to size. Attach the shelf tile (H) to the shelf with tile adhesive **(photo D),** then fasten the shelf frame to the shelf with 4d finish nails. Make sure the bottom frame edges are flush with the bottom edge of the shelf. The lower edge of the shelf should be 10" from the legs' bottom edges. Attach the shelf to the legs by driving 4d finish nails through the legs into the frame **(photo E).** Set the nails, and fill the holes with putty.

ATTACH THE TOP TILE. Use a power miter box to miter-cut

the top frame (F) to size. Attach the top tile (G) to the top tile base with adhesive, and nail the top frame in place against the top tile base **(photo F),** keeping the bottom edges flush. Be very careful when using the hammer; a misplaced strike could shatter the tile. When driving the nails be sure they line up with the top tile base, not the tile.

APPLY THE FINISHING TOUCHES. Sand the plant stand smooth, making sure to break the sharp edges on the bottom of the legs. Prime and paint the plant stand as desired. Coat it with two coats of satin-gloss polyurethane finish to protect it from scratches and marks.

(above) Use a lightweight tack hammer and 4d finish nails to install the top frame around the tile and top tile base.

(left) Drive 4d finish nails through the legs into the shelf.

Video/CD Rack

*Store your compact discs or videotapes, and find them
at a glance, in this sharp storage rack.*

CONSTRUCTION MATERIALS

Quantity	Lumber
1	1 × 10" × 8' pine
2	1 × 6" × 8' pine
1	1 × 4" × 2' pine
1	1 × 1" × 1' pine
1	¼" × 1 × 1' hardboard or plywood

Store your ever-expanding compact disc or video-tape collection on this convenient rack. The angled shelves have plenty of room even for a large collection, and you'll find the video/CD rack so simple and easy to make that, if you need more shelf space down the road, you can build another one in just a few hours.

The shelves are attached at an angle to keep the discs and tapes in the rack. The angle is easily determined with a triangular tracing guide, which you can construct easily from hardboard and scrap lumber. For extra stability, wooden brackets keep your video/CD collection braced firmly while not in use.

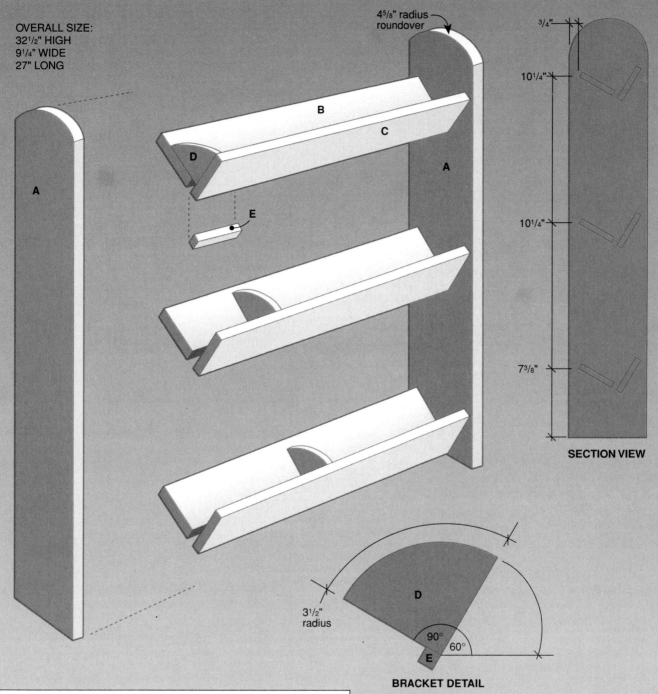

OVERALL SIZE:
32½" HIGH
9¼" WIDE
27" LONG

4⅝" radius roundover

¾"

10¼"

10¼"

7⅜"

SECTION VIEW

3½" radius

D

90° 60°

E

BRACKET DETAIL

Cutting List

Key	Part	Dimension	Pcs.	Material
A	Rack side	¾ × 9¼ × 32½"	2	Pine
B	Shelf back	¾ × 5½ × 25½"	3	Pine
C	Shelf front	¾ × 5½ × 25½"	3	Pine
D	Bracket	¾ × 3½ × 3½"	3	Pine
E	Slide	¾ × ¾ × 3½"	3	Pine

Materials: Wood glue, #6 × 2" wood screws, plugs, finishing materials.

Note: Measurements reflect the actual size of dimensional lumber.

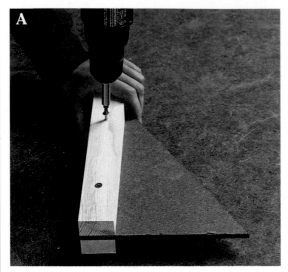

To lay out the shelf back and shelf front positions, make a guide with 1 × 2 pieces and hardboard.

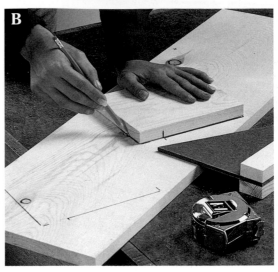

After you draw the guidelines for the back, mark the shelf position ¾" below the lowest back edge.

Directions:
Video/CD Rack

MAKE THE GUIDE. To position the shelves at the correct 60° angle, you need to draw accurate and precise guidelines along the rack sides. The easiest way to do this is to make a triangular guide to help you trace the lines. When you butt the guide against a rack side, simply trace a line along the angled edge. Use a 12 × 12 piece of square, flat hardboard or plywood to make this handy tool. Start by cutting a right triangle with one 12"-long leg, and one 7"-long leg. Cut along this line with a circular saw to make the triangular guide. Fasten two strips of 1 × 2 along both edges of the long side with wood screws to complete

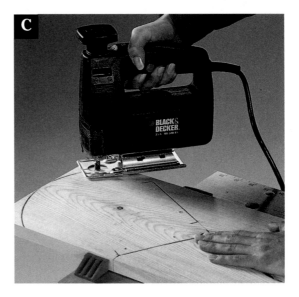

Use a jig saw to make the roundover cuts on the tops of the rack sides.

the tracing guide **(photo A).**

PREPARE THE SIDES. Before assembling the project, prepare to attach the shelf backs and shelf fronts to the rack sides. This involves some basic measuring and marking along the rack sides with a tape measure and the 60° triangular guide. Begin this step by cutting the rack sides (A) to size. You will use the triangular guide to lay out the position of the shelf

backs (B) and shelf fronts (C), but before drawing the guidelines you must measure and mark the height of the shelf back positions. Position the top rear corner of the shelf backs ¾" from the sides' back edges (see *Diagram* on page 63 for details on shelf back and shelf front). The top corners on the shelf backs should be spaced 10¼" away from each other at the following distances from the rack sides' bottom edges: 7⅜", 17⅞" and 27⅞". After mark-

TIP

Dimensional lumber is not the only option when building the video rack. If you don't mind rip-cutting the pieces, use MDF (medium density fiberboard). This composite material is inexpensive and reduces the risk of warping.

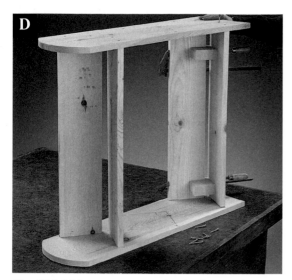

Use ¹³⁄₁₆"-thick spacers to maintain the gap between the shelf backs and shelf fronts.

Attach the brackets and slides, creating a stop for the discs or videotapes.

ing these points, use the triangular guide to draw the shelf back guidelines at these marks. Align the rear faces of the shelf backs flush with this guideline. Next, use a squared-up block of 6⁵⁄₁₆ × 5½" material, aligned carefully along the back guideline, to trace the shelf front positions **(photo B).** Like the shelf backs, the shelf fronts will be attached with their lower faces aligned with their guidelines. Maintain a ¹³⁄₁₆"-wide space between the shelf backs and shelf fronts. Finally, use a compass to draw a guideline with a 4⅝" radius along the side tops, and cut along the guidelines with a jig saw **(photo C).**

ATTACH THE SHELF FRONTS & SHELF BACKS. Start by cutting the shelf backs (B) and shelf fronts (C) to length. Drill ³⁄₁₆"-dia. pilot holes for #6 × 2" wood screws through the rack sides in position to fasten the shelf backs and shelf fronts. Glue the edges on the shelf backs, then fasten them between the rack sides with wood screws. Position the shelf fronts along the

guidelines, ¹³⁄₁₆" below the shelf backs. Trim some scrap 2 × 4 pieces to make ¹³⁄₁₆"-wide spacers to preserve the gap between the shelf fronts and shelf backs while you attach them to the rack sides **(photo D).** Apply glue, and attach the shelf fronts with wood screws driven through the rack sides into the shelf front edges.

BUILD THE BRACKETS & SLIDES. The brackets and slides keep your CD or video collection from falling over. If only a portion of the shelf is occupied, the brackets can be pushed against the videotapes or compact discs to hold the collection in place. The brackets and slides fit between the shelf fronts and shelf backs, inside the ¹³⁄₁₆"-wide gap that separates the two pieces. Begin by cutting the brackets (D) and slides (E) to size. Sand the brackets and slides to finished smoothness. Drill pilot holes through the slides into the brackets for wood screws. Apply glue to the

pieces and attach them with wood screws **(photo E).**

APPLY THE FINISHING TOUCHES. Fill all counterbored screw holes with plugs. Sand out rough edges with medium (150- or 120-grit) sandpaper, then finish-sand with fine-grit sandpaper. Finish the rack as desired. We primed the surfaces and used a high-gloss latex paint to complete the finish. Whether you're staining or painting, apply two thin coats of a satin-gloss polyurethane finish to protect your rack from scratches and marks.

TIP

Ensure a smooth finish by working in a well-ventilated, dust-free area. Airborne dust can ruin a painted finish. Avoid painting a project in an area where woodworking tools have recently been operated, and wipe off all sanded surfaces to completely remove dust.

Bookcase

This open-back bookcase combines straight, simple lines with a few graceful curves for an effect that is at home in any room.

PROJECT
POWER TOOLS

The spacious shelves and open-backed design of our bookcase give it an impressive style all its own without making it an over-whelming element in the room. The decorative arches on the sides and rails provide style without sacrificing strength or stability. The bookcase is built simply from one sheet of ply-wood. We used birch, but you can use oak or any other ply-wood you choose. The book-case is dressed up and finished off with the use of self-adhesive veneer tape which, when ap-plied to the plywood edges with a household iron, gives the bookcase the appearance of expensive solid hardwood instead of plywood.

The simple look and style will suit almost any room in your home, from bedroom to living room, and the project can easily support a full load of your favorite hardcover vol-umes. Our bookcase clearly proves that book storage doesn't have to be overly expensive, ornate or cumber-some. With a few quick and easy jig saw cuts, some edge tape and screws, you can build a long-lasting bookcase for your home that is as effective as it is attractive.

CONSTRUCTION MATERIALS

Quantity	Lumber
1	¾" × 4 × 8' birch plywood

OVERALL SIZE:
58" HIGH
12" WIDE
28" LONG

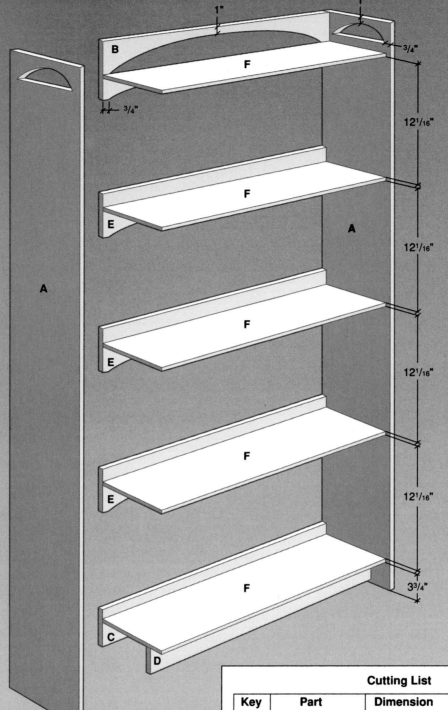

1"

1"

B

¾"

F

12¹/₁₆"

¾"

F

A

E

12¹/₁₆"

A

F

E

12¹/₁₆"

F

E

12¹/₁₆"

F

3¾"

C

D

Cutting List

Key	Part	Dimension	Pcs.	Material
A	Side	¾ × 12 × 58"	2	Plywood
B	Top rail	¾ × 6¼ × 26½"	1	Plywood
C	Bottom rail	¾ × 4½ × 26½"	1	Plywood
D	Front rail	¾ × 2¾ × 26½"	1	Plywood
E	Mid rail	¾ × 3¾ × 26½"	3	Plywood
F	Shelf	¾ × 11 × 26½"	5	Plywood

Materials: Wood glue, #8 × 2" wood screws, birch plugs, finishing materials.

Note: Measurements reflect the actual size of dimensional lumber.

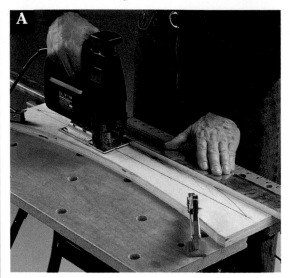

Cut the arch cutout in the top rail using a jig saw and a straightedge guide.

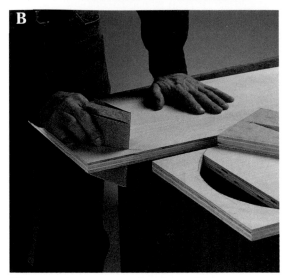

Wrap sandpaper around a piece of tin to create a sanding block that reaches into the cutout corners.

Directions: Bookcase

CUT THE PARTS. Begin by cutting the top rail (B), bottom rail (C), front rail (D) and mid rails (E) to size using a circular saw and straightedge. Cut the sides (A) to size from plywood material. Lay out the arches on the sides, three middle rails and the top rail. The arches are all centered on the rails, with the apex 1½" above the bottom edge. An easy way to draw the arches is to use a thin, flexible piece of metal, plastic or wood as a template, or tracing guide. Measure and mark points ¾" from each side edge. Tack a casing nail into the center of the rails, 1½" above the bottom edge. Also tack casing nails lightly into the marks at each end to hold the strip in place as you trace along it to draw the arch. Hook the flexible guide over the center nail, then flex each end to the marked points. Trace the arches, and then remove the nails. Cut along the guidelines with a jig saw to make the arches. Unlike the other rails, the top rail also has an arch cutout on the top. The top arch starts 3¼" from the top edge and extends upward to 1" from the top edge. Drill a pilot hole for the saw blade, then cut the arch cutout with a jig saw. Make the arch cutouts in the sides to match those in the top rail, using the same methods to draw the arches. Use a straightedge guide to cut the straight portion of the arches on the top rail and sides **(photo A).** A straightedge guide will ensure accurate, straight cuts once the arches have been cut. Sand the parts to 150-grit smoothness. Use a thin piece of metal or plastic backing to reach the corners of the arches when you sand the edges **(photo B).**

ATTACH THE VENEER STRIPS. We used adhesive-backed birch wood edge tape veneer along the visible edges on the bookcase. Apply the edge tape to the top edges of the top rail,

Use a heat gun to soften the adhesive on the veneer tape, then apply the tape to the inside edges of the cutout using a putty knife.

TIP

Veneer tape is often available in different types of wood species. Be sure to match the wood tape to the type of plywood you're using.

D

Use bar clamps to keep the top rail and shelf in place when you drive the screws. Keep the back and top edges flush with the sides.

E

Plug all screw holes prior to finishing. You can make the plugs or buy them at hardware or woodworkers' stores.

TIP

Although you can buy veneer edge trimmers in hardware stores, a block plane may work just as well. If you use a plane to trim the edges, however, remember to trim with the grain to avoid damaging the wood.

mid rails and sides with a common household iron. Also apply veneer tape on the arches and to the front edges of the sides. Apply veneer tape to the top rail arches and side arches by softening the veneer tape with a heat gun, and then use a putty knife to fit the tape into the arch corners **(photo C).** Cut the shelves (F) to size from plywood using a circular saw and straightedge, and apply veneer tape to the front edges of the shelves. When the tape is fully applied and cooled, trim and sand it to finished smoothness.

BUILD THE SHELF ASSEMBLIES. Begin this step by fastening the rails to the shelves with glue and wood screws. The top of the shelves should be ¾" from the top edge of the mid rails, with 3" separating the top shelf and the top edge of the top rail. The top edge of the bottom shelf is 1" from the top edge of the bottom rail.

ATTACH THE SHELVES. Use #8 × 2" counterbored wood screws to fasten the top rail and shelf to the sides **(photo D),** making sure the top and back edges of the rail are flush with the side top and edges (see *Diagram*, page 67). When properly assembled, the front edges of the shelves should be positioned ¼" from the sides' front edges. Next, attach the bottom shelf, front rail and bottom rail to the sides. Once again, keep the back edges flush, and position both rails so that their bottom edges are ¼" above the bottom side edges. This gap between the rails and the floor allows the bookcase to adapt slightly to an irregularity or curve in the floor, increasing its stability. Set the front rail ¼" back from the front side edges. To make sure the project is square, measure diagonally from corner to corner. To use bar clamps to draw the frame to square, position a bar clamp diagonally across the bookcase, and adjust it until the frame is pulled into square. Attach the remaining shelves and rails.

APPLY THE FINISHING TOUCHES. Fill all the screw holes by applying glue to the wood plugs and tapping them in with a mallet **(photo E).** Finish-sand the project with fine (150- or 180-grit) sandpaper, and finish it as desired. We applied two light coats of polyurethane.

Serving Trays

Serve your guests with our stylishly stackable serving trays—perfect for carrying drinks, snacks or plates.

CONSTRUCTION MATERIALS

Quantity	Lumber
1	1 × 3" × 8' oak
1	¾ × 14½ × 22½" oak plywood

Our serving tray is great for stylish entertaining at home. Serve your guests everything from drinks to dinner with a tray you made yourself. The graceful arches along the sides and ends lend our tray a refined appearance while giving you strong, built-in handles.

We used 1 × 3 oak for the sides and ends, and oak plywood for the bottom. Veneer edge tape along the visible tray bottom edges gives our tray the appearance of solid hardwood. Oak has always been prized for its strength, economy and versatility, and it doesn't disappoint on our tray. Build several of these beauties—they're designed to be stacked. Whether you're serving drinks at a party or snacks at an office meeting, our serving tray is dependable and beautiful.

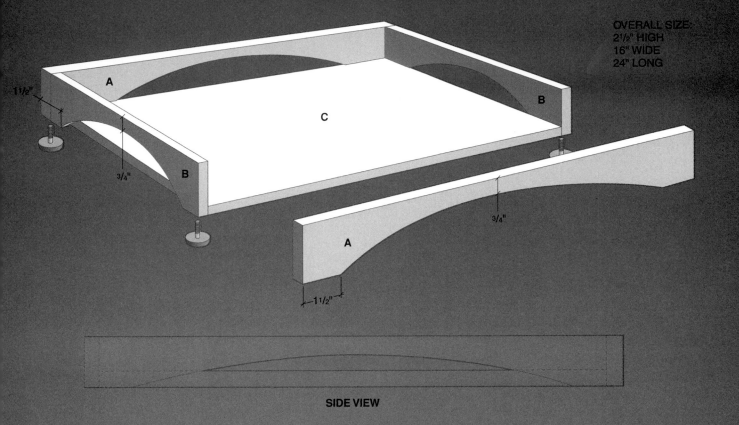

OVERALL SIZE:
2½" HIGH
16" WIDE
24" LONG

1½"

3/4"

B

A

C

B

A

3/4"

1½"

SIDE VIEW

Cutting List (one tray)				
Key	**Part**	**Dimension**	**Pcs.**	**Material**
A	Frame side	¾ × 2½ × 24"	2	Oak
B	Frame end	¾ × 2½ × 14½"	2	Oak
C	Tray bottom	¾ × 14½ × 22½"	1	Plywood

Materials: Wood glue, #6 × 1¼" wood screws, rubber feet, veneer edge tape, finishing materials.

Note: Measurements reflect the actual size of dimensional lumber.

Directions:
Serving Trays

MAKE THE FRAME SIDES & ENDS. Start by cutting the frame sides (A) and ends (B) to size from 1 × 3 oak. To mark the cutting lines for the arcs, draw starting points 1½" in from the end of each frame side edge, and ¾" in from each frame end edge. Mark a center point 1¾" up from the bottom edges on the sides and ends. Tack a casing nail into all the marks. Slip a thin strip of metal or plastic between the casing nails so the strip bows out to create a smooth arc. Trace the arc onto a frame side and frame end **(photo A),** then cut along the lines with a jig saw. Smooth the arcs with a drum sander and repeat the process with the other pieces. You can also use a piece with a finished arc as a template for marking and cutting the unfinished frame side and frame end.

ATTACH THE FRAME SIDES & ENDS. To construct the serving tray frame you must attach the frame ends between the frame sides. Make sure the outside faces of the frame ends are flush with the frame side ends. Fasten the frame sides to the ends with glue and evenly spaced, countersunk #6 × 1¼" wood screws **(photo B).** To prevent splitting, do not position the pilot holes within ⅜" from the top and bottom edges.

TIP

When you apply veneer edge tape, press a clean block of scrap wood against the strip as you go. This serves to flatten the tape and helps it cool for a strong adhesive bond.

Trace the arc on the frame side and frame end. Remove the metal strip and cut the arc with a jig saw.

Drive wood screws through the frame sides into the frame ends.

Fill the counterbored screw holes with glued plugs, and let the frame dry.

MAKE THE TRAY BOTTOM. The tray bottom is made from a piece of ¾"-thick oak plywood. To give the serving tray a finished appearance, you will need to apply veneer edge tape to the bottom edges before attaching the ends and sides. Veneer edge tape is available at any building center. Start by cutting the tray bottom (C) to size. Apply the edge tape to the tray bottom's side edges, making sure to avoid any visible

Drive wood screws through the frame sides and into the edges of the tray bottom.

as desired. We chose to stain the tray for a rich, dark-toned appearance. To protect the tray from spillage, consider applying a good, water-resistant top coat. When the finish is dry, attach rubber bumpers on the plywood base, just inside the oak frame edges. Rubber bumpers prevent tabletop scratches, and they act as registration pins if you build more than one tray and decide to stack them. Rubber bumpers are available at any building center. Build several serving trays; they look great when stacked **(photo D).**

seams in the tape. Cut the tape to length, and apply it with a household iron. After you have attached the veneer tape, trim and sand it to finished smoothness (for more information on applying and trimming edge tape, see *Bookcase*, page 69).

ATTACH THE BOTTOM. Fit the tray bottom between the frame sides and ends, making sure the bottom edges are resting flat on your worksurface. Measure and mark centerpoints 1" from each frame side edge, and fasten the tray bottom to the frame sides by driving counterbored #6 × 1¼" wood screws through these centerpoints into the bottom edges

(photo C). To prevent splitting, do not position the pilot holes within ⅜" from the top and bottom edges.

APPLY THE FINISHING TOUCHES. To make sure all the surfaces are smooth and consistent, fill any wood defects with wood filler. Sand the serving tray to finished smoothness, and soften any sharp edges or corners on the tray frame. Plug any exposed counterbored screw holes. Finish the serving tray

The rubber bumpers are spaced to fit inside the tray frame below when stacked.

Magazine Rack

Place our magazine rack by a favorite chair, desk or sofa to keep all your periodicals within arm's reach.

CONSTRUCTION MATERIALS

Quantity	Lumber
1	1 × 6" × 10' pine
1	1 × 4" × 6' pine
3	1 × 2" × 10' pine
1	¾" × 4 × 4' birch plywood

Our magazine rack is an indispensible piece of furniture next to a comfortable easy chair or bed, offering plenty of room to store those back issues that always seem to clutter up your home. With three shelves and a top surface for magazines and books, you shouldn't have a problem keeping your reading material neat and orderly. Our magazine rack is a great piece of furniture for any room in your home, and its simple lines are suitable for a contemporary or traditional setting. With the exception of the feet, which are easily cut following the diagram specifications on page 75, all the parts on our magazine rack can be made with straight cuts, ensuring a quick and easy project.

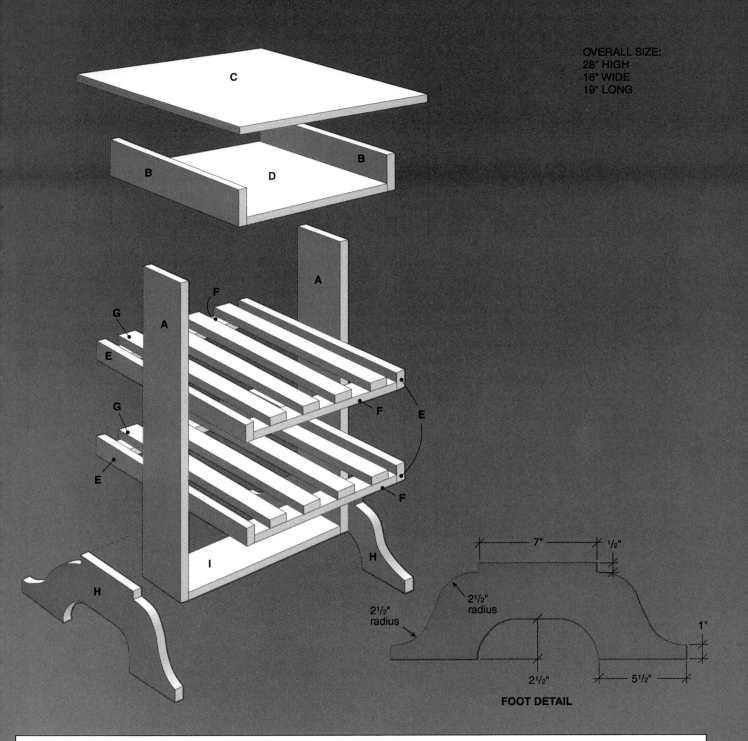

OVERALL SIZE:
28" HIGH
18" WIDE
19" LONG

FOOT DETAIL

7"   1/2"

2½"
radius

2½"
radius

2½"   5½"   1"

	Cutting List			
Key	**Part**	**Dimension**	**Pcs.**	**Material**
A	Leg	¾ × 5½ × 24½"	2	Pine
B	Side	¾ × 3½ × 16½"	2	Pine
C	Top	¾ × 18 × 19"	1	Plywood
D	Bottom	¾ × 14½ × 16½"	1	Plywood
E	Rail	¾ × 1½ × 18"	4	Pine

	Cutting List			
Key	**Part**	**Dimension**	**Pcs.**	**Material**
F	Stretcher	¾ × 1½ × 14½"	4	Pine
G	Slat	¾ × 1½ × 18"	8	Pine
H	Foot	¾ × 5½ × 16½"	2	Pine·
I	Spreader	¾ × 5½ × 16"	1	Pine

Materials: Wood glue, wood screws (#6 × 1¼, #6 × 1½, #6 × 2"), 1½" angle brackets, finishing materials.

Note: Measurements reflect the actual size of dimensional lumber.

Center the sides on the inside faces of the legs, and attach them with glue and deck screws.

Lay out their positions, then fasten the top to the sides with angle brackets.

Directions: Magazine Rack

ATTACH THE SIDES & LEGS. Attach a side (A) to the inside face of each leg (B). Start by cutting the legs and sides to size. Finish-sand the pieces with 150-grit sandpaper. Center the sides onto the legs, making sure the top edges are flush **(photo A).** Check to make sure the sides and legs are square, then fasten the pieces together with glue and countersunk #6 × 1¼" wood screws, driven through the sides into the legs.

BUILD THE TOP ASSEMBLY. Attach the magazine rack top and storage shelf to the sides. Cut the bottom (C) and top (D) to size from ¾"-thick birch plywood. Apply ¾"-wide birch veneer tape to the plywood edges, using a heat gun to activate the adhesive. Sand any rough surfaces until they are smooth. Use the bottom as a spacing guide to center the sides and legs against the top. Measure and mark the positions of the bottom and legs. Align the top, and fasten it to the sides with screws and

Fasten the stretchers to the rails to make the shelves.

1½ × 1½" angle brackets **(photo B).** These brackets allow you to attach the pieces without driving screws through the top surface. Once you have attached the top, fasten the bottom between the sides with glue and counterbored #6 × 2" wood screws driven through the sides. Make sure the bottom edges are flush. Plug the screw holes, and sand until the surfaces are completely smooth.

BUILD THE SHELVES. Our magazine rack contains two leg shelves for convenient storage of reading material. These shelves are easy-to-build frames that go together quickly with glue and wood screws. Begin by cutting the rails (E), stretchers (F) and slats (G) to length. Sand them smooth and then fasten the stretchers between the rails with glue and wood screws **(photo C).** Check to make sure the bottom edges are flush and the pieces are square. Cover the screw holes with glued plugs and sand the surfaces smooth. With the basic shelf frames now assembled, attach the slats to complete the assemblies (see *Diagram*, page 75). Place the slats over the stretchers, spaced evenly. Mark their locations, and remove them **(photo D).** Drill centered pilot holes through the stretchers at each slat location, and attach the slats with #6 × 1¼" wood screws, driven through the stretchers into the slats. Mark the shelf locations on the legs. Until you're ready to apply the finish, you should temporarily fasten the shelf assemblies between the legs with counterbored wood screws driven through the the legs. Use spacer blocks to hold the shelves in place as you fasten them to the legs **(photo E).**

ATTACH THE FEET & SPREADER. The feet (H) and spreader (I) provide structural stability and strength to the entire magazine rack. Cut the feet and spreader to size. The diagram on page 75 provides detailed information on how to make our pattern. Draw the cutlines and cut the feet to shape with a jig saw **(photo F).** Attach the spreader flush against the bottom edges of the legs with glue and wood screws. Glue the pieces and drive counterbored wood screws through the legs to attach the feet to the outside of the legs. The bottom edge of the leg should be 2¾" above the bottom edges of the feet. Plug the screw holes and sand the surfaces.

APPLY THE FINISHING TOUCHES. For a contrasted finish like the one shown here, remove the screws holding the shelves to the legs. Plug all exposed screw holes, and touch up the sur-

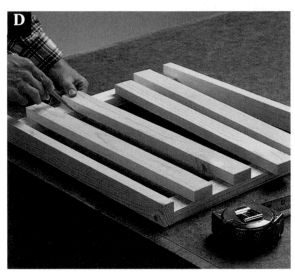

Mark the slat positions on the stretchers, and drill pilot holes for #6 × 1¼" wood screws.

faces as needed. Apply a clear finish to the shelves. Paint the legs and upper assembly as desired. Finally, add rubber pads or bumpers on the feet bottoms.

Use spacers to support the shelves as you attach them to the legs.

Use the first foot as a template for marking the second. Cut out with a jig saw.

Nightstand

A back rail adds style to our nightstand and keeps you from knocking bedside items to the floor. Put our night-stand at your bedside for a classic touch of bedroom beauty.

Our nightstand is a classic piece of furniture that will never go out of fashion. Ours is a simple nightstand with a solid, traditional look. The arched back rail and base pieces add some style and grace to the project, while the handy drawer gives you a great place to store some bedside items.

Assembling this little beauty is an easy process. You first build the box frame. The box frame is the central section of the nightstand, and decorative items are built around it. The box frame is made by attaching the sides, back and shelves. It is then topped off with a decorative back rail and wings. These pieces do more than dress up the nightstand—they reduce the risk of knocking over that insistent alarm clock when you lurch over to shut it off in the morning.

Once the top sections are complete, you then make the arched base and attach the two sections. The drawer comes next, and we avoided expen-sive metal track glides. Instead, we used friction reducing plastic bumpers and tack-on glides for easy installation and convenience.

Our nightstand is built from edge-glued "ponderosa" pine panels that you can purchase at most building centers. These panels come in varying widths, so be aware that the dimensions shown here are for ¾"-thick boards.

CONSTRUCTION MATERIALS

Quantity	Lumber
2	1 × 16" × 8' edge-glued pine
1	1 × 4" × 4' pine

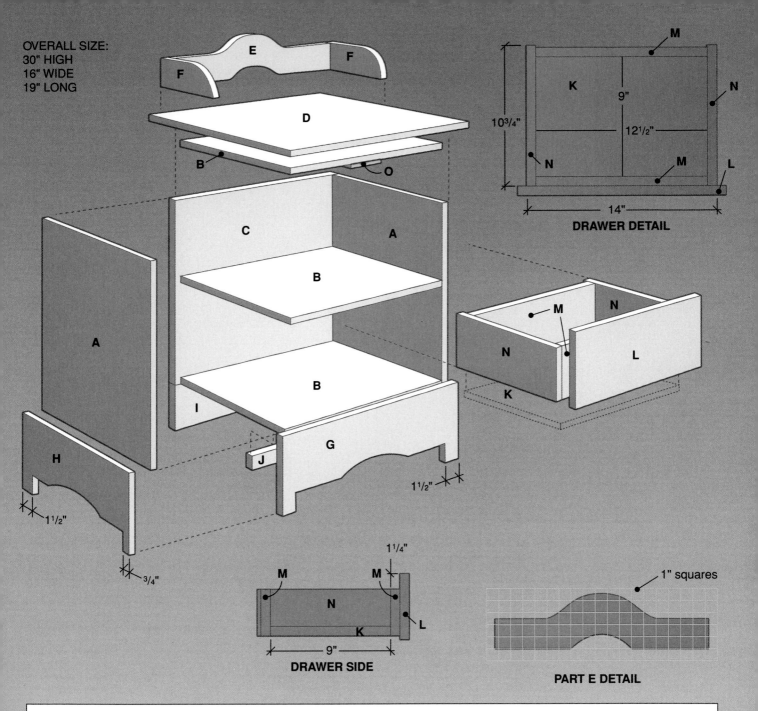

OVERALL SIZE:
30" HIGH
16" WIDE
19" LONG

DRAWER DETAIL

10³/₄"
9"
12¹/₂"
14"

DRAWER SIDE
1¹/₄"
9"

1¹/₂"
1¹/₂"
3/4"

PART E DETAIL
1" squares

Cutting List				
Key	**Part**	**Dimension**	**Pcs.**	**Material**
A	Side	¾ × 13¼ × 17"	2	Pine
B	Shelf	¾ × 13¼ × 14½"	3	Pine
C	Back	¾ × 16 × 17"	1	Pine
D	Top	¾ × 16 × 19"	1	Pine
E	Back rail	¾ × 4½ × 17½"	1	Pine
F	Wing	¾ × 2½ × 5½"	2	Pine
G	Base front	¾ × 8 × 17½"	1	Pine
H	Base side	¾ × 8 × 14"	2	Pine

Cutting List				
Key	**Part**	**Dimension**	**Pcs.**	**Material**
I	Base back	¾ × 4 × 16"	1	Pine
J	Base cleat	¾ × 2 × 16"	1	Pine
K	Drawer bottom	¾ × 9 × 12½"	1	Pine
L	Drawer front	¾ × 5 × 15¾"	1	Pine
M	Drawer end	¾ × 3½ × 12½"	2	Pine
N	Drawer side	¾ × 3½ × 10¾"	2	Pine
O	Stop cleat	¾ × 1½ × 3"	1	Pine

Materials: Glue, wood screws (1¼, 1½, 2"), ¾"-dia. wooden knobs, 4d finish nails, plastic drawer stop, tack-on drawer glides, stem bumpers, finishing materials.

Note: Measurements reflect the actual size of dimensional lumber.

Attach the back to one side, then check for square.

Trace the pattern, then cut the back rail to shape with a jig saw.

Directions: Nightstand

ATTACH THE SHELVES & SIDES. Start by cutting the sides (A) and shelves (B) to size. Sand the pieces to finished smoothness. Use glue and #6 × 2" countersunk wood screws to attach the top and bottom shelves flush with the top and bottom side edges. You will attach the middle shelf later in the assembly process. Make sure the screws are centered and the front and back shelf edges are flush with the side edges.

ATTACH THE BACK. Start by cutting the back to size. Sand the back to finished smoothness, then attach it to one side with glue and countersunk wood screws **(photo A).** Check the outside of the frame to be sure the sides are square with the shelves. If they are not square, you must apply pressure to one side to draw the pieces square. This can be done by hand or by attaching a bar clamp diagonally from one side to the other. When the

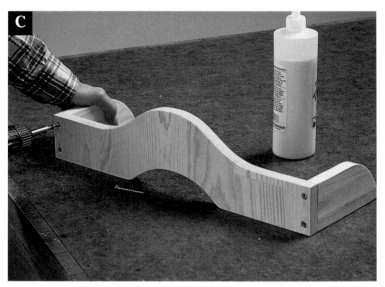

Fasten the wings to the back rail with glue and deck screws.

pieces are square, clamp them and continue to attach the back to the sides and shelves.

MAKE & ATTACH THE TOP ASSEMBLY. The top assembly consists of four pieces: the top (D), back rail (E) and wings (F). Start by cutting them to size. Transfer the grid on page 79 to a piece of stiff cardboard, making a cutting template for the back rail (see *Tip*, page 81). Trace the shape onto the back rail, and use a jig saw to cut it to finished shape **(photo B).**

Position the template you made for the back rail along the inside faces of the wing. Trace along the template arc to make a partial arc at the wing ends. Cut a smooth curve on the end of each wing. Make sure the curves on the wings are identical. Sand all the pieces to finished smoothness. Drill pilot holes in the back rail to attach the wings. The pilot holes should be positioned ⅜"

Draw the guidelines on the top, then drill the pilot holes and attach the back rail and wings.

TIP

When transferring a grid diagram, consider these options. You can enlarge the grid diagram on a copier, and trace it onto a piece of cardboard to form a tracing template. Or, you can grid your stock with 1" squares and draw the pattern directly onto the workpiece. Both options are easy and convenient.

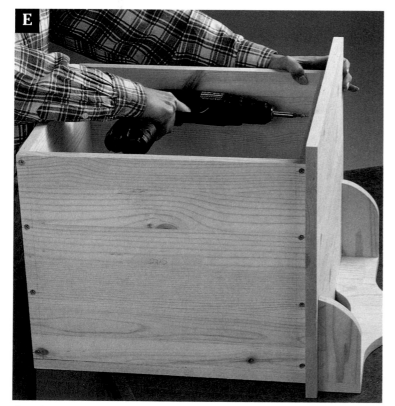

Attach the top assembly to the top shelf with glue and screws.

Finally, attach the back rail and wings to the top with wood screws and glue **(photo D).** Center the top assembly over the top shelf, with the back edges flush. Attach the top assembly by driving countersunk #6 × 1¼" wood screws through the top shelf into the top assembly **(photo E).**

ATTACH THE MIDDLE SHELF. Start by measuring and marking guidelines on the inside edges of the sides for the remaining shelf. Position the top of the middle shelf 5½" down from the tops of the sides. Fasten the shelf between the sides with screws and glue. This shelf will support the drawer, so make sure it is square to the sides. With the completion of this step, the nightstand box frame is complete.

MAKE THE BASE. Start by cutting the base front (G), base sides (H), base back (I) and base cleat (J) to size. Position the template made for the back rail onto the base front and base sides so that the top of the arc is 3" from the top of each piece. Center the template on the base front, but position it ¾" from the front edges on the sides (see *Diagram*, page 79).

from the outside edges. Fasten the wings to the back rail with glue and countersunk #6 × 1½" wood screws **(photo C).** Drill pilot holes along the back edge to attach the back rail. Position the back rail and wings onto the top with the back rail flush

with the top's back edge. Draw a 5½"-long line marking the outside edges of the wings. Make sure the distance between the wings' outside edges and the top edge is ¾". Drill pilot holes ⅜" inside each line on the top to attach each wing. Sand the top to finished smoothness.

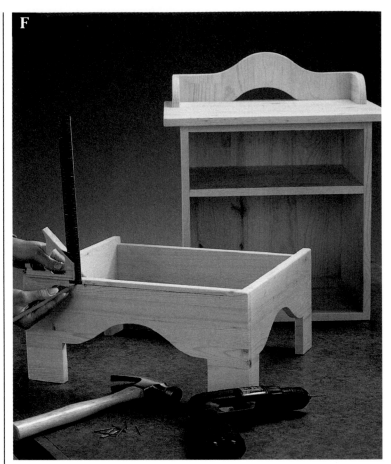

Use a combination square to mark the finish nail position on the base front.

Trace the arcs, and cut the designs from the pieces with a jig saw. Sand the parts smooth. Use glue and 4d finish nails to fasten the base front to the base sides. Fasten the base back between the base sides so that its top edge is ½" below the top edges of the base sides. Finally, attach the base cleat to the inside of the base front with #6 × 1¼" wood screws. Leave a ½" space between the top edge

of the cleat and the top edge of the base. Once you have attached the cleat, the base is complete.

ATTACH THE FRAME & BASE. Start by marking a guideline ¼" below the top edge of the base front and base sides **(photo F)**. Use a combination square to make it easy to scribe an accurate guideline. Carefully position the nightstand box frame into the base so that it rests on the base back and base cleat. Fasten the box frame to the base by driving finish nails along the guidelines through the base front and base sides, and into the edges of the bottom shelf.

BUILD THE DRAWER. Cut the drawer bottom (K), drawer front (L), drawer ends (M), and drawer sides (N). Measure and mark a line along the inside face of each drawer side, ¼" from the back edge, to mark the position of the rear drawer end. Drill pilot holes along the drawer ends, ⅜" above the bottom edges, and attach the drawer ends to the drawer bottom with counterbored wood screws and glue. Align the drawer sides so their front edges are flush with the front faces of the ends. Drill pilot holes through the sides, and fasten the sides to the bottom and ends with #6 × 1½" wood screws and glue **(photo G)**. Sand the drawer and drawer front to smooth the edges and prepare the surfaces for finish application.

ATTACH THE DRAWER FRONT. To align the drawer front with the drawer, you must measure and mark three lines. Mark a line along the inside face of the drawer front ¼" above the bottom edge. Mark another line down the center of the drawer front. Finally, mark a centerline on the top edge of the front drawer end. Fasten the drawer end to the drawer front so the bottom of the front is on the ¼" line, and the center marks are in line. Use countersunk #6 × 1¼" wood screws driven through the drawer end into the drawer front **(photo H)**.

INSTALL THE STOP CLEAT. When used in conjunction with a store-bought drawer stop, the stop cleat will prevent the drawer from falling out of the nightstand if you pull too hard. Start by cutting the stop cleat

(O) to size. Center the stop cleat beneath the top shelf, and attach it with glue and screws. The front edge of the stop cleat should be ¾" behind the front of the top shelf.

INSTALL THE HARDWARE. You have a number of options in making the drawer a functioning element of the nightstand. For instance, you can use metal glides that attach permanently to the drawer and frame. We used inexpensive plastic glides and stem bumpers. The Teflon®-coated glides have metal points and are installed like thumbtacks for easy application. Glue and insert the stem bumpers into drilled holes on the drawer bottom. You can buy these glides and bumpers at any building center. Always follow manufacturer's directions when installing the hardware, no matter what type you use. Start by fastening the wooden knobs to the drawer front. Be sure to space the wooden knobs evenly. Attach the glides. Finally, drill a ³⁄₁₆"-dia. hole on the rear drawer end for the drawer stop. A drawer stop is a small piece of plastic with a long stem that contacts the stop cleat when the drawer is opened, preventing it from sliding all the way out. Make the hole ½" below the drawer end's top edge. Glue and insert the drawer stop. Insert the drawer. With the drawer open slightly, reach in and turn the drawer stop until it is in position to touch the stop cleat.

APPLY FINISHING TOUCHES. Fill all the screw holes, and sand all the surfaces until they are completely smooth. Paint the nightstand inside and out, including the drawer, and apply a polyurethane topcoat to protect the painted finish.

TIP

Edge-glued pine paneling, sometimes known as "ponderosa paneling," is a fairly new product. Generally sold in 10-20" widths at building centers, these panels are often encased in plastic wrap and displayed with the shelving products.

(above) Fasten the drawer sides to the drawer ends and drawer bottom with glue and wood screws.

(left) Align the drawer front and attach the pieces by driving wood screws through the drawer end.

Mug Rack

Your everyday coffee mugs become decorative kitchen items when displayed on this original mug rack.

A mug rack gives you a great way to combine storage and decoration. Just put your mugs in this simple, convenient frame to display them on your kitchen countertop or hang them on a wall. The mugs will always be there when you need them, and instead of taking up valuable shelf space, they will become decorative kitchen items for all to see. Colorful mug designs look great against the beaded siding board backing on the rack. Paint the project to match your kitchen, or cover it with a clear finish to preserve the natural look of the wood. You can hang your mugs on Shaker pegs, which are easy to install with some glue and a portable drill. Fit the bottom and back of the mug rack with rubber bumpers for increased stability. With a minimum of work or cost, our mug rack will give you a decorative home accent you can be proud of.

CONSTRUCTION MATERIALS

Quantity	Lumber
1	1 × 4" × 10' pine
1	1 × 8" × 8' beaded siding board

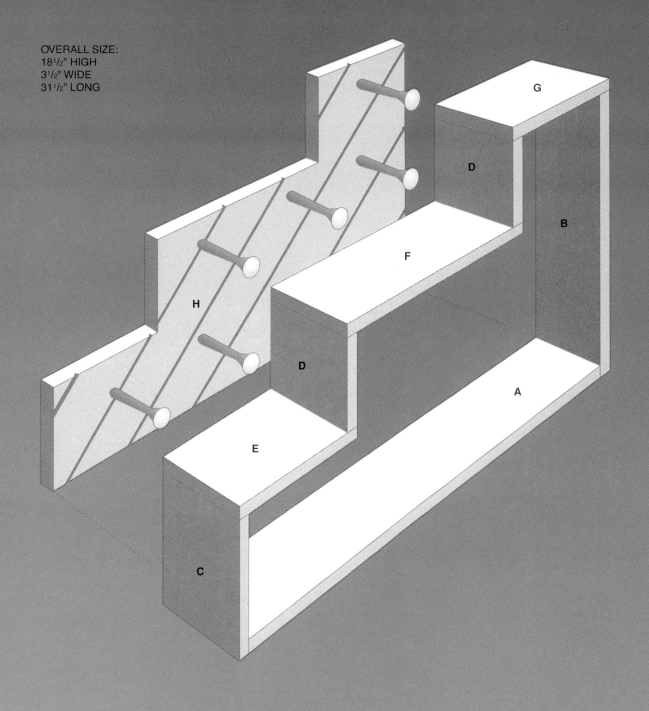

OVERALL SIZE:
18½" HIGH
3½" WIDE
31½" LONG

	Cutting List			
Key	**Part**	**Dimension**	**Pcs.**	**Material**
A	Frame bottom	¾ × 3½ × 29½"	1	Pine
B	Tall end	¾ × 3½ × 17¾"	1	Pine
C	Short end	¾ × 3½ × 9¾"	1	Pine
D	Divider	¾ × 3½ × 3¼"	2	Pine

	Cutting List			
Key	**Part**	**Dimension**	**Pcs.**	**Material**
E	Lower shelf	¾ × 3½ × 7½"	1	Pine
F	Middle shelf	1½ × 3½ × 15"	1	Pine
G	Top shelf	¾ × 3½ × 10½"	1	Pine
H	Backing	18½ × 31½"*	1	Siding

Materials: Wood glue, 4d finish nails, Shaker pegs (8), rubber feet (4), finishing materials.

Note: Measurements reflect the actual size of dimensional lumber.

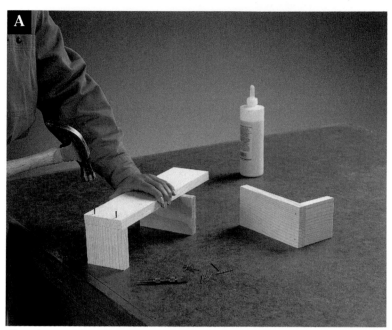

Use glue and finish nails to attach the dividers to the tops of the lower and middle shelves.

Fasten the top shelf to the middle shelf divider.

Directions: Mug Rack

ASSEMBLE THE FRAME. The mug rack frame is assembled completely with glue and finish nails. After you drive the finish nails into the wood, use a nail set to set the head below the wood surface. Remember to fill all the nail holes with wood putty. Start by cutting the frame bottom (A), tall end (B), short end (C), lower shelf (E) middle shelf (F), top shelf (G) and dividers (D) to size from 1 × 4 pine. Sand out any rough edges with medium (100- or 120-grit) sandpaper, then finish-sand with fine (150- or 180-grit) sandpaper. Fasten the ends to the bottom with glue and 4d finish nails, driven through the ends into the frame bottom edges. Make sure the

edges are flush. Next, attach the dividers to the tops of the lower and middle shelves with glue and finish nails **(photo A).** The end of each shelf should be flush with the end of each divider. Use support blocks to help you keep the pieces stationary on the worksurface. Once the dividers are attached, fasten the middle shelf to the top of the lower shelf divider. Make sure the divider edges and middle shelf edges are flush. Fasten the top shelf to the

> **TIP**
>
> *Siding is available in many different patterns such as tongue-and-groove, shiplap, or channel groove. Each pattern has a different joint pattern and appearance. These siding styles all cut easily with a circular saw or jig saw, but be careful of kick back, which can cause the material to jump off the table with dangerous force.*

middle shelf divider, once again keeping the edges flush **(photo B).** Finally, use glue and finish nails to fasten the shelves flush with the tall and

short ends to complete the mug rack frame.

BUILD & ATTACH THE BACKING. The backing (H) fits into the frame and holds the Shaker pegs. Make the backing from pieces of your favorite beaded siding. Join the pieces together as necessary to create an 18½ × 31½" panel that is treated as a single workpiece. Cut the backing, and place the mug rack frame on the pieces so their grooves run diagonally at about a 60° angle. The space inside the frame should be completely filled with the backing. Trace the cutting lines onto the back panel, following the inside of the frames **(photo C).** Glue the backing pieces together and let them dry. Next, turn the backing over, face-down. Turn the frame face-down on top of the backing,

Mark beaded siding positions for realignment.

Fasten the backing into the frame with finish nails, then set the nail holes.

and trace the inside of the frame. Remove the frame, then use a straightedge or square to retrace or straighten the lines. Cut the backing to shape with a straightedge guide and a jig saw. Test-fit the backing into the mug rack frame. If needed, trim it to fit the frame, and fasten the backing with 4d finish nails **(photo D),** driven through the frame and into the edges of the backing panel. Set and fill all the exposed nail holes.

ATTACH THE MUG PEGS. The main section of the project is now complete. For the final construction steps, you need to attach the mug pegs. The peg locations must be measured and marked carefully before any drilling is done. Start by measuring and marking a vertical line 4½" from the tall end, then draw three more vertical lines spaced 7¼" apart. Mark the peg centerpoints along the

lines. The first centerpoint should be 5½" from the bottom. The second should be 11" from the bottom. The third peg centerpoint should be 16½" from the bottom shelf. Use a power drill to make ½ × ⅝"-deep holes for the mug pegs at these centerpoints **(photo E).** Glue the pegs, and insert them into the holes. Wipe away any excess glue.

APPLY THE FINISHING TOUCHES. Make sure all the surfaces are sanded smooth, then paint or finish the mug rack as you see fit. We used a linseed oil finish on our mug rack. When the finish has dried, hang the mug rack on the wall, or install rubber bumpers on the bottom for stable countertop placement.

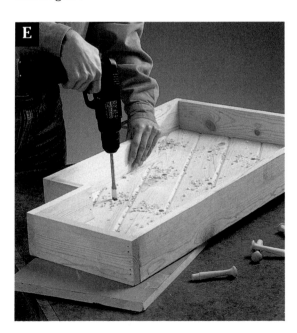

Measure and mark peg locations on the backing, then drill peg holes with a spade bit. Do not drill all the way through the backing.

Mission Lamp Base

The beauty and texture of oak combines with a simple style and charm in this traditional table lamp.

PROJECT
POWER TOOLS

This decorative lamp base provides just the right accent for a family room tabletop or bedside stand. It's made of red oak, and the design is simple and stylish. The clean vertical lines of the oak slats are rooted in the popular Mission style. Clearly, our lamp base will be an enjoyable project that you and your entire family can enjoy for a long time. The oak parts are joined with glue and nails, so the lamp base goes together with a minimum of time and fuss.

Once the base is assembled, just insert the lamp hardware, which you can buy at any local hardware store, and you're ready to turn it on. Lamp hardware kits include all the components you need to make your project functional—harp, socket, cord and tubing. Make sure you follow manufacturer's directions when installing the hardware. When you're finished, buy an attractive shade, either contemporary or classic, and set the lamp on a nightstand or table.

CONSTRUCTION MATERIALS

Quantity	Lumber
1	1 × 8" × 2' oak
2	1 × 2" × 10' oak
1	1 × 3 × 12" oak

OVERALL SIZE:
19¼" HIGH
8" WIDE
8" LONG

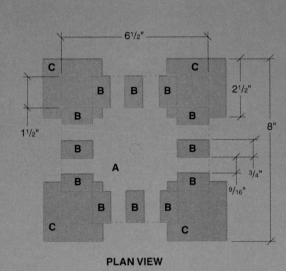

6½"

2½"

1½"

8"

¾"

9/16"

A

PLAN VIEW

Cutting List

Key	Part	Dimension	Pcs.	Material
A	Plate	¾ × 6½ × 6½"	2	Oak
B	Slat	¾ × 1½ × 17"	12	Oak
C	Foot	¾ × 2½ × 2½"	4	Oak

Materials: Wood glue, 6d finish nails, lamp hardware kit, finishing materials.

Note: Measurements reflect the actual size of dimensional lumber.

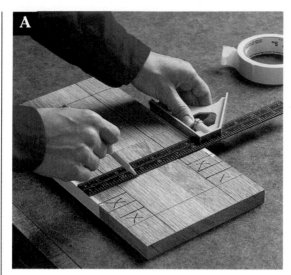

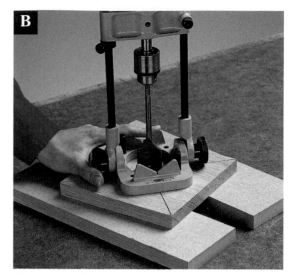

Tape the plates edge-to-edge and use a straight-edge to lay out and mark the slat positions.

Use a portable drill guide to make accurate center holes in the plates.

Drill pilot holes through the plates in position for 6d finish nails.

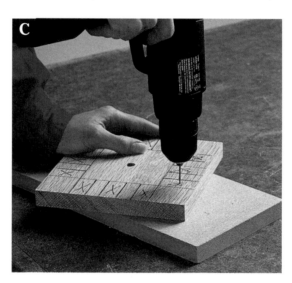

Directions: Lamp Base

PREPARE THE PLATES & SLATS. There aren't many parts in the lamp base, but you need to measure and mark accurately before assembling them. You must locate the exact centers of the bases, and position the slats so they are evenly spaced between them. Start by cutting

the plates (A) and slats (B) to size. Sand out rough edges with medium-grit (over 120) sandpaper, then finish-sand with fine-grit (150 or 180) sandpaper. Since only one side of each slat will be fully visible on the assembled project, make sure they have at least one clean, or knot-free, edge. Lay the plates edge-to-edge with their sides aligned, and tape or clamp them in place (see *Diagram*, page 89). Lay out the slat placement on the plates **(photo A).** Use a straightedge and pencil to draw lines diagonally from corner to corner on both plates

to locate their centers. Drill a 1-dia. × ¼"-deep counterbore hole on the bottom center of the lower plate **(photo B),** using a spade bit. This hole is made to make room for a washer when you assemble the lamp. Drill a ⅜"-dia. hole through the center of the ¼"-deep hole, and through the center of the other plate for the lamp tube. Use a drill with a ¹⁄₁₆"-dia. bit to make pilot holes for finish nails through the plates to secure the slats **(photo C).** Each slat should have two finish nails attaching it to the plates. To make sure all the holes in the plates are completely straight, use a portable drill guide, which keeps the drill stationary at the desired drilling angle.

ATTACH THE PLATES & SLATS. Attaching the plates and slats can be done quickly and easily with a few drops of glue and some 6d finish nails. Once all the slats have been attached to the plates, you need only attach the feet (C) to complete the lamp frame. Apply glue to the top edge of each slat and attach them, one at a time, to

---

TIP

Traditionally, Mission-style furnishings have a dark finish. If your goal is to create a true reproduction, use a dark walnut stain to finish your Mission-style projects.

the top plate. Fasten the slats to the plate by driving finish nails through the holes you drilled when preparing the parts **(photo D).** Use a nail set to set the finish nails deeper into the holes, and fill the holes with oak-tinted wood putty. For best results, fasten each slat with one nail, then check the positioning. Make any needed adjustments, and secure each slat with a second finish nail. Fasten the lower plate, with the 1"-dia. × ¼"-deep counterbore hole on the bottom, and repeat the nailing procedure. Set and fill the nail holes.

ATTACH THE FEET. Begin by cutting the feet (C) to size and sanding them to finished smoothness. For economy, we cut them from the same 1 × 8 board we used to make the plates. Measure and mark a line ¾" from the outside edge on two adjacent sides of each foot. These lines show where each plate corner is positioned on the feet (for more information on the feet placement, see *Diagram*, page 89). Like the slats, the feet are attached with finish nails and glue. Drill two holes for finish nails through each foot. Attach the feet to the plate with glue and nails, making sure the feet are properly aligned. Set and fill the nail holes, and sand the surfaces to finished smoothness.

INSTALL THE HARDWARE. Now that the lamp base is completely assembled, you need to insert the hardware that will make the project fully functional. You can buy a lamp socket kit at most hardware stores. The kit usually includes a harp for attaching a shade, a socket, lamp cord and a ⅜"-dia. threaded lamp tube. Begin by

Attach the slats to the top plate with glue and 6d finish nails.

Attach the threaded lamp tube with a washer and nut to secure the tube to the lamp frame.

cutting the lamp tube to length so that it extends from plate to plate. Insert the tube through the holes in the plates. Attach the harp to the top plate, and secure the tube to the bottom plate with a washer and nut **(photo E).** Thread the cord through the tube, and attach it according to manufacturer's directions.

APPLY THE FINISHING TOUCHES. The lamp is a decorative item, so you'll want to put a nice finish on the completed project. Finish the lamp as desired. We used light oak stain, then added two coats of wipe-on tung oil topcoat. Finally, apply felt pads to the bottom of the feet to prevent scratching on tabletop surfaces.

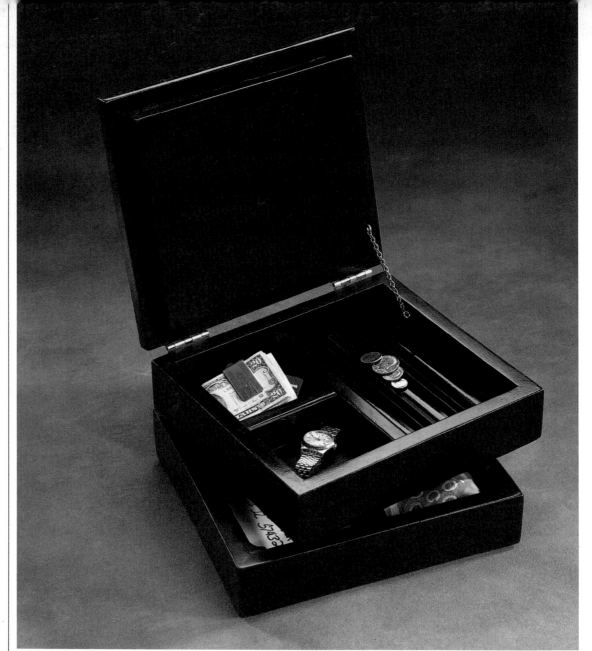

PROJECT
POWER TOOLS

Dresser Valet

Keep your personal items in order—with our convenient dresser valet,
you'll know where to find your watch or wallet every morning.

CONSTRUCTION MATERIALS	
Quantity	**Lumber**
1	1 × 10" × 4' pine
1	1 × 12" × 1' pine
1	1 × 3" × 8' pine
1	1 × 2" × 2' pine
1	¾ × 1¾"× 3' crown molding
1	½ × ½ × 6" cove molding

Our dresser valet makes it easy to just pull your things out of a pocket and drop them neatly into place. With our dresser valet, you'll never waste time turning a room upside down in search of that constantly missing watch, wallet or loose change. Your things will be right where you left them—organized and ready in your attractive dresser valet. The hinged lid flips up for easy access to everyday items, while the lower compartment is best used for items needed less frequently—just pivot the top compartment to the side to get in.

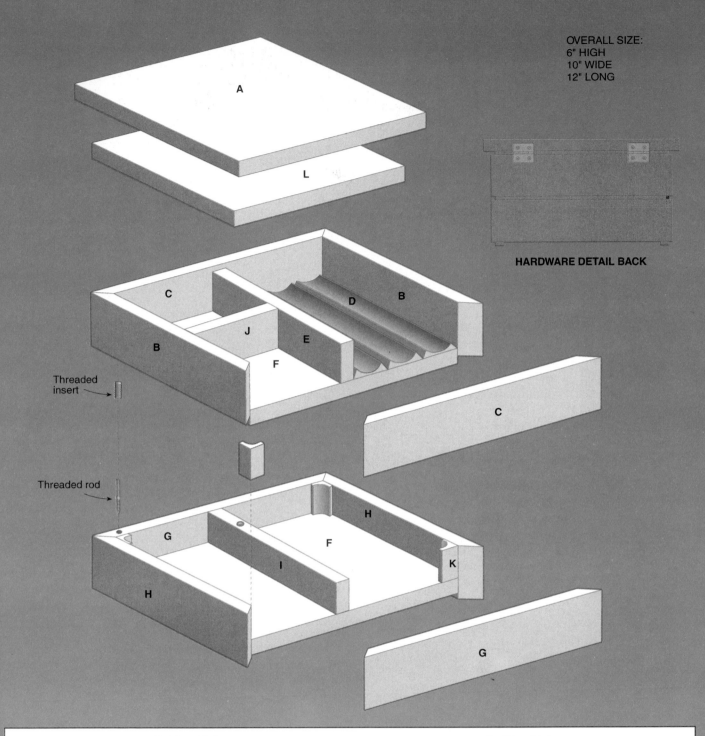

OVERALL SIZE:
6" HIGH
10" WIDE
12" LONG

HARDWARE DETAIL BACK

Threaded insert →

Threaded rod →

Cutting List				
Key	**Part**	**Dimension**	**Pcs.**	**Material**
A	Lid top	¾ × 10¾ × 12"	1	Pine
B	Top side	¾ × 2½ × 10¾"	2	Pine
C	Top end	¾ × 2½ × 12"	2	Pine
D	Tray molding	¾ × 1¾ × 9¼"	3	Molding
E	Long divider	¾ × 1½ × 9¼"	1	Pine
F	Tray bottom	¾ × 9¼ × 10½"	2	Pine

Cutting List				
Key	**Part**	**Dimension**	**Pcs.**	**Material**
G	Box side	¾ × 2½ × 12"	2	Pine
H	Box end	¾ × 2½ × 10¾"	2	Pine
I	Box divider	¾ × 1½ × 9¼"	1	Pine
J	Short divider	¾ × 1½ × 4½"	1	Pine
K	Corner brace	¾ × ½ × 1½"	4	Molding
L	Lid base	¾ × 9 × 10¼"	2	Pine

Materials: Wood glue, 4d finish nails, ¼" threaded insert, ¼"-dia. threaded rod, brass screw eyes, bullet catch, 4" brass chain, hinges, rubber bumpers, finishing materials.

Note: Measurements reflect the actual size of dimensional lumber.

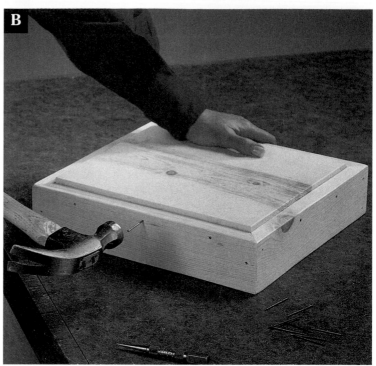

Miter-cut the top sides and top ends with a power miter box or a backsaw with miter box.

Fasten the tray bottom to the frame with 4d finish nails.

Directions: Dresser Valet

BUILD THE LID. The lid for our dresser valet is made of two ¾"-thick pieces of pine, face-glued together. The lid base is slightly smaller, creating a ¾"-wide lip around all sides. When assembled, the lid opens and closes smoothly onto the upper section of the dresser valet. Start by cutting the lid top (A) and lid base (L) to size. Soften the sharp corners and edges on these pieces with a sander or a router with a ¼" roundover bit. Carefully center the lid base on the top lid, and fasten the pieces with wood glue and 1¼" brads, driven through the lid base into the lid top.

BUILD THE TOP COMPART-MENT. The top compartment of our dresser valet is a mitered frame wrapped around a bottom board with several handy dividers between the frame sides. The frame is constructed by fastening four miter-cut

pieces together with glue and finish nails. Begin this step by cutting the top sides (B) and top ends (C) to size. Use a power miter box or a backsaw with a miter box to miter-cut the corners at a 45° angle **(photo A).** Apply glue to the mitered corners, and assemble the top frame. Keep the pieces firmly in place by attaching corner clamps. Once the glue has dried, reinforce the miter joints by driving 4d finish nails into the corners through each joint edge. To avoid visible nail heads when the project is completed, use a nail set to drive them below the surface of the wood.

> **TIP**
>
> Use 45° corner clamps when fastening the top sides and ends. These clamps are often used for making picture frames. They are inexpensive and highly effective for this kind of framing work.

BUILD THE TRAY DIVIDERS. In this step, you will make the tray bottom and insert it into the frame. Once the tray bottom is attached, you will fit it with dividers and molding to make the dresser valet a more effective storage unit. Start by cutting the tray molding (D) from cove molding, long divider (E), short divider (J) and tray bottoms (F) to size. Sand these pieces until they are completely smooth, then insert the tray bottom into the frame so that ¼" protrudes beyond the bottom frame edges. Attach the pieces with finish nails **(photo B).** When driving the finish nails through the frame to attach the bottom, place 2"-thick spacers inside the frame to keep the

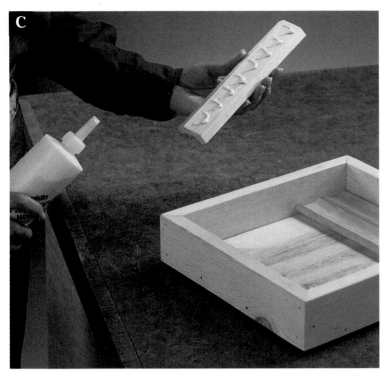

C

Glue and insert the tray molding, forming a new tray section.

bottom piece aligned correctly. Install the tray molding by applying glue to the bottom and setting the molding in place along one side of the tray bottom **(photo C).** Use glue to install the long divider so that it rests on the bottom and against the molding. The long divider's top edge should be ½" below the top edges of the frame. Install the short divider in position and allow to dry.

BUILD THE BOTTOM COMPARTMENT. Building the bottom compartment is easy. The methods used are similar to those in *Build the Top Compartment*, page 94. Start by cutting the box sides (G), box ends (H), corner braces (K) and box divider (I) to size. Use a power miter box to miter-cut the corners at a 45° angle. Apply glue to the mitered corners, and assemble the lower box frame. Keep the pieces firmly in place by attaching corner clamps

until the glue has dried. Reinforce the miter joints by driving 4d finish nails into the corners through each joint edge. Set the nails heads. Glue and attach the corner braces to the frame corners so their top edges are flush with the frame. Install the box divider so that the top edges are flush with the top edges of the frame, then install the bottom into the frame flush with the bottom frame edges. If the bottom is inserted correctly, it should be recessed ¼" up from the bottom edges of the frame.

INSTALL THE PIVOT. The pivot allows the top compartment to swing freely on top of the bottom compartment. Measure and mark centered points 1¾" from a corner on the top edges of the bottom compartment, and 1¾" from the corresponding corner on the bottom edges of the top compartment. Drill a ⅜"-dia. × ½"-deep hole into the

top compartment at the marked point, then drill a ¼"-dia. × 1"-deep hole into the corresponding point on the bottom compartment. The pivot holes must be perfectly straight on both compartments. Use a portable drill guide to ensure straight, accurate holes. Use a hex driver to screw a ¼" threaded insert into the hole in the top compartment. Screw a ¼"-dia. threaded rod into the bottom compartment **(photo D).** If you use a pair of pliers, pad the jaws of the pliers with masking tape to protect the threads on the rod. Once the hardware is inserted, thread the top compartment onto the threaded rod, and turn it until the bottom of the tray comes in contact with the top edges of the bottom compartment.

INSTALL THE BULLET CATCH. The bullet catch holds the top compartment in place when you pivot it. Install it on the top edge of the box divider by drilling a ¹¹⁄₃₂"-deep × ½"-dia. hole centered 1¼" from the

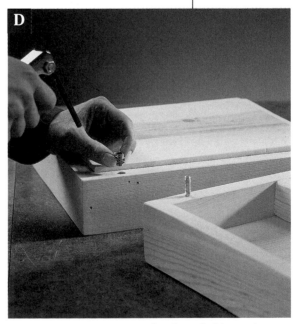

D

Use a hex driver to screw the threaded insert into the upper compartment.

Drill a hole to accept the bullet catch in the top compartment.

smooth, and paint the project as desired. We applied a black enamel finish to the dresser valet. Consider stenciling a design or initials onto the top of the valet **(photo F).** You can purchase a stencil pattern or cut one from plastic sheeting. Simply brush the desired color over the stencil pattern, and allow the paint to dry before removing it. Attach some rubber bumpers to the bottom of the box for stability, and attach hinges to the lid and top compartment. Attach brass screw eyes to a top side and the lid base, and connect them with a chain to hold the lid in an open position. Reinstall the top compartments on the threaded rod, and fill the dresser valet with valuables.

back side. Carefully insert the bullet catch, and turn the top compartment on the pivot a few times. The bullet catch should leave a small impression on the tray bottom. If not, dab a little lipstick on the bullet catch to mark the pivot arc. Swing the top compartment into the open position, and drill two $\frac{1}{4} \times \frac{1}{4}$"-deep holes along the arc to hold the catch. Drill one hole directly over the bullet catch when the valet is closed **(photo E).** Make the second hole over the catch to hold the top compartment in the open position.

APPLY THE FINISHING TOUCHES. Before you finish the dresser valet, you must separate the top and bottom compartments. Mask the threads of the threaded rod and the top of the bullet catch with tape. Fill all the nail holes with wood putty, sand the surfaces

Stencil your initials onto the top of the dresser valet.

Manual for

RADIATION ONCOLOGY NURSING PRACTICE AND EDUCATION

Third Edition

Edited by

Deborah Watkins Bruner, RN, PhD

Marilyn L. Haas, PhD, RN, CNS, ANP-C

Tracy K. Gosselin-Acomb, RN, MSN, AOCN®

Oncology Nursing Society

Pittsburgh, PA

ONS Publishing Division
Publisher: Leonard Mafrica, MBA, CAE
Director, Commercial Publishing/Technical Editor: Barbara Sigler, RN, MNEd
Production Manager: Lisa M. George, BA
Technical Editor: Judith A. DePalma, PhD, RN
Staff Editor: Lori Wilson, BA
Graphic Designer: Dany Sjoen

Manual for Radiation Oncology Nursing Practice and Education (Third Edition)

Library of Congress Control Number: 2004115283

ISBN 1-890504-51-3

Publisher's Note

This manual is published by the Oncology Nursing Society (ONS). ONS neither represents nor guarantees that the practices described herein will, if followed, ensure safe and effective patient care. The recommendations contained in this manual reflect ONS's judgment regarding the state of general knowledge and practice in the field as of the date of publication. The recommendations may not be appropriate for use in all circumstances. Those who use this manual should make their own determinations regarding specific safe and appropriate patient-care practices, taking into account the personnel, equipment, and practices available at the hospital or other facility at which they are located. The editors and publisher cannot be held responsible for any liability incurred as a consequence from the use or application of any of the contents of this manual. Figures and tables are used as examples only. They are not meant to be all-inclusive, nor do they represent endorsement of any particular institution by ONS. Mention of specific products and opinions related to those products do not indicate or imply endorsement by ONS.

ONS publications are originally published in English. Permission has been granted by the ONS Board of Directors for foreign translation. (Individual tables and figures that are reprinted or adapted require additional permission from the original source.) However, because translations from English may not always be accurate or precise, ONS disclaims any responsibility for inaccuracies in words or meaning that may occur as a result of the translation. Readers relying on precise information should check the original English version.

Printed in the United States of America

Oncology Nursing Society
Integrity • Innovation • Stewardship • Advocacy • Excellence • Inclusiveness

Contributors

Editors

Deborah Watkins Bruner, RN, PhD
Associate Member, Population Science and Radiation
   Oncology
Director, Prostate Cancer Risk Assessment Program
Director, Symptoms and Outcomes Research
Fox Chase Cancer Center
Cheltenham, Pennsylvania
*I—Clinical Practicum; IV, E—Distress/Coping; F—
Sexual Dysfunction; IX, D—Radioimmunotherapy
and Radionuclide Therapy*

Marilyn L. Haas, PhD, RN, CNS, ANP-C
Nurse Practitioner
Mountain Radiation Oncology
Asheville, North Carolina
*Evidence-Based Practice; IV, C—Skin Reactions; VII,
E—Intravascular Brachytherapy*

Tracy K. Gosselin-Acomb, RN, MSN, AOCN®
Clinical Operations Director
Department of Radiation Oncology
Duke University Health System
Durham, North Carolina
*VII, F—Intraoperative Radiation Therapy; VII, J—Total
Skin Irradiation*

Authors

Marylou S. Anton, MSN, RN, OCN®
Clinical Administrative Director
University of Texas M.D. Anderson Cancer Center
Houston, Texas
V, H—Female Pelvis

Pamela Baratti, RN
Research Radiation Oncology Staff Nurse
St. Jude Children's Hospital
Memphis, Tennessee
VIII—Special Populations: Pediatric Radiation Oncology

Andrea M. Barsevick, DNSc, RN, AOCN®
Director of Nursing Research
Fox Chase Cancer Center
Philadelphia, Pennsylvania
IV, B—Fatigue

Janye Laird Blivin, RN, MSN
Research Clinical Nurse Specialist
Department of Radiation Oncology
Duke University Medical Center
Durham, North Carolina
VII, K—Hyperthermia

Susan Bruce, RN, BSN, OCN®
Clinical Nurse IV Radiation Oncology
Duke University Health System
Durham, North Carolina
VII, L—Photodynamic Therapy

Jennifer Dunn Bucholtz, MS, CRNP, OCN®
Nurse Practitioner
Sidney Kimmel Comprehensive Cancer Center at Johns
   Hopkins
Baltimore, Maryland
III—Radiation Protection

Elise Carper, RN, MA, APRN-BC, AOCN®
Director of Nursing and Adult Nurse Practitioner
Continuum Cancer Centers of New York
New York, New York
VI, A—Sarcoma

Carrie Daly, RN, MS, AOCN®
Oncology Clinical Nurse Specialist
Radiation Oncology Department
St. Joseph Hospital
Chicago, Illinois
IX, B—Radioprotectors

Judith A. DePalma, PhD, RN
Associate Professor
Slippery Rock University
Slippery Rock, Pennsylvania
Evidence-Based Practice

Denise L. Dorman, RN, OCN®
Quality Control and Clinical Trial Coordinator
Nursing/Patient Education
Sarasota Oncology Center
Sarasota, Florida
XII, D—American Society for Therapeutic Radiology and Oncology

Maryann Dzibela, MSN, RNC, OCN®, CCRP
Radiation Oncology Research Coordinator
John F. Kennedy Medical Center
Edison, New Jersey
V, A—Brain and Central Nervous System Tumors; IX, D—Radioimmunotherapy and Radionuclide Therapy

Jacquelyn Fisher, RN, BSN, OCN®
Coordinator, Multidisiplinary Cancer Program
Oakwood Hospital and Medical Center
Dearborn, Michigan
X, C—Cancer Clinical Trials; D—Informed Consent

Elizabeth Gomez, RN, MSN
Director, Oncology Services
Putnam Hospital Center
Carmel, New York
Editor, ONS Web Site
Pittsburgh, Pennsylvania
XII, A—ONS Web Site; C—Personal Digital Assistant; E—National Comprehensive Cancer Network; F—National Cancer Institute

Donna Green, RN, BSN, BA, OCN®
Radiation Oncology Nurse Coordinator
Maine Medical Center
Portland, Maine
XI, B—Principles of Improving Organizational Performance

William Hogle, RN, BSN, OCN®
Clinical Manager
University of Pittsburgh Medical Center Passavant Hospital Cancer Center
Pittsburgh, Pennsylvania
V, G—Male Pelvis/Prostate; VII, C—Prostate Brachytherapy

Jean Holland, RN, MSN, AOCN®
Clinical Nurse—Radiation Oncology
Fox Chase Cancer Center
Philadelphia, Pennsylvania
V, E—Gastrointestinal/Abdomen

Melodie Homer, RN, MSN, AOCN®
Oncology Nurse Educator/Consultant
Marlton, New Jersey
IV, B—Fatigue

Joanne Frankel Kelvin, RN, MSN, AOCN®
Nurse Leader, Radiation Oncology
Memorial Sloan-Kettering Cancer Center
New York, New York
X, E—Nursing Management in Radiation Oncology; XII, B—American College of Radiology

Valerie Kogut, MA, RD, LDN
Research Dietitian
Department of Otolaryngology
University of Pittsburgh Physicians
Pittsburgh, Pennsylvania
IV, G—Nutrition

Eric Kuehn, MD
Radiation Oncologist
Mountain Radiation Oncology
Asheville, North Carolina
X, B—Nuclear/Radiologic Bioterrorism

C-M Charlie Ma, PhD
Professor and Director, Radiation Physicians
Radiation Oncology Department
Fox Chase Cancer Center
Philadelphia, Pennsylvania
II—Practice of Radiation Oncology

Beatrice Mautner, RN, MSN, OCN®
Manager, Oncology Medical Communications
Amgen Inc.
Thousand Oaks, California
XI, A—Joint Commission on Accreditation of Healthcare Organizations

Susan Mazanec, RN, MSN, AOCN®
Director, Office of Patient and Public Education
Ireland Cancer Center
University Hospitals of Cleveland
Cleveland, Ohio
IV, A—General Patient and Family Education

Christine A. Miaskowski, RN, PhD, FAAN
Professor and Chair, Department of Physiological Nursing
University of California
San Francisco, California
IV, D—Pain

Giselle Moore-Higgs, ARNP, MSN, AOCN®
Breast Center Coordinator
Shands Hospital at the University of Florida
Gainesville, Florida
*V, C—Breast; D—Thoracic; VII, D—Accelerated Partial
    Breast Irradiation; G—Stereotactic Radiosurgery/
    Radiotherapy*

Judith B. Nettleton, RN, BSN, OCN®
Staff Nurse, Radiation Oncology, and Neuro-Oncology
    Nurse Coordinator
West Michigan Cancer Center
Kalamazoo, Michigan
V, F—Bladder

Margaret Pierce, RN, BSN, OCN®
Nursing Resource Coordinator, Radiation Oncology
Northwestern Memorial Hospital
Chicago, Illinois
*VII, H—Total Body Irradiation; I—Total Nodal Irradia-
    tion*

Mary Ann Robbins, RN, BSN, OCN®
Clinical Nurse IV
Duke University Medical Center
Department of Radiation Oncology
Durham, North Carolina
VI, B—Lymphoma

Roberta A. Strohl, RN, MN, AOCN®
Senior Training Manager, Oncology
Schering Oncology Biotech
Kenilworth, New Jersey
VII, A—External Beam

Jayne S. Waring, RN, BSN, OCN®
Clinical Nurse IV, Radiation Oncology
Duke University Medical Center
Durham, North Carolina
*VII, B—LDR/HDR Brachytherapy; IX, D—
    Radioimmunotherapy and Radionuclide Therapy*

Linda Wilgus, RN, MSN, OCN®
Clinical Trials Coordinator
Lexington Clinic Cancer Center
Lexington, Kentucky
IX, A—Radiosensitizers; C—Concurrent Chemotherapy

Diane Williams, RN, MN
Advanced Practice Nurse, Palliative Radiation Oncology
    Program
Princess Margaret Hospital, University Health Network
Toronto, Ontario, Canada
X, A—Palliative Care and End-of-Life Issues

Mary Ellyn Witt, RN, MS, AOCN®
Clinical Research Nurse
University of Chicago Hospital
Chicago, Illinois
V, B—Head and Neck

Reviewers

Kathleen E. Bell, RN, MSN, OCN®
Clinical Nurse Specialist and Nurse Manager for Radia-
    tion Oncology Services
Spectrum Health
Grand Rapids, Michigan

Darla D. Gullikson, BSN
Department Director
Avera Sacred Heart Cancer Center
Yankton, South Dakota

Gloria A. Hagopian, RN, BSN, MSN, EdD
Professor Emeritus
University of North Carolina at Charlotte
Charlotte, North Carolina

James I. Hanus, RN, BSN, OCN®, MHA
Clinical Research Nurse and Practice Safety Manager
Kansas City Cancer Centers
Lenexa, Kansas

Denise A. Jeffery, RN, BSN
Clinical Leader, Radiation Oncology
Elliot Hospital
Manchester, New Hampshire

Table of Contents

List of Abbreviations

3DCRT: three-dimensional conformal radiotherapy

3DTPS: three-dimensional treatment planning system

5-FU: fluorouracil

AASECT: American Association of Sex Educators, Counselors, and Therapists

ACR: American College of Radiology

ACS: American Cancer Society

ADT: androgen deprivation therapy

AHRQ: Agency for Healthcare Research and Quality

ALARA: as low as reasonably achievable

ALND: axillary lymph node dissection

ANA: American Nurses Association

ANC: absolute neutrophil count

AP/PA: anteroposterior-posteroanterior

ASTRO: American Society for Therapeutic Radiology and Oncology

ATP: adenosine triphosphate

AUA: American Urology Association

AVM: arteriovenous malformations

BCG: Bacillus Calmette-Guérin

BCM: body cell mass

BEE: basal energy expenditure

BEV: beam's eye view

BFI: Brief Fatigue Inventory

BMI: body mass index

BMT: bone marrow transplant

Bq: becquerel

BUN: blood urea nitrogen

CAD: coronary artery disease

CBC: complete blood count

CBI: convergent beam irradiation

CDT: complex decongestive therapy

cGy: centigray

ci: curies

CNS: central nervous system

CPR: cardiopulmonary resuscitation

CSF: colony-stimulating factors

CT: computerized tomography

CTV: clinical target volume

CTZ: chemoreceptor trigger zone

DCIS: ductal carcinoma in situ

DNR: do not resuscitate

DPS: disintegration per second

DSB: double chromosomal strand break

DVH: dose volume histogram

DVT: deep vein thrombosis

EBP: evidence-based practice

EBRT: external beam radiation therapy

ECOG: Eastern Cooperative Oncology Group

EKG: electrocardiogram

FACT-F: Functional Assessment of Cancer Therapy–Fatigue

FDA: U.S. Food and Drug Administration

G-CSF: granulocyte–colony-stimulating factor

GI: gastrointestinal

GM-CSF: granulocyte macrophage–colony-stimulating factor

GTV: gross tumor volume

GU: genitourinary

GVHD: graft versus host disease

Gy: gray

GYN: gynecologic

HAMA: human anti-mouse antibodies

Hct: hematocrit

HD: Hodgkin's disease

HDR: high dose rate

HDR-IORT: high dose rate intraoperative radiation therapy

Hgb: hemoglobin

HLA: human leukocyte antigen

HSCT: hematopoietic stem cell transplant

HTLV-1: human T cell lymphotropic virus type 1

HVL: half-value layer

IBS: irritative bladder symptoms

IBW: ideal body weight

ICRP: International Commission on Radiation Protection

ICRU: International Commission on Radiation Units and Measures

IL: interleukin

IMRT: intensity-modulated radiotherapy

IOERT: intraoperative electron radiation therapy

IOP: improving organization performance

IORT: intraoperative radiation therapy

IT: information technology

IVBT: intravascular brachytherapy

JCAHO: Joint Commission on Accreditation of Healthcare Organizations

LDR: low dose rate

LET: linear energy transfer

LFS: Li-Fraumeni syndrome

LOH: loss of heterozygosity

M: mitosis

MAOI: monoamine oxidase inhibitors

MFI: multidimensional fatigue inventory

MLC: multileaf collimator

MR: milliroentgen

mrem: millirem

MRI: magnetic resonance imaging

MU: monitor units

NCCN: National Comprehensive Cancer Network

NCRP: National Council on Radiation Protection and Measurements

NHL: non-Hodgkin's lymphoma

NIH: National Institutes of Health

NK: neurokinin

NPO: nothing by mouth

NSAID: nonsteroidal anti-inflammatory drug

NSCLC: non-small cell lung cancer

OAR: organs at risk

ONS: Oncology Nursing Society

OR: operating room

ORN: osteoradionecrosis

PACU: post-anesthesia care unit

PBQ: Patent Benefit Questionnaire

PDA: personal digital assistant

PDT: photodynamic therapy

PET: positron emission tomography

PFS: Piper Fatigue Scale

PG-SGA: Patient-Generated Subjective Global Assessment

PICO: population, intervention, comparison, and outcome

POMS: Profile of Mood States

PPP: primary proliferative polycythemia

PRIME-MD: Primary Care Evaluation of Mental Disorders

PSCT: peripheral stem cell transplant

PTCA: percutaneous transluminal coronary angioplasty

PTV: planning target volume

QA: quality assurance

QOL: quality of life

RAD: radiation-absorbed dose

RSO: radiation safety officer

RT: radiation therapy

RTOG: Radiation Therapy Oncology Group

RU: research utilization

S: synthesis

SRS: stereotactic radiosurgery

SSRI: serotonin reuptake inhibitors

STS: soft tissue sarcoma

Sv: sievert

TBI: total body irradiation

TCA: tricyclic antidepressants

TLI: total lymphoid irradiation

TNF: tumor necrosis factor

TNI: total nodal irradiation

TNM: tumor node metastasis

TPN: total parenteral nutrition

TSH: thyroid-stimulating hormone

TSI: total skin irradiation

TURP: transurethral resection of prostate

USNRC: U.S. Nuclear Regulatory Commission

UTI: urinary tract infection

VHL: von Hippel-Lindau

VOD: veno-occlusive disease

WHO: World Health Organization

List of Brand Name Products

This list is not an assertion of trademark ownership or an endorsement of any product. This list is not comprehensive; more than one company may manufacture or market a product known by the same brand name. Every effort was made to ensure the accuracy of this information at press time. However, trademark ownership often changes, as do the names and locations of companies; therefore, the publisher and contributors disclaim responsibility for the accuracy of this list. Do not use this information without verifying it to ensure it is up-to-date. Cited trademark status pertains to the United States only. Not all the products listed are available in the United States.

Adriamycin®: Bedford Laboratories, Bedford, OH

Anzemet®: Aventis, Bridgewater, NJ

Aquaphor®: Beiersdorf, Hamburg, Germany

Astroglide®: Biofilm, Inc., Vista, CA

Bactrim®: Roche Pharmaceuticals, Nutley, NJ

Bexxar®: GlaxoSmithKline, Research Triangle Park, NC

Biafine®: Medix Pharmaceuticals Americas, Largo, FL

Bioclusive®: Johnson & Johnson, San Francisco, CA

Blenoxane®: Bristol-Myers Squib, Princeton, NJ

Boost®, Boost Plus®: Novartis Medical Nutrition, Minneapolis, MN

Carafate® Suspension: Aventis, Bridgewater, NJ

Cardura®: Pfizer, New York

Carnation Instant Breakfast®: Nestle, Vevey, Switzerland

Choice DM®: Bristol-Myers Squibb, Princeton, NJ

Compressure Comfort® Bra: Bellisse, South Burlington, VT

CyberKnife®: Accuracy Inc., Sunnyvale, CA

Dale Post-Surgical Bra®: Dale Medical, Plainville, MA

Decadron®: Merck, West Point, PA

Dilantin®: Pfizer, New York

Ditropan®: Alza Pharmaceuticals, Palo Alto, CA

Domeboro® Astringent Solution: Bayer, Morristown, NJ

Dove®: Unilever, London, England

DTIC-Dome®: Bayer, West Haven, CT

Duragesic®: Janssen Pharmaceutica, Titusville, NJ

Elmiron®: Alza Pharmaceuticals, Palo Alto, CA

Emend®: Merck, Whitehouse Station, NJ

Ensure®: Ross Laboratories, Columbus, OH

Ethyol®: MedImmune Oncology, Gaithersburg, MD

Eucerin®: Beiersdorf, Hamburg, Germany

Exu-Dry®: Smith & Nephew, Largo, FL

E-Z Flex®: Fluid Motion Biotechnologies, Columbia, NY

Flomax®: Abbott Laboratories, North Chicago, IL

Gamma Knife®: Elekta Instruments, Stockholm, Sweden

Gatorade®: Quaker Oats Company, Dallas, TX

Gengraf®: Abbott Laboratories, North Chicago, IL

Hytrin®: Abbott Laboratories, North Chicago, IL

Imodium® A-D: McNeil, Fort Washington, PA

Intrabeam® System: Zeiss, Oberkochen, Germany

Intron-A®: Schering, Kenilworth, NJ

Isocal®: Novartis Medical Nutrition, Minneapolis, MN

Isosource®: Novartis Medical Nutrition, Minneapolis, MN

Jeans Cream®: Jeans Cream, Peabody, MA

K-Y® Jelly: Johnson & Johnson, San Francisco, CA

Kytril®: Roche Pharmaceuticals, Nutley, NJ

Leucomax®: Novartis, East Hanover, NJ

Leukine®: Berlex Laboratories, Richmond, CA

Lomotil®: Pfizer, New York, NY

Lymphedema Alert® bracelet: National Lymphedema Network, Oakland, CA

Lymphoderm®: Advanced Therapists, West Palm Beach, FL

MammoSite® RTS: Texas MammoSite, San Antonio, TX

Marinol®: Solvay Pharmaceuticals, Brussels, Belgium

Matulane®: Sigma Tau Pharmaceuticals, Gaithersburg, MD

Megace®: Bristol-Myers Squibb, Princeton, NJ

Mesnex®: Bristol-Myers Squibb, Princeton, NJ

Mexate®: Bristol-Myers Squibb, Princeton, NJ

Mustargen®: Merck, West Point, PA

Neupogen®: Amgen, Thousand Oaks, CA

NuBasics®: Nestle Nutrition, Glendale, CA

OpSite®: Smith & Nephew, Largo, FL

Optimental®: Ross Laboratories, Columbus, OH

Osmolite®: Ross Laboratories, Columbus, OH

Peptinex®: Novartis Medical Nutrition, Minneapolis, MN

Photofrin®: Axcan Pharma, Birmingham, AL

Prograf®: Fujisawa Healthcare, Deerfield, IL

Prokine®: Hoechst Marion Roussel, Kansas City, MO

ProSure®: Ross Laboratories, Columbus, OH

Pyridium®: Warner Chilcott, Rockaway, NY

Quadramet®: Cytogen Corp., Princeton, NJ

RadiaPlex Rx™ Gel: MPM Medical, Irving, TX

Radiation Implant Briefs™: DM Medical, West Hyannisport, MA

Reglan®: Wyeth, Madison, NJ

ReidSleeve®: Peninsula Medical Supply, Scotts Valley, CA

Replens®: Parke-Davis, Morris Plains, NJ

Resource®: Novartis Medical Nutrition, Minneapolis, MN

Rheumatrex®: Stada Pharmaceuticals, Cranbury, NJ

Roferon-A®: Roche Pharmaceuticals, Nutley, NJ

Rowasa®: Ferring Pharmaceuticals, Suffern, NY

Salagen®: Pfizer, New York

Sandimmune®: Novartis, East Hanover, NJ

Sandoglobulin®: Novartis, East Hanover, NJ

Sandostatin®: Novartis, East Hanover, NJ

Tegaderm®: 3M, Maplewood, MN

Therabite®: Atos Medical Corp., Milwaukee, WI

TheraCare®: Emumagic, Nevis, MN

Thymoglobulin®: SangStat Medical, Fremont, CA

Urimax®: Integrity Pharmaceuticals, Indianapolis, IN

Urised®: Polymedica Pharmaceuticals, Woburn, MA

Urispas®: GlaxoSmithKline, Research Triangle Park, NC

Velban®: Eli Lilly, Indianapolis, IN

Zevalin™: Biogen IDEC, Cambridge, MA

Zofran®: GlaxoSmithKline, Research Triangle Park, NC

Zovirax®: GlaxoSmithKline, Research Triangle Park, NC

List of Generic Drugs and Brand Name Equivalents

This list is not comprehensive; more than one company may manufacture or market a product known by the same generic name. Although every effort was made to ensure the accuracy of this information at press time, product marketing changes frequently, as do brand names; therefore, the publisher and contributors disclaim responsibility for the accuracy of this list. Before using this information, verify it to ensure that it is up-to-date. Cited trademark status pertains to the United States only. Not all products listed are available in the United States.

acyclovir: Zovirax®

aluminum acetate: Domeboro® Astringent Solution

amifostine: Ethyol®

antithymocyte globulin: Thymoglobulin®

aprepitant: Emend®

atropine methenamine: Urised®

bleomycin: Blenoxane®

cyclosporine: Sandimmune®, Gengraf®

dacarbazine: DTIC-Dome®

dexamethasone: Decadron®

diphenoxylate atropine: Lomotil®

dolasetron: Anzemet®

doxazosin mesylate: Cardura®

doxorubicin hydrochloride: Adriamycin®

dronabinol: Marinol®

fentanyl: Duragesic®

filgrastim: Neupogen®

flavoxate hydrochloride: Urispas®

granisetron: Kytril®

ibritumomab tiuxetan: Zevalin™

interferon alpha: Intron-A®, Roferon-A®

intravenous immunoglobin: Sandoglobulin®

iodine-131 tositumomab: Bexxar®

loperamide hydrochloride: Imodium® A-D

megestrol acetate: Megace®

mesalamine: Rowasa®

methotrexate: Mexate®, Rheumatrex®

metoclopramide: Reglan®

nitrogen mustard: Mustargen®

octreotide acetate: Sandostatin®

ondansetron: Zofran®

oxybutynin: Ditropan®

pentosan polysulfate sodium: Elmiron®

phenazopyridine hydrochloride: Pyridium®

phenytoin: Dilantin®

pilocarpine: Salagen®

porfimer sodium: Photofrin®

procarbazine: Matulane®

samarium-153: Quadramet®

sargramostim: Leukine®, Prokine®, Leucomax®

sodium-2-mercaptoethane sulfonate: Mesnex®

sucralfate: Carafate® Suspension

tacrolimus: Prograf®

tamsulosin hydrochloride: Flomax®

terazosin hydrochloride: Hytrin®

trimethoprim sulfamethoxazole: Bactrim®

vinblastine: Velban®

Introduction

Each decade brings with it a new focus in health care. The last decade centered on cost containment, and although still continuing to be cost conscious, this decade has a focus on quality health care. This focus reaches all aspects of health care, including radiation oncology. As radiation oncology nurses, we participate in the delivery of high-quality health care in multiple ways. One way is to base our *practice* on scientific evidence. Evidence-based practice is defined as care that integrates best scientific evidence with clinical expertise, knowledge of pathophysiology and psychosocial issues, and decision-making preferences of patients (Rutledge & Grant, 2002). Another is to maintain the high level of our *art* through the physical and emotional support of both patients and families, for which cancer nurses are so well recognized. Yet another is to communicate and advocate for our role in delivering quality care to ensure that radiation oncology nursing services are available to those who need them. Cost containment frequently impinges on the quantity and quality of nursing services available in an institution, and it is only through self-promotion that other healthcare providers, administrators, and healthcare consumers will be made aware of the quality and necessity of the care radiation therapy nurses deliver.

In support of radiation oncology nurses' efforts to provide quality care, the Oncology Nursing Society is providing the third edition of the *Manual for Radiation Oncology Nursing Practice and Education*. As with past editions, this manual covers the role of the radiation oncology nurse and minimum qualifications for and the revised and expanded scope of radiation oncology nursing practice. This edition expands upon the last edition in terms of patient education, assessment, symptom management, documentation, radiation protection, and quality improvement. It also includes new sections on evidence-based practice, new technology, pediatrics, palliative care, nuclear and radiologic bioterrorism, clinical trials, and radiation oncology resources.

This manual provides specific guidelines for the education of nurses new to radiation oncology and for the practice of quality radiation oncology nursing care. This manual also can assist with articulation of the role of the radiation oncology nurse, justification of nursing staff positions in the department of radiation oncology, and the evaluation of radiation oncology nurses' performance.

This manual is not intended to serve as a comprehensive textbook but rather as an outline of the content necessary for the education and practice of the radiation oncology nurse.

Readers are encouraged to supplement this publication with the extensive reference lists provided in the text and to continue to seek out new knowledge that will provide the tools necessary for delivering high-quality, cost-effective patient care. Radiation oncology nurses also are strongly encouraged to identify gaps in current knowledge and initiate or participate in studies to fill those gaps that will help improve the quality of care delivered.

Rutledge, D.N., & Grant, M. (2002). Evidence-based practice in cancer nursing. Introduction. *Seminars in Oncology Nursing, 18,* 1–2.

Deborah Watkins Bruner, RN, PhD
Marilyn Haas, PhD, RN, CNS, ANP-C
Tracy K. Gosselin-Acomb, RN, MSN, AOCN®

Scope of Practice

The radiation oncology nurse is a registered professional nurse who functions independently and interdependently with the radiation oncology team in providing quality patient care. The radiation oncology nurse provides clinical care, education, and consultation. The radiation oncology nurse may participate in the leadership roles of clinician, educator, consultant, and/or researcher. Using an evidence-based model of practice, the radiation oncology nurse will provide assessment, diagnosis, outcome identification, planning, implementation, and evaluation, focusing on the continuum of care to support the patients receiving radiation therapy, their families, and caregivers.

Radiation oncology nursing practice is based on the philosophic tenets identified in the Oncology Nursing Society's (ONS's) *Statement on the Scope and Standards of Oncology Nursing Practice* (Brant & Wickham, 2004). These standards and the ONS *Statement on the Scope and Standards of Advanced Practice Nursing in Oncology* (Jacobs, 2003) provide the framework that delineates these roles. Critical components of professional practice are driven by the following core values: integrity, innovation, stewardship, advocacy, excellence, and inclusiveness (ONS, 2002). ONS encourages radiation oncology nurses to assign personal meaning to each of these values.

Currently, evidence-based practice (EBP) is the hallmark of 21st century nursing. EBP "defines care that integrates best scientific evidence with clinical expertise, knowledge of pathophysiology, knowledge of psychosocial issues, and decision making preferences of patients" (Rutledge & Grant, 2002, p. 1). Oncology nurses recognize that there are levels of evidence ranging from the highest level of well-designed and conducted meta-analyses or randomized controlled clinical trials to lower, yet valuable, levels of evidence, including expert opinion. The radiation oncology nurse evaluates the evidence based upon a hierarchy of evidence and will not limit his or her practice to only those sources that support a personal point of view. Radiation oncology nurses clearly cite sources of current evidence that exist in the topic area when developing policies, procedures, and guidelines for practice or publications.

It is *recommended* that minimal education for the radiation oncology nurse is a baccalaureate degree in nursing. *Preferred* nursing experience should include 2 years of oncology nursing; alternately, a 6–12 month didactic and clinically based preceptorship is highly *recommended*. Oncology nursing certification also is recommended.

The advanced practice nurse (APN) in radiation oncology is a master's or doctorally prepared nurse with specialized knowledge and skills acquired through study and supervised practice. Regardless of certification requirements, all oncology APNs must be licensed in their state as an RN and are subject to that state's legal restraints, regulations, and privileges for recognition and licensure of advanced practice nursing (Jacobs, 2003).

Standards of Care

"Standards of Care" pertain to professional nursing activities demonstrated by the radiation oncology nurse through the nursing process. The nursing process is the foundation of clinical decision making and encompasses all significant action taken by nurses in providing oncology care to all patients and families (Brant & Wickham, 2004). The overall goal is to influence patients' and families'/caregivers' overall health, well-being, and quality of life across the radiation therapy continuum.

Standard I. Assessment

The radiation oncology nurse assesses the needs of the patient and family throughout the continuum of care.

Standard II. Diagnosis

The radiation oncology nurse collaborates with other disciplines to analyze the assessment data and identify patient and family problems.

Standard III. Outcome identification

The radiation oncology nurse identifies expected, evidence-based nursing interventions, which will guide patient and family outcomes.

Standard IV. Planning

The radiation oncology nurse develops and communicates an individualized, comprehensive, measurable plan for interventions to attain expected outcomes.

Standard V. Implementation

The radiation oncology nurse uses evidence-based information to implement the plan of care to achieve the expected outcomes.

Standard VI. Evaluation

The radiation oncology nurse systematically evaluates patient and family responses to interventions and the process of care.

Standards of Professional Performance

"Standards of Professional Performance" describe a competent level of behavior in the professional nursing role. The radiation oncology nurse should be self-directed and purposeful in seeking the necessary knowledge and skills to enhance professional development and clinical outcomes (Moore-Higgs et al., 2003).

Standard I. Quality of care

The radiation oncology nurse systematically evaluates and documents the effectiveness of clinical care.

Standard II. Accountability

The radiation oncology nurse evaluates his or her own nursing practice in relation to professional practice standards, relevant statutes, and regulations.

Standard III. Education

The radiation oncology nurse, building upon the fundamentals of nursing, will participate in ongoing education activities and update knowledge pertaining to basic and behavioral sciences, technology, and information systems.

Standard IV. Leadership

The radiation oncology nurse serves as a leader, role model, and mentor for the professional development of peers and colleagues.

Standard V. Ethics

The radiation oncology nurse serves as a patient and family advocate, protecting personal health information and patient autonomy, dignity, and rights in a manner sensitive to spiritual, cultural, and ethnic practices.

Standard VI. Collaboration

The radiation oncology nurse collaborates and consults with patient and family, along with the multidisciplinary team, to enhance desired clinical outcomes.

Standard VII. Research

The radiation oncology nurse uses research as the scientific base for all nursing practice and participates in the conduct of research to improve patient outcomes.

Standard VIII. Resource utilization

The radiation oncology nurse strives to maintain the clinical aspect of the role, ensuring his or her expertise is primarily used for direct patient care, and healthcare institutions should recognize their expertise in allowing them to function at the highest level of patient care. Consideration will be given to patient and family safety, effectiveness of care, and securing of appropriate services and financial resources as needed.

References

Brant, J.M., & Wickham, R.S. (Eds.). (2004). *Statement on the scope and standards of oncology nursing practice.* Pittsburgh, PA: Oncology Nursing Society.

Jacobs, L.A. (Ed.). (2003). *Statement on the scope and standards of advanced practice nursing in oncology* (3rd ed.). Pittsburgh, PA: Oncology Nursing Society.

Moore-Higgs, G., Watkins-Bruner, D., Balmer, L., Johnson-Doneski, J., Komarny, P., Mautner, B., et al. (2003). The role of licensed nursing personnel in radiation oncology part A: Results of a descriptive study. *Oncology Nursing Forum, 30,* 51–58.

Oncology Nursing Society. (2002). *Core values of ONS and affiliated corporations.* Retrieved June 2, 2003, from http://www.ons.org/about/corevalues.shtml

Rutledge, D., & Grant, M. (2002). Evidence-based practice in cancer nursing: Introduction. *Seminars in Oncology Nursing, 18,* 1.

Evidence-Based Practice

I. Guideline development

A. Clinical practice guidelines are defined as "systematically developed statements to assist practitioner and patient decisions about appropriate health care for specific clinical circumstances" (Institute of Medicine [IOM], 1990, p. 27). The increased adherence to clinical practice guidelines, the availability of guidelines via the Internet, and the expectation of improved quality and cost-effectiveness of health care based upon guidelines (IOM) necessitates the evaluation of a guideline prior to adoption. Quality guidelines are those with a high degree of confidence in the method of development, the evidence-base, and the applicability and feasibility for practice (AGREE Collaboration, 2001).

B. A variety of tools or checklists exist to evaluate clinical practice guidelines. When these tools are compared, common points denote a quality guideline. A quality guideline should include
  1. Recommended interventions and the circumstances when most effective
  2. The extent, strength, and currency of evidence in support of the intervention (Cates et al., 2001)
  3. The role of patient preferences (AGREE Collaboration, 2001; Cates et al., 2001; Goolsby, 2001; Guyatt, Sinclair, Cook, & Glasziou, 1999; McSweeney, Spies, & Cann, 2001; Shaneyfelt, Mayo-Smith, & Rothwangl, 1999).

C. The Oncology Nursing Society (ONS) has implemented a policy to approach all revisions or new standards and guidelines from an evidence-based perspective and to adopt a format that clearly indicates the source and extent of evidence (ONS, 2003).

II. Definition and differences

A. Evidence-based practice (EBP) is solving clinical problems and delivering care based upon the best current evidence, applied with clinical expertise and an appreciation of the patient's values and expectations (Sackett, Straus, Richardson, Rosenberg, & Haynes, 2000).

B. The most credible evidence is that gained from research, but a broad definition of evidence can include a range from the "gold standard" of randomized controlled trials to expert opinion (Rutledge & Grant, 2002). See Figure 1 for an example of a hierarchy or levels of evidence.

C. EBP is a natural process for the inquiring radiation oncology nurse who wants to deliver the highest quality of care, but it is recognized that EBP is a time-consuming and resource-intensive process. Practice settings that value an environment of inquiry and the use of new, credible knowledge are most likely to provide the resources for access and application of that new knowledge (Rosswurm & Larrabee, 1999). The EBP process is similar to the nursing process because both involve similar steps. (More details about the steps in the EBP process can be found in DePalma & McGuire, 2005; Rosswurm & Larrabee, 1999; Rutledge et al., 2001; Stetler et al., 1998; Titler, 1998.)
  1. The clinical problem should emerge from clinical situations where a knowledge gap or uncertainty exists regarding the "best" response or intervention. Therefore, the problem is a statement of a question that needs to be answered or a situation that needs a solution. An ideal statement is succinct and includes the patient population, the setting, the intervention or treatment, and a desired outcome (Craig, 2002; Gibbs, 2003). The PICO (population, intervention, comparison, and outcome) framework can be helpful in formulating the statement because it serves as a reminder of the key aspects to include (Craig, 2002).
    a) Examples for a radiation therapy nurse
      (1) What type of smoking cessation program works best for patients with lung cancer who are undergoing outpatient thoracic irradiation and want to stop smoking?

Figure 1. Hierarchy or Levels of Evidence

Strongest Evidence

Meta-analysis of multiple controlled clinical trials

Individual trials or experiments

Integrative reviews of all types of research

Nonexperimental multiple studies, including descriptive, correlational, and qualitative research

Program evaluation, quality improvement data, or case reports

Opinions of experts—standards of practice, practice guidelines

Weakest Evidence

Note. From *Evidence-Based Practice Model Critique,* by Oncology Nursing Society, 1999, Pittsburgh, PA: Author. Retrieved May 21, 2004, from http://onsopcontent.ons.org/toolkits/ebp/process_model/critique/critique.htm#levels. Copyright 1999 by Oncology Nursing Society. Reprinted with permission.

(2) What are the "best interventions" to decrease the discomfort of peripheral neuropathy for patients receiving concurrent chemoradiation?

(3) What are the "best teaching strategies" (timeframe and format) for patients and their families when they begin their radiation treatments?

b) Searching for evidence: Radiation oncology nurses should elicit help from reference librarians or professional colleagues in planning and initiating the search for evidence. Initial searches often need to be refocused or expanded to locate a feasible amount of credible evidence to review. Ideal types of evidence are systematic reviews or meta-analyses (see Figure 1) that have already collected and synthesized relevant research studies and evidence-based clinical guidelines. Therefore, besides the general searching of bibliographic databases such as MEDLINE® and CINAHL®, sites that offer systematic reviews, clinical guidelines, or specialty-specific standards are valuable resources and should be included in the search strategy (see Table 1 for key re-

sources) (Hunt & McKibbon, 1997; McSweeney et al., 2001).

c) Evaluating the evidence: Although initially difficult, this step determines the scientific merit, feasibility, and utility of the evidence. The radiation oncology nurse must critically appraise the evidence for validity and its usefulness within the specific clinical practice or setting.

d) Synthesizing the evidence: This is combining the findings from all the sources of evidence and making a practice recommendation. Given the evidence, this is the "so what" step. Whether a practice change recommendation can be made is dependent upon the quality, amount, and currency of evidence. Decisions that can be made based upon the evidence include

(1) Sufficient credible evidence exists to make a clear practice recommendation.

(2) Contradictory evidence exists; therefore, the radiation nurse can make a decision about a practice change based upon his or her clinical expertise, knowledge of their patient population, and what is feasible within the setting.

Table 1. Evidence-Based Practice Web Sites

Site/URL	Description
Cochrane Library www.cochranelibrary.com/cochrane	Systematic reviews and guidelines. Generally medically oriented (Can browse titles and get abstracts for free but need to subscribe or pay a fee for documents) Examples: *Non-surgical interventions for late radiation cystitis in patients who have received radical radiotherapy to the pelvis,* Denton, A.S., Clarke, N.W., & Maher, E.J. (2003), Chichester, UK: Wiley & Sons.
Agency for Healthcare Research and Quality (AHRQ) www.ahcpr.gov	Evidence report topics, evidence technical reviews, and clinical guidelines
National Guideline Clearinghouse www.guideline.gov	A public resource for evidence-based clinical practice guidelines Example: *2002 update of recommendations for use of chemotherapy and radiotherapy protectants: Clinical practice guidelines of the American Society of Clinical Oncology.*
Database of Abstracts of Reviews of Effects (DARE) http://agatha.york.ac.uk/darehp.htm	Systematic reviews produced and maintained by the National Health System's Centre for Reviews and Dissemination
National Comprehensive Cancer Network www.nccn.org	Practice guidelines for clinicians and patients, most based on cancer type; also outcomes and resource links Example: *Distress Management in Cancer*
ONS EBP Online Resource Center http://onsopcontent.ons.org/toolkits/ebp/index.htm	Provides a list of integrated reviews pertinent to cancer care
Academic Center for Evidence-Based Nursing (ACE) www.acestar.uthscsa.edu	Comprehensive list of EBP resources targeting nurses
Centre for Health Evidence www.cche.net/che/home.asp	User's Guides for EBP series from *JAMA.* How to critique and use different types of evidence articles.

(3) Insufficient evidence exists upon which to base a clear practice recommendation. This situation may lead to a research project at the clinical setting to determine whether a particular intervention can improve outcomes.

(4) For example, given the research regarding the most effective skin care of the radiation site, what are the most critical steps to include in any skin care protocol or individual practice, and how may the current guidelines need to be altered based on the new findings?

e) Implementing the practice recommendation: Applying the results of the synthesis to actual practice often involves planning and making a change. Practice recommendations can be proposed as individual interventions or as protocols, guidelines, or pathways—whatever format will be most readily accepted by the clinicians—to be adopted by an entire program or setting. Whatever practice change systems exist within the healthcare setting should be employed to facilitate the change. Two key points are listed.

(1) Allow enough time for education of caregivers and patients.

(2) Develop the evaluation plan simultaneously with the implementation plan.

f) Evaluating the practice recommendation: Evaluation provides essential data for decision making and assists the multidisciplinary team members in determining whether the intervention should be continued, rejected, or modified.

(1) Data should include process issues as well as clinical outcomes and caregiver and organizational outcomes (Jennings, Staggers, & Brosch, 1999).

(2) For example, a change has been initiated to employ new patient education content regarding relaxation techniques aimed at improving breathlessness. Evaluation points would include the following.

(a) The percentage of radiation oncology nurses who are including the content in their patient education

(b) The percentage of breathless patients who have appropriate patient education documented

(c) Improvement of patient outcomes (e.g., breathlessness, activity levels, quality of life)

D. EBP and research utilization (RU) are similar in concept but differ in their philosophical underpinnings. RU and EBP are forms of knowledge utilization (Hunt, 2002), but EBP is more than RU (Jennings & Loan, 2001).

1. RU has been defined broadly by Stetler (1985) as "basing the practice, education, and management of nursing on research findings" (p. 40).

2. EBP is considered a total process beginning with the statement of the clinical question, through the evaluation of the effectiveness of the practice change and continual improvement of the process from the caregiver and patient perspective (DePalma, 2000; Goode & Piedalue, 1999; Pearson & Craig, 2002; White, 1997). This process has been discussed in more detail previously. EBP emphasizes research evidence but allows for the use of other levels of evidence, depending upon the adopted hierarchy or levels of evidence. EBP also addresses caregiver expertise and the patient's values and expectations, both of which foster the individualization of the application of the current best evidence.

E. Implications for practice

1. The importance of EBP is evident.

a) New requirements from regulatory and accrediting agencies have been created, such as the Joint Commission on Accreditation of Healthcare Organizations' (JCAHO) Core Measures phase of the ORYX initiative requirement that fosters evidence-based performance measures in healthcare settings (JCAHO, 2003).

b) Professional nursing organizations have included EBP in core competencies and standards of practice, especially related to the role of advanced practice nurses (American Association of Colleges of Nursing, 2002; American Nurses Association, 1996; National Organization of Nurse Practitioner Faculty & American Association of Colleges of Nursing, 2002).

2. The managed care environment, with the demands for quality care and cost-effectiveness with less staff and less patient contact, supports the adoption of an evidence approach to practice, because there is no time to be administering care that does not make a difference.

a) Evidence gives a strong foundation of understanding upon which to base the adaptation of nursing care.

b) Learning the principles of skin care helps radiation oncology nurses to *safely* adapt their approach to promote healing of moist desquamated wounds caused by radiation therapy (Haas & Kuehn, 2001).

3. Advance practice nurses are generally the perfect facilitators for EBP in any radiation therapy

setting because they possess the clinical expertise; the awareness of patient, family, and healthcare providers' needs; and knowledge of the particular clinical system to be able to negotiate for both the basic process and the resultant practice changes.

4. EBP is extremely relevant in radiation oncology nursing, where an emphasis has always existed on two of the components of the EBP process.

   a) Clinical expertise of the radiation therapy nurse

   b) Appreciation of the patient's and family's values and expectations

F. Advantages

1. Advantages of adopting an evidence-based approach to practice exist from administrative, clinical practice, regulatory, and legal perspectives.

2. Overall, EBP is

   a) Safe—Prevents errors caused by variation or lack of clarity in practice

   b) Therapeutic—Improves patient outcomes

   c) Ethical—Decreases variations in care based on patient populations or healthcare providers

   d) Cost effective in the long term—Controls resource utilization and impacts reimbursement

   e) Legally defensible—Limits liabilities because a rationale can be provided for "best" practice

   f) Satisfaction—Promotes patient and caregiver satisfaction.

References

AGREE Collaboration. (2001). *Appraisal of guidelines, research, and evaluation (AGREE) instrument.* Retrieved November 4, 2003, from http://www.agreecollaboration.org

American Association of Colleges of Nursing. (2002) *Position statement on nursing research.* Retrieved November 3, 2003, from http://www.aacn.org

American Nurses Association. (1996). *Scope and standards of advanced practice registered nurses.* Washington, DC: Author.

Cates, J.R., Young, D.N., Guerriero, D.J., Jahn, W.T., Armine, J.P., Korbett, A.B., et al. (2001). Evaluating the quality of clinical practice guidelines. *Journal of Manipulative and Physiological Therapeutics, 24*(3), 170–176.

Craig, J.V. (2002). How to ask the right question. In J.V. Craig & R.L. Smyth (Eds.), *Evidence-based practice manual for nurses* (pp. 21–44). Philadelphia: Churchill Livingstone.

DePalma, J.A. (2000). Evidence-based clinical practice guidelines. *Seminars in Perioperative Nursing, 9,* 115–120.

DePalma, J.A., & McGuire, D.B. (2005). Research. In A.B. Hamric, J.A. Spross, & C.M. Hanson (Eds.), *Advanced nursing practice: An integrative approach* (3rd ed., pp. 257–300). Philadelphia: Saunders.

Gibbs, L.E. (2003). *Evidence-based practice for the helping professions.* Toronto, Canada. Thomson Brooks/Cole.

Goode, C.J., & Piedalue, F. (1999). Evidence-based clinical practice. *Journal of Nursing Administration, 29*(5), 15–21.

Goolsby, M.J. (2001). Evaluating and applying clinical practice guidelines. *Journal of the American Academy of Nurse Practitioners, 13*(1), 3–6.

Guyatt, G.H., Sinclair, J., Cook, D.J., & Glasziou, P. (1999). Users' guides to the medical literature: XVI. How to use a treatment recommendation. *JAMA, 281,* 1836–1843.

Haas, M., & Kuehn, E. (2001). Teletherapy: External radiation therapy outcomes In D.W. Bruner, G. Moore-Higgs, & M. Haas (Eds.), *Radiation therapy: Multidisciplinary management* (pp. 55–66). Sudbury, MA: Jones and Bartlett.

Hunt, J.M. (2002). Future perspectives of evidence-based practice. *Seminars in Oncology Nursing, 18,* 79–81.

Hunt, D.L., & McKibbon, K.A. (1997). Locating and appraising systematic reviews. *Annals of Internal Medicine, 126,* 532–538.

Institute of Medicine. (1990). *Clinical practice guidelines: Directions for a new program.* Washington, DC: National Academy Press.

Jennings, B.M., & Loan, L.A. (2001). Misconceptions among nurses about evidence-based practice. *Image: Journal of Nursing Scholarship, 33,* 121–127.

Jennings, B.M., Staggers, N., & Brosch, L.R. (1999). A classification scheme for outcome indicators. *Image: Journal of Nursing Scholarship, 31,* 381–388.

Joint Commission on Accreditation of Healthcare Organizations. (2003). *Specification manual for national implementation of hospital core measures. Version 2.0.* Oakbrook Terrace, IL: Author.

McSweeney, M., Spies, M., & Cann, C.J. (2001). Finding and evaluating clinical practice guidelines. *Nurse Practitioner, 26*(9), 30, 33–34, 39, 43–47.

National Organization of Nurse Practitioners Faculties & American Association of Colleges of Nursing. (2002). *Nurse practitioner primary care competencies in specialty areas: Adult, family, gerontological, pediatric, and women's health.* Washington, DC: U.S. Department of Health and Human Services.

Oncology Nursing Society. (2003). *ONS evidence-based author guidelines.* Retrieved November 17, 2003, from http://onsopcontent.ons.org/toolkits/ebp/index.htm

Pearson, M., & Craig, J.V. (2002). In J.V. Craig & R.L. Smyth (Eds.), *Evidence-based practice manual for nurses* (pp. 3–20). Philadelphia: Churchill Livingstone.

Rosswurm, M.A., & Larrabee, J.H. (1999). A model for change to evidence-based practice. *Image: Journal of Nursing Scholarship, 31,* 317–322.

Rutledge, D., Cope, D., Haas, M., Hinds, P., Moore, K., & Van Gerpen, R. (2001). *EBP Process Model.* Retrieved October 4, 2003, from http://onsopcontent.ons.org/toolkits/ebp/index.htm

Rutledge, D.N., & Grant, M. (2002). Introduction. *Seminars in Oncology Nursing, 18,* 1–2.

Sackett, D.L., Straus, S.E., Richardon, W.S., Rosenberg, W., & Haynes, R.B. (2000). *Evidence-based medicine: How to practice and teach EBM* (2nd ed.). Philadelphia: Churchill Livingstone.

Shaneyfelt, T.M., Mayo-Smith, M.F., & Rothwangl, J. (1999). Are guidelines following guidelines? The methodological quality of clinical practice guidelines in the peer-reviewed medical literature. *JAMA, 281,* 1900–1905.

Stetler, C.B. (1985). Research utilization: Defining the concept. *Image: Journal of Nursing Scholarship, 17,* 40–44.

Stetler, C.B., Morsi, D., Rucki, S., Broughton, S., Corrigan, B., Fitzgerald, J., et al. (1998). Utilization-focused integrative reviews in nursing service. *Applied Nursing Research, 1,* 195–206.

Titler, M.G. (1998). Use of research in practice. In G. Lobiondo-Wood & J. Haber (Eds.), *Nursing research* (4th ed., pp. 467–498). St Louis, MO: Mosby.

White, S.J. (1997). Evidence-based practice and nursing. The new panacea? *British Journal of Nursing, 6,* 175–178.

Radiation Oncology Nursing Practice and Education

I. The clinical practicum

A. Course description: The didactic portion of this course is designed to prepare the registered nurse to practice in a radiation oncology setting. Course topics include the following.
 1. Principles and properties of ionizing radiation and radiobiology
 2. The purposes of radiation therapy (RT) as a cancer treatment modality
 3. General principles of patient and family education (radiation specific)
 4. Nursing assessment and management of general RT-related symptoms
 5. Nursing assessment and management of site-specific cancers and RT-related symptoms
 6. Description of modality-specific management, including brachytherapies, intraoperative radiotherapy, radiosurgery, hyperthermia, photodynamic therapy, and chemical modifiers
 7. Principles of radiation protection
 8. Current issues in RT, including palliative care, clinical trials research and informed consent, and nuclear/radiologic bioterrorism
 9. Quality improvement components
 10. Radiation oncology resources

B. Course objectives: At the completion of the didactic portion of this course, the nurse will be able to
 1. Discuss the principles and purposes of RT.
 2. Describe the principles of radiobiology.
 3. Assess patients undergoing RT for actual or potential problems and for general and site-specific side effects.
 4. Formulate a plan of care for a patient receiving RT, including patient assessment, evidence-based symptom management, patient/family education, measurable outcomes, and evaluation criteria.
 5. Teach the patient and family about the principles and procedures of RT and its potential side effects, and provide instruction in appropriate self-care measures.
 6. Describe the nursing management of the patient receiving external beam RT, interstitial brachytherapy, low-dose intracavitary brachytherapy, intravascular brachytherapy, intraoperative RT, stereotactic radiosurgery, hyperthermia, photodynamic therapy, and chemical modifiers.
 7. Describe evidence-based indications of palliative radiotherapy and the nursing manage-

ment of patients receiving palliative radiotherapy, including pain management.
 8. When appropriate (not all centers treat children), describe the nursing management for the special needs of children receiving radiotherapy including sedation, immobilization, comfort, and psychological support of patient and parents.
 9. Document key components of patient care basic to all radiotherapies.
 10. Describe radiation protection and safety precautions, procedures, and protocols, including policies and procedures to help prevent or assist in managing injuries caused in the event of bioterrorism.
 11. Identify components of a comprehensive quality improvement program.
 12. Describe the nurse's role in the informed consent process for clinical trials and the resources available to access clinical trials.

C. Clinical activities
 1. A qualified preceptor will supervise the nurse for a specified time period that is individualized, depending on the nurse's ability and skill in meeting the specific objectives and institutional standards.
 2. The preceptor and the nurse will establish specific objectives at the beginning of the clinical practicum to meet previously defined course objectives. The nurse and the preceptor may accomplish objectives by selecting a specific population of patients and providing the nurse with a period of supervised direct observation followed by independent responsibility for planning the care of these patients.
 3. The nurse will observe the role of the radiation therapist, dosimetrist, and physicist and understand the interdisciplinary nature of therapeutic planning and treatment.
 4. The nurse will demonstrate knowledgeable and effective patient and family teaching regarding the expected side effects of RT by disease site and modality. The nurse will instruct the patient and family in appropriate self-care measures to prevent and manage therapy-related side effects.

5. The nurse will perform histories and physicals during consultation, treatment, and follow-up appointments based upon the practice setting.
6. The nurse will perform targeted physical assessment as appropriate to symptom management.
7. The nurse will describe and document an appropriate plan of care and communicate the plan of care to the patient, family, and multidisciplinary team.
8. The nurse will initiate appropriate symptom management measures.
9. The nurse will make appropriate patient referrals (e.g., dietitian, pain management team, sexual counselor).
10. The nurse will evaluate and document the plan of care and revise the plan as needed.
11. The nurse will be able to verbalize principles of radiation protection and will be observed using appropriate radiation safety procedures.
12. The nurse will assist in identifying appropriate clinical trial options and will assume an appropriate role in the informed consent process for patients interested in clinical trials.

D. Evaluation
1. An evaluation tool based on the practicum course objectives and individual objectives set with the preceptor can be used to determine performance during consultation, treatment, and follow-up phases of care. The evaluation documents the nurse's
   a) Understanding of the principles of radiobiology and RT
   b) Knowledge of radiation side effects, patient assessment, and care management related to the treatment site and the radiotherapeutic modality used
   c) Ability to formulate individualized care plans for patients receiving RT
   d) Knowledge of patient-education principles, including patient literacy, mental ability to learn, and age-specific and cultural issues
   e) Knowledge of radiation protection and safety principles.
2. The activities indicated in Figure 2 should be performed at a satisfactory level. If the nurse has not had an opportunity to carry out a particular activity, indicate "N/A" (not applicable).

Figure 2. Clinical Practicum Evaluation Tool

Date of Performance:	Satisfactory		
	Yes	No	N/A
Consultation, Simulation, and Treatment Planning Phase			
1. Identifies self and nursing role to patient			
2. Checks patient identification			
3. Verifies that informed consent has been obtained			
4. Obtains nursing history and assessment			
5. Identifies patient's physical and psychosocial needs			
6. Assesses patient's literacy level and ability to learn			
7. Teaches patient and family about general and site-specific side effects of radiation therapy and self-care measures			
8. Solicits questions to be sure patient and family understand teaching			
9. Explains treatment protocols appropriate to patient (e.g., external beam radiation, brachytherapy, radiosensitizers, radioprotectors, hyperfractionation, total body irradiation, combined modality therapy)			
10. Reinforces discussion of appropriate clinical trials and assists in informed consent process			
11. Documents individualized plan of care			
12. Communicates plan of care to patient, family, and radiation therapy team			

(Continued)

Figure 2. Clinical Practicum Evaluation Tool *(Continued)*

	Satisfactory		
	Yes	No	N/A
Treatment Phase			
1. Assesses patient for general side effects of treatment (e.g., fatigue, skin changes)			
2. Assesses patient for acute site-specific or modality-specific side effects of treatment (e.g., alopecia, mucositis)			
3. Initiates measures to manage general side effects (e.g., dry desquamation, moist desquamation, anorexia)			
4. Initiates measures to manage site-specific side effects (e.g., mucositis)			
5. Teaches self-care measures to manage side effects of treatment			
6. Alerts patient to report potentially dangerous or uncomfortable symptoms immediately to nurse or physician			
7. Monitors patient's psychological status and coping skills			
8. Explains procedures and answers patient's questions			
9. Documents patient's response to treatment and symptom management			
10. Checks appropriate laboratory data and communicates results to other members of healthcare team as needed			
11. Institutes appropriate radiation safety precautions			
12. Consults and collaborates with other members of the healthcare team. Demonstrates effective communication skills			
13. Refers patients as needed to appropriate specialists (e.g., dietitian, pain management team, sexual counselor)			
14. Discusses discharge instructions with patient and family			
Follow-Up Phase			
1. Assesses patient for late effects of treatment			
2. Teaches or reinforces appropriate self-care measures			
3. Assesses patient for symptoms of recurrent disease			
4. Monitors patient's psychological status and coping skills			
5. Consults and collaborates with other members of the healthcare team as needed			
6. Checks appropriate laboratory and diagnostic data			
7. Reinforces need for patient to continue to report potentially dangerous or uncomfortable symptoms immediately to nurse or physician			
8. Evaluates and documents long-term response to therapy and side effects			
9. Refers patients as needed to appropriate specialists (e.g., dietitian, pain management team, sexual counselor)			
10. Instructs patient in cancer prevention and early detection measures			

II. The practice of radiation oncology

A. Principles of RT
  1. Definition of RT
      a) RT is the use of high-energy x-rays or particles to treat disease.
      b) Radiation with sufficient energy to disrupt atomic structures by ejecting orbital electrons is called ionizing radiation (Khan, 2003).
  2. Types of ionizing radiation commonly used in treatment (see Figure 3)
      a) Electromagnetic radiation: X-rays and gamma rays have the same characteristics but differ in origin.
        (1) X-rays: Photons (i.e., "packets" of energy generated from an electrical machine) (e.g., linear accelerator)
        (2) Gamma rays: Photons emitted from the nucleus of a radioactive source (e.g., cobalt-60, cesium-137, iridium-192).
      b) Particulate radiation: Consists of particles, including alpha particles, electrons, neutrons, and protons
        (1) Alpha particles: Large, positively charged particles with poor penetrating ability; emitted during disintegration (i.e., decay) of some radioactive source (e.g., radium); have a mass approximately 8,000 times that of an electron
        (2) Electrons: Small, negatively charged particles accelerated to high energies by an electrical machine
        (3) Beta particles: Electrons emitted during disintegration of radioactive sources
        (4) Protons: Large, positively charged particles that may be generated by an electrical machine; have a mass approximately 2,000 times that of an electron
        (5) Neutrons: Large, uncharged particles that may be generated by a large machine (e.g., cyclotron)
  3. Sources of radiation for treatment (see Figure 3) (Van Dyk, 1999)
      a) Megavoltage machines: Treatment machines used for external beam radiotherapy or teletherapy (treatment from a distance)
        (1) Linear accelerator: Machine generating ionizing radiation from electricity. These machines are commissioned to treat with x-rays (intermediate to deep depth of penetration and low to moderate skin dose) or electrons (shallow depth of penetration and high skin dose); depth of treatment varies with energy and type of radiation. Linear accelerators may have multiple energies of both x-rays and electrons, so depth of treatment may be selected for various tumor depths.
        (2) Cobalt-60 machine: Radioactive source (cobalt-60) emission of gamma rays; treatment depth is comparable to a 4 MeV x-ray beam (intermediate depth of penetration).
        (3) Cyclotron: Large, electrically powered machine that produces neutrons (large particles) or protons
      b) Radionuclides: Radioactive sources that emit radiation in the form of alpha and beta particles or gamma rays; each radionuclide emits particles and/or rays with energies that are characteristic of that specific radionuclide.

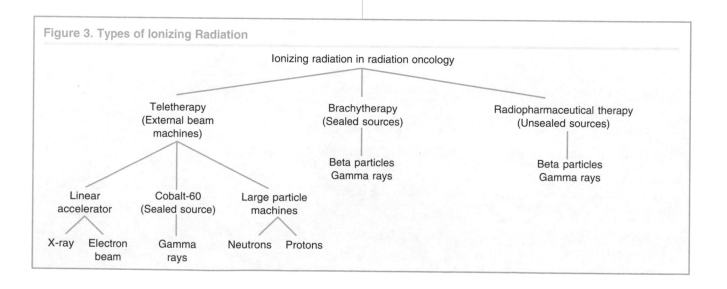

Figure 3. Types of Ionizing Radiation

(1) Brachytherapy (Therapy performed by placing radioactive material in or near the treatment volume. May be done with solid or liquid radioactive material): The therapeutic use of radionuclides that are sealed within metal containers; radioactive particles and/or rays penetrate the container to treat the disease. Sources are placed directly into (interstitial) or adjacent to (intracavitary, intraluminal surface) tumors. Small volumes of normal tissue and cancer can be irradiated to relatively high doses.

(a) Temporary: Sealed radioactive sources (e.g., iridium-192, cesium-137) are removed after the prescribed dose is reached in the calculated number of hours.

  i) High dose rate (HDR) treatment: One or several doses are administered and separated by at least six hours. Each dose is administered over a few minutes.

  ii) Low dose rate (LDR) treatment: Continuous LDR treatment is administered over several days.

(b) Permanent: Sealed radioactive source(s) are left permanently in the tissue. Sources used for permanent placement (e.g., iodine-125, gold-198, palladium) have relatively short half-lives and weak gamma emissions.

(2) Radiopharmaceutical therapy: Treatment with unsealed liquid radioactive sources that are ingested, injected, or instilled; each radionuclide has characteristics that determine where it can concentrate in the body. Oral iodine-131 is used to treat thyroid diseases. IV strontium-89 or samarium-153 is used to treat multiple bone metastases.

4. Radioactivity

a) Isotope: A nucleus contains protons and neutrons. The number of protons and neutrons determines which "element" it is. The number of neutrons determines which "isotope." An element may have both stable and radioactive isotopes (Khan, 2003).

b) Nuclei of radioactive elements have excess energy. Radioactive materials (also called radionuclides or radioactive sources/isotopes) decay and emit radiation in the form of alpha and beta particles and gamma rays until they become stable. Radioactivity, or radioactive decay, is the spontaneous emission (disintegration) of highly energetic particles or rays from the nuclei of an element. Radioactivity is measured in disintegration per second (DPS).

c) Half-life is the period of time required for a radioactive substance to lose one-half of its radioactivity through nuclear decay. The spontaneous decay or expulsion of particles and rays from a radionuclide occurs at a characteristic rate for each element.

d) A radioactive element radiates energy that is characteristic of that element. Some radioactive sources emit more penetrating radiation than others and, therefore, require more shielding to absorb the radiation. Fifty percent of the radioactivity from a source is absorbed by one half-value layer (HVL) of a substance, such as lead.

e) The characteristics of a radionuclide vary with the specific isotope. Table 2 shows the half-life, energy, and HVL of common elements.

Table 2. Characteristics of Radionuclides

Element	Half-Life	Energy	Half Value Layer[a] (lead [Pb])
Radium-226 (^{226}Ra)	1,620 years	1.0 MeV (gamma)	1.66 cm
Cesium-137 (^{137}Cs)	30.0 years	0.66 MeV (gamma)	0.65 cm
Cobalt-60 (^{60}Co)	5.2 years	1.25 MeV (gamma)	1.2 cm
Iridium-192 (^{192}Ir)	64.2 days	0.13–1.06 MeV (gamma)	0.6 cm
Iodine-131 (^{131}I)	8.0 days	0.36 MeV (gamma)	0.3 cm
Gold-198 (^{198}Au)	2.7 days	0.41 MeV (gamma)	0.33 cm
Iodine-125 (^{125}I)	60.2 days	0.02 MeV (gamma)	0.02 cm
Strontium-89 (^{89}Sr)	50.5 days	1.46 MeV (beta)	1 mm of lead blocks (100% of ^{89}Sr)

[a] One half value layer blocks 50% of the radiation.

Note. Based on information from Cember, 1996; St. Germain, 1993a, 1993b.

5. Measurement of radiation (see Figure 4) (Khan, 2003)

   a) Radiation-absorbed dose (RAD) is the amount of energy absorbed per unit mass. Radiation previously had been prescribed in RAD but is now prescribed in Gray (Gy). 1 Gy = 100 centiGray (cGy) = 100 RAD.

   b) Dose equivalent is used in radiation protection. Badge readings have been reported in millirem (mrem). Sievert (Sv) is the international unit for dose equivalent (100 rem = 1 Sv).

   c) Activity of radioactive sources has been measured in Curies (Ci). Becquerel (Bq) is the international unit. Both units are measured as DPS. 1 Ci = 3.7 x 10^{10} DPS. 1 Bq = 1 DPS = 2.7 x 10^{-11} Ci.

B. Radiobiology

1. Radiobiology is the study of events that occur after ionizing radiation is absorbed by a living organism. Ionizing radiation can result in breaking of chemical bonds and, eventually, in biologic change (see Figure 5). The nature and severity of effects and the time in which they appear depend on the amount and type of radiation adsorbed and the rate at which it is administered. Early and late responding tissues are affected differently by these factors. Interaction of radiation in cells is random and has no selectivity for any structure or site (Hall, 2000).

2. If critical sites are damaged by radiation, the probability of cell death is higher than if a noncritical site is damaged. DNA is considered to be the critical target for radiation damage. Cells can successfully repair much damage caused by ionizing radiation (Hall, 2000).

3. Response to ionizing radiation: Damage to DNA may lead to cell alteration or death. All living cells, whether normal or cancerous, are susceptible to the effects of radiation and may be injured or destroyed by RT. Injury generally is expressed at the time of cell division (reproductive death).

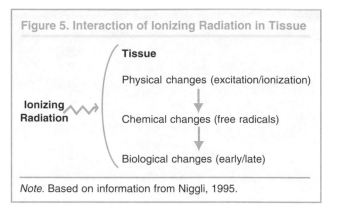

Figure 5. Interaction of Ionizing Radiation in Tissue

Ionizing Radiation →

Tissue

Physical changes (excitation/ionization)

↓

Chemical changes (free radicals)

↓

Biological changes (early/late)

Note. Based on information from Niggli, 1995.

   a) Physical stage: Excitation and ionization of atoms or molecules

   b) Radiochemical stage: Formation of free radicals, which are highly reactive

   c) Biologic stage: Damage to critical target (DNA, which is composed of two strands that form a double helix)

      (1) Single chromosomal strand breaks: These generally are repaired readily and have little biologic consequence (Rossi, 1996). Misrepair (incorrect repair) may result in mutation.

      (2) Double chromosomal strand break (DSB): DSBs are believed to be the most important damage produced in chromosomes by radiation and may result in cell death, mutation, or carcinogenesis. DSBs may activate an oncogene or inactivate a tumor suppressor gene (Hall & Cox, 1994).

4. Potential effects on a single cell in an irradiated volume of tissue (see Figure 6) include the following.

   a) No effect or no cell injury occurs in critical target.

   b) Radiation damage to critical target is repaired; cell continues to function and divide.

   c) Radiation damage to critical target is misrepaired and mutation occurs.

   d) Cell death occurs.

5. Radiation-induced chromosome aberration effects (Bender, 1995; Hall, 1994, 2000; Hall & Cox, 1994) include the following.

   a) Cell killing induced by radiation

      (1) Chromosome damage may cause reproductive failure (death at the time of cell division).

      (2) Apoptosis (programmed cell death), the process that occurs during normal development of organs and tissues, is enhanced by toxic treatments such as RT (Dewey, Ling, & Meyn, 1995).

Figure 4. Units of Measurement for Radiation

- Absorbed dose (Gray [Gy], radiation-absorbed dose [RAD]) (therapeutic doses)
  1 Gy = 100 RAD; 100 centigray (cGy) = 100 RAD

- Dose equivalent (Sievert [Sv], REM) (radiation protection)
  1 Sv = 100 REM

- Activity (Becquerel [Bq], Curie [Ci]) (activity of radionuclides)
  1 Bq = 2.7 x 10^{-11} Ci = 1 dps; 1 Ci = 3.7 x 10^{10} dps

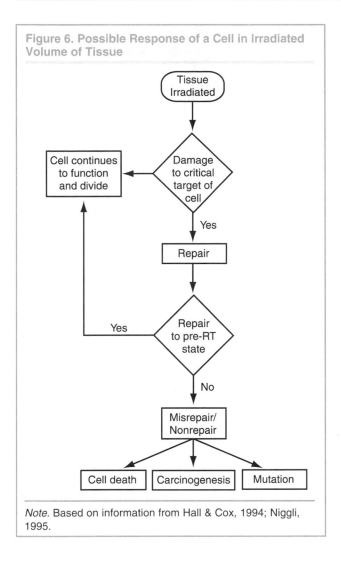

Figure 6. Possible Response of a Cell in Irradiated Volume of Tissue

Tissue Irradiated

Damage to critical target of cell

Cell continues to function and divide

Yes

Repair

Repair to pre-RT state

Yes

No

Misrepair/ Nonrepair

Cell death   Carcinogenesis   Mutation

Note. Based on information from Hall & Cox, 1994; Niggli, 1995.

b) Mutation (germ cells): Heritable change in genes expressed in later generations: A large variation in mutation types exists.

c) Carcinogenesis (somatic cells): Chromosome aberration that may cause oncogene activation or suppressor gene loss (Hall, 1994)

6. Radiosensitivity is the innate sensitivity of cells, tissues, or tumors to radiation. Both normal and cancer cells are affected by radiation. Cells vary in their expressed sensitivity to radiation. Generally, rapidly dividing cells are most sensitive (e.g., mucosa) and are referred to as radiosensitive. Nondividing or slowly dividing cells generally are less radiosensitive, or radioresistant (e.g., muscle cells, neurons). Exceptions include small lymphocytes and salivary gland cells, which are nondividing but are very radiosensitive. These may experience an interphase death (death prior to mitosis).

a) Manifestations of radiation effects occur at different times for different tissues (Hall & Cox, 1994).

(1) Acutely responding tissues demonstrate effects in hours to days and include the bone marrow, ovaries, testes, lymph nodes, salivary glands, small bowel, stomach, colon, oral mucosa, larynx, esophagus, arterioles, skin, bladder, capillaries, and vagina.

(2) Subacutely responding tissues demonstrate effects in weeks to several months after RT and include the lungs, liver, kidneys, heart, spinal cord, and brain.

(3) Late-responding tissues, including the lymph vessels, thyroid, pituitary gland, breasts, bones, cartilage, pancreas (endocrine), uterus, and bile ducts, rarely show acute effects and demonstrate effects months to years after RT.

b) Factors that influence radiation sensitivity include the following (Hall & Cox, 1994; Niggli, 1995).

(1) Cell-cycle phase: Cells in late G2 and mitosis (M) phases are more sensitive. Cells in the late synthesis (S) phase are most resistant to radiation.

(2) Oxygen: The presence of oxygen enhances radiation damage. When oxygen is not present, chemical damage in DNA may be repaired. Reoxygenation occurs as the tumor shrinks during RT, and previously hypoxic cells become better oxygenated. Hypoxia may contribute to radioresistance.

(3) Differentiation: Poorly differentiated tumors generally are more sensitive. Far more radiation is required to destroy the function of a differentiated cell than is required to destroy a dividing cell (Hall, 2000). However, poor differentiation of a tumor is associated with a poor disease-free survival rate, perhaps because of a more aggressive natural history (Bentzen, 1993).

(4) Proliferative capacity: Rapidly dividing cells generally are more sensitive to the effects of radiation. Nondividing or slowly dividing cells usually are less sensitive, or radioresistant.

(5) Repair of radiation damage: The greater the repair capability of the normal tissue, the greater the effectiveness of the radiation. DNA damage can be repaired to its original state or misrepaired with errors (mutation). Most repairs are believed to occur within six hours after a treatment.

(6) Tumor size: Tumor size is a major factor in dose-response outcomes of

RT. Larger tumors generally are more difficult to control than small tumors of the same type. Control of large tumor masses may require a radiation dose that would result in unacceptable damage to normal tissue. Often, the tumor bulk indicates a poorly oxygenated mass that, thus, is less radiosensitive.

(7) Fractionation: This is the division of a total prescribed dose into smaller daily doses, or fractions. Daily fractions generally are 1.8–2.0 Gy. Fraction size is the dominant factor in determining late effects on tissue, with large fractions causing an increase in late effects.

(a) Hyperfractionation: Multiple daily fractions (e.g., 1.2 Gy twice a day) are delivered, generally separated by at least six hours to allow for repair of damage to the normal tissues from the first dose before administering the second dose (Hall, 2000).

(b) The intent is to decrease late effects while achieving equal or improved tumor control and equal or slightly increased early effects. A higher total dose is administered.

(8) Quality of radiation: Energy of various types of radiation is distributed differently in tissues. Heavy particles (e.g., neutrons, alpha particles) ionize densely and quickly; light particles (e.g., electrons) ionize sparsely in tissues.

(a) Linear energy transfer (LET) is the distribution of energy along the ionization track in irradiated material. High LET radiation is densely ionizing and is less influenced by the presence of oxygen (i.e., more effective on hypoxic cells than low LET) and the cell-cycle phase. Less repair occurs with high LET radiation. Low LET radiation is sparsely ionizing.

(b) Relative biologic effectiveness of a radiation type is dependent on LET. High LET radiation is more biologically damaging than low LET radiation.

7. Effect of radiation on normal cells versus cancer cells (Hall & Cox, 1994)

a) Both normal cells and cancer cells are affected by radiation and are similar in their responses to RT. Only cancer cells are believed to undergo reoxygenation.

b) Malignant tumors differ greatly in radiosensitivity because of innate sensitivity, mitotic activity, hypoxic component, and blood supply.

c) Dividing a dose into multiple daily fractions spares normal tissues because of repair of damage between fractions and repopulation of cells if overall time is sufficient. Dose fractionation increases damage to cancer cells because of reoxygenation of the tumor and reassortment of cancer cells into more sensitive phases of the cell cycle.

d) Side effects are the result of radiation damage to normal cells.

C. Dose prescription, treatment planning, and simulation

1. Specification of dose and volume: The method of writing and interpreting a prescription is essential to the success of treatment.

a) The ICRU Report 50 (International Commission on Radiation Units and Measures [ICRU], 1993) definition of the treatment volume is separated into three distinct boundaries: (a) visible tumor, (b) a region to account for uncertainties in microscopic tumor spread, and (c) a region to account for positional uncertainties. These boundaries created three volumes (see Figure 7).

(1) Gross tumor volume (GTV): This is the gross extent of the malignant growth as determined by palpation or imaging study.

(2) Clinical tumor volume (CTV): This is the tissue volume that contains a GTV and/or subclinical microscopic malignant disease.

(3) Planning target volume (PTV): This volume is defined by specifying the margins that must be added around the CTV to compensate for the effects of organ, tumor, and patient movements and inaccuracies in beam and patient setup.

b) The ICRU Report 50 also defined two other dose volumes.

(1) Treated volume: This is the volume enclosed by an isodose surface that is selected and specified by the radiation oncologists as being appropriate to achieve the purpose of treatment (e.g., 95% isodose surface).

(2) Irradiated volume: This is the volume that receives a dose significant in relation to normal tissue tolerance (e.g., 50% isodose surface).

Figure 7. Schematic Illustration of the Boundaries of the Volumes Defined by ICRU 50

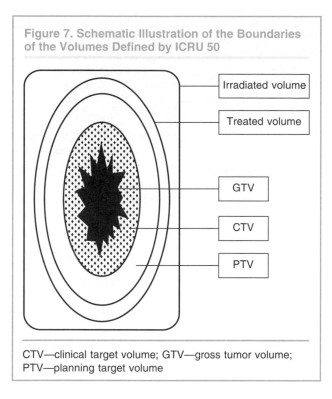

Irradiated volume

Treated volume

GTV

CTV

PTV

CTV—clinical target volume; GTV—gross tumor volume; PTV—planning target volume

c) Organs at risk (OAR) are defined as normal tissues whose radiation sensitivity may significantly influence treatment planning and/or prescribed dose.

d) ICRU 50 defines a series of doses including minimum, maximum, and mean dose for dose reporting purposes. Additionally, an ICRU reference dose is defined at the ICRU reference point. The ICRU reference point is chosen based on the following criteria: it must be clinically relevant, be defined in an unambiguous way, and be located where the dose can be accurately determined (not in a region where there are steep dose gradients). In general, this point should be in the central part of the PTV.

e) Dose volume histograms (DVHs) play an essential role in evaluating and in reporting three-dimensional radiotherapy dose distributions.

   (1) A cumulative DVH plots the fraction of a structure receiving at least a specified dose against the specified dose.

   (2) A differential DVH plots the fraction of a structure receiving a dose within a specified interval against the dose.

2. Treatment planning: Radiotherapy is a complex procedure that requires comprehensive treatment planning and quality assurance (QA). Treatment planning entails interactions among the radiation physicists, dosimetrists, radiation oncologists, residents, and radiation thera-

pists and the use of a large number of software programs and hardware devices for geometric and dosimetric planning and QA. The following are the steps in a treatment planning process (Fraass et al., 1998; Kutcher et al., 1994).

   a) Patient positioning and immobilization to ensure a consistent position during the course of imaging and treatment

   b) Patient data acquisition (computerized tomography [CT], magnetic resonance imaging [MRI], positron emission tomography [PET], manual contouring)

   c) Data transfer to treatment planning system

   d) Definition of treatment volume(s) and organs at risk (OARs)

   e) Treatment design (modality, beam arrangements, modifiers)

   f) Computation of dose distributions

   g) Plan evaluation (review of isodose distributions, DVHs, or other physical or biologic dosimetric parameters)

   h) Computation of monitor units or minutes based on the prescribed dose

   i) Production of blocks and beam modifiers

   j) Plan implementation (treatment simulation, data transfer to record, and verification of record and verify system)

   k) Patient-specific treatment planning QA (review of plan, chart, MU calculation, and port film and perform additional calculations or measurements to verify the dose)

3. Radiotherapy simulation: This is the process of aiming and defining the radiation beams to meet the goals of the prescribed therapy. It is mainly concerned with geometric aspects of a treatment, such as the orientation of beams, their sizes, the placement of field-shaping blocks, and the placement of marks on the patient to allow for reliable reproduction of treatment geometry from day to day. Unforeseeable problems with a patient setup or treatment technique also can be solved during simulation.

   a) A treatment simulator is an apparatus that uses a diagnostic x-ray tube but duplicates a radiation treatment unit in terms of its geometrical, mechanical, and optical properties.

   b) By radiographic visualization of internal organs, correct positioning of fields and shielding blocks can be obtained in relation to external landmarks (Farmer, Fowler, & Haggith, 1963; Greene, Nelson, & Gibb, 1964; Van Dyk, 1999).

4. A "virtual simulator" is a piece of software that performs treatment simulation based on a digital representation of the patient derived from serial CT or other tomographic images

(Sherouse, Mosher, Novins, Rosenma, & Chaney, 1987). Three-dimensional conformal radiotherapy (3DCRT): The goal of 3DCRT is to conform the spatial distribution of the prescribed radiation dose to the precise three-dimensional configuration of the treatment volume and, at the same time, to minimize the dose to the surrounding normal tissues (Smith & Purdy, 1991).

a) A three-dimensional treatment planning system (3DTPS) is needed to plan a radiotherapy treatment based on the three-dimensional treatment volume. A 3DTPS is generally characterized by acquisition of three-dimensional patient data, delineation of treatment portals based on a beam's eye view (BEV) projection of the PTV, calculation of dose in three-dimensional patient geometry, and display of dosimetric information in volumes.

b) 3DCRT is commonly delivered with megavoltage photon and electron beams using multileaf collimators (MLCs) or custom-designed blocks (cutouts) to shape uniform open fields (to match the BEV projection of the PTV) or using wedges or custom-designed compensators to account for the effect of surface irregularities and/or internal heterogeneities (to achieve uniform dose at a selected treatment depth, usually through the middle of the target volume).

5. Intensity-modulated radiotherapy (IMRT): IMRT is an advanced form of 3DCRT in which varying intensities (e.g., weights) of small subdivisions of beams (i.e., beamlets, field segments) are used to custom-design optimal radiation dose distributions (Webb, 2001). Because of the conformal dose distributions and steep dose gradients that can be achieved with IMRT, requirements for patient immobilization, target and structure delineation, treatment planning, beam delivery, and dose verification become more stringent (Boyer et al., 2000; Ma et al., 2000, 2002).

a) Special treatment planning software is needed to optimize the weights of individual beamlets (or field segments), via inverse planning (Bortfeld, Burkelbach, Boesecke, & Schlegel, 1990; Brahme, 1988; Webb, 1992) or forward planning (Galvin, Croce, & Bednarz, 2000; Xiao, Galvin, Hossain, & Valicenti, 2000), to achieve superior target coverage and normal tissue sparing, based on the specified dose requirements for the treatment volume(s) and dose constraints on the OARs.

b) Intensity-modulated radiation fields are commonly delivered using computer-controlled MLC (Convery & Rosenbloom, 1992; Ma, Boyer, Xing, & Ma, 1998; Spirou & Chui, 1994). However, beam intensity modulation also can be achieved using complex physical compensators.

D. Purpose of RT
1. RT is used to treat local or regional disease and, rarely, systemic disease. The aim is to destroy malignant cells in the treated volume of tissue while minimizing damage to normal tissues.
2. RT can be selected for various purposes (Haas & Kuehn, 2001).

a) Definitive treatment: RT is prescribed as the primary treatment modality, with or without chemotherapy, for the treatment of cancer. Examples can include cancer of the head/neck, lung, prostate, or bladder or Hodgkin's disease.

b) Neoadjuvant treatment: RT is prescribed prior to definitive treatment, usually surgery, to improve the chance of successful resection. Examples include esophageal or colon cancers.

c) Adjuvant treatment: RT is given after definitive treatment (either surgery or chemotherapy) to improve local control. Examples may include breast, lung, or high-risk rectal cancers.

d) Prophylaxis therapy: RT treats asymptomatic, high-risk areas to prevent growth of cancer. Examples are prophylactic cranial irradiation in lung cancer or central nervous system to prevent relapse of certain forms of leukemia.

e) Control: RT is given to limit the growth of cancer cells to extend the symptom-free interval for the patient. Examples may include pancreatic or lung cancers.

f) Palliation: RT is given to manage symptoms of bleeding, pain, airway obstruction, or neurologic compromise, alleviating life-threatening problems in noncurative patients or improving the patient's quality of life. Examples may include spinal cord compression, opening airways in patients with pneumonia, or bone metastases.

3. Tissue tolerance dose: The radiation dose to which a normal tissue can be irradiated and continue to function (see Table 3)

   a) Organs vary in their ability to tolerate radiation injury. Normal tissue tolerance to radiation depends on the ability of the dividing cells to produce enough mature cells to maintain function of the organ. The tolerance dose is the dose of radiation that results in an acceptable probability of a treatment complication (Hall, 2000).

   b) The amount of dose prescribed to eradicate a cancer ultimately is dependent on normal tissue tolerance of that dose.

4. Factors related to radiation-induced injury of normal tissue (Bentzen & Overgaard, 1994)

   a) Patient-related factors

      (1) Age

         (a) In children: Growth-related factors (e.g., growth retardation, endocrine changes)

         (b) In adults: Limited data available

      (2) Hemoglobin level

         (a) Low hemoglobin has been found to decrease local control probability in cancers such as squamous cell carcinoma of the head and neck (Fein et al., 1995; Regueiro, Millan, de la Torre, & Valcarcel, 1995), carcinoma of the cervix (Werner-Wasik et al., 1995), and transitional carcinoma of the bladder (Cole et al., 1995).

         (b) Little information is available concerning hemoglobin level related to normal tissue reactions.

      (3) Smoking: Can enhance some early and late side effects (Bentzen & Overgaard, 1994)

      (4) Tumor invasion: May interfere with normal tissue reactions

      (5) Infections: May increase normal tissue injury, especially when the immune system is compromised

   b) Intrinsic radiosensitivity

      (1) Genetic syndromes: Some are associated with increased sensitivity to RT (e.g., ataxia telangiectasia).

Table 3. Minimal and Maximal Tissue Tolerance to Radiotherapy Dose

Tissue	Dose-Related Injury	Minimal Tolerance Dose TD 5/5[a] (Gy)	Maximal Tolerance Dose TD 50/5[b] (Gy)	Amount of Tissue Treated (Field Size or Length)
Eye	Blindness			
	Retina	55	70	Whole
	Cornea	50	> 60	Whole
	Lens	5.0	12	Whole
Bone marrow	Aplasia, pancytopenia	2.5	4.5	Whole
		30	40	Segmental
Liver	Acute and chronic hepatitis	25	40	Whole
		15	20	Whole (strip)
Stomach	Perforation, ulcer, hemorrhage	45	55	100 cm²
Intestine	Ulcer, perforation, hemorrhage	45	55	400 cm²
		50	65	100 cm²
Brain	Infarction, necrosis	60	70	Whole
Spinal cord	Infarction, necrosis	45	55	10 cm
Heart	Pericarditis, pancarditis	45	55	60%
		70	80	25%
Lung	Acute and chronic pneumonitis	30	35	100 cm²
		15	25	Whole
Kidney	Acute and chronic nephrosclerosis	15	20	Whole (strip)
		20	25	Whole
Uterus	Necrosis, perforation	> 10	> 200	Whole
Vagina	Ulcer, fistula	90	> 100	Whole
Fetus	Death	2.0	4.0	Whole

[a] TD 5/5 = minimal tolerance dose; the dose, given to a population of patients under a standard set of treatment conditions, that will result in no more than a 5% rate of severe complications within five years after treatment.

[b] TD 50/5 = maximal tolerance dose; the dose, given to a population of patients under a standard set of treatment conditions, that will result in a 50% rate of severe complications within five years after treatment.

Note. Based on information from Bentel et al., 1989; Rubin et al., 1975.

(2) Autoimmune diseases (e.g., systemic lupus erythematosus)

5. Considerations for RT
   a) Diagnosis and staging: Tumor histology and extent of disease
   b) General condition of patient and comorbid conditions
   c) Tumor site: Are normal tissues included in treatment fields?
   d) Combination therapy (e.g., chemotherapy, hyperthermia, immunotherapy, biotherapy): The goal is to improve the therapeutic ratio relative to the use of a single modality of treatment (Hall & Cox, 1994).
   e) Available treatment facilities

6. Radioresponsiveness of normal tissue (see Figure 8)
   a) Expression of normal tissue injury varies greatly from patient to patient.
   b) Response of a tissue or organ primarily depends on the radiosensitivity of the cells and the kinetics of the population in which the cells are functioning.
   c) Treatment characteristics include total dose, dose per fraction or dose rate, and overall treatment time.
   d) With combined modality therapy (e.g., sequential/concomitant chemotherapy), interactions may substantially influence side effects of RT.

7. Side effects
   a) Early side effects
      (1) Occur during or immediately after RT
      (2) Depend on total dose, dose per fraction, and overall treatment time (Bentzen, 1993)
      (3) Do not predict for late side effects
   b) Late side effects
      (1) Occur months to years after RT and usually are a result of damage to the microcirculation
      (2) Depend highly on dose per fraction. High dose per fraction results in more severe late effects.

(3) The time from RT to a specific late effect is the latent period.

(4) Late injury expression is time dependent. Severity and percentage of patients expressing the injury increases over time (Bentzen, 1993).

References

Bender, M.A. (1995). Cytogenetics research in radiation biology. *Stem Cells, 13*(Suppl. 1), 172–181.

Bentel, G.C., Nelson, C.E., & Noell, K.T. (1989). *Treatment planning and dose calculation in radiation oncology.* Elmsford, NY: Pergamon Press.

Bentzen, S.M. (1993). Quantitative clinical radiobiology. *Acta Oncologica, 32,* 259–275.

Bentzen, S.M., & Overgaard, J. (1994). Patient-to-patient variability in the expression of radiation-induced normal tissue injury. *Seminars in Radiation Oncology, 4*(2), 68–80.

Bortfeld, T., Burkelbach, J., Boesecke, R., & Schlegel, W. (1990). Methods of image reconstruction from projections applied to conformation radiotherapy. *Physics in Medicine and Biology, 35,* 1423–1434.

Boyer, A.L., Mok, E., Luxton, G., Findley, D., Chen, Y., Pawlicki, T., et al. (2000). Quality assurance for treatment planning dose delivery by 3DCRT and IMRT. In A.S. Shiu & D.E. Mellenberg (Eds.), *General practice of radiation oncology physics in the 21st century* (pp. 187–230). Madison, WI: Medical Physics Publishing.

Brahme, A. (1988). Optimization of stationary and moving beam radiation therapy techniques. *Radiotherapy Oncology, 12,* 129–140.

Cember, H. (1996). *Introduction to health physics* (3rd ed.). New York: McGraw-Hill.

Cole, C.J., Pollack, A., Zagars, G.K., Dinney, C.P., Swanson, D.A., & von-Eschenback, A.C. (1995). Local control of muscle-invasive bladder cancer: Preoperative radiotherapy and cystectomy versus cystectomy alone. *International Journal of Radiation Oncology, Biology, Physics, 32,* 331–340.

Convery, D., & Rosenbloom, M.E. (1992). The generation of intensity modulated fields for conformal radiation therapy by dynamic collimation. *Physics in Medicine and Biology, 37,* 1359–1374.

Dewey, W.C., Ling, C.C., & Meyn, R.E. (1995). Radiation-induced apoptosis: Relevance to radiotherapy. *International Journal of Radiation Oncology, Biology, Physics, 33,* 781–796.

Farmer, F.T., Fowler, J.F., & Haggith, J.W. (1963). Megavoltage treatment planning and the use of xeroradiography. *British Journal of Radiology, 36,* 426–435.

Fein, D.A., Lee, W.R., Hanlon, A.L., Ridge, R.A., Langer, C.J., Curran, W.J., et al. (1995). Pretreatment hemoglobin level influences local control and survival of t1-t2 squamous cell carcinomas of the glottic larynx. *Journal of Clinical Oncology, 13,* 2077–2083.

Fraass, B., Doppke, K., Hunt, M., Kutcher, G., Starkschall, G., Stern, R., et al. (1998). American Association of Physicists in Medicine Radiation Therapy Committee Task Group 53: Quality assurance for clinical radiotherapy treatment planning. *Medical Physics, 25,* 1773–1829.

Galvin, J.M., Croce, R., & Bednarz, G. (2000). Advanced forward planning techniques; forward treatment planning is alive and well in the IMRT world. In A.S. Shiu & D.E. Mellenberg (Eds.), *General practice of radiation oncology physics in the 21st century* (pp. 73–100). Madison, WI: Medical Physics Publishing.

Greene, D., Nelson, K.A., & Gibb, R. (1964). The use of a linear accelerator "simulator" in radiotherapy. *British Journal of Radiology, 37,* 394–397.

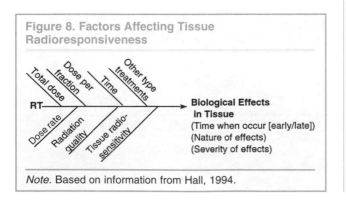

Figure 8. Factors Affecting Tissue Radioresponsiveness

RT → Biological Effects in Tissue
(Time when occur [early/late])
(Nature of effects)
(Severity of effects)

Total dose, Dose per fraction, Time, Other type treatments, Dose rate, Radiation quality, Tissue radiosensitivity

Note. Based on information from Hall, 1994.

Haas, M.L., & Kuehn, E.F. (2001). Teletherapy: External radiation therapy. In D.W. Bruner, G. Moore-Higgs, & M.L. Haas (Eds.), *Outcomes in radiation therapy: Multidisciplinary management* (pp. 55–66). Sudbury, MA: Jones and Bartlett.

Hall, E.J. (1994). Molecular biology in radiation therapy: The potential impact of recombinant technology on clinical practice. *International Journal of Radiation Oncology, Biology, Physics, 30,* 1019–1028.

Hall, E.J. (2000). *Radiobiology for the radiologist* (5th ed.). Philadelphia: Lippincott Williams & Wilkins.

Hall, E.J., & Cox, J.D. (1994). Physical and biologic basis of radiation therapy. In J.D. Cox (Ed.), *Moss' radiation oncology: Rationale, technique, results* (7th ed., pp. 3–65). St. Louis, MO: Mosby.

International Commission on Radiation Units and Measures. (1993). Report No. 50. *Prescribing, recording and reporting photon beam therapy.* Bethesda, MD: Author.

Khan, F.M. (2003). *Physics of radiation therapy* (3rd ed.). Philadelphia: Lippincott Williams & Wilkins.

Kutcher, G., Coia, L., Gillin, M., Hanson, W., Leibel, S., Morton, R., et al. (1994). Comprehensive QA for radiation oncology: Report of AAPM Radiation Therapy Committee Task Group 40. *Medical Physics, 21,* 581–618.

Ma, C.M., Pawlicki, T., Jiang, S.B., Mok, E., Kapur, A., Xing, L., et al. (2000). Monte Carlo verification of IMRT dose distributions from a commercial treatment planning optimization system. *Physics in Medicine and Biology, 45,* 2483–2495.

Ma, C.M., Price, R.A., McNeeley, S., Chen, L., Li, J.S., Wang, L., et al. (2002). Clinical implementation and quality assurance for intensity modulated radiation therapy. *Proceedings of the International Symposium on Standards and Codes of Practice in Medical Radiation Dosimetry.* Vienna: IAEA, IAEA-CA-96-120.

Ma, L., Boyer, A.L., Xing, L., & Ma, C.M. (1998) An optimized leaf-sequencing algorithm for beam intensity modulation using dynamic multileaf collimators. *Physics in Medicine and Biology, 43,* 1629–1643.

Niggli, H.F. (1995). 100 years of radiobiology: Implications for biomedicine and future perspectives. *Experientia, 51,* 652–664.

Regueiro, C.A., Millan, I., de la Torre, A., & Valcarcel, F.J. (1995). Influence of boost technique (external-beam radiotherapy or brachytherapy) on the outcome of patients with carcinoma of the base of the tongue. *Acta Oncologica, 34,* 225–233.

Rossi, H.H. (1996). Radiation physics and radiobiology. *Health Physics, 70,* 828–831.

Rubin, P., Cooper, R., & Phillips, T.L. (1975). *Radiation biology and radiation pathology syllabus, set RT 1: Radiation oncology.* Chicago: American College of Radiology.

Sherouse, G.W., Mosher, C.E., Novins, K.L., Rosenma, K.L., & Chaney, E.L. (1987). Virtual simulation: concept and implementation. In I.A.D. Bruinvis, P.H. van der Giessen, H.J. van Kleffens, & F.W. Wittkamper (Eds.), *Ninth international conference on the use of computers in radiation therapy* (pp. 433–436). Scheveningen, Netherlands: NorthHollan Publishing.

Smith, A.R., & Purdy, J.A. (Eds.). (1991). Three-dimensional photon treatment planning. Report of the collaborative working group on the evaluation of treatment planning for external photon beam radiotherapy. *International Journal of Radiation Oncology, Biology, Physics, 21,* 79–89.

Spirou, S.V., & Chui, C.S. (1994). Generation of arbitrary intensity profiles by dynamic jaws and multileaf collimators. *Medical Physics, 21,* 1031–1041.

St. Germain, J. (1993a). Personnel protection in medicine. In G.G. Eichholz & J.J. Shonka (Eds.), *Hospital health physics: Proceedings of the 1993 Health Physics Society Summer School* (pp. 91–102). Richland, WA: Health Physics Society.

St. German, J. (1993b). External monitoring within a medical environment. In G.G. Eichholz & J.J. Shonka (Eds.), *Hospital health physics: Proceedings of the 1993 Health Physics Society Summer School* (pp. 103–118). Richland, WA: Health Physics Society.

Van Dyk, J. (1999). *The modern technology of radiation oncology.* Madison, WI: Medical Physics Publishing.

Webb, S. (1992). Optimization by simulated annealing of three-dimensional conformal treatment planning for radiation fields defined by multi-leaf collimator: II. Inclusion of two-dimensional modulation of x-ray intensity. *Physics in Medicine and Biology, 37,* 1689–1704.

Webb, S. (2001). *Intensity-modulated radiation therapy.* Philadelphia: Institute of Physics Publishing.

Werner-Wasik, M., Schmid, C.H., Bornstein, L., Ball, H.G., Smith, D.M., & Madoc-Jones, H. (1995). Prognostic factors for local and distant recurrences in stage I and II cervical carcinoma. *International Journal of Radiation Oncology, Biology, Physics, 32,* 1309–1317.

Xiao, Y., Galvin, J., Hossain, M., & Valicenti, R. (2000). An optimized forward-planning technique for intensity modulated radiation therapy. *Medical Physics, 27,* 2093–2099.

III. Radiation protection

A. Diagnostic sources/types offered

1. Sources of potential radiation exposure in the medical setting

   a) X-rays from external radiograph studies (general x-rays, including portable x-ray units, fluoroscopy [e.g., C-arm fluoroscopic units], dental x-rays, CT scans, mammograms)

      (1) "Fluoroscopy for diagnostic imaging represents the largest source of occupational exposure in medicine because the operator must be present in the exam room and the x-ray tube used may be energized for considerable periods of time" (National Council on Radiation Protection and Measurements [NCRP], 1990, pp. 4–5).

      (2) General radiography poses little exposure if the operator is protected behind the shielded barrier (Bruner, Bucholtz, Iwamoto, & Strohl, 1998).

   b) Radiation emitted from radionuclides used in nuclear medicine studies (bone scan, thyroid scan, heart scan, radionuclide angiography, lymphoscintigraphy [sentinel lymph node localization])

   c) Radiation emitted from radionuclides used in laboratory departments (in-vitro studies on blood, urine, or cells and radioimmunoassays and laboratory research studies that use radionuclides)

2. Sources from therapeutic uses of ionizing radiation

a) External beam radiotherapy (teletherapy) sources (x-rays, gamma rays, electrons, protons, neutrons) (Bucholtz, 1994)
  (1) Because personnel are not permitted inside the treatment room for external beam radiotherapy, this source represents little exposure risk unless lower energy contact therapy orthovoltage sources are used and operated by personnel or if inadequate shielding is used for external beam equipment.
  (2) The patient receiving external beam radiation is not radioactive and poses no exposure risk to personnel, the public, or the family.
b) Radionuclide sources used in internal radiotherapy
  (1) Sealed sources (brachytherapy) (e.g., iodine-125, iridium-192, cesium-137 in the form of seeds or ribbons that are placed directly into tissues or applicators in body cavities)
  (2) Remote afterloading high dose rate brachytherapy: Radioactive sources (iridium-192) with a high specific activity that deliver a high dose rate of radiation in a short period of time. The radioactive source is housed in a shielded unit and poses no exposure risk to staff when inserted remotely into patients (Dunne-Daly, 1997).
  (3) Unsealed sources (oral, intravenous, radiopharmaceutical therapy) (e.g., iodine-131, strontium-89, yttrium-90)
B. Definitions concerning radiation protection
  1. ALARA (**as l**ow **as r**easonably **a**chievable) is a guideline used for radiation protection. The principle of ALARA is to minimize radiation exposure to workers, taking economic and social factors into account (NCRP, 1990). With this common sense approach, radiation exposure is kept lower than regulatory limits for workers and the general public (Health Physics Society, 2001).
  2. Dose equivalent is the quantity used to express irradiation incurred by exposed people on a common scale for all radiation. Because not all types of radiation have the same effect in humans, dose equivalent takes into account the type of radiation and the absorbed dose. For beta, gamma, and x-rays, the dose equivalent (expressed in rems or sieverts) is equal to the absorbed dose (expressed in RAD or Gray). For alpha radiation, the equivalent dose is assumed to be 20 times the absorbed dose (Health Physics Society, 2003).
  3. Dose equivalent limit (annual) is the annual dose equivalent limit defined by the degree to which radiation exposure should be controlled to achieve an acceptable level of risk for workers and the general public, taking into account both somatic and genetic effects of ionizing radiation (Bruner et al., 1998).
  4. Collective equivalent dose is the sum of the individual dose equivalents received in a given period of time by a specific population from exposure to a specified source of radiation (Bruner et al., 1998).
  5. Genetic effects are changes in the reproductive cells that may result in abnormal offspring of the person exposed to ionizing radiation (Bruner et al., 1998).
  6. Somatic effects are detrimental effects of radiation manifested in the person exposed to ionizing radiation (Bruner et al., 1998).
  7. Deterministic effects are somatic effects that increase in severity with the amount of radiation received by the individual above some threshold value. Deterministic effects usually occur at high doses of radiation exposure and can be acute (e.g., acute radiation syndrome seen in atomic bomb survivors in Japan in 1945 and Chernobyl nuclear power plant workers in 1986) or late (e.g., cataract induction from exposure to the lens of the eye) (Bruner et al., 1998).
  8. Stochastic effects are effects for which the probability of occurrence is a function of radiation dose without a threshold. The severity of the effects, according to this mechanism, occurs independent of the radiation dose (Bruner et al., 1998).
  9. Linear/no-threshold model is a conservative model for estimating radiation risk. It suggests that any increase in radiation dose, no matter how small, results in an incremental increase in risk. Although the acceptance of this model has been controversial in radiation protection scientific literature, NCRP's recent review concluded that no alternative dose-response

model is more plausible than the linear/no-threshold model (Upton, 2003).

C. Radiation protection standards and regulations
   1. Goals of radiation protection (Hendee, 1993)
      a) To prevent radiation-induced deterministic effects by keeping dose limits of exposed healthcare workers and the public below a certain threshold
      b) To limit the risk of stochastic effects to a reasonable level in relation to societal needs, values, and economic factors
         (1) Radiation protection standards have become more rigorous over the past 20 years.
         (2) An increased recognition of the effects of ionizing radiation, improved protection measures, improved exposure monitoring devices, an increase in the numbers of persons occupationally exposed to ionizing radiation, and a greater awareness of the risks of radiation exposure by society have contributed to strict radiation protection standards and practices (Hendee, 1993; Jankowski, 1992; Kocher, 1991).
         (3) There is an increased emphasis on protecting patients and workers from unnecessary ionizing radiation exposure.
         (4) Despite the theoretical risk factors, radiation studies (citations of these studies) of hundreds of thousands of occupationally exposed workers have not revealed any adverse health effect caused by normal exposure to artificial radiation. Dose limits applied to the public are only a small fraction of those for radiation workers (Health Physics Society, 2001).
   2. Organizations involved in radiation protection guidelines/standards that have no regulatory authority (Mossman, 2003)
      a) International Commission on Radiological Protection (ICRP)
         (1) An independent registered, nonprofit charity established in the United Kingdom to advance the science of radiation protection for the public benefit.
         (2) Involved with guidance on all aspects of radiation protection
      b) NCRP
         (1) Nongovernmental, nonprofit organization first chartered by the U.S. Congress in 1964
         (2) Composed of volunteer experts in radiation science
         (3) Performs many activities

      (a) Collects, analyzes, and disseminates recommendations about protection against radiation
      (b) Establishes radiation measurements, quantities, and units concerning radiation protection (NCRP, 1993)
      (c) Provides means by which organizations concerned with radiation protection can cooperate for effective utilization of combined resources
      (d) Cooperates with ICRP and other national and international organizations and governments concerned with radiation measurements and protection
      (e) Publishes guidelines concerning all aspects of radiation protection for both ionizing and nonionizing radiation exposure. Table 4 lists current NCRP limits of ionizing radiation exposure for radiation workers and the general public.

Type of Exposure	National Council on Radiation Protection Recommendations
Stochastic effects	
• Effective dose limits (cumulative)	10 mSv x age
• Effective dose limit (annual)	50 mSv
Deterministic effects	
• Dose equivalent limits for tissues and organs (annual)	
- Lens of eye	150 mSv
- Skin, hands, and feet	500 mSv
Embryo or fetus exposure	
• Effective dose limit	0.5 mSv/month
Public exposures (annual)	
• Effective dose limit, continuous or frequent exposure	1 mSv
• Effective dose limit, infrequent exposure	5 mSv
• Dose equivalent limit for skin and extremities	50 mSv
• Dose equivalent limit for lens of eye	15 mSv
Education and training exposures (annual)	
• Effective dose limit	1 mSv
• Dose equivalent limit for skin and extremities	50 mSv
• Dose equivalent limit for lens of eye	15 mSv
Negligible individual dose (annual)	0.01 mSv

Table 4. Summary of Recommended Dose Limits

Note. Based on information from National Council on Radiation Protection and Measurements, 1993.

3. Major agencies that have regulatory authority concerning medical uses of ionizing radiation
   a) U.S. Nuclear Regulatory Commission (USNRC)
      (1) Provides direct regulatory authority over the medical use of reactor-produced radionuclides (therapeutic and diagnostic)
      (2) Regulates use of byproduct materials (materials made radioactive in a reactor)
      (3) Regulates the use of radioactive materials used in medicine per the 10 Congressional Federal Register CFR Part 20, "Standards for Protection Against Radiation," including requirements for
         (a) Dose limits for radiation workers and the general public
         (b) Monitoring and labeling radioactive materials
         (c) Posting radiation areas
         (d) Reporting theft or loss of radioactive materials
         (e) Penalties for noncompliance with USNRC regulations
         (f) Tables of individual radionuclide exposure limits.
      (4) Issues broad medical licenses to individuals using radionuclides for medical use outside the hospital setting (Institute of Medicine, 1996)
      (5) Specifies what instructions should be given to nursing staff who care for brachytherapy patients as specified in 10 CFR Part 35
         (a) Size and appearance of the brachytherapy sources
         (b) Safe handling and shielding instructions in case of dislodged sources
         (c) Procedures for visitor control
         (d) Procedures for patient or human research control
         (e) Procedures for notifying the radiation safety officer if the patient has a medical emergency or dies (Institute of Medicine, 1996)
   b) U.S Food and Drug Administration (FDA)
      (1) Regulates the design and manufacture of radiation devices/equipment
      (2) Regulates the development of radiopharmaceuticals
   c) State radiation commission/agencies
      (1) States can be licensed by the USNRC or can be classified as agreement states. Agreement states, per state law, assign all responsibility for radiation protection to a state agency. Besides following USNRC guidelines, agreement states may require additional radiation protection practices. Figure 9 shows current USNRC and agreement states.
      (2) Individual states have their own radiation protection agencies that are responsible for setting state guidelines and enforcing the national standards and guidelines. Nurses are encouraged to become familiar with their individual state's guidelines.
   d) Institutional committees/individuals responsible for radiation protection
      (1) Institutional Radiation Safety Committee
         (a) Designated by hospital/institution administration and authorized by the state and/or USNRC to oversee and monitor the radiation protection program of an institution
         (b) Must meet four times per year to review the hospital's/institution's radiation protection program and must have a nursing representative (Institute of Medicine, 1996).
      (2) Radiation safety officer (RSO) responsibilities
         (a) Implements and monitors the institution's radiation protection program
         (b) Trains personnel, including nurses, in radiation protection practices
         (c) Serves as the primary resource person regarding the institutional radiation protection practices/issues
         (d) Monitors radiation exposure of institution's employees who work in radiation setting

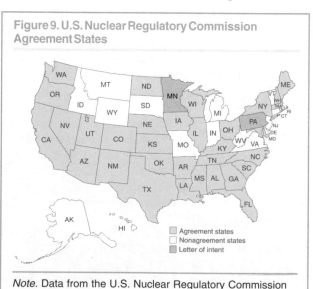

Figure 9. U.S. Nuclear Regulatory Commission Agreement States

Note. Data from the U.S. Nuclear Regulatory Commission Web site, http://www.hsrd.ornl.gov/nrc. Current as of September 14, 2004.

(e) Monitors radiation exposure from patients who are receiving internal RT in both inpatient and outpatient settings

(f) Determines radiation isolation discharge (Institute of Medicine, 1996)

D. Radionuclide factors that determine the type and amount of radiation protection measures

1. Type and energy of radiation emission from radionuclide (e.g., alpha, beta, gamma). Radionuclides can give off one, two, or three of these emissions depending on the specific radionuclide.

   a) Alpha: Particles of radiation composed of two protons and two neutrons that travel at great speed but have poor penetrating abilities (Bucholtz, 1994)

   (1) Maximum distance is less than 5 cm in air.

   (2) Because of poor penetrating ability, pure alpha emitters are not used in therapy.

   (3) A sheet of paper, clothes, or a distance of greater than 5 cm is adequate to shield a person from external alpha particle radiation.

   (4) Alpha particle sources inside the human body in high quantities (i.e., radon gas) can pose an internal hazard.

   b) Beta: Particles of radiation, similar to electrons, with greater penetration than alpha particles. Beta particles travel only about one-half inch inside human tissue and are not capable of penetrating something as thin as a pad of paper (Bucholtz, 1994).

   (1) Pure beta particle radionuclides used in therapy (phosphorus-32, yttrium-90, strontium-89) can be shielded by thick plastic.

   (2) Once a beta radionuclide is instilled or injected into the body, the patient's body will supply adequate shielding.

   (3) If a certain dose of some beta emitters is used systemically, the patient's body fluids may be temporarily radioactive.

   c) Gamma: Rays of radiation given off by a radionuclide as an unstable nucleus decays (Bucholtz, 1994)

   (1) Gamma rays have a wide range of energies and penetrating abilities. The higher the energy, the thicker the material needed to shield gamma radiation.

   (2) High-energy gamma-emitting radionuclides require both specified distances and shielding to reduce one's exposure.

   (3) Patients receiving high-energy gamma radionuclides (e.g., cesium-137, radium-226, iridium-192) may be required to be in radiation isolation and behind lead shields.

   (4) Low-energy gamma emitters, such as iodine-125 and palladium-103, do not require these same precautions.

2. Half-life: The time required by a radioactive material to reduce to one-half of its radioactivity by radioactive decay. No chemical or physical operation can alter the decay rate of a radioactive substance (Bucholtz, 1994).

   a) Sealed radionuclides are chosen for either permanent implants (short half-life, low emissions) or temporary implants, which may have long half-lives.

   b) Concern is given to the storage of the source if dislodged or if spills or contamination occurs. Policies related to these incidents are based on the radionuclide's half-life.

   c) Contaminated radioactive waste may require storage for decay for a time equal to 10 times the half-life. For example, if the half-life is 8 days, this storage requirement would be 80 days.

3. Amount of energy of the specific radionuclide used

   a) In general, the greater the amount of the source used for high energy radionuclides, the greater the amount of radiation safety protection measures are needed.

   b) The amount required for radiation isolation is determined by regulatory agencies, such as USNRC, from guidelines established by the NCRP.

4. Radionuclide form: The two basic forms of radionuclides used are sealed (e.g., rods, ribbons, needles, seeds), which are surgically

implanted into tumor tissues or in special applicators placed in body cavities, or unsealed (e.g., liquids, capsules, colloids), which can be ingested, injected, or instilled into the body.

   a) Sealed sources (Bucholtz, 1994)

      (1) With sealed sources, the source, not the patient, is radioactive. The radioactive material is encapsulated, and safety measures are based on the source itself and the likelihood the source will become dislodged. The patient and his or her body fluids are not radioactive. For temporary implants, once the source has been removed and returned to safe storage and the area surveyed and checked for any dislodged sources, no further radiation protection measures are required.

      (2) With permanent implants, such as iodine-125 seeds, dislodged source precautions may be in place for a specified period of time.

   b) Unsealed sources (Bucholtz, 1994)

      (1) With unsealed sources, the patient and his or her body fluids may be radioactive for a specified period of time, which is determined by the energy of the radionuclide, the amount used, and its half-life.

      (2) Radiation safety measures will be based on the patient and the possibility of contamination from the patient's body fluids (e.g., sweat, saliva, urine).

E. Principles of radiation protection

   1. Time: The amount of exposure received is directly related to the amount of time spent near the radioactive source. Nurses should continue to provide needed patient care while minimizing the time spent in close contact with the patient receiving gamma radionuclide therapy, which poses a radiation expo-

sure risk. The time limit per direct patient contact per nursing shift should be posted on the patient's hospital room door. Time limit for patient visitors also should be posted. Examples of strategies to minimize time include the following (Dow, 1992).

   a) Provide necessary patient education before the procedure and teach the patient important self-care measures.

      (1) Observe and document the patient's ability to perform self-care measures (e.g., taking routine medications, performing daily hygiene) before the procedure.

      (2) Evaluate the patient's understanding of the rationale to limit nursing care, staff contact, and family visitors.

   b) Provide the maximum amount of direct nursing care before the radioactive source is placed or administered.

   c) Assemble all necessary equipment/supplies in the patient's room before the procedure to avoid unnecessary trips and ensure that equipment (e.g., telephone, television) in the patient's room works properly before the radioactive source is administered.

   d) Check frequently on the patient via the intercom or telephone; anticipate the patient's needs; and encourage the patient to communicate any problems or concerns to the staff via the intercom or telephone.

   e) Use time efficiently when in contact with the patient. Nurses caring for patients with specific radioactive procedures may want to practice routine care activities (e.g., log rolling the patient from side to side, visually checking the position of the gynecologic applicator, emptying a urine Foley bag) required in an inpatient setting.

   f) Rotate the nursing/ancillary staff caring for the patient receiving radioactive implants and reassure the family that care is a priority and the patient will not be neglected.

   2. Distance: The amount of radiation exposure one receives is inversely related to the distance one is from the radioactive source (inverse square law). By doubling the distance from the source, exposure is decreased by a factor of four (two squared). For example, an exposure rate of 40 mrem/hour at one meter would decrease to an exposure rate of 10 mrem/hour at a distance of two meters (see Figure 10). The following are examples of nursing care measures that maximize distance from a radioactive source. With direct patient contact, stand as far away from the sealed radioactive source

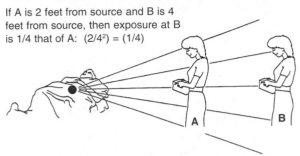

Figure 10. The Inverse Square Law for Distance

If A is 2 feet from source and B is 4 feet from source, then exposure at B is 1/4 that of A: $(2/4^2) = (1/4)$

Note. From "Radiotherapy" (p. 225) by L.J. Hilderley in S.L. Groenwald, M.H. Frogge, M. Goodman, and C.H. Yarbro (Eds.), *Cancer Nursing: Principles and Practice*, 1992, Sudbury, MA: Jones and Bartlett. Copyright 1992 by Jones and Bartlett. Reprinted with permission.

as possible. For example, stand at the head of the bed to take vital signs when in the room with a patient who has a gynecologic implant. Talk to the patient from the doorway versus inside the room (Dunne-Daly, 1997).

    a) Assist the patient with needed tasks (e.g., unwrapping food tray items) from a distance versus next to the source.

    b) Reinforce teaching of self-care activities at a distance from the patient.

  3. Shielding: The amount of radiation exposure received from a specified radioactive source can be decreased by the use of an absorbing material (shield) placed between the source and the person receiving the exposure. The amount of exposure decreased by shielding will vary with the energy of the source and the thickness of the shielding material. HVL refers to the thickness of a material required to reduce radiation exposure to one-half of its original exposure amount. For example, the HVL of cesium-137 is 6 mm of lead or 10 cm of concrete. Following are common suggestions for using shielding to reduce exposure (Dunne-Daly, 1997).

    a) Keep the shielding between the source and the person exposed. Build shields into the walls and floors of treatment rooms that are used for radioactive procedures that use high-energy gamma sources.

    b) Continue to use principles of time and distance, even with shields, to further reduce radiation exposure.

    c) Consider that maneuvering the shield may require increased nursing time in the room, making some uses of shields unwarranted.

    d) Select the correct material for shielding based on the type of emitters (i.e., lead for high-energy gamma sources, plastic for pure beta sources).

    e) Use more shielding in institutions that perform large numbers of gamma-emitting radioactive procedures.

F. Radiation monitoring devices

  1. General information

    a) Even though ionizing radiation cannot be detected by the human senses, detection devices can measure the amounts of radiation exposure received by an individual through the use of a personal monitoring device or survey monitor.

    b) Monitoring devices do not offer any radiation exposure protection. They only physically measure levels or amounts of exposure.

  2. Types of personal dosimetry monitors

    a) Film badge: An individual monitoring device that contains a piece of a special film, which is periodically read (i.e., monthly, three times per year). The optical density of the film changes when it is exposed to ionizing radiation. An individual's film then is compared to a known amount of exposure to obtain the periodic amount of radiation exposure received. Film badges are recommended for individuals who need constant radiation exposure monitoring in the occupational setting. Film badge guidelines are as follows (Dunne-Daly, 1997).

      (1) Badge should be worn consistently at work during the time of potential and actual exposure (should not be worn outside of work).

      (2) Badge is not to be shared or exchanged with other staff.

      (3) Badge should not be exposed to excessive heat or moisture.

      (4) Badge should not remain on lab coat or placed in a room using radiation sources when not worn.

      (5) Badge should be worn on the area of the body that the highest deep, shallow, and eye-dose equivalent is expected to be received (in general, this is on the front of the body between the waist and collar of the individual). For specialized work where the highest dose is at the head level, such as in fluoroscopy, the dosimeter should be worn at the collar.

      (6) Badge should be read according to the institutional time schedule for read-

ings and the cumulative record of badge readings be kept on file at the institution.

b) Ring badge: An individual monitoring device similar to a film badge but worn on the finger that is used by personnel who are handling radioactive material. Guidelines are similar to those of a film badge (Dunne-Daly, 1997).

c) Pocket ion chamber dosimeter: A lightweight radiation measurement instrument that gives similar readouts of radiation exposure as a film badge that individuals use who do not need continual radiation exposure monitoring but periodic monitoring for scheduled radioactive procedures. Unlike a film badge, different personnel can share pocket dosimeters. The amount of radiation exposure received is known immediately for each person who wears the monitoring device. Pocket dosimeters are especially useful for nursing/healthcare staff and family members in contact with persons who are cared for on inpatient or outpatient units that infrequently use diagnostic or therapeutic radioactive materials. Pocket ion dosimeters should (Dunne-Daly, 1997)

(1) Be left at the nurse's station or outside the patient's room with the exposure dose record sheet that keeps track of individual exposure amounts. These devices should not be kept near the radioactive source.

(2) Be worn the same place as a personal film badge, where the highest dose may be received.

(3) Be read before entering the patient's room and then again after leaving the patient's room and recorded on the dose record sheet. Information to be recorded includes the name of the person exposed, date, time, dosimeter readouts, time spent in the room, and reading before entering and then after leaving the room.

(4) Be handled gently. If dropped, tapped, or knocked, pocket ion chamber dosimeters can show inaccurate readings and may need to be recalibrated by the radiation safety staff or radiation oncology dosimetry staff.

(5) Be read by holding them up toward the light, in a horizontal position, and reading the point at which the hairline crosses the numbered scale.

(6) Have their records kept on file and monitored by the RSO/radiation protection staff.

G. Recognition of radiation-restricted areas: Federal and state laws require the posting of appropriate radiation protection warning signs in areas containing potential and real radiation exposure (NCRP, 1989).

1. Radiation caution signs (NCRP, 1989) (see Figure 11)

a) Contain a yellow background with magenta lettering and should specify the specific radionuclide source and radiation precautions

b) Should be placed on the door of the room once a source is present and until the source is removed or until exposure risk is no longer present

c) May be placed as stickers on a patient's identification wristband

2. Therapeutic radionuclide information sheets

a) Should be placed in the patient's chart

b) Document radionuclide information (e.g., type of radiation, length of use, specific restrictions, emergency contacts, dislodgment precautions).

H. Special radiation protection considerations and issues involved in specific radiation procedures

1. Yttrium-90 labeled antibody (anti-CD20 radiolabeled antibody) (Hendrix, 2004; Wagner et al., 2002); strontium-89 for painful bony metastases (Silberstein, Buscombe, McEwan, & Taylor, 2003)

a) Because yttrium-90 is a pure beta emitter, administration is safely performed on an outpatient basis. Some patients need to be treated as inpatients for medical reasons, not because of radiation protection needs. Strontium-89, also a pure beta emitter,

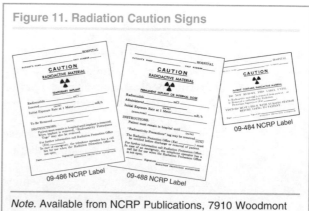

Figure 11. Radiation Caution Signs

09-486 NCRP Label   09-488 NCRP Label   09-484 NCRP Label

Note. Available from NCRP Publications, 7910 Woodmont Avenue, Suite 400, Bethesda, MD 20814-3095; 800-229-2652, ext. 25.

can be given as an outpatient injection (Silberstein et al., 2003; Wagner et al., 2002).

b) There is minimal radiation exposure risk to patients' family members and healthcare workers in contact with the patient.

c) Healthcare staff need to follow universal precautions. Bags, vials, and tubes that are used and contain yttrium-90 absorb any radiation that may be present.

d) Patients receiving yttrium-90–labeled antibodies can be discharged immediately after treatment, and no patient activity limits or dose rate limit measurements need to be taken (Wagner et al., 2002).

e) The person administering the radiolabeled antibody should wear gloves and use a plastic syringe cover over the radiolabeled medication and be careful to not spray or drip the medication.

f) Patient should be encouraged to use regular toilet facilities, avoid urine leakage, and double flush the toilet. Anyone handling the patient's urine, especially in first 24 hours post-injection, should wear gloves.

g) Condoms are recommended for sexual relations for one week post-injection (Hendrix, 2004).

h) After discharge, patients should clean up any spilled urine and dispose of any urine- or blood-contaminated material (e.g., flush it down the toilet; place it in plastic bag in household trash) to prevent its being handled by others.

2. Radioiodine-131 for thyroid cancer/hyperthyroidism (Meier et al., 2002)

a) In 1997, the USNRC revised its patient release regulations, allowing for larger activities of radioactive iodine-131 to be given as an outpatient administration. Previously, the USNRC required any individual receiving 30 or greater millicuries of radioactive iodine-131 to be an inpatient in radiation isolation and discharged after an exposure rate of < 5 mR (milliroentgen)/hour at one meter was obtained. The new regulation allows patients to be released if the total effective dose equivalent to any other individual is not likely to exceed 5.0 mSv (Grigsby, Siegel, Baker, & Eichling, 2000).

b) Studies have shown that the amount of radiation exposure received by household members of patients discharged after receiving iodine-131 have been below the limit (5.0 mSv) mandated by current USNRC regulations (Grigsby et al., 2000; Ryan et al., 2000).

3. Iodine-125 and palladium-103 prostate seed implants (Michalski, Mutic, Eichling, & Ahmed, 2003; Smathers et al., 1999)

a) Prostate implants can be done as an outpatient procedure. Once the seeds are in place, there is little radiation exposure risk to others.

b) USNRC guidelines allow discharge of patients if the exposure rate at one meter is at or below 0.01 mSv/hour for iodine-125 and 0.03 mSv/hour for palladium-103.

c) A study involving radiation exposure to family members of men who received iodine-125 seeds showed that spouses received an average of 14 mrem and other family members received less than 8 mrem over a course of one year. With palladium-103, spouses received 6 mrem and other family members essentially 0 mrem. (To put things into perspective, a person flying from New York to Tokyo receives 20 mrem, and someone flying from New York to Los Angeles receives 5 mrem.)

d) Discharge instructions to patients who received iodine-125 or palladium-103 vary per institution but usually include avoidance of holding young infants, young children, or pregnant women on one's lap and using a condom for several months.

4. Special radiation protection considerations: In a freestanding, non–hospital-associated facility, it is recommended that the local fire/EMS/police are aware of radiation hazards. All freestanding facilities also are regulated by NRC/state radiation control organizations.

5. Special populations: Radiation exposure of pregnant employees (NCRP, 1994)

a) Embryos/fetuses are the most radiosensitive living tissues.

b) The most radiosensitive period of a fetus is in the first trimester.

c) Because of the radiosensitivity of the embryo, a pregnant woman has a dose limit of 5 mSv (0.5 rem) during pregnancy per NCRP guidelines.

d) Many institutions recommend that pregnant women and men and women who are trying to conceive not provide care to patients who are receiving radionuclide therapy; however, by law, pregnant women cannot be restricted from providing this care, as long as NCRP guidelines for exposure limits are followed.

e) The pregnant woman assumes all responsibility for the exposure of the fetus until the pregnancy is officially declared. Once a pregnancy is declared, the supervisors/ RSO are responsible for ensuring the pregnant woman's monitored radiation exposure does not exceed the 5 mSv (0.5 rem) dose limit. The RSO also is required to evaluate the work area and recommend further procedures to reduce exposure.

6. Emergency procedures: General guidelines for emergency procedures, including radioactive spills and loss or rupture of a sealed radioactive source, can be found in *NCRP Report No. 105*, Appendix A (1989).

   a) Dislodged source guidelines

      (1) Notify the radiation oncologist and RSO regarding any dislodged source as soon as it is discovered.

      (2) Have a lead storage container available to store any dislodged source and have long-handled forceps available to pick up the source. Only individuals with training in handling radioactive sources should be permitted to handle dislodged sources. Bare hands should never be used to pick up a radioactive source.

      (3) The patient also should be instructed to never pick up a dislodged radioactive source but to immediately contact the staff if a dislodged source is suspected.

      (4) The time the source became dislodged should be recorded and communicated to the radiation oncology team to determine the therapeutic radiation dose received by the patient.

      (5) Radiation safety staff should survey all applicators/dressings/linen that may contain a dislodged source before removing them from the room.

      (6) A patient receiving a permanent iodine-125 seed implant should be instructed to contact the radiation safety staff immediately if a seed is found dislodged. The radiation safety staff should counsel the patient regarding disposal of the seed(s).

   b) Cardiopulmonary resuscitation (CPR) of patients who have received radionuclide therapy.

      (1) CPR in patients with sealed radionuclides

         (a) Begin CPR immediately.

         (b) Notify someone immediately who can properly remove the sealed source and place it in a lead/safe container.

         (c) Once the source is removed and properly stored and the area is surveyed, no additional risk of exposure is present.

      (2) CPR in patients with unsealed sources (iodine-131) (Health Physics Society, 2004)

         (a) Begin CPR immediately.

         (b) Notify radiation safety personnel/ radiation oncologist.

         (c) Realize that the priority is the patient, and staff exposure is likely to be minimal. (Thirty minutes of resuscitation of a patient with 100 millicuries of iodine-131 would result in approximately 100 mrem exposure at one foot, 200 mrem/ hour exposure rate.)

         (d) People performing CPR should wear gloves, gown, and shoe covers.

         (e) All equipment used for CPR should be surveyed for radiation contamination before removal from the room.

         (f) All personnel involved in CPR should remain in the immediate location of the patient's room and be cleared to leave the area by radiation safety personnel.

   c) Periodic in-service instruction regarding radiation protection

      (1) Regulations require that nurses caring for patients receiving radionuclides be instructed in radiation protection measures. Some regulations require yearly in-services.

      (2) Institutions may want to establish a competency-based, yearly radiation protection exam (see Figure 12).

I. Related Web sites

   1. National Council on Radiation Protection and Measurements—www.ncrp.org

Figure 12. Radiation Protection Self-Learning Examination

True or False

1. The acronym ALARA, used in radiation protection, stands for as low as reasonably achievable.   ___True ___False

2. Radioactive yttrium-90 is a pure beta emitter and can be safely given in the outpatient setting.   ___True ___False

3. The body fluids of a patient who receives a sealed iridium-192 source for a soft tissue sarcoma will be temporarily radioactive.   ___True ___False

4. Radiation-measuring film badges can be shared between healthcare providers.   ___True ___False

5. No chemical or physical operation can alter the decay of a radioactive substance.   ___True ___False

Multiple Choice

6. The international unit of dose equivalent that corresponds to 100 rem is
   1. 10 Sv
   2. 100 mSv
   3. 1 Sv
   4. 10 mSv

7. To minimize the amount of radiation exposure a nurse receives from a high-energy gamma radioactive source of cesium-137, the nurse should
   a. Maximize the distance from the source when talking with the patient.
   b. Minimize the time spent in close proximity to the source when providing patient care.
   c. Stay behind the lead shield when entering the patient's room to remove a food tray.
   d. Sit next to the patient at the bedside to review the plan of care.

   1. a, b
   2. a, b, d
   3. a, b, c
   4. All of the above

8. The NCRP's recommended annual dose limit for continuous or frequent exposure for the public is
   1. 1 mSv (100 mrem)
   2. 10 mSv (1 rem)
   3. 100 mSv (10 rem)
   4. 5 mSv (0.5 rem)

9. If a nurse notices that a sealed radioactive source has become dislodged from a patient's implant applicator, which of the following actions are **not** recommended?
   a. Note the time that the source was dislodged.
   b. Immediately place the source back into the patient.
   c. Notify the radiation safety officer and radiation oncologist as soon as possible.
   d. Advise the patient to place the radioactive sealed source into the lead container in the room.

   1. a, b
   2. a, b, c
   3. b, d
   4. a, c, d

10. Factors that determine the amount and type of radiation protection measures recommended in the care of patients receiving radionuclides include
    a. The dose-specific activity of the radionuclide used.
    b. The half-life of the radionuclide used.
    c. The type of radionuclide emission(s) (i.e., alpha, beta, gamma radiation).
    d. The method of radionuclide delivery.

    1. a, b
    2. a, b, c
    3. b, c, d
    4. All of the above

Answers		
1. True	4. False	7. 3	10. 4
2. True	5. True	8. 1	
3. False	6. 3	9. 3	

2. International Commission on Radiological Protection—www.icrp.org
3. U.S. Food and Drug Administration—www.fda.gov
4. U.S. Nuclear Regulatory Commission—www.nrc.gov
5. American Association of Physicists in Medicine—www.aapm.org
6. Radiological Society of North America—www.rsna.org
7. Health Physics Society ("Ask the Experts")—www.hps.org

References

Bruner, D.W., Bucholtz, J.D., Iwamoto, R., & Strohl, R. (Eds.). (1998). *Manual for radiation oncology nursing practice and education.* Pittsburgh, PA: Oncology Nursing Society.

Bucholtz, J. (1994). Radiation therapy. In J. Gross & B.L. Johnson (Eds.), *Handbook of oncology nursing* (pp. 35–55). Sudbury, MA: Jones and Bartlett.

Dow, K.H. (1992). Principles of brachytherapy. In K.H. Dow & L.J. Hilderley (Eds.), *Nursing care in radiation oncology* (pp. 16–29). Philadelphia: Saunders.

Dunne-Daly, C. (1997). Principles of brachytherapy. In K.H. Dow, J.D. Bucholtz, R. Iwamoto, V.K. Fieler, & L.J. Hilderley (Eds.), *Nursing care in radiation oncology* (pp. 21–35). Philadelphia: Saunders.

Grigsby, P.W., Siegel, B.A., Baker, S., & Eichling, J.O. (2000). Radiation exposure from outpatient radioactive iodine (I-131) therapy for thyroid carcinoma. *JAMA, 283,* 2272–2274.

Health Physics Society. (2001). *Position statement. Occupational radiation safety standards and regulations are sound.* Retrieved July 16, 2003, from http://www.hps.org/documents/

Health Physics Society. (2003). *Radiation fact sheets.* Retrieved July 16, 2003, from http://www.hps.org/publicinformation/radfactsheets

Health Physics Society. (2004). *Answer to question #1753 submitted to "Ask the experts."* Retrieved September 14, 2004, from http://hps.org/publicinformation/atc/q1753.html

Hendrix, C. (2004). Radiation safety guidelines for radioimmunotherapy with yttrium 90 ibritumomab tiuxetan. *Clinical Journal of Oncology Nursing, 8,* 31–34.

Hendee, W.R. (1993). History, current status and trends in radiation protection standards. *Medical Physics, 20,* 1303–1314.

Institute of Medicine. (1996). *Radiation medicine. A need for regulatory reform.* Washington, DC: National Academy of Sciences.

Jankowski, C.B. (1992). Radiation protection for nurses: Regulations and guidelines. *Journal of Nursing Administration, 22,* 30–34.

Kocher, D.C. (1991). Perspective on the historical development in radiation protection standards. *Health Physics, 61,* 519–527.

Meier, D.A., Brill, D.A., Becker, D.V., Clarke, S., Silberstein, E.B., Royal, H.D., et al. (2002). *Society of Nuclear Medicine procedure guideline for therapy of thyroid disease with iodine-131 (sodium iodide)* [Version 1.0]. Reston, VA: Society of Nuclear Medicine.

Michalski, J., Mutic, S., Eichling, J., & Ahmed, S.N. (2003). Radiation exposure to family and household members after prostate brachytherapy. *International Journal of Radiation Oncology, Biology, Physics, 56,* 764–768.

Mossman, K.L. (2003). The role of advisory organizations in ionizing radiation protection science and policy: A proposal. *Medical Physics, 30,* 1229–1234.

National Council on Radiation Protection and Measurements. (1989). *NCRP Report No. 105. Radiation protection for medical and allied health personnel.* Bethesda, MD: Author.

National Council on Radiation Protection and Measurements. (1990). *NCRP Report No. 107. Implementation of the principle of as low as reasonably achievable (ALARA) for medical and dental personnel.* Bethesda, MD: Author.

National Council on Radiation Protection and Measurements. (1993). *NCRP Report No. 116. Limitation of exposure to ionizing radiation.* Bethesda, MD: Author.

National Council on Radiation Protection and Measurements. (1994). *NCRP Commentary No. 9. Considerations regarding the unintended radiation exposure of the embryo, fetus, or nursing child.* Bethesda, MD: Author.

Ryan, M.T., Spicer, K.M., Frei-Lahr, D., Samei, E., Frey, G.D., Hargrove, H., et al. (2000). Health physics consequences of outpatient treatment of non-Hodgkin's lymphoma with 131I-radiolabeled antibody and antiB1 antibody. *Health Physics, 79*(Suppl. 5), S52–S55.

Silberstein, E.B., Buscombe, J.R., McEwan, A., & Taylor, A.T. (2003). *Society of Nuclear Medicine procedure guideline for palliative treatment of painful bony metastases* [Version 3.0]. Albuquerque, NM: Society of Nuclear Medicine.

Smathers, S., Wallner, K., Korssjoen, T., Bergsagel, C., Hudson, R.H., Sutlief, S., et al. (1999). Radiation safety parameters following prostate brachytherapy. *International Journal of Radiation Oncology, Biology, Physics, 45,* 397–399.

Upton, A.C. (2003). The state of the art in the 1990's: NCRP Report No. 136 on the scientific bases for linearity in the dose-response relationship for ionizing radiation. *Health Physics, 85,* 15–22.

Wagner, H.N., Wiseman, G.A., Marcus, C.S., Nabi, H.A., Nagle, C.E., Fink-Bennett, D.M., et al. (2002). Administration guidelines for radioimmunotherapy of non-Hodgkin's lymphoma with 90-Y-labeled anti-CD20 monoclonal antibody. *Journal of Nuclear Medicine, 43,* 267–272.

IV. General symptom management

A. General patient and family education
1. Definition: Patient education is a planned, systematic process that uses various techniques such as teaching, counseling, and behavior modification to assist people to learn health-related behaviors (e.g., knowledge, skills, attitudes, values) (Barlett, 1985; Bastable, 2003b). Patient education is a dynamic and interactive process between the teacher and learner.
2. Learning theories provide a framework for patient education (see Table 5) (Doak, Doak, & Root, 1996).
3. Components of the patient education process include assessment, planning, implementation, and evaluation (Bastable, 2003b; Redman, 2001).
4. Historically, patient education has been a core role component of the radiation oncology nurse

Table 5. A Summary of Key Education and Behavior Theories and Their Applications

Theory Name	Proponents	Description	Application
Health Belief Model	Hochbaum Becker Rosenstock Greene	Explains people's health behaviors: why they may accept preventative health services or adopt healthy behaviors	A behavior research tool, but can imply best content and topic sequence for educational materials.
Self-Efficacy	Bandura Adams Beyer	People are more likely to adopt a health behavior if they think they can do it.	Intervention should give people confidence by building up to behavior step by step. Give them many little "successes" in the behavior change process.
Locus of Control Theory	Wollston	People who believe *they* are in control of their own health status are more likely to change behaviors in response to health education facts. The converse is also true.	For people who believe they are *not* in control, build more support into health education programs.
Cognitive Dissonance Theory	Festinger Lewin	A high level of unhappiness (dissonance) is more likely to lead to behavior change. Theory points to readiness to change, and how to cut probability of relapse.	Design intervention to foster unhappiness with present behavior status. To reduce relapse, reinforce to keep dissonance low.
Diffusion Theory	Rogers Shoemaker Preston	Some people will adopt new behaviors early, some late. Early adopters can influence others. Applies to a community or population.	Foster early adoption by making intervention consistent with beliefs, values, social system of target population.
Stages of Readiness	Prochaska	A person goes through stages of readiness to adopt and to maintain a new health behavior. Education interventions work best if they match a person's stage of readiness.	Design interventions to fit the stage of readiness of your client population. If many stages are present, the intervention may need several different messages.
Adult Education Theories	Bruner Bradford Coleman Knowles	Main concern of adults is solving and managing their own problems. They care about self-fulfillment. Adults need active participation. Adults are less interested in facts about health as a subject.	1. Design education intervention to address the solution to their health problems. Give less information about other topics. 2. Build on adult's experiences. 3. "Talk it out," teach via demonstrations, discussion, and examples.

Note. From *Teaching Patients With Low Literacy Skills* (2nd ed., p. 13), by C.C. Doak, L.G. Doak, and J.H. Root, 1996, Philadelphia: Lippincott. Copyright 1996 by Lippincott. Reprinted with permission.

(Bruner, 1993; Hilderley, 1980; Moore-Higgs et al., 2003; Shepard & Kelvin, 1999; Strohl, 1988).

5. Rationale for patient education

   a) Patient's Bill of Rights establishes a patient's right to information about diagnosis, treatment, prognosis, procedures, medical consequences, personnel, and the hospital (American Hospital Association, 1973). The ONS position statement *Patients' Bill of Rights for Quality Cancer Care* (ONS, 2002) outlines patients' rights to information throughout the cancer care continuum.

   b) State Nurse Practice Acts and the American Nurses Association's (ANA's) *Standards of Clinical Nursing Practice* (ANA, 1998) define the scope of nursing practice and designate health or patient education as an independent function of the professional nurse (Smeltzer & Bare, 2000).

   c) Accreditation organizations, such as the Joint Commission on Accreditation of Healthcare Organizations (JCAHO), have delineated patient care standards that include education components.

   d) Although there are many anecdotal reports of the benefits of patient education, there are few empirical studies of the efficacy of informational interventions for patients receiving radiotherapy (Ream & Richardson, 1996).

e) In randomized studies by D'Haese et al. (2000), Haggmark et al. (2001), and Poroch (1995), preparatory patient education significantly increased satisfaction in patients undergoing RT. However, their findings did not concur regarding the effect of patient education on anxiety reduction.

  (1) Studies of patient education and radiation oncology often explore a specific intervention and its impact. Hagopian (1996) found that patients who listened to informational audiotapes practiced more helpful self-care behaviors than those in the control group. Patients were noted to perform more self-care behaviors after receiving systematic information about side-effect management techniques (Dodd, 1987).

  (2) In another study, the helpfulness or number of self-care behaviors was not impacted by structured patient education in the form of a newsletter (Hagopian, 1991). Two randomized trials describe conflicting results regarding the impact of a preparatory videotape on reducing general anxiety. Although Thomas, Daly, Perryman, and Stockton (2000) reported that a video improved satisfaction and reduced treatment-related anxiety, Harrison et al. (2001) found that the additional provision of videotape did not significantly reduce pretreatment worry.

f) Assessment

  (1) Learning needs are gaps in knowledge, skills, or attitudes (Kitchie,

2003). Most patients want information primarily so they can be active participants in their RT (Hinds, Streater, & Mood, 1995). Ongoing assessment is essential as informational needs change over time (Hinds et al.; Treacy & Mayer, 2000) and exist across the continuum of cancer care (Chelf et al., 2001).

(2) Readiness to learn is the time when the patient is both receptive and willing to learn and occurs in four realms of physical readiness, emotional readiness, experiential readiness, and knowledge readiness (Kitchie, 2003).

(3) Learning style is defined as the way that the patient perceives and processes information (Moss, 1994). Many learning styles exist. One approach to describing learning styles uses the senses.

  (a) Visual learner

  (b) Auditory learner

  (c) Tactile learner

  (d) Vocal learner

  (e) Kinesthetic learner

(4) Literacy level: The definition of literacy is broad in scope: "an individual's ability to read, write, speak in English, and compute and solve problems at levels of proficiency necessary to function on the job, in the family of the individual, and in society" (U.S. Congress, 1991). Low literacy is a barrier to patient education and may adversely impact informed consent, treatment outcomes, and quality of life (Davis, Williams, Marin, Parker, & Glass, 2002; Merriman, Ades, & Seffrin, 2002).

  (a) Assessment of functional competency levels (levels 1–5) instead of grade levels is a more recent method to define literacy skills, with individuals in levels 1 and 2 lacking sufficient basic skills to function adequately (Doak et al., 1996). Twenty percent of adult Americans are functionally illiterate (level 1) and read at or below a 5th grade level (Doak et al., 1996).

  (b) Literacy skills vary widely. Patients may be able to read but have poor reading comprehension (Fisher, 1999). A descriptive study by Cooley et al. (1995) found that

the educational grade completed was higher than actual reading levels of the patients studied.

(c) Tools for assessing literacy level in the clinical setting are outlined in Table 6 (Quirk, 2000).

(d) Informal, subtle cues that may indicate low literacy include lack of interest, expression of frustration, slow reading speed, desire to let someone else read first, claims to have forgotten glasses, and inability to complete forms completely (Davis et al., 2002).

g) Planning: Formulate patient teaching plan with goals that are realistic, measurable, and congruent with the patient, treatment plan, and phase of illness (Johnson & Johnson, 1998). Patients require sensory, procedural, and self-care information (Poroch, 1995) that is tailored to the individual (Chelf et al., 2001). The teaching plan may include the following topics (adapted from ONS's *Manual for Radiation Oncology Nursing Practice and Education*) (Bruner, Bucholtz, Iwamoto, & Strohl, 1998):

(1) Goal of treatment (cure versus control versus palliation)

(2) Type of treatment (teletherapy, brachytherapy, radiotherapy, intraoperative, hyperthermia, photodynamic therapy, radioimmunotherapy)

(3) Simulation
   (a) Purpose
   (b) Preparation (e.g., disrobing, use of contrast material, laxative, enema)
   (c) Description of procedure (e.g., duration, staff present, oral contrast, positioning, immobilization devices, x-rays, computerized CT scan, tattoos)
   (d) Post-simulation care (e.g., laxative)

(4) External beam treatment schedule
   (a) Monday through Friday (e.g., once or twice daily)
   (b) Total number of fractions and days
   (c) Days to be seen in status check with physician and nurse
   (d) Days to receive lab work, if necessary
   (e) Timing of concurrent chemotherapy, if necessary

(5) External beam treatment experience
   (a) Staff administering treatment
   (b) Positioning
   (c) Video and audio monitoring system
   (d) Sensory aspects (e.g., size of machine, sounds of machine, temperature of the room)
   (e) Duration
   (f) Port films

(6) Possible side effects
   (a) General and site-specific side effects that may occur
   (b) Causes of symptoms
   (c) Expected onset and duration
   (d) Use of medications
   (e) Reassurance that patient is not radioactive with external beam radiotherapy

(7) Self-care measures

Table 6. Literacy Screening Tools

Tool	Type	Time to Administer	Strengths	Limitations
WRAT	Word recognition	5 minutes	Accurate in determining appropriate grade equivalent	Only English-speaking patients. Does not test vocabulary or comprehension
TOFHLA	Reading comprehension	22 minutes	Available in Spanish and English	Better research tool than clinical tool
REALM	Word recognition	2–3 minutes	Measures ability to read medical and health-related vocabulary. Simple scoring. Less time to administer	Does not test for comprehension. Only available in English

Note. From "Screening for Literacy and Readability: Implications for the Advanced Practice Nurse," by P.A. Quirk, 2000, *Clinical Nurse Specialist, 14*(1), p. 28. Copyright 2000 by Lippincott Williams & Wilkins. Reprinted with permission.

(a) Preventive measures to initiate at start of treatment

(b) Interventions to initiate as symptoms develop

(c) Use of complementary therapies

(d) Activity and nutrition recommendations

(8) Physician and nurse contact information

(a) Indications for calling

(b) Telephone numbers to call during business hours, evenings, and weekends

(9) Resources for assistance (e.g., support groups, dietitian, social worker, spiritual care counselor, community agencies)

(10) Discharge instructions

(a) Self-care

(b) Indications for calling prior to scheduled follow-up visit

(11) Instructions during follow-up phase

(a) Signs and symptoms of late effects

(b) Self-care

(c) Cancer prevention measures/healthy lifestyle

(d) Cancer screening guidelines

h) Implementation

(1) Include significant others in teaching.

(2) Build a trusting relationship.

(3) Use teaching strategies appropriate for the developmental stage of the learner (Bastable & Rinwalske, 2003) (see Table 7). Teaching techniques to optimize learning in the older adult include rest periods, pacing, rehearsing, positive reinforcement, cueing, and setting personalized goals (Rendon, Davis, Gioiella, & Tranzillo, 1986).

(4) Schedule time for patient education to occur.

(5) Create an effective learning environment that is private, quiet, and free from distractions.

(6) Attend to patient's comfort needs prior to initiating teaching session.

(7) Provide verbal instructions.

(a) Avoid using medical or technical terminology.

(b) Divide complex information or tasks into smaller subunits of instruction.

(c) Use advanced organizers or simple category names that are meaningful to the patient (Redman, 2001).

(d) Tailor or personalize the instruction.

(e) Allow time for questions and answers.

(f) Provide telephone numbers of staff.

(8) Use tools to reinforce verbal instructions.

(a) Print materials should be matched to the reading skills of the patient.

(b) Video tapes

(c) Audio tapes

(d) Computer-assisted instruction

(e) Internet

(f) Flip charts

(g) Models

(h) Calendars or journals

(9) Use various methods of teaching.

(a) Personal session

(b) Group instruction or class

(c) Family conference

(d) Role-play

(e) Demonstration

(10) Strategies for teaching patients with low-literacy skills include using multiple teaching methods and tools; partitioning information into small pieces; using vivid visuals; encouraging interaction during educational session; offering examples or testimonials; and using videotapes (Bastable, 2003a; Doak, Doak, Friedell, & Meade, 1998; Meade, 1996).

i) Evaluation

(1) Obtain verbal feedback from patient.

(2) Observe return demonstration.

(3) Provide immediate feedback to the learner to increase motivation or the desire to learn (Moss, 1994). Feedback consists of positive reinforce-

Table 7. Stage-Appropriate Teaching Strategies

Learner	General Characteristics	Teaching Strategies	Nursing Interventions
Infancy–toddlerhood • Approximate age: Birth–3 yr. • Cognitive stage: Sensorimotor • Psychosocial stage: Trust versus mistrust (Birth–12 months) • Autonomy versus shame and doubt (1–3 yr.)	Dependent on environment Needs security Explores self and environment Natural curiosity	Orient teaching to caregiver. Use repetition and imitation of information. Stimulate all senses. Provide physical safety and emotional security. Allow play and manipulation of objects.	Forge alliances. Encourage physical closeness. Provide detailed information. Answer questions and concerns. Ask for information on child's strengths/limitations and likes/dislikes.
Preschooler • Approximate age: 3–6 yr. • Cognitive stage: Preoperational • Psychosocial stage: Initiative versus guilt	Egocentric Thinking precausal, concrete, punitive Limited sense of time Fears bodily injury Cannot generalize Animistic thinking (objects possess life or human characteristics) Centration (focus is on one characteristic of an object) Separation anxiety Motivated by curiosity Active imagination, prone to fears Play is his/her work.	Use warm, calm approach. Build trust. Use repetition of information. Allow manipulation of objects and equipment. Give care with explanation. Reassure not to blame self. Explain procedures simply and briefly. Provide safe, secure environment. Encourage questions to reveal perceptions/feelings. Use simple drawings and stories. Use play therapy, with dolls and puppets. Stimulate senses: visual, auditory, tactile, motor.	Welcome active involvement. Forge alliances. Encourage physical closeness. Provide detailed information. Answer questions and concerns. Ask for information on child's strengths/limitations and likes/dislikes.
School-aged childhood • Approximate age: 6–12 yr. • Cognitive stage: Concrete operations • Psychosocial stage: Industry versus inferiority	More realistic and objective Understands cause and effect Deductive/inductive reasoning Wants concrete information Able to compare objects and events Variable rates of physical growth Reasons syllogistically Understands seriousness and consequences of actions Subject-centered focus Immediate orientation	Encourage independence and active participation. Be honest, allay fears. Use logical explanation. Allow time to ask questions. Use analogies to make invisible processes real. Establish role models. Relate care to other children's experiences; compare procedures. Use subject-centered focus. Use play therapy. Provide group activities. Use drawings, models, dolls, painting, audio- and videotapes.	Welcome active involvement. Forge alliances. Encourage physical closeness. Provide detailed information. Answer questions and concerns. Ask for information on child's strengths/limitations and likes/dislikes.
Adolescence • Approximate age: 12–18 yr. • Cognitive stage: Formal operations • Psychosocial stage: Identity versus role confusion	Abstract, hypothetical thinking Can build on past learning Reasons by logic and understands scientific principles Future orientation Motivated by a desire for social acceptance Peer group important Intense personal preoccupation, appearance extremely important (imaginary audience) Feels invulnerable, invincible/immune to natural laws (personal fable)	Establish trust, authenticity. Know their agenda. Address fears/concerns about outcomes of illness. Identify control focus. Include in plan of care. Use peers for support and influence. Negotiate changes. Focus on details. Make information meaningful to life. Ensure confidentiality and privacy. Arrange group sessions. Use audiovisuals, role-play, contracts, reading materials. Provide for experimentation and flexibility.	Explore emotional and financial support. Determine goals and expectations. Assess stress levels. Respect values and norms. Determine role responsibilities and relationships. Allow for 1:1 teaching without parents present, but with adolescent's permission; inform family of content covered.

(Continued on next page)

Table 7. Stage-Appropriate Teaching Strategies *(Continued)*

Learner	General Characteristics	Teaching Strategies	Nursing Interventions
Young adulthood • Approximate age: 18–40 yr. • Cognitive stage: Formal operations • Psychosocial stage: Intimacy versus isolation	Autonomous Self-directed Uses personal experiences to enhance or interfere with learning Intrinsic motivation Able to analyze critically Makes decisions about personal, occupational, and social roles Competency-based learner	Use problem-centered focus. Draw on meaningful experiences. Focus on immediacy of application. Encourage active participation. Allow to set own pace, be self-directed. Organize material. Recognize social role. Apply new knowledge through role-playing and hands-on practice.	Explore emotional and financial support. Assess motivational level for involvement. Identify potential obstacles and stressors.
Middle-aged adulthood • Approximate age: 40–60 yr. • Cognitive stage: Formal operations • Psychosocial stage: Generativity versus self-absorption and stagnation	Sense of self well-developed Concerned with physical changes At peak in career Explores alternative lifestyles Reflects on contributions to family and society Reexamines goals and values Questions achievements and successes Has confidence in abilities Desires to modify unsatisfactory aspects of life.	Focus on maintaining independence and reestablishing normal life patterns. Assess positive and negative past experiences with learning. Assess potential sources of stress due to midlife crisis issues. Provide information to coincide with life concerns and problems.	Explore emotional and financial support. Assess motivational level for involvement. Identify potential obstacles and stressors.
Older adulthood • Approximate age: 65 yr. and over • Cognitive stage: Formal operations • Psychosocial stage: Ego integrity versus despair	Cognitive changes Decreased ability to think abstractly, process information Decreased short-term memory Increased reaction time Increased test anxiety Stimulus persistence (afterimage) Focuses on past life experiences	Use concrete examples. Build on past life experiences. Make information relevant and meaningful. Present one concept at a time Allow time for processing/response (slow pace). Use repetition and reinforcement of information. Avoid written exams. Use verbal exchange and coaching. Establish retrieval plan (use one or several clues). Encourage active involvement. Keep explanations brief. Use analogies to illustrate abstract information.	Involve principal caregivers. Encourage participation. Provide resources for support (respite care). Assess coping mechanisms. Provide written instructions for reinforcement. Provide anticipatory problem solving (what happens if . . .).
	Sensory/motor deficits Auditory changes Hearing loss, especially high-pitched tones, consonants (S, Z, T, F, and G), and rapid speech Visual changes Farsighted (needs glasses to read) Lenses become opaque (glare problem) Smaller pupil size (decreased visual adaptation to darkness) Decreased peripheral perception	Speak slowly, distinctly. Use low-pitched tones. Face client when speaking. Minimize distractions. Avoid shouting. Use visual aids to supplement verbal instruction. Avoid glares, use soft white light. Provide sufficient light. Use white backgrounds and black print. Use large letters and well-spaced print. Avoid color coding with blues, greens, purples, and yellows.	

(Continued on next page)

Table 7. Stage-Appropriate Teaching Strategies *(Continued)*

Learner	General Characteristics	Teaching Strategies	Nursing Interventions
Older adulthood *(cont.)*	Yellowing of lenses (distorts low-tone colors: blue, green, violet) Distorted depth perception Fatigue/decreased risk taking Selective learning Intimidated by formal learning	Increase safety precautions/provide safe environment. Ensure accessibility and fit of prostheses (i.e., glasses, hearing aid). Keep sessions short. Provide for frequent rest periods. Allow for extra time to perform. Establish realistic short-term goals. Give time to reminisce. Identify and present pertinent material. Use informal teaching sessions. Demonstrate relevance of information to daily life. Assess resources. Make learning positive. Identify past positive experiences. Integrate new behaviors with formerly established ones.	

Note. From *Nurse as Educator. Principles of Teaching and Learning for Nursing Practice* (2nd ed., p. 122), by S.B. Bastable and M.A. Rinwalske, 2003, Sudbury, MA: Jones and Bartlett. Copyright 2003 by Jones and Bartlett. Reprinted with permission.

ment or suggestions for improvement (Smeltzer & Bare, 2000).

   (4) Reinforce learning at subsequent patient visits.

  j) Documentation: Use the ONS *Radiation Therapy Patient Care Record* (Catlin-Huth, Haas, & Pollock, 2002)

   (1) Assessment: Document identified learning needs and any factors that may influence patient's learning in the medical record.

   (2) Planning: Document learning objectives.

   (3) Implementation: Document person(s) taught, topics, and methods used.

   (4) Evaluation: Document patient's response to teaching, and plan for reinforcement and further evaluation.

  k) Selected online resources

   (1) American Cancer Society—www .cancer.org

   (2) Combined Health Information Database—http://chid.nih.gov

   (3) National Cancer Institute (NCI)—http://cancer.gov

   (4) National Center for Complementary and Alternative Medicine— http://nccam.nih.gov

   (5) National Coalition for Cancer Survivorship—www.canceradvocacy.org

   (6) National Institute for Literacy—http://novel.nifl.gov

   (7) National Library of Medicine—www .medlineplus.gov

   (8) Oncology Nursing Society—www .ons.org

   (9) PBS Literacy Link—www.pbs.org/adultlearning/literacy

References

American Hospital Association. (1973). *Statement on a Patient's Bill of Rights*. Chicago: Author.

American Nurses Association. (1998). *Standards of clinical nursing practice*. Washington, DC: Author.

Barlett, E.E. (1985). At last, a definition. *Patient Education and Counseling, 7,* 323–324.

Bastable, S.B. (2003a). Literacy in the adult patient population. In S.B. Bastable (Ed.), *Nurse as educator. Principles of teaching and learning for nursing practice* (2nd ed., pp. 189–231). Sudbury, MA: Jones and Bartlett.

Bastable, S.B. (2003b). Overview of education in health care. In S.B. Bastable (Ed.), *Nurse as educator. Principles of teaching and learning for nursing practice* (2nd ed., pp. 3–20). Sudbury, MA: Jones and Bartlett.

Bastable, S.B., & Rinwalske, M.A. (2003). Developmental stages of the learner. In S.B. Bastable (Ed.), *Nurse as educator. Principles of teaching and learning for nursing practice* (2nd ed., pp. 119–159). Sudbury, MA: Jones and Bartlett.

Bruner, D.W. (1993). Radiation oncology nurses: Staffing patterns and role development. *Oncology Nursing Forum, 20,* 651–655.

Bruner, D.W., Bucholtz, J.D., Iwamoto, R., & Strohl, R. (Eds.). (1998). *Manual for radiation oncology nursing practice and education.* Pittsburgh, PA: Oncology Nursing Society.

Catlin-Huth, C., Haas, M., & Pollock, V. (2002). *Radiation therapy patient care record: A tool for documenting nursing care.* Pittsburgh, PA: Oncology Nursing Society.

Chelf, J.H., Agre, P., Axelrod, A., Cheney, L., Cole, D.D., Conrad, K., et al. (2001). Cancer-related patient education: An overview of the last decade of evaluation and research. *Oncology Nursing Forum, 28,* 1139–1147.

Cooley, M.E., Moriaty, H., Berger, M.S., Selm-Orr, D., Coyle, B., & Short, T. (1995). Patient literacy and the readability of written cancer educational materials. *Oncology Nursing Forum, 22,* 1345–1351.

Davis, T.C., Williams, M.V., Marin, E., Parker, R.M., & Glass, J. (2002). Health literacy and cancer communications. *CA: A Cancer Journal for Clinicians, 52,* 134–149.

D'Haese, S., Vinh-Hung, V., Bijdekerke, P., Spinnoy, M., De Beukeleer, M., Lochie, N., et al. (2000). The effect of timing of the provision of information on anxiety and satisfaction of cancer patients receiving radiotherapy. *Journal of Cancer Education, 15,* 223–227.

Doak, C.C., Doak, L.G., Friedell, G.H., & Meade, C.D. (1998). Improving comprehension for cancer patients with low literacy skills: Strategies for clinicians. *CA: A Cancer Journal for Clinicians, 48,* 151–162.

Doak, C.C., Doak, L.G., & Root, J.H. (1996). *Teaching patients with low literacy skills* (2nd ed.). Philadelphia: Lippincott.

Dodd, M.J. (1987). Efficacy of proactive information on self-care in radiation therapy patients. *Heart and Lung, 16,* 538–544.

Fisher, E. (1999). Low literacy levels in adults: Implications for patient education. *Journal of Continuing Education in Nursing, 30,* 56–61.

Haggmark, C., Bohman, L., Ilmoni-Brandt, K., Naslund, I., Sjoden, P., & Nilsson, B. (2001). Effects of information supply on satisfaction with information and quality of life in cancer patients receiving curative radiation therapy. *Patient Education and Counseling, 45,* 173–179.

Hagopian, G.A. (1991). The effects of a weekly radiation therapy newsletter on patients. *Oncology Nursing Forum, 18,* 1199–1203.

Hagopian, G.A. (1996). The effects of informational audiotapes on knowledge and self-care behaviors of patients undergoing radiation therapy. *Oncology Nursing Forum, 23,* 697–700.

Harrison, R., Dey, P., Slevin, N.J., Eardley, A., Gibbs, A., Cowan, R., et al. (2001). Randomized controlled trial to assess the effectiveness of a videotape about radiotherapy. *British Journal of Cancer, 84,* 8–10.

Hilderley, L.J. (1980). The role of the nurse in radiation oncology. *Seminars in Oncology, 7,* 39–47.

Hinds, C., Streater, A., & Mood, D. (1995). Functions and preferred methods of receiving information related to radiotherapy. *Cancer Nursing, 18,* 374–384.

Johnson, M.B., & Johnson, J.L. (1998). The education process. In J.K. Itano & K.N. Taoka (Eds.), *Core curriculum for oncology nursing* (3rd ed., pp. 727–733). Philadelphia: Saunders.

Kitchie, S. (2003). Determinants of learning. In S.B. Bastable (Ed.), *Nurse as educator. Principles of teaching and learning for nursing practice* (2nd ed., pp. 75–118). Sudbury, MA: Jones and Bartlett.

Meade, C.D. (1996). Producing videotapes for cancer education: Methods and examples. *Oncology Nursing Forum, 23,* 837–846.

Merriman, B., Ades, T., & Seffrin, J.R. (2002). Health literacy in the information age: Communicating cancer information to patients and families. *CA: A Cancer Journal for Clinicians, 52,* 130–133.

Moore-Higgs, G.J., Watkins-Bruner, D., Balmer, L., Johnson-Doneski, J., Komarny, P., Mautner, B., et al. (2003). The role of licensed nursing personnel in radiation oncology. Part B: Integrating the ambulatory care nursing conceptual framework. *Oncology Nursing Forum, 30,* 59–64.

Moss, V.A. (1994). Assessing learning abilities, readiness for education. *Seminars in Perioperative Nursing, 3,* 113–120.

Oncology Nursing Society. (2002). *Patients' bill of rights for quality cancer care.* Retrieved September 17, 2004, from http://www.ons.org/publications/positions/PatientsBillofRights.shtml

Poroch, D. (1995). The effect of preparatory patient education on the anxiety and satisfaction of cancer patients receiving radiation therapy. *Cancer Nursing, 18,* 206–214.

Quirk, P.A. (2000). Screening for literacy and readability: Implications for the advanced practice nurse. *Clinical Nurse Specialist, 14,* 26–32.

Ream, E., & Richardson, A. (1996). The role of information in patients' adaptation to chemotherapy and radiotherapy: A review of the literature. *European Journal of Cancer Care, 5,* 132–138.

Redman, B.K. (2001). *The practice of patient education.* St. Louis, MO: Mosby.

Rendon, D.C., Davis, D.K., Gioiella, E.C., & Tranzillo, M.J. (1986). The right to know, the right to be taught. *Journal of Gerontological Nursing, 12*(12), 33–38.

Shepard, N., & Kelvin, J.F. (1999). The nursing role in radiation oncology. *Seminars in Oncology Nursing, 15,* 237–249.

Smeltzer, S.C., & Bare, B.G. (2000). *Brunner & Suddarth's textbook of medical-surgical nursing* (9th ed.). Philadelphia: Lippincott.

Strohl, R.A. (1988). The nursing role in radiation oncology: Symptom management of acute and chronic reactions. *Oncology Nursing Forum, 15,* 429–434.

Thomas, R., Daly, M., Perryman, B., & Stockton, D. (2000). Forewarned is forearmed—benefits of preparatory information on videocassette for patients receiving chemotherapy or radiotherapy—a randomized controlled trial. *European Journal of Cancer, 36,* 1536–1543.

Treacy, J.T., & Mayer, D.K. (2000). Perspectives on cancer patient education. *Seminars in Oncology Nursing, 16,* 47–56.

U.S. Congress. (1991). *Public law 102-73, the National Literacy Act of 1991.* Retrieved July 22, 2003, from http://www.nifl.gov/nifl/public-law.html

B. Fatigue
1. Pathophysiology
   a) The underlying mechanism of fatigue in patients receiving RT remains inconclusive; however, several hypotheses have been suggested (Morrow, Andrews, Hickok, Roscoe, & Matteson, 2002).
      (1) The anemia hypothesis: Anemia may be present in patients with cancer because of bleeding, hemolysis, or bone marrow infiltration. Although patients receiving radiation treatment may not experience the levels of fatigue associated with chemotherapy, fatigue is

highly prevalent in this subgroup of patients with cancer.

(2) The ATP hypothesis: ATP (adenosine triphosphate) provides the energy required for cellular function. With consistent food intake, ATP synthesis can occur. Many patients with cancer, however, will experience difficulty with chewing, swallowing, nausea, vomiting, food aversion, and/or anorexia. This decreases the amount of glucose needed for ATP production. If ATP cannot be replenished, decreased cellular functioning may lead to physical fatigue.

(3) The vagal afferent hypothesis: Afferent C-fibers may be stimulated by substances such as 5-HT, substance P, cytokines, and prostaglandins, which are released in response to the cancer and/or its treatment. This may lead to a reflex decrease in skeletal muscle tonc, which, in turn, can cause a decrease in physical energy.

(4) The hypothalamic pituitary axis, cytokines, and 5-HT hypothesis: Cytokines, specifically tumor necrosis factor (TNF), interleukin (IL)-1, and IL-6, are released in response to ionizing radiation. Additional cytokines follow, which may be associated with acute and chronic effects of radiation. 5-HT has the ability to alter the central nervous system (CNS) by causing changes in the hypothalamic pituitary axis. TNF-α can interrupt the production of serotonin by allowing high levels of 5-HT to be released. Low levels of serotonin can contribute to depression and possibly fatigue.

b) Risk factors

(1) Anemia may develop when treatment includes the sternum and pelvis: radiation to large sites with active bone marrow may reduce the oxygen-carrying capacity of the blood. Lower hemoglobin levels are consistent with higher levels of fatigue (Magnan & Mood, 2003).

(2) Severity of pain is associated with poor sleep quality; morning fatigue increases when pain severity increases (Miaskowski & Lee, 1999).

(3) Psychological distress includes depression, anxiety, confusion, and anger. The literature is mixed, with no clear consensus on the relationship between fatigue and depression.

(a) A study by Visser and Smets (1998) did not identify a strong cause and effect between fatigue and depression in patients receiving radiation.

(b) A relationship between fatigue and depression in patients with cancer has been identified in prior research (Hopwood & Stephens, 2000; Loge, Abrahamsen, Ekeberg, & Kaasa, 2000).

(c) Although distress is identified as a significant predictor of fatigue, further research is needed to determine the mechanism of this relationship (Irvine, Vincent, Graydon, & Bubela, 1998).

(d) Sleep disturbance is a significant predictor of severe fatigue in patients with cancer. Patients with difficulty falling asleep, nighttime awakenings, and awakening too early are more likely to report high levels of fatigue (Anderson et al., 2003).

(e) Nutritional deficits develop because of anorexia, taste changes, nausea, vomiting, stomatitis, esophagitis, mucositis, xerostomia, gastritis, and diarrhea; poor nutrition and weight loss, dehydration, and/or electrolyte imbalance may result (Beach, Siebeneck, Buderer, & Ferner, 2001).

(f) Combination therapy with surgery, chemotherapy, or biotherapy in addition to RT can lead to cumulative fatigue and may continue after completion of treatment (Morrow et al., 2002).

(g) Non-cancer comorbidities, including infection, hypothyroidism, malnutrition, and cardiac, pulmonary, renal, hepatic, neurologic, and/or endocrine function, should be treated appropriately, lessening possibility of additional sources of fatigue (Mock et al., 2003).

(h) Medications commonly used during cancer treatment may contribute to fatigue. Opioids, antiemetics, antidepressants, antihistamines, and beta blockers may cause patients to experience side effects, including lethargy, drowsiness, and/or weakness (Mock et al., 2003).

(i) Reduced functional status may occur because of physical and emotional factors. Daily trips for radiation treatment can cause increased physical fatigue and a decreased ability to maintain normal daily activities (Mock et al., 1997; Sitton, 1997).

(j) Disease progression and pattern of fatigue is unpredictable (Mock et al., 2003). Fatigue and pain can have a synergistic effect, resulting in a much worse overall symptom experience, especially in elderly patients with cancer (Given, Given, Azzouz, Kozachik, & Stommel, 2001).

2. Incidence: Fatigue occurs in 65%–100% of patients who receive radiation (Monga, Kerrigan, Thornby, & Monga, 1999; Nail & Jones, 1995). Differences in incidence and severity are affected by age, gender, stage of disease, and functional ability (Schwartz et al., 2000).

3. Assessment

a) Screening: The presence and severity of fatigue needs to be determined. The following three questions can provide this initial information:

(1) Are you experiencing fatigue?

(2) If so, on a scale of 0–10, 0 being no fatigue and 10 being the most severe fatigue, how would you rate it?

(3) How has this fatigue impacted your daily life? (Piper et al., 1998)

b) Information should be given on fatigue management, even when fatigue is mild or absent at the time of screening.

c) Comprehensive assessment

(1) Objective data

(a) Medical history

(b) Review of systems

(c) Physical examination

(d) Laboratory values: complete blood count (CBC), electrolytes, additional testing as appropriate

(2) Subjective information

(a) Severity and pattern of fatigue

(b) Effects on mood

(c) Ability to concentrate

(d) Exacerbating factors

(e) Cultural issues

d) Fatigue assessment tools

(1) The ONS fatigue scale (1999) provides a 5-point scale, with 1 indicating no fatigue and 5 representing the worst fatigue possible (see Appendix A).

(2) The revised Piper Fatigue Scale (PFS) includes four dimensions: mood/cognition, affective meaning, sensory, and behavioral/severity. This tool has 27 items and is used for screening and outcome assessment (Piper et al., 1998).

(3) The Brief Fatigue Inventory (BFI) has nine items and is useful for distinguishing severe fatigue but is less reliable for assessing mild to moderate fatigue (Mendoza et al., 1999).

(4) The Functional Assessment of Cancer Therapy–Fatigue (FACT-F) has 13 items, identifies physical and psychological aspects of fatigue, and can be used for screening and outcome assessment (Cella, 1997, 1998).

(5) The Multidimensional Fatigue Inventory (MFI-20) has 20 items and distinguishes general, physical, mental, reduced motivation and activity parameters, captures physical and psychological data, and can be used for screening and assessment of outcomes (Smets, Garssen, Bonke, & De Haes,

1995; Smets, Garssen, Cull, & de Haes, 1996).

(6) The Profile of Mood States (POMS) contains 65 items and measures tension-anxiety, anger-hostility, vigor-activity, fatigue-inertia, and confusion-bewilderment. This tool captures only psychological information and because of its length, it is too cumbersome for screening (McNair, Lorr, & Droppleman, 1992).

e) Follow-up assessment

(1) Determine the effectiveness of fatigue management strategies. Although fatigue may resolve after treatment, some patients experience chronic fatigue, which can lead to psychological distress and depression and is negatively associated with quality of life (Jereczek-Fossa, Marsiglia, & Orecchia, 2002; Visser & Smets, 1998; Vordermark, Schwab, Flentje, Sailer, & Kolbl, 2002).

(2) Provide self-assessment information; encourage discussion of concerns at follow up visits (Mock et al., 2003).

4. Management of treatable causes

a) Pharmacologic management

(1) Anemia: At least five nonexperimental, open-label, community-based trials provide evidence that treating anemia reduces fatigue (Crawford et al., 2002; Demetri, Kris, Wade, Degos, & Cella, 1998; Gabrilove, Einhorn, Livingston, Winer, & Cleeland, 1999; Glaspy et al., 1997; Quirt et al., 2001). The National Comprehensive Cancer Network (NCCN) guidelines panel on fatigue recommended that anemia be treated according to its cause (Mock et al., 2003).

(a) Iron or folic acid deficiencies should be restored.

(b) Blood loss can be replaced by transfusion.

(c) Use recombinant human erythropoietin to treat anemia caused by chronic disease and/or treatment toxicity. Intervention is recommended before hemoglobin drops below 10 g/dl (Magnan & Mood, 2003).

(2) Pain: The Agency for Healthcare Research and Quality (AHRQ) (2001) convened an expert panel that employed an explicit science-based methodology and expert clinical judgment to develop cancer pain management guidelines (Jacox, Carr, & Payne, 1994). The World Health Organization (WHO, 1990) Analgesic Ladder is recommended for titrating therapy for cancer pain.

(a) Use acetaminophen, aspirin, or a nonsteroidal anti-inflammatory drug (NSAID) for mild or moderate pain.

(b) If pain persists or increases, add opioids, such as codeine, or hydrocodone.

(c) If pain is persistent or moderate/severe at outset, increase opioid potency or use higher doses.

(d) For persistent pain, administer medication around-the-clock, with additional doses as needed for breakthrough pain.

(3) Depression: At least two systematic reviews support the pharmacologic treatment of depression (Berber, 1999; Guaiana, Barbui, & Hotopf, 2003). These reviews did not cite patients with cancer explicitly. Three well-known classes of drugs are used to treat depression (Barsevick & Much, 2004).

(a) Selective serotonin reuptake inhibitors (SSRIs), including paroxetine, sertraline, and fluoxetine, slow the reabsorption of the neurotransmitter serotonin after release into the synapse.

(b) Tricyclic antidepressants (TCAs), such as amitriptyline, doxepin, imipramine, and nortriptyline, increase the availability of the neurotransmitters norepinephrine and serotonin.

(c) Monoamine oxidase inhibitors (MAOIs), such as phenelzine, tranylcypromine, and isocarboxazid, block the enzyme monoamine oxidase that normally breaks down norepinephrine and serotonin.

   (4) Sleep disturbance: Morin (1993) summarized the research on the pharmacologic treatment of insomnia (National Institutes of Health [NIH], 1984, 1991). Several classes of drugs are used to manage insomnia (Mills & Graci, 2003).

     (a) Nonbenzodiazepine hypnotics, including zaleplon and zolpidem, have a short half-life, so they induce sleep with few residual effects.

     (b) Benzodiazepines, such as triazolam, temazepam, and lorazepam, have a longer half-life and are associated with residual effects, including daytime fatigue and impairment of cognitive and psychomotor functioning.

     (c) Antidepressants with sedative effects, such as trazodone, amitriptyline, and doxepin, may be used to treat insomnia.

   (5) Nutrition: Appetite stimulants, including megesterol acetate and dexamethasone, are effective in stimulating appetite and weight gain and improving well-being according to a systematic review (Brown, 2002).

   (6) Comorbidities: A clinically based recommendation of the NCCN panel is to review comorbidities to determine if they are managed optimally. Stabilization may require the introduction of new medications, titration of current drugs, or both (Mock et al., 2003).

 b) Nonpharmacologic management

   (1) Information: Numerous clinical trials have demonstrated that providing concrete objective information is effective in preparing individuals for a variety of healthcare experiences. Providing a description of physical sensations, causes, patterns, and consequences of a problem such as fatigue enables the individual and family to plan for it and maintain a sense of control over their experience (Diefenbach & Leventhal, 1996; Johnson, Fieler, Jones, Wlasowicz, & Mitchell, 1997; Reuille, 2002).

     (a) Physical sensations: Fatigue is the subjective feeling of being tired that persists and interferes with functioning. A person can feel mentally and/or physically fatigued. Fatigue may persist despite adequate rest or sleep (Barsevick, Whitmer, & Walker, 2001; Berger & Farr, 1999).

     (b) Potential causes of fatigue (see Section IV, B—Fatigue)

     (c) Patterns

       i) Fatigue pattern during RT: Fatigue increases gradually over a five- to six-week course of therapy to a high point at the end of treatment, then gradually declines (Beck & Schwartz, 2000; Christman, Oakley, & Cronin, 2001).

       ii) Fatigue pattern after completion of radiotherapy: It is estimated that up to 40% of individuals treated for cancer with radiotherapy could suffer from chronic fatigue; almost 20% have characterized their fatigue as severe (Jereczek-Fossa et al., 2002; Vordermark et al., 2002). The duration of fatigue after treatment is unknown.

     (d) Consequences of fatigue may include loss of capacity for physical performance (Mock, 2001) or decreased ability to function in usual activities (Barsevick et al., 2001). Consequences of successful fatigue management include reduced fatigue and ability to maintain valued activities despite fatigue.

   (2) Energy conservation: One systematic review and two pilot studies demonstrated that energy conservation is effective in managing fatigue (Barsevick

et al., 2004; Barsevick, Whitmer, Sweeney, & Nail, 2002; Tiesinga, Dassen, Halfens, & van den Heuvel, 1999). Energy conservation is the planned management of energy resources to prevent or reduce fatigue.

(a) Goal: To maintain valued activities through a balance of rest and activity

(b) Strategies: Use of rest periods, priority setting, delegation of less important activities, pacing oneself, and performing demanding activities at times of peak energy

(c) Techniques

   i) Make a priority list of usual activities and delegate low priority activities to others.

   ii) Keep a daily diary to learn fatigue patterns and use as a basis for scheduling valued activities.

(3) Attention restoration: One clinical trial has demonstrated that attention restoration reduced attentional fatigue in patients with cancer. Attention restoration is a self-care activity used to deal with mental fatigue, distraction, and difficulty concentrating (Cimprich, 1992, 1993).

(a) Goal: To prevent or reduce mental fatigue

(b) Characteristics of attention-restoring activities

   i) Captures and holds one's attention.

   ii) Provides a change from one's usual routine.

   iii) Provides a sense of being removed from one's current environment.

(c) Techniques

   i) Select a restorative activity that is of personal interest (e.g., sitting, walking, observing a natural environment, tending plants, caring for a pet, reading, working on a craft project)

   ii) Engage in the restorative activity for a minimum of 20 minutes per day at least three times per week.

   iii) Keep a record of the time spent performing the restorative activity, as well as fatigue level before and after.

(4) Sleep education/hygiene: Interventions focused on cognitive, behavioral, and informational factors known to play a role in insomnia have been developed for healthy people with chronic insomnia. These techniques are used to modify maladaptive sleep habits, reduce arousal, and educate about healthy sleep practices (Hauri & Wisbey, 1994; Morin, 1993). However, these techniques have not been tested in patients with cancer (Savard & Morin, 2001). One pilot study of a sleep promotion plan for patients with cancer has demonstrated the feasibility of this approach (Berger et al., 2002).

(a) Prevention of sleep problems through healthy sleep habits

   i) Establish and maintain a regular bedtime/wake time.

   ii) Stay in bed only for intended hours of sleep.

   iii) Avoid eating, watching TV, or reading in bed.

   iv) Avoid taking naps that could interfere with nighttime sleep.

   v) Exercise regularly at least four hours prior to bedtime.

   vi) Keep rooms fully illuminated during the day; reduce illumination at night.

(b) Self-care interventions for sleep disturbance

   i) Relaxation techniques

   ii) Meditation

(5) Cognitive behavioral therapies, especially relaxation techniques, have been widely tested during cancer treatment and demonstrated efficacy in reducing symptoms, including pain, nau-

sea/vomiting, insomnia, and anxiety (Jacobsen & Hann, 1998). Several types of relaxation techniques can be used singly or in combination (Jacobsen & Hann; Mills & Graci, 2003).

(a) Progressive muscle relaxation: Flex and relax each body part several times in succession until all areas of the body are relaxed.

(b) Guided imagery: Imagine a restful or peaceful scene with all the senses and use this scene to become relaxed.

(c) Diaphragmatic breathing: Take slow, deep breaths while expanding the whole diaphragm and pushing out the stomach.

(d) Body scan: Sit or lie in a comfortable position and pay attention to each body part for 20–30 seconds without judgment.

(e) Meditation: Focus on a word, sound, or object while clearing all other thoughts from the mind.

(6) Behavioral management of nutritional deficits: It is well known that cancer treatment can impair nutritional status resulting in fatigue. Behavioral interventions using relaxation techniques have demonstrated efficacy in improving physical well-being during cancer treatment (Fleishman, 1998; Jacobsen & Hann, 1998). However, there is no evidence that these approaches improve nutritional status. A variety of clinically based behavioral suggestions may be used (Cunningham, 2004).

(a) Eat small meals during the day.

(b) Keep food and nutritional supplements close at hand.

(c) Avoid foods that have become unpalatable because of treatment.

(d) Unless there is a medical contraindication, "indulge" in previously avoided high-fat, high-cholesterol foods.

(e) Use social rituals, such as eating with others or drinking wine.

(7) Exercise

(a) A pilot study and a clinical trial of exercise for patients with breast cancer receiving radiotherapy has demonstrated fatigue reduction (Mock et al., 1997, 2001). Several other studies have documented efficacy during and/or after chemotherapy, biotherapy, and stem cell transplant (Dimeo, 2001; Dimeo et al., 1996; Dimeo, Fetscher, Lange, Mertelsmann, & Keul, 1997; Dimeo, Rumberger, & Keul, 1998; Dimeo, Stieglitz, Novelli-Fischer, Fetscher, & Keul, 1999; Mock et al., 1997; Schwartz, Mori, Gao, Nail, & King, 2001; Schwartz, Thompson, & Masood, 2002). A regular program of aerobic exercise (walking, bicycling, or self-selected exercise) has been found to be beneficial.

(b) Clinically based recommendations by NCCN (Mock et al., 2003)

i) An exercise program should be individualized to the person's age, gender, and fitness level (Mock et al., 2000; Nail, 2002).

ii) Exercise recommendations should include type of exercise, intensity, duration, and frequency; guidance also should be provided about starting level and rate of progression to higher levels.

iii) Safety precautions
   • An individual with appropriate expertise should prescribe exercise.
   • For the individual with specific comorbidities (such as bone metastases) or in a deconditioned state, referral to a rehabilitation program or physical medicine may be appropriate.
   • The individual should be advised to avoid exercising one to two days after receiving chemotherapy

and during periods of neutropenia, low platelets, anemia, or fever.
- The individual should be told to discontinue exercise and seek medical attention if he or she has shortness of breath, chest pain, dizziness, nausea/vomiting, or pain during activity.

5. Documentation
   a) Fatigue rating (Catlin-Huth, Haas, & Pollock, 2002)
      (1) No fatigue
      (2) Mild fatigue
      (3) Moderate fatigue
      (4) Extreme fatigue
      (5) Worst fatigue
   b) Additional documentation (Catlin-Huth et al., 2002)
      (1) Probable causes of fatigue
      (2) Impact on daily activities
      (3) Planned interventions
      (4) Subsequent outcomes
6. Patient and family education outcomes
   a) Adequate knowledge about fatigue
   b) Demonstration of fatigue management skills
   c) Self-report of decreased fatigue
   d) Ability to accomplish important activities despite fatigue
   e) Evaluation of self-intervention strategies and continued utilization of interventions for chronic fatigue
   f) Overall improvement in psychological well-being when patients are able to reach realistic goals based on information received, self-esteem, and confidence (Irvine et al., 1998; Ream & Richardson, 1999)
7. Teaching tools
   a) Symptom diary (Nail, 2002): Individuals rate fatigue and 14 other symptoms daily on a 0–10 scale. The purpose of these ratings is to document the pattern of fatigue and other symptoms.
   b) Self-care instructions (Nail, 2002): This self-care guide provides important factual information about fatigue as well as self-care instructions.
   c) Web sites: Many healthcare-related Web sites now contain accurate, updated information about fatigue.
      (1) American Cancer Society—www.cancer.org (800-ACS-2345)
      (2) National Comprehensive Cancer Network—www.nccn.org (888-909-NCCN)
      (3) Cancer Care Network—www.cancercare.org
      (4) Oncology Nursing Society—www.ons.org (866-257-4667)

References

Agency for Healthcare Research and Quality. (2001). *Management of cancer pain.* Washington, DC: U.S. Department of Health and Human Services.

Anderson, K.O., Getto, C.J., Mendoza, T.R., Palmer, S.N., Wang, X.S., Reyes-Gibby, C.C., et al. (2003). Fatigue and sleep disturbance in patients with cancer, patients with clinical depression, and community-dwelling adults. *Journal of Pain Symptom Management, 25,* 307–318.

Barsevick, A., Dudley, W., Beck, S., Sweeney, C., Whitmer, K., & Nail, L. (2004). A randomized clinical trial of energy conservation for patients with cancer-related fatigue. *Cancer, 100,* 1302–1310.

Barsevick, A., & Much, J. (2004). Depression. In C.H. Yarbro, M.H. Frogge, & M. Goodman (Eds.), *Cancer symptom management* (3rd ed., pp. 668–684). Sudbury, MA: Jones and Bartlett.

Barsevick, A.M., Whitmer, K., Sweeney, C., & Nail, L.M. (2002). A pilot study examining energy conservation for cancer treatment-related fatigue. *Cancer Nursing, 25,* 333–341.

Barsevick, A.M., Whitmer, K., & Walker, L. (2001). In their own words: Using the common sense model to analyze patient descriptions of cancer-related fatigue. *Oncology Nursing Forum, 28,* 1363–1369.

Beach, P., Siebeneck, B., Buderer, N.F., & Ferner, T. (2001). Relationship between fatigue and nutritional status in patients receiving radiation therapy to treat lung cancer. *Oncology Nursing Forum, 28,* 1027–1031.

Beck, S.L., & Schwartz, A.L. (2000). Unrelieved pain contributes to fatigue and insomnia. *Oncology Nursing Forum, 27,* 350.

Berber, M.J. (1999). Pharmacological treatment of depression. Consulting with Dr. Oscar. *Canadian Family Physician, 45,* 2663–2668.

Berger, A.M., & Farr, L. (1999). The influence of daytime inactivity and nighttime restlessness on cancer-related fatigue. *Oncology Nursing Forum, 26,* 1663–1671.

Berger, A.M., VonEssen, S., Khun, B.R., Piper, B.F., Farr, L., Agrawal, S., et al. (2002). Feasibility of a sleep intervention during adjuvant breast cancer chemotherapy. *Oncology Nursing Forum, 29,* 1431–1441.

Brown, J.K. (2002). A systematic review of the evidence on symptom management of cancer-related anorexia and cachexia. *Oncology Nursing Forum, 29,* 517–532.

Catlin-Huth, C., Haas, M., & Pollock, V. (2002). *Radiation therapy patient care record: A tool for documenting nursing care.* Pittsburgh, PA: Oncology Nursing Society.

Cella, D. (1997). The Functional Assessment of Cancer Therapy–Anemia (FACT-An) Scale: A new tool for the assessment of outcomes in cancer anemia and fatigue. *Seminars in Hematology, 34*(3 Suppl. 2), 13–19.

Cella, D. (1998). Factors influencing quality of life in cancer patients: Anemia and fatigue. *Seminars in Oncology, 25*(3 Suppl. 7), 43–46.

Christman, N.J., Oakley, M.G., & Cronin, S.N. (2001). Developing and using preparatory information for women undergoing radiation therapy for cervical or uterine cancer. *Oncology Nursing Forum, 28,* 93–98.

Cimprich, B. (1992). Attentional fatigue following breast cancer surgery. *Research in Nursing and Health, 15*(3), 199–207.

Cimprich, B. (1993). Development of an intervention to restore attention in cancer patients. *Cancer Nursing, 16*(2), 83–92.

Crawford, J., Cella, D., Cleeland, C.S., Cremieux, P.Y., Demetri, G.D., Sarokhan, B.J., et al. (2002). Relationship between changes in hemoglobin level and quality of life during chemotherapy in anemic cancer patients receiving epoetin alfa therapy. *Cancer, 95,* 888–895.

Cunningham, R.S. (2004). The anorexia-cachexia syndrome. In C.H. Yarbro, M.H. Frogge, & M. Goodman (Eds.), *Cancer symptom management* (3rd ed., pp. 137–167). Sudbury, MA: Jones and Bartlett.

Demetri, G.D., Kris, M., Wade, J., Degos, L., & Cella, D. (1998). Quality-of-life benefit in chemotherapy patients treated with epoetin alfa is independent of disease response or tumor type: Results from a prospective community oncology study. Procrit study group. *Journal of Clinical Oncology, 16,* 3412–3425.

Diefenbach, M.A., & Leventhal, H. (1996). The Common-Sense Model of Illness representation: Theoretical and practical considerations. *Journal of Social Distress and Homeless, 5*(1), 11–38.

Dimeo, F.C. (2001). Effects of exercise on cancer-related fatigue. *Cancer, 92*(Suppl. 6), 1689–1693.

Dimeo, F.C., Bertz, H., Finke, J., Fetscher, S., Mertelsmann, R., & Keul, J. (1996). An aerobic exercise program for patients with haematological malignancies after bone marrow transplantation. *Bone Marrow Transplantation, 18,* 1157–1160.

Dimeo, F.C., Fetscher, S., Lange, W., Mertelsmann, R., & Keul, J. (1997). Effects of aerobic exercise on the physical performance and incidence of treatment-related complications after high-dose chemotherapy. *Blood, 90,* 3390–3394.

Dimeo, F.C., Rumberger, B.G., & Keul, J. (1998). Aerobic exercise as therapy for cancer fatigue. *Medicine and Science in Sports and Exercise, 30,* 475–478.

Dimeo, F.C., Stieglitz, R.D., Novelli-Fischer, U., Fetscher, S., & Keul, J. (1999). Effects of physical activity on the fatigue and psychologic status of cancer patients during chemotherapy. *Cancer, 85,* 2273–2277.

Fleishman, S. (1998). Cancer cachexia. In J.C. Holland & W. Breitbart (Eds.), *Psycho-oncology* (pp. 468–475). New York: Oxford University Press.

Gabrilove, J.L., Einhorn, L.H., Livingston, R.B., Winer, E., & Cleeland, C.S. (1999). Once-weekly dosing of epoetin alfa is similar to three-times-weekly dosing in increasing hemoglobin and quality of life [Abstract]. *Proceedings of the American Society of Clinical Oncology, 15,* 574a.

Given, C.W., Given, B., Azzouz, F., Kozachik, S., & Stommel, M. (2001). Predictors of pain and fatigue in the year following diagnosis among elderly cancer patients. *Journal of Pain and Symptom Management, 21,* 456–466.

Glaspy, J., Bukowski, R., Steinberg, D., Taylor, C., Tchekmedyian, S., & Vadhan-Raj, S. (1997). Impact of therapy with epoetin alfa on clinical outcomes in patients with nonmyeloid malignancies during cancer chemotherapy in community oncology practice. Procrit study group. *Journal of Clinical Oncology, 15,* 1218–1234.

Guaiana, G., Barbui, C., & Hotopf, M. (2003). Amitriptyline versus other types of pharmacotherapy for depression. *Cochrane Database of Systematic Reviews, 2,* CD004186.

Hauri, P., & Wisbey, J. (1994). Actigraphy and insomnia: A closer look. Part 2. *Sleep, 17,* 408–410.

Hopwood, P., & Stephens, R.J. (2000). Depression in patients with lung cancer: Prevalence and risk factors derived from quality-of-life data. *Journal of Clinical Oncology, 18,* 893–903.

Irvine, D.M., Vincent, L., Graydon, J.E., & Bubela, N. (1998). Fatigue in women with breast cancer receiving radiation therapy. *Cancer Nursing, 21*(2), 127–135.

Jacobsen, P., & Hann, D. (1998). Cognitive-behavioral interventions. In J.C. Holland & W. Breitbart (Eds.), *Psycho-oncology* (pp. 717–729). New York: Oxford University Press.

Jacox, A., Carr, D.B., & Payne, R. (1994). New clinical practice guidelines for the management of pain in patients with cancer. *New England Journal of Medicine, 330,* 651–655.

Jereczek-Fossa, B.A., Marsiglia, H.R., & Orecchia, R. (2002). Radiotherapy-related fatigue. *Critical Review of Oncology Hematology, 41,* 317–325.

Johnson, J., Fieler, V., Jones, L., Wlasowicz, G., & Mitchell, M. (1997). *Self-regulation theory: Applying theory to your practice.* Pittsburgh, PA: Oncology Nursing Society.

Loge, J.H., Abrahamsen, A.F., Ekeberg, O., & Kaasa, S. (2000). Fatigue and psychiatric morbidity among Hodgkin's disease survivors. *Journal of Pain and Symptom Management, 19,* 91–99.

Magnan, M.A., & Mood, D.W. (2003). The effects of health state, hemoglobin, global symptom distress, mood disturbance, and treatment site on fatigue onset, duration, and distress in patients receiving radiation therapy [Online]. *Oncology Nursing Forum, 30,* E33–E39.

McNair, D.M., Lorr, M., & Droppleman, L.F. (1992). *Profile of Mood States manual* (2nd ed.). San Diego, CA: Educational and Industrial Testing Service.

Mendoza, T.R., Wang, X.S., Cleeland, C.S., Morrissey, M., Johnson, B.A., Wendt, J.K., et al. (1999). The rapid assessment of fatigue severity in cancer patients: Use of the Brief Fatigue Inventory. *Cancer, 85,* 1186–1196.

Miaskowski, C., & Lee, K.A. (1999). Pain, fatigue, and sleep disturbances in oncology outpatients receiving radiation therapy for bone metastasis: A pilot study. *Journal of Pain and Symptom Management, 17,* 320–332.

Mills, M., & Graci, G. (2004). Sleep disturbances. In C.H. Yarbro, M.H. Frogge, & M. Goodman (Eds.), *Cancer symptom management* (3rd ed., pp. 111–128). Sudbury, MA: Jones and Bartlett.

Mock, V. (2001). Fatigue management: Evidence and guidelines for practice. *Cancer, 92*(Suppl. 6), 1699–1707.

Mock, V., Atkinson, A., Barsevick, A., Cella, D., Cimprich, B., Cleeland, C., et al. (2000). NCCN practice guidelines for cancer-related fatigue. *Oncology, 14*(11A), 151–161.

Mock, V., Atkinson, A., Barsevick, A., Cella, D., Cimprich, B., Cleeland, C., et al. (2003). NCCN 2003 cancer-related fatigue clinical practice guidelines in oncology. *Journal of the National Comprehensive Cancer Network, 1,* 308–331.

Mock, V., Dow, K.H., Meares, C.J., Grimm, P.M., Dienemann, J.A., Haisfield-Wolfe, M.E., et al. (1997). Effects of exercise on fatigue, physical functioning, and emotional distress during radiation therapy for breast cancer. *Oncology Nursing Forum, 24,* 991–1000.

Mock, V., Pickett, M., Ropka, M.E., Muscari, E.L., Stewart, K.J., Rhodes, V.A., et al. (2001). Fatigue and quality of life outcomes of exercise during cancer treatment. *Cancer Practice, 9*(3), 119–127.

Monga, U., Kerrigan, A.J., Thornby, J., & Monga, T.N. (1999). Prospective study of fatigue in localized prostate cancer patients undergoing radiotherapy. *Radiation Oncology Investigations, 7*(3), 178–185.

Morin, C.M. (1993). *Insomnia: Psychological assessment and management.* New York: Guilford.

Morrow, G.R., Andrews, P.L., Hickok, J.T., Roscoe, J.A., & Matteson, S. (2002). Fatigue associated with cancer and its treatment. *Supportive Care in Cancer, 10,* 389–398.

Nail, L.M. (2002). Fatigue in patients with cancer. *Oncology Nursing Forum, 29,* 537.

Nail, L.M., & Jones, L.S. (1995). Fatigue as a side effect of cancer treatment: Impact on quality of life. *Quality of Life: A Nursing Challenge, 4,* 8–13.

National Institutes of Health. (1984). Drugs and insomnia: The use of medications to promote sleep. *JAMA, 18,* 2410–2414.

National Institutes of Health. (1991). Consensus development conference statement: The treatment of sleep disorders of older people. *Sleep, 14,* 169–177.

Oncology Nursing Society. (1999). *ONS fatigue scale.* Retrieved May 11, 2004, from http://64.233.167.104/custom?q=cache: kJUsbMZIgDIJ:www.ons.org/images/Library/ons_publications/ onf/2001/January_February/fatigue/24.pdf+ONS+fatigue +scale&hl=en

Piper, B.F., Dibble, S.L., Dodd, M.J., Weiss, M.C., Slaughter, R.E., & Paul, S.M. (1998). The revised Piper Fatigue Scale: Psychometric evaluation in women with breast cancer. *Oncology Nursing Forum, 25,* 677–684.

Quirt, I., Robeson, C., Lau, C.Y., Kovacs, M., Burdette-Radoux, S., Dolan, S., et al. (2001). Epoetin alfa therapy increases hemoglobin levels and improves quality of life in patients with cancer-related anemia who are not receiving chemotherapy and patients with anemia who are receiving chemotherapy. *Journal of Clinical Oncology, 19,* 4126–4134.

Ream, E., & Richardson, A. (1999). From theory to practice: Designing interventions to reduce fatigue in patients with cancer. *Oncology Nursing Forum, 26,* 1295–1303.

Reuille, K.M. (2002). Using self-regulation theory to develop an intervention for cancer-related fatigue. *Clinical Nurse Specialist, 16,* 312–319.

Savard, J., & Morin, C.M. (2001). Insomnia in the context of cancer: A review of a neglected problem. *Journal of Clinical Oncology, 19,* 895–908.

Schwartz, A.L., Mori, M., Gao, R., Nail, L.M., & King, M.E. (2001). Exercise reduces daily fatigue in women with breast cancer receiving chemotherapy. *Medical Science Sports Exercise, 33,* 718–723.

Schwartz, A.L., Nail, L.M., Chen, S., Meek, P., Barsevick, A.M., King, M.E., et al. (2000). Fatigue patterns observed in patients receiving chemotherapy and radiotherapy. *Cancer Investigation, 18*(1), 11–19.

Schwartz, A.L., Thompson, J.A., & Masood, N. (2002). Interferon-induced fatigue in patients with melanoma: A pilot study of exercise and methylphenidate [Electronic version]. *Oncology Nursing Forum, 29,* E85–E90.

Sitton, E. (1997). Managing side effects of skin changes and fatigue. In K.H. Dow, J.D. Bucholtz, R. Iwamoto, V.K. Fieler, & L.J. Hilderley (Eds.), *Nursing care in radiation oncology* (2nd ed., pp. 79–100). Philadelphia: Saunders.

Smets, E.M., Garssen, B., Bonke, B., & De Haes, J.C. (1995). The Multidimensional Fatigue Inventory (MFI) psychometric qualities of an instrument to assess fatigue. *Journal of Psychosomatic Research, 39,* 315–325.

Smets, E.M., Garssen, B., Cull, A., & de Haes, J.C. (1996). Application of the multidimensional fatigue inventory (MFI-20) in cancer patients receiving radiotherapy. *British Journal of Cancer, 73,* 241–245.

Tiesinga, L.J., Dassen, T.W., Halfens, R.J., & van den Heuvel, W.J. (1999). Factors related to fatigue: Priority of interventions to reduce or eliminate fatigue and the exploration of a multidisciplinary research model for further study of fatigue. *International Journal of Nursing Studies, 36,* 265–280.

Visser, M.R., & Smets, E.M. (1998). Fatigue, depression and quality of life in cancer patients: How are they related? *Supportive Care in Cancer, 6*(2), 101–108.

Vordermark, D., Schwab, M., Flentje, M., Sailer, M., & Kolbl, O. (2002). Chronic fatigue after radiotherapy for carcinoma of the prostate: Correlation with anorectal and genitourinary function. *Radiotherapy Oncology, 62,* 293–297.

World Health Organization. (1990). Cancer pain relief and palliative care. Report of a WHO expert committee. *World Health Organization Technical Report Series, 804,* 1–75.

C. Skin reactions
   1. Pathophysiology
      a) Skin composed of two main layers
         (1) Epidermis (superficial layer)—during normal skin regeneration, superficial cells are shed through normal desquamation, and new cells are formed in the basal layer of the epidermis and continuously replace those that are lost. The basal layer of the epidermis proliferates rapidly; therefore, it is particularly sensitive to radiotherapy.
         (2) Dermis (deep layer containing blood vessels, glands, nerves, and hair follicles)—provides the supportive structure required for the epidermis to renew.
      b) Ionizing radiation damages the mitotic ability of stem cells within the basal layer, thus preventing the process of repopulation and weakening the integrity of the skin. Repeated radiation impairs the cell division within the basal layer, and skin reaction develops (Archambeau, Pezner, & Wasserman, 1995).
      c) The skin is very sensitive to RT. Basal cell loss begins at 20–25 Gy (visible at two to three weeks) and maximum depletion occurs at 50 Gy (usually peaking at the end of treatment) (Chao, Perez, & Brady, 2001).
      d) Hair loss—temporary and partial hair loss occurs at 30 Gy, and permanent hair loss can occur at 55 Gy (Chao et al., 2001).
   2. Incidence
      a) Increasing use of concomitant chemotherapy and high-dose radiotherapy means that skin reactions are still a major problem for patients.

b) Incidence rate is difficult to predict and monitor, as the severity and occurrence is not well documented. Specific anatomic sites have been quoted in the literature.

c) Impacting factors

    (1) Treatment related: Type of energy (electrons versus photons), use of tangential fields (higher doses received within thinner areas), use of parallel opposed fields (two skin surfaces are proximal), skin bolus (gel-like sheets build up skin to ensure higher dose), skin types (scalp has a higher tolerance than trunk or groin), more oxygenated cells than hypoxic cells, or previous radiation exposure (Chao et al., 2001)

    (2) Non–treatment related: General skin condition, moist areas of the body causing friction (axilla, inframammary areas, groin, or perineum), age, nutritional status (hydration), exposure to prior chemotherapy agents known as "radiation recall" (i.e., doxorubicin), and underlying medical conditions (scleroderma, lupus) (Chao et al., 2001)

3. Staging/assessment of symptoms

  a) Radiation-induced skin reactions are dependent on time-dose factors rather than on the total dose delivered (Archambeau, 1987).

  b) Radiation-induced skin reactions range from erythema, where different shapes of redness occur from the release of histamine-like substances from damaged germinal cells, to dry desquamation (dry, flaky, or scaly skin) because the sweat and sebaceous glands have been damaged, or to moist desquamation where blistering, peeling, and sloughing of the skin occur. Damage to the hair follicles and sweat glands can be permanent. Rarely seen is necrosis, which involves damage to the deeper layers of the skin.

  c) NCI (2003) has a four-point scale of color stages or skin patterns; however, the patient's feeling is missing in this scale. Further assessment could include subjective pain (0–10 scale), sensation feeling (burning, prickly, or pruritus), and interference with activities of daily living.

  d) Assessment should include treatment fields and exit sites.

4. Acute effects

  a) The major acute side effects to the skin while receiving RT are erythema, dry desquamation, moist desquamation, and ulceration. The overall goal is to keep the skin intact by minimizing scratching and rubbing and keeping the skin moisturized. If moist desquamation develops, the goal is to support epithelial recovery and avoid superinfections.

  b) Interventions

    (1) During treatment planning, special positioning devices may be used to reduce skin folds.

    (2) All surgical wounds should be healed before initiating RT.

    (3) Very few randomized studies have been conducted to evaluate skin care products; most are anecdotal. No standardized protocols are available on skin care products (Moore-Higgs & Amdur, 2001; Pazdur, Coia, Hoskins, & Wagman, 2003). Although not an exhaustive list, available products for erythema include

      (a) Aquaphor® (Beiersdorf, Hamburg, Germany)*

      (b) Eucerin® (Biersdorf)*

      (c) TheraCare™ (Emumagic, Nevis, MN* (pure lanolin cream)

      (d) Vitamin A & E ointment/cream*

      (e) Biafine® (Medix Pharmaceuticals Americas, Largo, FL) (RTOG 97-13 demonstrated no prophylactic capability [Fisher et al., 2000].)

      (f) Aloe vera gels* (No skin differences were seen with aloe vera gels [Williams, Burk, & Loprinzi, 1996].)

      (g) Natural skin care gel*

      (h) Chamomile and almond oil (Skin changes appeared later [Maiche, Grohn, & Maki-Hokkonen, 1991].) (* Indicates no studies found on product)

(4) For moist desquamation
  (a) Normal saline compresses or modified Burow's solution soaks for 15–20 minutes, three times a day (Pazdur et al., 2003)
  (b) Use moisture vapor permeable dressings (e.g., Tegaderm™ [3M, Maplewood, MN], OpSite® [Smith & Nephew, Largo, FL], Bioclusive™ [Johnson & Johnson, San Francisco, CA]) or hydrocolloid dressings. Do not use dry dressings.
  (c) Vaseline petrolatum gauze provides a moisture barrier, easy to take off prior to treatment.
(5) Historically, use of topical agents (e.g., lotions, deodorants) prior to RT is discouraged. Recent studies indicate only a small amount (1%–5%) of skin dose increased when products were used prior to treatment. The only contraindications were the chemical irritants in the products (Burch, Parker, Vann, & Arazie, 1997).
(6) Use of cornstarch is debatable. Instructions vary from not recommending its use, especially with moist desquamation (because of potential for fungal infections), to recommending its use instead of baby powder.

5. Long-term effects
  a) Major late side effects: Telangiectasias, fibrosis, and/or necrosis can occur after receiving therapy. The goal is to improve skin texture and elasticity.
  b) Interventions
    (1) Keep the skin moist and supple with moisturizing lotions.
    (2) Use sunblocks.
6. Documentation: Use *Radiation Therapy Patient Care Record* (Catlin-Huth, Haas, & Pollock, 2002).
  a) Use the NCI Skin Toxicity Scale when documenting the skin reaction. It is a vital component of nursing care that reflects changes over time, responses to interventions, and wound healing.
  b) Include patients' subjective feelings about the reaction to pain, pruritus, or burning.
  c) Document any serous drainage (e.g., type, amount, odor), topical fungal, or other infections.
7. Patient and family education outcomes
  a) Teach overall general skin care (Haas, 2004).

(1) Gently wash the skin with tepid water, using a soft washcloth and non-deodorant soap. Studies demonstrated that Dove® (Unilever, London, England) is a good nonirritating soap (Fortin & Larochelle, 2001; Frosch & Klingman, 1979). Avoid removing any temporary marks. Pat dry.
(2) Wear loose-fitting natural-fiber clothing (e.g., silk, 100% cotton).
(3) Avoid perfumed skin products and powders.
(4) Use only the recommended skin care products, avoiding makeup in the treatment fields.
(5) Avoid scratching the skin. Seek advice from healthcare professional for possible steroid cream.
(6) Use electric razor instead of wet shaving.
(7) Protect skin from wind, sun, and extreme temperatures. SPF 30 sunblock with UVA/UVB protection is recommended for irradiated skin.
(8) Avoid putting anything hot or cold, such as heating pads or ice packs, directly on the treated skin.
(9) Seek advice of healthcare professional in regard to swimming.
(10) Extra adhesive tapes or bandages should not be used within the treatment fields.
(11) Try using gentle detergents to wash clothes, and avoid starching the clothes you would wear over treatment areas.
  b) Teach patient/family members when to expect skin reactions.
  c) Teach patient/family members how to care for all stages of skin breakdown. Report any signs of infection.

References

Archambeau, J. (1987). Relative radiation sensitivity of the integumentary system dose response of the epidermal, microvascular, and dermal population. *Advances in Radiation Biology, 12,* 147–203.

Archambeau, J., Pezner, R., & Wasserman, T. (1995). Pathophysiology of irradiated skin and breast. *International Journal of Radiation Oncology, Biology, Physics, 31,* 1171–1185.

Burch, S.E., Parker, S.A., Vann, A.M., & Arazie, J.C. (1997). Measurement of 6-MV x-ray surface dose when topical agents are applied prior to external beam irradiation. *International Journal of Radiation Oncology, Biology, Physics, 38,* 447–451.

Catlin-Huth, C., Haas, M., & Pollock, V. (2002) *Radiation therapy patient care record: A tool for documenting nursing care.* Pittsburgh, PA: Oncology Nursing Society.

Chao, R., Perez, C., & Brady, L. (2001). *Radiation oncology management decisions.* Philadelphia: Lippincott Williams & Wilkins.

Fisher, J., Scott, C., Stevens, R., Marconi, B., Champion, L., Freedman, G.M., et al. (2000). Randomized phase III study comparing best supportive care to Biafine as a prophylactic agent for radiation-induced skin toxicity for women undergoing breast irradiation: RTOG 97-113. *International Journal of Radiation Oncology Biology Physics, 48,* 1307–1310.

Fortin, R., & Larochelle, M. (2001). The impact of skin washing with water and soap during breast irradiation: A randomized study. *Radiotherapy Oncology, 58,* 333–339.

Frosch, P., & Klingman, A. (1979). The Soap Chamber: A new method for assessing the irritancy of soaps. *Journal of the American Academy of Dermatology, 1*(1), 35–41.

Haas, M. (2004). Radiation therapy. In C.G. Varrichio (Ed.), *A cancer source for nurses* (8th ed., pp. 131–147). Sudbury, MA: Jones and Bartlett.

Maiche, A., Grohn, P., & Maki-Hokkonen, H. (1991). Effect of chamomile cream and almond ointment on acute radiation skin reaction. *Acta Oncologica, 30,* 395–396.

Moore-Higgs, G., & Amdur, R.J. (2001). Sustained integrity of protective mechanisms (skin, oral, immune systems). In D.W. Bruner, G. Moore-Higgs, & M. Haas (Eds.), *Outcomes in radiation therapy: Multidisciplinary management* (pp. 493–518). Sudbury, MA: Jones and Bartlett.

National Cancer Institute. (2003). *Common terminology criteria for adverse advents* (Version 3.0). Bethesda, MD: Author.

Pazdur, R., Coia, L., Hoskins, W., & Wagman, L. (2003). *Cancer management: A multidisciplinary approach.* Melville, NY: The Oncology Group.

Williams, M., Burk, M., & Loprinzi, C. (1996). Phase III double-blind evaluation of an aloe-vera gel as a prophylactic agent for radiation-induced skin toxicity. *International Journal of Radiation Oncology, Biology, Physics, 36,* 345–349.

D. Pain
  1. Pathophysiology: Cancer pain can be acute or chronic (more than three months in duration) and occur as a result of the cancer or its treatment. Pain can be classified as nociceptive or neuropathic based on its underlying pathophysiologic mechanism (Miaskowski et al., 2004).
    a) Nociceptive pain occurs as a result of tissue injury.
      (1) RT-induced causes of nociceptive pain include mucositis, skin reactions, enteritis, and proctitis.
      (2) Disease-related causes of nociceptive pain include bone metastasis and obstruction of a hollow viscus.
    b) Neuropathic pain results from nerve injury.
      (1) RT-induced causes of neuropathic pain include cervical, brachial, or lumbosacral plexopathies and polyneuropathies.
      (2) Disease- and treatment-related causes of neuropathic pain include epidural spinal cord compression, tumor-induced plexopathies, and postherpetic neuralgia.
  2. Pain occurs in approximately 50% of patients who are receiving treatment for cancer (Caraceni & Portenoy, 1999) and in 80%–90% of patients during the terminal phases of the disease (Chiu, Hu, & Chen, 2000; Potter, Hami, Bryan, & Quigley, 2003).
  3. Assessment is the cornerstone of effective pain management. All patients with cancer should be screened for pain at each encounter with the healthcare system. If the patient reports pain during the universal screening procedure, a comprehensive pain assessment should be conducted to evaluate for persistent and breakthrough pain and to diagnose the cause of the pain. Ongoing assessments should be performed to determine the effectiveness of the pain management plan.
    a) Comprehensive pain assessment—Determines the cause of the patient's pain
      (1) Persistent pain—Constant pain that lasts for long periods of time
        (a) Onset
        (b) Description
        (c) Location
        (d) Intensity/severity (rated using a 0 [no pain] to 10 [worst pain imaginable] numeric rating scale)
        (e) Aggravating and relieving factors
        (f) Previous and current treatments and their effectiveness
        (g) Associated symptoms—Fatigue, insomnia, depression, changes in appetite (Miaskowski et al., 2004)
      (2) Breakthrough pain—Sudden severe flare-ups of pain that come and go (Hwang, Chang, & Kasimis, 2003; Mercadente et al., 2002)
        (a) Presence of breakthrough pain
        (b) Frequency and duration of the episodes of breakthrough pain
        (c) Intensity
        (d) Occurrence of the painful episode—Spontaneous, incident

(e) Previous and current treatments and their effectiveness

(3) Physical examination

    (a) General examination

    (b) Focused neurologic examination

(4) Appropriate diagnostic tests—Pain medication should be administered to facilitate the diagnostic workup.

b) Ongoing pain assessments—Should determine if the pain management plan is effective.

(1) Evaluation of pain intensity

(2) Evaluation of pain relief

(3) Evaluation of the impact of pain on functional status and quality of life

(4) Evaluation of patient's level of adherence with the pain management plan

4. Documentation

a) Document the results of universal screening for pain at each patient visit.

b) Document the findings from the comprehensive pain assessment in the patient's medical record.

c) Document ratings of pain intensity at each visit.

5. Collaborative management

a) Use appropriate combinations of non-opioid, opioid, and co-analgesics, depending on the cause and the severity of the patient's pain (Miaskowski et al., 2004).

(1) Nonopioid analgesics (e.g., acetaminophen, NSAIDs)

    (a) Indicated for mild to moderate pain

    (b) Have a narrow therapeutic window and a ceiling effect

(2) Opioid analgesics

    (a) Indicated for moderate to severe pain

    (b) Doses and schedules should be adjusted to produce maximal analgesia with minimal side effects.

(3) Co-analgesics are medications that do not have a primary indication for pain but produce analgesia. These medications often are used in the management of neuropathic pain.

b) Chronic persistent pain should be managed with a long-acting opioid that is administered on a regular schedule. Breakthrough pain should be managed with a short-acting opioid that is administered on an as-needed basis.

c) Side effects of nonopioid, opioid, and co-analgesics should be monitored and managed to improve adherence with the pain management plan.

d) Nonpharmacologic strategies should be used to supplement pharmacologic strategies in the management of cancer pain.

(1) Relaxation

(2) Distraction

(3) Guided imagery

e) Pain from bone metastasis may be treated with RT or radiopharmaceuticals (e.g., strontium-89, samarium-153). Analgesic regimens may require adjustment following the administration of these therapies.

6. Patient and family education

a) Discuss concerns about and differences in tolerance, physical dependence, and psychological addiction.

b) Teach patients how to aggressively manage the side effects of analgesic medication to improve adherence with the pain management plan (Miaskowski et al., 2001).

c) Teach patients how to use a pain management diary to record changes in pain intensity and medication use (West et al., 2003).

d) Teach patients how to communicate unrelieved pain to clinicians (West et al., 2003).

References

Caraceni, A., & Portenoy, R.K. (1999). An international study of cancer pain characteristics and syndromes. IASP Task Force on Cancer Pain. *Pain, 82,* 263–274.

Chiu, T.Y., Hu, W.Y., & Chen, C.Y. (2000). Prevalence and severity of symptoms in terminal cancer patients: A study in Taiwan. *Supportive Care in Cancer, 8,* 311–313.

Hwang, S.S., Chang, V.T., & Kasimis, B. (2003). Cancer breakthrough pain characteristics and responses to treatment in a VA medical center. *Pain, 101*(1–2), 55–64.

Mercadente, S., Radbruch, L., Caraceni, A., Cherny, N., Kassa, S., Nauck, F., et al. (2002). Episodic (breakthrough) pain: Consensus conference of an expert working group of the European Association for Palliative Care. *Cancer, 94,* 832–839.

Miaskowski, C., Cleary, J., Burney, R., Coyne, P.J., Finley, R., Foster, R., et al. (2004). *Management of cancer pain in adults and children: Clinical practice guidelines.* Glenview, IL: American Pain Society.

Miaskowski, C., Dodd, M.J., West, C., Paul, S.M., Tripathy, D., Koo, P., et al. (2001). Lack of adherence with the analgesic regimen: A significant barrier to effective cancer pain management. *Journal of Clinical Oncology, 19,* 4275–4279.

Potter, J., Hami, F., Bryan, T., & Quigley, C. (2003). Symptoms in 400 patients referred to palliative care services: Prevalence and patterns. *Palliative Medicine, 17,* 310–314.

West, C.M., Dodd, M.J., Paul, S.M., Schumacher, K., Tripathy, D., Koo, P., et al. (2003). The PRO-SELF® Pain Control Program: An effective approach for cancer pain management. *Oncology Nursing Forum, 30,* 65–73.

E. Distress/coping
  1. Pathophysiology
    a) Acute
      (1) Emotional distress, most frequently expressed as anxiety or depression, is commonly associated with cancer and the side effects of related therapies, including RT.
      (2) Anxiety can be defined as vague uneasy and unpleasant feelings of potential harm or distress (Gobel, 2003).
      (3) Depression can be defined as a feeling of gloom, emptiness, numbness, or despair (Barsevick & Much, 2003).
      (4) Depression has been strongly linked to cancer progression and mortality (Hjerl et al., 2003; Spiegel & Giese-Davis, 2003).
      (5) A recent study of disease-specific stress in patients with different tumor types before, at the end of, and six weeks after the end of radiotherapy found that, in 265 patients (157 male, 108 female; median age 58.6 years), the most common stressor was physical functioning, without significant changes during and after therapy (Sehlen et al., 2003).
        (a) Significant increases in stress were observed for anxiety, pain, and information at six weeks.
        (b) Women showed significantly higher stress from before radiotherapy to six weeks after therapy.
        (c) Younger patients displayed a decrease in anxiety, whereas elderly patients demonstrated an increase.
        (d) Patients with breast cancer had the highest stress levels.
        (e) Predictors of distress were tumor stage, addiction to alcohol or nicotine, metabolic disorder, marital status, and age.
      (6) In an earlier study of patients undergoing external beam radiotherapy (Andersen & Tewfik, 1985)
        (a) Those with a high level of pretreatment anxiety reported a significant reduction post-treatment, although they remained the most anxious subgroup.
        (b) Patients with a moderate level of pretreatment anxiety reported no change.
        (c) Patients with low levels of anxiety reported significant increases in anxiety.
        (d) Patients who were either low or high in state anxiety also exhibited more anger or hostility than patients with moderate anxiety.
      (7) Significant associations have been found among post-treatment fatigue and diagnosis, physical distress, functional disability, quality of sleep, psychological distress, and depression (Smets et al., 1998).
    b) Late
      (1) Many cancer survivors experience symptoms of post-traumatic stress (hyperarousal, avoidance, and intrusiveness), and some live with the constant fear that the cancer may return (Deimling, Kahana, Bowman, & Schaefer, 2002).
      (2) In addition, many patients who experience a recurrence blame themselves (Lee-Jones, Humphris, Dixon, & Hatcher 1997).
      (3) Some studies have documented significant anxiety and/or depression as a problem in long-term survivors of various cancers, including testicular, uri-

nary bladder, ovarian, and colorectal cancers (Bodurka-Bevers et al., 2000; Fossa, Dahl, & Loge, 2003; Henningsohn et al., 2003; Ramsey, Berry, Moinpour, Giedzinska, & Andersen, 2002).

(4) Other studies of various tumor types, breast and prostate cancers, have found that cancer survivors either do not differ in levels of distress or may have better self-reported quality of life than non-cancer controls (Bruner et al., 1999; Ellman & Thomas, 1995; Olweny et al., 1993).

2. Incidence
   a) Estimates suggest that approximately one-third of patients with cancer experience clinically significant distress (Cwikel & Behar, 1999).
   b) Only 10%–25% of those at high risk for psychosocial problems will eventually use psychosocial oncology services (Cwikel & Behar, 1999; Holland, 1997).
   c) The prevalence of anxiety and depression may be nearly 50% in patients undergoing RT (Leopold et al., 1998), but the literature is sparse and conflicting.
   d) Studies in the United States indicate that depressive disorders vary by gender and generally are more common in women than in men (Strouse, 1997).

3. Assessment
   a) Risk factors associated with distress and problems coping with cancer
      (1) Cancer site—More depression has been documented among patients with specific tumor types.
         (a) Patients with head and neck cancers have reported high levels of depression usually linked to lifestyle behaviors and lack of social support (de Leeuw et al., 2000).
            i) A recent study showed that although other measures of quality of life improved over time for patients treated with radiotherapy for head and neck cancers, emotional functioning and depression did not improve by one month post-treatment (Rose & Yates, 2001).
            ii) However, other studies have shown improvement in depressive symptoms of head and neck patients at 12 months post-radiotherapy (de Graeff et al., 1999a, 1999b; de Graeff et al., 2000).
         (b) Patients with breast cancer also have high levels of documented anxiety and depression.
            i) One study documented that 14% of women referred for adjuvant radiotherapy following surgery had morbid anxiety (Maraste, Brandt, Olsson, & Ryde-Brandt, 1992).
               • Significant depression was recorded for only 1.5% of patients, but severe anxiety was recorded in 19% of patients with mastectomies versus 10% of those treated with breast-conserving surgery
               • In a subgroup aged 50–59 years, morbid anxiety was significantly more common among patients with mastectomies (44%) than among patients treated with breast-conserving surgery and radiotherapy (4%)
               • The results suggest that at the start of adjuvant radiotherapy, emotional distress is characterized by anxiety rather than depression, and the risk of serious anxiety is especially high for women with mastectomies in their 50s.
            ii) In a study of women with early-stage breast cancer who were referred for adjuvant

radiotherapy (Mose et al., 2001)

- 53% of the women felt distressed because cancer affected the breast.
- 48% were initially afraid of radiotherapy.
- 36% never had their anxiety reduced during treatment.

iii) Predictors of high levels of distress in women with breast cancer include (Mose et al., 2001)

- Age 58 years or younger
- Initial anxiety
- Being negatively affected by environmental factors
- Those who did not find distraction helpful.

(2) Age: Younger age has been associated with higher levels of anxiety/depression (Compas et al., 1999; Epping-Jordan et al., 1999).

(3) Poor pretreatment coping ability has been associated with post-treatment maladaptive coping (Dropkin, 1997; Holland, 1997).

(4) History of psychiatric problems is associated with an increased risk of poor coping (Leopold et al., 1998).

(5) High levels of social support have been shown to be associated with better coping; conversely, low levels of social support are associated with poorer coping with cancer (Akechi et al., 1998; Penninx et al., 1998; Sollner et al., 1999).

b) Assessment measures: Few reports in the literature exist of the testing of clinically relevant and easy-to-use assessment tools for anxiety and depression in the outpatient radiation oncology setting.

(1) One RT-specific study (Leopold et al., 1998) found a short, structured interview procedure, Primary Care Evaluation of Mental Disorders (PRIME-MD), that allowed radiation oncologists to quickly and reliably identify mood disorders in their patients.

(a) A diagnosis of a depressive or anxiety disorder by PRIME-MD was made in 59 of the 122 patients (48%) (Leopold et al., 1998).

(b) PRIME-MD has had extensive testing in other patient settings (Spitzer, Kroenke, & Williams, 1999).

(2) Many tools for the assessment of anxiety and depression are available, and more comprehensive reviews can be found elsewhere (Barsevick & Much, 2004; Bruner & Diefenbach, 2001; Gobel, 2004).

(a) Spielberger State-Trait Anxiety Inventory

(b) Hospital Anxiety and Depression Scale

(c) Center for Epidemiological Studies Depression Scale

(d) Impact of Event Scale

(e) Medical Outcomes Study–Depression Scale

(3) Documentation should include

(a) Risk factors for distress described previously

(b) For those at risk, screening and/or diagnosis of anxiety/depression should be documented with one of the assessment tools described.

(c) Because most radiotherapy departments do not conduct such screening or diagnostic assessments, documentation of referral to appropriate medical personnel (social worker, psychologist, psychiatrist, mental health nurse practitioner) *is essential.*

(d) The ONS *Radiation Therapy Patient Care Record* (Catlin-Huth, Haas, & Pollock, 2002): Emotional alterations—Coping

i) 0—Effective

ii) 1—Ineffective

4. Acute and late effects and evidence-based management

a) Major barriers exist to implementation of effective strategies to improve coping because of

(1) Lack of knowledge of the multifaceted nature of cancer distress

(2) Outmoded attitudes of patients, staff, and institutions about psychological issues

(3) Stigmatizing labels for those who access psychological therapy (Bruner & Diefenbach, 2001)

b) Guidelines for the treatment of distress related to cancer have been developed for evaluation, treatment, and follow-up of the general patient with cancer, as well as specific information for the management of patients with

(1) Adjustment disorders

(2) Major depressive disorder

(3) Delirium

(4) Anxiety

(5) Dementia

(6) Substance abuse disorder

(7) Personality disorders (National Comprehensive Cancer Network, 1999)

c) Although depression is rarely if ever helpful, certain levels of anxiety followed by problem-focused coping strategies have been associated with more effective post-treatment coping in patients treated with and without RT (Dropkin, 1997).

d) The nursing challenge with such a complex, multifaceted problem as distress is finding strategies that are realistic within the primarily outpatient radiotherapy department. Something as simple as a brief orientation program has been shown to reduce anxiety, depressive symptoms, and overall distress in outpatients with cancer.

(1) One study (McQuellon et al., 1998) assigned 150 patients to an intervention (a clinic tour, general information about clinic operations, and a question and answer session with an oncology counselor) or usual care control group.

(2) The intervention group had lower state anxiety, lower overall distress, and fewer patients reporting depressive symptoms (McQuellon et al., 1998).

e) Behavioral management

(1) Relaxation training and guided imagery have shown positive results in patients with anxiety and, in some cases, depression.

(a) The feeling of anxiety is associated with muscle tension and increased heart rate (the fight or flight response) and is theorized to be unable to exist in the process of progressive muscle relaxation (Jacobson, 1964; Mcguigan, 1993).

(b) In a study of 82 outpatients who were undergoing curative (73 patients) or palliative (9 patients) radiotherapy assigned to either relaxation training or a control condition that included education and counseling along with the RT, significant reductions were noted in the treatment group in tension, depression, anger, and fatigue (Decker, Cline-Elsen, & Gallagher, 1992).

(2) Music therapy

(a) Music therapy has been shown to decrease anxiety in patients receiving chemotherapy.

(b) The only reported music therapy study specifically tested in patients receiving RT showed no significant difference in anxiety levels between the group assigned to music therapy during radiotherapy and the control group. However, further analyses identified changes and trends in state anxiety scores, suggesting a possible benefit of music therapy during radiotherapy, thus requiring more research (Smith, Casey, Johnson, Gwede, & Riggin, 2001).

(3) Success of distraction techniques, including imagery or music therapy, is highly individual and related to the patient's past use and perceived credibility. Patients' preference for their use should be assessed and not assumed (Kwekkeboom, 2001, 2003).

(4) Group therapy may decrease distress and improve coping for patients with cancer undergoing radiotherapy.

　(a) In a study of 48 patients receiving radiotherapy, subjects assigned to the psychotherapy group (six patients per group, 90-minute weekly sessions for 10 weeks) showed significant decreases in both emotional and physical symptoms, and the decreases were greater at four weeks after the end of radiotherapy compared to the control group (Forester, Kornfeld, Fleiss, & Thompson, 1993).

　(b) In one study (Evans & Connis, 1995), 72 patients with cancer who were diagnosed with depression were randomly assigned to one of three conditions: cognitive-behavioral treatment, social support, and a no-treatment control condition. Both the cognitive-behavioral and social support therapies resulted in less depression, hostility, and symptoms versus the control group. The social support intervention also resulted in fewer psychiatric symptoms and reduced maladaptive interpersonal sensitivity and anxiety. The social support groups demonstrated more changes that were evident at the six-month follow-up.

(5) Cognitive therapy

　(a) Interest in biofeedback waxes and wanes, and no positive studies in the literature are RT- or cancer outpatient–specific. Much of cognitive therapy currently centers on distraction.

　(b) A recent study showed that a virtual reality distraction intervention for women aged 50 and older decreased anxiety levels immediately following chemotherapy treatments. There was a trend toward improved symptoms at 48 hours following completion of chemotherapy. For this study, a head-mounted display (Sony PC Glasstron PLM-S700®) was used to display encompassing images and block competing stimuli during chemotherapy infusions (Schneider, Ellis, Coombs, Shonkwiler, & Folsom, 2003).

(6) Medical management

　(a) Psychotherapy and pharmacotherapy combined are more effective than either alone in treating emotional distress, as well as in preventing the relapse of distress in patients with cancer (Twillman & Manetto, 1998). Patients should receive appropriate referrals.

　(b) Pharmacotherapy alone (For more comprehensive lists, drug interactions, and evidence-based management, see Barsevick & Much, 2004; Bruner & Diefenbach, 2001; Gobel, 2004.)

　　i) Benzodiazepines (e.g., diazepam, alprazolam)—Most commonly used for acute and chronic anxiety

　　ii) SSRIs (e.g., paroxetine, fluoxetine)—Most commonly used for depression caused by cancer

　　　• Demonstrated efficacy in treating cancer-related depressive symptoms, at least in women with cancer (Holland, Romano, Heiligenstein, Tepner, & Wilson, 1998; Pezzella, Moslinger-Gehmayr, & Contu, 2001)

　　　• May be better suited for use in depressed patients with cancer because they lack the significant adverse anticholinergic and cardiovascular effects of TCAs

　　iii) TCAs (e.g., amitriptyline, doxepin)

　　iv) Lithium

v) MAOIs (e.g., phenelzine, tranylcypromine)

(c) Herbal therapies (e.g., ginseng, St. John's wort)—more commonly used for anxiety than depression; little evidence of effectiveness exists. (For a more comprehensive list, see Gobel, 2004.) Patients always should discuss use with their physician, because some herbal therapies may interfere with prescribed medications.

5. Patient and family education and outcomes
   a) Education
   (1) Discuss with patient and family the potential for a traumatic event, such as distress caused by cancer.
   (2) Instruct the patient and family that open communication is the best way of dealing with distress, and the patient should inform his or her nurse, doctor, and family of this symptom.
   (3) Reassure the patient and family that there are strategies to help anxiety and depression if they are severe or last longer than a few days.
   (4) Several self-care guides for dealing with anxiety and depression exist and can be copied directly and given to the patient. They include
      (a) Relaxation and guided imagery (Gobel, 2004)
      (b) Depression (Barsevick & Much, 2004)
      (c) Taking antidepressant medications (Barsevick & Much, 2004).
      (d) Side effects of antidepressant medications (Barsevick & Much, 2004)
      (e) Depression self-care data log (Barsevick & Much, 2004)
   b) Resources
   (1) The Internet is a rich resource for cancer-related information. All sites do not contain the same level of accuracy, so before recommending anything to a patient, the nurse should be aware of what the Web site contains.
   (2) American Cancer Society (ACS)
      (a) General Web site—www.cancer.org or refer to local office by telephone
      (b) ACS cancer survivors Web site—www.acscsn.org

(3) NCI-sponsored CancerNet—http://cancer.gov/cancerinformation
(4) National Institute of Mental Health—www.nimh.nih.gov
(5) National Mental Health Association—www.nmha.org

c) Outcomes
(1) The patient and family will demonstrate adequate knowledge about distress through communication or seeking medical assistance and support.
(2) The patient will demonstrate adaptive coping.
(3) The patient will report a decrease in distress.
(4) The patient will be able to function mentally and emotionally.

References

Akechi, T., Kugaya, A., Okamura, H., Nishiwaki, Y., Yamawaki, S., & Uchitomi, Y. (1998). Predictive factors for psychological distress in ambulatory lung cancer patients. *Supportive Care in Cancer, 6,* 281–286.

Andersen, B.L., & Tewfik, H.H. (1985). Psychological reactions to radiation therapy: Reconsideration of the adaptive aspects of anxiety. *Journal of Personality and Social Psychology, 48,* 1024–1032.

Barsevick, A.M., & Much, J.K. (2004). Depression. In C.H. Yarbro, M.H. Frogge, & M. Goodman (Eds.), *Cancer symptom management* (3rd ed., pp. 668–692). Sudbury, MA: Jones and Bartlett.

Bodurka-Bevers, D., Basen-Engquist, K., Carmack, C.L., Fitzgerald, M.A., Wolf, J.K., de Moor, C., et al. (2000). Depression, anxiety, and quality of life in patients with epithelial ovarian cancer. *Gynecologic Oncology, 78*(3 Pt. 1), 302–308.

Bruner, D.W., & Diefenbach, M. (2001). Distress/coping. In D.W. Bruner, G. Moore-Higgs, & M. Haas (Eds.), *Outcomes in radiation therapy: Multidisciplinary management* (pp. 563–589). Sudbury, MA: Jones and Bartlett.

Bruner, D.W., Ross, E., Raysor, S., Hanlon, A., James, J., Grumet, S., et al. (1999). Men treated with radiotherapy have better global quality of life outcomes despite decrements in site-specific quality of life domains than men at increased risk but without prostate cancer [Abstract]. *International Journal of Radiation Oncology, Physics, Biology, 45*(Suppl. 2), 432.

Catlin-Huth, C., Haas, M., & Pollock, V. (2002). *Radiation therapy patient care record: A tool for documenting nursing care.* Pittsburgh, PA: Oncology Nursing Society.

Compas, B.E., Stoll, M.F., Thomsen, A.H., Oppedisano, G., Epping-Jordan, J.E., & Krag, D.N. (1999). Adjustment to breast cancer: Age-related differences in coping and emotional distress. *Breast Cancer Research Treatments, 54*(3), 195–203.

Cwikel, J.G., & Behar, L.C. (1999). Organizing social work services with adult cancer patients: Intergrating empirical research. *Social Work in Health Care, 28*(3), 55–76.

Decker, T.W., Cline-Elsen, J., & Gallagher, M. (1992). Relaxation therapy as an adjunct in radiation oncology. *Journal of Clinical Psychology, 48,* 388–393.

Deimling, G.T., Kahana, B., Bowman, K.F., & Schaefer, M.L. (2002). Cancer survivorship and psychological distress in later life. *Psycho-oncology, 11,* 479–494.

de Graeff, A., de Leeuw, R.J., Ros, W.J., Hordijk, G.J., Battermann, J.J., Blijham, G.H., et al. (1999a). A prospective study on quality of life of laryngeal cancer patients treated with radiotherapy. *Head and Neck, 21,* 291–296.

de Graeff, A., de Leeuw, J.R., Ros, W.J., Hordijk, G.J., Blijham, G.H., & Winnubst, J.A. (1999b). A prospective study on quality of life of patients with cancer of the oral cavity or oropharynx treated with surgery with or without radiotherapy. *Oral Oncology, 35*(1), 27–32.

de Leeuw, J.R., de Graeff, A., Ros, W.J., Blijham, G.H., Hordijk, G.J., & Winnubst, J.A. (2000). Prediction of depressive symptomatology after treatment of head and neck cancer: The influence of pre-treatment physical and depressive symptoms, coping, and social support. *Head and Neck, 22,* 799–807.

Dropkin, M.J. (1997). Coping with disfigurement/dysfunction and length of hospital stay after head and neck cancer surgery. *ORL-Head and Neck Nursing, 15*(1), 22–26.

Ellman, R., & Thomas, B.A. (1995). Is psychological well-being impaired in long-term survivors of breast cancer? *Journal of Medical Screening, 2*(1), 5–9.

Epping-Jordan, J.E., Compas, B.E., Osowiecki, D.M., Oppedisano, G., Gerhardt, C., Primo, K., et al. (1999). Psychological adjustment in breast cancer: Processes of emotional distress. *Health Psychology, 18,* 315–326.

Evans, R.L., & Connis, R.T. (1995). Comparison of brief group therapies for depressed cancer patients receiving radiation treatment. *Public Health Report, 110,* 306–311.

Forester, B., Kornfeld, D.S., Fleiss, J.L., & Thompson, S. (1993). Group psychotherapy during radiotherapy: Effects on emotional and physical distress. *American Journal of Psychiatry, 150,* 1700–1706.

Fossa, S.D., Dahl, A.A., & Loge, J.H. (2003). Fatigue, anxiety, and depression in long-term survivors of testicular cancer. *Journal of Clinical Oncology, 21,* 1249–1254.

Gobel, B.H. (2004). Anxiety. In C.H. Yarbro, M.H. Frogge, & M. Goodman (Eds.), *Cancer symptom management* (3rd ed., pp. 651–667). Sudbury, MA: Jones and Bartlett.

Henningsohn, L., Wijkstrom, H., Pedersen, J., Ahlstrand, C., Aus, G., Bergmark, K., et al. (2003). Time after surgery, symptoms and well-being in survivors of urinary bladder cancer. *British Journal of Urology, 91,* 325–330.

Hjerl, K., Andersen, E.W., Keiding, N., Mouridsen, H.T., Mortensen, P.B., & Jorgensen, T. (2003). Depression as a prognostic factor for breast cancer mortality. *Psychosomatics, 44*(1), 24–30.

Holland, J.C. (1997). Preliminary guidelines for the treatment of distress. *Oncology, 11*(11A), 109–114.

Holland, J.C., Romano, S.J., Heiligenstein, J.H., Tepner, R.G., & Wilson, M.G. (1998). A controlled trial of fluoxetine and desipramine in depressed women with advanced cancer. *Psycho-oncology, 7,* 291–300.

Jacobson, E. (1964). *Anxiety and tension control: A physiological approach.* Philadelphia: Lippincott.

Kwekkeboom, K.L. (2001). Outcome expectancy and success with cognitive-behavioral interventions: The case of guided imagery. *Oncology Nursing Forum, 28,* 1125–1132.

Kwekkeboom, K.L. (2003). Music versus distraction for procedural pain and anxiety in patients with cancer. *Oncology Nursing Forum, 30,* 433–440.

Lee-Jones, C., Humphris, G., Dixon, R., & Hatcher, M.B. (1997). Fear of cancer recurrence—a literature review and proposed cognitive formulation to explain exacerbation of recurrence fears. *Psycho-oncology, 6,* 95–105.

Leopold, K.A., Ahles, T.A., Walch, S., Amdur, R.J., Mott, L.A., Wiegand-Packard, L., et al. (1998). Prevalence of mood disorders and utility of the PRIME-MD in patients undergoing radiation therapy. *International Journal Radiation Oncology, Biology, Physics, 42,* 1105–1112.

Maraste, R., Brandt, L., Olsson, H., & Ryde-Brandt, B. (1992). Anxiety and depression in breast cancer patients at start of adjuvant radiotherapy. Relations to age and type of surgery. *Acta Oncologica, 31,* 641–643.

Mcguigan, F.J. (1993). Progressive muscle relaxation: Origins, principles, and clinical applications. In P.M. Lerhrer, & R.I. Woolfolk (Eds.), *Principles and practice of stress management* (2nd ed., pp. 17–52). New York: Guilford Press.

McQuellon, R.P., Wells, M., Hoffman, S., Craven, B., Russell, G., Cruz, J., et al. (1998). Reducing distress in cancer patients with an orientation program. *Psycho-oncology, 7,* 207–217.

Mose, S., Budischewski, K.M., Rahn, A.N., Zander-Heinz, A.C., Bormeth, S., & Bottcher, H.D. (2001). Influence of irradiation on therapy-associated psychological distress in breast carcinoma patients. *International Journal Radiation Oncology, Biology, Physics, 51,* 1328–1335.

National Comprehensive Cancer Network. (1999). NCCN practice guidelines for the management of psychosocial distress. *Oncology, 13*(5A), 113–147.

Olweny, C., Juttner, C., Rofe, P., Barrow, G., Esterman, A., Waltham, R., et al. (1993). Long-term effects of cancer treatment and consequences of cure: Cancer survivors enjoy quality of life similar to their neighbors. *European Journal of Cancer, 29A,* 826–830.

Penninx, B.W., van Tilburg, T., Boeke, A.J., Deeg, D.J., Kriegsman, D.M., & van Eijk, J.T. (1998). Effects of social support and personal coping resources on depressive symptoms: Different for various chronic diseases. *Health Psychology, 17,* 551–558.

Pezzella, G., Moslinger-Gehmayr, R., & Contu, A. (2001). Treatment of depression in patients with breast cancer: A comparison between paroxetine and amitriptyline. *Breast Cancer Research Treatments, 70*(1), 1–10.

Ramsey, S.D., Berry, K., Moinpour, C., Giedzinska, A., & Andersen, M.R. (2002). Quality of life in long term survivors of colorectal cancer. *American Journal of Gastroenterology, 97,* 1228–1234.

Rose, P., & Yates, P. (2001). Quality of life experienced by patients receiving radiation treatment for cancers of the head and neck. *Cancer Nursing, 24,* 255–263.

Schneider, S.M., Ellis, M., Coombs, W.T., Shonkwiler, E.L., & Folsom, L.C. (2003). Virtual reality intervention for older women with breast cancer. *Cyberpsychology Behavior, 6,* 301–307.

Sehlen, S., Hollenhorst, H., Schymura, B., Herschbach, P., Aydemir, U., Firsching, M., et al. (2003). Psychosocial stress in cancer patients during and after radiotherapy. *Strahlentherapie Onkologie, 179*(3), 175–180.

Smets, E.M., Visser, M.R., Willems-Groot, A.F., Garssen, B., Oldenburger, F., van Tienhoven, G., et al. (1998). Fatigue and radiotherapy: Experience in patients undergoing treatment. *British Journal of Cancer, 78,* 899–906.

Smith, M., Casey, L., Johnson, D., Gwede, C., & Riggin, O.Z. (2001). Music as a therapeutic intervention for anxiety in patients receiving radiation therapy. *Oncology Nursing Forum, 28,* 855–862.

Sollner, W., Zschocke, I., Zingg-Schir, M., Stein, B., Rumpold, G., Fritsch, P., et al. (1999). Interactive patterns of social support and individual coping strategies in melanoma patients and their correlations with adjustment to illness. *Psychosomatics, 40*(3), 239–250.

Spiegel, D., & Giese-Davis, J. (2003). Depression and cancer: Mechanisms and disease progression. *Biologic Psychiatry, 54,* 269–282.

Spitzer, R.L., Kroenke, K., & Williams, J.B. (1999). Validation and utility of a self-report version of PRIME-MD: The PHQ primary care study. Primary care evaluation of mental disorders. Patient health questionnaire. *JAMA, 282,* 1737–1744.

Strouse, T. (1997). Identifying and treating depression in women with cancer: A primary care approach. *Medscape Women's Health, 2*(9), 3–5.

Twillman, R.K., & Manetto, C. (1998). Concurrent psychotherapy and pharmacotherapy in the treatment of depression and anxiety in cancer patients. *Psycho-oncology, 7,* 285–290.

F. Sexual dysfunction
1. Pathophysiology
   a) General
      (1) Three phases of the sexual response cycle—desire, arousal, and orgasm—can be affected by cancer and cancer therapies (Wilmoth & Bruner, 2002).
         (a) Desire often is affected by factors such as anger, pain, body image, and disease processes and medications.
         (b) Arousal causes vasodilation and vasocongestion with subsequent erection in men and vaginal lubrication in women. Surgery may cut through the vessels, or radiotherapy may cause sclerosis of the vessels necessary for these functions.
         (c) Orgasm is mediated by the sympathetic nervous system, and therapies such as surgery, radiotherapy, and chemotherapy may have an adverse effect on the nerves involved in this portion of the sexual response cycle (Wilmoth & Bruner, 2002).
   b) Acute
      (1) Denuding of the vaginal epithelium in females and the urethral epithelium in males and females and inflammation account for the majority of acute effects related to sexual intercourse during RT (Shield, 1995).
      (2) Disease may affect libido, or it may be related to decreased or ablated ovarian or testicular function that may occur at doses as low as 6 Gy (Howell & Shalet, 1998).
   c) Late
      (1) Narrowing and obliteration of the small pelvic vessels and circumferential fibrosis of the perivaginal tissue contribute to vaginal stenosis in women treated with pelvic radiotherapy and are more pronounced in those receiving brachytherapy (Grigsby et al., 1995), which increases the surface dose to the vagina.
      (2) The vaginal epithelium may appear thin, pale, and atrophic over time and may be traumatized by intercourse or masturbation.
      (3) In males, RT accelerates atherosclerotic changes in the pelvis that eventually interfere with the arterial blood supply of the penis, decreasing voluntary erectile capacity. Fibrosis of the neurovascular bundles further decreases erectile capacity. RT accelerates atherosclerotic disease (Goldstein, Feldman, Deckers, Babayan, & Krane, 1984).
2. Incidence
   a) Pelvic cancer: Some degree of sexual dysfunction has been reported in most patients treated for pelvic cancers with radiotherapy, depending on the site, volume treated, and dose (Bruner, 2001).
   b) Breast cancer: Sexual dysfunction in women treated for breast cancer has been estimated at 21%–39%, regardless of treatment modality (Lamb, 1995). Women treated with external beam RT in combination with lumpectomy for breast cancer may experience disruption in sexual activity, probably as a result of temporary effects of skin discomfort and fatigue (Bruner & Berk, 2003). However, an advantage of partial mastectomy over breast reconstruction was documented in terms of maintain-

ing pleasure and frequency of breast caressing during sexual activity (Schover et al., 1995).

c) Head and neck cancer: One study of sexual functioning in 55 patients with head and neck cancer following RT ± surgery found that 58% were no longer having intercourse, although 85% were still interested in sex. The majority reported arousal problems, and 58% had orgasmic problems, yet 49% were satisfied with their current sexual functioning (Monga, Tan, Ostermann, & Monga, 1997).

d) Cervical cancer: Radiotherapy versus surgery generally has been associated with higher rates of sexual dysfunction in women treated for cervical carcinoma (Schover, Fife, & Gersheson, 1989; Seibel, Graves, & Freeman, 1980), with the exception of a recent report indicating that surgery and not radiotherapy accounted for the majority of risk of vaginal stenosis as well as insufficient lubrication and reduced vaginal elasticity (Bergmark, Avall-Lundqvist, Dickman, Henningsohn, & Steineck, 1999).

e) Endometrial cancer: Little research has been conducted to report the degree of sexual dysfunction after RT for endometrial cancer. Vaginal stenosis has been reported in up to 72% of women treated with intracavitary radiation for endometrial cancer and 88% of women treated for cervical cancer (Bruner, Keegan, Corn, Martin, & Hanks, 1993).

f) Prostate cancer: Most studies of men older than age 65 reported a 50% potency rate after RT; however, a recent study of potency post-RT ± androgen deprivation therapy (ADT) in men age 50–65, as compared to age-matched controls, reported a 67% overall potency rate in the RT group. Potency was 73% post-RT for those who were potent pretreatment. Overall RT +

ADT potency was 41%, compared to 85% for age-matched controls. Potency increased to 55% for those who had RT + ADT but were off ADT for six months or more (Bruner, Nicolaou, Hanlon, & Hanks, 1997). Preliminary studies of interstitial radiation implants and cryosurgical ablation carry a 45% and 90% risk of impotence, respectively (Chaikin et al., 1996).

g) Bladder cancer: Very little research has been conducted on sexual dysfunction after treatment for bladder cancer. In a rare study of sexual function in males treated with RT for bladder cancer, 71% felt their sex life was worse following RT, but only 56% were concerned about the deterioration (Little & Howard, 1998).

h) Testicular cancer: RT for testicular cancer has been associated with reduced semen volume (60%), reduced erectile potential (48%), premature ejaculation (40%), reduced intensity of orgasm (38%), loss of sexual desire (17%), and an inability to ejaculate (5%), yet only 8% of the men treated with RT reported a decrease in sexual satisfaction from prior to therapy (Arai, Kawakita, Okada, & Yoshida, 1997).

i) Anorectal cancer: The ability to have an orgasm after multimodality therapy (preoperative radiotherapy followed by surgery) has been reported to disappear in 50% of both male and female patients, in 45% of patients after locally advanced primary, and in 57% after locally recurrent rectal cancer treatments (Mannaerts et al., 2001). Treatment may interfere significantly with homosexual relationships, and homosexuals are at an elevated risk for anal cancers (Frisch, Smith, Grulich, & Johansen, 2003; Goldstone, Winkler, Ufford, Alt, & Palefsky, 2001).

3. Assessment

a) Risk factors: Sexual activity pretreatment appears to be the best predictor of sexual function post-treatment (Andersen, Cyranowski, & Espindle, 1999). Pretreatment dysfunction needs to be assessed because it leads to a greater risk of sexual problems post-RT.

b) Sexual history: For a comprehensive sexual history, see Bruner and Berk, 2003.

(1) Age: Especially important in assessing sexual function because changes occur frequently with age as a result of comorbidities (Burns-Cox & Gingell, 1997).

(2) Cultural/ethnic background: Sexual values and norms vary widely among

cultures (Meston, Trapnell, & Gorzalka, 1996; Wyatt et al., 1998).

(3) History of sexual activity, including sexual orientation, age at first intercourse, number of partners, marital discord, and problems with desire, arousal, or orgasm

(4) History of sexual abuse: An estimated 300,000 women are raped each year (U.S. Department of Justice, 2002); it has been estimated that 16% of women treated for gynecologic malignancies have been sexually abused (Bergmark et al., 1999).

(5) Frequency of sexual activity over past six months

(6) Satisfaction with sexual ability and frequency

(7) Medications that may interfere with sexual function (e.g., antihypertensives, antidepressants)

(8) Female issues
   (a) Dyspareunia
   (b) Vaginal dryness

(9) Male issues
   (a) Erectile ability
   (b) Retrograde ejaculation

c) Physical examination
   (1) Female
      (a) Check skin over vulva and around anus for breakdown, lesions, or inflammation.
      (b) Check for vaginal stenosis.
      (c) Check for vaginal discharge or bleeding.
   (2) Male
      (a) Check skin over the penis and scrotum for breakdown, lesions, or inflammation.
      (b) Check anal area for breakdown, fissures, or lesions.

d) Documentation (in addition to above) (Catlin-Huth, Haas, & Pollock, 2002)
   (1) Sexual alteration
      (a) 0—Absent
      (b) 1—Present
   (2) Vaginal drainage
      (a) 0—Absent
      (b) 1—Present

4. Acute effects and evidence-based management
   a) Psychological—Prepare the patient for the possible effects of treatment on sexual function.
   b) Behavioral
      (1) Discuss need for patient to manage symptoms (e.g., pain) before trying to engage in sexual activity.

      (2) Encourage communication between the patient and partner concerning fears regarding continued sexual function.
   c) Medical
      (1) A recent structured review of the literature found the strongest evidence of treatment benefit for acute radiation vaginal changes to be topical estrogens and benzydamine (Denton & Maher, 2003).
      (2) The structured literature review also found evidence to support the use of vaginal dilators to maintain vaginal patency (Denton & Maher, 2003)
      (3) Use of dilators should begin as soon as patient can tolerate it to prevent adhesions from forming.
         (a) Patient can begin during radiotherapy if she can tolerate it.
         (b) A condom stuffed with cotton balls and tied at the bottom, used with ample lubricant, may make the experience more tolerable.

5. Long-term effects and evidence-based management
   a) Psychological
      (1) Support the patient with concerns regarding sexual function.
      (2) Refer patients with history of sexual abuse or marital problems to a social worker, family therapist, or sex counselor.
   b) Behavioral
      (1) Encourage communication between the patient and partner concerning fears regarding continued sexual function.
      (2) Teach proper positioning for continued sexual activity that would prevent discomfort depending on the therapy or problem (Bruner & Berk, 2003).
   c) Medical

(1) Women need to continue to have something (penis or vaginal dilator) dilate the vagina at least three times per week for life.

(2) Vaginal dryness can be managed with water-soluble lubricants (Bruner & Berk, 2003).

(3) Medications such as sildenafil have been shown to improve erectile function post-RT for prostate cancer (Kedia, Zippe, Agarwal, Nelson, & Lakin, 1999; Merrick et al., 1999; Valicenti et al., 2001; Weber, Bieri, Kurtz, & Miralbell, 1999; Zelefsky, McKee, Lee, & Leibel, 1999).

(4) Refer men to a urologist. For men who are not candidates for oral medications to improve erections, other potential treatments include penile implants, injectable medications, or vacuum devices. Positive outcomes have been reported with some erectile aids (Litwin et al., 1999).

(5) Refer women to a urologist or sex therapist.

(6) Sildenafil may improve both subjective and physiologic parameters of the female sexual response (Berman et al., 2001), although this has not been tested in women with sexual dysfunction related to cancer therapies.

(7) Fertility issues after RT are beyond the scope of this outline, and readers are referred elsewhere (Bruner, 2001).

6. Patient and family education

a) Teach patient and partner about the potential impact on sexual function caused by pelvic irradiation (see Schover, 1999). The expected outcome is that they will be able to verbalize an understanding of potential sexual dysfunction and will discuss issues with their nurse/physician.

b) Teach patient and partner methods to minimize sexual discomfort and/or dysfunction (see Bruner and Berk, 2003, for more in-depth instructions). The expected outcome is that patient (and partner) will comply with methods to minimize sexual dysfunction.

c) Teach women to use a vaginal dilator to prevent vaginal stenosis post–intracavitary implant (Bruner & Berk, 2003). The expected outcome is that the patient will maintain vaginal patency.

d) Teach men how to use erectile aids, if needed. The expected outcome is that the patient will maintain erectile function.

e) Discuss with patient and partner about when to resume intercourse and/or masturbation after therapy. The expected outcome is that the patient will not act too soon and risk pain or performance anxiety and that he or she will not wait too long so as to build up a fear of returning to normal function.

f) Teach the patient and partner to report continued sexual dysfunction to the nurse or physician.

g) Assure patient that, if needed, he or she can be referred to specialists in sexual dysfunction such as urologists or psychologists if physical, psychological, or relationship problems persist.

(1) The American Association of Sex Educators, Counselors, and Therapists (AASECT), a not-for-profit, interdisciplinary professional organization includes sex educators, counselors, and therapists, as well as physicians, nurses, social workers, psychologists, allied healthcare professionals, clergy members, lawyers, sociologists, marriage and family counselors and therapists, family planning specialists, and researchers.

(2) The AASECT directory lists members by state for patients looking to self refer (www.aasect.org/directory .cfm).

h) Related Web sites

(1) For a site that contains links to cancer site-specific sexuality Web pages as well as general sex education sites: www.bigeye.com/sexeducation/ index.html

(2) For the American Cancer Society site "Sexuality for Women and Their Partners": www.cancer.org/docroot/ MIT/MIT_7_1x_Sexuality forWomenandTheirPartners.asp

(3) For the American Cancer Society site "Sexuality for Men and Their

Partners":www.cancer.org/docroot/
MIT/MIT_7_1x_SexualityforMen
andTheirPartners.asp?sitearea=&level=

(4) For a site that has a discussion of sexuality and breast cancer therapy: http://bcresources.med.unc.edu/posttreat.htm#sexuality

(5) For a site that has information on the effects chemotherapy have on sexuality: www.ellisfischel.org/chemo/sexuality.shtml

Suggested Readings

Alterowitz, R., & Alterowitz, B. (1999). *The lovin' ain't over: The couple's guide to better sex after prostate disease.* Westbury, NY: Health Education Literary Publisher.

Kahane, D.H. (1995). *No less a woman: Femininity, sexuality and breast cancer* (2nd ed.). Alameda, CA: Hunter House.

Schover, L.R. (1997). *Sexuality and fertility after cancer.* New York: John Wiley & Sons.

References

Andersen, B.L., Cyranowski, J.M., & Espindle, D. (1999). Men's sexual self-schema. *Journal of Personality and Social Psychology, 74,* 645–666.

Arai, Y., Kawakita, M., Okada, Y., & Yoshida, O. (1997). Sexuality and fertility in long-term survivors of testicular cancer. *Journal of Clinical Oncology, 15,* 1444–1448.

Bergmark, K., Avall-Lundqvist, E., Dickman, P.W., Henningsohn, L., & Steineck, G. (1999). Vaginal changes and sexuality in women with a history of cervical cancer. *New England Journal of Medicine, 340,* 1383–1389.

Berman, J.R., Berman, L.A., Lin, H., Flaherty, E., Lahey, N., Goldstein, I., et al. (2001). Effect of sildenafil on subjective and physiologic parameters of the female sexual response in women with sexual arousal disorder. *Journal of Sex Marital Therapy, 27,* 411–420.

Bruner, D.W. (2001). Maintenance of body image and sexual function. In D.W. Bruner, G. Moore-Higgs, & M. Haas (Eds.), *Outcomes in radiation therapy: Multidisciplinary management* (pp. 611–636). Sudbury, MA: Jones and Bartlett.

Bruner, D.W., & Berk, L. (2004). Altered body image and sexual health. In C.H. Yarbro, M.H. Frogge, & M. Goodman (Eds.), *Cancer symptom management* (3rd ed., pp. 596–603). Sudbury, MA: Jones and Bartlett.

Bruner, D.W., Keegan, M., Corn, B., Martin, E., & Hanks, G. (1993). Vaginal stenosis and sexual function following intracavitary radiation for the treatment of cervical and endometrial carcinoma. *International Journal of Radiation Oncology, Biology, Physics, 27,* 825–830.

Bruner, D.W., Nicolaou, N., Hanlon, A., & Hanks, G. (1997). Sexual function after radiotherapy + androgen deprivation for clinically localized prostate cancer in younger men (age 50–65). *Oncology Nursing Forum, 24,* 327.

Burns-Cox, N., & Gingell, C. (1997). The andropause: Fact or fiction? *Postgraduate Medical Journal, 73,* 553–556.

Catlin-Huth, C., Haas, M., & Pollock, V. (2002). *Radiation therapy patient care record: A tool for documenting nursing care.* Pittsburgh, PA: Oncology Nursing Society.

Chaikin, D.C., Broderick, G.A., Malloy, T.R., Malkowicz, S.B., Whittington, R., & Wein, A.J. (1996). Erectile dysfunction following minimally invasive treatments for prostate cancer. *Urology, 48,* 100–104.

Denton, A.S., & Maher, E.J. (2003). Interventions for the physical aspects of sexual dysfunction in women following pelvic radiotherapy. *Cochrane Database of Systematic Reviews, 1,* CD003750.

Frisch, M., Smith, E., Grulich, A., & Johansen, C. (2003). Cancer in a population-based cohort of men and women in registered homosexual partnerships. *American Journal of Epidemiology, 157,* 966–972.

Goldstein, I., Feldman, M., Deckers, P., Babayan, R., & Krane, R. (1984). Radiation associated impotence: A clinical study of its mechanism. *JAMA, 251,* 903–910.

Goldstone, S.E., Winkler, B., Ufford, L.J., Alt, E., & Palefsky, J.M. (2001). High prevalence of anal squamous intraepithelial lesions and squamous-cell carcinoma in men who have sex with men as seen in a surgical practice. *Diseases of the Colon and Rectum, 44,* 690–698.

Grigsby, P.W., Russell, A., Bruner, D., Eifel, P., Koh, W.J., Spanos, W., et al. (1995). Late injury of cancer therapy on the female reproductive tract. *International Journal of Radiation Oncology, Biology, Physics, 31,* 1281–1299.

Howell, S., & Shalet, S. (1998). Gonadal damage from chemotherapy and radiotherapy. *Endocrinology and Metabolism Clinics of North America, 27,* 927–943.

Kedia, S., Zippe, C.D., Agarwal, A., Nelson, D.R., & Lakin, M.M. (1999). Treatment of erectile dysfunction with sildenafil citrate (Viagra) after radiation therapy for prostate cancer. *Urology, 54,* 308–312.

Lamb, M.A. (1995). Effects of cancer on the sexuality and fertility of women. *Seminars in Oncology Nursing, 11,* 120–127.

Little, F.A., & Howard, G.C. (1998). Sexual function following radical radiotherapy for bladder cancer. *Radiotherapy and Oncology, 49*(2), 157–161.

Litwin, M.S., Flanders, S.C., Pasta, D.J., Stoddard, M.L., Lubeck, D.P., & Henning, J.M. (1999). Sexual function and bother after radical prostatectomy or radiation for prostate cancer: Multivariate quality-of-life analysis from CaPSURE. Cancer of the Prostate Strategic Urologic Research Endeavor. *Urology, 54,* 503–508.

Mannaerts, G.H., Schijven, M.P., Hendrikx, A., Martijn, H., Rutten, H.J., & Wiggers, T. (2001). Urologic and sexual morbidity following multimodality treatment for locally advanced primary and locally recurrent rectal cancer. *European Journal of Surgical Oncology, 27,* 265–272.

Merrick, G.S., Butler, W.M., Lief, J.H., Stipetich, R.L., Abel, L.J., & Dorsey, A.T. (1999). Efficacy of sildenafil citrate in prostate brachytherapy patients with erectile dysfunction. *Urology, 53,* 1112–1116.

Meston, C.M., Trapnell, P.D., & Gorzalka, B.B. (1996). Ethnic and gender differences in sexuality: Variations in sexual behavior between Asian and non-Asian university students. *Archives of Sexual Behavior, 25*(1), 33–72.

Monga, U., Tan, G., Ostermann, H., & Monga, T. (1997). Sexuality in the head and neck cancer patient. *Archives of Physical Medicine and Rehabilitation, 78,* 298–304.

Schover, L.R. (1999). Counseling cancer patients about changes in sexual function. *Oncology, 13,* 1585–1591.

Schover, L.R., Fife, M., & Gersheson, D. (1989). Sexual dysfunction and treatment for early stage cervical cancer. *Cancer, 63,* 204–212.

Schover, L.R., Yetman, R.J., Tuason, L.J., Meisler, E., Esselstyn, C.B., Hermann, R.E., et al. (1995). Partial mastectomy and breast reconstruction. A comparison of their effects on psychosocial adjustment, body image, and sexuality. *Cancer, 75,* 54–64.

Seibel, M.M., Graves, W.L., & Freeman, M.G. (1980). Carcinoma of the cervix and sexual function. *Obstetrics and Gynecology, 55,* 484–487.

Shield, P.W. (1995). Chronic radiation effects: A correlative study of smears and biopsies from the cervix and vagina. *Diagnostic Cytopathology, 13*(2), 107–119.

U.S. Department of Justice. (2002). *Sourcebook of criminal justice statistics.* Retrieved June 16, 2004, from http://www.albany.edu/sourcebook

Valicenti, R.K., Choi, E., Chen, C., Lu, J.D., Hirsch, I.H., Mulholland, G.S., et al. (2001). Sildenafil citrate effectively reverses sexual dysfunction induced by three-dimensional conformal radiation therapy. *Urology, 57,* 769–773.

Weber, D.C., Bieri, S., Kurtz, J.M., & Miralbell, R. (1999). Prospective pilot study of sildenafil for treatment of postradiotherapy erectile dysfunction in patients with prostate cancer. *Journal of Clinical Oncology, 17,* 3444–3449.

Wilmoth, M., & Bruner, D.W. (2002). Including sexuality into cancer nursing practice: Tips and techniques. *Oncology Nursing Updates, 9,* 1–14.

Wyatt, G.E., Desmond, K.A., Ganz, P.A., Rowland, J.H., Ashing-Giwa, K., & Meyerowitz, B.E. (1998). Sexual functioning and intimacy in African American and white breast cancer survivors: A descriptive study. *Women's Health, 4,* 385–405.

Zelefsky, M.J., McKee, A.B., Lee, H., & Leibel, S.A. (1999). Efficacy of oral sildenafil in patients with erectile dysfunction after radiotherapy for carcinoma of the prostate. *Urology, 53,* 775–778.

G. Nutrition
1. Pathophysiology
   a) Effect of RT on healthy tissue can cause changes in normal physiological function, which may eventually decrease a patient's nutrition status by interfering with the ingestion, digestion, or absorption of nutrients (Donaldson, 1977).
   b) Patients with aerodigestive tract tumors are most at risk for developing nutrition-related side effects (Chencharick & Mossman, 1983; Darbinian & Coulston, 1990; Polisena, 2000). Examples from various sites tumor sites could include
      (1) CNS (brain, spinal column)
         (a) Acute: Nausea, vomiting
         (b) Chronic: Dysphagia, weight loss, hyperglycemia
      (2) Head and neck areas (larynx, pharynx, tonsils, tongue, nasopharynx, salivary gland)
         (a) Acute: Mucositis, sore mouth and throat, dysphagia, odynophagia, xerostomia, dysgeusia, dysosmia, anorexia
         (b) Chronic: Cachexia, xerostomia, dysgeusia, dental caries, ulcers, osteoradionecrosis, trismus
      (3) Thorax areas (esophagus, lung)
         (a) Acute: Anorexia, dysphagia, gastric reflux
         (b) Chronic: Fibrosis, stenosis, perforations, fistula
      (4) Abdominal and pelvic areas (cervical, prostate, pancreatic, uterine, colon, rectal)
         (a) Acute: Anorexia, nausea, vomiting, diarrhea, gas and bloating, acute colitis and enteritis, choleretic enteropathy
         (b) Chronic: Diarrhea, maldigestion, malabsorption, chronic colitis and enteritis, ulcer, stricture, obstruction, perforation, fistula
   c) Acute side effects begin approximately the second or third week of treatment. Symptoms peak about two-thirds of the way through treatment and may continue two to three weeks after treatment is completed. Taste and saliva changes caused by head and neck radiation can take months to improve and may never return to baseline (Polisena, 2000).
   d) Chronic radiation injury is especially likely to adversely affect nutrition. Chronic indications, however, may not occur for months to years after treatment and frequently are irreversible (Donaldson, 1977; Kokal, 1985).
2. Incidence
   a) CNS: Approximately 20% of patients experience persistent nausea or anorexia (or both) throughout their treatment (Ross, 1990).
   b) Head and neck areas: Patients reported a 50% taste loss involving all four tastes, up to an accumulated 30 Gy (Conger, 1973; Silverman, 1999). A dose of 60 Gy may cause permanent taste loss in 90% of patients (Madeya, 1996). Diminished salivary flow may persist for more than five years after radiation. Forty to 60% of patients with head and neck cancer experienced swallowing difficulties because of RT. In one study (Chencharick & Mossman, 1983; Jensen, Pederson, Reibel, & Nauntofte, 2003), xerostomia was reported in 25% of 74 patients with head and neck cancer before radiotherapy and in 80% of patients by the fourth week of radiation treatment. Taste changes were reported in 14% of patients with head and neck cancer before radiotherapy and in 84% of patients by the fifth week of treatment.

c) Thorax areas: Irradiation of thoracic malignancies commonly causes esophagitis. Therefore, patients may complain of dysphagia two to three weeks after the initiation of therapy. Symptoms may continue for the duration of therapy and for several weeks after the completion of therapy (Donaldson, 1977; Donaldson & Lenon, 1979; Werner-Wasik, Yu, Marks, & Shultheiss, 2004). Anorexia has been reported in 60% of patients by the fourth week of treatment (King, Nail, Kreamer, Strohl, & Johnson, 1985).

d) Abdominal and pelvic areas: Three to 11% of patients receiving radiotherapy to the abdomen and pelvic regions have reported nutrition problems. The incidence of nutrition problems is higher among patients receiving both chemotherapy and radiotherapy (Donaldson, 1984).

3. Assessment
   a) Risk factors
      (1) Poor or inadequate dietary intake prior to treatment (Polisena, 2000)
      (2) Weight loss ≥ 5% in one month, ≥ 10% in six months (Polisena, 2000)
      (3) Alcohol and tobacco use (Polisena, 2000)
      (4) Vitamin and mineral supplementation—No recommended minimum or maximum level of antioxidants exists during radiation treatment for patients with cancer. However, megadoses are discouraged, as they may decrease the effectiveness of cancer therapy (Mayer & Ferguson, 2002).
      (5) Herbal supplement use may delay cancer treatment or interact with certain types of cancer treatment (Montbriand, 1999; Spaulding-Albright, 1997)
      (6) Medical history—Concurrent illnesses/diseases (diabetes, coronary artery disease [CAD], dementia, depression) (Polisena, 2000)
      (7) Social situations—Poverty, diminished self-care ability or lack of caretaker (Polisena, 2000)
      (8) Concurrent therapies (e.g., aggressive chemotherapy) (Polisena, 2000)
   b) Clinical manifestations of RT affecting nutrition (Darbinian & Coulston, 1990; Dow, Bucholtz, Iwamoto, Fieler, & Hilderley, 1997)
      (1) CNS: Headaches, seizures, altered mental status, nausea, vomiting
      (2) Head and neck areas: Dry mouth, taste changes, weight loss, dysphagia, pain, decrease in the width of mouth opening, sore throat, changes in saliva production, chewing problems
      (3) Thorax areas: Dysphagia, indigestion, early satiety, weight loss, pain, shortness of breath
      (4) Abdomen and pelvis: Nausea, vomiting, diarrhea, bloating, flatulence, constipation
   c) Physical examination (Decker, Gecsedi, Kogut, Scott, & Snyder, 2003; Dow et al., 1997)
      (1) Baseline data
         (a) Physical exam (e.g., height/weight, body mass index [BMI])
         (b) Basal energy expenditure (BEE), vital signs
         (c) Estimating energy needs
         (d) Estimating protein needs
         (e) Laboratory data (e.g., albumin, hemoglobin, transferrin, hematocrit, white blood cell count, electrolytes, liver function tests)
         (f) Patient-Generated Subjective Global Assessment (PG-SGA)—Ottery (2001) modified it for use in an oncology population (see Appendix B).
            i) 0—Minimal impact on nutritional status (stage A)
            ii) 1—Mild impact
            iii) 2—Moderate impact (stage B)
            iv) 3—Potentially severe impact
            v) 4—Potentially life threatening (stage C)
         (g) Interpretation of total scores—Ottery (2001) recommended
            i) 0–1—No intervention; reassess on a regular basis
            ii) 2–3—Patient/family teaching by nurse, dietitian, or other

clinician; pharmacologic intervention as needed; laboratory assessment may be warranted

    iii) 4–8—Dietitian intervention necessary, together with nurse or physician to manage nutritional impact symptoms

    iv) ≥ 9—Critical need for improved symptom management and/or nutritional intervention

(2) Examination: Assessment

  (a) General appearance

  (b) Karnofsky Performance Status (see www2.mc.duke.edu/depts/hospital/9200bmt/Karnofsky.htm)

  (c) Oral cavity: Infections, dental condition

  (d) Nutritional intake: Fluids, calories, and proteins

  (e) Skin turgor

  (f) Edema

  (g) "Quick Guide to Estimating Energy Needs in Adults" (Dempsey & Mullen, 1985)

  (h) "Quick Guide to Estimating Protein Needs in Adults" (Dempsey & Mullen, 1985)

  (i) Scored PG-SGA (see Appendix B)

(3) Knowledge of alternative mode of feeding (tube feeding), if indicated

4. Documentation (Catlin-Huth, Haas, & Pollock, 2002)

  a) Weight loss (NCI, 2003)

    (1) Grade 1—5% to < 10% from baseline

    (2) Grade 2—10% to < 20% from baseline

    (3) Grade 3—> 20% from baseline

  b) Anorexia (NCI, 2003)

    (1) 1—Loss of appetite without alteration in eating habits

    (2) 2—Oral intake altered without significant weight loss or malnutrition; oral nutrition supplements indicated

    (3) 3—Associated with significant weight loss or malnutrition (e.g., inadequate oral caloric and/or fluid intake); IV fluids, tube feedings, or TPN indicated

    (4) 4—Life-threatening consequences

    (5) 5—Death

c) Nausea (NCI, 2003)

    (1) 1—Loss of appetite without alteration in eating habits

    (2) 2—Oral intake decreased without significant weight loss, dehydration, or malnutrition; IV fluids indicated < 24 hours.

    (3) 3—Inadequate oral caloric or fluid intake; IV fluids, tube feedings, or TPN indicated ≥ 24 hours.

    (4) Life-threatening consequences

    (5) 5—Death

d) Vomiting (NCI, 2003)

    (1) 1—One episode in 24 hours

    (2) 2—Five episodes in 24 hours

    (3) 3—More than six episodes in 24 hours; need for IV fluids

    (4) 4—Requiring parenteral nutrition; physiologic consequences requiring intensive care; hemodynamic collapse; life-threatening consequences

    (5) 5—Death

e) Diarrhea (NCI, 2003)

    (1) 1—Increase of less than four stools/day over baseline

    (2) 2—Increase of four to six stools/day

    (3) 3—Increase of more than seven stools/day or incontinence; need for parenteral support for dehydration

    (4) 4—Physiologic consequences requiring intensive care; hemodynamic collapse

    (5) 5—Death

f) Salivary gland changes (NCI, 2003)

    (1) 1—Slightly thickened saliva; may have slightly altered taste (e.g., metallic); additional fluids may be required

    (2) 2—Thick, ropy, sticky saliva; markedly altered taste; alteration in diet required

    (3) 3—Symptoms leading to inability to adequately aliment orally; IV fluids, tube feedings, or TPN indicated

g) Taste disturbance (NCI, 2003)

    (1) 1—Slightly altered; no change in diet

    (2) 2—Markedly altered with change in diet; noxious or unpleasant taste; loss of taste

h) Constipation (NCI, 2003)
  (1) 1—Requiring stool softener or dietary modification
  (2) 2—Requiring laxatives
  (3) 3—Obstipation requiring manual evacuation or enema
  (4) 4—Obstruction or toxic megacolon
  (5) 5—Death
i) Dyspepsia and/or heartburn (NCI, 2003)
  (1) 1—Mild
  (2) 2—Moderate
  (3) 3—Severe

5. Collaborative management
  a) Early nutritional intervention is key. Preventing cancer-induced weight loss and other symptoms helps to promote better tolerance to treatment and a better quality of life.
  b) Instruct the patient on consuming a high-calorie/high-protein diet and commercial nutrition supplements to maintain proper nutritional intake (Ross, 1990).
  c) Instruct the patient about the importance of exercise to enhance tolerance of cancer treatments and to stimulate appetite.
  d) Instruct the patient and caregiver on bland, moist, soft, nonacidic, low-lactose, and low-residue foods.
  e) Consult with clinical dietitian or speech pathologist for patients at risk for aspiration.
  f) Encourage the use of enteral nutrition. Enteral nutrition, also referred to as tube feeding, is indicated for patients who are unable to ingest adequate calories, protein, vitamins, minerals, and fluid by mouth yet have a functional GI tract. Indications for enteral nutrition support include states of hypermetabolism, as in sepsis, burns, or trauma, neurologic disease, such as stroke or dysphagia, GI disease, oncologic disease, psychiatric disease, and organ system failure. Contraindications for enteral nutrition are a malfunctioning GI tract, mechanical obstruction or ileus, severe GI hemorrhage, intractable vomiting or diarrhea, and high-output GI tract (Mercadante, 1998). Think of parenteral nutrition as the last resort to maintain gut mobility. If TPN is truly indicated, observe for refeeding syndrome. Refeeding syndrome is characterized by fluid retention leading to cardiac decompensation and rapid drop in serum levels of phosphorus, magnesium, and potassium (Hearing, 2004).
  g) Counseling early in a patient's course of treatment is necessary. The importance of maintaining good nutrition, curtailing further weight loss, and discussing the anticipated eating difficulties all should be reviewed with the patient and family.
  h) Encourage oral health examination (see section V, B—Head and Neck).
  i) Encourage the importance of eating small, frequent meals.
  j) Monitor hydration closely and replace electrolytes as needed.
  k) Suggest bulking agents and pectin to control diarrhea in patients receiving radiation to the pelvis (Walker & Masino, 1998).
  l) Anticipate the need to start appetite stimulants early. Pharmacologic management can include
    (1) Megestrol acetate—Progestational agent, stimulates appetite and weight gain but mostly as fat; dose dependent; hypogonadism (impotence, muscle loss); decreases glucose tolerance and GI tolerance (nausea/vomiting/diarrhea, gas, dry mouth) (Bruera, 1998)
    (2) Dronabinol—Appetite maintained long-term (improves mood, decreased nausea, increased weight); no adverse GI side effects; no development of tolerance to therapeutic effects/no toxicity; no addiction, side effects (seem to be age-related; decreasing dose may eliminate/lessen adverse effects, 2.5 mgs bid) (Von Roenn, 2002)
    (3) Corticosteroids (dexamethasone)—Short-lived appetite, no real weight gain; muscle loss/weakness, osteoporosis, fluid retention, high blood sugar, electrolyte disturbances, insomnia, gastric irritation (nausea/vomiting) (Von Roenn, 2002)
    (4) Cyproheptadine—Antiserotonergic, antihistamine approved in the United

States for treatment of allergic disorders. Studies have been conducted with patients with cancer, AIDS, dry mouth, and drowsiness and urination difficulties; limited efficacy (most patients stop before three months because of clinical deterioration) (Bruera, 1998).

(5) Hydrazine sulfate—Evaluated because of ability to inhibit gluconeogenesis; in vitro data suggest it inhibits tumor necrosis factor cytolytic activity; well tolerated, no toxicity but no appetite gains or weight gains (Bruera, 1998)

(6) Anabolic agents—Testosterone derivatives; well studied in patients with AIDS but not those with cancer; cannot be used in some cancers; need for more studies (Bruera, 1998)

(7) Metoclopramide—Treats early satiety; delayed gastric emptying may occur in up to 60% of patients with cancer; patients with dysmotility will benefit the most, usually at 10 mg qid; side effects respond to dose reduction (diarrhea and hyperactivity); use in combination with narcotic analgesic (Bruera, 1998).

6. Patient/family education: Sessions in which behavioral topics are covered may vary according to patient's readiness, skills, resources, and need for lifestyle changes.

   a) Dry mouth or thick saliva (Feber, 1995; Walker & Masino, 1998; Wilkes, 2003)

     (1) Frequent oral care every two hours

     (2) Drink 8–12 cups of liquid a day to help loosen mucus.

     (3) Use a straw to drink liquids.

     (4) Include soft, bland-tasting foods that are at room temperature. Consider use of pureed fruits and vegetables, as well as ice pops or shaved ice.

     (5) Use broth, soup, or sauces to moisten foods.

     (6) Avoid citrus and dry foods and alcohol or alcohol-containing products.

     (7) Suck on sugarless or sour candy.

     (8) Use artificial salvia or other mouth lubricants.

     (9) Make a salt water rinse (1 teaspoon baking soda and ½ teaspoon salt dissolved in 1 quart boiling water); use mixture at room temperature at least four to five times per day.

   b) Taste changes or loss of taste (Polisena, 2000; Sherry, 2002; Stubbs, 1989; Wilkes, 2003)

     (1) Use plastic utensils to reduce metallic taste.

     (2) Experiment with cold or cool-temperature foods that have less taste or aroma.

     (3) Try unflavored nutrition supplements intended for tube feeding, such as Isocal® (Novartis Medical Nutrition), Osmolite® (Ross Laboratories, Columbus, OH), or Isosource® (Novartis Medical Nutrition).

     (4) Try tart or spicy foods, if oral mucosa is not distressed.

     (5) Eat a few pineapple chunks to get rid of bad taste or to change taste sensations between eating different foods.

   c) Dysphagia (D'Angelo, 2000; Polisena, 2000; Wilkes, 2003)

     (1) Add gravy or sauces to foods to increase moisture.

     (2) Eat blended foods. Warm foods before blending for best results.

     (3) Accept the importance of nutrition supplements or milkshake recipes for calorie and protein intake.

     (4) If aspiration is a risk, sit upright when eating.

     (5) If dysphagia is related to brain metastases, a referral to a speech language pathologist may help to prevent secondary aspiration risk.

   d) Diarrhea (Meier, Burri, & Steurwald, 2003; Polisena, 2000; Wilkes, 2003)

     (1) Avoid raw fruits and vegetables, whole-grain bread and cereals, nuts, popcorn, skins, and seeds.

     (2) Follow a bland diet. Try pectin-containing foods such as potatoes, applesauce, oatmeal, bananas, cooked carrots, and rice.

     (3) Do not drink large quantities of fruit juice and sweetened fruit drinks.

(4) Replace fluid losses with one cup of water for each episode of diarrhea. Avoid caffeine and lactose fluids.

(5) Consume foods and beverages high in sodium and potassium, such as soups, bananas, potatoes, bouillon, and Gatorade® (Quaker Oats Company, Dallas, TX).

(6) May want to use products containing glutamine, such as Resource® (Novartis Medical Nutrition), GlutaSolve® (Novartis Medical Nutrition), Impact® Glutamine (Novartis Medical Nutrition) (Klimberg, 1996).

e) Gas and bloating (Eagle et al., 2001; Polisena, 2000)

(1) Avoid gas-producing beverages (carbonated products), additives (artificial sweeteners), and foods (broccoli, cabbage, cauliflower, beans, lentils, and eggs).

(2) Use an enzyme product to help digest the carbohydrates in gas-producing foods.

(3) Eat five to six small meals a day.

f) Nausea and vomiting (Darbinian & Coulston, 1990; Osoba, Zee, & Pater, 1997; Polisena, 2000; Walker & Masino, 1998)

(1) Schedule a light meal before or after treatment and/or carry food with you to eat after treatment.

(2) Try dry foods, such as crackers, toast, or bread sticks, every few hours during the day.

(3) Choose foods that do not have a strong odor, and eat cold foods instead of hot ones.

(4) Avoid foods that are overly sweet, fatty, fried, or spicy.

g) Sore mouth and throat (Polisena, 2000; Wojtaszek, 2000)

(1) Use buttermilk as a rinse to coat mouth.

(2) Use liquid or pureed foods for the term of the treatment.

(3) Consider nutrition supplements and milkshake recipes if unable to consume solid foods in adequate quantities.

(4) Drink nectars instead of apple, grape, or acidic juices.

h) Fat malabsorption (Koch et al., 1996; Polisena, 2000; Ross, 1990)

(1) Use medium chain triglyceride oil (e.g., Peptinex® [Novartis Medical Nutrition], Optimental® [Ross Laboratories]) if necessary.

(2) Try a low-fat diet while maintaining sufficient calorie intake if pancreatic enzymes do not help.

(3) Switch to elemental or defined formula diet if necessary.

(4) Begin TPN if intestinal function is so impaired as to prohibit enteral provision of nutrients or if severe malnutrition cannot be corrected by enteral nutrition support.

i) Anorexia/cachexia (Darbinian & Coulston, 1990; Jatoi & Loprinzi, 2001; Rust & Kogut, 2001)

(1) For energy needs
(a) 20 kcal/kg—Initial refeeding of patients who are malnourished or depleted
(b) 21–25 kcal/kg—Obese patients for maintenance
(c) 25–30 kcal/kg—Maintenance/ standard
(d) 30–35 kcal/kg—Malnourished and/or extensive treatment or bone marrow transplant
(e) 35–45 kcal/kg—Depleted and/or hypermetabolic state

(2) For protein needs
(a) 0.5–0.8 g/kg—Hepatic or renal compromise
(b) 0.8–1.0 g/kg—Recommended dietary allowance for adults
(c) 1.0–1.5 g/kg—Most patients with cancer
(d) 1.5 g/kg—Bone marrow transplant recipients
(e) 1.5–2.0 g/kg—Patients with cancer who are depleted of protein

(3) Encourage small, frequent meals.

(4) Encourage liquids between meals.

(5) Encourage high-protein foods or enhance protein content of diet.

(6) Use specialized commercial nutrition supplements containing Omega-3 fatty acids and essential amino acids to promote weight gain, build muscle, and support immune function.

(7) Nutrient-dense supplements

  (a) ProSure®, Ensure®, Ensure Plus® (Ross Laboratories)

  (b) Boost®, Boost Plus® (Novartis Medical Nutrition), Choice DM® (Bristol-Myers Squibb)

  (c) Resource® Support™, Impact® (Novartis Medical Nutrition) NuBasics® soups (Nestlé Nutrition, Glendale, CA)

  (d) Fortified milk/yogurts

j) Expected clinical outcomes of ideal/goal values (American Dietetic Association, 1998)

(1) Albumin 3.5–5.0 mg/dl

(2) Prealbumin 19–43 mg/dl

(3) Hemoglobin (Hgb) > 12 g/dl (female) Hgb > 14 g/dl (male)

(4) Hematocrit (HCT) > 38 volume percentage (female) HCT > 44 volume percentage (male)

(5) Complete metabolic profile within normal limits

(6) Maintain weight ≥ 85% UBW

k) Web sites

(1) *A Dietitian's Cancer Story*—www.cancerrd.com—Contents include recipes, menus, information about soy, and nutritional strategies to use during treatment or recovery.

(2) Oncology Nutrition Dietetic Practice Group of the American Dietetic Association—www.oncologynutrition.org—Contents include research information and nutrition tips.

(3) NCI—http://cancer.gov—Contents include *Eating Hints: Recipes and Tips for Better Nutrition During Treatment*, recipes and nutrition for patients with cancer (PDQ document)—version for patients and healthcare professionals, nutritional implications of cancer therapies, nutritional suggestions for symptom management, and a table on herbs and possible food/drug interactions.

(4) American Cancer Society—www.cancer.org—Contents include tips for symptom management of nutrition-related problems.

(5) American Institute for Cancer Research—www.aicr.org—Contents include recipes, information for cancer prevention and cancer survivors, serving size finder, and research updates.

References

American Dietetic Association. (1998). *Medical nutrition therapy across the continuum of care* (2nd ed.). Chicago: Author.

Bruera, E. (1998). Pharmacological treatment of cachexia: Any progress? *Supportive Care in Cancer, 6,* 109–113.

Catlin-Huth, C., Haas, M., & Pollock, V. (2002). *Radiation therapy patient care record: A tool for documenting nursing care.* Pittsburgh, PA: Oncology Nursing Society.

Chencharick, J.D., & Mossman, K.L. (1983). Nutritional consequences of the radiotherapy for head and neck cancer. *Cancer, 51,* 811–815.

Conger, A. (1973). Loss and recovery of taste acuity in patients irradiated to the oral cavity. *Radiation Research, 53,* 338–347.

D'Angelo, C.R. (2000). Nutrition in the cancer patient. *Topics in Clinical Nutrition, 15*(2), 20–23.

Darbinian, J.A., & Coulston, A.M. (1990). Impact of radiation therapy on the nutrition status of the cancer patient: Acute and chronic complications. In A.S. Bloch (Ed.), *Nutrition management of the cancer patient* (pp. 181–197). Rockville, MD: Aspen Publications.

Decker, G., Gecsedi, R., Kogut, V., Scott, G., & Snyder, A. (2003). *The current role of nutrition in patients with cancer* [Monograph]. Minneapolis, MN: Novartis.

Dempsey, D., & Mullen, J. (1985). Macronutrient requirements in the malnourished cancer patient: How much of what and why? *Cancer, 55,* 290–294.

Donaldson, S.S. (1977). Nutritional consequences of radiotherapy. *Cancer Research, 37,* 2407–2413.

Donaldson, S.S. (1984). Nutritional support as an adjunct to radiation therapy. *Journal of Parenteral and Enteral Nutrition, 8,* 302–310.

Donaldson, S.S., & Lenon, R.A. (1979). Alterations of nutritional status: Impact of chemotherapy and radiation therapy. *Cancer, 43,* 2036–2052.

Dow, K.H., Bucholtz, J.D., Iwamoto, R., Fieler, V., & Hilderley, L. (Eds.). (1997). *Nursing care in radiation oncology* (2nd ed.). Philadelphia: Saunders.

Eagle, D.A., Gian, V., Lauwers, G.Y., Manivel, J.C., Moreb, J.S., Mastin, S., et al. (2001). Gastroparesis following bone marrow transplantation. *Bone Marrow Transplantation, 28,* 59–62.

Feber, T. (1995). Mouth care for patients receiving oral irradiation. *Professional Nurse, 10,* 666–670.

Hearing, S.D. (2004). Refeeding syndrome. *BMJ, 328,* 908–909.

Jatoi, A., & Loprinzi, C.L. (2001). Current management of cancer-associated anorexia and weight loss. *Oncology, 15,* 497–510.

Jensen, S.B., Pedersen, A.M. Reibel, J., & Nauntofte, B. (2003). Xerostomia and hypofunction of the salivary glands in cancer therapy. *Supportive Care in Cancer, 11,* 207–225.

King, K.B., Nail, L.M., Kreamer, K., Strohl, R.A., & Johnson, J.E. (1985). Patients' descriptions of the experience of receiving radiation therapy. *Oncology Nursing Forum, 12*(4), 55–62.

Klimberg, V.S. (1996). How glutamine protects the gut during irradiation. *ICCN, 3,* 21.

Koch, J., Garcia-Shelton, Y.L., Neal, E.A., Chan, M.F., Weaver, K.E., & Cello, J.P. (1996). Steatorrhea: A common manifestation in patients with HIV/AIDS. *Nutrition, 12,* 507–510.

Kokal, W.A. (1985). The impact of antitumor therapy on nutrition. *Cancer, 55,* 273–278.

Madeya, M. (1996). Oral complications from cancer therapy: Part 1—Pathophysiology and secondary complications. *Oncology Nursing Forum, 23,* 801–807.

Mayer, K., & Ferguson, M. (2002). Antioxidant use during radiation or chemotherapy: A summary. Association of Community Cancer Centers. *Integrating Nutrition into Your Cancer Program, 17*(Suppl. 2), 24–32.

Meier, R., Burri, E., & Steurwald, M. (2003). The role of nutrition in diarrhea syndromes. *Current Opinion in Clinical Nutrition and Metabolic Care, 6,* 563–567.

Mercadante, S. (1998). Parenteral versus enteral nutrition in cancer patients: Indications and practice. *Supportive Care in Cancer, 6,* 85–93.

Montbriand, M.J. (1999). Past and present herbs used to treat cancer: Medicine, magic, or poison? *Oncology Nursing Forum, 26,* 49–60.

National Cancer Institute. (2003). *Common terminology criteria for adverse events* (Version 3.0). Bethesda, MD: Author.

Osoba, D., Zee, B., & Pater, J. (1997). Determinants of post-chemotherapy nausea and vomiting in patients with cancer. *Journal of Clinical Oncology, 15,* 116–123.

Ottery. F. (2001). *Nutritional oncology: Planning a winning strategy.* Online presentation given June 28, 2001, in a live chat. Retrieved June 13, 2004, from http://www.cancersource.com/ppt/22311ppt/Ross_files/frame.htm

Polisena, C.G. (2000). Nutrition concerns with the radiation therapy patient. In P.D. McCallum & C.G. Polisena (Eds.), *The clinical guide to oncology nutrition* (pp. 70–78). Chicago: American Dietetic Association.

Ross, B.T. (1990). The impact of radiation therapy on the nutrition status of the cancer patient: An overview. In A.S. Bloch (Ed.), *Nutrition management of the cancer patient* (pp. 173–180). Rockville, MD: Aspen Publications.

Rust, D.M., & Kogut, V.J. (2001). Anorexia and cachexia. In J. Yasko (Ed.), *Nursing management of symptoms associated with chemotherapy* (5th ed., pp. 41–62). West Conshohocken, PA: Meniscus Health Care Communications.

Sherry, V.W. (2002). Taste alterations among patients with cancer. *Clinical Journal of Oncology Nursing, 6,* 73–77.

Silverman, S., Jr. (1999). Oral cancer: Complications of therapy. *Oral Surgery, Oral Medicine, Oral Pathology, Oral Radiology, and Endodontics, 88,* 122–126.

Spaulding-Albright, N. (1997). A review of some herbal and related products commonly used by cancer patients. *Journal of the American Dietetic Association, 10*(Suppl. 2), 208–215.

Stubbs, L. (1989). Taste changes in cancer patients. *Nursing Times, 85*(3), 49–50.

Von Roenn, J.H. (2002). *Integrating nutrition into your cancer program.* Rockville, MD: Association of Community Cancer Centers.

Walker, M.S., & Masino, K. (1998). *Oncology nutrition: Patient education materials.* Chicago: American Dietetic Association.

Werner-Wasik, M., Yu, X., Marks, L.B., & Schultheiss, T.E. (2004). Normal-tissue toxicities of thoracic radiation therapy: Esophagus, lung, and spinal cord as organs at risk. *Hematology-Oncology Clinics of North America, 18,* 131–160.

Wilkes, G. (2003). Nutrition issues facing lung cancer individuals. In M. Haas (Ed.), *Contemporary issues in lung cancer: A nursing perspective* (pp. 153–173). Sudbury, MA: Jones and Bartlett.

Wojtaszek, C.A. (2000). Management of chemotherapy-induced stomatitis. *Clinical Journal of Oncology Nursing, 4,* 263–269.

V. Site-specific management

A. Brain and central nervous system

1. Categories (Kepes, 1990)

(*Note.* All malignant tumors are marked by *.)

a) Neuroepithelial

(1) *Astrocytic tumors: Derived from astrocytes. Functions of astrocytes include physical and biochemical support, insulation of the receptive surface of neurons, interactions with capillary endothelial cells in the establishment, and maintenance of the blood-brain barrier (Robbins, Cotran, & Kumar, 1989). Tumors are divided histopathically into three grades of malignancies:

(a) Grade II astrocytoma (survival up to five years)

(b) Grade III anaplastic astrocytoma (survival up to three years)

(c) Grade IV glioblastoma multiforme (survival < two years)

(2) *Oligodendroglial tumors: Derived from oligodendrocytes. Principal function is the production and maintenance of the CNS myelin (Robbins et al., 1989).

(a) First brain tumor for which molecular genetic analysis has practical ramifications (Levin, Leibel, & Gutin, 2001). Molecular genetic alterations are determined by loss of heterozygosity (LOH) analysis on chromosome 1 p and chromosome 19 q, a finding suggesting a synergistic effect of both genetic alterations in tumor growth (Kleihues & Cavenee, 2000).

(b) Chromosome 1p and 19q loss is chemosensitive 50% of the time and has a neuroradiologic response (Cox, 1994).

(c) Lack of chromosome 1p and 19q loss is chemosensitive 25% of the time and rarely has neuroradiologic response.

(d) Tumors are divided into oligodendroglioma and anaplastic oligodendroglioma.

(3) Ependymomas: In the first two decades of life, this tumor typically occurs in the fourth ventricle; in midlife, the spinal cord. Ependymomas usually present with hydrocephalus secondary to obstruction of the fourth ventricle. Because of its location, it is difficult to be completely excised. They are slow growing, usually benign, and difficult to eradicate (Robbins et al., 1989).

(a) Myxopapillary (associated with a five-year survival rate)

(b) *Anaplastic ependymoma

(c) *Ependymoblastoma has a propensity to disseminate throughout the CNS.

(4) *Mixed gliomas: Tumors composed of admixtures of neoplastic cells are problematic in treating (Gonzales, 1995). They are divided into

(a) Oligoastrocytoma

(b) Anaplastic.

(5) Choroid plexus tumors: Marked by atypia, brisk mitotic activity, and extensive necrosis. They are most common in children and young adults.

(a) Related to patients with Li-Fraumeni syndrome (LFS), an autosomal dominant disorder characterized by multiple primary neoplasms in children and young adults, including soft tissue sarcomas, osteosarcomas, breast cancer, brain tumors, leukemia, and adrenocortical carcinoma. The majority of LFS is caused by a TP53 germline mutation and von Hippel-Lindau disease (VHL), which is inherited through an autosomal dominant trait and characterized by the development of capillary hemangioblastomas of the CNS and retina, clear cell renal carcinoma, phaeochromocytoma, and pancreatic and inner ear tumors. VHL is caused by germline mutations of the VHL tumor suppressor gene (Kleihues & Cavenee, 2000).

(b) Disease is associated with a five-year survival.

(6) Neuroepithelial tumors of uncertain origin have poor cell differentiation. Three tumors are listed in this category: astroblastoma, polar spongioblastoma, and gliomatosis cerebri (Gonzales, 1995).

(7) *Neuronal and mixed neuronal-glial tumors are gangliocytoma, ganglioma, malignant ganglioma, dysplastic gangliocytoma, desmoplastic infantile ganglioma, and dysembryoplastic neuroepithelial tumors (Gonzales, 1995).

(8) *Pineal tumors: The pineal gland is located in the posterior portion of the third ventricle. These tumors are rare, < 1% of intracranial tumors, and divided into pineocytoma and pineoblastoma (Gonzales, 1995).

(9) *Embryonal tumors: Neuroblastoma, retinoblastoma, ependymoblastoma, and primitive neuroectodermal (Gonzales, 1995).

b) Peripheral nerve tumors

(1) Schwannoma: Benign tumor of the peripheral nerve sheath. Vestibular schwannoma (acoustic neuroma). Treatment options include surgery and Gamma Knife® (Elekta Instruments, Stockholm, Sweden) radiosurgery. Radiosurgery, a noninvasive procedure, is associated with a high rate of tumor control and low morbidity (Flickinger, Kondziolka, Niranjan, & Lunsford, 2001) (see

section VII, G—Stereotactic Radiosurgery [SRS]).

(2) Neurofibroma: Benign tumor

c) Meningioma: Tumors arising from the lining of the brain, usually arachnoid, associated with slow growth (Robbins et al., 1989).

d) *Hemopoietic tumors

(1) Primary malignant lymphoma: Majority of CNS lymphomas are non-Hodgkin's tumors of B cell lineage. CNS lymphoma is also a complication of immunocompromised patients with HIV infection (Gonzales, 1995).

(2) Plasmacytomas usually occur in vertebrae and skull bones.

(3) Granulocytic sarcoma, previously known as chloroma, is regarded as a manifestation of a systemic myeloproliferative disorder (Gonzales, 1995).

e) *Germ cell tumors: May respond best to radiation, although pre-chemotherapy may have a role (Levin et al., 2001).

f) Cysts and tumor-like lesions, nonmalignant

g) Pituitary tumors
(1) Adenoma
(2) *Carcinoma

h) Local extensions of regional CNS tumors

i) *Metastatic tumors: The most common form of brain cancer (Armstrong & Gilbert, 2000)

(1) The most common malignancies that metastasize to the brain are lung, breast, cutaneous malignant melanoma, renal, and colon (Levin et al., 2001).

(2) Histology of primary cancer is the most important risk factor for the development of brain metastases (Armstrong & Gilbert, 2000).

2. Incidence and epidemiology

a) An estimated 18,400 new brain and CNS cases and 12,690 estimated deaths will occur in 2004 (Jemal et al., 2004).

b) Exposure to pesticides, herbicides, fertilizers, various petrochemical industries, and vinyl chloride increases brain tumor risk (gliomas) (Levin et al., 2001).

c) Viruses, such as Epstein-Barr, can be linked to CNS tumors (Geddes, Bhattacharjee, Savage, Scaravilli, & McLaughlin, 1992). DNA viruses, adenovirus, SV-40, and papovavirus are known to be inducers of neoplasia (Gonzales, 1995).

d) Electromagnetic field studies, to date, have not suggested an increased risk of brain tumors (Wrench, Yost, & Miike, 1999).

e) Family history of cancer carries an increased risk (Gonzales, 1995).

3. Molecular genetics: Most common alteration—chromosome 17 mutation associated with tumor suppressor gene p53 and chromosome 1p and 19q LOH (Cox, Stetz, & Pajak, 1995).

4. Routinely irradiated tumors (Karim, 1995)

a) Anaplastic gliomas, grades 3 and 4

b) Medulloblastomas, ependymomas, malignant pineal tumors

c) Primary malignant lymphomas, malignant meningiomas, primitive neuroectodermal tumors

d) Cerebral metastases

e) Pituitary nonhormone active adenomas

f) Pituitary hormone active tumors resistant to surgical and medical intervention

g) Tumors with threatening symptomatology

h) Craniopharyngioma

i) Deep seated, inoperable tumors

5. Symptoms of cranial irradiation

a) Cerebral edema

(1) Pathophysiology: Radiation-induced edema occurs most commonly in larger doses of radiation to the brain. Changes from capillary permeability and increased intracranial pressure from primary or metastatic growths contribute to cerebral edema (Levin et al., 2001).

(2) Incidence

(a) Conventional daily fractions of 1.8–2.0 Gy or hyperfractionated schedules of 0.9–1.2 Gy two times a day are well tolerated. Incidence increases with higher doses per fraction (Levin et al., 2001).

(b) Sheline, Wara, and Smith (1980) suggested that the threshold doses for brain injury are approximately 35 Gy in 10 fractions, 60 Gy in 35 fractions, and 76 Gy in 60 fractions. Doses of 50 Gy to whole brain in 1.8–2 Gy are well tolerated, and in children, the threshold dose is 30–35 Gy (Costine, Williams, Morris, Rubin, & Okunieff, 2004).

(c) Edema may occur if patient is not on steroid medication (Karim, 1995).

(d) Edema may occur if steroids are tapered quickly (Bucholtz, 1997).

(3) Assessment

   (a) Clinical manifestations (Bucholtz, 1997)

     i) Generalized edema
- Headache
- Nausea and vomiting
- Changes in mentation

     ii) Focal signs
- Weakness of extremities
- Visual changes
- Seizures
- Speech problems
- Cranial neuropathy

   (b) Physical and neurologic exam

(4) Documentation (Catlin-Huth, Haas, & Pollock, 2002)

   (a) Karnofsky Performance Scale: 0–100

   (b) Pain location—Identify location

   (c) Pain intensity—0–10

   (d) Pain intervention
     i) 0—None
     ii) 1—Over-the-counter medication
     iii) 2—NSAIDs or nonopioids
     iv) 3—Opioids
     v) 4—Adjuvant medication
     vi) 5—Complementary methods

   (e) Effectiveness of pain intervention
     i) 0—No relief
     ii) 1—Pain relieved 25%
     iii) 2—Pain relieved 50%

     iv) 3—Pain relieved 75%
     v) 4—Pain relieved 100%

   (f) CNS alteration: Depressed level of consciousness
     i) 0—Normal
     ii) 1—Somnolence or sedation not interfering with function
     iii) 2—Somnolence or sedation interfering with function but not interfering with activities of daily living
     iv) 3—Obtundation or stupor; difficult to arouse; interfering with activities of daily living
     v) 4—Coma

   (g) Orientation to person, place, and time

   (h) Neuropathy—Motor
     i) 0—Normal
     ii) 1—Subjective weakness but no objective findings
     iii) 2—Mild objective weakness interfering with function but not interfering with activities of daily living
     iv) 3—Objective weakness interfering with daily living
     v) 4—Paralysis

   (i) Ataxia
     i) 0—Absent
     ii) 1—Present

   (j) Speech impairment
     i) 0—Normal
     ii) 1—
     iii) 2—Awareness of receptive or expression aphasia, does not impair ability to communicate
     iv) 3—Receptive or expressive dysphasia, impairs ability to communicate
     v) 4—Inability to communicate

   (k) Seizures
     i) 0—None
     ii) 1—
     iii) 2—Seizure(s) self-limited and consciousness is preserved
     iv) 3—Seizures(s) in which consciousness is altered
     v) 4—Seizures of any type that are prolonged, repetitive, or difficult to control (e.g., status epilepticus, intractable epilepsy)

   (l) Sensory alteration: Ocular/visual
     i) 0—Normal

ii) 1—Mild

iii) 2—Moderate

iv) 3—Severe

v) 4—Unilateral or bilateral loss of vision (blindness)

(m) Nausea

i) 0—None

ii) 1—Able to eat

iii) 2—Oral intake significantly decreased

iv) 3—No significant intake

v) 4—

(n) Vomiting

i) 0—None

ii) 1—One episode in 24 hours over pretreatment

iii) 2—Two to five episodes in 24 hours over pretreatment

iv) 3—More than six episodes in 24 hours over pretreatment or need for IV fluids

v) 4—Requiring parenteral nutrition, physiologic consequences requiring intensive care, hemodynamic collapse

(o) Thrush

i) 0—Absent

ii) 1—Present

(p) Dyspepsia and/or heartburn

i) 0—None

ii) 1—Mild

iii) 2—Moderate

iv) 3—Severe

(5) Collaborative management for acute effects of cerebral edema

(a) Steroids: Synthetic glucocorticoids: Dexamethasone or methylprednisone

i) Vasogenic edema from tumor can contribute to neurologic dysfunction.

ii) Steroids reduce capillary permeability in as early as one hour after a single dose (Shapiro, Hiesiger, & Cooney, 1990).

iii) Patients improve clinically when steroids are given (Chang et al., 1992).

iv) Dexamethasone incompatibilities: Contraindicated with daunorubicin, doxorubicin, metaraminol, and vancomycin (Karch, 2003).

v) Standard care is to monitor mucous membrane for oral fungal infections, such as thrush (from steroid use); maintain good oral hygiene (Karch, 2003).

vi) Monitor patient for stomach irritation (from steroid use) (Karch, 2003).

(b) Pain medication for headaches

i) The brain is anesthetic. Traction on the dura or the blood vessels within the brain causes headache or pressure (Armstrong & Gilbert, 2000).

ii) Headaches develop as a presenting symptom or develop during the course of the disease. Persistent headaches may occur more commonly in patients for whom headaches were a presenting symptom (Levin et al., 2001).

iii) Administer medication, as prescribed, for relief of pain.

(c) Anticonvulsant therapy

i) Seizures develop as a consequence of metastatic disease to brain or leptomeninges (Quinn & DeAngelis, 2000).

ii) Monitor antiepileptic therapy with serum drug level, liver function, and CBC (Armstrong & Gilbert, 2000).

iii) Monitor for skin rash and the more extreme exfoliative rash/ toxic epidermal necrolysis (Stevens-Johnson syndrome) with administration of phenytoin (Karch, 2003). Phenytoin is associated with a reported 20%–30% risk of rash (Armstrong, Gilbert, & Movas, 2001).

iv) Assess for focal neurologic symptoms: Weakness, hemiparesis, hemiplegia, or loss of communication.

(6) Patient and family education

(a) Provide written and verbal instructions for signs and symptoms of cerebral edema.

(b) Provide written and verbal instructions for use of steroid and antiepileptic medication; emphasize the importance of maintaining schedule; and do not initiate abrupt cessation of either drug (Karch, 2003).

(c) Instruct patient and family in side effects of prolonged steroid use (Bucholtz, 1997). Also instruct the patient not to abruptly stop taking steroids because of withdrawal side effects; use steroid taper.

i) Gastrointestinal: Stomach irritation and abdominal distention. Instructions in use of antacids to be given with steroid dose to prevent peptic ulcers.

ii) Endocrine: Increased blood sugar (requires close monitoring of diabetic patients), cushingoid state, growth retardation, menstrual irregularities, and decreased carbohydrate tolerance

iii) Fluid and electrolyte disturbance: Sodium retention, potassium loss, hypertension, and moon faces

iv) Nervous system: Mood swings, restlessness, insomnia, vertigo, psychoses, headaches, euphoria, intracerebral hemorrhage, cataracts, and increased intraocular pressure

v) Dermatologic effects: Acne, impaired wound healing, hirsutism, thin and fragile skin, atrophy, petechiae, and bruising

vi) Musculoskeletal: Proximal steroid myopathy (especially thigh muscles, then upper arms) and osteoporosis

vii) Infection: Increased susceptibility, especially to Candida; also may mask signs of infection (Karch, 2003)

viii) Intracranial tumors: Devastating because of their growth and spread to vital brain centers of emotion, speech, personality, vision, balance, and other neurologic functions that make patients "people" (Strickler & Lipsky-Phillips, 2000). Patients' families need to be aware of personality changes that occur and report changes to their nurse and physician.

ix) Long-term steroid use affects the patient's quality of life and self-image as a result of fluid retention, weight gain, leg weakness, insomnia, diabetes, and delayed wound healing. Restrictions on driving, employment, and recreational activities may be mandatory for patients at risk for seizures (Armstrong & Gilbert, 2000).

(7) Follow-up for cerebral edema includes symptom assessment and neuroimaging (Mendenhall & Moore-Higgs, 2001).

(8) Tools

(a) Karnofsky Performance Scale: Unidimensional measure of physical functioning (Armstrong & Gilbert, 2000)

(b) Quality-of-life assessments

i) FACT-Brain: Measures quality of life in patients undergoing treatment for brain tumors (Weitzner, Myers, Gelke, Cella, & Levin, 1995).

ii) Mini-Mental Status Evaluation: Includes orientation, registration, attention and calculation, recall, language, and level of consciousness.

b) Acute alopecia
  (1) Pathophysiology: Hair follicles and glands are radiosensitive. Radiosensitivity is due to the relatively high rate of growth (mitotic activity); thus, these follicles are more susceptible to radiation damage. Radiation causes premature conversion of hair follicle cells from the anagen to the telogen (resting phase), which results in new hairs being shed at an increased rate (Goodman, Hilderley, & Purl, 1997).
  (2) Incidence (Goodman et al., 1997)
      (a) Epilation occurs in doses as low as 5 Gy but is temporary.
      (b) Higher doses (45 Gy or greater) may produce permanent alopecia or delayed regrowth for over a year.
      (c) Alopecia occurs regionally or in patches, only in the direct path of the radiation beam.
      (d) Complete scalp hair loss occurs with whole brain RT for primary or metastatic brain cancer.
  (3) Assessment
      (a) Scalp evaluation for complications of acute side effects of brain irradiation including dry scalp, radiation dermatitis, hyperpigmentation, and alopecia (Sawaya & Bindal, 1995).
      (b) Use the ONS *Radiation Therapy Patient Care Record* (Catlin-Huth et al., 2002) and the Radiation Therapy Oncology Group (RTOG) grading system for acute and late radiation side effects.
  (4) Documentation (Catlin-Huth et al., 2002)
      (a) Skin sensation
          i) 0—No problem
          ii) 1—Pruritus
          iii) 2—Burning
          iv) 3—Painful
      (b) Radiation dermatitis
          i) 0—None
          ii) 1—Faint erythema or dry desquamation
          iii) 2—Moderate or brisk erythema or patchy moist desquamation, mostly confined to skin folds and creases or moderate edema
          iv) 3—Confluent moist desquamation > 1.5 cm in diameter and not confined to skin folds; pitting edema
          v) 4—Skin necrosis or ulceration of full thickness dermis; may include bleeding not induced by minor trauma or abrasion
      (c) Alopecia
          i) 0—Normal
          ii) 1—Mild hair loss
          iii) 2—Pronounced hair loss
  (5) Collaborative management for acute effects of alopecia (Goodman et al., 1997)
      (a) Gently wash hair with mild shampoo one to two times a week.
      (b) Use head covering to protect scalp from wind, cold, and sun.
      (c) Apply a sunscreen with an SPF 15 or more on face and scalp and cover with a shading hat.
      (d) Use water-soluble lubricant on scalp (see section IV, C—Skin Reactions).
      (e) Check behind ears in folds for moist desquamation.
      (f) Use a soft-bristle brush to reduce stress on hair shaft.
      (g) Avoid hair dyes and permanents.
  (6) Patient and family education
      (a) Instruct patient that radiation alopecia is limited to the radiotherapy portals. Inform patient that hair thinning usually begins to occur after two to three weeks of treatment (Bucholtz, 1997).
      (b) Hair regrowth takes three to six months (Bucholtz, 1997).
      (c) Hair may return a different color or consistency (Bucholtz, 1997).
      (d) Hair loss may be permanent at a radiation dose of 55 Gy (Bucholtz, 1997).
      (e) Patient education precedes initiation of RT and promotes self-care

behaviors and optimal outcomes (Goodman et al., 1997).

(f) Provide literature regarding wigs (types, where to purchase, insurance reimbursement, wig alternatives).

(g) Assistance from community-based organizations
  i) The American Cancer Society, which provides "Look Good . . . Feel Better" program—www.cancer.org
  ii) American Brain Tumor Association—www.abta.org
  iii) Brain Tumor Society—www.tbts.org
  iv) National Brain Tumor Foundation—www.braintumor.org
  v) NCI—http://cancer.gov

c) Acute radiation myelopathy
  (1) Pathophysiology: Attributed to transient demyelination caused by radiation-induced inhibition of myelin-producing oligodendroglial cells in the irradiated cord segment. Radiation induces a transient disruption of the blood–spinal cord barrier resulting in vasogenic edema, which, in turn, leads to demyelination (Levin et al., 2001).

  (2) Incidence
    (a) Radiation myelopathy may be present as transient, early delayed, or late delayed. Acute is clinically manifested by momentary electric shock-like paresthesias and numbness radiating from neck to the extremities, which is precipitated by neck flexion (Lhermitte's sign) (Pearlman & Shaw, 2000).
    (b) Radiation dose of 45 Gy in 22 fractions over five weeks is safe, with the risk of myelopathy being

less than 0.2%. Doses 57–61 Gy (1.8–2.0 Gy, five days/week) is 5%. Doses 68–73 Gy may be as high as a 50% risk (Schultheiss, Kun, Ang, & Stephens, 1995).

    (c) Early delayed myelopathy typically develops one to six months after irradiation (Pearlman & Shaw, 2000).

  (3) Assessment (Pearlman & Shaw, 2000)
    (a) Assess patient for Lhermitte's sign in early acute radiation myelopathy.
    (b) Assess CNS alteration for neuropathy (Catlin-Huth et al., 2002).

  (4) Collaborative management of acute effects of myelopathy (Pearlman & Shaw, 2000)
    (a) Instruct patient not to flex head briskly.
    (b) Instruct patient that this syndrome only lasts a few weeks and is not associated with chronic progressive myelitis (Michalski, 2004).

  (5) Patient and family education
    (a) Adequate preparatory education with sensory and procedural information will reduce the anxiety and fear of the patient with cancer who is facing life-threatening illness (Poroch, 1995).
    (b) Describe signs and symptoms of Lhermitte's sign and avoid neck flexion.
    (c) Stress temporary nature of this side effect.
    (d) Early myelopathy resolves within 6–12 months (Levin et al., 2001).

d) Late radiation myelopathy
  (1) Pathophysiology: Permanent demyelination of sensory neurons leading to permanent irreversible weakness and progressive functional loss from the radiation portal down (Levin et al., 2001)

  (2) Incidence
    (a) More severe effects in late radiation myelopathy. Generally occurs 13–29 months following RT (Michalski, 2004).
    (b) Chances increase with larger doses of radiation and larger fields of treatment.

  (3) Assessment/documentation: CNS alteration assessment for neuropathy (Catlin-Huth et al., 2002)

  (4) Collaborative management with urologist and pain management team. Per-

manent myelopathy is characterized by progressive motor weakness, paresthesias, loss of pain and temperature sensation, loss of bladder control, bowel control, and sensory and motor function loss (Michalski, 2004).

(5) Patient and family education

(a) Instruct family to maintain safe environment.

(b) Encourage physical therapy for prevention of deep vein thrombosis (DVT) and pneumonia.

(c) If necessary, instruct family member in urinary catheterization technique, bladder training, or bowel regimen.

(d) Localized spine pain or referred pain must be carefully assessed to rule out epidural spinal cord compression, an oncologic emergency. Pain can be managed, but myelopathy is not reversible (McCaffery & Pasero, 1999).

(e) Refer to support groups.

e) Acute somnolence syndrome

(1) Pathophysiology (Shaw, 2000)

(a) Radiation effects to the oligodendroglial or myelin-producing cells result in an interruption of myelin synthesis. Myelin forms a concentric sheath that surrounds the axons or nerve fibers. In the brain, this reaction produces somnolence, increased irritability, loss of appetite, and sometimes an exacerbation of tumor-associated symptoms.

(b) When these symptoms occur in children, it is called "somnolence syndrome."

(2) Incidence

(a) Early delayed transient reactions lasting several weeks to six months that do not predict subsequent injury (Michalski, 2004)

(b) In a study conducted by Faithfull (1991), 100% of patients receiving cranial irradiation reported a somnolence syndrome of excessive sleep, drowsiness, lethargy, and anorexia.

(3) Assessment (Pearlman & Shaw, 2000)

(a) Assess for subjective signs and symptoms of sleepiness, sensory changes, lethargy, ataxia, and severe fatigue.

(b) A positron emission tomography (PET) scan or magnetic resonance imaging (MRI) test may be indicated.

(c) Level of consciousness and neurologic examination may be necessary.

(4) Documentation (Catlin-Huth et al., 2002): Depressed level of consciousness

(a) 0—Normal

(b) 1—Somnolence or sedation not interfering with function

(c) 2—Somnolence or sedation interfering with function but not interfering with activities of daily living

(d) 3—Obtundation or stupor; difficult to arouse

(e) 4—Coma

(5) Collaborative management of acute effects of somnolence syndrome—Acute

(a) Decreases all aspects of patients' quality of life (Armstrong & Gilbert, 2001).

(b) Administer steroids as prescribed for acute phase.

(c) A somnolence syndrome of increased fatigue also can appear one to four months after treatment (Sawaya & Bindal, 1995).

(6) Patient and family education

(a) Patient is unable to continue with normal routine of activities of daily living. Role reversal often occurs during this time, including loss of role function within family and workplace (Faithful, 1991). Elevated distress may be observed.

(b) Worsening of neurologic symptoms and increased tumor edema may be observed.

f) Radiation necrosis—Late

(1) Pathophysiology (Shaw, 2001)

(a) Necrosis is tissue damage to the white matter of the brain or spinal cord.

(b) The underlying mechanisms of late delayed radiation reactions to control

(c) Nervous system tumors include the following.

    i) Injury to the capillary endothelium leading to the narrowing or obliteration of the arteries supplying blood to the brain or spinal cord (Shaw, 2001)

    ii) Direct damage to its tissues

(2) Incidence

(a) Seen in increased radiation doses in CNS tumors; late delayed reactions are irreversible (Shaw, 2001).

(b) Five percent incidence with doses above 55 Gy (Shaw, 2001)

(c) Onset is typically between six months and two years post-therapy (Schultheiss et al., 1995).

(3) Assessment

(a) Progression to necrosis usually is observed as a mass lesion producing increased intracranial pressure (Karim, 1995).

(b) Symptoms

    i) Visible symptoms of increased intracranial pressure (Catlin-Huth et al., 2002)

    ii) Focal clinical symptomatology (e.g., epilepsy, motor, sensory, speech disturbances) (Karim, 1995)

    iii) Severe diffuse injury may impair intellectual function causing loss of memory and confusion.

(4) Documentation

(a) Assessment parameters and common toxicity criteria according to the ONS *Radiation Therapy Patient Care Record* (CNS alteration) (Catlin-Huth et al., 2002)

(b) Diagnostic: Angiography and PET imaging may be necessary to distinguish tumor from radiation necrosis (Schultheiss et al., 1995).

(5) Collaborative management

(a) Steroids reduce capillary permeability and may temporarily reduce symptoms.

(b) No intervention currently exists to halt or reverse the late effects of RT (Karim, 1995).

(6) Patient and family education

(a) Neurologic changes in patient must be reported.

(b) Complementary therapies for radiation symptom distress should be reviewed.

    i) Therapeutic massage may decrease pain, anxiety, and symptom distress; increase relaxation; and enhance comfort and sleep (Smith, Kemp, Hemphill, & Vojir, 2002).

    ii) Other types of complementary therapies are aromatherapy and music therapy.

    iii) Support services, such as hospice consultation, may be helpful.

g) Cerebral atrophy—Late

(1) Pathophysiology

(a) Exact pathophysiology is unknown.

(b) Cerebral cortical atrophy occurs in 17%–50% of patients treated for brain tumors (Narayana & Leibel, 2004).

(c) Cerebral cortical atrophy is more severe with larger treatment volumes, higher doses, older age, and longer intervals after radiation and chemotherapy (Narayana & Leibel, 2004).

(d) Related to cranial irradiation and high-dose methotrexate, demonstrating ventricular enlargement and cerebral atrophy (Cox, 1994).

(2) Incidence (Cox, 1994)

(a) Occurs more often in patients who receive more than 30 Gy whole brain radiation.

(b) Increased incidence in pediatric patients.

(c) Begins six months to one year post-RT.

(d) High-dose methotrexate and cranial irradiation increase risk.

(3) Assessment (Cox, 1994): Clinical manifestations

(a) Cerebral changes can mimic recurrent tumor with mass effect on CT.

(b) White matter changes are well defined by MRI studies.

(c) Recognize symptoms of neurologic deterioration.

(4) Documentation

(a) Assessment parameters and common toxicity criteria according to the ONS *Radiation Therapy Patient Care Record* (CNS alteration) (Catlin-Huth et al., 2002)

(b) Diagnostic evaluation

(5) Collaborative management

(a) If communicating hydrocephalus is present, a ventriculoperitoneal shunt may be placed.

(b) Mental status evaluation (Regine, Scott, Murray, & Curran, 2001)

i) Observation and questioning of the patient with a CNS tumor. (Note behavior, affect, facial expressions, timing of answers, orientation, general simple knowledge, questions, memory, and motor function.)

ii) The Mini-Mental Status Examination is a tool used for mental status evaluation in patients with brain tumors.

iii) RTOG clinical brain studies mandate that essential baseline mental status assessments be done prior to radiation treatments. This first assessment will provide the basic knowledge of the patient's mental status. Neurocognitive morbidity is an important endpoint in RTOG cancer trials.

(6) Patient and family education

(a) Communicate importance of mental status evaluations to patient and family.

(b) Educate on the importance of safety with developing gait abnormalities.

(c) See support services for patients with brain tumors.

h) Cranial neuropathies—Late

(1) Pathophysiology (Gordon, Char, & Sagerman, 1995)

(a) Radiation optic neuropathy occurs secondary to vascular injury.

(b) Vascular damage to small blood vessels may lead to optic neuropathy.

(c) Daily fraction size is an important determinant in the development of optic neuropathy.

(d) Damage to the cochlear-vestibular nerve may cause hearing loss.

(2) Incidence (Gordon et al., 1995)

(a) Uncommon

(b) Associated with high total doses (more than 65 Gy)

(c) Increased incidence with concomitant chemotherapy and larger doses of RT

(d) Optic neuropathy occurs most often 12–18 months after RT.

(e) Optic neuropathy is a complication of stereotactic radiosurgery. A single dose of 70 Gy can lead to demyelination of a segment of the optic nerve.

(3) Assessment (Gordon et al., 1995)

(a) Optic neuropathies present as a progressive visual loss that may progress to blindness.

(b) Subjective symptom of hearing loss

(c) Suggest physical and neurologic exams, including cranial nerve testing.

(d) Recommend a consultation with ophthalmologist.

(e) Recommend a consultation for audiogram.

(4) Documentation (Catlin-Huth et al., 2002)

(a) Ocular/visual
  i) 0—Normal
  ii) 1—Mild
  iii) 2—Moderate
  iv) 3—Severe
  v) 4—Unilateral or bilateral loss of vision

(b) Middle ear/hearing
  i) 0—Normal
  ii) 1—Serous otitis without subjective decrease in hearing
  iii) 2—Serous otitis or infection requiring medical intervention; subjective decrease in hearing; rupture of tympanic membrane with discharge
  iv) 3—Otitis with discharge, mastoiditis, or conductive hearing loss
  v) 4—Necrosis of the canal soft tissue or bone

(5) Patient and family education
  (a) Written information concerning long-term side effects
  (b) Side effects and safety measures of anticoagulant therapy
  (c) Baseline audiogram
  (d) Enroll in monitoring program.

i) Endocrinopathies—Late
(1) Pathophysiology: Radiation or a combination of radiation and chemotherapy damage can cause decreased levels of hormones.
  (a) When the hypothalamic pituitary axis is in the field of radiation to the nasopharynx, a variety of neuroendocrine disturbances can occur (Sklar & Constine, 1995).
  (b) Growth hormone deficiency can occur following doses of 18 Gy (Sklar & Constine, 1995).
  (c) The Childhood Cancer Survivor Study collected data from 1,607

patients who survived their disease for five or more years. Risks of hormone deficiency were consistently elevated for those treated with radiation, surgery, and chemotherapy. Overall, 43% of cases reported one or more endocrine-related medical conditions (Gurney et al., 2003).

(2) Incidence (Sklar & Constine, 1995)
  (a) Growth hormone deficiency is one of the most common long-term endocrine consequences of radiation to the CNS in children.
  (b) Diagnosis and treatment of hypothyroidism in children is required for growth, cognition, and progression to puberty.
  (c) Growth impairment and decreased linear growth rate has been found in 50%–100% of children with brain tumors who receive cranial or craniospinal radiation. This generally occurs within the first five years after treatment.
  (d) Hypothalamic pituitary axis. RT > 24 Gy: Hypothalamic dysfunction

(3) Assessment
  (a) Hypothyroid: Cold intolerance, fatigue, constipation, decreased stamina, and weight gain
  (b) Addison's crisis: Amenorrhea, hypertension, and decreased libido
  (c) Diabetes insipidus: Polyuria, polydipsia
  (d) Retarded bone age: Growth hormone deficiency, poor linear growth
  (e) Sexual hormone deficiency or early sexual maturation
  (f) Physical examination

(4) Documentation
  (a) Growth and development adverse event: Bone growth, puberty delayed, and stature (NCI, 2003)
  (b) Emotional alteration: Coping (Catlin-Huth et al., 2002)
    i) 0—Effective
    ii) 1—Ineffective

(5) Collaborative management
  (a) Height at three- to six-month intervals to plot on standard growth charts
  (b) Hand x-ray for bone assessment (Sklar & Constine, 1995)

(c) Thyroid function tests and routine blood studies to exclude major organ dysfunction

(6) Patient and family education

(a) Parents need specific written and verbal instructions on the importance of growth hormones.

(b) Patients and their families require information about late effects of treatment. To reduce anxiety and enhance self-care, the information should include presentation, prevalence, and duration of side effects (Wengstrom & Forsberg, 1999).

References

Armstrong, T.S., & Gilbert, M.R. (2000). Metastatic brain tumors: Diagnosis, treatment, and nursing interventions. *Clinical Journal of Oncology Nursing, 4,* 5.

Armstrong, T.S., Gilbert, M.R., & Movas, B. (2001). Brain malignancies. In D.W. Bruner, G. Moore-Higgs, & M. Haas (Eds.), *Outcomes in radiation therapy: Multidisciplinary management* (pp. 137–178). Sudbury, MA: Jones and Bartlett.

Belford, K. (2000). Central nervous system cancers. In C.H. Yarbro, M.H. Frogge, M. Goodman, & S.L. Groenwald (Eds.), *Cancer nursing: Principles and practice* (5th ed., pp. 1048–1097). Sudbury, MA: Jones and Bartlett.

Bucholtz, J.D. (1997). Central nervous system tumors. In K.H. Dow, J.D. Bucholtz, R. Iwamoto, V. Fieler, & L.J. Hilderley (Eds.), *Nursing care in radiation oncology* (2nd ed., pp. 136–146). Philadelphia: Saunders.

Catlin-Huth, C., Haas, M., & Pollock, V. (2002). *Radiation therapy patient care record: A tool for documenting nursing care.* Pittsburgh, PA: Oncology Nursing Society.

Chang, D.B., Yang, P.C., Luh, K.T., Kuo, S.H., Hung, R.L. & Lee, L.N. (1992). Late survival of non-small cell lung cancer patients with brain metastases. Influence of treatment. *Chest, 101,* 1293–1297.

Costine, L.S., Williams, J.P., Morris, M., Rubin, R., & Okunieff, P. (2004). Late effects of cancer treatment. In C.A. Perez, L.W. Brady, E.C. Halperin, & R.K. Schmidt-Ullrich (Eds.), *Principles and practice of radiation oncology* (4th ed., pp. 357–365). Philadelphia: Lippincott Williams & Wilkins.

Cox, J.D. (Ed.). (1994). *Moss' radiation oncology.* St. Louis, MO: Mosby.

Cox, J.D., Stetz, J., & Pajak, T.F. (1995). Toxicity criteria of the Radiation Therapy Oncology Group and European Organization for Research and Treatment of Cancer. *International Journal of Radiation Oncology, Biology, Physics, 31,* 1341–1346.

Faithfull, S. (1991). Patients' experience following cranial radiotherapy: A study of somnolence syndrome. *Journal of Advanced Nursing, 16,* 939–946.

Flickinger, J.C., Kondziolka, D., Niranjan, A., & Lundsford, M. (2001). Results of acoustic neuroma radiosurgery: Analysis of 5 years' experience using current methods. *Journal of Neurosurgery, 94,* 1–6.

Geddes, J.F., Bhattacharjee, M.B., Savage, F., Scaravilli, F., & McLaughlin, J.E. (1992). Primary cerebral lymphoma: A study of 47 cases probed for Epstein-Barr virus genome. *Journal of Clinical Pathology, 45,* 587–590.

Gonzales, M. (1995). Classification and pathogenesis of brain tumors. In A.H. Kaye & E.R. Laws (Eds.), *Brain tumors* (pp. 31–45). New York: Churchill Livingstone.

Goodman, M., Hilderley, L.J., & Purl, S. (1997). Integumentary and mucous membrane alterations. In S.L. Groenwald, M.H. Frogge, M. Goodman, & C.H. Yarbro (Eds.), *Cancer nursing: Principles and practice* (4th ed., pp. 768–789). Sudbury, MA: Jones and Bartlett.

Gordon, K.B., Char, D.H., & Sagerman, R.H. (1995). Late effects of radiation on the eye and ocular/adnexa. *International Journal of Radiation Oncology, Biology, Physics, 31,* 1123–1139.

Gurney, J.G., Kadan-Lottic, M.S., Packer, R.J., Meglia, J.P., Sklar, C.A., Punyko, J.A., et al. (2003). Endocrine and cardiovasular late effects among adult survivors of childhood brain tumors. *Cancer, 97,* 663–673.

Jemal, A., Tiwari, R., Murray, T., Ghafoor, A., Samuels, A., Ward, E., et al. (2004). Cancer statistics, 2004. *CA: A Cancer Journal for Clinicians, 54,* 8–29.

Karch, A.M. (Ed.). (2003). *2003 Lippincott's nursing drug guide.* Philadelphia: Lippincott Williams & Wilkins.

Karim, A.B.M. (1995) Radiation therapy and radiosurgery for brain tumors. In A.H. Kaye & E.R. Laws (Eds.), *Brain tumors* (pp. 331–348). New York: Churchill Livingstone.

Kepes, J.J. (1990, September). *Review of the WHO's proposed new classification of brain tumors.* Proceedings of the XIth International Congress of Neuropathology, Japanese Society of Neuropathology, Kyoto, Japan.

Kleihues, P., & Cavenee, W.K. (2000). *Pathology and genetics of tumours of the nervous system.* Lyon, France: IARC Press.

Levin, H.A., Leibel, S.A., & Gutin, P.H. (2001). Neoplasms of the central nervous system. In V.T. DeVita, S. Hellman, & S.A. Rosenberg (Eds.), *Cancer: Principles and practice of oncology* (6th ed., pp. 461–520, 2100–2160). Philadelphia: Lippincott.

McCaffery, M., & Pasero, C. (1999). *Pain: Clinical manual.* St. Louis, MO: Mosby.

Mendenhall, W., & Moore-Higgs, G. (2001). Stereotactic radiosurgery and radiotherapy. In D.W. Bruner, G. Moore-Higgs, & M. Haas (Eds.), *Outcomes in radiation therapy: Multidisciplinary management* (pp. 89–101). Sudbury, MA: Jones and Bartlett.

Michalski, J.M. (2004). Spinal canal. In C.A. Perez, L.W. Brady, E.C. Halperin, & R.K. Schmidt-Ullrich (Eds.), *Principles and practice of radiation oncology* (4th ed., pp. 869–874). Philadelphia: Lippincott Williams & Wilkins.

Narayana, A., & Leibel, D. (2004). Primary and metastatic brain tumors in adults. In S.A. Leibel & T.L. Phillips (Eds.), *Textbook of radiation oncology,* (2nd ed., pp. 463–495). Philadelphia: Saunders.

National Cancer Institute. (2003). *Common terminology criteria for adverse events* (Version 3.0). Bethesda, MD: Author.

Pearlman, A., & Shaw, E.G, (2000). Spinal cord tumors. In L.L. Gundersen & J.E. Tepper (Eds.), *Clinical radiation oncology* (pp. 395–410). New York: Churchill Livingstone.

Poroch, D. (1995). The effect of preparatory patient education on the anxiety and satisfaction of cancer patients receiving radiation therapy. *Cancer Nursing, 18,* 206–214.

Quinn, J.A., & DeAngelis, L.M. (2000). Neurological emergencies in the cancer patient. *Seminars in Oncology, 27,* 311–321.

Regine, W.F., Scott, C., Murray, K., & Curran, W. (2001). Neurocognitive outcome in brain metastases patients treated with accelerated-fractionation vs. accelerated-hyperfractionation radiotherapy: An analysis from RTOG 91-04. *International Journal of Radiation Oncology, Biology, Physics, 51,* 711–717.

Robbins, S.L., Cotran, R.S., & Kumar, V.K. (1989). The nervous system. In J.H. Morris (Ed.), *Robbin's pathologic basis of disease* (4th ed., pp. 1385–1450). Philadelphia: Saunders.

Sawaya, R., & Bindal, R.E. (1995). Metastatic brain tumors. In A.H. Kaye & E.R. Laws (Eds.), *Brain tumors* (pp. 923–942). New York: Churchill Livingstone.

Schultheiss, T.E., Kun, L.E., Ang, K.K., & Stephens, L.C. (1995). Radiation response of the central nervous system. *International Journal of Radiation Oncology, Biology, Physics, 31,* 1093–1112.

Shapiro, W.R., Hiesiger, E.M., Cooney, G.A., Basler, G.A., Lipschutz, L.E., & Posner, J.B. (1990). Temporal effects of dexamethasone on the blood-to-brain and blood-to-tumor transport of 14C-alpha-aminoisobutyric acid in rat C6 gliomas. *Journal of Neurooncology, 8,* 197–202.

Shaw, E.G. (2000). Central nervous system tumors. In L.L. Gunderson & J.E. Tepper (Eds.), *Clinical radiation oncology* (pp. 314–354). New York: Churchill Livingstone.

Sheline, G., Wara, W., & Smith, V. (1980). Therapeutic irradiation and brain injury. *International Journal of Radiation Oncology, Biology, Physics, 9,* 1215–1228.

Sklar, C.A., & Constine, L.S. (1995). Chronic neuroendocrinological sequelae of radiation therapy. *International Journal of Radiation Oncology, Biology, Physics, 31,* 1113–1121.

Smith, M.C., Kemp, J., Hemphill, L., & Vojir, C.P. (2002). Outcomes of therapeutic massage for hospitalized cancer patients. *Image: Journal of Nursing Scholarship, 34,* 257–262.

Strickler, R., & Lipsky-Phillips, M. (2000). Astrocytomas: The clinical picture. *Clinical Journal of Oncology, 4,* 4.

Weitzner, M.A., Myers, C.A., Gelke, C.K., Cella, D.F., & Levin, V.A. (1995). The Functional Assessment of Cancer Therapy (FACT) scale. Development of a brain subscale and revalidation of the general version (FACT-G) in patients with primary brain tumors. *Cancer, 75,* 1151–1161.

Wengstrom, Y., & Forsberg, C. (1999). Justifying radiation oncology nursing practice. *Oncology Nursing Forum, 26,* 741–750.

Wrench, M., Yost, M., & Miike, R. (1999). Adult glioma in relation to residential power frequency electromagnetic field exposures in the San Francisco Bay area. *Epidemiology, 10,* 523.

B. Head and neck
   1. Stomatitis/mucositis/pharyngitis/esophagitis (upper one-third esophagus)
      a) Pathophysiology: Stomatitis/mucositis is the inflammation and ulceration of the oral mucosa (Biron et al., 2000). Radiotherapy in the head and neck field causes a temporary reduction in epithelial cell renewal, thereby impacting the division of dividing cells in the oral basal epithelium resulting in painful and debilitating atrophy and ulcerations. Four stages include
         (1) Inflammatory or vascular phase—Asymptomatic redness and erythema
         (2) Epithelial phase—Solitary, white desquamative patches that are slightly painful
         (3) Ulcerative or bacteriologic phase—Large contiguous acutely painful lesions with associated dysphagia and decreased oral intake
         (4) Healing phase—Renewal of epithelial proliferation (Berger & Kilroy, 2001; Biron et al., 2000; Sonis, 1989).
      b) Incidence and risk factors
         (1) Incidence is radiation dose dependent and exacerbated by concurrent chemotherapy. Patients receiving concurrent treatment may develop symptoms after one week, and the healing phase may not be resolved until one to three months after treatment completion (Haas & Kuehn, 2001).
         (2) Risk factors that may lead to worsening of symptoms include smoking and alcohol consumption; damage from ill-fitting dental prosthesis; periodontal disease; salivary gland dysfunction; immunosuppression; and bacterial, viral, or fungal infection (Berger & Kilroy, 2001).
      c) Assessment
         (1) Oral assessment for baseline and a referral to dentistry should occur before treatment begins. Poor oral hygiene and poor dentition should be addressed before initiation of treatment to prevent worsening of problems during and after treatment.
         (2) Oral assessment and intervention should occur weekly or more frequently if patient complains of mouth tenderness, pain, or dysphagia. Weekly weights are included in assessment.
         (3) Physical examination: Examine lips, tongue, gingiva, and oral cavity for color, moisture, integrity, and presence of stomatitis or infection (see Table 8).
         (4) Assess whether patient has tracheostomy; metal tracheostomy cannula must be removed during treatment if within the treatment field.
      d) Documentation (Catlin-Huth, Haas, & Pollock, 2002)
         (1) Mucositis due to radiation
            (a) 0—None
            (b) 1—Erythema of the mucosa
            (c) 2—Patchy pseudomembranous reaction (patches generally ≤ 1.5 cm in diameter and noncontiguous)
            (d) 3—Confluent pseudomembranous reaction (contiguous patches generally > 1.5 cm in diameter)

Table 8. Oral Assessment Guide

Category	Tools for Assessment	Methods of Measurement	Numerical and Descriptive Ratings 1	2	3
Voice	Auditory	Converse with patient.	Normal	Deeper or raspy	Difficulty talking or painful
Swallow	Observation	Ask patient to swallow. To test gag reflex, gently place tongue blade on back of tongue and depress.	Normal swallow	Some pain on swallow	Unable to swallow
Lips	Visual/palpatory	Observe and feel tissue.	Smooth, pink, and moist	Dry or cracked	Ulcerated or bleeding
Tongue	Visual/palpatory	Feel and observe appearance of tissue.	Pink, moist, and papillae present	Coated or loss of papillae with a shiny appearance with or without redness	Blistered or cracked
Saliva	Tongue blade	Insert blade into mouth, touching the center of the tongue and the floor of the mouth.	Watery	Thick or ropey	Absent
Mucous membranes	Visual	Observe appearance of tissue.	Pink and moist	Reddened or coated (increased whiteness without ulcerations)	Ulcerations with or without bleeding
Gingiva	Tongue blade and visual	Gently press tissue with tip of blade.	Pink, stippled, and firm	Edematous with or without redness	Spontaneous bleeding or bleeding with pressure
Teeth or dentures (or denture-bearing area)	Visual	Observe appearance of teeth or denture-bearing area.	Clean and no debris	Plaque or debris in localized areas (between teeth if present)	Plaque or debris generalized along gum line or denture-bearing area

Note. Reprinted with permission of June Eilers, RN, MSN, CS, University of Nebraska Medical Center, Omaha, NE.

      (e) 4—Necrosis or deep ulceration; may include bleeding not induced by minor trauma or abrasion
  (2) Thrush (Catlin-Huth et al., 2002)
      (a) 0—Absent
      (b) 1—Present
  (3) Pharynx and esophagus (Catlin-Huth et al., 2002)
      (a) 0—No change over baseline
      (b) 1—Mild dysphagia or odynophagia; may require topical anesthetic or non-narcotic analgesic; may require soft diet

      (c) 2—Moderate dysphagia or odynophagia; may require narcotic analgesics; may require puree or liquid diet
      (d) 3—Severe dysphagia or odynophagia with dehydration or weight loss (> 15% from pretreatment baseline) requiring gastric feeding tube, IV fluids, or hyperalimentation
      (e) 4—Complete obstruction, ulceration, perforation, or fistula
  (4) Pain location and intensity (Catlin-Huth et al., 2002)

(a) Document location of pain.

(b) Record patient's subjective rating of degree of pain, with ratings ranging from 0 (no pain) to 10 (severe pain).

(5) Pain intervention (Catlin-Huth et al., 2002)

(a) 0—None

(b) 1—Over-the-counter medications

(c) 2—NSAIDs or nonopioids

(d) 3—Opioids

(e) 4—Adjuvant medications (e.g., neuroleptics)

(f) 5—Complementary and/or alternative methods

(6) Effectiveness of pain intervention (Catlin-Huth et al., 2002)

(a) 0—No relief

(b) 1—Pain relieved 25%

(c) 2—Pain relieved 50%

(d) 3—Pain relieved 75%

(e) 4—Pain relieved 100%

e) Collaborative management of stomatitis/mucositis/pharyngitis/esophagitis

(1) Prevention

(a) Shih, Miaskowski, Dodd, Stotts, and MacPhail (2002) reviewed more then 50 published papers aimed at prevention, palliation, or reduction of RT–induced oral mucositis. Studies involving antimicrobial, coating, and anti-inflammatory agents did not demonstrate decreased severity of radiation-induced oral mucositis. Seven studies that included the use of the cytokine granulocyte macrophage–colony-stimulating factor (GM-CSF) in mouthwashes concluded they may facilitate healing.

(b) Recommendations for optimal care include (Haas & Kuehn, 2001; Shih et al., 2002; Symonds, 1998)

i) Schedule dental evaluation for optimal care of existing teeth or necessary dental extraction before radiation begins. Fluoride treatments initiated and continued post-treatment.

ii) Avoid irritants such as alcohol, cigarettes, alcohol-based mouthwashes, spicy foods, and rough toothbrushes.

iii) Brush teeth and prosthetics with soft toothbrush after each meal and at bedtime.

iv) Use saline mouth rinses, lasting one to two minutes, four to six times daily (see section IV, G—Nutrition).

v) Maintain hydration and a diet high in calories and protein. Nutrition supplemental drinks (Ensure® [Ross Laboratories]), Carnation Instant Breakfast® [Nestle, Vevey, Switzerland]) are encouraged.

(2) Intervention when mouth and throat tenderness occurs (Biron et al., 2000; Haas & Kuehn, 2001; Shih et al., 2002)

(a) Follow recommendations for optimal care (see section (1) *(b)* above).

(b) Perform more frequent mouth assessments to evaluate possible infection. Bacterial and fungal infections should be treated with appropriate medications.

(c) Assess weight and hydration biweekly. Feeding tube may be necessary if aspiration, hydration, or rapid weight loss are a concern.

(d) Minimize use of dentures.

(e) Use a topical anesthetic; swish and spit or swish and swallow are safe recommendations for patients who do not aspirate. When lesions are confined to a limited area, application of anesthetic may be applied with a cotton swab.

(f) Oral pain medication or pain medication put through a feeding tube should be used to relieve discomfort and pain.

(g) Recommendation should be made based on patient's ability to swallow, compatibility with other medications, and level of pain.

Patients with neutropenia should be warned that anti-inflammatory medication may mask a fever. Suggestions for mild pain include nonopioid analgesics or NSAIDs. Moderate pain can be controlled with medications that include hydrocodone or codeine. Severe pain should be managed with narcotics that include a fentanyl transdermal system (fentanyl), hydromorphone, oxycodone hydrochloride, or morphine sulfate elixir (see section IV, D—Pain).

f) Patient and family education
   (1) Instruct patient and family about oral care regimen and need for routine follow-up with a dentist.
   (2) Instruct patient on oral assessment and symptoms to monitor and report to the healthcare provider.

2. Dysphagia
   a) Pathophysiology: Dysphagia is defined as difficulty in eating (Camp-Sorrell, 2004). Adults with head and neck cancer experience dysphagia when one or more of the following occur (Camp-Sorrell; Witt, 1999).
      (1) Tumor interrupts or damages the co-ordinated process needed to swallow.
      (2) Surgical resection impedes the swallowing process.
      (3) Stomatitis/esophagitis—acute effect
      (4) Radiation fibrosis—late effect
   b) Incidence and risk factors
      (1) Incidence is dependent upon tumor size, tumor location, radiation dose, which will be exacerbated by concurrent chemotherapy, and late effect of radiation fibrosis.
         (a) Tumor size and location—Highest risk are patients with T3 and T4 lesions. Locations of highest risk are the oral cavity, pharynx, and larynx. Pauloski et al. (2000) studied 352 patients with head and neck cancer; 41% complained of dysphagia before treatment began.
         (b) Acute side effect from radiation—Concomitant patients may experience dysphagia after one week of treatment; confluent reactions frequently occur beyond 50 Gy (Abitbol, Friedland, Lewin, Rodrigues, & Mishra, 1999).
         (c) Radiation fibrosis—Kendall, McKenzie, Leonard, and Jones (1998) reported on patients one year post-radiation. All 20 patients functioned adequately in terms of nutrition requirements, but no one had a completely normal swallowing study. Tissue fibrosis decreased mobility in vital swallowing structures and altered ability to swallow. Vokes et al. (2003) reported in a concomitant study of patients with T3/T4 lesions that 14 of 57 patients had feeding tubes at 12 months; 3 were able to eat and had tubes removed over the next 6 months; 6 kept their tube to supplement their eating; and 5 were unable to take anything by mouth.
      (2) Risk factors—Tumor size and location, treatment modality, lack of therapeutic management of dysphagia before, during, and after treatment (Camp-Sorrell, 2004; Witt, 1999)
   c) Assessment
      (1) Perform oral assessment for baseline and evaluate range of motion of lips, tongue, and jaw. Assess cough reflex and gag reflex.
      (2) Refer patient to speech pathologist for swallowing evaluation. The radiographic swallowing evaluation visualizes the timing of the swallowing phases and extent of aspiration. Make a recommendation for a gastrostomy tube if the patient aspirates.
      (3) Nutritional assessment—Evaluate laboratory values and physical indications of dehydration and malnutrition, and question patient on intake.
      (4) Pain assessment—Painful swallowing may be related to infection, tumor

infiltration, or inflammation from radiation.

    (5) Swallowing assessment (nonradiologic), pain assessment, and weight should be evaluated weekly during treatment.

  d) Documentation

    (1) Pharynx and esophagus (Catlin-Huth et al., 2002)

      (a) 0—No change over baseline

      (b) 1—Mild dysphagia or odynophagia; may require topical anesthetic or non-narcotic analgesic; may require soft diet.

      (c) 2—Moderate dysphagia or odynophagia; may require narcotic analgesics; may require puree or liquid diet.

      (d) 3—Severe dysphagia or odynophagia with dehydration or weight loss (15% from pretreatment baseline) requiring gastric feeding tube, IV fluids, or hyperalimentation.

      (e) 4—Complete obstruction, ulceration, perforation, or fistula

    (2) Pain location and intensity (Catlin-Huth et al., 2002)

      (a) Document location of pain.

      (b) Record patient's subjective rating of degree of pain, with ratings ranging from 0 (no pain) to 10 (severe pain).

    (3) Pain intervention (Catlin-Huth et al., 2002)

      (a) 0—None

      (b) 1—Over-the-counter medications

      (c) 2—NSAIDs or nonopioids

      (d) 3—Opioids

      (e) 4—Adjuvant medications (e.g., neuroleptics)

      (f) 5—Complementary and/or alternative methods

    (4) Effectiveness of pain interventions (Catlin-Huth et al., 2002)

      (a) 0—No relief

      (b) 1—Pain relieved 25%

      (c) 2—Pain relieved 50%

      (d) 3—Pain relieved 75%

      (e) 4—Pain relieved 100%

    (5) Thrush (Catlin-Huth et al., 2002)

      (a) 0—Absent

      (b) 1—Present

  e) Collaborative management of dysphagia

    (1) Acute side effects—Goal is to optimize hydration, nutrition, comfort, and swallowing safety.

      (a) Pain management—Treatment of painful oral lesions, xerostomia, and infection will improve swallowing.

      (b) Swallowing therapy and direct swallowing exercises—Fibrosis after radiation occurs (Kendall et al., 1998). Presently, no studies have proven early intervention decreases fibrosis. Intervention with swallowing exercises are encouraged to strengthen musculature, increase range of motion, and develop compensatory strategies (Barbour, 1999).

      (c) Gastrostomy tube should be placed if aspiration occurs or when patient cannot maintain hydration and nutrition.

      (d) Assess patient biweekly or if new complaints emerge during manifestation of acute side effects.

    (2) Long-term risk for dysphagia—Goal is to optimize swallowing technique. Most patients post-radiotherapy will be able to maintain nutrition without a gastrostomy tube, but the risk for problems with fibrosis exists (Kendall et al., 1998; Vokes et al., 2003). Optimal swallowing interventions include the following.

      (a) Good oral hygiene—Evaluate for good dentition and proper fitting dentures or prosthesis; encourage comfort measures for xerostomia, meticulous oral hygiene, and fluoride treatments; promote and encourage good nutrition.

      (b) Evaluation by swallowing pathologist—Patients with post-treatment dysphagia should be evaluated annually. Evaluation may detect specific problems with

dysphagia and encourage preventive measures for safe eating and decreasing fibrosis.

(c) Long-term follow-up should include an assessment for changes in nutrition intake, assessment for symptoms of aspiration, and assessment for compliance with exercises and/or swallowing techniques recommended by the swallowing pathologist. A radiographic swallowing study and follow-up with the swallowing pathologist should be ordered when changes in nutrition or complaint of dysphagia are noted.

f) Patient and family education

(1) Instruct patient and family on maintaining good nutrition, managing dysphagia, and the need for follow-up with oncologist and swallowing pathologist.

(2) Instruct patient on symptoms of dysphagia/aspiration and which symptoms to monitor and report to the healthcare provider.

3. Xerostomia

a) Pathophysiology: Xerostomia is the subjective complaint of a dry mouth, correlated with objective salivary gland dysfunction (Guchelaar, Vermes, & Meerwaldt, 1997). Salivary gland tissue is acutely radiosensitive. When major salivary glands are in the treatment field, a 50%–60% decrease in saliva flow occurs the first week (Guchelaar et al., 1997).

(1) The loss of salivary parenchyma is the most probable cause of decreased saliva. Sodium and chloride levels of saliva rise, suggesting that reabsorption is defective. Salivary bicarbonate is decreased, resulting in a more acidic saliva (Guchelaar et al., 1997).

(2) When saliva production decreases, saliva changes from a thin to thick consistency.

(3) Thick, acidic saliva causes food and bacteria to adhere to teeth, resulting in plaque formation. This altered mouth environment leads to periodontal disease and altered quality of life issues (Iwamoto, 1999).

b) Incidence and risk factors

(1) Radiation-induced xerostomia is affected by the radiation field, dose, use of IMRT, concomitant chemotherapy, and use of a radioprotectant. Most patients do not return to their pretreatment level of saliva production (Chao et al., 2001; Schuchter, 2002).

(2) Xerostomia is exacerbated by surgical excision of the salivary gland, oral infections of the mouth, use of medications that cause xerostomia (anticholinergics, antidepressants, antihistamines, and antispasmotics), and a climate of low humidity (Maher, 2004).

c) Assessment

(1) Clinical manifestations: Patient may complain of pain, thick saliva, or dryness (Maher, 2004).

(2) Quality of life: Address how the xerostomia is affecting their ability to swallow, eat, taste, speak, and sleep (Haas & Kuehn, 2001). Intimacy may be affected secondary to decreased lubrication when kissing.

(3) Physical examination

(a) Inspect the oral cavity. The mouth may appear dry with furrowing of the tongue. Debris may adhere to the surface. Oral secretions may be thick, ropey, or absent. Assess for signs of infection or irritation from dentures or prosthesis (Maher, 2004).

(b) Monitor weight. Weight loss may occur because of difficulty eating or swallowing.

d) Documentation: Salivary gland changes (Catlin-Huth et al., 2002)

(1) 0—None

(2) 1—Slightly thickened saliva; may have slightly altered taste; additional fluids may be required.

(3) 2—Thick, ropey, sticky saliva; markedly altered taste; alterations in diet required.

(4) 3—

(5) 4—Acute salivary necrosis

e) Collaborative management of xerostomia

(1) Prevention

(a) IMRT—When a radiation facility is able to treat patients with head and neck cancer with IMRT, the incidence of xerostomia can be significantly reduced. Chao et al. (2001) reviewed 430 patients who received radiation for oropharynx cancer. Conclusion: Patients treated without IMRT, 60%–75%, experienced grade II or higher chronic xerostomia. Oropharynx radiation treatments using IMRT, 17%–30%, had chronic xerostomia of grade II or higher.

(b) Radiotherapy protectant—Brizel et al. (2000) reported a randomized study of 315 patients, half of whom received radiation only and half of whom received radiation and amifostine. At one-year follow-up, chronic xerostomia occurred in 34% of patients who received amifostine versus 57% in those who did not receive amifostine (see section IX, B—Radioprotectors).

(c) Pilocarpine is a cholinergic drug that acts at the level of receptors that have the potential to increase saliva from residual salivary glands. Guchelaar el al. (1997) reported it to be effective in increasing salivary flow and reducing the symptom of xerostomia. It should be used with caution in patients with other comorbidities, and if ineffective after several months, the drug should be discontinued.

(2) Acupuncture for chronic xerostomia—Johnstone, Niemtzow, and Riffenburgh (2002) reported a 68% response rate, and Blom, Dawidson, Fernberg, Johnson, and Angmar-Mansson (1996) reported that many patients experienced thinner saliva and improved taste. Both studies delivered acupuncture using different techniques. Blom and Lunderberg (2000) concluded that 24 acupuncture treatments resulted in improvement up to six months; patients who continued with acupuncture, at three-year follow-up, maintained improvement.

(3) Therapeutic self-care measures (Maher, 2004)

(a) Take frequent sips of water.

(b) Perform mouth care before and after meals and at bedtime to refresh the mouth and make eating more comfortable.

(c) Avoid mouthwashes with alcohol. Normal saline mouth rinse is recommended.

(d) Soft, moist foods are easier to consume. Avoid dry and sticky foods.

(e) Commercial artificial saliva substitutes and lubricants may provide relief.

(f) Add humidity to environment, especially the bedroom.

(g) Use of sugar-free hard candy and gum may increase saliva production.

(h) Cigarette smoking and alcohol consumption will enhance xerostomia. Educate patient about cessation and seeking support for addiction.

(i) Recommendations, without evidence, include papaya juice (liquefies thick saliva), rinse and expectorate solution of meat tenderizer and water (dissolves thick saliva), and smear olive oil on tongue before bedtime.

(4) Therapeutic measures involving a dentist (Maher, 2004)

(a) Fluoride treatments are a lifelong recommendation for prevention of tooth decay. The dentist may provide fluoride trays.

(b) Evaluate dentures/prosthesis. If irritation is problematic, refer to dentistry and limit use.

(c) Frequent follow-up (three to four times per year) with dentistry for optimal dental health

f) Patient and family education
  (1) Teach family about xerostomia and how to alleviate dryness and prevent injury to fragile mucosa.
  (2) Instruct patient and family that xerostomia may be a permanent side effect, and meticulous care is a lifelong recommendation.

4. Taste changes
  a) Pathophysiology: Taste changes are defined as a reduction in taste sensitivity (hypogeusia), an absence of taste sensation (ageusia), or a distortion of normal taste (dysgeusia). Radiotherapy to the head and neck field results in taste changes from a direct pathologic effect of radiation on taste buds. There is a reduction in the number of buds on the tongue, reduction in the number of cells per bud, and damage to the microvilli of the taste cells (Ripamonti et al., 1998).
  b) Incidence and risk factors
    (1) Taste changes are radiation dose dependent. Changes are not noticed until radiation doses of 20 Gy have been administered, and a dose of 60 Gy causes a loss of taste in more than 90% of patients. Alterations to the taste of salty and bitter foods are the most pronounced, whereas the taste of sweet is least affected. Loss of taste is usually temporary but can last two to six months after treatment completion (Haas & Kuehn, 2001; Harris, 2000; Ripamonti et al., 1998).
    (2) Risk factors that may lead to worsening of symptoms include concomitant chemotherapy, direct effect of the tumor itself, oral infection, antibiotic therapy, or surgery (Tait, 1999).
  c) Assessment
    (1) Clinical manifestations
      (a) Patient reports taste changes.
      (b) Assess the type of taste change experienced. Can patient taste sweet, salty, sour, and bitter?
      (c) Note foods that are avoided or not eaten.
    (2) Physical examination
      (a) Monitor weight.
      (b) Examine mouth.
  d) Documentation: Taste disturbances (Catlin-Huth et al., 2002)
    (1) 0—Normal
    (2) 1—Slightly altered
    (3) 2—Markedly altered
  e) Collaborative management of taste changes

    (1) Intervention with zinc sulfate
      (a) Ripamonti et al. (1998) conducted a randomized study with zinc sulfate tablets or placebo with patients receiving radiation for head and neck cancer.
      (b) Zinc sulfate administration slowed down the worsening and accelerated the improvement of taste acuity in a clinically and statistically relevant way for some of the taste qualities.
    (2) Therapeutic measures from the American Cancer Society (2002) include
      (a) Rinse mouth with tea, ginger ale, salt water, or water with baking soda before eating to help clear the taste buds.
      (b) Flavor foods with onion, garlic, mustard, and herbs. If stomatitis is resolved, may use ketchup, barbecue sauce, citrus fruits, vinegar, and chili powder.
      (c) Increase the sugar in foods to increase their pleasant taste and decrease salty, bitter, or acid tastes.
      (d) Lemon drops, mints, or gum may help rid unpleasant tastes that linger after eating.
      (e) Serve foods cold or at room temperature. This can decrease the foods' tastes and smells, making them easier to tolerate.
      (f) Freeze and eat foods such as cantaloupe, grapes, oranges, and watermelon.
      (g) Fresh vegetables may be more appealing than canned or frozen.
  f) Patient and family education
    (1) Instruct patient and family about taste changes, when and how long they may last.

(2) Teach patient and family measures on how to cope with taste changes.
  (a) Explain that taste changes may be long-lasting. Return of taste is individualized.
  (b) Nutritional intake should be monitored to prevent weight loss.
5. Laryngitis—Changes in voice quality
  a) Pathophysiology: Laryngitis is defined as an inflammation of the larynx resulting in changes in voice quality. RT for head and neck cancer often includes the larynx in the field of treatment. Larynx cartilage becomes edematous, leading to impaired mobility of the vocal cords, resulting in temporary hoarseness (Haas & Kuehn, 2001).
  b) Incidence and risk factors
    (1) Incidence for laryngitis is variable and can be influenced by concomitant chemotherapy. Verdonck-de-Leeuw et al. (1999) demonstrated that it may be influenced by total dose and delivery. Post-treatment voice was better in patients treated with 60 Gy in 25 fractions versus 60 Gy in 30 fractions.
    (2) Risk factors include tumor location (patients with larynx cancer often present with hoarseness), initial biopsy procedure, smoking, and age. Verdonck-de-Leeuw et al. (1999) demonstrated that the increasing age of the speaker increased the nonvibratory portion of the vocal cord.
  c) Assessment
    (1) Clinical manifestations—Note voice quality before, during, and after treatment. Assess level of hoarseness.
    (2) Physical examination—Indirect laryngoscopy reveals vocal cord edema, erythema, and paralysis.
  d) Documentation: Voice changes/stridor/larynx (Catlin-Huth et al., 2002)

(1) 0—Normal
(2) 1—Mild or intermittent hoarseness
(3) 2—Persistent hoarseness but able to vocalize; may have mild to moderate edema.
(4) 3—Whispered speech, not able to vocalize; may have marked edema.
(5) 4—Marked dyspnea/stridor requiring tracheostomy or intubation
  e) Collaborative management
    (1) Avoid straining the voice to minimize irritation to the vocal cords.
    (2) Avoid use of alcohol, tobacco, and spicy and acidic foods.
    (3) Warm saline gargle can be soothing.
    (4) Consult pain management if needed.
    (5) Occasionally, steroids or alpha-adrenergic agents may become necessary if edema becomes severe. In rare instances, a tracheostomy is necessary because of airway compromise (Haas & Kuehn, 2001).
  f) Patient and family education
    (1) Instruct patient and family on measures to preserve voice and soothe throat.
    (2) Instruct patient and family regarding symptoms of airway obstruction and how to get emergency care.
6. Hearing changes
  a) Pathophysiology: Hearing changes are defined as an altered perception in the ability to hear. Decreased hearing occurs when the auditory structures are in the radiation treatment field, resulting in the loss of hearing on the affected side (Haas & Kuehn, 2001).
  b) Incidence and risk factors
    (1) The incidence is rare. Treatment for nasopharynx cancer or skin cancer of the ear may cause hearing loss.
    (2) The main risk factor is having the middle ear in the treatment field. Patients should be evaluated for baseline hearing loss and hardened cerumen (Haas & Kuehn, 2001).
  c) Assessment (Andresen et al., 1998)
    (1) Clinical manifestations: Decreased hearing acuity is reported.
    (2) Physical examination
      (a) Inspect the ear canal and, using an otoscope, note the presence of ear wax and debris. A tuning fork may be used to assess for air and bone conduction.
      (b) The tympanic membrane should appear opalescent; if the mem-

brane appears bulging, erythematous, or punctured or if drainage or blood is present, an otolaryngologist needs to perform a further evaluation.

   d) Documentation of hearing changes (Bruner, Bucholtz, Iwamoto, & Strohl, 1998)

     (1) 0—None

     (2) 1—Mild tinnitus; slightly reduced hearing

     (3) 2—Moderate tinnitus; moderately reduced hearing

     (4) 3—Hearing loss interfering with function but correctable with hearing aid and/or medications

     (5) 4—Complete hearing loss

   e) Collaborative management

     (1) Administer pseudoephedrine, as directed, if fluid has accumulated in the middle ear.

     (2) Administer antibiotics, as directed, for ear infections.

     (3) Arrange for immediate evaluation with an otolaryngologist if any sudden, acute hearing loss occurs.

     (4) Arrange for removal of cerumen by trained staff in otolaryngology.

   f) Patient and family education

     (1) Instruct patient and family to monitor for hearing changes.

     (2) Advise patient to report any sudden, acute changes in hearing immediately.

7. Osteoradionecrosis (ORN)

   a) Pathophysiology: ORN is the decrease in bone density caused from radiation-induced cellular injury. Occurrence is predominantly in the mandible. Aitasalo, Niinikoski, Grenman, and Virolainen (1998) described mandibular radionecrosis as the result of radiation-induced obliteration of the alveolar artery, leading to necrosis of the bone.

   b) Incidence and risk factors

     (1) Incidence of mandibular osteoradionecrosis has varied widely in the literature, from 0.4%–56% (Jereczek-Fossa & Orecchia, 2002).

     (2) Numerous factors that may lead to ORN are total radiotherapy dose, field and fraction size, and volume of mandible treated to a high dose.

     (3) Risk factors for ORN include poor oral hygiene, alcohol and tobacco use, bone inflammation, poor fitting oral/dental prosthesis, proximity of tumor to bone, and dental extractions after radiotherapy (Jereczek-Fossa & Orecchia, 2002).

   c) Assessment

     (1) Evaluate risk factors.

     (2) Clinical manifestations

       (a) Oral, jaw, or facial pain

       (b) Mandibular fracture

     (3) Physical examination

       (a) Assess oral cavity, especially the condition of the teeth and buccal mucosa.

       (b) Assess for infection, nonhealing wounds, and condition of mandible.

   d) Documentation (Catlin-Huth et al., 2002)

     (1) Pain location and intensity

       (a) Document location of pain.

       (b) Record patient's subjective rating of degree of pain, with ratings ranging from 0 (no pain) to 10 (severe pain).

     (2) Pain intervention

       (a) 0—None

       (b) 1—Over-the-counter medications

       (c) 2—NSAIDs or nonopioids

       (d) 3—Opioids

       (e) 4—Adjuvant medications (e.g., neuroleptics)

       (f) 5—Complementary and/or alternative methods

     (3) Effectiveness of pain interventions

       (a) 0—No relief

       (b) 1—Pain relieved 25%

       (c) 2—Pain relieved 50%

       (d) 3—Pain relieved 75%

       (e) 4—Pain relieved 100%

   e) Collaborative management of ORN (acute and long-term)

     (1) Prevention

       (a) Consult with dentistry prior to radiation to optimize oral health and repair poor-fitting oral/dental prosthesis.

(b) Administer antibiotics as prescribed for oral infections and prior to extractions.

(c) Continue meticulous oral care and use of fluoride to prevent dental caries.

(d) Instruct patient to minimize oral irritants

(e) Maintain good nutritional status.

(2) Intervention when ORN occurs

(a) Conservative modalities include saline irrigations, antibiotics during infectious periods, and topically applied antiseptics (Jereczek-Fossa & Orecchia, 2002).

(b) When conservative measures are not effective, intervention to remove loosened bone elements and treatment with hyperbaric oxygen is effective. Radical surgery is reserved for persistent ORN.

(c) Successful surgery includes using hyperbaric oxygen pre- and postoperatively and resection of the mandible with reconstruction, often using the tibia (Aitasalo et al., 1998; Jereczek-Fossa & Orecchia, 2002).

f) Patient and family education

(1) Instruct patient and family about ORN, including risk factors, signs and symptoms, and measures of prevention.

(2) Instruct patient and family to continue meticulous mouth care and routine evaluations by dentistry.

8. Trismus

a) Pathophysiology: Trismus is defined as tonic contractions of the pterygoid muscles in the mouth. Radiation to temporomandibular joint and pterygoid muscle may result in fibrosis, causing trismus. Mandibular dysfunction appears to worsen with increased doses of radiation to the pterygoid muscle (Goldstein, Maxymiw, Cummings, & Woods, 1999).

b) Incidence and risk factors

(1) Patients with radiation to pterygoid muscle and temporomandibular joint are at risk for trismus. Patients with severe trismus may open the mouth no more then a few millimeters (Goldstein et al., 1999).

(2) Risk increases in patients who had previous mouth and neck surgery and/or in patients who do not perform mouth exercises.

c) Assessment

(1) Clinical manifestations

(a) Patient reports difficulty opening mouth.

(b) Patient reports difficulty chewing.

(2) Physical examination: Ability to open mouth is limited.

d) Documentation

(1) Assessment for trismus is performed by measuring the amount of millimeters a patient can open the mouth.

(2) Effectiveness of intervention for trismus is documented by recording the changes in number of millimeters a patient can open the mouth. Patients' comments regarding ability to chew are a measurement of treatment effectiveness.

e) Collaborative management of trismus

(1) Prevention: Encourage patient to exercise mouth regularly with chewing exercises to prevent fibrosis (Haas & Kuehn, 2001).

(2) Interventions when trismus occurs

(a) Consult with a physical therapist and speech therapist for evaluation of a supplemental device to expand movement. Therabite® (Atos Medical Corporation, Milwaukee, WI) and E-Z Flex® (Fluid Motion Biotechnologies, Columbia, New York) are two recommendations. Buchbinder, Currivan, Kaplan, and Urken (1993) reported improvement with the Therabite system as compared to unassisted exercise and exercise with tongue blades. E-Z Flex is a newer device with no comparison data in the literature. E-Z Flex is based on a hydraulic approach to mobilization but does not apply the same amount of force to the jaw as Therabite.

(b) Encourage the intake of nutritional supplements while patient has trismus.

f) Patient and family education

(1) Inform patient and family regarding risks for trismus and to report changes in mouth mobility.

(2) Instruct patient and family about mouth and chewing exercises to prevent fibrosis.

9. Skin reactions (see section IV, C—Skin Reactions)

References

Abitbol, A., Friedland, J., Lewin, A., Rodrigues, M., & Mishra, V. (1999). Radiation therapy in oncologic management with special emphasis on head and neck carcinoma. In P. Sullivan & A. Guilford (Eds.), *Swallowing intervention in oncology* (pp. 47–62). San Diego, CA: Singular.

Aitasalo, K., Niinikoski, J., Grenman, R., & Virolainen, E. (1998). A modified protocol for early treatment of osteomyelitis and osteoradionecrosis of the mandible. *Head and Neck, 20,* 411–417.

American Cancer Society. (2002). *Nutrition for the person with cancer.* Atlanta, GA: Author.

Andressen, H., Cyr, M., Guadagnini, J., Hickey, M., Higgins, T., Huntoon, M., et al. (1998). General history, risk factors, and normal physical assessment. In L. Harris & M. Huntoon (Eds.), *Core curriculum for otorhinolaryngology and head-neck nursing* (pp. 31–61). New Smyma Beach, FL: Society of Otorhinolaryngology and Head-Neck Nurses.

Berger, A., & Kilroy, T. (2001). Oral complications. In V.T. DeVita, S. Hellman, & S.A. Rosenberg (Eds.), *Cancer: Principles and practice of oncology* (6th ed., pp. 2881–2893). Philadelphia: Lippincott Williams & Wilkins.

Biron, P., Sebban, C., Gourmet, R., Chvetzoff, G., Philip, I., & Blay, J.Y. (2000). Research controversies in management of oral mucositis. *Supportive Care in Cancer, 8,* 68–71.

Blom, M., Dawidson, I., Fernberg, J., Johnson, G., & Angmar-Mansson, B. (1996). Acupuncture treatment of patients with radiation-induced xerostomia. *European Journal of Oral Cancer, 32B*(3), 182–190.

Blom, M., & Lunderberg, T. (2000). Long-term follow-up of patients treated with acupuncture for xerostomia and the influence of additional treatment. *Oral Diseases, 6,* 15–24.

Brizel, D.M., Wasserman, T., Henke, M., Strnad, V., Rudat, V., Monnier, A., et al. (2000). Phase III randomized trial of amifostine as a radioprotector in head and neck cancer. *Journal of Clinical Oncology, 18,* 3339–3345.

Bruner, D.W., Bucholtz, J.D., Iwamoto, R., & Strohl, R. (Eds.). (1998). *Manual for radiation oncology nursing practice and education.* Pittsburgh, PA: Oncology Nursing Society.

Buchbinder, D., Currivan, R.B., Kaplan, A.J., & Urken, M.L. (1993). Mobilization regimens for the prevention of jaw hypomobility in radiated patient: A comparison of three techniques. *Journal of Oral and Maxillofacial Surgery, 51,* 863–867.

Camp-Sorrell, D. (2004). Dysphagia. In C.H. Yarbo, M.H. Frogge, & M. Goodman (Eds.), *Cancer symptom management* (3rd ed., pp. 168–178). Sudbury, MA: Jones and Bartlett.

Catlin-Huth, C., Haas, M., & Pollock, V. (2002). *Radiation therapy patient care record: A tool for documenting nursing care.* Pittsburgh, PA: Oncology Nursing Society.

Chao, K.S., Majhail, N., Huang, C., Simpson, J., Perez, C., Haughey, B., et al. (2001). Intensity-modulated radiation therapy reduces late salivary toxicity without compromising tumor control in patients with oropharyngeal carcinoma: A comparison with conventional techniques. *Radiotherapy and Oncology, 61,* 275–280.

Goldstein, M., Maxymiw, W.G., Cummings, B.J., & Woods, R.E. (1999). The effects of antitumor irradiation on mandibular opening and mobility: A prospective study of 58 patients. *Oral Surgery, Oral Medicine, Oral Pathology, Oral Radiology, and Endodontics, 88,* 365–373.

Guchelaar, H.J., Vermes, A., & Meerwaldt, J.H. (1997). Radiation-induced xerostomia: Pathophysiology, clinical course, and supportive treatment. *Supportive Care in Cancer, 5,* 281–288.

Haas, M., & Kuehn, E. (2001). Head and neck cancers. In D.W. Bruner, G. Moore-Higgs, & M. Haas (Eds.), *Outcomes in radiation therapy: Multidisciplinary management* (pp. 195–213). Sudbury, MA: Jones and Bartlett.

Harris, L. (2000). Head and neck malignancies. In C.H. Yarbo, M.H. Frogge, M. Goodman, & S.L. Groenwald (Eds.), *Cancer nursing: Principles and practice* (5th ed., pp. 1210–1243). Sudbury, MA: Jones and Bartlett.

Jereczek-Fossa, B., & Orecchia, R. (2002). Radiotherapy-induced mandibular bone complications. *Cancer Treatment Review, 28*(1), 65–74.

Johnstone, P., Niemtzow, R., & Riffenburgh, R. (2002). Acupuncture for xerostomia. *Cancer, 94,* 1151–1156.

Kendall, K., McKenzie, S., Leonard, R., & Jones, C. (1998). Structural mobility in deglutition after single modality treatment of head and neck carcinoma with radiotherapy. *Head and Neck, 8,* 720–725.

Maher, K. (2004). Xerostomia. In C.H. Yarbo, M.H. Frogge, & M. Goodman (Eds.), *Cancer symptom management* (3rd. ed., pp. 215–229). Sudbury, MA: Jones and Bartlett.

Pauloski, B., Rademaker, A., Logemann, J., Stein, D., Beery, Q., Newman, L., et al. (2000). Pretreatment swallowing function in patients with head and neck cancer. *Head and Neck, 22,* 474–482.

Ripamonti, C., Zecca, E., Brunelli, C., Fulfaro, F., Villa, S., Balzarini, A., et al. (1998). A randomized, controlled clinical trial to evaluate the effects of zinc sulfate on cancer patients with taste alterations caused by head and neck irradiation. *Cancer, 82,* 1938–1945.

Schuchter, L, Hensley, M., Meropol, N., & Winer, E. (2002). 2002 update of recommendations for the use of chemotherapy and radiotherapy protectants: Clinical practice guidelines of the American Society of Clinical Oncology. *Journal of Clinical Oncology, 20,* 2895–2903.

Shih, A., Miaskowski, C., Dodd, M., Stotts, N., & MacPhail, L. (2002). A research review of the current treatments for radiation-induced oral mucositis in patients with head and neck cancer. *Oncology Nursing Forum, 29,* 1063–1077.

Sonis, S.T. (1989). Oral complications of cancer therapy. In V.T. DeVita, S. Hellman, & S.A. Rosenberg (Eds.), *Cancer: Principles and practice of oncology* (pp. 2144–2152). Philadelphia: Lippincott.

Symonds, R.P. (1998). Treatment-induced mucositis: An old problem with new remedies. *British Journal of Cancer, 77,* 1689–1695.

Tait, N. (1999). Anorexia-cachexia syndrome. In C.H. Yarbo, M.H. Frogge, & M. Goodman (Eds.), *Cancer symptom management* (2nd ed., pp. 183–195). Sudbury, MA: Jones and Bartlett.

Verdonck-de-Leeuw, I., Hilgerrs, F., Keus, R., Koopmans-van Beinum, F., Greven, J., De-Jong, J., et al. (1999). Multidimensional assessment of voice characteristics after radiotherapy for early glottic cancer. *International Journal of Radiation Oncology, Biology, Physics, 44,* 1071–1078.

Vokes, E., Stenson, K., Rosen, F., Kies, M., Rademaker, A., Witt, M.E., et al. (2003). Weekly carboplatin and paclitaxel followed by concomitant paclitaxel, fluorouracil, and hydroxyurea chemoradiotherapy: Curative and organ-preserving therapy for advanced head and neck cancer. *Journal of Clinical Oncology, 21,* 320–326.

Witt, M.E. (1999). Food for life: Management of swallowing-related issues in head and neck cancer. *Developments in Supportive Cancer Care, 3*(2), 43–45.

C. Breast
  1. Skin reactions
     a) Definition: Inflammatory process that occurs in the skin of the treatment area
     b) Pathophysiology: In human skin, ionizing radiation affects the rapidly dividing cells of the epidermis, hair follicles, and sebaceous glands and follows a predictive pattern of acute and late skin reactions. Skin reactions result from the depletion of actively proliferating cells in a renewing cell population (Archambeau, 1987). In the treatment of breast cancer, this may include the skin of the breast, nipple, and areola after breast conservation surgery or the chest wall after mastectomy. The axilla and skin of the supraclavicular area (neck and shoulder) also may be involved. Radiation-induced skin reactions can be classified as acute (first six months) or late (second six months) (Perez & Brady, 1992).
        (1) Acute radiation reactions typically appear between 10 and 14 days from commencement of radiotherapy and continue to increase in severity until the completion of treatment (Porock, Kristjanson, Nikoletti, Cameron, & Pedler, 1998). They depend more on time dose factors than on total dose delivered. Manifests as erythema, pruritus, hyperpigmentation, and dry desquamation. May proceed to moist desquamation (Porock et al., 1998).
        (2) Late radiation reactions appear six months to many years after completion of radiotherapy. They may manifest as hypo- and/or hyperpigmentation of the skin, telangiectasia, pruritus, increased vulnerability to injury secondary to atrophy (thinning of the skin), and fibrosis (loss of elasticity). Moderate to severe fibrosis of the skin as well as postoperative scarring may result in decreased mobility of the muscles of the chest wall and shoulder (McDonald, 1992).
        (3) Disease-related skin problems may be seen during radiation treatment in patients with inflammatory breast cancer, a large fungating tumor of the breast or chest wall, or Paget's disease (dermatitis of nipple or areola).
     c) Incidence (McDonald, 1992)
        (1) The incidence is dose dependent and may be exacerbated by previous or concurrent chemotherapy.
        (2) Risk factors for severe skin reactions include the integrity of the skin at initiation of treatment, age, weight, breast size, nutritional status, presence of comorbid disease, tobacco use, previous RT in the same field, and patient compliance with recommendations for daily skin care. Use caution with patients who have a history of collagen vascular disease (e.g., scleroderma, active lupus erythematosus).
        (3) Skin changes, such as pruritus and mild erythema, are evident in most individuals during the third week of treatment or at a dose of approximately 30 Gy.
        (4) Moist desquamation most commonly occurs in regions of friction such as the inframammary fold or axilla at doses of 45–60 Gy. It also may occur on the chest wall at these doses.
     d) Assessment
        (1) Pretreatment skin status
           (a) Assess for evidence of surgical wound breakdown, rashes, or areas that appear irritated from clothing.
           (b) Conduct global assessment for evidence of non–treatment-related factors that may increase risk of skin reactions, including age, nutritional status, presence of coexisting disease, drug therapy, chemotherapy, smoking (impaired oxygenation), skin color and condition, UV exposure (skin only), and site (Porock, 2002).
        (2) Careful visual examination of the skin within the treatment fields (including exit sites) should be performed once a week during treatment and during regular follow-up examinations.

e) Documentation (Catlin-Huth, Haas, & Pollock, 2002)
   (1) Skin sensation
      (a) 0—No problem
      (b) 1—Pruritus
      (c) 2—Burning
      (d) 3—Painful
   (2) Radiation dermatitis
      (a) 0—None
      (b) 1—Faint erythema or dry desquamation
      (c) 2—Moderate to brisk erythema or patchy moist desquamation, mostly confined to skin folds and creases; or moderate edema
      (d) 3—Confluent moist desquamation ≥ 1.5 cm diameter and not confined to skin folds; pitting edema
      (e) 4—Skin necrosis or ulceration of full-thickness dermis; may include bleeding not induced by minor trauma or abrasion
   (3) Comfort alteration (pain) also should be assessed on a scale of 0 (no pain) to 10 (severe pain)
   (4) Drainage (Catlin-Huth et al., 2002)
      (a) 0—Absent
      (b) 1—Present
   (5) Drainage odor (Catlin-Huth et al., 2002)
      (a) 0—Absent
      (b) 1—Present
f) Collaborative management for skin reactions
   (1) Acute effects
      (a) Prevention
         i) Identify factors that may increase the skin reaction, and take measures to reduce impact of each factor.
         ii) Use special positioning devices to reduce appositional skin folds.
         iii) Delay treatment until surgical wound has completely healed.
         iv) Obtain a nutritional evaluation by a dietitian, if needed.
         v) Obtain an evaluation by an internist to maximize stability of comorbid disease, especially diabetes.
         vi) If skin integrity is compromised by the presence of tumor in the treatment field, a plan should be initiated for minimizing further trauma and irritation, preventing infection, absorbing exudate, and decreasing odor.
      (b) Intervention
         i) Dry desquamation
            • A number of products have been used to prevent and treat acute skin reactions (see section IV, C—Skin Reactions). Biafine® may delay or prevent reactions in large-breasted women (Fisher et al., 2000).
            • Avoid lotions that contain heavy metal. Avoid having lotion on skin during the radiation treatment, as the lotion can increase skin reaction. Remove excess lotion with a soft washcloth before treatment.
         ii) Pruritus: The following interventions may be helpful (McDonald, 1992; Wickline, 2004).
            • Dry cornstarch (controversial) (see section IV, C—Skin Reactions)
            • Oatmeal colloidal soap applied to the affected area for 5–10 minutes and then rinsed
            • Oatmeal colloidal lotion applied after treatment and before bed
            • Pure aloe gel applied after treatment and before bed
            • Mild topical steroid applied once a day
         iii) Moist desquamation: The treatment of moist desquama-

tion has changed as a result of the research available on wound healing.

- Current wound healing policy is to support the wound with protective dressing and moisture rather than to leave the wound to air dry.
- Several key factors must be considered before selecting a wound care plan for an individual patient.
  - Size and site of the wound
  - Presence of infection
  - Radiation treatment plan
  - Ability of the patient to comply with wound care plan
- Cleanse the wound.
  - Small bleeding points can be controlled with silver nitrate sticks.
  - Apply wound care products.
  - For patients who are continuing with treatment, use a product that absorbs and does not provide a "bolus" effect (e.g., hydroactive gels [95% water with 5% gel-forming polymers]).
  - For patients who are not continuing with treatment, use a product that provides moisture with or without an antibacterial or antifungal effect (e.g., silver sulfadiazine [effective against gram-positive and gram-nega-

tive organisms and *Candida albicans*]).

- Apply protective dressing. A nonstick absorbent dressing (e.g., Exu-Dry® [Smith & Nephew, Largo, FL], telfa pad) should be applied. A hydrocolloid, occlusive, and moisture vapor–permeable dressing may be used. However, they must be removed before daily treatment and therefore may cause more desquamation and pain.
- Treat infection if present.
- Control pain with appropriate medication.
- If tumor is present in the wound, a chronic wound care program should be initiated that includes cleansing the wound, debridement, controlling bleeding, controlling odor, protecting the wound from further damage, and controlling pain.
- Metronidazole 0.8% gel, charcoal dressings, a suspension of aluminum hydroxide/magnesium hydroxide, or yogurt may be applied to the wound to reduce the odor. Silver nitrate sticks or a sucralfate paste (1 g sucralfate tablet crushed into 2–3 ml of hydrogel) may reduce oozing sites of blood. If dressings become stuck to the wound, soak them off with normal saline.
- Aluminum hydroxide/magnesium hydroxide suspension or yogurt applied to an ulcerated area often will relieve burning sensations (Waller & Caroline, 1996).

(2) Late effects: Late skin reactions progress slowly and subclinically from six months to many years later. Each patient needs an individualized plan to improve skin texture and elasticity as well as to reduce risks for trauma.

(a) Prevention and intervention

i) Skin texture and elasticity
- Apply moisturizing lotion that includes vitamin E or aloe vera gel to the treatment field at least once a day.
- Avoid exposure to the sun or generously apply an appropriate sunscreen and repeat during sun exposure.
- Initiate physical therapy with gentle massage or myofascial release to increase elasticity and reduce fibrosis and scar formation.

ii) Reduce risk for trauma
- Avoid activities that increase risk of skin break or bruising.
- Avoid scratching, the use of adhesive tape, and other activities that increase skin friction.

(b) If skin breakdown or necrosis occurs, a local recurrence of the cancer should be ruled out before referral to a chronic wound care specialist.

g) Patient and family education
(1) Acute effects
(a) Inform patient and family that skin reactions are expected to become noticeable in approximately the third week of treatment.
(b) Instruct patient and family on which sites are at risk for skin reactions.
(c) Avoid applying skin care products (perfume, deodorant, body powder, and lotion) in treatment field.
(d) If departmental protocol includes use of a specific product to reduce symptoms of skin reaction, discuss appropriate use of product, including cleansing to remove it before treatments. Provide schedule of appropriate times to perform skin care that do not conflict with treatment time.
(e) Wash gently with mild soap and water, rinse thoroughly with tepid water, and dry with gentle patting motions using a soft towel. Frosch and Kligman (1979) rated soaps in terms of irritant qualities and found that Dove® soap was the only one classified as mild. Campbell and Illingworth (1992) conducted a randomized controlled trial to determine whether patients should wash the skin within the treatment field during and shortly after RT. The findings suggested that patients using a mild soap and water to cleanse the skin each day did not change the skin's reactions in treatment fields receiving up to 40 Gy. This study has not been repeated, nor has it been conducted for patients receiving higher doses of radiotherapy.
(f) Teach patients to minimize skin trauma by reducing friction to the skin. Patients should avoid tight clothing, including bras, and clothing that increases skin moisture (nylon) and should use an electric razor in the axilla. Some individuals may benefit from wearing a sports bra that is one to two sizes larger than what they normally wear, or a cotton camisole or T-shirt may provide gentle support.
(g) Avoid sun exposure and temperature extremes.
(h) Maintain adequate nutritional and fluid intake.
(i) Teach patient and family the difference between dry desquamation and moist desquamation so that they can report side effects to the nurse or physician when appropriate and that they know what to expect.
(2) Late effects

(a) Inform patient of the potential for permanent skin changes as an outcome of treatment.

(b) Instruct patient on ways to protect the skin from further injury.

  i) Avoid exposure of treated skin to the sun or tanning booths.

  ii) Moisturize the skin daily.

  iii) Avoid clothes that cause friction or rub the treated skin.

  iv) Avoid products with harsh chemicals that may irritate the skin (i.e., hair removal products).

(c) Inform patient that residual breast swelling, firmness, and retraction of the breast may occur as late reactions. Some treatment options include

  i) Referral to massage therapist or lymphedema program for gentle tissue massage of the breast or chest wall, shoulder, and axilla.

  ii) Use of a compression bra designed to reduce edema, such as the Compressure Comfort® Bra (Bellisse, South Burlington, VT) or the Dale Post-Surgical Bra® (Dale Medical, Plainville, MA).

2. Lymphedema

  a) Definition: The accumulation of fluid in the interstitial tissues caused by disruption in the regional lymphatic system (National Lymphedema Network [NLN], 2004)

  b) Pathophysiology: Lymphedema develops when lymphatic vessels are missing or impaired (primary) or when lymph vessels are damaged or removed (secondary) (NLN, 2004).

(1) Radiation-related (i.e., scarring of the chest wall, breast, or axilla can limit the lymphatic circulation)

(2) Disease-related (i.e., tumor infiltration of lymphatic channels or tumor compression can block fluid returning to circulation from the arm)

(3) Treatment-related (i.e., surgical disruption of lymphatics during removal of axillary lymph nodes)

  c) Incidence and risk factors

(1) Axillary lymph node dissection (ALND) is associated with acute complication rates of 20%–55%, including lymphedema, sensory nerve damage, hemorrhage, and seroma formation and chronic lymphedema rates of 7%–56% (Gerber et al., 1992; Ivens et al., 1992; Kissin, Querci della Rovere, & Easton, 1986).

(2) Lymphedema increases with the addition of radiation to the axilla or supraclavicular area after lymph node dissection (Larson et al., 1986; Mazanec, 1997).

(3) More conservative surgical procedures (i.e., sentinel lymph node biopsy) and the decreased use of irradiation after dissection has reduced the incidence of lymphedema (Horsley & Styblo, 1991).

(4) Recent studies (Blanchard, Donohue, Reynolds, & Grant, 2003; Cheville et al., 2003) have shown that the risk of lymphedema still exists despite significant advances in both surgery and radiation technique.

  d) Assessment

(1) Measure bilateral circumference at standard points at each follow-up visit (i.e., 10 cm above and below the alcrenon) (Petrek, Pressman, & Smith, 2000)

(2) Lymphedema develops in a number of stages, from mild to severe (referred to as stages 1, 2, and 3) (Thiadens, 2000).

  (a) Stage 1 (spontaneously reversible): Tissue is still at the "pitting" stage, which means that when pressed by fingertips, the area indents and holds the indentation. Usually, upon waking in the morning, the limb(s) or affected area is normal or almost normal size.

  (b) Stage 2 (spontaneously irreversible): The tissue now has a spongy

consistency and is "nonpitting," meaning that when pressed by fingertips, the tissue bounces back without any indentation forming. Fibrosis found in stage 2 lymphedema marks the beginning of the hardening of the limbs and increasing size.

    (c) Stage 3 (lymphostatic elephantiasis): At this stage, the swelling is irreversible and usually the limb(s) is/are very large. The tissue is hard (fibrotic) and unresponsive; some patients consider undergoing reconstructive surgery called "debulking" at this stage.

e) Documentation

  (1) Measurements of both arms on patient care record (Catlin-Huth et al., 2002)

  (2) Lymphatics (NCI, 2003)

    (a) 0—None

    (b) 1—Mild lymphedema

    (c) 2—Moderate lymphedema requiring compression; lymphocyst

    (d) 3—Severe lymphedema limiting function; lymphocyst requiring surgery

    (e) 4—Severe lymphedema limiting function with ulceration

f) Collaborative management of lymphedema

  (1) Compression garment—An elastic sleeve or ReidSleeve® (Peninsula Medical Supply, Scotts Valley, CA) worn on the affected arm to encourage fluid to move out of the arm.

  (2) Complex decongestive therapy (CDT)—This therapy includes (NLN, 2004)

    (a) Manual lymphatic drainage—A gentle massage that stimulates collateral lymphatic channels to move the fluid out of the arm

    (b) Compression bandaging—Helps lymph flow and prevents refilling of the arm between treatment sessions while encouraging the skin to reshape to a smaller size

    (c) Individualized exercise program—Used with compression bandaging to help lymphatic drainage and build strength, flexibility, endurance, and function

    (d) Patient education—About skin care, self-massage, diet, exercise, and continued prevention methods

  (3) Assess and manage signs/symptoms of lymphangitis (infection) in the arm, shoulder, or breast, including rash; red, blotchy skin or discoloration of the skin; itching of the arm, under the arm, or breast; increased swelling; skin feels warmer than the other side; heavy sensation in the arm (more so than usual); pain, and in some cases, high fever and chills (NLN, 2004).

g) Patient and family education

  (1) Instruct the patient at risk for lymphedema about preventive measures including the following (Breastcancer.org, 2002; Lymphoedema Association of Australia, 1998; NLN, 2004).

    (a) Keep the entire arm, under the arm, and breast spotlessly clean. Gentle cleansing products should be used. Dry the skin with a towel gently. Pay special attention to creases in the skin and the areas between fingers.

    (b) Make sure all fabric that comes in contact with the skin is regularly washed. This includes bandages and compression garments.

    (c) Carry packages, purses, or briefcases only on the unaffected side.

    (d) Use a moisturizing lotion to help keep the skin from cracking. The lotion should not contain alcohol, dyes, lanolin, mineral oil, petroleum products, talc, or perfumes. (Note that pure essential oils have a fragrance but are not considered perfumes.) The lotion should also have antiseptic properties and the correct pH (e.g., Lymphoderm® [Advanced Therapists, West Palm Beach, FL] therapeutic body lotion, Eucerin®). Apply the lotion to

the arm after a bath or shower, and if lymphedema is present, apply it before applying bandages or compression garments and again after they are removed.

(e) Avoid chemical hair removers. If possible, use a well-maintained electric razor, replacing the heads regularly. Because of the danger of cuts and nicks, it is not recommended that a regular razor be used.

(f) Avoid extreme temperature changes when bathing, showering, and swimming; washing dishes, mopping floors, or doing laundry; receiving therapeutic treatments; or at the gym—do not use the sauna or hot tub.

(g) Protect the arm from weather extremes: In hot weather seek air conditioning and keep the arm cool; in cold weather seek central heating. If you must go out, have the arm and shoulder well bundled, but not sweaty. In sunny weather, protect the arm, shoulder, and breast with sunscreen and/or clothing.

(h) Avoid all tight clothing, jewelry, and elastic bands on the affected arm, including watches, rings, and binding stockings.

(i) Be careful cutting nails. Do not nick skin or cut cuticles. When having a manicure, make sure technician knows about the risk of lymphedema. If the cuticles must be pushed back, use a cuticle stick covered with cotton. The use of acrylic or other nail products may increase the risk of infection.

(j) Medical care, such as injections, blood pressure measurement, drawing blood, and allergy tests, should be performed on an unaffected limb. (Note: A leg often can be used if both arms are at risk.) Any procedure that punctures the skin in the arm, under the arm, or breast is to be avoided, including acupuncture. Wear a Lymphedema Alert® bracelet (NLN, Oakland, CA).

(k) Avoid all types of trauma such as cuts, scrapes, bruises, burns (including sunburns, sports injuries, insect bites, all animal bites and scratches), and forceful impact. Be sensible and protect yourself; use seatbelts, use a thimble when sewing, and wear rubber gloves when washing dishes or gardening. Wear insect repellent when outdoors.

(l) Exercise is important. However, if the affected arm begins to ache or feels tired, rest it immediately, and elevate it if possible. Consult a lymphedema specialist before proceeding with an exercise routine. Safe exercises include walking, swimming, and water exercise. If lymphedema is present, it is important to be bandaged or wear a compression garment during exercise.

(m) Avoid any repetitive movements, especially those against resistance. Never do anything to the point of exhaustion. The arm and shoulder will fatigue more quickly than the rest of the body and will take longer to recover from physical exertion. If your arm begins to ache, rest and elevate the arm. If elevation does not make the symptoms better, call your physician.

(n) Barometric pressure is reduced at high altitudes and can lead to the onset of lymphedema or make the condition worse. Therefore, wearing a compression garment is extremely important during airplane travel or vacation in high altitudes. This is recommended even if lymphedema is not present. (Over-the-counter garments are available for a modest cost.)

(o) Wear soft pads under bra straps, particularly if the breasts are large. Avoid wearing a heavy prosthesis or underwire bras.

(p) Patients who live in a humid climate should try dusting the skin with cornstarch. Keeping the skin dry helps reduce fungi, which may cause infection.

(q) Drink plenty of water. The recommended amount of water is one ounce for every two pounds of body weight.

(r) Maintain ideal weight through a well-balanced, low-sodium, high-fiber diet. Avoid smoking and alcohol. The diet should contain easily digested protein (e.g., chicken, fish, tofu). Eat 10%–30% of total calorie intake as protein.

(s) Patients with lymphedema should wear a well-fitted compression sleeve during all waking hours. See the therapist for follow-up at least every four to six months. If the sleeve is too loose, most likely the arm circumference has reduced or the sleeve is worn.

(2) Infections can be very serious and require immediate medical attention. An infection in the arm, shoulder, or breast could be the beginning or worsening of lymphedema. If a rash, itching, redness, pain, fever, or increased arm swelling is noticed, the patient should see the physician immediately.

3. Brachial plexopathy

a) Definition: The brachial plexus is a major neural structure, providing motor and sensory innervation to the upper extremity. Brachial plexopathies develop when lesions occur anywhere along the course of the brachial plexus. These lesions often are caused by primary or secondary tumors, radiation fibrosis, or trauma (Wittenberg & Adkins, 2000).

b) Pathophysiology

(1) Radiation-related: Most common in patients who undergo RT to the axillary region. Neurologic damage after RT may be observed several months to years after therapy, and it is most likely to occur in patients who have received radiation doses in excess of 60 Gy (Moore et al., 1990). This damage generally occurs 5–30 months after completion of RT, with a peak at 10–20 months (Kori, Foley, & Posner, 1989). Common symptoms include paresthesias, hyperesthesias, pain, and weakness (Kori et al., 1989; Moore et al., 1990).

(2) Disease-related: Tumors may metastasize to the brachial plexus. Breast cancer is the most likely to metastasize because major lymphatic drainage routes for the breast course through the apex of the axilla (Wittenberg & Adkins, 2000).

c) Incidence and risk factors

(1) Brachial plexopathy is considered unusual after radiation and is associated with high doses to the axilla and supraclavicular area (Salner et al., 1981).

(2) Radiation-induced brachial plexopathy is related to radiation dose; 73% occur with doses greater than 55 Gy; 15% occur with doses greater than 51 Gy (Shields, Raque, & Gardner, 1996).

d) Assessment: Symptoms typically occur in an upper trunk distribution, with weakness of the arm flexors and shoulder abductors (Wilburn, 1993).

(1) Paresthesias

(2) Hyperthesias

(3) Pain

(4) Weakness

e) Documentation

(1) Sensory changes

(2) Functional changes

(3) Pain

f) Collaborative management of brachial plexopathy

(1) Provide pain control.

(2) If related to tumor compression, treatment with either local (radiation) or systemic therapy (chemotherapy or hormonal therapy)

(3) Consult with physical therapist for arm/shoulder mobilization exercises.

g) Patient and family education

(1) Provide patient and family with information about signs and symptoms of brachial plexopathy.

(2) Inform patient and family about potential injury resulting from changes in sensory and motor function.

4. Second malignancies

a) Definition: A radiation-induced second malignancy is a new malignancy that occurs within the previously irradiated tissue.

b) Pathophysiology

(1) Radiation-related: Exact mechanisms and radiation dose are unknown; may involve radiation, multimodality therapy, and patient-related factors.

(2) Disease-related: Current theories focus on genetic predisposition and lifestyle factors.

c) Incidence and risk factors

(1) Angiosarcoma arising in the irradiated breast after breast-conserving therapy has been reported with increasing frequency over a similar time period. Although angiosarcoma after breast-conserving therapy is uncommon (approximately 100 cases are reported in the literature), the incidence has increased as more women are treated with segmental mastectomy and radiotherapy (Monroe, Feigenberg, & Mendenhall, 2003).

(2) Postmastectomy RT has been found to provide a moderate increase in risk for ipsilateral lung carcinoma starting 10 years after exposure; this increased risk is reported to persist to at least 20 years. Postlumpectomy RT does not appear to incur an increased risk (Zablotska & Neugut, 2003).

(3) Primary esophageal squamous cell carcinoma also has been found in patients treated with RT and who had a follow-up period of greater than 10 years. A less definite trend was seen for esophageal adenocarcinoma (Ahsan & Neuget, 1998).

d) Assessment

(1) Family history

(2) Lifestyle risk factors currently under investigation

(a) Smoking

(b) Diet

(c) Alcohol

e) Documentation: Document assessment findings.

f) Collaborative management for second malignancies

(1) Follow American Cancer Society guidelines for recommending routine screening studies, including mammograms, Pap smears, chest x-rays, and colonoscopy.

(2) Refer for genetic counseling, if appropriate.

g) Patient and family education

(1) Instruct patient on the importance of routine follow-up care including breast self-examination, clinical breast examination, and mammogram as a means of early detection of second malignancy.

(2) Counsel patient on lifestyle behaviors to prevent other primary malignancies (e.g., smoking, diet/weight control).

5. Breast edema

a) Definition: Swelling of the treated breast tissue commonly found in women treated with breast conservation RT; can occur in women during RT, especially larger-breasted women, within the first couple of weeks of RT.

b) Pathophysiology: The onset of breast swelling is gradual and continues until completion of treatment. It is commonly associated with mild discomfort and breast tenderness. Resolution of the swelling is also gradual. The time course of breast edema has not been fully characterized.

c) Incidence and risk factors: Most women experience some degree of swelling during RT. In a prospective assessment of late changes in the breast, Moody et al. (1994) found only 6% of women with small breasts developed moderate or severe late changes, as compared with 22% of women with moderate-sized breasts and 39% with large breasts (p < 0.001). A significant correlation was found between breast size and dose in homogeneity, which may account for the marked changes in breast appearance in the larger breast.

    d) Assessment

      (1) Physical examination

      (2) Careful inspection for evidence of erythema, skin changes (similar to peau d'orange), warmth, and/or discoloration of the breast that may indicate cellulitis.

    e) Collaborative management of breast edema

      (1) Referral to massage therapist or lymphedema program for gentle tissue massage of the breast or chest wall, shoulder, and axilla.

      (2) Use of a compression bra designed to reduce edema, such as the Compressure Comfort Bra.

      (3) Intermittent aches and pains in the treated breast is a common acute side effect that can be managed with NSAIDs.

    f) Patient and family education

      (1) Educate the patient on the importance of wearing a supportive bra or compression bra to reduce the edema.

      (2) Teach the patient the signs and symptoms of infection, including erythema, warmth, and increased swelling.

6. Rib fracture

    a) Definition: A fracture of one or more ribs within the treatment field

    b) Pathophysiology: Radiation can result in alterations in the soft tissue and bones of the chest wall, increasing the risk of a rib fracture because of weakness.

    c) Incidence and risk factors: Spontaneous rib fractures occur in approximately 10% of patients who receive radiation to the chest wall following mastectomy (Mendenhall, Fletcher, & Million, 1987). Fractures may be asymptomatic and only found on chest x-ray or bone scan, or they may be quite painful. Typically, the fractures heal spontaneously within six to eight weeks. Overgaard (1988) found that patients treated with a large dose per fraction had a significantly higher incidence of late bone damage (19%) than patients treated with a standard dose per fraction (6%).

    d) Assessment

      (1) Symptoms may include chest wall pain with deep respiratory inspiration and/or cough, pain with movement, or sudden onset of chest wall pain. Low-grade fever is observed in patients with pneumonitis.

      (2) X-ray of the ribs

    e) Collaborative management of rib fracture: Pain management

    f) Patient and family education

      (1) Educate the patient on the importance of avoiding activities that include pressure against the chest wall, such as contact sports.

      (2) Teach the patient appropriate sitting and lying positions that can reduce the pain associated with the rib fracture.

      (3) Educate the patient on the signs and symptoms that should be reported immediately, including sudden shortness of breath, hemoptysis, or worsening pain.

7. Cardiac toxicity

    a) Incidence: RT has been associated with an increased risk of cardiac mortality and morbidity in early-stage left-sided breast cancer. The anterior left ventricle is frequently included in the treatment fields (Mendenhall et al., 1987). Cardiac mortality has been found to positively correlate with cardiac dose-volume (Gyenes, Rutqvist, Liedberg, & Fornander, 1998).

    b) Patients who receive high dose-volumes appear to have an increased mortality from ischemic heart disease but not myocardial infarctions (Gyenes et al., 1998). With modern technology, including CT simulation, it is possible to decrease the volume of heart in the irradiation of the left breast. Immobilization devices are used to passively "shift" the heart out of place to minimize the heart exposure.

8. Pulmonary toxicity

    a) Incidence—Pulmonary complications following radiation for breast cancer are relatcd to radiation dose, technique, and volume of lung included in the treatment field. Depending on patient anatomy and treatment technique, a variable amount of lung is always irradiated when the breast, chest wall, or regional lymphatics are treated (Mendenhall et al., 1987).

b) Acute pneumonitis is more likely when larger volumes of lung are irradiated (see section V, D—Thoracic). Asymptomatic pulmonary fibrosis, limited to the treatment volume, usually is seen on chest x-ray and CT imaging, including the apical region when the supraclavicular/axillary region is irradiated (see section V, D—Thoracic).

References

Ahsan, H., & Neuget, A.I. (1998). Radiation therapy for breast cancer and increased risk for esophageal carcinoma. *Annals of Internal Medicine, 128,* 114–117.

Archambeau, J.O. (1987). Relative radiation sensitivity of the integumentary system dose response of the epidermal, microvascular, and dermal populations. In J. Lett & K. Altman (Eds.), *Advances in radiation biology* (pp. 147–203). San Diego, CA: Academic Press.

Blanchard, D.K., Donohue, J.H., Reynolds, C., & Grant, C.S. (2003). Relapse and morbidity in patients undergoing sentinel lymph node biopsy alone or with axillary dissection for breast cancer. *Archives of Surgery, 138,* 482–488.

Breastcancer.org. (2002). *Arm lymphedema—Prevention and management.* Retrieved June 16, 2004, from http://www.breastcancer.org

Campbell, I.R., & Illingworth, M.H. (1992). Can patients wash during radiotherapy to the breast or chest wall? A randomized controlled trial. *Clinical Oncology, 4*(2), 78–82.

Catlin-Huth, C., Haas, M., & Pollock, V. (2002). *Radiation therapy patient record: A tool for documenting nursing care.* Pittsburgh, PA: Oncology Nursing Society.

Cheville, A.L., McGarvey, C.L., Petrek, J.A., Russo, S.A., Taylor, M.E., & Thiadens, S.R. (2003). Lymphedema management. *Seminars in Radiation Oncology, 13,* 290–301.

Fisher, J., Scott, C., Stevens, R., Marconi, B., Champion, L., Freedman, G.M., et al. (2000). Randomized phase III study comparing best supportive care to Biafine as a prophylactic agent for radiation-induced skin toxicity for women undergoing breast irradiation: RTOG 97–113. *International Journal of Radiation Oncology, Biology, Physics, 48,* 1307–1310.

Frosch, P., & Kligman, A. (1979). The soap chamber: A new method for assessing the irritancy of soaps. *Journal of the American Academy of Dermatology, 1*(1), 35–41.

Gerber, L., Lampert, M., Wood, C., Duncan, M., D'Angelo, T., Schain, W., et al. (1992). Comparison of pain, motion, and edema after modified radical mastectomy vs local excision with axillary dissection and radiation. *Breast Cancer Research and Treatment, 2,* 139–145.

Gyenes, G., Rutqvist, L.E., Liedberg, A., & Fornander, T. (1998). Long-term cardiac morbidity and mortality in a randomized trial of pre- and post-operative radiation therapy versus surgery alone in primary breast cancer. *Radiotherapy and Oncology, 48*(2), 185–190.

Horsley, J.S., & Styblo, T. (1991). Lymphedema in the postmastectomy patient. In K.B. Copeland & E. Copeland (Eds.), *The breast: Comprehensive management of benign and malignant diseases* (pp. 701–706). Philadelphia: Saunders.

Ivens, D., Hoe, A.L., Podd, T.J., Hamilton, C.R., Taylor, I., & Royle, G.T. (1992). Assessment of morbidity from complete axillary dissection. *British Journal of Cancer, 66,* 136–138.

Kissin, M.W., Querci della Rovere, G., & Easton, D. (1986). Risk of lymphoedema following the treatment of breast cancer. *British Journal of Surgery, 73,* 580–584.

Kori, S.H., Foley, K.M., & Posner, K. (1989). Brachial plexus lesions in patients with cancer: 100 cases. *Neurology, 39,* 450–451.

Larson, D., Weinstein, M., Goldberg, I., Silver, B., Recht, A., Cady, B., et al. (1986). Edema of the arm as a function of the extent of axillary surgery in patients with stage I–II carcinoma of the breast treated with primary radiotherapy. *International Journal of Radiation Oncology, Biology, Physics, 12,* 1575–1582.

Lymphoedema Association of Australia. (1998). *Treatment of lymphedema.* Retrieved June 16, 2004, from http://www.lymphoedema.org.au

Mazanec, S.R. (1997). Breast cancer. In K.H. Dow, J.D. Bucholtz, R. Iwamoto, V. Fieler, & L.J. Hilderley (Eds.), *Nursing care in radiation oncology* (2nd ed., pp. 101–135). Philadelphia: Saunders.

McDonald, A. (1992). Altered protective mechanisms. In K.H. Dow & L. Hilderley (Eds.), *Nursing care in radiation oncology* (pp. 96–109). Philadelphia: Saunders.

Mendenhall, N.P., Fletcher, G.H., & Million, R.R. (1991). Adjuvant radiation therapy following modified radical or radical mastectomy. In K.I. Bland & E.M. Copeland (Eds.), *The breast: Comprehensive management of benign and malignant diseases* (pp. 770–780). Philadelphia: Saunders.

Moody, A.M., Mayles, W.P., Bliss, J.M., A'Hern, R.P., Owen, J.R., Regan, J., et al. (1994). The influence of breast size on late radiation effects and association with radiotherapy dose in homogeneity. *Radiotherapy and Oncology, 33*(2), 106–112.

Moore, N.R., Dixon, A.K., Wheeler, T.K., Freer, C.E., Hall, L.D., & Sims, C. (1990). Axillary fibrosis or recurrent tumor: An MRI study in breast cancer. *Clinical Radiology, 42,* 42–46.

Monroe, A.T., Feigenberg, S.J., & Mendenhall, N.P. (2003). Angiosarcoma after breast-conserving therapy. *Cancer, 97,* 1832–1840.

Nation Cancer Institute. (2003). *Common terminology criteria for adverse events* (Version 3.0). Bethesda, MD: Author.

National Lymphedema Network. (2004). *Lymphedema: A brief overview.* Retrieved June 16, 2004, from http://www.lymphnet.org/whatis.html

Overgaard, M. (1988). Spontaneous radiation-induced rib fractures in breast cancer patients treated with postmastectomy irradiation. A clinical radiobiological analysis of the influence of fraction size and dose-response relationships on late bone damage. *Acta Oncologica, 27*(2), 117–122.

Perez, C., & Brady, L. (1992). Overview. In C. Perez & L. Brady (Eds.), *Principles and practice of radiation oncology* (2nd ed., p. 7). Philadelphia: Lippincott.

Petrek, J.A., Pressman, P.I., & Smith, R. (2000). Lymphedema: Current issues in research and management. *CA: A Cancer Journal for Clinicians, 50,* 292–307.

Porock, D. (2002). Factors influencing the severity of radiation skin and oral mucosal reactions: Development of a conceptual framework. *European Journal of Cancer Care, 11*(1), 33–43.

Porock, D., Kristjanson, L., Nikoletti, S., Cameron, F., & Pedler, P. (1998). Predicting the severity of radiation skin reactions in women with breast cancer. *Oncology Nursing Forum, 25,* 1019–1029.

Salner, A.I., Botnick, L.E., Herzog, A.G., Goldstein, M.A., Harris, J.R., Levene, M.B., et al. (1981). Reversible brachial plexopathy following primary radiation therapy for breast cancer. *Cancer Treatment Reports, 65,* 797–802.

Shields, C.B., Raque, G.H., & Gardner, P.K. (1996). Neurologic aspects of breast cancer. In W.L. Donegan & J.S. Spratt (Eds.), *Cancer of the breast* (pp. 717–727). Philadelphia: Saunders.

Thiadens, S.R.J. (2000). *Lymphedema: An information booklet* (6th ed.). Oakland, CA: National Lymphedema Network.

Waller, A., & Caroline, N.L. (1996). *Handbook of palliative care in cancer.* Boston: Butterworth-Heinemann.

Wilburn, A.J. (1993). Brachial plexus. In P.J. Dyck & P.K. Thomas (Eds.), *Peripheral neuropathy* (3rd ed., pp. 911–950). Philadelphia: Saunders.

Wickline, M.M. (2004). Continuing education: Prevention and treatment of acute radiation dermatitis: A literature review. *Oncology Nursing Forum, 31,* 237–247.

Wittenberg, K.H., & Adkins, M.C. (2000). MR imaging of nontraumatic brachial plexopathies: Frequency and spectrum of findings. *Radiographics, 20,* 1023–1032.

Zablotska, L.B., & Neugut, A.I. (2003). Lung carcinoma after radiation therapy in women treated with lumpectomy or mastectomy for primary breast carcinoma. *Cancer, 97,* 1404–1411.

D. Thoracic
1. Radiation pneumonitis and fibrosis
    a) Definition: Radiotherapy of tumors located within or around the thoracic cavity usually results in partial irradiation of the surrounding normal lung tissue. Lung damage after radiotherapy has been reported in the treatment of breast cancer, Hodgkin's lymphoma, and esophageal and lung cancers. Radiation-induced respiratory toxicity ranges from asymptomatic impairment of lung function to radiation pneumonitis and fibrosis (De Jaeger et al., 2003).
    b) Pathophysiology: Radiation pneumonitis is an interstitial pulmonary inflammation. Several cell populations of the lung, among them alveolar macrophages, type II cells, fibroblasts, and endothelial cells, are involved in a network of interactions leading to inflammation and pulmonary fibrosis (Abratt & Morgan, 2002).
        (1) Initial injury: Damage to the pneumocytes and endothelial cells and to the interstitium lead to a release of surfactant and exudate into the alveoli and also to interstitial edema. This occurs over the first month and is termed the early phase of the latent period (Abratt & Morgan, 2002).
        (2) Second phase: There is continuing inflammatory response with capillary obstruction and increase in leukocytes, plasma cells, macrophages, fibroblasts, and collagen fibers. The alveolar septa become thickened, and the alveolar space becomes smaller. This phase lasts from one to several months and is termed the intermediate or acute pneumonitis phase (Abratt & Morgan, 2002).
        (3) Late phase: Fibrosis develops together with loss of capillaries, increase in the thickness of the alveolar septa, and obliteration of the alveolar space. This occurs six months or later (Abratt & Morgan, 2002).
    c) Incidence and risk factors
        (1) There are currently no well-established means for predicting the risk of developing RT-induced lung injury.
        (2) Symptomatic pneumonitis occurs in 5%–15% of patients irradiated for mediastinal lymphoma, lung cancer, and breast cancer (Knopp, 1997).
        (3) Interstitial pneumonitis occurs in 50% of patients receiving single-fraction total body irradiation (TBI) and is the reason why fractionated TBI is the treatment of choice (Knopp, 1997).
        (4) Risk factors that have been associated with an increased risk of developing pneumonitis include a low performance status, decreased pretreatment pulmonary function, history of smoking, once-daily radiotherapy dose fractionation, radiotherapy combined with chemotherapy, and larger radiation doses (> 2.67 Gy) per fraction (Inoue et al., 2001).
        (5) A combination of chemotherapy and radiation can increase the extent of lung injuries, especially with certain chemotherapeutic agents (McDonald, Rubin, Phillips, & Marks, 1995).
            (a) Bleomycin
            (b) Methotrexate
            (c) Mitomycin
            (d) Nitrosoureas
            (e) Alkylating agents
            (f) Cytosine
            (g) Arabinoside
            (h) Vinca alkaloids
            (i) Procarbazine
            (j) Doxorubicin
            (k) Dactinomycin
        (6) Clinically significant radiation pneumonitis occurs in an estimated 13%–37% of patients treated for lung cancer

with combination chemotherapy and irradiation (Rodrigues, Lock, D'Souza, Yu, & Van Dyk, 2004).

(7) Fibrosis usually is asymptomatic if it is limited to less than 50% of one lung (McDonald et al., 1995).

d) Assessment of pneumonitis
  (1) Clinical manifestations (Abratt & Morgan, 2002)
    (a) Occur up to three months after a fractionated course of irradiation
    (b) Symptoms usually resolve in six to eight weeks without any long-term effects.
    (c) Symptoms may include
      i) Nonproductive cough
      ii) Low-grade fever
      iii) Tachycardia
      iv) Dyspnea
      v) Pleuritic chest pain
  (2) Physical examination
    (a) Low-grade fever
    (b) Shortness of breath
    (c) Nonproductive cough
    (d) Blood-tinged sputum
    (e) Consolidation in region corresponding to radiation field, although less evident as area contracts with fibrosis (Cox & Komaki, 1994; McDonald et al., 1995).
    (f) Tachycardia
  (3) Radiographic findings (McDonald et al., 1995)
    (a) Chest x-ray—Diffuse infiltrate corresponding to the RT field. Not always evident.
    (b) CT scan—Evidence of increased lung density and discrete and solid consolidation in corresponding RT field
  (4) Pulmonary function studies (Abratt & Morgan, 2002).

    (a) Most objective evaluation of the functional late effects of radiation lung toxicity
    (b) No gross abnormalities for four to eight weeks after treatment
    (c) The volume of lung irradiated may affect the pattern of decreases of the different lung volumes.
    (d) Measurements need to include both lung volumes and the transfer factor (diffusion capacity of the lung for carbon monoxide).

e) Assessment of fibrosis
  (1) Clinical manifestations
    (a) Can occur 6–12 months after treatment is completed (Nicolaou, 2003)
    (b) Symptoms are proportional to the extent of lung parenchyma involved and the preexisting pulmonary reserve.
    (c) Symptoms are minimal if fibrosis is limited to < 50% of one lung.
    (d) Fibrosis develops insidiously and usually stabilizes in one to two years
    (e) If symptoms are present, they are usually dyspnea associated with progressive chronic cor pulmonale.
  (2) Physical examination
    (a) Tachypnea
    (b) Dyspnea
  (3) Radiographic findings
    (a) Scarring and reduction of lung volume (Abratt & Morgan, 2002)
    (b) Retraction of the involved lung with elevation of the hemidiaphragm is the predominant finding (Nicolaou, 2003).
    (c) CT imaging is the preferred study.
  (4) Pulmonary function studies
    (a) May show mild deterioration as fibrosis develops
    (b) Maximum breathing capacity reduced

f) Documentation (Catlin-Huth, Haas, & Pollock, 2002)
  (1) Cough
    (a) 0—Absent
    (b) 1—Mild, relieved by nonprescription medication
    (c) 2—Requiring narcotic antitussive
    (d) 3—Severe cough or coughing spasms, poorly controlled or unresponsive to treatment
  (2) Hemoptysis
    (a) 0—None

(b) 1—Specks of blood in mucus

(c) 2—Pink-tinged mucus

(d) 3—Small clots of blood in mucus

(e) 4—Frank blood in mucus

(3) Mucus color

   (a) 0—Clear

   (b) 1—White

   (c) 2—Yellow

   (d) 3—Green

   (e) 4—Brown

   (f) 5—Red (hemoptysis)

(4) Dyspnea

   (a) 0—Normal

   (b) 1—Dyspnea on exertion

   (c) 2—Dyspnea at normal level of activity

   (d) 3—Dyspnea at rest or requiring ventilator support

(5) O_2 saturation level

g) Collaborative management

(1) Prevention: The use of cytoprotective agents such as amifostine may reduce radiation-induced lung toxicity (Antonadou et al., 2001; Komaki et al., 2002; Vujaskovic et al, 2002) (see section IX, B—Radioprotectors).

(2) Interventions

   (a) Corticosteroids: Corticosteroids remain the treatment of choice for radiation pneumonitis. They provide symptomatic relief, do not reverse or prevent fibrosis, and may be contraindicated.

   (b) Bronchodilators

   (c) Expectorants, humidifier, increased hydration, antitussives

   (d) Bed rest

   (e) Supplemental oxygen

   (f) Delanian, Porcher, Balla-Mekias, and Lefaix (2003) suggested that six months of pentoxifylline and tocopherol (vitamin E) may stimulate the regression of superficial radiation-induced fibrosis.

(3) Management of other symptoms

   (a) Fatigue (see section IV, B—Fatigue)

   (b) Anorexia (see section IV, G—Nutrition)

(4) Coordination of symptom management

   (a) Share information about symptom management (e.g., home health, medical oncology, hospice) with all nurses caring for the patient.

   (b) Provide a safe home environment through continuity of care.

(5) Patient and family education

   (a) Acute

     i) Inform patient and family about interventions to manage cough and shortness of breath.

     ii) Teach patient and family the signs and symptoms of pneumonitis.

     iii) Instruct patient to alternate rest and activity.

     iv) Advise patient to avoid irritants (e.g., tobacco, pollutants).

     v) Teach patient and family signs and symptoms (e.g., fever, cough, dyspnea) to report to the healthcare team.

     vi) Provide written steroid taper instructions for the patient to follow.

   (b) Late

     i) Teach patient and family signs and symptoms of fibrosis.

     ii) Teach patient and family methods to avoid further respiratory compromise.

2. Radiation myelopathy

a) Definition: Radiation myelopathy is a rare, well-described, serious complication of spinal cord irradiation. Recovery from radiation-induced motor sequelae is rare, whereas the regeneration of sensory losses is relatively frequent (Esik et al., 2003).

(1) Among the sensory radiogenic injuries of the spinal cord, Lhermitte's sign is most frequent. It is characterized by a sensation similar to an electric shock passing down the spine in the cervico-caudal direction. It may

be felt in the upper or lower limbs (Esik et al., 2003).

  (2) The risk of radiation myelopathy sometimes limits delivery of the dose necessary for tumor control or for reirradiation.

b) Pathophysiology: Spinal cord changes in radiation myelopathy may include white matter lesions, vasculopathies, and glial reactions (Schultheiss, Kun, Ang, & Stephens, 1995).

c) Incidence and risk factors: When RT is given in a conventional fractionation schedule of 2 Gy per day, the incidence of radiation myelopathy is less than 1% for total doses 50–55 Gy and up to 5% for total doses 55–60 Gy (Aristizabal, Caldwell, & Avila, 1977). The dose per fraction, total dose, and absolute length of cord irradiated play an important role in determining whether radiation damage to the spinal cord occurs (Atkins & Tretter, 1966).

d) Assessment

  (1) Clinical manifestations: Symptoms may develop after a latent period from six months and on (Schultheiss et al., 1995). They may be subtle initially. Severity of symptoms is often progressive.

    (a) Paresthesia or sensory deficits (either unilateral or bilateral)

    (b) Leg weakness

    (c) Clumsiness

    (d) Diminished proprioception

    (e) Lhermitte's sign may preceed permanent myelopathy.

    (f) Paralysis

    (g) Bladder or anal dysfunction/incontinence

  (2) Physical examination (Schultheiss et al., 1995)

    (a) Complete neurologic examination

    (b) Patterns of paresthesias

    (c) Upper or lower extremity weakness

    (d) Gait spasticity (foot drop)

    (e) Hemiparesis

    (f) Brown Sequard syndrome

    (g) Pain

    (h) Hyperreflexia and Babinski reflex often are found.

  (3) Radiographic findings

    (a) CT scan—Rarely abnormal (Schultheiss et al., 1995)

    (b) MRI—May show cord swelling with decreased intensity of T1-weighted images and increased intensity on T2-weighted images (Wang, Shen, & Jan, 1992)

  (4) Other studies

    (a) Myelogram—May be normal or may show slight widening of the spinal cord (Schultheiss et al., 1995)

    (b) Cerebral spinal fluid—Usually normal. May have a slight elevation of total protein, basic protein, and lymphotcytes (Paulson & Quenemoen, 1984)

    (c) Nerve conduction studies—Decreased spinal conduction velocities (Dorfman et al., 1992; Snooks & Swash, 1985)

e) Documentation (Catlin-Huth et al., 2002)

  (1) Neuropathy—Motor

    (a) 0—Normal

    (b) 1—Subjective weakness but no objective findings

    (c) 2—Mild objective weakness interfering with function, but not with activities of daily living

    (d) 3—Objective weakness interfering with activities of daily living

    (e) 4—Paralysis

  (2) Ataxia

    (a) 0—Absent

    (b) 1—Present

  (3) Urinary incontinence

    (a) 0—Absent

    (b) 1—Present

  (4) Bowel incontinence

    (a) 0—Absent

    (b) 1—Present

  (5) Additional evaluations may include sensory (numbness), spincter control, pain, and neurologic function.

f) Collaborative management for radiation myelopathy

  (1) Prevention: Careful dose calculation and administration of RT

(2) Interventions
  (a) Evaluate for other etiologies, including tumor progression, infection, or trauma.
  (b) Administer corticosteroid.
  (c) Provide a referral to rehabilitation in an attempt to maximize function.
g) Patient and family education
  (1) Educate patient and family on neurologic symptoms to report.
  (2) Instruct patient on injury prevention secondary to neurologic and sensory deficits, including fall prevention.
  (3) Instruct patient and family on corticosteroid administration and taper as well as potential side effects.
  (4) Progression of symptoms depends upon the degree to which the lesion transects the spinal cord and the level of injury.
3. Cardiac injury
  a) Definition: Acute inflammation and progressive fibrosis of the pericardial, myocardial, and endocardial (valvular and arterial) tissues (Brosius, Waller, & Roberts, 1981; Stewart, Cohn, Fajardo, & Hancock, 1967; Stewart & Fajardo, 1971; Veinot & Edwards, 1996).
  b) Pathophysiology
    (1) Certain cytokines and growth factors, such as TGF-beta1 and IL-1 beta, may stimulate radiation-induced endothelial proliferation, fibroblast proliferation, collagen deposition, and fibrosis leading to advanced lesions of atherosclerosis (Basavaraju & Easterly, 2002).
    (2) Pericardial disease is one of the most common manifestations of radiation-induced cardiac injury. Acute pericarditis may occur early in the course of treatment, but constrictive or effusive pericarditis also may develop months to years after therapy (Brosius et al., 1981; Stewart & Fajardo, 1984; Veinot & Edwards, 1996).
    (3) Other late complications include myocardial fibrosis and cardiomyopathy, accelerated coronary artery disease, conduction abnormalities, and valvular dysfunction (Lund et al., 1996; McEniery, Doristi, Schiavone, Pedrick, & Sheldon, 1987; Slama et al., 1991; Stewart & Fajardo, 1984).
    (4) The risk of cardiac damage correlates with radiation dose-volume and fractionation.

c) Incidence and risk factors
  (1) The overall incidence of clinically detectable heart injury after thoracic irradiation is approximately 30%, although patients treated with mantle radiation for Hodgkin's disease are at highest risk for developing cardiac complications because of the proximity of the radiation field to cardiac structures (Veinot & Edwards, 1996).
  (2) The risk of radiation-induced cardiac injury may be further increased by the concomitant use of anthracycline-based chemotherapy, especially when larger cumulative doses of doxorubicin (> 450 mg/m^2) are used, when radiation and chemotherapy are given concurrently, and when high dose-volumes of cardiac radiation are administered (Eltringham, Fajardo, & Stewart, 1975; Shapiro et al., 1998; Valagussa et al., 1994).
  (3) A significantly higher risk of death from ischemic heart disease has been reported for patients treated with radiation for Hodgkin's disease and breast cancer (Basavaraju & Easterly, 2002).
  (4) Other known cardiac risk factors such as tobacco use, hypertension, and hyperlipidemia further increase the risk of coronary atherosclerosis, myocardial infarction, and sudden death (Amronin & Solomon, 1965; Glanzmann, Kaufman, Jenni, Hess, & Huguenin, 1998).
  (5) Little is known about the prevalence of heart disease present prior to the initiation of RT.
d) Assessment
  (1) Clinical manifestations
    (a) Shortness of breath
    (b) Chest pain

(c) Fatigue
(d) Lower extremity swelling
(e) Syncope
(2) Physical examination
    (a) Arrhythmias
    (b) Altered respiratory status
    (c) Lower extremity edema
(3) Cardiac function studies
    (a) Electrocardiogram (EKG)
    (b) Resting echocardiograph and/or exercise echocardiography
    (c) CT or MRI
e) Collaborative management for cardiac injuries
(1) Prevention
    (a) Use treatment strategies that use lower total radiation doses and minimize cardiac exposure.
    (b) Avoid concurrent cardiotoxic chemotherapeutic agents when possible.
(2) Early detection
    (a) Perform routine cardiac evaluation during follow-up examinations.
    (b) Provide a referral to cardiology for recommendations to reduce the degree of initial cardiac injury and slow the progression of vascular, myocardial, and valvular fibrosis.
       i) Regular EKG and echocardiograms
       ii) Antibiotic prophylaxis for significant valve disease
       iii) Aggressive treatment of cardiac risk factors, especially hyperlipidemia, both at the time of cardiac therapy and during follow-up
f) Patient and family education
(1) Importance of routine cardiac examinations

(2) Compliance with recommendations for cardiac health, including diet, maintaining an ideal weight, and exercise
(3) Signs and symptoms of heart disease to report

4. Esophageal injury
a) Definition: Abnormalities included abnormal motility with and without mucosal edema, stricture, ulceration and pseudodiverticulum, and fistula. Abnormal motility occurred 4–12 weeks following radiotherapy alone and as early as 1 week after therapy when concomitant chemotherapy had been given. Strictures may develop 4–8 months following completion of radiotherapy. Ulceration, pseudodiverticulum, and fistula formation do not develop in a uniform time frame. Radiation-induced esophageal injury is more frequent when radiotherapy and chemotherapy are combined than it is with radiotherapy alone (Lepke & Libshitz, 1983).
b) Pathophysiology: Each abnormality is directly related to the tissue injury that occurs with high-dose radiation and the subsequent healing process.
c) Incidence and risk factors: Although rare complications occur, the exact incidence of these abnormalities is not well documented in the literature.
d) Assessment
(1) Clinical manifestations
    (a) Dysphagia
    (b) Hemoptysis with ulceration
    (c) Weight loss
    (d) Chest pain
(2) Physical examination
    (a) Weight loss
    (b) Difficulty in swallowing solid foods
(3) Additional studies: Upper endoscopy
e) Documentation: Nutritional alteration (Catlin-Huth et al., 2002)
(1) Anorexia
    (a) 0—None
    (b) 1—Loss of appetite
    (c) 2—Oral intake significantly decreased
    (d) 3—Requiring IV fluids
    (e) 4—Requiring feeding tube or parenteral nutrition
(2) Nausea
    (a) 0—None
    (b) 1—Able to eat
    (c) 2—Oral intake significantly decreased

(d) 3—No significant intake, requiring IV fluids

(e) 4—

(3) Dyspepsia and/or heartburn

    (a) 0—None

    (b) 1—Mild

    (c) 2—Moderate

    (d) 3—Severe

    (e) 4—

f) Collaborative management for esophageal injury

  (1) Depends on the specific injury.

  (2) Referral to a gastroenterologist may be appropriate for esophageal dilation, cauterization of bleeding, or placement of a stent.

g) Patient and family education

  (1) Dietary suggestions and restrictions

  (2) Signs and symptoms to report

References

Abratt, R.P., & Morgan, G.W. (2002). Lung toxicity following chest irradiation in patients with lung cancer. *Lung Cancer, 35*(2), 103–109.

Amronin, G.D., & Solomon, R.D. (1965). Production of arteriosclerosis in the rabbit. *Archives of Pathology, 75,* 219.

Antonadou, D., Coliarakis, N., Synodinou, M., Athanassiou, H., Kouveli, A., Verigos, C., et al. (2001). Randomized phase III trial of radiation treatment +/- amifostine in patients with advanced-stage lung cancer. *International Journal of Radiation Oncology, Biology, Physics, 51,* 915–922.

Aristizabal, S., Caldwell, W.L., & Avila, J. (1977). The relationship of time-dose fractionation factors to complications in the treatment of pituitary tumors by irradiation. *International Journal of Radiation Oncology, Biology, Physics, 2,* 667–673.

Atkins, H.L., & Tretter, P. (1966). Time-dose considerations in radiation myelopathy. *Acta Radiologica: Therapy Physics Biology, 5,* 79–94.

Basavaraju, S.R., & Easterly, C.E. (2002). Pathophysiological effects of radiation on atherosclerosis development and progression, and the incidence of cardiovascular complications. *Medical Physics, 29,* 2391–2403.

Brosius, F.C., Waller, B.F., & Roberts, W.C. (1981). Radiation heart disease. Analysis of 16 young (aged 15 to 33 years) necropsy patients who received over 3,500 rads to the heart. *American Journal of Medicine, 70,* 519–529.

Catlin-Huth, C., Haas, M., & Pollock, V. (2002). *Radiation therapy patient care record: A tool for documenting nursing care.* Pittsburgh, PA: Oncology Nursing Society.

Cox, J., & Komaki, R. (1994). The lung and thymus. In J. Cox (Ed.), *Radiation oncology rationale, technique, results* (pp. 320–355). St. Louis, MO: Mosby.

De Jaeger, K., Seppenwoolde, Y., Boersma, L.J., Muller, S.H., Baas, P., Belderbos, J.S., et al. (2003). Pulmonary function following high-dose radiotherapy of non-small cell lung cancer. *International Journal of Radiation Oncology, Biology, Physics, 55,* 1164–1165.

Delanian, S., Porcher, R., Balla-Mekias, S., & Lefaix, J.L. (2003). Randomized, placebo-controlled trial of combined pentoxifylline and tocopherol for regression of superficial radiation-induced fibrosis. *Journal of Clinical Oncology, 21,* 2545–2550.

Dorfman, L.S., Donaldson, S.S., Gupta, P.R., & Bosley, T.M. (1992). Electrophysiologic evidence of subclinical injury to the posterior columns of the human spinal cord after therapeutic radiation. *Cancer, 50,* 2815–2819.

Eltringham, J.R., Fajardo, L.F., & Stewart, J.R. (1975). Adriamycin cardiomyopathy: Enhanced cardiac damage in rabbits with combined drug and cardiac irradiation. *Radiology, 115,* 471–472.

Esik, O., Csere, T., Stefanits, K., Lengyel, Z., Safrany, G., Vonoczky, K., et al. (2003). A review on radiogenic Lhermitte's sign. *Pathology Oncology Research, 9*(2), 115–120.

Glanzmann, C., Kaufman, P., Jenni, R., Hess, O.M., & Huguenin, P. (1998). Cardiac risk after mediastinal irradiation for Hodgkin's disease. *Radiotherapy Oncology, 46*(1), 51–62.

Inoue, A., Kunitoh, H., Sekine, I., Sumi, M., Tokuuye, K., & Saijo, N. (2001). Radiation pneumonitis in lung cancer patients: A retrospective study of risk factors and the long-term prognosis. *International Journal of Radiation Oncology, Biology, Physics, 49,* 649–655.

Knopp, J.M. (1997). Lung cancer. In K.H. Dow, J.D. Bucholtz, R. Iwamoto, V. Fieler, & L.J. Hilderley (Eds.), *Nursing care in radiation oncology* (2nd ed., pp. 293–315). Philadelphia: Saunders.

Komaki, R., Lee, J.S., Kaplan, B., Allen, P., Kelly, J.F., Liao, Z., et al. (2002). Randomized phase III study of chemoradiation with or without amifostine for patients with favorable performance status inoperable stage II–III non-small cell lung cancer: Preliminary results. *Seminars in Radiation Oncology, 12*(1 Suppl. 1), 46–49.

Lepke, R.A., & Libshitz, H.I. (1983). Radiation-induced injury of the esophagus. *Radiology, 148,* 375–378.

Lund, M.B., Ihlen, H., Voss, B.M.R., Abrahamsen, A.F., Nome, O., Kongerud, J., et al. (1996). Increased risk of heart valve regurgitation after mediastinal radiation for Hodgkin's disease: An echocardiographic study. *Heart, 76,* 591–595.

McDonald, S., Rubin, P., Phillips, T., & Marks, B. (1995). Injury to the lung from cancer therapy: Clinical syndromes, measurable endpoints and potential scoring systems. *International Journal of Radiation Oncology, Biology, Physics, 3,* 1187–1205.

McEniery, P.T., Doristi, K., Schiavone, W.A., Pedrick, T.J., & Sheldon, W.C. (1987). Clinical and angiographic features of coronary artery disease after chest irradiation. *American Journal of Cardiology, 60,* 1020–1024.

Nicolaou, N. (2003). Prevention and management of radiation toxicity. In R. Pazdur, L.R. Coia, W.J. Hoskins, & L.D. Wagman (Eds.), *Cancer management: A multidisciplinary approach* (7th ed., pp. 909–939). New York: The Oncology Group.

Paulson, G.W., & Quenemoen, L.R. (1984). Radiation myelopathy. *Ohio State Medical Journal, 80,* 387–389.

Rodrigues, G., Lock, M., D'Souza, D., Yu, E., & Van Dyk, J. (2004). Prediction of radiation pneumonitis by dose-volume histogram parameters in lung cancer—A systematic review. *Radiotherapy Oncology, 71*(2), 127–138.

Schultheiss, T.E., Kun, L.E., Ang, K.K., & Stephens, L.C. (1995). Radiation response of the central nervous system. *International Journal of Radiation Oncology, Biology, Physics, 31,* 1093–1112.

Shapiro, C.L., Hardenbergh, P.H., Gelman, R., Blanks, D., Hauptman, P., Recht, A., et al. (1998). Cardiac effects of adjuvant doxorubicin and radiation therapy in breast cancer patients. *Journal of Clinical Oncology, 16,* 3493–3501.

Slama, M.S., Le Guludec, D., Sebag, C., Leenhardt, A.R., Davy, J.M., Pellerin, D.E., et al. (1991). Complete atrioventricular block following mediastinal irradiation: A report of six cases. *Pacing and Clinical Electrophysiology, 14,* 1112–1118.

Snooks, S.J., & Swash, M. (1985). Motor conduction velocity in the human spinal cord: Slowed connection in multiple sclerosis and radiation myelopathy. *Journal of Neurology, Neurosurgery, and Psychology, 48,* 1135–1139.

Stewart, J.R., Cohn, K.E., Fajardo, L.F., & Hancock, E.W. (1967). Radiation-induced heart disease: A study of 25 patients. *Radiology, 89,* 302–310.

Stewart, J.R., & Fajardo, L.F. (1971). Radiation-induced heart disease. Clinical and experimental aspects. *Radiologic Clinics of North America, 9,* 511–531.

Stewart, J.R., & Fajardo, L.F. (1984). Radiation-induced heart disease: An update. *Progress in Cardiovascular Diseases, 27*(3), 173–194.

Valagussa, P., Zambetti, M., Biasi, S., Moliterni, A., Zucali, R., & Bonadonna, G. (1994). Cardiac effects following adjuvant chemotherapy and breast irradiation in operable breast cancer. *Annals of Oncology, 5,* 209–216.

Veinot, J.P., & Edwards, W.D. (1996). Pathology of radiation-induced heart disease: A surgical and autopsy study of 27 cases. *Human Pathology, 27,* 766–773.

Vujaskovic, Z., Feng, Q.F., Rabbani, Z.N., Samulski, T.V., Anscher, M.S., & Brizel, D.M. (2002). Assessment of the protective effect of amifostine on radiation-induced pulmonary toxicity. *Experimental Lung Research, 28,* 577–590.

Wang, P.Y., Shen, W.C., & Jan, J.S. (1992). MR imaging in radiation myelopathy. *AJNR: American Journal of Neuroradiology, 13,* 1049–1058.

E. Gastrointestinal/abdomen
  1. Anorexia
    a) Pathophysiology
      (1) Radiation to the abdomen produces alterations in GI function.
      (2) Sustained stimulation of GI receptors leads to early satiety and decreased appetite (Hogan, 1990).
    b) Incidence
      (1) As many as 31%–87% of patients with cancer are affected by anorexia/cachexia (Tait, 1999).
      (2) At the time of diagnosis, 80% of patients with upper GI cancers and 60% of patients with lung cancer have experienced significant weight loss (Bruera, 1997).
      (3) Patients who experience weight loss during treatment have a decreased response to and tolerance of chemotherapy and RT (Cunningham & Bell, 2000; Jatoi & Loprinzi, 2001).
      (4) Treatment side effects such as mucositis, nausea, vomiting, and diarrhea contribute to anorexia and weight loss.
    c) Assessment
      (1) Preexisting conditions that contribute to anorexia and weight loss are age,
      nicotine use, medical conditions (e.g., severe chronic obstructive pulmonary disease, diseases affecting metabolism), malignant symptoms, and socioeconomic conditions, such as living alone and low income (Brown, 2002). Other symptoms also associated with weight loss are depression, infection, dyspnea, pain, fatigue, and the cumulative effect of several symptoms (McMahon & Brown, 2000).
      2) Weight change: Compare usual weight with present weight, time interval that weight loss occurred, and weight at each visit. Weight loss of 2%–5% is considered severe (McMahon & Brown, 2000).
      (3) Nutritional screening tools are available, such as the PG-SGA (Ottery, 1994).
      (4) Dietary intake: Three-day food diary, including one weekend day (Brown, 2002)
      (5) Functional status, such as decreased ability to care for self and maintain nutritional status, as measured by the Karnofsky Performance Status and Eastern Cooperative Oncology Group (ECOG) performance status (McMahon & Brown, 2002)
      (6) Physical examination findings to evaluate signs of malnutrition, such as weakness, loss of body fat, loss of muscle mass, and fluid status (McMahon & Brown, 2002)
      (7) Symptoms affecting nutrition, such as pain, mucositis, infection, fatigue, and depression
    d) Collaborative management of anorexia
      (1) Acute effects
        (a) Deficits in calories, protein, zinc, iron and iodine, and vitamin B_{12} (Doerr et al., 1997; Lindsey, Larson, Dodd, Brecht, & Packer, 1994)
        (b) Decreased quality of life, including physical, psychological, and social functioning (Brown, 2002; Lai & Perng, 1998)
        (c) Management
          i) Nutritional counseling: Individualized or structured nutritional teaching program; regular and frequent nutritional counseling (Ovesen, Allingstrup, Hannibal, Mortensen, & Hansen, 1993)

ii) Oral liquid supplement interventions (Ovesen & Allingstrup, 1992; McCarthy & Weihofen, 1999)

iii) Enhance calorie intake (small, frequent meals, calorie-dense foods); limit beverage intake around mealtime; take advantage of time of day when patient has best appetite.

iv) Supplement diet with eicosapentaenoic acid, a polyunsaturated fatty acid found in fish oil (e.g., ProSure® [Ross Laboratories]), no more than two cans per day (Ross Laboratories, 2003; Tisdale, 1996; Wigmore, Barber, Ross, Tisdale, & Fearon, 2000).

v) Symptom management (nausea, vomiting, pain, constipation, depression)

vi) Exercise may improve physical functioning, body composition, and muscle strength (Brown, 2002).

vii) Goal is weight loss of less than 5% during treatment (Ottery, 1994).

(2) Pharmacologic treatment: Progestational agents

(a) Megestrol acetate 160–800 mg/day (Bruera, MacMillan, Kuehn, Hanson, & MacDonald, 1990; Fietkaw, Riepl, & Kettner, 1997; Gagnon & Bruera, 1998; Kornblith et al., 1993; Loprinzi et al., 1993, 1994)

(b) Medroxyprogesterone acetate 300–1,000 mg/day (Brown, 2002)

(c) Potential adverse effects of progestational agents: Thromboembolic events, breakthrough bleeding, peripheral edema, hyperglycemia, hypertension, Cushing's syndrome, and alopecia (Maltoni et al., 2001)

(d) Corticosteroids improve appetite, food intake, performance status, and quality of life. No change in body weight. Symptom management for up to four weeks (Gagnon & Bruera, 1998).

(e) Metoclopramide 5 mg prior to meals enhances gastric motility and is useful for managing nausea and vomiting (Rust & Gill, 1997).

e) Documentation of anorexia (Catlin-Huth, Haas, & Pollock, 2002)

(1) 0—None

(2) 1—Loss of appetite

(3) 2—Oral intake significantly decreased

(4) 3—Requiring IV fluids

(5) 4 Requiring feeding tube or parenteral nutrition

f) Patient and family education (Cunningham, 2004)

(1) Education on general information about nutrition: Fundamentals of good nutrition

(2) Sources of nutritious calories and protein

(3) Teach how to complete food diaries.

(4) Symptoms to report that affect food intake

(5) Patient and family participation in development and implementation of the plan for nutrition

(6) Related Web sites

(a) CancerSymptoms.org—www.cancersymptoms.org/symptoms/anorexia

(b) CancerCare—www.cancercare.org

(c) Yale–New Haven Medical Center—http://info.med.yale.edu (managing side effects)

2. Nausea and vomiting

a) Pathophysiology

(1) Acute effects—Physiologic causes of nausea

(a) Studies carried out in animals during the 1950s led to the concept of a "vomiting center" located in the dorsolateral reticular formation and a chemoreceptor trigger zone (CTZ) within or near the area postrema (Harding, Young, & Anno, 1993).

(b) Vomiting center and vagal nuclei are stimulated by radiation or chemical mediators (American Society of Health-System Pharmacists, 1999; Wickham, 2003).

(c) Activation of neurotransmittal receptors—serotonin, substance P, dopamine, neurokinin 1 (NK-1), and other receptors that stimulate the CTZ in the area postrema in the brain (Frankel-Kelvin, 1997; Wickham, 2003)

(d) Stimulation of enterochromaffin cells by abdominal radiation yields liberation of serotonin (5-HT) that binds to 5HT3 receptors on vagal terminals, which activates the CTZ (Roberts & Priestman, 1993; Spitzer, 1995; Wickham, 2003)

(e) Local inflammation, release of histamine and prostaglandins (American Society of Health-System Pharmacists, 1999; Frankel-Kelvin, 1997)

(f) Radiation to the brain can directly affect the CTZ (Hogan & Grant, 1997).

   i) Nausea is mediated by the CNS, cerebral cortex, and autonomic nervous system (Wickham, 2003).

   ii) The stomach relaxes and gastric acid secretion is inhibited. A contraction of the small intestine causes the alkaline contents of the small bowel to be propelled into the stomach (Murphy-Ende, 2000).

(g) Vomiting—Mediated through the vomiting center and activated by several inputs, including the CTZ, cerebral cortex, limbic region, and afferent vagal and visceral nerves (Rhodes, Johnson, & McDaniel, 1995; Wickham, 2003).

(2) Late effects: Result from a combination of vascular damage and loss of parenchymal cells (Hall, 2000)

(a) Stomach—Ulceration and submucosal fibrosis can lead to antral fibrosis.

(b) Small intestine—Stenosis, serosal breakdown, and adhesion formation can lead to perforation, obstruction, nausea and vomiting, as well as abdominal cramping, chronic diarrhea, malabsorption with weight loss, and chronic blood loss (Coia, 1998; Crane & Janjan, 2003).

(c) Doses greater than 50 Gy may produce gastric ulcers two or more months following completion of radiation (Coia, 1998).

b) Incidence

(1) Acute effects

(a) Dependent upon the treatment field, treatment volume, dose, and fractionation (American Society of Health-System Pharmacists, 1999; Wickham, 1999).

(b) Onset may be within 10–15 minutes following TBI and hemibody radiation (Harding et al., 1993).

(c) Approximately 50% of people who receive conventionally fractionated radiation to the abdomen have onset of symptoms within 40–90 minutes (American Society of Health-System Pharmacists, 1999).

(d) Highest risk with TBI (Gralla et al., 1999).

(e) Intermediate risk with hemibody, upper abdomen, abdominal-pelvic, mantle, and craniospinal irradiation and cranial radiosurgery (Gralla et al., 1999)

(f) Low risk for RT alone with head and neck, extremities, breast, cranium only, pelvis, and thorax (Gralla et al., 1999); risk increases with concomitant chemotherapy.

(2) Chronic effects

(a) Gastric atrophy and ulceration may occur after doses of 45 Gy or more (Coia, 1998; Engelking, 2004).

(b) Symptoms may present months to years after cessation of treatment.

c) Assessment
  (1) Risk factors
    (a) Incidence and severity of past nausea and vomiting, precipitating factors
    (b) Age—More likely in patients younger than 50 years (Goodman, 1997; Morrow & Rosenthal, 1996)
    (c) Gender—More likely in menstruating women (Wickham, 2003).
    (d) Susceptibility to motion sickness (Hickock, Roscoe, & Morrow, 2001)
    (e) Unsuccessful past treatment of nausea and vomiting
    (f) Other possible causes—Concurrent chemotherapy, emetic potential of chemotherapy, other drugs (e.g., opioids), infection, constipation, intestinal obstruction, hypercalcemia, electrolyte abnormalities, and increased intracranial pressure (Wickham, 2003)
    (g) Anxiety—Patient expectation for nausea (Jacobsen et al., 1988)
  (2) Symptom assessment
    (a) Occurrence, frequency, intensity, onset, and duration of nausea and vomiting. Use patient report such as diaries, journals, and logs (Rhodes, 1997).
    (b) Signs of dehydration (e.g., poor skin turgor, electrolyte imbalance, increased weakness or fatigue, concentrated urine, orthostatic pressure, oral cavity moisture)
    (c) Physical examination
      i) Height and weight
      ii) CBC: Rule out associated infection and dehydration.
      iii) Electrolytes: Rule out dehydration—chloride and potassium due to loss in emesis (Wickham, 1999), blood urea nitrogen (BUN), creatinine ratio, CO_2 (Wickham, 2003); Calcium—rule out hypercalcemia (Iwamoto, 1992).
      iv) Oral intake over last 24-hour period
d) Collaborative management of nausea and vomiting
  (1) Pharmacologic
    (a) 5HT3 receptor antagonists block the stimulation of 5HT3 receptors at various points in the body and are useful to prevent radiation-induced emesis (Bey et al., 1996; Feyer, Stewart, & Titbach, 1998; Franzen et al., 1996; Prentice et al., 1995; Roberts & Priestman, 1993; Tramer, Reynolds, Stoner, Moore, & McQuay, 1998).
      i) May need prophylactic prevention of constipation (Goodman, 1997).
      ii) Headache, lightheadedness, and sedation are other common side effects.
      iii) Ondansetron, granisetron, and dolasetron have similar efficacy (Gralla et al., 1999).
      iv) Some patients have successful control with a second 5HT3 antagonist, despite inadequate control with a first (de Wit et al., 2001; Fayer et al., 1998).
    (b) Dopamine receptor antagonists bind to D2 and other receptors to vomiting impulses.
      i) At risk for extrapyramidal symptoms: More common in children and young adults.
      ii) May use prophylactic diphenhydramine
      iii) D2 receptor antagonists include phenothiazines, the most commonly used being prochlorperazine, butyrophenone, haloperidol, and substituted benzamides (metoclopramide) (Wickham, 2003).
    (c) Controlled-release metoclopramide, 20–80 mg every 12 hours for a maximum period of 12 weeks, has demonstrated a 40%–60% decrease in the severity of nausea

over the first two weeks of treatment and an approximate 50% reduction in severity of vomiting over the first four weeks of treatment (Wilson et al., 2002).

(d) Corticosteroids (e.g., dexamethasone, prednisone, prednisolone)—Mechanism is unclear. Possible inhibition of prostaglandin synthesis. May cause insomnia, anxiety, or euphoria (Goodman, 1997; Kirkbride et al., 2000).

(e) Benzodiazepines—Anxiolytics and amnesics may be useful for treatment of anticipatory nausea and vomiting (Malik et al., 1995).

(f) NK-1 antagonists are a new class of antiemetics that block the NK-1 receptor. The NK-1 receptor antagonist is more effective in prevention of delayed emesis. When added to the best current antiemesis drug, acute emesis also was decreased. Aprepitant is approved for prevention of acute and delayed emesis with highly emetogenic chemotherapy (Hesketh et al., 1999).

(g) High risk for radiation-induced nausea and vomiting—TBI and combination therapy with emetogenic chemotherapy (Gralla et al., 1999)

   i) 5HT3 antagonists give complete control rates of 50%–90% (Gralla et al., 1999).

   ii) Addition of corticosteroids may be beneficial.

   iii) Use serotonin receptor antagonist with or without corticosteroid before each fraction and for at least 24 hours afterward (American Society of

Health-System Pharmacists, 1999; Feyer et al., 1998; Gralla et al., 1999).

   iv) Patients receiving concurrent chemo-radiation should be given an antiemetic agent based on the level of emetogenicity of chemotherapy and risk factors associated with radiation-induced emesis (American Society of Health- System Pharmacists, 1999).

(h) Intermediate risk for radiation-induced nausea and vomiting: Hemibody, upper abdomen, abdominal-pelvic, mantle, craniospinal irradiation, and cranial radiosurgery

   i) Use serotonin receptor antagonist or dopamine receptor antagonist before each fraction.

   ii) Serotonin receptor antagonist is more effective. Efficacy may decrease after the first week.

   iii) Dopamine receptor antagonist may be more appropriate for patient receiving craniospinal or lower half-body radiation. Dexamethasone has efficacy similar to 5HT3 antagonists for patients receiving treatment to upper abdomen (Gralla et al., 1999).

(i) Low risk for radiation-induced nausea and vomiting: Radiation to cranium only, breast, head and neck, extremities, pelvis, thorax; treatment on as-needed basis. Use daily pretreatment dopamine antagonist, 5HT3 antagonist for rescue (Gralla et al, 1999).

(2) Nonpharmacologic management

   (a) Use in combination with prescribed antiemetic therapy.

   (b) May be effective by producing physiologic relaxation, which may decrease nausea and vomiting, serve as distractions, and enhance control.

      i) Self-hypnosis: State of altered consciousness and total body relaxation to an idea (King, 1997)

      ii) Biofeedback (King, 1997)

iii) Progressive contraction and relaxation of various muscle groups (King, 1997)

iv) Imagery: Mentally take self away by focusing on images of a relaxing place (Troesch, Rodehaver, Delaney, & Yanes, 1993).

v) Distraction: Learn to divert attention. Use videos, games, or puzzles (Vasterling, Jenkins, & Tope, 1993).

e) Documentation (Catlin-Huth et al., 2002)

(1) Nausea

(a) 0—None

(b) 1—Able to eat

(c) 2—Oral intake significantly decreased

(d) 3—No significant intake, requiring IV fluids

(2) Vomiting

(a) 0—None

(b) 1—One episode in 24 hours over pretreatment

(c) 2—Two to five episodes in 24 hours over pretreatment

(d) 3—More than or equal to six episodes in 24 hours over pretreatment or need for IV fluids

(e) 4—Requiring parenteral nutrition or physiologic consequences requiring intensive care; hemodynamic collapse

f) Patient and family education

(1) Teach patients at high or intermediate risk to self-administer antiemetics pretreatment on a daily basis.

(2) Instruct the patient to record nausea and vomiting in a diary.

(3) If the patient is vomiting, the patient should check weight daily.

(4) Teach symptoms of dehydration, such as excessive thirst, dizziness, palpitations, and fever.

(5) Practice dietary modifications such as small, frequent meals, foods that are cold or at room temperature, avoidance of favorite foods to avoid food aversions, and avoidance of fatty, spicy, salty, and sweet foods that may aggravate nausea (Wickham, 1999)

(6) Meal preparation when not feeling nauseous; share cooking with family members.

(7) Instruct nonpharmacologic methods to alleviate nausea.

(8) Use self-care guidelines for nausea and vomiting from RT (Wickham, 2003)

(9) Related Web sites

(a) CancerNausea.com—www.cancernausea.com

(b) National Comprehensive Cancer Network—www.nccn.org

(c) American Cancer Society—www.cancer.org

(d) NCI—http://cancer.gov

(e) American Society of Clinical Oncology patient Web site—www.peoplelivingwithcancer.org

3. Diarrhea/proctitis

a) Pathophysiology

(1) Acute effects

(a) Radiation affects the rapidly dividing cells of the small and large bowel.

i) Crypt stem cells responsible for cellular replacement are affected, resulting in denudement and atrophy of villi in the small bowel and flattening of the epithelial surface in the large bowel (Engelking, 2004).

ii) Loss of epithelial absorptive function results in loss of water, electrolytes, protein, and blood. Conjugated bile salts are not absorbed, enter the colon, and are deconjugated by bacterial flora resulting in water retention and diarrhea (Engelking, 2004).

iii) Decreased lactase causes accumulation of lactose (Engelking, 2004; Mercadante, 1995; Saclarides, 1997).

(b) Diarrhea occurs as a result of hypermotility of bowels, loss of absorptive surface with decreased absorption of nutrients and bile salts, and decreased or absent lactose resulting in lactose intolerance (Engelking, 2004).

(c) Symptoms may include nausea, vomiting, abdominal cramping, watery diarrhea, bleeding, and anemia. Symptoms of proctitis include mucoid rectal discharge, rectal pain, and rectal bleeding (Saclarides, 1997).

(d) Quality of life can be significantly affected by diarrhea, with physical and psychosocial consequences (Engelking, 2004).

(e) Symptoms usually resolve in two to three months (Saclarides, 1997).

(2) Chronic effects

(a) Median onset of 8–12 months to up to 15 years post-radiation. Result of vascular insufficiency due to damaged cells in blood vessels and connective tissue in the bowel wall (Engelking, 2004; Saclarides, 1997).

(b) Findings may include chronic bleeding, stricture, ulceration, obstruction, abscess formation, fistula formation, perforation, and diarrhea (Cascinu, 1995; Classen et al., 1998; Martz, 1999).

(c) The volume of small bowel in the field impacts the incidence and type of complications seen (Saclarides, 1997).

(d) The small intestine is sensitive to late effects and is a dose-limiting structure in the treatment of the abdomen and pelvis.

b) Incidence and risk factors

(1) Acute

(a) Most patients undergoing radiation to the abdomen, pelvis, or rectum will show signs of acute enteritis (Saclarides, 1997).

(b) Increased incidence with higher dose fraction, larger treatment volume, concomitant chemotherapy, radiation, prior abdominal or pelvic surgery, history of colitis, ileitis, and irritable bowel syndrome (Engelking & Sauerland, 2000)

(c) Usually occurs between 10–30 Gy (Engelking, 2004; Martz, 1999; Perez & Brady, 1998)

(2) Chronic effects

(a) Occurs in 5%–15% of patients treated with lower abdominal/pelvic irradiation (Engelking & Sauerland, 2000)

(b) In patients treated with chemoradiotherapy for rectal cancer, small bowel obstruction occurred in 5%–10% of patients, radiation enteritis in 4%, and rectal stricture formation in 5% (Ooi, Tjandra, & Green, 1999).

c) Assessment

(1) Individual risk factors

(a) Prior abdominal surgery

(b) History of pelvic inflammatory disease or colitis

(c) History of cardiovascular disease, hypertension, or diabetes (Frankel-Kelvin, 1997)

(2) Usual pattern of elimination

(3) Change in bowel pattern: Onset, frequency, amount and character of stools, blood in stool (Cancer.gov, 2003a, 2003b)

(4) Presence of other symptoms such as flatus, cramping, nausea, and abdominal distension (Cancer.gov, 2003a, 2003b)

(5) Nutritional status: Weight and height, change in eating habits, amount of residue in diet (Cancer.gov, 2003a, 2003b)

(6) Signs of dehydration: Poor skin turgor for age, serum electrolyte imbalance, increased weakness, orthostatic hypotension, and weight loss (Hogan, 1998)

(7) Level of stress, coping patterns, impact of symptoms on usual lifestyle (Hogan, 1998)

(8) Inflamed hemorrhoids

(9) Elevated temperature

(10) Comorbid conditions can exaggerate side effects (diabetes, lactose in-

tolerance, baseline chronic GI abnormalities) (Engelking, 2004; Hogan, 1998).

(11) Assess for over-the-counter medications, as some can exacerbate diarrhea.

d) Collaborative management of acute and chronic diarrhea

(1) Dietary modification

   (a) Include low-residue foods such as baked, broiled, or steamed meat, fish, and poultry; refined grains; cooked vegetables; canned fruit and applesauce; bananas; juices and nectars (McCallum & Polisena, 2000).

   (b) Include potassium-rich foods (Hogan, 1998).

   (c) Avoid fried and fatty foods, lactose products, foods high in fiber, strong spices and herbs, caffeine, alcohol, and tobacco.

   (d) Avoid foods that are too hot or cold (Hogan, 1998). Evaluate on a case-by-case basis (Engelking, 2004).

(2) Drink 3,000 cc of fluid a day (Hogan, 1998). Some fluids should contain some salt and sugar, such as clear broth, gelatin desserts, and sports drinks or soft drinks with some carbonation removed (Saltz, 2003).

(3) Pharmacologic management: Goals are inhibition of intestinal motility, reduction in intestinal secretions, and promotion of absorption.

   (a) Bulk-forming agents—Methylcellulose and pectin, which absorb water and enhance stool bulk (may cause abdominal discomfort and bloating in some people) (Engelking, 2004; Hogan, 1998)

   (b) Loperamide HCL slows GI peristalsis, which increases GI transit time and promotes water reabsorption. Start with 4 mg at the first episode of diarrhea, followed by 2 mg after each unformed stool, with a maximum of 12–16 mg in 24 hours (Wilkes, Ingwersen, & Barton-Burke, 2002).

   (c) Diphenoxylate/atropine slows GI transit time. Appears to have similar efficacy to loperamide in mild to moderate diarrhea (Saltz, 2003). It is associated with more CNS side effects, including dizziness, nausea, vomiting, and blurred vision (Engelking, 2004). Dose is one to two tablets every four hours as needed, not to exceed eight tablets in 24 hours (Cancer.gov, 2003a).

   (d) Paregoric may be used alternating with loperamide. Usual dose: 1 teaspoon qid as needed (Cancer.gov, 2003a).

   (e) Cholestyramine is a bile salt sequestering agent. Dose is one package after each meal and at bedtime (Cancer.gov, 2003a; Cascinu, 1995; Frankel-Kelvin, 1997).

   (f) Donnatal, an anticholinergic/antispasmodic agent, is used to alleviate bowel cramping. Dose is one to two tablets every four hours as needed (Cancer.gov, 2003a).

   (g) Mucosal prostaglandin inhibitors, such as aspirin or sulfasalazine, may be useful for radiation-induced diarrhea (Cancer.gov, 2003a; Coia, Myerson, & Tepper, 1995; Kilic, Egenhan, Ozenirler, & Dursun, 2000).

   (h) Steroid foam given rectally for proctitis

   (i) Narcotics may be needed for relief of abdominal pain.

   (j) Prior to beginning radiation to the pelvis, barium studies should be done to determine the extent of small bowel descent within the pelvis.

e) Documentation (Catlin-Huth et al., 2002)

(1) Diarrhea (patients without colostomy)

   (a) 0—None

   (b) 1—Increase of less than four stools/day over pretreatment

   (c) 2—Increase of four to six stools/day or nocturnal stools

(d) 3—Increase of seven or more stools/day or incontinence; need for parenteral support for dehydration

(e) 4—Physiologic consequences requiring intensive care or hemodynamic collapse

(2) Diarrhea (patient with colostomy)

(a) 0—None

(b) 1—Mild increase in loose, watery colostomy output compared with pretreatment

(c) 2—Moderate increase in loose, watery colostomy output compared with pretreatment but not interfering with normal activity

(d) 3—Severe increase in loose, watery colostomy output compared with pretreatment, interfering with normal activity

(e) 4—Physiologic consequences requiring intensive care or hemodynamic collapse

f) Patient and family education

(1) Educate the patient and family about expected side effects prior to therapy.

(2) Teach diarrhea management.

(a) Record number and consistency of daily bowel movements and when to seek medical attention (e.g., rectal spasms, excessive cramping, watery or bloody stools, continued diarrhea not relieved by treatment) (Engelking, 2004; Hogan, 1998).

(b) Teach signs and symptoms of dehydration, such as excessive thirst, fever, dizziness or lightheadedness, and palpitations (Hogan, 1998).

(c) Teach dietary modifications.

(d) Give specific instructions on how to take antidiarrheal medications.

(e) Give recommendations for proper skin care: Sitz baths, moisture barrier creams, and ointments

(f) Instruct the patient to report symptoms such as change in stools, rectal bleeding, or pain in follow-up.

(g) Related Web sites

i) NCI—http://cancer.gov

ii) American Society of Clinical Oncology patient Web site— www.peoplelivingwithcancer .org

iii) Abramson Cancer Center of the University of Pennsylvania—www.oncolink.upenn .edu

iv) CancerSource—www .cancersource.com

References

American Society of Health-System Pharmacists. (1999). ASHP therapeutics guidelines on the pharmacologic management of nausea and vomiting in adult and pediatric patients receiving chemotherapy or radiation therapy or undergoing surgery. *American Journal of Health-System Pharmacy, 56,* 729–764.

Bey, P., Wilkinson, P., Resbeat, M., Bourdin, S., Le Floch, O., Hahne, W., et al. (1995). A double-blind, placebo-controlled trial of IV dolasetron mesilate in the prevention of radiotherapy-induced nausea and vomiting in cancer patients. *Supportive Care in Cancer, 4,* 378–383.

Brown, J.K. (2002). A systematic review of the evidence on symptom management of cancer-related anorexia and cachexia. *Oncology Nursing Forum, 29,* 517–530.

Bruera, E. (1997). ABCs of palliative care: Anorexia, cachexia, and nutrition. *BMJ, 315,* 1219–1222.

Bruera, E., MacMillan, K., Kuehn, N., Hanson, J., & MacDonald, N., (1990). A controlled trial of megestrol acetate on appetite, calorie intake, nutritional status, and other symptoms in patients with advanced cancer. *Cancer, 66,* 1279–1282.

Cancer.gov. (2003a). *Gastrointestinal complications* (PDQ®). Retrieved March 18, 2003, from http://cancerinfo/pdq/ supportivecare/gastrointestinalcomplications/healthprofessional

Cancer.gov. (2003b). *Radiation enteritis* (PDQ®). Retrieved July 16, 2003, from http://cancerinfo/pdq/supportivecare/ radiationenteritis/healthprofessional

Cascinu, S. (1995). Drug therapy in diarrheal disease in oncology and hematology patients. *Critical Reviews in Oncology/Hematology, 18,* 37–50.

Catlin-Huth, C., Haas, M., & Pollock, V. (2002). *Radiation therapy patient care record: A tool for documenting nursing care.* Pittsburgh, PA: Oncology Nursing Society.

Classen, J., Belka, C., Paulsen, F., Budach, W., Hoffmann, W., & Bamberg, M. (1998). Radiation-induced gastrointestinal toxicity: Pathophysiology, approaches to treatment and prophylaxis. *Strahenther Onkology, 174*(Suppl. III), 82–84.

Coia, L. (1998). Gastrointestinal cancer. In L.R. Coia & D.J. Moylan (Eds.), *Introduction to clinical radiation oncology* (pp. 243–283). Madison, WI: Medical Physics Publishing.

Coia, L.R., Myerson, R.J., & Tepper, J.E. (1995). Late effects of radiation therapy on the gastrointestinal tract. *International Journal of Radiation Oncology, Biology, Physics, 31,* 1213–1236.

Crane, C.H., & Janjan, N.A. (2003). The stomach and small intestine. In J.D. Cox & K.K. Ang (Eds.), *Radiation oncology* (pp. 444–464). St. Louis, MO: Mosby.

Cunningham, R. (2004). The anorexia-cachexia syndrome. In C.H. Yarbro, M.H. Frogge, & M. Goodman (Eds.), *Cancer symptom management* (3rd ed., pp. 137–155). Sudbury, MA: Jones and Bartlett.

Cunningham, R.S., & Bell, R. (2000). Nutrition in cancer: An overview. *Seminars in Oncology Nursing, 16,* 90–98.

deWit, R., deBoer, A., Linden, G., Stoter, G., Sparreboon, A., & Verweij, J. (2001). Effective crossover to granisetron after failure to ondansetron: A randomized double blind study in patients failing ondansetron plus dexamethasone during the first 24 hours following highly emetogenic chemotherapy. *British Journal of Cancer, 85,* 1099–1101.

Doerr, T.D., Prasad, A.S., Marks, S.C., Beck, F.W., Shamsa, F.H., Penny, H.S., et al, (1997). Zinc deficiency in head and neck cancer patients. *Journal of the American College of Nutrition, 16,* 418–422.

Engelking, C. (2004). Diarrhea. In C.H. Yarbro, M.H. Frogge, & M. Goodman (Eds.), *Cancer symptom management* (3rd ed., pp. 528–550). Sudbury, MA: Jones and Bartlett.

Engelking, C., & Sauerland, C. (2000). Maintenance of normal elimination. In D.W. Bruner, G. Moore-Higgs, & M. Haas (Eds.), *Outcomes in radiation therapy: Multidisciplinary management* (pp. 530–562). Sudbury, MA: Jones and Bartlett.

Feyer, P.C., Stewart, A.L. & Titbach, O.J. (1998). Aetiology and prevention of emesis induced by radiotherapy. *Supportive Care in Cancer, 6,* 253–260.

Fietkaw, R., Riepl, M., & Kettner, H. (1997). Supportive use of megestrol acetate in patients with head and neck cancer during radio(chemo)therapy. *European Journal of Cancer, 33,* 75–79.

Frankel-Kelvin, J. (1997). Gastrointestinal cancers. In K.H. Dow, J.D. Bucholtz, R. Iwamoto, V. Fieler, & L. Hilderley (Eds.), *Nursing care in radiation oncology* (pp. 152–183). Philadelphia: Saunders.

Franzen, L., Nyman, J., Hagberg, H., Jakobsson, M., Sorbe, B., Nyth, A., et al. (1996). A randomized placebo controlled study with ondansetron in patients undergoing fractionated radiotherapy. *Annals of Oncology, 7,* 587–592.

Gagnon, G., & Bruera, E. (1998). A review of the drug treatment of cachexia associated with cancer. *Drugs, 55,* 675–688.

Goodman, M. (1997). Risk factors and antiemetic management of chemotherapy-induced nausea and vomiting. *Oncology Nursing Forum, 24*(Suppl. 7), 20–32.

Gralla, R.J., Osoba, D., Kris, M., Kirkbride, P., Hesketh, P., Chinnery, L., et al. (1999). Recommendations for the use of antiemetics: Evidence-based, clinical practice guidelines. *Journal of Clinical Oncology, 17,* 2971–2994.

Hall, E.J. (2000). *Radiobiology for the radiologist.* Philadelphia: Lippincott Williams & Wilkins.

Harding, R., Young, R., & Anno, G. (1993). Radiotherapy-induced emesis. In P.L.R. Andrews & G.J. Sanger (Eds.), *Emesis in anticancer therapy: Mechanisms and treatment* (pp. 163–178). London: Chapman and Hall Medical.

Hesketh, P., Gralla, R., Webb, R., Veno, W., Delprete, S., Bachinsky, M., et al. (1999). Randomized phase II study of neurokinin 1 receptor antagonist CJ—11,974 in the control of cisplatin-induced emesis. *Journal of Clinical Oncology, 17,* 338–343.

Hickok, J.T., Roscoe, J.A., & Morrow, G.R. (2001). The role of patients' expectations in the development of anticipatory nausea related to chemotherapy for cancer. *Journal of Symptom Management, 22,* 843–850.

Hogan, C. (1990). Advances in management of nausea and vomiting. *Nursing Clinics of North America, 25,* 475–495.

Hogan, C.M. (1998). The nurses' role in diarrhea management. *Oncology Nursing Forum, 25,* 879–886.

Hogan, C., & Grant, M. (1997). Physiologic mechanisms of nausea and vomiting in patients with cancer. *Oncology Nursing Forum, 24*(Suppl. 7), 8–12.

Iwamoto, R. (1992). Altered nutrition. In K.H. Dow & L. Hilderley (Eds.), *Nursing care in radiation oncology* (pp. 69–95). Philadelphia: Saunders.

Jacobsen, P.B., Andrykowski, M.A., Redd, W.H., Die-Trill, M., Hakes, T.B., Kaufman, R.J., et al. (1988). Nonpharmacologic factors in the development of posttreatment nausea with adjuvant chemotherapy for breast cancer. *Cancer, 61,* 379–385.

Jatoi, A., & Loprinzi, C. (2001). Current management of cancer-associated anorexia and weight loss. *Oncology, 15,* 497–508.

Kilic, D., Egenhan, I., Ozenirler, S., & Dursun, A. (2000). Double-blinded randomized, placebo-controlled study to evaluate the effectiveness of sulphasalazine in preventing acute gastrointestinal complications due to radiotherapy. *Radiotherapy Oncology, 57,* 125–129.

King, C. (1997). Nonpharmacologic management of chemotherapy-induced nausea and vomiting. *Oncology Nursing Forum, 24*(Suppl. 7), 41–48.

Kirkbride, P., Bezjak, A., Pater, J., Zee, B., Palmer, M.J., Wong, R., et al. (2000). Dexamethasone for the prophylaxis of radiation-induced emesis: A National Cancer Institute of Canada Clinical Trials Group phase III study. *Journal of Clinical Oncology, 18,* 1960–1966.

Kornblith, A., Hollis, D., Zuckerman, E., Lyss, A., Canelles, G., Cooper, R., et al. (1993). Effect of megestrol acetate on quality of life in a dose-response trial in women with advanced breast cancer. *Journal of Clinical Oncology, 11,* 2081–2089.

Lai, S.L., & Perng, R.P. (1998). Impact of nutritional status on the survival of lung cancer patients. *Chinese Medical Journal, 61,* 134–140.

Lindsey, A.M., Larson, P.J., Dodd, M.J., Brecht, M.L., & Packer, A. (1994). Comorbidity, nutritional intake, social support, weight and functional status over time in older cancer patients receiving radiotherapy. *Cancer Nursing, 17,* 113–124.

Loprinzi, C., Bernath, A., Schaid, D., Mailliard, J., Athmann, L., Michalak, J., et al. (1994). Phase III evaluation of 4 doses of megestrol acetate as therapy for patients with cancer anorexia and/or cachexia. *Oncology, 51*(Suppl. 1), 2–7.

Loprinzi, C., Michalak, J., Schaid, D., Mailliard, J., Athmann, L., Goldberg, R., et al. (1993). Phase III evaluation of four doses of megestrol acetate as therapy for patients with cancer anorexia and/or cachexia. *Journal of Clinical Oncology, 11,* 762–767.

Malik, I., Khan, W., Qazilbash, M., Ata, E., Butt, A., & Khan, M. (1995). Clinical efficacy of lorazepam in prophylaxis of anticipatory, acute, and delayed nausea and vomiting induced by high doses of cisplatin. *American Journal of Clinical Oncology, 18,* 170–175.

Maltoni, M., Nanno, O., Scarpi, E., Rossi, D., Serra, P., & Amadon, D.F. (2001). High dose progestins for the treatment of cancer anorexia-cachexia syndrome: A systematic review of randomized clinical trials. *Annals of Oncology, 12,* 289–300.

Martz, C.H. (1999). Diarrhea. In C.H. Yarbro, M.H. Frogge, & M. Goodman (Eds.), *Cancer symptom management* (2nd ed., pp. 522–536). Sudbury, MA: Jones and Bartlett.

McCallum, P.O., & Polisena, C.G. (2000). *The clinical guide to oncology nutrition.* Chicago: American Dietetic Association.

McCarthy, D., & Weihofen, D. (1999). The effect of nutritional supplements on food intake in patients undergoing radiotherapy. *Oncology Nursing Forum, 26,* 897–900.

McMahon, K., & Brown, J. (2000). Nutritional screening and assessment. *Seminars in Oncology Nursing, 16,* 106–112.

Mercadante, S. (1995). Diarrhea in terminally ill patients: Pathophysiology and treatment. *Journal of Pain and Symptom Management, 10,* 298–309.

Morrow, G., & Rosenthal, S. (1996). Models, mechanisms and management of anticipatory nausea and emesis. *Oncology, 53*(Suppl. 1), 4–7.

Murphy-Ende, K. (2000). Nausea and vomiting. In D. Camp-Sorrell & R. Hawkins (Eds.), *Clinical manual for the oncology advanced practice nurse* (pp. 379–397). Pittsburgh, PA: Oncology Nursing Society.

Ooi, B.S., Tjandra, J.J., & Green, M.D. (1999). Morbidities of adjuvant chemotherapy and radiotherapy for resectable rectal cancer: An overview. *Diseases of the Colon and Rectum, 42,* 403–418.

Ottery, F. (1994). Rethinking nutritional support of the cancer patient: The new field of nutritional oncology. *Seminars in Oncology, 21,* 770–778.

Ovesen, L., & Allingstrup, L. (1992). Different quantities of two commercial liquid diets consumed by weight-losing cancer patients. *Journal of Parenteral and Enteral Nutrition, 16,* 275–278.

Ovesen, L., Allingstrup, L., Hannibal, J., Mortensen, E.L., & Hansen, O.P. (1993). Effect of dietary counseling on food intake, body weight, response rate, survival and quality of life in cancer patients undergoing chemotherapy. A prospective, randomized study. *Journal of Clinical Oncology, 11,* 2043–2049.

Perez, C.A., & Brady, L.W. (1998). *Principles and practices of radiation oncology* (3rd ed.). Philadelphia: Lippincott-Raven.

Prentice, H.G., Cunningham, S., Gandhi, L., Cunningham, J., Collis, C., & Hamon, M. (1995). Granisetron in the prevention of irradiation-induced emesis. *Bone Marrow Transplantation, 15,* 445–448.

Rhodes, B. (1997). Criteria for assessment of nausea, vomiting, and retching. *Oncology Nursing Forum, 24*(Suppl.), 13–19.

Rhodes, V., Johnson, M., & McDaniel, R. (1995). Nausea, vomiting, and retching. The management of the symptom experience. *Seminars in Oncology Nursing, 11,* 256–265.

Roberts, J.T., & Priestman, T.J. (1993). A review of ondansetron in the management of radiotherapy-induced emesis. *Oncology, 50*(3), 173–179.

Ross Laboratories. (2003). ProSure [product information]. Retrieved June 10, 2004, from http://www.prosure.com/

Rust, D., & Gill, C. (1997). Nutritional support. In R. Gates & R. Fink (Eds.), *Oncology nursing secrets* (pp. 262–276). Philadelphia: Haney & Belfus.

Saclarides, T.J. (1997). Radiation injuries of the gastrointestinal tract. *Surgical Clinics of North America, 77,* 261–268.

Saltz, L. (2003). Understanding and managing chemotherapy-induced diarrhea. *Journal of Supportive Oncology, 1*(1), 35–46.

Spitzer, T. (1995). Clinical evidence for 5-HT3-receptor antagonist efficacy in radiation-induced emesis. In D.J.M. Reynolds, P.L.R. Andrews, & C.J. Davis (Eds.), *Serotonin and the scientific basis of antiemetic therapy* (pp. 84–89). Philadelphia: Oxford Clinical Communications.

Tait, N. (1999). Anorexia-cachexia syndrome. In C.H. Yarbro, M.A. Frogge, & M. Goodman (Eds.), *Cancer symptom management* (2nd ed., pp. 183–197). Sudbury, MA: Jones and Bartlett.

Tisdale, M.J. (1996). Inhibition of lipolysis and muscle protein degradation by EPA in cancer cachexia. *Nutrition, 12*(Suppl.), 31–33.

Tramer, M.R., Reynolds, D.J., Stoner, N.S., Moore, R.A., & McQuay, H.J. (1998). Efficacy of 5-HT3 receptor antagonists in radiotherapy-induced nausea and vomiting: A quantitative systematic review. *European Journal of Cancer, 34,* 1836–1844.

Troesch, L., Rodehaver, D., Delaney, E., & Yanes, B. (1993). The influence of guided imagery on chemotherapy-related nausea and vomiting. *Oncology Nursing Forum, 20,* 1179–1185.

Vasterling, J., Jenkins, R., & Tope, D. (1993). Cognitive distraction and relaxation training for the control of side effects due to cancer chemotherapy. *Journal of Behavioral Medicine, 16,* 65–80.

Wickham, R. (1999). Nausea and vomiting. In C.H. Yarbro, M.H. Frogge, & M. Goodman (Eds.), *Cancer symptom management* (2nd ed., pp. 228–253). Sudbury, MA: Jones and Bartlett.

Wickham, R. (2004). Nausea and vomiting. In C.H. Yarbro, M.H. Frogge, & M. Goodman (Eds.), *Cancer symptom management* (3rd ed., pp. 187–207). Sudbury, MA: Jones and Bartlett.

Wigmore, S.J., Barber, M.D., Ross, J.A., Tisdale, M.J., & Fearon, K.C. (2000). Effect of oral eicosapentaenoic acid on weight loss in patients with pancreatic cancer. *Nutrition and Cancer, 36,* 177–184.

Wilkes, G.M., Ingwersen, K., & Barton-Burke, M. (2002). *Oncology nursing drug handbook.* Sudbury, MA: Jones and Bartlett.

Wilson, J., Plourde, J.Y., Marshall, D., Yoshida, S., Chow, W., Harsanvi, Z., et al. (2002). Long-term safety and clinical effectiveness of controlled-release metoclopramide in cancer-associated dyspepsia syndrome: A multicenter evaluation. *Journal of Palliative Care, 18,* 84–91.

F. Bladder
1. RT is used as part of multimodality therapy for invasive bladder cancer in combination with surgery and chemotherapy. It is therefore important for the nurse to understand the role and side effects associated with combined modality therapy (Bruner & Horwitz, 2001; Martin, 2001).
   a) Bacillus Calmette-Guérin (BCG) is the most effective intravesical treatment for superficial bladder cancer. However, 30%–40% of tumors are refractory (Punnen, Chin, & Jewett, 2003).
   b) BCG failure is usually an indication for cystectomy, but several salvage intravesical strategies have been proposed, including combination RT (National Comprehensive Cancer Network, 2004).
   c) Chemotherapy has been used extensively in metastatic cancer of the bladder and urinary tract (Raghavan, 2003).

(1) Transitional cell carcinomas are the tumors most responsive to chemotherapy (Raghavan, 2003).

(2) Standard single agents (e.g., methotrexate, doxorubicin, mitomycin, ifosfamide, vinblastine, cisplatin) have produced objective response rates of 15%–25%, and combination chemotherapy (e.g., taxanes, gemcitabine) has resulted in a regression in 40%–75% of cases (Raghavan, 2003).

d) A recent meta-analysis (Widmark, Flodgren, Damber, Hellsten, & Cavallin-Stahl, 2003) reported the evidence for use of RT in treatment of bladder cancer.

(1) Moderate evidence shows that hyperfractionated RT provides a survival benefit at 5 and 10 years and an increased local control rate compared with conventional fractionation.

(2) Some evidence shows that preoperative RT followed by cystectomy does *not* provide any significant survival benefit compared to cystectomy alone.

(3) Moderate evidence shows that palliative RT of invasive bladder carcinoma can rapidly provide tumor-related symptom relief.

(4) Moderate evidence shows that palliative hypofractionated RT, 3 fractions in 1 week, gives the same relief of symptoms as 10 fractions in 2 weeks.

(5) Conclusive information on use of RT, optimal doses, and combination therapy for bladder cancer is lacking, and large randomized trials are needed.

2. Irritative bladder symptoms (IBS)

a) Pathophysiology

(1) IBS is a group of symptoms that includes dysuria, frequency, nocturia, and urgency. These symptoms may occur as acute or early symptoms and can be seen during and up to 12 months after treatment. This complex of symptoms is called IBS (Marks, Carroll, Dugan, & Anscher, 1995).

(2) Because of the nature of bladder cancer, it may be difficult to differentiate if the symptoms are from the tumor or from the RT (Sengelov & von der Masse, 1999).

(3) Early or acute urinary symptoms are a result of injury and inflammation of the epithelial layer of the bladder mucosa to the ionizing radiation (Muruve, 2001).

(4) Submucosal inflammation eventually may lead to fibrosis, perineural inflammation, and surface ulceration (Muruve, 2001).

(5) Side effects from RT may vary because of the amount of irradiated bladder volume, field setup, beam quality, fraction size, total dose, previous surgeries, and overall condition of the patient (Sengelov & von der Masse, 1999).

(6) Long-term effects (> 12 months) are mainly fibrovascular and include luminal occlusion, vascular ectasia, and necrosis of the vessel's walls. These changes lead to ischemia and fibrosis, leading to loss of muscle tone with dysfunctional voiding (Muruve, 2001).

(7) With conformal radiation, higher doses can be given to the target tissue, while giving lower doses to normal tissue. Side effects usually are decreased when normal tissue is spared. In bladder cancer, because of the proximity of the bladder neck and exposure to the urethra, side effects are not decreased (Muruve, 2001).

b) Incidence

(1) Occurrence of urinary symptoms that appear during radiation can vary from 23%–80% (Marks et al., 1995).

(2) Symptoms of IBS occur in 2%–12% of patients whose whole bladder radiation doses reach 50–60 Gy. Partial treatment of the bladder using 50–75 Gy has a 5%–20% complication rate for IBS (Muruve, 2001).

(3) Symptoms usually subside anywhere from several weeks to one year after completion of radiation but have been present as late as 48 months afterward (Marks et al., 1995).

c) Assessment: Includes urologic voiding pattern related to frequency of urination, urgency, nocturia, dysuria, and time of day it is better or worse. If symptoms are moderate to severe, have patient keep bladder diary (Berry, 2003).

d) Collaborative management of IBS
  (1) Acute effects
      (a) Encourage patient to increase fluid intake to 2–3 liters (unless contraindicated for cardiac or other medical reasons) to keep urine more diluted, which is less irritating to the bladder mucosa and helps to wash out clots that can cause an obstruction of urine flow (Kelly & Miaskowski, 1996).
      (b) Encourage patient to avoid caffeine and spicy drinks and food because they can be irritative to the bladder mucosa (Kelly & Miaskowski, 1996).
      (c) Administer pharmacologic agents as prescribed to relieve symptoms (Berry, 2003).
          i) Phenazopyridine hydrochloride has analgesic and anesthetic effects on the urinary tract. Useful for irritative effects of RT. Warn the patient that this drug will color the urine orange.
          ii) Urimax® (Integrity Pharmaceuticals, Indianapolis, IN) (contains hyoscyamine sulfate) is indicated for treatment of irritative voiding and pain of the urinary tract.
          iii) Flavoxate hydrochloride is an antispasmodic for urgency, frequency, nocturia, suprapubic pain, and incontinence associated with cystitis.

  (2) Long-term effects
      (a) Long-term effects that can occur years after initial therapy include contracted bladder, ulcer formation, fistulas, and bladder dysfunction (mainly IBS) (Muruve, 2001).
      (b) For persistent symptoms of slight to moderate IBS, continue to have patient obtain prescriptions for medications.
      (c) For symptoms that cause severe IBS, refer patient to urologist for possible surgical intervention.
      (d) For suspected ulcer of fistula, refer patient to urologist for possible surgical intervention.

3. Urinary tract infection (UTI)
   a) Pathophysiology
     (1) UTI or whole bladder infection can occur as an early or late side effect from radiation to the bladder. It is not a common acute side effect of RT but can occur as a secondary symptom because of the nature of bladder cancer (Muruve, 2001).
     (2) Inflammatory changes in the bladder mucosa can occur with exposure of subepithelial tissues to the caustic effects of urine.
   b) Incidence: Occurrence of UTI is 9%–22%, including both early and late symptoms (Henningsohn, Wijkstrom, Dickman, Bergmark, & Steineck, 2002).
   c) Assessment (Kelly & Miaskowski, 1996)
     (1) Obtain urinalysis, with microscopic analysis and culture and sensitivity if indicated for symptom. Check urine for color, clarity, and odor.
     (2) Check temperature.
     (3) Check patient for diaphoresis or chills.
     (4) Assess patient for lower abdominal or flank pain.
     (5) Obtain a CBC to rule out an elevated white blood count, which may indicate an infection.
   d) Collaborative management of UTI
     (1) Administer antibiotic for UTI as directed by the urine culture and sensitivity, such as sulfamethoxazole/trimethoprim, ciprofloxacin, or nitrofurantoin (Berry, 2003).
     (2) Monitor patient for signs and symptoms of allergic reaction from the antibiotic.
     (3) Patient may need to admitted to the hospital for IV antibiotic therapy if oral antibiotics do not relieve infection.

4. Hemorrhagic cystitis with irritative or hemorrhagic symptoms
   a) Pathophysiology
      (1) Vascular changes can occur along with endothelial edema and thickening, with a progressive depletion of a blood supply to the irradiated tissue or frank hematuria (Muruve, 2001).
      (2) Concurrent chemotherapy may increase the damaging effects of irradiation, as seen with cyclophosphamide and ifosfamide, which can cause hemorrhagic cystitis with gross hematuria, irritative voiding symptoms, and bladder contracture (Muruve, 2001).
   b) Incidence: Slight to moderate IBS along with hematuria were reported by 19%–49% of patients and more severe IBS plus hematuria in 33%–48% of patients (Muruve, 2001).
      (1) Symptoms of acute cystitis usually subside two to eight weeks after treatment (Volpe, 2000).
      (2) The trigone of the bladder is more sensitive to radiation side effects than is the dome of the bladder (Muruve, 2001).
      (3) Doses that are greater than 75–80 Gy can cause serious bladder injury (Marks et al., 1995).
   c) Assessment (Kelly & Miaskowski, 1996)
      (1) Monitor for signs of bleeding (e.g., patient complaining of dizziness or lightheadedness, decrease in blood pressure, weak pulse, fatigue).
      (2) Monitor for signs of fluid volume loss (e.g., poor skin turgor).
      (3) Monitor presence of blood in the urine. Obtain a urinalysis with microscopic analysis; observe for color, clarity, and odor.
      (4) Monitor for anemia. Obtain a CBC; check if hemoglobin and hematocrit are within normal limits.
      (5) Monitor patient's intake and output (Lind, 1998).
      (6) Obtain physician order for prothrombin time and international normalized ratio to assess bleeding tendencies.
      (7) Check frequency of urination; clots may obstruct urinary flow. Patient should void every two hours.
      (8) Obtain order for a type and crossmatch for blood transfusion as needed.
   d) Collaborative management
      (1) Acute effects
         (a) If patient is unable to void, may need to obtain order to catheterize patient. Patient may need bladder irrigations with saline performed by a physician.
         (b) Obtain order for blood transfusion (packed red cells) if hemoglobin and hematocrit are low.
         (c) Conjugated estrogens have been shown to normalize the prolonged bleeding time found in patients with hemorrhagic cystitis, which improves homeostasis (Liu et al., 1990).
         (d) Pentoxifylline, which is useful in providing relief from radiation fibrosis, enhances blood flow, enhancing oxygenation of the tissue. Normal dose is 400 mg tid po for six weeks (Muruve, 2001).
         (e) Pentosan polysulfate sodium is useful in treating the pain or discomfort of interstitial cystitis. Normal dose is 100 mg tid po. Alert the patient that this drug is a weak anticoagulant; contraindicated in patients on anticoagulant therapy (Physician's Desk Reference, 2003).
         (f) Flavoxate hydrochloride is an antispasmodic for urgency, frequency, nocturia, suprapubic pain, and incontinence associated with cystitis.
         (g) If patient is concurrently receiving chemotherapeutic agents that can cause hemorrhagic cystitis, administer sodium-2-mercaptoethane sulfonate for the prevention of hemorrhagic cystitis. The compound is given to detoxify acrolein, the byproduct of cyclophosphamide,

which causes the hemorrhagic cystitis (Liu et al., 1990; Marks et al. 1995).

(2) Long-term effects

(a) Hyperbaric oxygen—The breathing of 100% oxygen is thought to increase vascular density, which stimulates angiogenesis leading to the repair of tissue damaged from radiation (Corman, McClure, Pritchett, Kozlowski, & Hampson, 2003).

(b) Alum can be instilled intravesically for the treatment of hemorrhagic cystitis. Alum controls the hemorrhage by causing protein precipitation in the interstitial spaces and cell membranes, which leads to contraction of bleeding vessels (Goswami, Mahajan, Nath, & Sharma, 1993).

5. Obstructive symptoms (Muruve, 2001)

a) Pathophysiology: A decrease in force or caliber of flow, including urinary retention, decrease in caliber of urinary stream, leakage, or dribbling

(1) Normal smooth muscle may be replaced by fibroblasts and collagen deposition, causing severe scarring known as fibrosis.

(2) Fibrosis leads to tissue hypoxia (ischemia) and necrosis. Mucosal ischemia and epithelial damage compound, as these tissues develop more submucosal fibrosis as they are further exposed to the caustic effects of urine. Clinical findings show ulcer formation, radiation neuritis, and post-radiation fibrosis.

b) Incidence of severe obstructive complications has been reported at 9% (Sengelov & von der Masse, 1999).

c) Assessment

(1) Pain, discomfort

(2) Decrease in bladder capacity

(3) Change in caliber or flow of urine, such as weak stream

(4) Loss of control of urine

(5) Inability to void

(6) Draw blood for electrolytes, BUN, and creatinine to assess renal function.

d) Collaborative management

(1) Acute effects

(a) Oxybutynin chloride is an antispasmodic indicated for neurogenic bladder problems such as retention, urinary overflow, incontinence, nocturia, urinary frequency, or urgency.

(b) Tamsulosin hydrochloride

(c) Antihypertensives are useful for obstructive urinary symptoms because they help to relax the smooth muscles in the body that may help improve urinary flow. Additional antihypertensive medications should not be perscribed if patient is taking one (Spratto & Woods, 2003).

i) Terazosin hydrochloride

ii) Doxazosin mesylate

(2) Long-term effects

(a) For obstructive urinary symptoms unrelieved with medications, patient may need to have an indwelling catheter placed or be taught to self-catheterize.

(b) Obstructive urinary symptoms unrelieved with oral pharmacologic management may require cystectomy.

6. Assessment: Other diagnostic tests that may be useful in determining extent of radiation side effects (Muruve, 2001)

a) IV pyelogram is useful in evaluating anatomic abnormalities such as strictures, fistula formation, and renal calcifications in the genitourinary tract.

b) A computerized axial tomography scan can be useful in diagnosing bladder fistulas, bladder wall thickening, viewing the bladder intravesically with air or contrast, or detecting extraluminal masses.

c) Urodynamics may be helpful in assessing bladder volume, flow rate, decreased bladder compliance, and post-void residual urine caused by injury to the innervation of the bladder.

d) Cystoscopy may be useful in confirming acute radiation changes seen in the bladder mucosa, such as telangiectasia, diffuse erythema, increase in submucosal vascularity, and mucosal edema (Muruve, 2001).

7. Documentation (Catlin-Huth, Haas, & Pollock, 2002)

a) Urinary frequency/urgency
  (1) 0—Normal
  (2) 1—Increase in frequency or nocturia up to twice as normal
  (3) 2—Increase > twice as normal but < hourly
  (4) 3—Hourly or more with urgency, requiring catheter
  (5) 4—

b) Dysuria
  (1) 0—None
  (2) 1—Mild symptoms requiring no intervention
  (3) 2—Symptoms relieved with therapy
  (4) 3—Symptoms not relieved despite therapy
  (5) 4—

c) Urinary retention
  (1) 0—Absent
  (2) 1—Present

d) Urinary incontinence
  (1) 0—Absent
  (2) 1—Present

e) Skin sensation
  (1) 0—No problem
  (2) 1—Pruritus
  (3) 2—Burning
  (4) 3—Painful

f) Mucous membrane alteration
  (1) Drainage
    (a) 0—Absent
    (b) 1—Present
  (2) Drainage odor
    (a) 0—Absent
    (b) 1—Present

8. Patient and family education

a) Instruct patient about the possibility of bladder irritation from pelvic irradiation.

b) Instruct the patient to drink 2–3 liters of fluid per day to help decrease irritation to the bladder mucosa (Berry, 2003).

c) Instruct patient to void frequently every two to four hours, empty bladder before sleep, and drink fluids during the night if awakened to help decrease irritation of the bladder mucosa caused by the urine being in the bladder (Kelly & Miaskowski, 1996).

d) Instruct patient to call physician if symptoms go unrelieved or persist even with pain medications or oral antibiotics.

e) Instruct patient to take medications as prescribed to relax bladder muscles and to call

for a refill when 5–10 tablets are left (Berry, 2003).

f) Instruct patient about signs and symptoms of bladder infection such as burning or stinging on urination, increased frequency of urination, pain in the abdomen over the bladder, low back pain, low-grade fever, foul-smelling urine, blood in urine, increased urge to urinate, and painful sexual intercourse and to call a nurse or healthcare provider when they occur.

g) Instruct patient to take temperature daily and to call physician if temperature is 100°F or higher.

h) Instruct patient on how to urinate on schedule until frequency and urgency decrease to manageable interval.

i) Instruct patient to practice pelvic floor exercises, called Kegels. Instruct patient to tighten and relax the muscles that are used to stop and release urine flow. These exercises can help to strengthen muscles to regain control of urination (American Cancer Society, 2001).

j) For incontinence or leakage, instruct patient on options to help manage, such as the use of incontinence pads, use of a penile clamp, and use of a Texas catheter with leg bag.

k) Instruct patient on how to self-catheterize if instructed to do so by the physician.

l) Instruct patient in perineal skin care (Berry, 2003).
  (1) Keep skin in perineum and genital area clean with soap and water.
  (2) Use a moisture barrier on the skin, if needed, to protect the skin from excoriation.
  (3) Wear loose clothing to help prevent moisture buildup on the skin.
  (4) Wear incontinence pads to absorb moisture and change frequently to prevent skin excoriation.

(5) Call the nurse if skin becomes reddened or irritated.

9. Related Web sites

   a) Managing Side Effects in RT—www.soch.com/cli_pat_can_rad_abdomen.html

   b) American Foundation for Urologic Disease—www.afud.org/conditions/bladdercancer.asp

   c) University of Pittsburgh Medical Center: Bladder Cancer—www.upmccancercenters.com/cancer/bladder/recurrent_prof.cfm

   d) NCI Cancer.gov: What You Need to Know About Bladder Cancer—http://cancer.gov/cancerinfo/wyntk/bladder

   e) Oncology Channel: Bladder Cancer—www.oncologychannel.com/bladdercancr/index.shtml

   f) ASCO Patient Web site—www.peoplelivingwithcancer.org

   g) Bladder Cancer Web Cafe: Information resources support—http://blcwebcafe.org/urinaryph.asp

   h) Understanding Bladder Cancer and What You Should Know About Its Diagnosis and Treatment—http://telescan.nki.nl/bladder2/html

   i) Consult Doctors: Bladder infection—www.consultdrs.com/infectious.html

References

American Cancer Society. (2001). *Sexuality and cancer: For the woman who has cancer and her partner*. Atlanta, GA: Author.

Berry, D. (2004). Bladder disturbances. In C.H. Yarbro, M.H. Frogge, & M. Goodman (Eds.), *Cancer symptom management* (3rd ed., pp. 505–511). Sudbury, MA: Jones and Bartlett.

Bruner, D.W., & Horwitz, M. (2001). Bladder cancer. In D.W. Bruner, G. Moore-Higgs, & M. Haas (Eds.), *Outcomes in radiation therapy: Multidisciplinary management* (pp. 331–350). Sudbury, MA: Jones and Bartlett.

Catlin-Huth, C., Haas, M., & Pollock, V. (2002). *Radiation therapy patient care record: A tool for documenting nursing care*. Pittsburgh, PA: Oncology Nursing Society.

Corman, J.M., McClure, D., Pritchett, R., Kozlowski, P., & Hampson, N.B. (2003) Treatment of radiation induced hemorrhagic cystitis with hyperbaric oxygen. *Journal of Urology, 169*, 2200–2202.

Goswami, A.K., Mahajan, R.K., Nath, R., & Sharma, S.K. (1993). How safe is 1% alum irrigation in controlling intractable vesical hemorrhage. *Journal of Urology, 149*, 264–267.

Henningsohn, L., Wijkstrom, H., Dickman, P.W., Bergmark, K., & Steineck, G. (2002). Distressful symptoms after radical radiotherapy for urinary bladder cancer. *Radiotherapy and Oncology, 62*, 215–225.

Kelly, L.P., & Miaskowski, C. (1996). An overview of bladder cancer: Treatment and nursing implications. *Oncology Nursing Forum, 23*, 459–469.

Lind, J. (1998). Nursing care of the client with cancer of the urinary system. In J.K. Itano & K.N. Taoka (Eds.), *Core curriculum of oncology nursing* (pp. 434–437). Philadelphia: Saunders.

Liu, Y.K., Harty, J.I., Steinbock, G.S., Holt, H.A., Jr., Goldstein, D.H., & Amin, M. (1990). Treatment of radiation or cyclophosphamide induced hemorrhagic cystitis using conjugated estrogen. *Journal of Urology, 144*, 41–43.

Marks, L.B., Carroll, P.R., Dugan, T.C., & Anscher, M.S. (1995). The response of the urinary bladder urethra and ureter to radiation and chemotherapy. *International Journal of Radiation Oncology, Biology, Physics, 31*, 1257–1280.

Martin, C.W. (2001). Combined modality treatments. In D.W. Bruner, G. Moore-Higgs, & M. Haas (Eds.), *Outcomes in radiation therapy: Multidisciplinary management* (pp. 121–133). Sudbury, MA: Jones and Bartlett.

Muruve, N.A. (2001). *Radiation cystitis*. Retrieved May 27, 2004, from http://www.emedicine.com/med/topic2869.htm

National Comprehensive Cancer Network. (2004). *Clinical practice guidelines in oncology. Bladder cancer: Including upper tract tumors and transitional cell carcinoma and prostate*. Retrieved May 27, 2004, from http://www.nccn.org

Physician's Desk Reference. (2003). *Pentosan polysulfate sodium*. Montvale, NJ: Medical Economics.

Punnen S.P., Chin, J.L., & Jewett, M.A. (2003). Management of Bacillus Calmette-Guerin (BCG) refractory superficial bladder cancer: Results with intravesical BCG and interferon combination therapy. *Canadian Journal of Urology, 10*, 1790–1795.

Raghavan, D. (2003). Progress in the chemotherapy of metastatic cancer of the urinary tract. *Cancer, 97*(Suppl. 8), 2050–2055.

Sengelov, L., & von der Masse, H. (1999). Radiotherapy in bladder cancer [Review]. *Radiotherapy and Oncology, 52*, 1–14.

Spratto, G.R., & Woods, A. (Eds.). (2003). *PDR nurse's drug handbook*. Clifton Park, NY: Delmar Learning.

Volpe, H.M. (2000). Radiation therapy. In J. Held-Warmkessel (Ed.), *Contemporary issues in prostate cancer: A nursing perspective* (pp. 150–157). Sudbury, MA: Jones and Bartlett.

Widmark, A., Flodgren, P., Damber, J.E., Hellsten, S., & Cavallin-Stahl, E. (2003). A systematic overview of radiation therapy effects in urinary bladder cancer. *Acta Oncologica, 42*(5–6), 567–581.

G. Male pelvis/prostate

   1. Urinary dysfunction (frequency, urgency, retention, dysuria, nocturia)

      a) Pathophysiology

         (1) Acute—Urinary frequency/urgency results from changes in the urinary bladder and prostate gland. The exact mechanism causing early and temporary changes in bladder function is not fully understood (Maher, 1997).

            (a) Normal function depends upon the successful interaction of the bladder wall mucosa, muscle layers, and supporting neurovascular structures. Smooth muscle edema occurring early in radiotherapy can contribute to early changes in reservoir function (Marks, Carroll,

Dugan, & Anscher, 1995). This causes an increase in urinary frequency, urgency, nocturia, and dysuria.

(b) Radiation to the prostate can contribute to the described associated urinary morbidity. Chronic inflammatory changes of the prostate gland itself occur in 37% of patients treated with RT (Gaudin, Zelefsky, Leibel, Fuks, & Reuter, 1999).

(2) Late—Interstitial fibrosis occurs in irradiated tissue, which can be accompanied by obliterative endarteritis and telangiectasia.

(a) Thin-walled dilated vessels may rupture resulting in painless hematuria.

(b) Epithelial tissue appears thin, pale, and atrophic and may ulcerate (Bruner, Bucholtz, Iwamoto, & Strohl, 1998).

b) Incidence

(1) Noninfectious cystitis is mild and intermittent initially, usually starting after three to five weeks. Infections may occur during the first week or less than 10 treatments if bacteria were introduced during simulation (Bruner et al., 1998; Maher, 1997).

(2) Males with enlarged prostates are at risk for increased urinary obstructive symptoms secondary to swelling of the gland, which can start at any point throughout the treatment course (Forman, Keole, Bolton, & Tekyi-Mensah, 1999).

(3) Incidence rates are dependent upon specific treatment planning and modality.

(4) Approximately 1%–2% of patients receiving RT will develop a urinary tract infection (Roberts, Murphy, & Ludgate, 1990).

(a) 3-D conformal and conventional therapy to the prostate (see Table 9)

(b) IMRT to the prostate (see Table 10)

c) Assessment

(1) Presence of urinary urgency, frequency, dysuria, hematuria, and nocturia

Table 9. 3-D Conformal and Conventional Therapy to the Prostate: Incidence of Urinary Side Effects

Grade	Description	Percentage
Acute		
Grade 0	No change	38%–62%
Grade 1	Frequency of urination or nocturia twice pretreatment habit/dysuria, urgency not requiring medication	53%–59%
Grade 2	Frequency of urination or nocturia that is less than every hour. Dysuria, urgency, or bladder spasm requiring local anesthetic.	20%–23%
Grade 3	Frequency with urination and nocturia hourly or more frequently or dysuria, pelvis pain or bladder spasm requiring regular, frequent narcotic/gross hematuria with or without clot passage	1%–3%
Grade 4	Hematuria requiring transfusion/acute bladder obstruction not secondary to clot passage, ulceration, or necrosis	—
Late		
Grade 0–1	Grade 0—None Grade 1—Slight epithelial atrophy, minor telangiectasia (microscopic hematuria)	83%
Grade 2	Moderate frequency, generalized telangiectasia, intermittent macroscopic hematuria	5%–37%
Grade 3	Severe frequency and dysuria, severe generalized telangiectasia (often with petechiae), frequent hematuria, reduction in bladder capacity (< 150 cc)	0.1%–2%
Grade 4	Necrosis/contracted bladder, capacity < 100 cc, severe hemorrhagic cystitis	—
Grade 5	Death related to radiation	—

Note. Based on information from Chism et al., 2003; Dearnaley et al., 1999; Michalski et al., 2000; Zelefsky, Cowen, et al., 1999; Zelefsky, Wallner, et al., 1999.

Table 10. IMRT to the Prostate: Incidence of Urinary Side Effects	
Grade	**Percentage**
Acute	
Grade 0	33%
Grade 1	38%
Grade 2	28%–34%
Grade 3	< 0.5%
Late	
Grade 0	74%
Grade 1	16%
Grade 2	9.5%
Grade 3	0.5%

Note. Based on information from Shu et al., 2001; Zelefsky et al., 2002.

(2) Examination of distended bladder (retention)
(3) Reports of weakened urinary stream, obstructive symptoms, urge or stress incontinence
(4) Elevated temperature
(5) Discolored or cloudy urine
(6) Bladder spasms
(7) Physical examination
    (a) Palpate and percuss abdomen and suprapubic area to assess for bladder distention or tenderness.
    (b) Allow symptoms (fever, pain, cloudy urine, or hematuria) to indicate what testing should be performed (e.g., a urinalysis and/or urine culture to detect the presence of bacteria and red and white blood cells).
d) Documentation (Catlin-Huth, Haas, & Pollock, 2002)
    (1) Urinary frequency/urgency
        (a) 0—Normal
        (b) 1—Increase in frequency or nocturia up to two times greater than normal
        (c) 2—Increase greater than two times normal but less than hourly
        (d) 3—Hourly or more with urgency, requiring catheter
        (e) 4—
    (2) Urinary incontinence
        (a) 0—Absent
        (b) 1—Present
    (3) Urinary retention
        (a) 0—Absent
        (b) 1—Present
    (4) Dysuria
        (a) 0—None

    (b) 1—Mild symptoms requiring no intervention
    (c) 2—Symptoms relieved with therapy
    (d) 3—Symptoms not relieved despite therapy
    (e) 4—
e) Collaborative management
    (1) Acute effects of urinary symptoms
        (a) Maintain hydration (one to two liters) throughout daytime (Iwamoto & Maher, 2001) while decreasing fluid intake in the evening to reduce the incidence of nocturia (Bruner et al., 1998).
        (b) Avoid caffeinated products. Although studies are not available specific to postradiation in patients with prostate cancer, some evidence suggests eliminating caffeine may assist in decreasing bothersome urinary symptoms (Abel et al., 1999; Albertsen, 1997; Gray, 2001).
        (c) Administer appropriate medication as prescribed.
            i) Ibuprofen—400–800 mg three to four times daily, relieves pain by inhibiting prostaglandin synthesis (Deglin & Vallerand, 2003)
            ii) Oxybutynin chloride—5 mg two to three times daily, not to exceed 5 mg daily or 10–15 mg daily as extra large tablets. Inhibits the action of acetylcholine and has antispasmolytic action on smooth muscle. Inform patients this medication may cause drowsiness or blurred vision (Deglin & Vallerand, 2003).
            iii) Phenazopyridine—200 mg up to three times daily, acts on urinary mucosa to produce an analgesic effect. Caution patients that urine will turn a reddish/orange color (Deglin & Vallerand, 2003; Iwamoto & Maher, 2001).
            iv) Tamsulosin hydrochloride—0.4 mg once daily, can be increased to 0.8 mg daily if ineffective. Decreases contractions of smooth muscle within the prostatic capsule by binding to alpha-1 receptors

(Deglin & Vallerand, 2003; Prosnitz et al., 1999).

    v) Terazosin hydrochloride—1 mg or may be increased to 5–10 mg daily. Decreases contractions of smooth muscle within prostatic capsule by binding to alpha-1 receptors (Deglin & Vallerand, 2003). This drug was found to be effective in treating benign prostatic obstruction (Wilt, Howe, & MacDonald, 2002), although some controversy exists whether it is more effective than other alpha blockers (Kaplan, 2002).

    vi) Doxazosin mesylate—1–8 mg daily with gradual dose escalation. Decreases contractions of smooth muscle within prostatic capsule by binding to alpha-1 receptors (Deglin & Vallerand, 2003).

    (d) Temporary suspension of RT may be considered.

(2) Long-term effects of urinary symptoms

    (a) Late effects generally are managed by long-term administration of urinary analgesics, antispasmodics, or alpha-1 receptor–blocking agents mentioned under acute effects.

    (b) If long-term effects are a result of decreased bladder capacity or urethral strictures, surgical or endoscopic evaluation at intervention may be necessary (Maher, 1997).

f) Patient and family education

(1) Inform patient and family of potential for urinary side effects from pelvic irradiation.

(2) Educate patient and family as to signs and symptoms of urinary tract infection and radiation-induced cystitis.

(3) Instruct patient and family to report first signs and/or symptoms of radiation-induced cystitis.

(4) Instruct patient in dietary interventions, and promote adequate hydration.

(5) Reassure patient as to the availability of medications should symptoms become problematic. Thoroughly review side effect profile and possible drug interactions with patient as appropriate.

2. Proctitis/diarrhea

  a) Pathophysiology: See section V, E—Gastrointestinal/Abdomen

  b) Incidence of lower GI side effects: Rates are dependent on treatment planning and technique.

    (1) With 3-D conformal RT (see Table 11)

      (a) Acute

      (b) Chronic

    (2) With IMRT (see Table 12)

      (a) Acute (see Table 13)

      (b) Late (see Table 14)

  c) Assessment of symptoms (see section V, E—Gastrointestinal/Abdomen)

  d) Documentation

    (1) Elimination alteration (Catlin-Huth et al., 2002)

      (a) Diarrhea (patients without colostomy) (see section V, E—Gastrointestinal/Abdomen)

      (b) Diarrhea (patients with colostomy) (see section V, E—Gastrointestinal/Abdomen)

      (c) Proctitis (RTOG Morbidity Grading Scale)

        i) 0—None

        ii) 1—Increased stool frequency and occasional blood-streaked stools or rectal discomfort (including hemorrhoids) not requiring medication

        iii) 2—Increased stool frequency, bleeding, mucous discharge,

Table 11. Incidence of Lower GI Side Effects With 3-D Conformal Radiation Therapy

Grade	Percentage
Acute	
Grade 0	45%–62%
Grade 1	21%–31%
Grade 2	16%–24%
Grade 3	0–1%
Grade 4	0
Chronic	
Grade 0–1	90%
Grade 2	9%–14%
Grade 3	0.75%–3%
Grade 4	0

Percentage ranges can vary widely, as toxicity often is related to radiation dose, field size, and anatomic inclusions within the prescribed field.

Note. Based on information from Chism, et al., 2002; Michalski et al., 2000; Zelefsky, Cowen, et al., 1999; Zelefsky & Eid, 1998; Zelefsky, Wallner, et al., 1999.

Table 12. Incidence of Lower GI Side Effects With IMRT

Grade	Percentage
Acute	
Grade 0–1	–
Grade 2	4.5%
Grade 3	0
Grade 4	0
Chronic	
Grade 0–1	–
Grade 2	1.5%
Grade 3	0.1%
Grade 4	0

Note. Based on information from Zelefsky et al., 2002.

or rectal discomfort requiring medication; anal fissure

    iv) 3—Symptoms not relieved despite therapy. Increased stool frequency/diarrhea requiring parenteral support; rectal bleeding requiring transfusion; or persistent mucous discharge necessitating sanitary pads

    v) 4—Perforation, bleeding, necrosis, or other life-threatening complication requiring surgical intervention (e.g., colostomy)

  (d) Other factors
    i) Daily weight
    ii) Compliance with dietary recommendations and fluid intake
    iii) May be helpful to use a daily documentation of dietary intake and bowel pattern sheet

(2) Skin sensation (see section IV, C—Skin Reactions)

e) Collaborative management

(1) Acute effects of diarrhea (see section V, E—Gastrointestinal/Abdomen)

  (a) Dietary management: Goal is to minimize diarrhea and abdominal cramping and initiate dietary interventions at start of treatment (Kelvin, 1997).
    i) Low fiber to decrease irritation of mucosa and GI motility
    ii) Low lactose to handle lactase deficiency
    iii) Low fat, to prolong transit time

    iv) May consider adding psyllium as a bulk-forming agent (Bliss et al., 2001; Murphy, Stacey, Crook, Thompson, & Panetta, 2000)

    v) If severe diarrhea continues, eliminate any fruits and vegetables, except for bananas and applesauce.
      • If symptom still continues, treatment break may be required.
      • Consult a dietitian.

  (b) Fluid and nutrient balance: Goal is adequate amounts of fluid and nutrients to prevent dehydration, electrolyte imbalance, and weight loss.
    i) Clear juices, broth, and decaffeinated tea
    ii) Juices high in electrolytes (e.g., Gatorade®)
    iii) Lactose-free liquid supplements

  (c) Skin alteration from diarrhea (see sections IV, C—Skin Reactions; V, E—Gastrointestinal/Abdomen)
    i) If appropriate, suggest the use of sanitary pads or adult incontinence briefs for rectal discharge or stool incontinence.

Table 13. Acute RTOG Lower GI, Including Pelvis Morbidity Grading Scale

Grade	Criteria
Grade 0	No change
Grade 1	Increased frequency or change in quality of bowel habits not requiring medication. Rectal discomfort not requiring medication.
Grade 2	Diarrhea requiring parasympatholytic drugs (e.g., diphenoxylate HCL). Mucous discharge not necessitating sanitary pads. Rectal or abdominal pain requiring analgesics.
Grade 3	Diarrhea requiring parenteral support. Severe mucous or bloody discharge necessitating sanitary pads. Abdominal distention (flat plate radiograph demonstrates distended bowel loops).
Grade 4	Acute or subacute obstruction, fistula, or perforation; GI bleeding requiring transfusion; abdominal pain or tenesmus requiring tube decompression or bowel diversion.

Note. Based on information from RTOG, 2003.

Table 14. Late RTOG Small/Large Intestine Morbidity Grading Scale

Grade	Criteria
Grade 0	None
Grade 1	Mild diarrhea, mild abdominal cramping, bowel movement five times daily, slight rectal discharge or bleeding
Grade 2	Moderate diarrhea and colic bowel movements more than five times daily. Excessive rectal mucus or intermittent bleeding.
Grade 3	Obstruction or bleeding requiring surgery
Grade 4	Necrosis/perforation/fistula

Note. Based on information from RTOG, 2003.

    ii) Aggressive personal and anal hygiene (Boyd & Berardi, 2002)

(d) Medications/pharmacologic: After three or more watery bowel movements a day, initiation should begin (Kelvin, 1997).

    i) Initial treatment: Anticholinergic medications (see section V, E—Gastrointestinal/Abdomen)

    ii) If experiencing proctitis, consider administering appropriate medication as prescribed.

- Hydrocortisone preparations (creams, ointments, suppository, or foam) can be used up to four times daily (Boyd & Berardi, 2002; Donjon & Goeckner, 1999).
- Topical lidocaine—Apply as needed, not to exceed 30 g per day
- Aluminum acetate—Powder or tablets dissolved in tepid water and soaks applied three to four times daily for one week (Donjon & Goeckner, 1999). May be used with sitz baths.
- Sucralfate—1 g qid or 2 g bid by mouth (Deglin & Vallerand, 2003; Sasai et al., 1998). May also be used in an enema preparation (Melko, Turco, Phelan, & Sauers, 1999)

- Mesalamine—Rectal suppository or suspension enema one bottle per rectum at night; however, this may cause diarrhea (Deglin & Vallerand, 2003; Goldstein & DiMarino, 2000).

    iii) If no response to pharmacologic interventions

- Consult proctologist/gastroenterologist if diarrhea or rectal bleeding is unresolved by pharmacologic interventions.
- Send stool for *Clostridium difficile* toxin if early into treatment or not responding to pharmaceuticals (can be caused by chemotherapy, RT, prolonged hospitalization, and high doses of antibiotics) (Blot et al., 2003).
- Treatment breaks may be considered during therapy.

(2) Long-term effects of diarrhea

    (a) Maintain low-fiber diet (Iwamoto & Maher, 2001).

    (b) Maintain aggressive anal/personal hygiene (Boyd & Berardi, 2002).

    (c) Continue the use of sanitary pads or adult incontinence briefs as needed.

    (d) Long-term use of medications for both urinary morbidity as described above and antidiarrheal/proctitis medications also as described above with the possible addition of the following.

      i) Hydrocortisone enemas (Gul, Prasannan, Jabar, Shaker, & Moissin, 2002)

      ii) Sucralfate enemas (Gul et al., 2002)

    (e) Close follow-up with proctologist/gastroenterologist if indicated who may recommend the following.

      i) Laser treatment to cauterize bleeding vessels within the rectum (Kaassis, Oberti, Burtin, & Boyer, 2000; Taieb et al., 2001)

      ii) Formalin instillation or applied topically for chronic hemorrhagic proctitis (Counter, Froese, & Hart, 1999; Luna-Perez & Rodriguez-Ramirez, 2002; Ouwendijk et al., 2002).

iii) Hyperbaric oxygen treatments (Warren, Feehan, Slade, & Cianci, 1997).

f) Patient and family education (see section V, E—Gastrointestinal/Abdomen)

(1) Inform patient that diarrhea is an expected side effect of radiation to the pelvis and that it usually occurs after 2.5–3 weeks of treatment.

(2) Teach dietary modifications.

(3) Instruct patient and family in comfort measures (e.g., sitz bath, tepid water cotton cloth soaks).

(4) Explain protocol for perianal hygiene (mild soap, do not rub, pat dry).

(5) Describe signs and symptoms of dehydration.

(6) Instruct patient to keep a log of number and consistency of bowel movements per day.

(7) Inform patient and family members of medications available to alleviate treatment-related side effects. Thoroughly review side effect profile and possible drug interactions. Instruct in appropriate use of any suppositories, foams, ointments, or enemas if prescribed.

(8) Post-treatment, late effects: Instruct patient on reporting symptoms, including changes in stools and rectal bleeding or pain, and those to report at follow-up visits or when to call physician.

(9) Teaching tools

3. Sexual dysfunction (see section IV, F—Sexual Dysfunction)

a) Pathophysiology—radiation can result in erectile dysfunction by accelerating microvascular angiopathy in the arteriolar system supplying the corporal muscles causing cavernosal fibrosis or stenosis of the pelvic arteries, thereby leading to impotence (Bruner et al., 1998; Zelefsky, Leibel, et al., 1998). It also is reported that higher doses of radiation to the neurovascular bundle can influence the degree of impotence (Zelefsky, Valicenti, Goodman, & Perez, 2004).

b) Incidence

(1) Sexual dysfunction can pertain not only to impotence, but also to a number of other physical and psychological factors. "A sexual dysfunction is characterized by a disturbance in the process that characterizes the sexual response cycle or by pain associated with sexual intercourse" (American Psychiatric Association, 2000, p. 535).

(a) Anejaculation

(b) Impotence

(c) Retrograde ejaculation

(d) Premature ejaculation

(e) Lack of sexual desire

(f) Depression (Incrocci, Slob, & Levendag, 2002; Kao et al., 2000; Teloken, 2001)

(2) The literature is lacking in data on incidence for specific types of sexual dysfunction as experienced by men after having received RT. The exception to this, however, is impotence. Impotence is considered a late effect of RT, as it often occurs six to eight months after the completion of treatment (Incrocci et al., 2002).

(a) With 3-D conformal treatment to the prostate, impotence is 41%–85% (Teloken, 2001).

(b) With IMRT to the prostate, impotence rates are not yet available. Treatment may result in improved potency rates over 3-D conformal treatment (Sethi, Mohideen, Leybovich, & Mulhall, 2003).

c) Assessment (Bruner et al., 1998; Maher, 1997; Teloken, 2001)

(1) Baseline dysfunction prior to initiation of treatment

(2) Baseline sexual activity level

(3) Baseline satisfaction/dissatisfaction with intercourse

(4) Medications or comorbid conditions (hypertension, diabetes, peripheral vascular disease, neuropathy)

(5) Decreased ability to achieve erection

(6) Decreased sensation during intercourse

(7) Retrograde ejaculation

(8) Decreased ability to achieve orgasm

d) Documentation (in addition to baseline and existing symptoms) (see section IV, F—Sexual Dysfunction)

e) Collaborative management

(1) Acute effects of sexual dysfunction (see section IV, F—Sexual Dysfunction) (Bruner et al., 1998; Teloken, 2001)

   (a) Factors such as stress and impaired coping may contribute to acute onset of impotence.

   (b) Interventions for acute onset of impotence would not significantly differ from those carried out under long-term effects (refer to interventions below).

(2) Long-term effects of sexual dysfunction (see section IV, F—Sexual Dysfunction) (Bruner et al., 1998)

   (a) Patient and spouse may need to be referred for professional counseling regarding the physical and psychological effects of sexual dysfunction.

   (b) Referral to urology for other alternative treatments

     i) Other nonsurgical approaches include urethral suppositories, intracavernous injections, and vacuum devices.

     ii) Penile prostheses have yielded satisfaction rates of up to 85% (Mulcahy, 2000).

f) Patient and family education

(1) Sexual issues must be incorporated into the general discussion of side effects of treatment, rather than being raised as a separate issue, to reduce any embarrassment and provide permission for the men to raise sexual issues in future discussions (Stead, 2003).

(2) Patient should verbalize understanding of importance of communication between both partners regarding concerns/issues of sexual dysfunction.

(3) Patient should verbalize understanding of side effects of RT as it relates to sexual dysfunction.

(4) Instruct patient and significant other about alternative medical and surgical interventions that may be available to them.

(5) Inform patient of the availability of medications to treat some forms of sexual dysfunction. Thoroughly review side-effect profile and drug interactions of prescribed medications.

(6) Patient and partner are informed about resuming intercourse and/or sexual activity after therapy.

(7) Patient and partner should inform nurse and/or physician of continued sexual dysfunction

(8) Teaching tools for specific site

References

Abel, L.J., Blatt, H.J., Stipetich, R.L., Fuscardo, J.A., Zeroski, D., Miller, S.E., et al. (1999). Nursing management of patients receiving brachytherapy for early-stage prostate cancer. *Clinical Journal of Oncology Nursing, 3,* 7–15.

Albertsen, P.C. (1997). Urologic nuisances: How to work up and relieve men's symptoms. *Geriatrics, 52,* 46–50.

American Psychiatric Association. (2000). *Diagnostic and statistical manual of mental disorders* (4th ed., text revision). Washington, DC: Author.

Bliss, D.Z., Jung, H.J., Savik, K., Lowry, A., Lemoine, M., Jensen, L., et al. (2001). Supplementation with dietary fiber improves fecal incontinence. *Nursing Research, 50,* 203–213.

Blot, E., Escande, M.C., Besson, D., Barbut, F., Granpeix, C., Asselain, B., et al. (2003). Outbreak of clostridium difficile-related diarrhea in an adult oncology unit: Risk factors and microbiological characteristics. *Journal of Hospital Infection, 53,* 187–192.

Boyd, E.L., & Berardi, R. (2002). Anorectal disorders. In R.R. Berardi, E.M. DeSimone, G.D. Newton, M.A. Oszko, N.G. Popovich, C.J. Rollins, et al. (Eds.), *Handbook of nonprescription drugs* (13th ed., pp. 361–380). Washington, DC: American Pharmaceutical Association.

Bruner, D.W., Bucholtz, J.D., Iwamoto, R., & Strohl, R. (Eds.). (1998). *Manual for radiation oncology nursing practice and education.* Pittsburgh, PA: Oncology Nursing Society.

Catlin-Huth, C., Haas, M., & Pollock, V. (2002). *Radiation therapy patient care record: A tool for documenting nursing care.* Pittsburgh, PA: Oncology Nursing Society.

Chism, D.B., Horwitz, E.M., Hanlon, A.L., Pinover, W.H., Mitra, R.K., & Hanks, G.E. (2003). Late morbidity profiles in prostate cancer patients treated to 79–84 Gy by a simple four-field coplanar beam arrangement. *International Journal of Radiation Oncology, Biology, Physics, 55,* 71–77.

Counter, S.F., Froese, D.P., & Hart, M.J. (1999). Prospective evaluation of formalin therapy for radiation proctitis. *American Journal of Surgery, 177,* 396–398.

Dearnaley, D.P., Khoo, V.S., Norman, A.R., Meyer, L., Nahum, A., Tait, D., et al. (1999). Comparison of radiation side effects of conformal and conventional radiotherapy in prostate cancer: A randomized trial. *Lancet, 353,* 267–272.

Deglin, J.H., & Vallerand, A.H. (2003). *Davis's drug handbook for nurses* (8th ed.). Philadelphia: F.A. Davis.

Donjon, R.P., & Goeckner, B.J. (1999). *Mosby's OTC drugs.* St. Louis, MO: Mosby.

Dow, K.H., Bucholtz, J.D., Iwamoto, R.R., Fieler, V.K., & Hilderley, L.J. (Eds.). (1997). *Nursing care in radiation oncology* (2nd ed.). Philadelphia: Saunders.

Forman, J.D., Keole, S., Bolton, S., & Tekyi-Mensah, S. (1999). Association of prostate size with urinary morbidity following mixed conformal neutron and photon irradiation. *International Journal of Radiation Oncology, Biology, Physics, 45,* 871–875.

Gaudin, P.B., Zelefsky, M.J., Leibel, S.A., Fuks, Z., & Reuter, V.E. (1999). Histopathologic effects of three dimensional conformal external beam radiation therapy on benign and malignant prostate tissues. *American Journal of Surgical Pathology, 23,* 1021–1041.

Goldstein, F., & DiMarino, A.J. (2000). Diarrhea as a side effect of mesalamine treatment for inflammatory bowel disease. *Journal of Clinical Gastroenterology, 31,* 60–62.

Gray, M. (2001). Caffeine and urinary continence. *Journal of Wound, Ostomy, and Continence, 28,* 66–69.

Gul, Y.A., Prasannan, S., Jabar, F.M., Shaker, A.R., & Moissin, K. (2002). Pharmacotherapy for chronic hemorrhagic radiation proctitis. *World Journal of Surgery, 26,* 1499–1502.

Incrocci, L., Slob, A.K., & Levendag, P.C. (2002). Sexual dysfunction after radiotherapy for prostate cancer. *International Journal of Radiation Oncology, Biology, Physics, 52,* 681–693.

Iwamoto, R.R., & Maher, K.E. (2001). Radiation therapy for prostate cancer. *Seminars in Oncology Nursing, 17,* 90–100.

Jemal, A., Murray, T., Samuels, A., Ghafoor, A., Ward, E., & Thun, M.J. (2003). Cancer statistics, 2003. *CA: A Cancer Journal for Clinicians, 53,* 5–26.

Kaassis, M., Oberti, E., Burtin, P., & Boyer, J. (2000). Argon plasma coagulation for the treatment of hemorrhagic radiation proctitis. *Endoscopy, 32,* 673–676.

Kao, T.C., Cruess, D.F., Garner, D., Foley, J., Seay, T., Friedrichs, P., et al. (2000). Multicenter patient self-reporting questionnaire on impotence, incontinence, and stricture after radical prostatectomy. *Journal of Urology, 163,* 858–864.

Kaplan, S.A. (2002). Terazosin for treating symptomatic benign prostatic obstruction: A systematic review of efficacy and adverse effects. *Journal of Urology, 168,* 1657–1658.

Kelvin, J.F. (1997). Gastrointestinal cancers. In K.H. Dow, J.D. Bucholtz, R. Iwamoto, V. Fieler, & L. Hilderley (Eds.), *Nursing care in radiation oncology* (2nd ed., pp. 152–183). Philadelphia: Saunders.

Luna-Perez, P., & Rodriguez-Ramirez, S.E. (2002). Formalin instillation for refractory radiation-induced hemorrhagic proctitis. *Journal of Surgical Oncology, 80,* 41–44.

Maher, K.E. (1997). Male genitourinary cancers. In K.H. Dow, J.D. Bucholtz, R. Iwamoto, V. Fieler, & L. Hilderley (Eds.), *Nursing care in radiation oncology* (2nd ed., pp. 184–219). Philadelphia: Saunders.

Marks, L.B., Carroll, P.R., Dugan, T.C., & Anscher, M.S. (1995). The response of the urinary bladder, urethra, and ureter to radiation and chemotherapy. *International Journal of Radiation Oncology, Biology, Physics, 31,* 1257–1280.

Melko, G.P., Turco, T.F., Phelan, T.F., & Sauers, N.M. (1999). Treatment of radiation-induced proctitis with sucralfate enemas. *Annals of Pharmacotherapy, 33,* 1274–1276.

Michalski, J.M., Purdy, J.A., Winter, K., Roach, M., Srinivasan, V., Sandler, H.M., et al. (2000). Preliminary report of toxicity following 3-D radiation therapy for prostate cancer on 3DOG/RTOG 9406. *International Journal of Radiation Oncology, Biology, Physics, 46,* 391–402.

Mulcahy, J.J. (2000). Erectile function after radical prostatectomy. *Seminars in Urologic Oncology, 18,* 71–75.

Murphy, J., Stacey, D., Crook, J., Thompson, B., & Panetta, D. (2000). Testing control of radiation-induced diarrhea with a psyllium bulking agent: A pilot study. *Canadian Journal of Oncology Nursing, 10,* 96–100.

Owendijk, R., Tetteroo, G.W., Bode, W., & deGraaf, E.J. (2002). Local formalin instillation: An effective treatment for uncontrolled radiation-induced hemorrhagic proctitis. *Digestive Surgery, 19,* 25–55.

Prosnitz, R.G., Schneider, L., Manola, J., Rocha, S., Loffredo, M., Lopes, L., et al. (1999). Tamsulosin palliates radiation-induced urethritis in patients with prostate cancer: Results of a pilot study. *International Journal of Radiation Oncology, Biology, Physics, 45,* 563–566.

Radiation Therapy Oncology Group. (2003). *RTOG morbidity grading scale.* Retrieved May 20, 2003, from http://www.rtog.org/members/toxicity/acute.html

Roberts, F.J., Murphy, J., & Ludgate, C. (1990). The value and significance of routine urine cultures in patients referred for radiation therapy of prostatic malignancy. *Clinical Oncology, 2,* 18–21.

Rullier, E., Goffre, B., Bonnel, C., Zerbib, F., Caudry, M., & Saric, J. (2001). Preoperative radio-chemotherapy and sphincter-saving resection for T3 carcinomas of the lower third of the rectum. *Annals of Surgery, 234,* 633–640.

Sasai, T., Hiraishi, H., Suzuki, Y., Masuyama, H., Ishida, M., & Terano, A. (1998). Treatment of chronic post-radiation proctitis with oral administration of sucralfate. *American Journal of Gastroenterology, 93,* 1593–1595.

Sethi, A., Mohideen, N., Leybovich, L., & Mulhall, J. (2003). Role of IMRT in reducing penile doses in dose escalation for prostate cancer. *International Journal of Radiation Oncology, Biology, Physics, 55,* 970–978.

Shu, H.G., Lee, T.T., Vigneauly, E., Xia, P., Pickett, B., Phillips, T.L., et al. (2001). Toxicity following high dose three-dimensional conformal and intensity modulated radiation therapy for clinically localized prostate cancer. *Urology, 57,* 102–107.

Stead, M.L. (2003). Sexual dysfunction after treatment for gynecologic and breast malignancies. *Current Opinion in Obstetrics and Gynecology, 15*(1), 57–61.

Taieb, S., Rolachon, A., Cenni, J.C., Nancey, S., Bonvoisin, S., Descos, L., et al. (2001). Effective use of argon plasma coagulation in the treatment of severe radiation proctitis. *Diseases of the Colon and Rectum, 44,* 1766–1771.

Teloken, C. (2001). Management of erectile dysfunction secondary to treatment for localized prostate cancer. *Cancer Control, 8,* 540–545.

Warren, D.C., Feehan, P., Slade, J.B., & Cianci, P.E. (1997). Chronic radiation proctitis treated with hyperbaric oxygen. *Undersea Hyperbaric Medicine, 3,* 181–184.

Wilt, T.J., Howe, W., & MacDonald, R. (2002). Terazosin for treating symptomatic benign prostatic obstruction: A systematic review of efficacy and adverse effects. *British Journal of Urology, 89,* 214–225.

Zelefsky, M.J., Cowen, D., Fuks, Z., Shike, M., Burman, C., Jackson, A., et al. (1999). Long term tolerance of high dose three-dimensional conformal radiotherapy in patients with localized prostate carcinoma. *Cancer, 85,* 2460–2468.

Zelefsky, M.J., & Eid, J.F. (1998). Elucidating the etiology of erectile dysfunction after definitive therapy for prostate cancer. *International Journal of Radiation Oncology, Biology, Physics, 40,* 129–133.

Zelefsky, M.J., Fuks, Z., Hunt, M., Yamada, Y., Marion, C., Ling, C.C., et al. (2002). High dose intensity modulated radiation therapy for prostate cancer: Early toxicity and biochemical outcome in 772 patients. *International Journal of Radiation Oncology, Biology, Physics, 53,* 1111–1116.

Zelefsky, M.J., Leibel, S.A., Gaudin, P.B., Kutcher, G.J., Fleshner, N.E., Venkatramen, E.S., et al. (1998). Dose escalation with three dimensional conformal radiation therapy affects the outcome in prostate cancer. *International Journal of Radiation Oncology, Biology, Physics, 41,* 491–500.

Zelefsky, M.J., Valicenti, R.K., Goodman, K., & Perez, C.A. (2004). Male genitourinary tumors. In C.A. Perez, L.W. Brady, E.C. Halperin, & R.K. Schmidt-Ullrich (Eds.), *Principles and practice of radiation oncology* (4th ed., pp. 1692–1762). Philadelphia: Lippincott.

Zelefsky, M.J., Wallner, K.E., Ling, C.C., Raben, A., Hollister, T., Wolfe, T., et al. (1999). Comparison of the five-year outcome and morbidity of three-dimensional conformal radiotherapy versus transperineal permanent iodine 125 implantation for early stage prostatic cancer. *Journal of Clinical Oncology, 17,* 517–522.

H. Female pelvis
  1. Introduction
      a) Pelvic RT is used to treat gynecologic cancers (cervical, endometrial, ovarian, vaginal, and vulvar), bladder cancer, and colon cancer.
      b) Gynecologic cancer incidence: For 2004, the estimated new cases for female genital cancers are 82,550, with an estimated 28,720 deaths (ACS, 2004).
      c) Typical daily dose of external radiation to pelvic fields is 18–20 Gy. Intracavitary radiation (see section VII, B—LDR/HDR Brachytherapy), also known as brachytherapy, may consist of
          (1) Applicators—tandem and ovoids: Fletcher-suit and Manchester
          (2) Vaginal cylinder
  2. Skin changes
      a) Pathophysiology
          (1) Acute
              (a) Patient may experience itchy, dry, and possibly flaky skin in the genital area known as dry desquamation. Occurs at doses of about 3 Gy (Dow, Bucholtz, Iwamoto, Fieler, & Hilderley, 1997; Mayer, 1997; Sitton, 1997).
              (b) May progress to moist desquamation (see section IV, C—Skin Reactions)
          (2) Late: Classified as occurring six or more months after RT and include vaginal fibrosis, atrophy, ulceration, pigmentation changes, thinning, and telangiectasia (Dow et al., 1997; Mayer, 1997; Sitton, 1997)
      b) Incidence: Tissue disruption occurs when bacteria affects the production of ammonia from urinary urea and increases the skin pH, skin permeability, and fecal enzyme activity (Brown & Sears, 1993).
      c) Staging/assessment of symptoms
          (1) Risk factors
              (a) Skin folds in perineum within the treatment field
              (b) Concomitant use of chemotherapy/radiosensitizing agents before, during, or after radiation
              (c) Autoimmune diseases or other comorbid conditions
              (d) Medications: Steroids
          (2) Clinical manifestations
              (a) Pruritus
              (b) Pain
          (3) Physical examination (see section IV, C—Skin Reactions)
          (4) Documentation (see sections IV, B—Fatigue; IV, C—Skin Reactions; and IV, D—Pain)
              (a) Use assessment tools developed (Catlin-Huth, Haas, & Pollock, 2002).
              (b) In addition, document any changes in vaginal discharge (i.e., amount, color, odor).
      d) Collaborative management
          (1) Acute effects (see section IV, C—Skin Reactions)
          (2) Late effects (see section IV, C—Skin Reactions)
      e) Patient and family education
          (1) Perform nutritional evaluation and education to ensure proper diet to enhance tissue healing.
          (2) Instruct on signs and symptoms of infection, enforce need to report them (e.g., fever, chills, drainage, odor).
          (3) Instruct on use of pain medications and antipruritic medications.
          (4) Minimize friction: Wash area with hands, not with a washcloth; pat area dry with a soft, clean towel or blow dry with hair dryer on cool setting; wear loose-fitting, soft clothing (preferably

cotton because it is absorbent and allows evaporation of moisture).

(5) Avoid scratching.

(6) Avoid rubbing vigorously and massaging.

(7) Avoid use of tape in area.

(8) Avoid extreme temperatures (e.g., heating pads, ice packs).

(9) Avoid irritants (e.g., soaps, perfumes, powders [other than those recommended by the physician or nurse]).

(a) Wash skin with mild soap and lukewarm water.

(b) Keep skin folds dry.

3. Urinary frequency/dysuria

a) Pathophysiology

(1) Acute

(a) Symptoms that may occur during RT can include pain with urination, urinary frequency, urgency, hesitancy, and an increase in nocturia.

(b) Urinary symptoms occur as a result of radiation-induced inflammation and edema of the bladder mucosa (Strohl, 1990).

(c) The bladder is relatively tolerant to radiation. Therapeutic doses > 60–70 Gy over a six- to seven-week period generally result in cystitis.

(2) Late

(a) Over the course of time, the epithelium of the bladder thins and appears pale and atrophic and can ulcerate with or without trauma or infection.

(b) Interstitial fibrosis occurs in areas that received high doses of radiation. Telangiectasia formation and thin-walled dilated blood vessels may rupture, resulting in a painless hematuria (Bruner, Bucholtz, Iwamoto, & Strohl, 1998).

b) Incidence

(1) Incidence varies widely, depending on factors related to radiation timing, dose, and volume. Acute symptoms subside within several weeks following RT (Nicolaou, 2001).

(2) Acute symptoms can vary from 23%–80% among patients receiving pelvic irradiation for a variety of tumors (Maduro, Pras, Willemse, & de Vries, 2003).

(3) Because of the various sites of treatment, doses, and fractionation schedules, late effects to the bladder differ. Ten percent of serious injury to the bladder is associated with 70–80 Gy doses.

(4) Severe effects include hemorrhagic cystitis, incontinence, fistula, and conditions requiring surgery to tumors (Maduro et al., 2003).

(5) Hemorrhagic cystitis can occur 6 months to 10 years after pelvic RT, with moderate to severe persistent rates of hematuria as 3%–5% after radiotherapy for pelvic malignancies (Corman, McClure, Pritchett, Kozlowski, & Hampson, 2003).

(6) Chronic cystitis may occur 6–18 months after treatment and produces chronic bladder changes (e.g., decreased capacity, hemorrhagic changes within mucosa). One to two percent of patients may experience hemorrhagic cystitis after pelvic RT (Mathews, Rajan, & Josefson, 1999).

(7) Cervical cancer: For moderate to severe sequelae, the range is 1%–2%. Acute urologic toxicity (all grades) is reported in 27% of patients. Adding chemotherapy to radiation increases acute effects (Maduro et al., 2003).

(8) Endometrial cancer: In a five-year evaluation of 233 patients with stage IB grades 1 and 2 endometrial cancer treated with adjuvant high dose rate intravaginal brachytherapy, less than 1% of patients developed grade 3 genitourinary toxicity (Alektiar et al., 2002).

(9) An evaluation of patients with endometrial cancer was completed on 317 consecutive patients with endometrial cancer who were treated with surgery and adjuvant radiotherapy. Severe acute urinary bladder complications were seen in 1% of patients.

The severity of acute bowel and bladder toxicity did not correlate with the time to occurrence of late toxicity in these areas (Jereczek-Fossa, Jassem, & Badzio, 2002).

c) Assessment of symptoms
  (1) Clinical
    (a) Symptoms indicative of bladder irritation (i.e., changes from baseline, including urinary frequency, dysuria, urgency, nocturia, and hematuria)
    (b) Urge incontinence (occurs at the time of sensation of bladder fullness associated with the immediate desire to urinate)
    (c) Stress incontinence associated with activity
    (d) Obstructive symptoms (e.g., decrease in flow, force of flow)
  (2) Physical examination
    (a) Palpate and percuss abdomen and suprapubic area to assess for bladder distention or tenderness.
    (b) As indicated by symptoms, conduct a urinalysis and/or urine culture (fever, pain, cloudy urine, or hematuria) to detect the presence of bacteria and red and white cells.

d) Documentation: Elimination alteration (Catlin-Huth et al., 2002)
  (1) Urinary frequency/urgency
    (a) 0—Normal
    (b) 1—Increase in frequency or nocturia up to two times the normal
    (c) 2—Increase more than two times the normal but less than hourly
    (d) 3—Hourly or more with urgency, requiring catheter
    (e) 4—
  (2) Urinary incontinence
    (a) 0—Absent
    (b) 1—Present
  (3) Urinary retention
    (a) 0—Absent
    (b) 1—Present
  (4) Dysuria
    (a) 0—None
    (b) 1—Mild symptoms requiring no intervention
    (c) 2—Symptoms relieved with therapy
    (d) 3—Symptoms not relieved despite therapy
    (e) 4—
  (5) Drainage: Fistula recto-vaginal
    (a) 0—Absent
    (b) 1—Present
  (6) Type of drainage
    (a) Fecal
    (b) Urinary

e) Collaborative management
  (1) Acute effects of urinary frequency/dysuria: Interventions for acute effects of urinary symptoms
    (a) Instruct patient to drink one to three liters of fluids per day while decreasing fluid intake in the evening to reduce the incidence of nocturia (Bruner et al., 1998).
    (b) Encourage patient to avoid caffeine products (e.g., coffee, tea, cola), alcohol, spices, chocolate, and tobacco products (Dow et al., 1997)
    (c) Send urine specimen for urinalysis and cultures to rule out infectious process that may be contributing to symptoms.
    (d) Administer appropriate medication as prescribed.
      i) Ibuprofen—400–800 mg three to four times daily, relieves pain by inhibiting prostaglandin synthesis (Deglin & Vallerand, 2003)
      ii) Use of antispasmodics—Provide relief from symptoms of dysuria
        • Phenazopyridine hydrochloride
        • A combination of antiseptic and parasympatholytics
      iii) Use of antispasmodics—Provide relief from bladder spasms (relax the bladder smooth muscle by inhibiting

the muscarinic effect of acetylcholine)
- Oxybutynin chloride
- Flavoxate hydrochloride
- Tamsulosin hydrochloride—0.4 mg once daily, can be increased to 0.8 mg daily if ineffective. Decreases contractions of smooth muscle within the prostatic capsule by binding to alpha-1 receptors (Deglin & Vallerand, 2003).

(e) Use of antihypertensive medication (Relaxation of smooth muscle can be produced by blockade of alpha-1 adrenergic adrenoreceptors in the bladder.)
  i) Terazosin hydrochloride
  ii) Doxazosin mesylate—use with caution in patients on hypertensive medication.
  iii) Treatment break may be considered.

(2) Long-term effects of urinary frequency/dysuria
(a) A long-term complication of vesicovaginal fistula usually requires a urinary diversion until the fistula heals.
  i) Requires multidisciplinary approach including surgery
  ii) May require TPN to reduce bowel content and provide adequate calories to promote healing
  iii) Hyperbaric oxygen therapy may be necessary (Williams, Clarke, Dennis, Dennis, & Smith, 1992).
(b) Radiation fibrosis causing the formation of urethral strictures may

require the placement of urethral stents.
f) Patient and family education
  (1) Inform patient and family of potential for urinary side effects from pelvic irradiation.
  (2) Educate patient and family as to signs and symptoms of urinary tract infection and radiation-induced cystitis.
  (3) Instruct patient and family to report first signs and/or symptoms of radiation-induced cystitis.
  (4) Instruct patient in dietary interventions and promote adequate hydration.
  (5) Reassure patient as to the availability of medications should symptoms become problematic. Thoroughly review side-effect profile and possible drug interactions with patient as appropriate.

4. Diarrhea/proctitis
  a) Pathophysiology (see section V, E—Gastrointestinal/Abdomen)
  b) Incidence
    (1) Cervical cancer: A 15%–25% incidence of severe small intestinal injury occurs with 50–55 Gy administered to para-aortic nodes and pelvis (Perez et al., 1991)
    (2) Occurrence of late intestinal side effects (mainly diarrhea) assessed three to four years after pelvic radiotherapy for carcinoma of the endometrium and cervix, found to be significantly higher in women treated than controls as was pain in the lower back, hips, and thighs (Bye, Trope, Loge, Hjermstad, & Kaasa, 2000).
    (3) RT is not typically used in ovarian cancer. This is because radiation would need to be given to the entire abdomen and pelvis, increasing its toxicity. Radiation is sometimes useful to treat isolated areas of tumor that are causing pain and are no longer responsive to chemotherapy.
  c) Assessment of symptoms (see section V, E—Gastrointestinal/Abdomen)
  d) Documentation
    (1) Elimination alteration (Catlin-Huth et al., 2002)
      (a) Diarrhea (patient without colostomy) (see section V, E—Gastrointestinal/Abdomen)
      (b) Diarrhea (patients with colostomy) (see section V, E—Gastrointestinal/Abdomen)

(c) Proctitis (RTOG Morbidity Grading Scale)
  i) 0—None
  ii) 1—Increased stool frequency, occasional blood-streaked stools, or rectal discomfort (including hemorrhoids) not requiring medication
  iii) 2—Increased stool frequency, bleeding, mucus discharge, or rectal discomfort requiring medication; anal fissure
  iv) 3—Increased stool frequency/diarrhea requiring parenteral support; rectal bleeding requiring transfusion; or persistent mucus discharge necessitating pads
  v) 4—Perforation, bleeding, necrosis, or life-threatening complication requiring surgical intervention (e.g., colostomy)
(d) Other factors
  i) Documentation of daily weight
  ii) Compliance with dietary recommendations and fluid intake: May be helpful to use a daily documentation of dietary intake and bowel pattern sheet
(e) "Weekly Bowel Pattern Recording Sheet: Self-Care Guide" (Engelking, 2004, p. 551).
(2) Skin sensation (see section IV, C—Skin Reactions)
e) Collaborative management
  (1) Acute effects of diarrhea (see section V, E—Gastrointestinal/Abdomen)
    (a) Dietary management: Minimize diarrhea and abdominal cramping, initiate dietary interventions at start of treatment.
      i) Low fiber to decrease irritation of mucosa and GI motility
      ii) Low lactose to handle lactase deficiency
      iii) Low fat to prolong transit time
      iv) If severe diarrhea continues, eliminate any fruits and vegetables, except bananas and applesauce.
        • If symptom still continues, treatment break may be required.

• Consult a dietitian (Dow et al., 1997; Nelson, Moxness, Jensen, & Gastineaus, 1994; Woodtli & VanOrt, 1991).
(b) Fluid and nutrient balance: Adequate amounts of fluid and nutrients to prevent dehydration, electrolyte imbalance, and weight loss
  i) Encourage clear juices, broth, decaffeinated tea, sports drinks high in electrolytes (e.g., Gatorade®), and lactose-free liquid supplements.
  ii) IV hydration and electrolyte replacement during daily visits may be necessary (Dow et al., 1997; Hassey, 1987; Nelson et al., 1994; Sitton, 1992).
(c) Medications/pharmacologic: After three or more days, note watery bowel movements and day of initiation.
  i) Initial treatment is anticholinergic medications (see section V, E—Gastrointestinal/Abdomen).
  ii) If not effective at full dose, opium derivatives can be used.
  iii) Bulk laxatives absorb fluid and increase stool bulk (should be taken with less liquid than when used for constipation).
  iv) Ongoing dietitian involvement (Dow et al., 1997)
(2) Long-term effects of diarrhea
  (a) Possibility of radiation-induced fistula: Most frequent major sequelae at 1.5% in patients receiving irradiation alone versus 1.6%

in patients treated with irradiation plus surgery for cervical cancer (Perez et al., 1995).

    i) Caused by two factors—Recurrent disease or radiation-induced. If recurrent disease is ruled out, treatment must be very aggressive to promote healing.

    ii) Small bowel and rectovaginal fistulas are very painful and usually require a temporary colostomy. This allows bowel to rest and to promote healing. Once fistula has healed, colostomy can be reversed.

  (b) Small bowel obstruction

    i) 1.8% in patients receiving irradiation alone versus 4.2% in patients treated with irradiation plus surgery for cervical cancer (Perez et al., 1995)

    ii) Increased chances of obstruction with continued radiation to pelvis and abdominal surgeries

    iii) If obstruction occurs, patient may need to be on clear liquid diet to rest bowel or may need to perform colostomy or ileostomy to relieve obstruction. May occur several years after completion of treatment.

  (c) Perforation: May develop if obstruction is not acted upon. Colostomy is necessary to rest bowel and promote healing of anastomosis of bowel after surgery. Usually temporary but dependent on site of perforation.

 f) Patient and family education (see section V, E—Gastrointestinal/Abdomen)

(1) Inform patient that diarrhea is an expected side effect of radiation to the pelvis and usually occurs after 2.5–3 weeks of treatment.

(2) Teach dietary modifications.

(3) Instruct patient and family in comfort measures (e.g., sitz bath, tepid water cotton cloth soaks).

(4) Explain protocol for perianal hygiene (mild soap, do not rub, pat dry).

(5) Describe signs and symptoms of dehydration.

(6) Instruct patient to keep a log of number and consistency of bowel movements per day.

(7) Inform patient and family members of medications available to alleviate treatment-related side effects. Thoroughly review side-effect profile and possible drug interactions. Instruct in appropriate use of any suppositories, foams, ointments, or enemas if prescribed.

(8) Post-treatment late effects: Instruct patient on reporting symptoms, including changes in stools, rectal bleeding, or pain at follow-up visits or to call physician.

 g) Teaching tools for specific site

5. Sexual dysfunction (see section IV, F—Sexual Dysfunction)

 a) Pathophysiology

  (1) Acute

    (a) Denuding of the vaginal epithelium and the urethral epithelium and inflammation account for the majority of acute effects related to sexual dysfunction during RT (Pitkin & Van Vorrhis, 1971).

    (b) Libido may be affected by the disease itself or the decreased or ablation of ovarian function by radiation doses as low as 6 Gy.

  (2) Late

    (a) Vaginal stenosis is increased in those who received increased surface dose to the vagina during brachytherapy (Grigsby et al., 1995).

    (b) The vaginal epithelium is affected similarly as the bladder epithelium. The radiation causes thinning and pale atrophic changes over time and may be traumatized by intercourse and/or masturbation.

 b) Incidence

  (1) 25%–100% of all patients treated with radiation for pelvic cancers have re-

ported sexual dysfunction, depending on site, dose, and volume treated (Bruner & Iwamoto, 1996).

(2) Cervical cancer: Sexual dysfunction has been reported in 55%–78% of women treated with both external beam and intracavitary radiation (Abitol & Davenport, 1974; Bruner et al., 1993).

(3) Endometrial cancer: Vaginal stenosis has been reported in up to 72% of women treated for endometrial cancer after intracavitary radiation (Abitol & Davenport, 1974; Bruner et al., 1993).

c) Assessment of symptoms
  (1) Risk factors
    (a) Sexual dysfunction needs to be assessed prior to start of radiation because it may lead to a greater risk for sexual problems post-therapy.
    (b) Sexual activity pretreatment appears to be the best predictor of post-treatment sexual activity (Anderson, Woods, & Cryanowski, 1994).
    (c) Pre–radiation treatment surgical intervention(s)
  (2) Clinical
    (a) Sexual history: Pretreatment history of sexual activity should include sexual preference, age at first intercourse, number of sexual partners, marital relationship, and any problems with desire, arousal, or orgasm. The nurse must have an open mind and accept the couple's sexual practice (Cartwright-Alcarese, 1995).
    (b) Frequency of sexual activity over past 6–12 months
    (c) Satisfaction with ability
    (d) Satisfaction with frequency
    (e) Dyspareunia
    (f) Decrease in vaginal lubrication and sensation
  (3) Physical examination
    (a) Check external genitalia and perineum for skin changes over vulva and around anus for lesions, inflammation, or skin breakdown.
    (b) Examine patient for vaginal stenosis.
    (c) Check for vaginal discharge or vaginal bleeding.
  (4) Psychological
    (a) History of sexual abuse

    (b) Body image: Radiation will cause either temporary or permanent gonadal failure as well as changes in body image (Cartwright-Alcarese, 1995).

d) Collaborative management
  (1) Acute effects of sexual dysfunction (see section IV, F—Sexual Dysfunction)
    (a) Prepare the patient for the acute effects radiation treatment will cause to sexual function.
      i) Support the patient on concerns of sexual dysfunction.
      ii) Encourage open communication between patient and partner. The most difficult aspect of discussing sexuality with patients is getting started. A simple question such as "How are things going sexually?" may be all it takes to initiate a conversation that can be a very positive influence on the patient's postdiagnosis sexual relationship(s) (Auchincloss, 1990).
      iii) Refer patient with history of sexual abuse or marital problems to a social worker, family counselor, or sex therapist.
    (b) Educate patient in use of pain medication prior to sexual activity to help manage symptoms (e.g., pain) prior to engaging in activity. Teach proper positioning for continued sexual activity to prevent discomfort, depending on therapy or problem (Bruner & Iwamoto, 1996).
    (c) Radiotherapy can cause vaginal dryness and vaginal stenosis, but these symptoms can be improved

by the use of vaginal dilators and lubricants (Stead, 2003).

(2) Long-term effects of sexual dysfunction (see section IV, F—Sexual Dysfunction)

    (a) Vaginal stenosis: To prevent vaginal stenosis, teach women to use a vaginal dilator following intracavitary implant (Bruner & Iwamoto, 1996).

    (b) Vaginal dryness: Educate patient on the use of vaginal lubricants during sexual activity (Bruner & Iwamoto, 1996).

        i) K-Y® Jelly (Johnson & Johnson, Fort Washington, PA)

        ii) Astroglide® (Biofilm, Inc., Vista, CA)

        iii) Replens® (Parke-Davis, Morris Plains, NJ)

e) Documentation (Catlin-Huth et al., 2002)

(1) Sexuality alteration (see section IV, F—Sexual Dysfunction)

(2) Mucous membrane alteration

    (a) Drainage

        i) 0—Absent

        ii) 1—Present

    (b) Drainage odor

        i) 0—Absent

        ii) 1—Present

    (c) Vaginal bleeding

        i) 0—None

        ii) 1—Spotting requiring two pads per day

        iii) 2—Requiring ≥ 2 pads every day, but not requiring transfusion

        iv) 3—Requiring transfusion

        v) 4—Catastrophic bleeding, requiring major nonelective intervention

f) Patient and family education

(1) Sexual issues must be incorporated into the general discussion of side effects of treatment, rather than being raised as a separate issue, to reduce any embarrassment while at the same time providing permission for the women to raise sexual issues in future discussions (Stead, 2003).

(2) Patient and partner should be able to verbalize a good understanding of the potential impact of pelvic irradiation on sexual function.

(3) Patient and partner should be made aware of alternative techniques for sexual intercourse to minimize sexual discomfort and/or dysfunction.

(4) Patient and partner are informed about resuming intercourse and/or masturbation after therapy.

(5) Patient and partner should inform nurse and/or physician of continued sexual dysfunction.

g) Teaching tools for specific site

References

Abitol, M., & Davenport, J. (1974). Sexual dysfunction after therapy for cervical carcinoma. *American Journal for Obstetrics and Gynecology, 199,* 119–189.

Alektiar, K.M., McKee, A, Venkatraman, E., McKee, B., Zelefsky, M.J., Mychalczak, et al. (2002). Intravaginal high-dose-rate brachytherapy for Stage IB (FIGO Grade 1, 2) endometrial cancer. *International Journal of Radiation Oncology, Biology, Physics, 53,* 707–713.

American Cancer Society. (2004). *Cancer facts and figures 2004.* Atlanta, GA: Author.

Anderson, B.L., Woods, X., & Cryanowski, J. (1994). Sexual self-schema as a possible predictor of sexual problems following cancer treatment. *Canadian Journal of Human Sexuality, 3*(2), 165–170.

Auchincloss, S. (1990). Sexual dysfunction in cancer patients: Issues in evaluation and treatment. In J.C. Holland & J.H. Holland (Eds.), *Handbook of psycho-oncology: Psychological care of the patient with cancer* (pp. 383–413). New York: Oxford University Press.

Berry, D. (2004). Bladder disturbances. In C.H. Yarbro, M.H. Frogge, & M. Goodman (Eds.), *Cancer symptom management* (3rd ed., pp. 505–511). Sudbury, MA: Jones and Bartlett.

Brown, D., & Sears, M. (1993). Perineal dermatitis: A conceptual framework. *Ostomy/Wound Management, 39*(7), 28–30.

Bruner, D.W., Bucholtz, J.D., Iwamoto, R., & Strohl, R. (Eds.). (1998). *Manual for radiation oncology nursing practice and education.* Pittsburgh, PA: Oncology Nursing Society.

Bruner, D.W., & Iwamoto, R. (1996). Altered sexual health. In S.L. Groenwald, M.H. Frogge, M. Goodman, & C.H. Yarbro (Eds.), *Cancer symptom management* (pp. 523–551). Sudbury, MA: Jones and Bartlett.

Bruner, D.W., Lanciano, R., Keegan, M., Corn, B., Martin, E., & Hanks, G. (1993). Vaginal stenosis and sexual dysfunction following intracavitary radiation therapy for the treatment of cervical and endometrial carcinoma. *International Journal of Radiation Oncology, Biology, Physics, 27,* 825–830.

Bye, A., Trope, C., Loge, J.H., Hjermstad, M., & Kaasa, S. (2000). Health-related quality of life and occurrence of intestinal side effects after pelvic radiotherapy—Evaluation of long-term effects of diagnosis and treatment. *Acta Oncologica, 39*(2), 173–180.

Cartwright-Alcarese, F. (1995). Addressing sexual dysfunction following radiation therapy for gynecological malignancies. *Oncology Nursing Forum, 22,* 1227–1232.

Catlin-Huth, C., Haas, M., & Pollock, V. (2002). *Radiation therapy patient care record: A tool for documenting nursing care.* Pittsburgh, PA: Oncology Nursing Society.

Corman, J.M., McClure, D., Pritchett, R., Kozlowski, P., & Hampson, N.B. (2003). Treatment of radiation-induced hemorrhagic cystitis with hyperbaric oxygen. *Journal of Urology, 169,* 2200–2202.

Deglin, J.H., & Vallerand, A.H. (2003). *Davis's drug handbook for nurses* (8th ed.). Philadelphia: F.A. Davis.

Dow, K.H., Bucholtz, J.D., Iwamoto, R.R., Fieler, V.K., & Hilderley, L.J. (Eds.). (1997). *Nursing care in radiation oncology* (2nd ed.). Philadelphia: Saunders.

Grisgby, P., Russell, A., Bruner, D., Eifel, P., Koh, W., Spanos, W., et al. (1995). Late injury of cancer therapy on the female reproductive tract. *International Journal of Radiation Oncology, Biology, Physics, 31,* 1281–1299.

Hassey, K.M. (1987). Radiation therapy for rectal cancer and the implications for nursing. *Cancer Nursing, 10,* 311–318.

Jereczek-Fossa, B.A., Jassem, J., & Badzio, A. (2002). Relationship between acute and late normal tissue injury after postoperative radiotherapy in endometrial cancer. *International Journal of Radiation Oncology, Biology, Physics, 52,* 476–482.

Maduro, J.H., Pras, E., Willemse, P.H.B., & de Vries, E.G.E. (2003). Acute and long-term toxicity following radiotherapy alone or in combination with chemotherapy for locally advanced cervical cancer. *Cancer Treatment Reviews, 129,* 471–488.

Mathews, R., Rajan, N., & Josefson, L. (1999). Hyperbaric oxygen therapy for radiation induced hemorrhagic cystitis. *Journal of Urology, 161,* 435–437.

Mayer, D. (1997). Skin integrity alterations associated with radiation therapy. In S. Baird (Ed.), *Decision-making in oncology nursing* (pp. 112–113). Philadelphia: Becker.

Nelson, J.K., Moxness, K.E., Jensen, M.D., & Gastineaus, C.F. (1994). *Mayo Clinic diet manual: A handbook of nutritional practices* (7th ed.). St. Louis, MO: Mosby.

Nicolaou, N. (2003). Prevention and management of radiation toxicity. In R. Pazdur, L. Coia, W. Hoskins, & L. Wagman (Eds.), *Cancer management: A multidisciplinary approach* (7th ed., pp. 909–939). New York: The Oncology Group.

Perez, C.A., Fox, S., Lockett, M.A., Grigsby, P.W., Camel, H.M., Galakatos, A., et al. (1991). Impact of dose in outcome if irradiation alone in carcinoma of the uterine cervix: Analysis of two different methods. *International Journal of Radiation Oncology, Biology, Physics, 21,* 885–898.

Perez, C.A., Grigsby, P.W., Camel, H.M., Galakatos, A.E., Mutch, D., & Lockett, M.A. (1995). Irradiation alone or combined with surgery in stage IB, IIA, and IIB carcinoma of uterine cervix: Update of a nonrandomized comparison. *International Journal of Radiation Oncology, Biology, Physics, 31,* 703–716.

Pitkin, R., & Van Vorrhis, L. (1971). Postirradiation vaginitis: An evaluation of prophylaxis with topical estrogen. *Radiology, 99,* 417–421.

Sitton, E. (1992). Early and late radiation-induced skin alternations. Part II: Nursing care of irradiated skin. *Oncology Nursing Forum, 19,* 907–912.

Sitton, E. (1997). Hodgkin's disease and non-Hodgkin's lymphoma. In K.H. Dow, J.D. Bucholtz, R.R. Iwamoto, V.K. Fieler, & L.J. Hilderley (Eds.), *Nursing care in radiation oncology* (2nd ed., pp. 261–292). Philadelphia: Saunders.

Stead, M.L. (2003). Sexual dysfunction after treatment for gynecologic and breast malignancies. *Current Opinion in Obstetrics and Gynecology, 15*(1), 57–61.

Strohl, R.A. (1990). External beam radiation therapy in gynecologic cancers. *Clinical Issues in Perinatal and Women's Health Nursing, 1,* 525–531.

Williams, J.A., Jr., Clarke, D., Dennis, W.A., Dennis, E.J., & Smith, S.T. (1992). The treatment of pelvic soft tissue radiation necrosis with hyperbaric oxygen. *American Journal of Obstetrics and Gynecology, 167,* 412–415.

Woodtli, A.M., & VanOrt, S. (1991). Nursing diagnosis and functional health patterns in patients receiving external radiation therapy: Cancer of the digestive organs. *Nursing Diagnosis, 4,* 15–25.

VI. Disease-specific management

A. Sarcoma

1. Introduction and overview of disease

   a) Sarcomas are categorized as arising from the soft tissues, bone, or viscera. Sarcomas are named for the tissue of origin. Visceral sarcomas arising from connective tissues within the stroma can be found in all organs and are extremely rare. Treatment of visceral sarcomas is based on the organ of origin (Graham, 2001).

   b) Soft tissue sarcomas (STS) are malignant tumors that arise primarily from connective tissues and also rarely from endothelium and mesothelium. Connective tissue is found almost everywhere in the body, and sarcomas can arise from any of these sites. The most common sites are the extremities, trunk/retroperitoneum, and areas of the head and neck. Treatment approaches for soft tissue sarcomas are predicated on the tissue of origin. Examples of tumor types include liposarcoma, leiomyosarcoma, rhabdomyosarcoma, hemangiosarcoma, Kaposi's sarcoma, angiosarcoma, synovial sarcoma, schwannoma, and neuroblastoma (O'Sullivan et al., 1999).

   c) Sarcomas of bone arise from the skeletal system and are extremely rare, comprising only 0.2% of all new cancers in the United States. The two most common subtypes are osteosarcoma and Ewing's sarcoma, both considered cancers of childhood and adolescence. Less common are spindle cell sarcomas such as fibrosarcoma, chondrosarcoma, and malignant fibrous histiocytoma (Forscher & Casciato, 2000).

   d) Pathologic differentiation of sarcomas is imprecise and complex. The most important predictive features are the grade (cellular differentiation) and amount of necrosis present in a specimen. These pathologic features determine both how the tumor will behave and how it should be treated (Forscher & Casciato, 2000; Zagars et al., 2003).

2. Incidence and risk factors (Forscher & Casciato, 2000)

a) The U.S. incidence of all new cases of STS is 0.7%, but in children younger than 15, the incidence is higher: 6.5%.

b) Sarcomas of bone comprise only 0.2% of all new cancers in the United States.

3. Radiation treatment

a) Treatment is usually directed with curative intent.

b) Management of STS of the extremity has changed dramatically from the days when amputation was the rule. Curative treatment in extremity sarcomas now emphasizes limb-sparing surgery and function-sparing radiotherapy (Alektiar, Leung, Zelefsky, Healey, & Brennan, 2002). Use of intraoperative RT after removal of retroperitoneal sarcomas, followed by external beam radiotherapy, may improve outcomes in this difficult setting (Hu & Harrison, 2000). Head and neck sarcomas present unique challenges because of the heterogeneity of tumor types and presentations. However, surgical resection, with as wide a margin as is possible, followed by external beam RT (EBRT) is the standard of care, and concomitant chemotherapy may be used (Kraus, Harrison, & O'Malley, 1999; Sturgis & Potter, 2003).

c) Palliative radiation is sometimes given when a sarcoma causes significant pain, loss of mobility, and diminished quality of life. However, tumorcidal doses of radiation are not usually tolerated in this setting, and the amount of radiation that can be delivered safely is ineffective more than 50% of the time. Chemotherapy is a more common palliative treatment, or in the case of extremity sarcoma, a palliative amputation may be used (Forscher & Casciato, 2000).

d) EBRT is the primary means of delivering radiation. Sequencing of preoperative versus postoperative RT varies. Treatment outcomes (overall survival, local control) are essentially the same, but a small increase in RT-related complications after post-operative RT was noted in one recent study (Zagars & Ballo, 2003).

e) Postoperative RT often involves radiation to a flap or graft used to close the surgical wound following resection. A recent review (Spierer, Alektiar, Zelefsky, Brennan, & Cordiero, 2003) from one institution analyzed 43 patients who underwent limb-sparing surgery and reconstruction of the surgical defect followed by RT. Five of 43 patients developed wound complications necessitating surgery, but the majority (95%) tolerated the RT without difficulty.

f) Low dose rate (LDR) brachytherapy can be used alone or in conjunction with EBRT following surgery. This usually involves placement of after-loading catheters into the tumor bed following surgical excision of the tumor. These catheters are later "loaded" with radioactive seeds for three to five days. The seeds and catheters then are removed, prior to the patient's discharge from the hospital. For more detail on brachytherapy, see section VII of this manual. A 5-year local control rate of 84% with an overall survival rate of 70% was reported in one institution's nearly 15-year experience with brachytherapy alone following surgical excision for high-grade primary STS. Poorer outcomes were noted with shoulder locations, upper extremity sarcomas, and in cases with positive margins (Alektiar et al., 2002) (see section VII).

g) Intraoperative RT (IORT) uses electrons (IOERT) or HDR photons (HDR-IORT) during surgery and provides focused radiation to the bed of resected tumors, such as retroperitoneal sarcomas (see section VII, F—Intraoperative). This delivery method focuses intense radiation to the surgical bed or area at risk, while minimizing radiation injury to normal tissues (bowel, bladder). Following recovery from surgery, additional radiation often is given via external beam up to normal tissue tolerance. The combination of EBRT and IORT provides tumorcidal doses with acceptable morbidity (Dunne-Daly, 1997; Hu & Harrison, 2000; Mackenzie, Reid, Barrett, & O'Dwyer, 2003) (see section VII, F—Intraoperative).

4. Acute effects

a) Acute reactions include skin reaction, pain, difficulty in coping, changes in sexuality, fatigue, nausea, diarrhea, and marrow suppression. (The assessment and management of all but marrow suppression are discussed in other sections of this manual.)

b) Marrow suppression is an acute effect of RT whenever significant bone marrow is in the field of treatment, as in extremity sarcoma. Mild neutropenia can occur but usually is self-limiting and does not require colony-stimulating support. As in any marrow suppression, patients must be given detailed neutropenia precautions. Weekly CBCs should be assessed as well (Shelton, 2003).

c) Abdominal RT may cause nausea and/or diarrhea. Premedication with an antiemetic is important from start of treatment to minimize the development of anticipatory nausea. Dietary changes to decrease intake of fat, lactose, and fiber may be helpful, and patients should obtain an antidiarrheal to keep in the home in case diarrhea develops (Kelvin, 1997).

5. Late effects

a) Lymphedema may be present following surgery and exacerbated by RT. However, radiation-related lymphedema is more commonly seen in the weeks to months following completion of treatment. It is more likely to occur when a large area of an extremity is radiated and with longer portals, > 35 cm. Efforts are made during treatment planning to spare at least 33% of the circumference of the extremity from direct radiation, minimizing risk of impaired lymph and vascular flow post-treatment (Stinson et al., 1991).

b) Joints also are spared from direct radiation whenever possible. A retrospective review (Stinson et al., 1991) of 145 patients, performed by the Radiation Oncology branch of NCI, found that if 50% or more of a joint was irradiated, contracture was much more common. Physical therapy is encouraged throughout treatment to maximize flexibility and function of limbs.

c) When the growth plate of an extremity or epiphysis is radiated, there is a possibility of impaired growth of that extremity with resultant deformity or dysfunction. Again, every effort is made during treatment planning to avoid direct radiation to this area, but occasionally it is necessary. In that case, a thorough discussion during consultation is crucial to ensure patient/caregiver understanding of possible treatment sequelae. This is of particular importance when treating a still-growing child (Stinson et al., 1991).

6. Patient and family education

a) Assess patient/caregiver understanding of the disease process, treatment proposed, and patient/caregiver ability and readiness to learn.

b) Review the RT treatment procedure(s) to be used—IORT, brachytherapy, and/or EBRT.

c) Review the treatment schedule; give a patient calendar if undergoing several stages of treatment (i.e., IORT plus EBRT for retroperitoneal sarcoma).

d) Review expected acute side effects and their management. This may include skin reaction, pain, difficulty in coping, changes in sexuality, fatigue, and marrow suppression. When an extremity sarcoma is being treated, teach patients and caregivers to elevate the extremity if swelling/edema occurs.

e) Near completion of treatment, review follow-up care and appointment schedules with patients and caregivers. Review the possible late effects and the importance of timely follow-up care.

f) Document all of the above in the patient's record.

7. Follow-up management

a) Recurrence is seen in up to one-third of all patients treated with multimodality therapies following an 18-month disease-free interval.

b) Whenever possible, surgical resection is done, with or without postoperative RT. Meticulous follow-up by the radiation oncologist and surgeon is required (Graham, 2001).

(1) Perform a thorough history and complete physical at each follow-up visit,

typically every three to four months the first year following treatment, extending over time to semiannually, to annually by the fifth year post-treatment. Evaluate the site of disease as well as associated nodal chains.

(2) An annual chest radiograph is standard. Any abnormalities found are evaluated by chest CT or PET scan.

References

Alektiar, K.M., Leung, D., Zelefsky, M.J., Healey, J.H., & Brennan, M.F. (2002). Adjuvant brachytherapy for primary high-grade soft tissue sarcoma of the extremity. *Annals of Surgical Oncology, 9*(1), 48–56.

Dunne-Daly, C. (1997). Principles of brachytherapy. In K.H. Dow, J.D. Buckholtz, R. Iwamoto, V.K. Fieler, & L.J. Hilderley (Eds.), *Nursing care in radiation oncology* (2nd ed., pp. 21–35). Philadelphia: Saunders.

Forscher, C.A., & Casciato, D.A. (2000). Sarcomas. In D.A. Casciato & Lowitz, B.B. (Eds.), *Manual of clinical oncology* (4th ed., pp. 349–362**)**. Philadelphia: Lippincott Williams & Wilkins.

Graham, D. (2001). Management of soft tissue sarcoma. *Nursing Clinics of North America, 36,* 553–565.

Hu, K.S., & Harrison, L.B. (2000). Adjuvant RT of retroperitoneal sarcoma: The role of intraoperative radiotherapy (IORT). *Sarcoma, 4,* 11–16.

Kelvin, J.F. (1997). Gastrointestinal cancers. In K.H. Dow, J.D. Buckholtz, R. Iwamoto, V.K. Fieler, & L.J. Hilderley (Eds.), *Nursing care in radiation oncology* (2nd ed., pp. 152–183). Philadelphia: Saunders.

Kraus, D., Harrison, L., & O'Malley, B. (1999). Soft tissue and bone sarcomas of the head and neck. In L.B. Harrison, R.B. Sessions, & W.K. Hong (Eds.), *Head and neck cancer: A multidisciplinary approach* (pp. 871–895). Philadelphia: Lippincott-Raven.

Mackenzie, S., Reid, R., Barrett, A., & O'Dwyer, P.J. (2003). Management of soft tissue sarcomas of the abdomen and pelvis. *Colorectal Disease, 5*(2), 129–132.

O'Sullivan, B., Wylie, J., Catton, C., Gutierrez, E., Swallow, C.J., Wunder, J., et al. (1999). The local management of soft tissue sarcoma. *Seminars in Radiation Oncology, 9,* 328–348.

Shelton, B.K. (2003). Evidence-based care for the neutropenic patient with leukemia. *Seminars in Oncology Nursing, 19,* 133–141.

Spierer, M.M., Alektiar, K.M., Zelefsky, M.J., Brennan, M.F., & Cordiero, P.G. (2003). Tolerance of tissue transfers to adjuvant RT in primary soft tissue sarcoma of the extremity. *International Journal of Radiation Oncology, Biology, Physics, 56,* 1112–1116.

Stinson, S.F., DeLaney, T.F., Greenberg, J., Yang, J.C., Lampert, M.H., Hicks, J.I., et al. (1991). Acute and long-term effects on limb function of combined modality limb sparing therapy for extremity soft tissue sarcoma. *International Journal of Radiation Oncology, Biology, Physics, 21,* 1493–1499.

Sturgis, E.M., & Potter, B.O. (2003). Sarcomas of the head and neck region. *Current Opinions in Oncology, 15,* 239–252.

Zagars, G.K., & Ballo, M.T. (2003). Sequencing radiotherapy for soft tissue sarcoma when re-resection is planned. *International Journal of Radiation Oncology, Biology, Physics, 56,* 21–27.

Zagars, G.K., Ballo, M.T., Pisters, P.W., Pollock, R.E., Patel, S.R., Benjamin, R.S., et al. (2003). Prognostic factors for patients with localized soft-tissue sarcoma treated with conservation surgery and RT: An analysis of 225 patients. *Cancer, 97,* 2530–2525.

B. Lymphoma
1. Introduction and overview of disease
  a) Diverse group of neoplasms arising from uncontrolled growth of lymphocytes in lymph nodes and lymphoid tissues (Groenwald, Frogge, Goodman, & Yarbro, 1995). The lymph system is made up of thin tubes that branch, like blood vessels, into all parts of the body. Lymph nodes are groups of small, bean-shaped organs that make and store infection-fighting cells. Clusters of lymph nodes are found in the underarms, pelvis, neck, and abdomen. The spleen, the thymus, and the tonsil also are part of the lymph system (NCI, 2002).
  b) Appearance of the cells and the pattern in which they grow within the lymph node or bone marrow are critical for the correct diagnosis. Lymphomas demonstrating the Reed-Sternberg cells were classified as Hodgkin's disease (HD) and those without were classified as non-Hodgkin's lymphoma (NHL) (Groenwald et al., 1995).
  c) HD accounts for only 1% of all cancers diagnosed. Patients usually present with painless lymphadenopathy. One-third of patients with HD present with one of the three B symptoms: fever, night sweats, and weight loss. Patients who have both weight loss and fevers have a particularly poor prognosis. HD generally spreads from one lymph node group to an immediately adjacent lymph node group. More than 80% of the patients with HD present with cervical lymph node involvement, and more than 50% have mediastinal disease (Chao, Perez, & Brady, 1999).
  d) NHL is diagnosed 6 times as often as HD, and its death rate is 13 times greater. It is the fifth most common malignancy in the United States and accounts for 4.5% of all cancers (Molina, 2001). NHL is characterized by the type of malignant cell that is involved, the patterns in which they grow, and how fast the cells divide and the tumor progresses. NHL has a propensity for skipping to noncontiguous lymph node groups. NHL has a marked increase in the incidence of bone marrow and mesenteric

lymph node involvement. The histopathologic classification of NHL has been a challenge for decades to both pathologists and clinicians (Gospondarowicz & Wasserman, 1998) (see Figure 13).

2. Incidence and risk factors

a) Gender: Overall incidence of lymphoma is slightly higher in men than women (Jemal et al., 2004).

b) Age: HD has a bimodal peak. The early peak is from 25–30 years of age, and the second peak is from ages 75–80. HD is rare in children younger than 10 years of age (Hoppe, 1998). The incidence of NHL rises steadily with age, starting in the fourth or fifth decade.

c) Race: More prevalent in whites than African Americans and Asian Americans (Molina, 2001).

d) Socioeconomic: More common in middle-class than in lower-class families and more common in developed than in underdeveloped countries.

e) Environmental factors (Molina, 2001)

(1) Occupations: farmers, pesticide applicators, grain (flour) millers, meat workers, wood and forestry workers, chemists, painters, mechanics, machinists, and printers

(2) Chemicals: pesticides and herbicides, solvents, wood preservatives, and dusts

(3) Radiation

(a) Survivors of atomic bombs and nuclear reactor accidents

(b) Prior RT and chemotherapy

f) Viruses/bacteria

(1) Epstein-Barr virus is associated with Burkitt's lymphoma.

(2) Human T cell lymphotropic virus type I (HTLV-1) responsible for adult T cell leukemia/lymphoma. Most common in some parts of Japan and in the Caribbean region. Same family of viruses as HIV and is spread through sexual intercourse; contaminated blood can be passed to children through breast milk (ACS, 2004).

(3) Human herpes virus 8

(4) Hepatitis C virus

(5) *Helicobacter pylori* (bacteria) are associated with lymphomas of the stomach.

(6) Simian virus 40 (SV40) is being closely studied. The virus was present in polio vaccines from 1955 until 1963. It was removed from the vaccine in 1963. Some doctors think this may have contributed to the rapid increase in non-Hodgkin's lymphoma incidence that began in the 1970s (ACS, 2004).

g) Immunodeficiency (Molina, 2001)

(1) HIV infection

(2) Iatrogenic immunosuppression (transplant recipients)

(3) Collagen vascular and autoimmune diseases

3. Radiation treatment

a) Hodgkin's disease treatment includes the involved and contiguous lymphatic chains. This encompasses the clinically apparent disease and the contiguous nodal regions at risk for subclinical disease (Hull & Mendenhall, 2001).

(1) Mantle field includes all of the major lymph mode regions above the diaphragm. The field extends from the inferior portion of the mandible almost to the level of the insertion of the diaphragm. Individually contoured lung block is designed to conform to the patient's anatomy and tumor distribution (Hoppe, 1998).

(2) Preauricular field is used when the primary site of enlarged nodes may

Figure 13. Major Lymph Node Groups

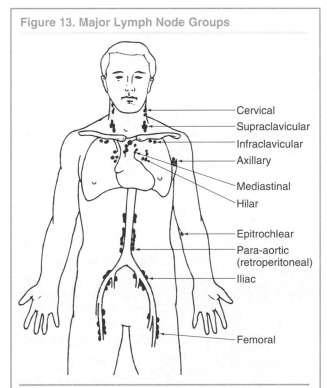

Cervical
Supraclavicular
Infraclavicular
Axillary
Mediastinal
Hilar
Epitrochlear
Para-aortic (retroperitoneal)
Iliac
Femoral

Note. From "Lymphomas" by C.H. Yarbro in S.L. Groenwald, M.H. Frogge, M. Goodman, and C.H. Yarbro (Eds.), *The Care of Individuals With Cancer* (p. 1331), 2000, Sudbury, MA: Jones and Bartlett. Copyright 2000 by Jones and Bartlett. Reprinted with permission.

include bulky high cervical nodes, extending very near the upper border of the typical mantle field (Chao et al., 1999).

(3) Sub-diaphragmatic field is the inverted Y, includes para-aortic nodes and bilateral pelvic, inguinal, and femoral nodal regions (see Figure 14) (ports used for total nodal irradiation). The spleen also may be included (Hull & Mendenhall, 2001).

(4) Total lymphoid irradiation (TLI) refers to sequential treatment to a mantle and inverted Y field. When the sub-diaphragmatic field does not include the pelvis, the term used is

subtotal lymphoid irradiation (Chao et al., 1999) (see section VII, I—TMI).

b) RT for NHL is based on the location of the tumor, which defines the treatment volume, critical organs, and dose-limiting structures (Gospondarowicz & Wasserman, 1998).

(1) Involved field irradiation is most commonly used for localized lymphomas and implies treatment to the involved nodal regions with adequate margins or to the extranodal site and its immediate lymph node drainage area (Gospondarowicz & Wasserman, 1998).

(2) Consolidative radiation after chemotherapy to areas of bulk disease

(3) Relapse treatment is individualized based on prior chemotherapy or radiation treatment.

(4) Total skin irradiation (TSI) of cutaneous T cell lymphoma (see section VII, J—Total Skin Electron Beam Therapy).

4. Mantle field irradiation

a) Acute effects (Lymphoma Information Network, 2000; Sitton, 1992)

(1) Fatigue

(2) Hair loss

(3) Skin reaction

(a) Skin reactions result from the depletion of actively proliferating cells in a renewing cell population.

(b) See section IV, C—Skin Reactions

(4) Changes in taste

(a) The taste buds are radiosensitive, and the changes may include blunting or increased sensitivity to certain tastes. Normal taste may return months after treatment is completed.

(b) Have the patient perform oral care prior to eating.

(c) Add spices and seasoning to food if not treating the mantle field.

(d) Try out different foods.

(e) See section V, B—Head and Neck

(5) Mucositis (see section V, B—Head and Neck)

(6) Xerostomia

(a) Xerostomia occurs when the salivary glands are treated with radiation. The saliva becomes thick and ropey. It occurs at 10 Gy and

Figure 14. Ports Used for Total Nodal Irradiation

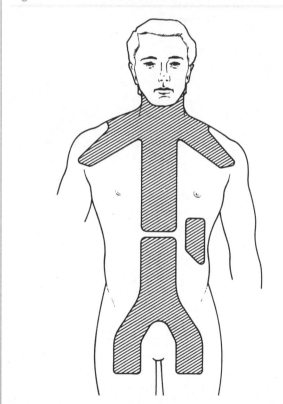

The upper port, called a mantle, extends from the mandible to the diaphragm and includes cervical, axillary, supraclavicular, infraclavicular, and mediastinal node chains. The heart and lungs are protected, in part, by lead shields. The lower port, called an inverted Y, extends from the diaphragm to the lower pelvis and includes para-aortic, iliac, inguinal, and femoral node chains. The small left lateral port, called splenic port, includes the spleen and splenic hilar nodes.

Note. From "Lymphomas" by C.H. Yarbro in S.L. Groenwald, M.H. Frogge, M. Goodman, and C.H. Yarbro (Eds.), *The Care of Individuals With Cancer* (p. 1338), 2000, Sudbury, MA: Jones and Bartlett. Copyright 2000 by Jones and Bartlett. Reprinted with permission.

is permanent at 40 Gy (Bruce, 2004).

   (b) Frequent prophylactic dental care

   (c) Fluoride treatment

   (d) See section V, B—Head and Neck

(7) Dysphagia/esophagitis

   (a) It is caused by irritation of the membranes lining the throat and esophagus. Usually seen after the second or third week of treatment and may continue for months after treatment.

   (b) Eat soft, bland foods such as puddings, custards, and yogurt.

   (c) Take dietary supplements.

   (d) Avoid irritants such as citrus and alcohol.

   (e) Medicate with viscous xylocaine, liquid antacids, or narcotics.

   (f) See section V, D—Thoracic

(8) Nausea and vomiting

   (a) Nausea and vomiting occur when neurotransmitters are stimulated and an impulse is sent to the autonomic nervous system, causing nausea, and to the somatic and visceral system to produce vomiting (Murphy-Ende, 2000).

   (b) Take antiemetic prior to treatment and as needed.

   (c) Schedule treatment at the end of the day.

   (d) Avoid eating just prior to treatment.

(9) Decreased blood counts

   (a) Thrombocytopenia occurs from deficient production of platelets or an accelerated platelet destruction (Lynch, 2000).

   (b) Neutropenia is caused by decreased neutrophils in the body resulting in an increased risk of infection (Lynch, 2000).

   (c) Check CBC weekly during treatment and hold treatment as needed.

  b) Long-term effects

(1) Thyroid dysfunction

   (a) Subclinical hypothyroidism develops in approximately 50% of the patients with HD. It is manifested by an elevation of the thyroid-stimulating hormone (TSH), even with a normal thyroxine level (Chao et al., 1999).

   (b) Thyroid profile (blood work) with follow-up visits

   (c) Thyroid hormonal replacement as needed

(2) Radiation pneumonitis

   (a) May develop within 6–12 weeks after completing treatment. Associated with lung inflammation that is characterized by a mild, nonproductive cough, low-grade fever, and difficult breathing with exertion. Occurs in 1% or less of patients receiving mantle field irradiation. The risk may increase if the chemotherapy drug bleomycin was used in combination with RT (Hoppe, 1998).

   (b) Fewer than 5% of patients develop symptomatic pneumonitis, manifested by cough, fever, pleuritic chest pain, and infiltrate on chest radiograph that often conforms to the irradiation fields. Symptomatic management usually is sufficient; however, a small proportion of patients require treatment with corticosteroids (Chao et al., 1999).

(3) Cardiovascular disease

   (a) Mediastinal radiation predisposes patients to premature coronary artery disease and pericardial and myocardial fibrosis, but modification to treatment techniques have decreased the dose of radiation to the heart (Hancock, Tucker, & Hoppe, 1993).

   (b) Refer to a cardiologist if symptomatic.

(4) Radiation pericarditis (Hoppe, 1998)

   (a) Occurs in fewer than 5% of patients. It presents as an acute febrile syndrome with chest pain

and friction rub; it usually clears within a few weeks.

(b) Routine echocardiogram

(c) Analgesics and NSAIDs

(d) Refer to a cardiologist if symptomatic.

(e) Tamponade or constrictive pericarditis is more serious. It is seen in less than 1% of patients and may require surgical correction (Hoppe, 1998).

(5) Infection

(a) Herpes zoster can occur during treatment or within the first two years after treatment in 10%–15% of patients (Hoppe, 1998).

(b) Initiate acyclovir.

(6) Lhermitte's sign

(a) Develops in approximately 10%–15% of patients and is caused by transient demyelinization of the spinal cord.

(b) Occurs one to two months after treatment and spontaneously resolves after two to six months (Chao et al., 1999).

(7) Secondary malignancies

(a) The mean 15-year actuarial risk for any secondary malignant neoplasm in survivors of HD or NHL is 17.6% compared with 2.6% in the general population (Fernsler & Fanuele, 1998).

(b) The following are the most common secondary malignancies in HD or NHL.

i) Leukemia

ii) Breast cancer

iii) Thyroid cancer (peaks 15–19 years post-radiation treatment)

iv) Lung cancer (great risk among those who smoked at the time of diagnosis and who continued smoking after treatment)

(8) Para-aortic and spleen field

(a) Acute effects

i) Nausea and vomiting

ii) Diarrhea (Lymphoma Information Network, 2000)

- Low-residue diet
- Antidiarrheal medication

iii) Decreased blood counts

iv) Fatigue

(b) Long-term effects

i) Post-splenectomy sepsis (Chao et al., 1999)

- Can be caused by *Streptococcus pneumoniae*, meningococcus, and *Haemophilus* strains.
- This can be minimized by prior immunization against these organisms.

ii) Preventive care (Young, Bookman, & Longo, 1990)

- Pneumococcal vaccine every five years
- Influenza vaccine every year
- Prompt treatment of febrile disease

(9) Pelvic node fields

(a) Acute effects

i) Diarrhea

ii) Decreased blood counts

iii) Fatigue

(b) Long-term effects (Sitton, 1992)

i) Sterility in males

- Sperm production may be reduced or stopped during therapy. It may return to normal in three to five years. Sterility may be permanent if the patient received alkylating agents as part of his chemotherapy regimen.
- Suggest sperm banking prior to starting RT for men who wish to have children.

ii) Sterility in females

- The use of inverted Y irradiation to the pelvic lymph nodes can cause early menopause as a result of ovarian exposure to radiation (Bruner, 2001).
- Surgical manipulation of ovaries out of radiation field (oophoropexy)
- Freezing embryos prior to radiation treatment
- Androgens have been shown to improve low libido in some women who have undergone menopause (Bruner, 2001).

(10) Psychosocial and economic: Most challenging effect by both the survivors and healthcare providers. Severity of the problems is related to the developmental stage of the survivor (Fernsler & Fanuele, 1998).

(a) Anxiety/fear of recurrence

(b) Denial of insurance

(c) Denial of job offers or rejection by the military

(d) Body image

(11) Importance of healthy lifestyle

(a) Diet

(b) Exercise

(c) Not smoking

(d) Limit sun exposure

(e) Breast self-exam

5. Patient and family education

a) Teach patient and family about the required treatment and length of treatment depending upon treatment site.

b) Teach patient/family about the acute and late effects of treatment that they may experience depending upon their individual treatment site.

c) Teach patient and family about medications that may be used to minimize side effects of treatment.

d) Teach patient and family about appropriate healthcare risks associated with treatment and lifestyle modifications.

e) Teach patient and family about the need for long-term follow-up.

6. Follow-up management (Young et al., 1990)

a) Patients who are seen in follow-up may have appropriate diagnostic tests performed, including chest x-ray, thyroid panel, and CBC.

b) Patients should receive appropriate vaccinations, as necessary.

References

American Cancer Society. (2004). *How is non-Hodgkin's lymphoma diagnosed?* Retrieved June 1, 2004, from http://www.cancer.org/docroot/CRI/content/CRI_2_4_3X_How_is_non-Hodgkins_lymphoma_diagnosed_32.asp

Bruce, S. (2004). Radiation-induced xerostomia: How dry is your patient? *Clinical Journal of Oncology Nursing, 8,* 61–67.

Bruner, D.W. (2001). Maintenance of body image and sexual function. In D.W. Bruner, G. Moore-Higgs, & M. Haas (Eds.), *Outcomes in radiation therapy: Multidisciplinary management* (pp. 611–636). Sudbury, MA: Jones and Bartlett.

Chao, K.S., Perez, C., & Brady, L. (1999). *Radiation oncology: Management decisions.* Philadelphia: Lippincott-Raven.

Fernsler, J., & Fanuele, J. (1998). Lymphomas: Long-term sequelae and survivorship issues. *Seminars in Oncology Nursing, 14,* 321–328.

Gospondarowicz, M., & Wasserman, T. (1998). Non-Hodgkin's lymphomas. In C.A. Perez & L.W. Brady (Eds.), *Principles and practice of radiation oncology* (3rd ed., pp. 1987–2001). Philadelphia: Lippincott-Raven.

Groenwald, S., Frogge, M., Goodman, M., & Yarbro, C. (1995). *Comprehensive cancer nursing review* (2nd ed.). Sudbury, MA: Jones and Bartlett.

Hancock, S., Tucker, M., & Hoppe, R. (1993). Factors affecting late mortality from heart disease after treatment of Hodgkin's disease. *JAMA, 270,* 1949–1955.

Hoppe, R.T. (1998). Hodgkin's disease. In C.A. Perez & L.W. Brady (Eds.), *Principles and practice of radiation oncology* (3rd ed., pp. 1963–1986). Philadelphia: Lippincott-Raven.

Hull, M., & Mendenhall, N. (2001). The role of radiation therapy in Hodgkin's lymphoma. *Oncology Spectrums, 2,* 720–726.

Jemal, A., Tiwari, R.C., Murray, T., Ghafoor, A., Samuels, A., Ward, E., et al. (2004). Cancer statistics, 2004. *CA: A Cancer Journal for Clinicians, 54,* 8–29.

Lymphoma Information Network. (2000, April 7). *Lymphoma radiotherapy—Side effects.* Retrieved July 7, 2003, from http://www.lymphomainfo.net?therapy/radiotherapy/side-effects.html

Lynch, M.P. (2000). Neutropenia and thrombocytopenia. In D. Camp-Sorrell & R. Hawkins (Eds.), *Clinical manual for the oncology advanced practice nurse* (pp. 693–707). Pittsburgh, PA: Oncology Nursing Society.

Molina, A. (2001). Non-Hodgkin's lymphoma. In R. Pazdur, L. Coia, W. Hoskins, & L. Wagman (Eds.), *Cancer management: A multidisciplinary approach* (5th ed., pp. 585–622). Melville, NY: PRR Inc.

Murphy-Ende, K. (2000). Nausea and vomiting. In D. Camp-Sorrell & R. Hawkins (Eds.), *Clinical manual for the oncology advanced practice nurse* (pp. 379–385). Pittsburgh, PA: Oncology Nursing Society.

National Cancer Institute. (2002). *Primary CNS lymphoma (PDQ®): Treatment.* Retrieved July 7, 2003, from http://www.nci.nih.gov/cancerinfo/pdq/treatment/primary-CNS-lymphoma/patient/

Sitton, E. (1992). Hodgkin's disease and non-Hodgkin's lymphoma. In K.H. Dow, J.D. Bucholtz, R. Iwamoto, V.K. Fieler, & L.J. Hilderley (Eds.), *Nursing care in radiation oncology* (2nd ed., pp. 261–291). Philadelphia: Saunders.

Young, R., Bookman, M., & Longo, D. (1990). Late complications of Hodgkin's disease management. *Journal of the National Cancer Institute Monographs, 10,* 55–60.

VII. Modality-specific management

A. External beam

1. Procedure description

a) Delivery of radiation from a specified distance to a defined target volume to cure (definitive, neoadjuvant, adjuvant), control, or palliate tumor within the defined field or in special cases prophylactically (Haas & Kuehn, 2001).

b) Also referred to as "teletherapy" or therapy from a distance

c) The external beam treatment machine consists of a radiation source, a collimating system that forms and directs the beam, a shielding system, a control system to turn the beam on and off, a light field that delineates the field, a means to rotate the beam, and a support assembly for the patient (Bourland, 2000).

d) Delivers a daily fractionated (single dose of ionizing radiation) radiation dose to a defined target

e) Allows delivery of a cumulative dose to the tumor within tolerance of the surrounding normal tissue

f) Delivers radiation to the tumor site and draining lymphatics (Zelman, 2000) in a dose determined by the tumor type, site, and size.

2. Indications

a) External beam therapy is indicated in almost all cancers. It is estimated that 50%–60% of all individuals with cancer will receive radiation at some point in the treatment of their cancer (Chao, Perez, & Brady, 2002).

b) External beam treatment may be indicated throughout the cancer trajectory. It is used curatively for definitive, neoadjuvant, or adjuvant (e.g., early-stage Hodgkin's disease, head and neck or cervical cancer), palliative to alleviate pain from bone metastases, or prophylactically in patients with small cell lung cancer to prevent brain metastasis (Rubin & Williams, 2001).

c) External beam therapy may be indicated as a single modality or in combination with other cancer therapies.

d) Persons receiving external beam therapy must be able to lie still on the treatment table during therapy. Although treatment may last only several minutes, the fact that the patient is alone in the room on an elevated table requires assessment of their ability to do so. Children, individuals who are confused or have psychiatric disorders, or critically ill or ventilated patients can safely receive external beam treatment with appropriate assessment and prior planning (Bucholtz, 1994). This will avoid the risk of injury during therapy.

e) Individuals with multiple sites of disease are typically not candidates for radiation, as their disease cannot be encompassed in a radiation field. Specific sites may be

treated but systemic therapy such as chemotherapy may be indicated (Chao et al., 2002).

3. Treatment

a) Simulation (Schell, Maurer, Seibert, & Fang-Fang, 2001)

(1) The patient is placed on the simulator table or CT simulation table in a position that allows for treatment of the tumor volume without treating significant normal tissue. Supine is the most common position.

(2) An immobilization device may be made to assist in maintaining the treatment position. Examples of these devices include casts, head holders, bite blocks, thermoplastic face masks, and/or vacuum bags.

(3) Physical exam, CT scan, MRI, and surgical reports are used to define the target with the simulator's isocenter, and films are taken to determine if the target is correct.

(4) Information documented during simulation includes gantry angle, collimator angle, table position, and field size.

(5) Temporary or permanent marks are placed on the skin or immobilization device to be used in daily treatment setup.

(6) Computer-aided simulation uses a volumetric image of the patient in the treatment position with the entire process taking place within the computer using software tools to identify normal tissue and delineate treatment fields. This allows for more precise definition of the target volume and location of critical normal structures.

b) Treatment planning (Schell et al., 2001)

(1) Ensures that an adequate dose is delivered to the tumor while not exceeding normal tissue tolerance

(2) Information from simulation is used by the dosimetry staff to develop a plan, which is offered to the physician for approval.

(3) Treatment plan includes the number of treatments, dose per fraction, energy, prescription point location, and total dose. Treatment portals must cover the tumor volume with a margin.

(4) GTV includes the gross disease and abnormally enlarged regional nodes.

(5) CTV includes GTV plus regions considered to potentially have microscopic disease.

(6) PTV includes a margin around the CTV, which considers motion such as respiration and variations in the setup.

c) Treatment

(1) Before the first treatment, a verification or portal film is taken to confirm setup is accurate. Port films are repeated on a weekly basis. The physician may check the patient on the machine before the first treatment is given.

(2) Patients lay on the table for approximately 15 minutes or longer depending on the complexity of the setup, although the beam is only on for a few minutes (Bourland, 2000).

(3) Treatments are given daily, Monday–Friday. If patients have twice-a-day treatment, at least six hours must elapse before giving the next dose (Rubin & Williams, 2001).

4. Collaborative management

a) Acute effects

(1) General side effects, such as fatigue and anorexia, are experienced during EBRT.

(2) Site-specific side effects (acute and late) are determined by the area treated, the total dose, and the influence of other modalities, such as surgery and/or chemotherapy. See the specific treatment sites.

(3) Emotional reactions to therapy may also occur. Fears related to "being radioactive," and perceptions of therapy require ongoing assessment and intervention (Strohl, 1999).

b) Late effects

(1) Late effects of EBRT are related to the total dose given, the energy of the beam used, and the treatment site. Late effects may include hypo- or hyper-pigmentation of the skin, atrophy and/or fibrosis of the skin and superficial tissues, and fibrosis of the deep tissue or organs. Tissue necrosis also may occur, resulting in an open skin wound and/or fistulae formation (Williams, Keng, & Sutherland, 2001).

(2) Second malignancies (e.g., breast cancer following treatment for Hodgkin's disease) also may develop as late effects.

c) Management

(1) Assess for comorbid factors such as smoking, recent surgery, and concurrent or recent chemotherapy, as these factors may alter tolerance and increase the incidence or severity of side effects (Rubin & Williams, 2001).

(a) Assess the patient's ability to tolerate treatment, both from the side effects as well as the social issues (e.g., transportation).

(b) Obtain pretreatment nutritional assessment in patients with evidence of anorexia, significant weight loss, or obvious cachexia.

(c) If patients have cardiac pacemakers/implantable defibrillators, contact the manufacturer before initiating radiation. Cardiac monitoring before, during, and afterward may be required (Haas & Kuehn, 2001; Hogle, 2002).

(d) Careful treatment planning should be used to reduce both acute and late effects.

(2) Plan for at least once-weekly assessment during therapy.

d) Patient and family education

(1) Educate the patient and family about the following aspects of RT. Describing the process of therapy as well as the anticipated side effects of treatment helps to prepare patients for therapy (Rutledge & McGuire, 2004).

(a) What radiation is and how it works

(b) Simulation and treatment planning process

(c) Goal of therapy (prophylaxis, curative, palliative)

(d) Importance of patient compliance with positioning. Sometimes analgesics may be ordered prior to treatment.

(e) Anticipated side effects and methods to reduce effects

(f) Role of communication between the radiation oncology staff regarding any side effects the patient experiences

(2) Preparing patients for therapy includes addressing fears about being irradiated. This is a modality that is difficult for most people to comprehend. The fact that an invisible beam of energy can destroy tumor cells seems unreal. The mystery associated with the therapy may lead to doubt and fear (Strohl, 1999).

(3) Repeated teaching needs to emphasize that persons receiving EBRT are not radioactive and that late effects are the result of biologic effects of radiation (Strohl, 1999).

References

Bourland, J. (2000). Radiation oncology physics. In L. Gunderson & J. Tepper (Eds.), *Clinical radiation oncology* (pp. 64–119). New York: Churchill Livingstone.

Bucholtz, J. (1994). Comforting children during radiation therapy. *Oncology Nursing Forum, 21,* 987–994.

Chao, K., Perez, C., & Brady, L. (2002). *Radiation oncology: Management decisions* (2nd ed.). Philadelphia: Lippincott Williams and Wilkins.

Haas, M., & Kuehn, E.F. (2001). Teletherapy: External radiation therapy. In D.W. Bruner, G. Moore-Higgs, & M. Haas (Eds.), *Outcomes in radiation therapy: Multidisciplinary management* (pp. 55–66). Sudbury, MA: Jones and Bartlett.

Hogle, W.P. (2002). Implantable defibrillator malfunctions should not be overlooked. *Clinical Journal of Oncology Nursing, 6,* 252.

Rubin, P., & Williams, J. (2001). Principles of radiation oncology and cancer radiotherapy. In P. Rubin (Ed.), *Clinical oncology: A multidisciplinary approach for physicians and students* (8th ed., pp. 99–125). Philadelphia: Saunders

Rutledge, D., & McGuire, C. (2004). Evidence-based symptom management. In C.H. Yarbro, M.H. Frogge, & M. Goodman (Eds.), *Cancer symptom management* (3rd ed., pp. 3–15). Sudbury, MA: Jones and Bartlett.

Schell, M., Maurer, C., Seibert, J., & Fang-Fang, Y. (2001). Radiation physics as applied to clinical radiation oncology. In P. Rubin (Ed.), *Clinical oncology: A multidisciplinary approach for physicians and students* (8th ed., pp. 126–146). Philadelphia: Saunders.

Strohl, R. (1999). Radiation therapy. In C. Miaskowski & P. Buchsel (Eds.), *Oncology nursing: Assessment and clinical care* (pp. 59–83). St. Louis, MO: Mosby.

Williams, J., Keng., P., & Sutherland, R. (2001). Basic principles of radiobiology. In P. Rubin (Ed.), *Clinical oncology: A multidisciplinary approach for physicians and students* (8th ed., pp. 75–79). Philadelphia: Saunders.

Zeman, E. (2000). Biologic basis of radiation oncology. In L. Gunderson & J. Tepper (Eds.), *Clinical radiation oncology* (pp. 1–42). New York: Churchill Livingstone.

B. LDR/HDR brachytherapy

1. Procedure description: Brachytherapy is the temporary or permanent placement of a radioactive source into a body cavity (intracavitary), into the tissue (interstitial), or on the surface of the body (e.g., plaque, custom bolus) (Bruner, Bucholtz, Iwamoto, & Strohl, 1998). It also is used by placing catheters into the airway, GI tract, or blood vessel (intraluminal or intravascular). Brachytherapy may be used by itself or as an adjunctive treatment in combination with external beam therapy to increase the total dose to a specified target. It is clear that brachytherapy is the optimum way of delivering conformal radiotherapy tailored to the shape of the tumor while sparing surrounding normal tissues (DeVita, Hellman, & Rosenberg, 2001). Knowledge of specific radionuclide types is essential to the radiation oncology nurse. The patient is not radioactive with temporary sealed sources, only the source is radioactive. Once the implanted source is removed, the patient no longer needs to be treated with any special precautions (Bruner, Moore-Higgs, & Haas, 2001).

a) With LDR brachytherapy treatments, approximately 0.4–2 Gy are given in an hour, requiring treatment times of 24 to 144 hours. LDR has the advantage of being radiobiologically more sound, allowing curative doses to tumors, and sparing normal tissues better (Bruner et al., 2001). LDR brachytherapy enhances radiation effect by taking advantage of repair, redistribution, and repopulation principles even in poorly oxygenated tissue (Yarbro, Frogge, Goodman, & Groenwald, 2000).

b) With HDR brachytherapy treatments, approximately 0.2 Gy are delivered per minute, with a treatment time of a few minutes. HDR brachytherapy's advantage is that the dose is delivered quickly, resulting in improved patient comfort, more reliable positioning of the source, less dose to ancillary personnel, and an ability to perform the procedure as an outpatient (Bruner et al., 2001).

2. Indications

a) Brachytherapy delivers a high radiation treatment dose to a specified tumor volume with a rapid fall-off in radiation dose to adjacent normal tissue (Bruner et al., 1998).

b) Common diseases treated with LDR/HDR are gynecologic cancers, such as cancers of the cervix, vulva, vagina, and endometrium; breast cancer; bronchogenic tumors; esophageal cancer; head and neck tumors; brain tumors; prostate cancer; choroidal melanoma, retinoblastoma, and others (Bruner et al., 1998; Fieler, 1997; Gosselin & Waring, 2001).

  c) LDR/HDR brachytherapy may be used as a "boost" in conjunction with EBRT.

3. Potential risks

  a) Acute and late effects of brachytherapy are those caused by effects of ionizing radiation (Bruner et al., 1998).

    (1) Invasive brachytherapy procedures to various body sites carry risks of complications, such as perforation, infection, or bleeding (Bruner et al., 1998).

    (2) Complications associated with bed rest and catheterization include thrombophlebitis, pulmonary embolus, and urinary sepsis, especially for LDR brachytherapy (Bruner et al., 1998).

  b) Incidence: The majority of patients undergoing brachytherapy experience site-specific side effects related to the implant. In addition, the patients may have unresolved acute side effects of EBRT at the time of the implant because brachytherapy often is administered during or soon after the course of external beam treatment (Bruner et al., 1998; Velji & Fitch, 2001). Elderly or debilitated patients are more vulnerable to complications (Bruner et al., 1998).

  c) Assessment and management (see site-specific assessment and management for each implant site).

4. Procedure history and uses

  a) Used since early 1900s following discovery of radium by Marie Curie (Dunne-Daly, 1997; Eifel, 1997; Hogle, Quinn, & Heron, 2003; Wright, Jones, Whelan, & Lukka, 1994)

  b) First used as surface applicators of radium to treat skin lesions (Dunne-Daly, 1997)

  c) 1950s—development of afterloaders (Dunne-Daly, 1997)

    (1) Source holders (applicators) placed in outpatient clinic or while in surgery

    (2) Source loaded when patient was in radiation procedure room or returned to radiation-safe inpatient room

    (3) Reduced exposure to healthcare provider

  d) 1960s–70s—decline in use because of the development of linear accelerators

  e) 1980s—renewed interest (Dunne-Daly, 1997)

    (1) Single modality

    (2) Combination with other modalities (external beam, hyperthermia)

  f) Currently widely used (Dunne-Daly, 1997)

    (1) Knowledge of long-term effects

    (2) Improved safety and protection techniques

    (3) Increased knowledge regarding care of implant patients (DeVita et al., 2001). Brachytherapy requires the expertise of a team of trained personnel (physician, physicist, dosimetrist, radiation therapist, RT nurse, and radiation safety officer) to implement the individualized treatment plan designed by the radiation oncologist.

      (a) Brachytherapy has a variety of current uses alone or in combination with other therapies and in specific cancers.

      (b) Brachytherapy is used to improve local tumor control.

        i) Gynecologic cancers (Dunne-Daly, 1997; Eifel, 1992, 1997; Fieler, 1997; Gosselin & Waring, 2001; Gupta et al., 1998; Holland, 2001; Mock, Kucera, Fellner, Knocke, & Potter, 2003; Velji & Fitch, 2001; Wright et al., 1994)

         • Vaginal cylinder/stump

         • Tandem and ovoids

         • Interstitial needles and template

        ii) Head and neck (Devine & Doyle, 2000; Dunne-Daly, 1997; Kremer, Klimek, Andreopoulos, & Mosges, 1998)

         • Intracavitary catheters

         • Interstitial catheters

        iii) Lung (Bruner et al., 1998; Dunne-Daly, 1997; Fieler, 1997; Powell, 1999)

- Endobronchial catheters
- Interstitial catheters
iv) Breast (Dunne-Daly, 1997; Hogle et al., 2003)
  - Interstitial catheters
  - Applicators
  - Inflatable catheters
v) Prostate
  - Radioactive seed implant (permanent/LDR)
  - Radioactive seed implant (temporary/HDR)

g) Brachytherapy irradiates small volumes and can potentially minimize complications (Nag, Sasha, Janjan, Petersen, & Saider, 2001). Brachytherapy is used to preserve vital organ function.
  (1) Soft tissue sarcoma
  (2) Oropharyngeal cancers
  (3) Intraocular melanoma, retinoblastoma
  (4) Meningiomas
  (5) Malignant brain tumors (Bruner et al., 1998)

h) Brachytherapy is used to treat recurrent or inoperable cancers.
  (1) Lung cancer (bronchogenic)
  (2) Esophageal cancer (Bruner et al., 1998)

i) Brachytherapy is used to control disease in previously radiated sites.
  (1) Recurrent gynecologic (GYN) cancers
  (2) Head and neck cancers
  (3) GI malignancies (Bruner et al., 1998)

j) Isotopes and techniques used with various cancers: Most current brachytherapy performed with reactor-produced radionuclides (Bruner et al., 1998)
  (1) Safer
  (2) Easier to use
    (a) Cesium-137
    (b) Iridium-192
    (c) Iodine-125
    (d) Palladium-103

  (e) Gold-198
(3) Mechanism of action (Dunne-Daly, 1997)
  (a) Alpha, beta, and gamma rays transfer energy to living matter.
  (b) Ionization of molecules in cells
  (c) Cellular reproduction process altered
  (d) Irradiated cells destroyed instantly
  (e) Irradiated cell unable to reproduce
  (f) Extent of injury related to capabilities of isotope
(4) Isotopes and techniques used in brachytherapy (see Table 15)

k) LDR/HDR brachytherapy
(1) Conventional LDR brachytherapy involves an operative procedure with anesthesia for placement of a hollow applicator device or catheter into body tissues or cavities. Radioactive sources are manually afterloaded into the applicators after the patient has returned to the designated hospital room (Bruner et al., 1998; Dunne-Daly, 1997). With post-op soft tissue sarcomas, no radiation is administered for at least five days to allow for wound healing (Carrubba, Jankowski, & Kunsman, 1999).
  (a) Hospitalization and specialized nursing care are required while the implant remains in place, which may be from one to several days.
  (b) Bed rest is required for gynecologic, some prostate, and rectal implants.
  (c) LDR brachytherapy also can be performed using remote afterloading techniques.
  (d) Strict room confinement is required for all inpatient brachytherapy (see section III of this manual).

Table 15. Isotopes Used in Brachytherapy

Cancer	Technique	Isotope
Endometrial	Intracavitary	Cesium-137, Iridium-192
Cervical	Intracavitary or interstitial	Iridium-192, Cesium-137, Radium-226, Cobalt-60
Prostate	Interstitial	Iodine-125, Palladium-103
Breast	Interstitial	Iridium-192
Eye (melanoma)	Plaque therapy	Cobalt-60, Iodine-125, Iridium-192
Head and neck	Interstitial or intracavitary	Iridium-192, Cesium-137, Radium-226, Cobalt-60
Rectal	Interstitial	Iridium-192, Cesium-137
Esophageal	Intraluminal	Iridium-192, Cesium-137
Bronchogenic	Endobronchial or interstitial	Iridium-192

Note. Based on information from Dunne-Daly, 1997.

(e) Invasive brachytherapy procedures to various body sites carry risks of complications such as perforation, infection, and bleeding (Bruner et al., 1998).

(2) HDR brachytherapy involves the use of an automated remote afterloading device for the placement of the radioactive source into the applicators, which have been placed in the tumor/cavity (see Figure 15). Sources are loaded from a storage safe that is in the afterloader and delivered via source guide tubes that connect the afterloader to the patient's treatment device, which are attached to the applicators inside the patient (Bruner et al., 1998).

(3) HDR brachytherapy allows patients to be treated with a high dose of radiation in a short period of time as outpatients, with minimal radiation exposure to healthcare providers (Dow, Bucholtz, Iwamoto, Fieler, & Hilderley, 1997). Generally, the HDR treatments are repeated until the desired dose has been delivered (Holland, 2001).

(a) The use of HDR treatment is possible in virtually all sites treated by conventional LDR therapy and by intracavitary, interstitial, intravascular, mold, percutaneous, or intraoperative techniques, with advantages for pediatric or adult patients. In selected instances, HDR appears to be well tolerated and as effective as LDR (Mock et al., 2003). Patients state a variety of reasons (traveling distance most often sited) for preferring LDR or HDR, when given the option (Wright, Jones, Whelan, & Lukka, 1994).

(b) Anesthesia or sedation may be required depending on the site, applicator, and age/comprehension of the patient; however, these procedures generally are performed on an outpatient basis with or without sedation/anesthesia (Eifel, 1992).

(c) Treatment times are shorter, but more treatments may be needed. Caregivers and visitors are not subject to radiation exposure after the patient is discharged (Brandt, 1991).

5. Collaborative management

a) Gynecologic implants, LDR: Applicators include intracavitary tandem and ovoids,

Figure 15. High Dose Rate Brachytherapy Treatment Unit and Control Console

Note. Photos courtesy of Duke University Health System.

vaginal cylinders, and transperineal interstitial vaginal template and needles (for advanced gynecologic malignancies) (Gupta et al., 1999).

(1) Pretreatment bowel preparation regimen per institution (i.e., enema morning of implant)

(2) Strict bed rest with log roll for care is mandatory to prevent possible dislodgment of applicator(s). In addition, a Foley catheter is inserted. Moistened vaginal packing is used to secure the position of the applicators and to pack the bladder and rectum away from the vaginal sources (Eifel, 1997). The applicator also may be held in place with radiation briefs and/or by suturing. Bowel management with antidiarrheal medication is given; low-residue diet

(with finger foods) for nutrition is provided; head of bed should be raised no higher than 30°. Check position of implant every shift and as necessary; modify bathing and linen change. Instruct patient on care guidelines and rationale while on bed rest (Gosselin & Waring, 2001).

(3) Prevent complications of immobility by use of compression stockings, coughing/deep breathing postoperatively, isometric exercises, and anticoagulants, if ordered (Bruner et al., 1998).

(4) Promote patient's comfort and decrease procedure-related pain with use of analgesics (oral, IV, patient-controlled analgesia, transdermal, epidural). Evaluate pain control each shift and more frequently if needed. Strong analgesia required ½–1 hour prior to removal of applicators (especially the interstitial needles and template, which could cause more pain during removal than other applicators). Pressure and ice applied to perineum for five minutes or longer after removal of needles to minimize bleeding and improve comfort (Bruner et al., 1998; Gosselin & Waring, 2001).

(5) Decrease social isolation; keep items within reach (call bell, hydration, tissues); answer call light promptly, check on patient often; educate patient per rationale of isolation.

(6) Address issues of long-term effects of vaginal stenosis. Prescribe and educate patient per use of vaginal dilator. Address concerns regarding sexuality. Patients receiving brachytherapy have a variety of informational needs and prefer to be fully informed about their conditions (Brandt, 1991).

(7) Refer to institutional radiation safety guidelines for exposure limits for staff, family, and other visitors (see section III—Radiation Protection).

(8) Provide patient with discharge instructions and contact telephone numbers. Report any excessive bleeding from bladder, vagina, or rectum; excessive pain; foul odor of urine or vaginal drainage; temperature above 101°F, increased urinary frequency or dysuria; inability to void after four hours; and diarrhea not controlled with diet or antidiarrheal medications (Gosselin & Waring, 2001).

(9) Educate staff caring for patient about the applicator, source, and rationale.

Lack of knowledge of staff members can contribute to fear on the caregivers' part (Gosselin & Waring, 2001; Stajduhar, 2000; Sticklin, 1994; Velji & Fitch, 2001).

b) Gynecologic implants, HDR: Applicators include tandem and ovoids and ring type or vaginal cylinders/stumps.

(1) Teach patient and family what to expect during the treatment. The aspects of treatment context, symptomatology, and passage of time are important to address during and after brachytherapy (Velji & Fitch, 2001).

(2) Provide special instructions, if any, such as eat light breakfast, take regular medications, and take antidiarrheal medication if necessary.

(3) Brachytherapy applicators need to be stabilized/anchored in place to ensure accuracy of placement of sources. There are several ways to accomplish this. With gynecologic patients using tandem and ovoid applicators, the applicators are stabilized after insertion with gauze packing to minimize movement while transporting patient. After packing is complete, the device should be further stabilized by suturing the labia or using a more humane approach, such as Radiation Implant Briefs™ (see Figure 16).

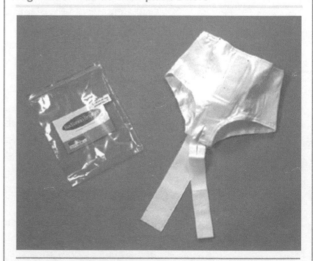

Figure 16. Radiation Implant Briefs™

Note. From "Nursing Management of Patients Receiving Brachytherapy for Gynecologic Malignancies," by T.K. Gosselin and J.S. Waring, 2001, *Clinical Journal of Oncology Nursing, 5,* p. 60. Copyright 2001 by the Oncology Nursing Society. Reprinted with permission.

(4) Assess and prepare the patient upon arrival to the clinic. Have the patient put on a pair of Radiation Implant Briefs. A Foley catheter and rectal tube will be inserted prior to the applicator being placed. Premedicate with oral pain medication and antianxiety medication, if necessary.

(5) The patient should be monitored throughout the preparation and procedure.

(6) Instruct the patient upon discharge about problems to report (e.g., increased urinary frequency or dysuria, foul odor of urine or vaginal discharge, fever, increased pain, heavy bleeding) (Gosselin & Waring, 2001) (see Table 16).

(7) Educate per pelvic site–specific management, such as vaginal stenosis and sexuality issues (see Figure 17).

c) Head and neck implants, LDR: Plastic catheters are afterloaded with iridium seeds.

(1) Prevent respiratory or cardiovascular complications by encouraging routine post-op exercises (e.g., deep breathing, changing position in bed, ambulating inside room), if appropriate.

(2) Prior to implant, patient to receive aggressive bowel regimen to decrease chance of dislodging radioactive sources while straining during bowel movement (Devine & Doyle, 2001).

(3) Have tracheostomy set in room; tracheostomy may be performed for airway obstruction resulting from edema (Bruner et al., 1998).

(4) Prior to implant, teach patient techniques for self-suctioning, oral hygiene, and tracheostomy care if indicated (Bruner et al., 1998; Devine & Doyle, 2001).

(5) Provide nutrition and fluids during implant with soft or liquid diet, nasogastric tube, or IV hydration

Table 16. Acute Side Effects of Treatment

Side Effect	Symptoms	Nursing Intervention
Urinary tract infection or bladder/urethral inflammation	Dysuria, frequency, and foul odor	Obtain urine specimen for urine analysis and culture and sensitivity. Monitor and report results to physician or advanced practice nurse (APN). Consult with physician or APN regarding antibiotics or other medications.
Vaginal infection	Elevated temperature and pain, malodorous vaginal discharge	Patient should report to emergency room or clinic for evaluation.
Vaginal stenosis	Difficulty with sexual intercourse, difficulty with gynecologic examination	Review use of vaginal dilator and lubricant. Provide American Cancer Society booklet on sexuality.
Perineal discomfort	Pain, erythema, and moist desquamation	Consult with physician or APN regarding pain relief. Educate patient on pain medications and side effects. Review use of sitz baths. Review use of topical anesthetics in treatment field.
Constipation	Absence of bowel movement	Review laxative protocol. Provide and review dietary modifications.
Diarrhea	Increased frequency of liquid stool	Review dietary modifications. Provide and review with patient a low-residue diet sheet. Consult with physician or APN regarding use of antidiarrheal medications. Encourage oral fluids.
Fatigue	Decreased ability to perform activities of daily living.	Monitor hematocrit and hemoglobin. Review energy conservation techniques. Review dietary needs.

Note. From "Nursing Management of Patients Receiving Brachytherapy for Gynecologic Malignancies," by T.K. Gosselin and J.S. Waring, 2001, *Clinical Journal of Oncology Nursing, 5,* p. 63. Copyright 2001 by the Oncology Nursing Society. Reprinted with permission.

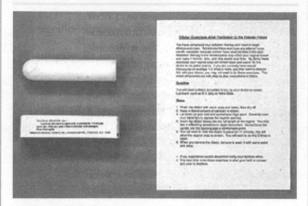

Figure 17. Vaginal Dilator and Patient Instruction Sheet

Note. From "Nursing Management of Patients Receiving Brachytherapy for Gynecologic Malignancies," by T.K. Gosselin and J.S. Waring, 2001, *Clinical Journal of Oncology Nursing, 5,* p. 63. Copyright 2001 by the Oncology Nursing Society. Reprinted with permission.

(Bruner et al., 1998). Although some patients receiving head and neck implants can be allowed to sip a liquid formula through a straw, most are fed through a nasogastric tube (Perez & Brady, 1998).

(6) Promote comfort by medicating as needed with NSAIDs or narcotic analgesics. Avoid overmedication, which can result in suppression of cough reflex or respirations.

(7) Prior to implant, assess patient's ability to read and write. Provide tools for communication if needed (e.g., pen, paper, white board with marker). If patient is illiterate, provide alternate communication strategies (e.g., cards with commonly needed items or nursing care procedures pictured). Intensive patient and family education reduces stress about procedure (Devine & Doyle, 2001).

(8) Inspect implant site every shift for intactness. Discourage patient from touching site. Exact placement of the applicator is crucial for the result of radiotherapy (Kremer et al., 1999).

d) Lung implants, HDR or LDR: Treatment—Endobronchial catheters are placed during fiberoptic bronchoscopy, and iridium-192 seed ribbons are temporarily applied (Bruner et al., 1998) (see Figure 18).

(1) HDR is an outpatient procedure.

(a) The patient is NPO (nothing by mouth) for 8–12 hours before the procedure. Vital signs and oxygen saturation are monitored and an IV is started.

(b) The nurse prepares the patient for bronchoscopy through which a catheter is guided to the tumor area.

(c) IV sedation (e.g., diazepam, versed, fentanyl), a local anesthetic (e.g., topical lidocaine [aerosol or viscous]), and additional medications (atropine, epinephrine) may be administered to keep patient comfortable and minimize gag reflex during procedure (Powell, 1999).

(d) The patient may be discharged to a responsible party when vital signs are stable, gag reflex returns, and patient is able to ambulate (Powell, 1999).

(2) LDR is an inpatient procedure.

(a) The patient receiving LDR requires hospitalization for two to seven days, depending on the radioactive source strength (Dow et al., 1997).

(b) After bronchoscopy and placement of the catheter, the patient is placed in a radiation safety–approved room (see section III of this manual) where the radioactive source is loaded.

(c) The RN monitors for complications such as bleeding, infection,

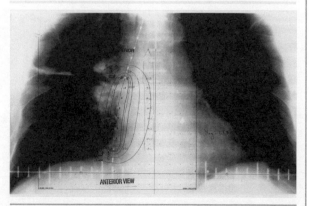

Figure 18. Localization Film of Endobronchial Iridium Seed Implant for Brachytherapy: Isodose Curves Superimposed

Note. Photo courtesy of City of Hope Medical Center.

and/or respiratory compromise. Cough suppressant medication may be needed.

    (d) Patient is discharged after radioactive source and catheter are removed and the patient is stable.

e) Eye plaques: Used in retinoblastoma, most common in pediatric patients and young adults; ocular/choroidal melanoma is most common in adults (Halperin, Constine, Tarbell, & Kun, 1999). Plaque radiotherapy is effective in the management of cases that otherwise would have been managed with enucleation (Shields, Naseripour, Shields, Freire, & Caer, 2003).

    (1) LDR

    (2) Performed in operating room with ophthalmologic surgeon (adult, pediatric)

    (3) Radiation physicist also present

    (4) Equipment for I-125 ocular plaque construction and placement includes a dummy plaque to aid in the placement of the necessary retention sutures, a gold backing with lug holes for sutures, and a plastic insert to hold the radioactive I-125 seeds (Halperin et al., 1999) (see Figure 19).

    (5) Other types of plaques using various isotopes also are available.

    (6) Patient (pediatric) with retinoblastoma is hospitalized 40–50 hours (35–40 Gy)

    (7) Patient (adult) with ocular melanoma is hospitalized two to five days (85 Gy to the prescriptive point) (DeVita et al., 2001).

    (8) Special care for both adult and pediatric patients would be to protect affected eye from trauma (creative, occlusive bandaging for the pediatric patient).

    (9) Acute effects are pain and operative infection.

    (10) Long-term effects are cataracts.

6. Patient and family education

    a) Educate patient and family on type of implant, rationale, procedure, preparation, sensory information, availability of pain medication, and care during treatment specific to type of implant (Bruner et al., 1998). Intensive patient and family education about the brachytherapy procedure, necessary visitation restrictions, and the anticipation of potential patient problems is instrumental in preventing complica-

Figure 19. Equipment for I-125 Ocular Plaque Construction and Placement

Equipment for I-125 ocular plaque construction and placement includes, from left to right, a dummy plaque to aid in the placement of the necessary retention sutures, a gold backing with lug holes for sutures, and a plastic insert to hold the radioactive I-125 seeds.

Note. From *Pediatric Radiation Oncology* (3rd ed., p. 137), by E.C. Halperin, L.S. Constine, M.J. Tarbell, and L.E. Kun, 1999, Philadelphia: Lippincott Williams & Wilkins. Copyright 1999 by Lippincott Williams & Wilkins. Reprinted with permission.

tions (Devine & Doyle, 2001). Patients receiving HDR brachytherapy experience side effects similar to those caused by external radiation treatments, with fatigue being the most often reported symptom (Fieler, 1997).

    b) Discuss rationale and methods for radiation protection, self-care during implant, and limitations on staff and visitor time in room (see section III of this manual).

    c) Provide verbal and written discharge instructions with guidelines for activity, bathing, skin or wound care, diet, smoking restrictions (bronchoscopy), alcohol restrictions, medication guidelines, and symptoms to report to a doctor or nurse. Be sure to include telephone numbers for daytime and after hours.

    d) Instruct per early and late side effects, address specific questions and concerns, and provide follow-up appointment information.

7. Brachytherapy for benign disease

    a) Pterygium: An elastotic degeneration of collagen that produces a fleshy mass in the bulbar conjunctiva that grows across the cornea, interfering with vision (Dow et al., 1997)

    b) Caused by repeated irritation to the eyes (e.g., welding, woodwork, sun, sand)

      (1) Treatment

        (a) Strontium-90, surface application

        (b) 10 Gy weekly, for six weeks (Paryani et al., 1994)

      (2) Rationale (Dunne-Daly, 1997; Paryani et al., 1994)

(a) Primary treatment is surgery.

(b) High rate of regrowth with surgery

(c) Brachytherapy can decrease recurrence rates.

8. Related Web sites

a) American Brachytherapy Society—www.americanbrachytherapy.org

b) American Society for Therapeutic Radiology and Oncology—www.astro.org

c) Oncology Nursing Society—www.ons.org

References

Brandt, B. (1991). Informational needs and selected variables in patients receiving brachytherapy. *Oncology Nursing Forum, 18,* 1221–1229.

Bruner, D.W., Bucholtz, J.D., Iwamoto, R., & Strohl, R. (Eds.). (1998). *Manual for radiation oncology nursing practice and education.* Pittsburgh, PA: Oncology Nursing Society.

Bruner, D.W., Moore-Higgs, G., & Haas, M. (Eds.). (2001). *Outcomes in radiation therapy: Multidisciplinary management.* Sudbury, MA: Jones and Bartlett.

Carrubba, D.M., Jankowski, C.B., & Kunsman, J. (1999). Nursing management of soft tissue sarcomas of the extremities. *Clinical Journal of Oncology Nursing, 3,* 168–179.

Devine, P., & Doyle, T. (2001). Brachytherapy for head and neck cancer: A case study. *Clinical Journal of Oncology Nursing, 5,* 55–57.

DeVita, V.T., Hellman, S., & Rosenberg, S.A. (Eds.). (2001). *Cancer: Principles and practice of oncology* (6th ed.). Philadelphia: Lippincott Williams & Wilkins.

Dow, K.H., Bucholtz, J.D., Iwamoto, R., Fieler, V., & Hilderley, L. (Eds.). (1997). *Nursing care in radiation oncology* (2nd ed.). Philadelphia: Saunders.

Dunne-Daly, C. (1997). Principles of brachytherapy. In K.H. Dow, J.D. Bucholtz, R. Iwamoto, V.K. Fieler, & L.J. Hilderley (Eds.), *Nursing care in radiation oncology* (2nd ed., pp. 21–35). Philadelphia: Saunders.

Eifel, P.J. (1992). High-dose-rate brachytherapy for carcinoma of the cervix: High tech or high risk? *International Journal of Radiation Oncology, Biology, Physics, 24,* 383–386.

Eifel, P.J. (1997). Intracavitary brachytherapy in the treatment of gynecologic neoplasms. *Journal of Surgical Oncology, 66,* 141–147.

Fieler, V.K. (1997). Side effects and quality of life in patients receiving high dose rate brachytherapy. *Oncology Nursing Forum, 24,* 545–553.

Gosselin, T.K., & Waring, J.S. (2001). Nursing management of patients receiving brachytherapy for gynecological malignancies. *Clinical Journal of Oncology Nursing, 5,* 59–63.

Gupta, A.K., Vincini, F.A., Frazier, A.J., Barth-Jones, D.C., Edmundson, G.K., Mele, E., et al. (1999). Iridium-192 transperineal interstitial brachytherapy for locally advanced or recurrent gynecological malignancies. *International Journal of Radiation Oncology, Biology, Physics, 43,* 1055–1060.

Halperin, E., Constine, L., Tarbell, N., & Kun, L. (Eds.). (1999). *Pediatric radiation oncology* (3rd ed.). Philadelphia: Lippincott Williams & Wilkins.

Hogle, W.P., Quinn, A.E., & Heron, D.E. (2003). Advances in brachytherapy: New approaches to target breast cancer. *Clinical Journal of Oncology Nursing, 7,* 324–328.

Holland, J. (2001). New treatment modalities in radiation therapy. *Journal of Intravenous Nursing, 24,* 95–101.

Kremer, B., Klimek, L., Andreopoulos, D., & Mosges, R. (1999). A new method for the placement of brachytherapy probes in paranasal sinus and nasopharynx neoplasms. *International Journal of Radiation Oncology, Biology, Physics, 43,* 995–1000.

Mock, U., Kucera, H., Fellner, C., Knocke, T.H., & Potter, R. (2003). High-dose-rate (HDR) brachytherapy with or without external beam radiotherapy in the treatment of primary vaginal carcinoma: Long-term results and side effects. *International Journal of Radiation Oncology, Biology, Physics, 56,* 950–957.

Nag, S., Sasha, D., Janjan, N., Petersen, I., & Saider, M. (2001). The American Brachytherapy Society's recommendations for brachytherapy of soft tissue sarcomas. *International Journal of Radiation Oncology, Biology, Physics, 49,* 1033–1043.

Paryani, S.B., Scott, W.P., Wells, J.W., Johnson, D.W., Chobe, R.J., Kuruvilla, A., et al. (1994). Management of pterygium with surgery and radiation therapy. The North Florida Pterygium Study Group. *International Journal of Radiation Oncology, Biology, Physics, 28,* 101–103.

Perez, C.A., & Brady, L.W. (Eds.). (1998). *Principles and practice of radiation oncology* (3rd ed.). Philadelphia: Lippincott-Raven.

Powell G. (1999). High dose rate brachytherapy endobronchial treatments: Adjunctive medications and discharge instructions. *Canadian Oncology Nursing Journal, 9*(3), 143–144.

Shields, C.L., Naseripour, M., Shields, J.A. Freire, J., & Caer, J. (2003). Custom-designed plaque radiotherapy for nonresectable iris melanoma in 38 patients: Tumor control and ocular complications. *American Journal of Ophthalmology, 135,* 648–656.

Stajduhar, K.I., Neithercut, J., Chu, E., Pham, P., Rohde, J., Sicotte, A., et al. (2000). Thyroid cancer: Patients' experiences of receiving iodine-131 therapy. *Oncology Nursing Forum, 27,* 213–218.

Sticklin, L.A. (1994). Strategies for overcoming nurses' fear of radiation exposure. *Cancer Practice, 2,* 275–278.

Velji, K., & Fitch, M. (2001). The experience of women receiving brachytherapy for gynecological cancer. *Oncology Nursing Forum, 28,* 743–751.

Wright, J., Jones, G., Whelan, T., & Lukka, H. (1994). Patient preference for high or low dose rate brachytherapy in carcinoma of the cervix. *Radiotherapy and Oncology, 33,* 187–194.

Yarbro, C.H., Frogge, M.H., Goodman, M., & Groenwald, S.L. (Eds.). (2000). *Cancer nursing: Principles and practice* (5th ed.). Sudbury, MA: Jones and Bartlett.

C. Prostate brachytherapy

1. Procedure description: Also referred to as interstitial implantation, for the purpose of eradicating malignant cells from within the prostate gland. LDR and HDR implants can be used as monotherapy or as a boost in combination with EBRT and/or androgen ablation (Abel et al., 1999; Held-Warmkessel, 2001; Kaplan, 2000). Brachytherapy has the advantage of delivering higher doses to tumor with reduced toxicity to normal tissues. The practice of prescribing LDR versus HDR brachytherapy for prostate malignancies can be driven by patient preference or physician preference/training.

2. Indications: Differs according to LDR and HDR

a) Candidates for LDR prostate brachytherapy include patients whose cancer is clinically confined to the prostate (T1 or T2 tumors) and have a life expectancy of greater than five years (Merrick, Butler, Farthing, Dorsey, & Adamovich, 1998).

(1) Some clinicians treat T3 lesions with the addition of EBRT to bring surrounding tissues to a higher therapeutic dose (Pellizzon et al., 2003), although others have treated T3 lesions with brachytherapy alone (Ragde, Grado, & Nadir, 2001).

(2) Palladium is frequently used to treat high-grade lesions, which are characterized by a Gleason score of 7–10. It is presumed that because of palladium's shorter half-life and higher initial dose it is better suited to treat high-grade prostate tumors (Merrick et al., 1998).

(3) Conversely, iodine is used to treat lower grade tumors, a Gleason score of 2–6 (Merrick et al., 1998). Retrospective studies have not shown a consistent difference in cure rates or morbidity between iodine and palladium (Wallner et al., 2002). However, some studies have shown patients implanted with palladium recovered from urinary-related problems more quickly than their iodine counterparts (Gelblum et al., 1999; Wallner et al., 2002).

b) Candidates for HDR prostate brachytherapy include patients with both favorable (stage < T2a) and unfavorable (stage T2B or higher) disease (Martinez et al., 2000, 2001).

3. Treatment

a) LDR: Consists of inserting needles directly into the prostate gland under the guidance of transrectal ultrasound. This is an operative procedure during which the patient can undergo either general or epidural anesthesia, although there are reports of patients having undergone the procedure with local anesthesia (Smathers, Wallner, Simpson, & Roof, 2000). Small radioactive seeds then are placed into the gland through the needles.

(1) Sources most commonly used include the following radioactive isotopes (Iwamoto & Maher, 2001).

(a) Iodine 125 (I-125)—having a 60-day half-life.

(b) Palladium 103 (Pd-103)—having a 17-day half-life.

(2) The number of needles used depends on the size of the prostate gland. Typically, 18–30 needles are inserted and immediately removed following the procedure. A typical prostate will receive 70–100 seeds (University of Pittsburgh Medical Center [UPMC], 2003).

b) HDR

(1) An operative procedure during which a template is secured to the perineum, and, under the guidance of transrectal ultrasound, needles are inserted through the holes in the template and into the prostate gland. As the needles are removed, plastic catheters are left in place and secured by way of the template.

(2) After radiation planning is complete, the catheters are secured to an HDR afterloader, and the radiation source is directed into and out of each catheter. Iridium dwell time varies according to source strength and radiation plan.

(3) Typically, treatments are given in three fractions at approximately 6 Gy each, although some clinicians administer HDR treatments in two or four fractions at doses ranging from 5.5–10.5 Gy (Martinez et al., 2000, 2001).

(4) This procedure requires overnight inpatient hospitalization and interstitial catheter care to be administered by either radiation oncology nurses or inpatient staff nurses (Cancer Treatment Centers of America, 2003; Martinez et al., 2000, 2001).

(5) The most commonly used isotope is iridium-192.

4. Side effects: Acute and late side effects from prostate brachytherapy can be influenced by a number of different factors that include prostate size > 60 g; history of transurethral resection of prostate (TURP); higher pretreatment American Urology Association (AUA) scores; addition of EBRT (Han et al., 2001; Kaplan, 2002; Wallner et al., 2002).

a) Acute side effects

(1) Side effects during the acute phase are caused by procedural trauma, and later effects are a result of urethral irritation from radiation exposure (Abel, Dafoe-Lambie, Butler, & Merrick, 2003).

(2) Urinary frequency/urgency is a result of changes in both the prostate and the urinary bladder. Exact mechanisms causing early and temporary changes in bladder function are not fully understood (Maher, 1997). Normal function depends upon the successful interaction of the bladder wall mucosa, muscle layers, and supporting neurovascular structures. When smooth muscle edema occurs early in the course of radiotherapy, this may contribute to early changes in reservoir function (Marks, Carroll, Dugan & Anscher, 1995). This can cause an increase in urinary frequency, urgency, nocturia, and dysuria.

(3) Changes can occur to the bladder causing urinary urgency, frequency, retention/distended bladder, dysuria, nocturia, hematuria, weakened stream/obstructive symptoms, urge incontinence, stress incontinence, and discolored or cloudy urine (Maher, 1997; Marks et al., 1995).

(4) Changes can occur to the bowels: softer, more frequent stools, night-time bowel frequency, diarrhea, abdominal cramping, bloating, flatulence, bowel urgency, feeling of incomplete bowel evacuation, incontinence of stools, rectal irritation/ulceration (proctitis), rectal bleeding, rectal discharge, and tenesmus (Maher, 1997; Saclarides, 1997).

(5) Inflamed hemorrhoids

(6) Skin ulceration in the gluteal folds

b) Late side effects

(1) Chronic inflammatory changes of the prostate gland itself occur in 37% of patients treated with RT (Gaudin, Zelefsky, Leibel, Fuks, & Reuter, 1999).

(2) Interstitial fibrosis occurs in radiated tissue, which can be accompanied by obliterative endarteritis and telangiectasia. Thin-walled dilated vessels may rupture, resulting in painless hematuria. Eventually, epithelial tissue will appear thin, pale, and atrophic and may ulcerate (Bruner, Bucholtz, Iwamoto, & Strohl, 1998).

(3) Urinary symptoms vary significantly and can persist for up to two years postoperatively (Zelefsky, Cowen, et al., 1999; Zelefsky, Wallner, et al., 1999). Statistics vary as to how many men will develop long-term cystitis from RT.

(4) Changes can continue with bladder symptoms (Merrick, Butler, Lief, & Galbreath, 2001; Zelefsky, Cowen, et al., 1999; Zelefsky, Wallner, et al., 1999): urinary urgency; urinary retention, 2%–22% experience urinary retention; weakened urinary stream, 5%–12% experience urethral strictures; and 1% experience incontinence, 6%–12% have incontinence with previous TURP (Ragde et al., 1997; Wallner et al., 2002).

(5) After a six-year follow-up, 39% of patients post-implant maintained potency sufficient enough for vaginal penetration. Factors leading to decreased potency rates include poor pre-implant erectile function, use of supplemental EBRT, and a history of diabetes (Merrick et al., 2002).

(6) Late-onset proctitis usually occurs between one to two years post-implant. This often is demonstrated by rectal bleeding. Rectal ulceration and fistula formation are exceedingly rare (Abel et al., 2003; Howard, et al., 2001).

(7) Erectile dysfunction occurs in as many as 61% of men after prostate brachytherapy with or without additional EBRT (Merrick et al., 2001). Assess baseline dysfunction prior to initiation of treatment (baseline sexual activity level, satisfaction/dissatisfaction with intercourse, medications, or comorbid conditions), then after treatment (decreased ability to achieve erection, decreased sensation during intercourse, retrograde ejaculation, decreased ability to achieve orgasm) (see Tables 17–20).

5. Collaborative management for LDR: Predominantly outpatient procedure
   a) Acute effects
      (1) Educate patients about the differences between palladium and iodine implant (half-life, exposure precautions).
      (2) Inform patient and family of acute and late effects.
      (3) Indwelling catheter may be required until acute postoperative swelling of

smooth muscle decreases and urinary obstructive symptoms subside.
      (4) Collect and monitor urine for the first 24 hours following implant (Perez, Zwickler, & Williamson, 2004).
      (5) If a displaced seed is found, place in a container and return to radiation oncology department as soon as possible.
      (6) Educate patient and family about exposure precautions as indicated by institutional policy (see patient/family education).
      (7) Administer and educate about side effects of medications prescribed to alleviate urinary or bowel morbidity.
      (8) Urinary-specific management (see section V, G—Male Pelvis/Prostate)
      (9) Bowel management (see section V, G—Male Pelvis/Prostate)
      (10) Proctitis (see section V, G—Male Pelvis/Prostate)
   b) Late
      (1) Patient and spouse may need to be referred for professional counseling regarding the physical and psychological effects of sexual dysfunction.
         (a) Encourage communication regarding fears/concerns of sexual dysfunction (Bruner et al., 1998).
         (b) Identify resources that may be helpful in managing the effects of sexual dysfunction (e.g., sex therapist, counselor, physician, books, pamphlets) (Barsevick, Much, & Sweeney, 2000).
      (2) Administer appropriate medication as prescribed.
         (a) Sildenafil—25–100 mg 30 minutes to 4 hours before sexual activity. A phosphodiesterase-5 (PDE5) inhibitor, this drug works

Table 18. Incidence of Urinary Toxicity

Gelblum et al. (1999)	Kang et al. (2001)
Acute (less than two months) Grade 1—37% Grade 2—41% Grade 3—2%	**Acute** (less than two months) Grade 1—23% Grade 2—45% Grade 3—20%
Chronic (less than four months) Grade 1—21% Grade 2—13%	**Chronic** (less than one year) Grade 1—12% –

Table 17. RTOG Urinary Morbidity Grading Scale

Grade	Description
Acute	
0	No change
1	Frequency of urination or nocturia twice pretreatment habit/dysuria, urgency not requiring medication
2	Frequency of urination or nocturia that is less than every hour. Dysuria, urgency, or bladder spasm requiring local anesthetic.
3	Frequency with urination and nocturia hourly or more frequently/dysuria; pelvis pain or bladder spasm requiring regular, frequent narcotic/gross hematuria with or without clot passage
4	Hematuria requiring transfusion/acute bladder obstruction not secondary to clot passage, ulceration, or necrosis

Note. Based on information from RTOG, 2004a.

Grade	Description
Late	
0	None
1	Slight epithelial atrophy, minor telangiectasia (microscopic hematuria)
2	Moderate frequency, generalized telangiectasia, intermittent macroscopic hematuria
3	Severe frequency and dysuria, severe generalized telangiectasia (often with petechiae), frequent hematuria, reduction in bladder capacity (< 150 cc)
4	Necrosis/contracted bladder, capacity < 100 cc, severe hemorrhagic cystitis
5	Death related to radiation

Note. Based on information from RTOG, 2004b.

Table 19. RTOG Lower GI, Including Pelvis Morbidity Grading Scale

Grade	Description
Acute	
0	No change
1	Increased frequency or change in quality of bowel habits not requiring medication. Rectal discomfort not requiring medication.
2	Diarrhea requiring parasympatholytic drugs (e.g., diphenoxylate hydrochloride). Mucous discharge not necessitating sanitary pads. Rectal or abdominal pain requiring analgesics.
3	Diarrhea requiring parenteral support. Severe mucous or bloody discharge necessitating sanitary pads. Abdominal distention (Flat plate radiograph demonstrates distended bowel loops.)
4	Acute or subacute obstruction, fistula, or perforation; GI bleeding requiring transfusion; abdominal pain or tenesmus requiring tube decompression or bowel diversion

Note. Based on information from RTOG, 2004a.

Grade	Description
Late	
0	None
1	Mild diarrhea, mild abdominal cramping, bowel movement five times daily, slight rectal discharge or bleeding
2	Moderate diarrhea and colic bowel movements more than five times daily. Excessive rectal mucous or intermittent bleeding.
3	Obstruction or bleeding requiring surgery
4	Necrosis/perforation/fistula

Note. Based on information from RTOG, 2004b.

by enhancing the effects of nitric oxide released during sexual stimulation, which eventually promotes smooth muscle relaxation of the corpus cavernosum, thereby promoting increased blood flow and subsequent erection (Deglin & Vallerand, 2003). Teloken (2001) reported successful treatment with sildenafil among patients who have received RT to the prostate has ranged from 70%–80%.

(b) Other PDE5 inhibitors, such as tadalafil or vardenafil HCl, work similarly to sildenafil and may be useful in treating impotence. However, no studies currently are known that have examined the effectiveness of tadalafil or vardenafil among patients treated with RT.

(3) Referral to urology for other alternative treatments

(a) Other nonsurgical approaches include urethral suppositories, intracavernous injections, and vacuum devices.

(b) Penile prostheses have yielded satisfaction rates of up to 85% (Mulcahy, 2000).

6. Collaborative management for HDR prostate brachytherapy (brachytherapy catheter care)
a) Keep area open to air as much as possible.
b) Keep perineal template as clean as possible.
c) Some discharge may occur while catheters are in place; frequent pad changes may be necessary to maintain patient hygiene and comfort.
d) Decrease bowel movements while catheters/template in place.
(1) Loperamide hydrochloride (see information presented earlier for dosing)
(2) Low-fiber diet (Iwamoto & Maher, 2001)
e) Minimize patient activity to avoid brachytherapy catheter displacement and maintain patency of indwelling urinary catheter.
f) Collect and monitor urine for the first 24 hours post-implant (Perez et al., 2004).
g) Inpatient staff nurses need to be aware that patient is not radioactive and exposure precautions are unnecessary for HDR prostate brachytherapy patients as long as they are not connected to the remote afterloader for treatment administration.
h) Administer pain medications as needed for postoperative discomfort, acute and late urinary and bowel morbidity, as well as late effect potency issues.
7. Patient and family education
a) For brachytherapy
(1) Teach patient and family that side effects from brachytherapy are similar to those used for EBRT.
(2) Teach patient and family about dietary modifications: Maintaining hydration (1–2 liters) throughout day-

Table 20. Incidence of Lower GI Toxicity

Acute Effects (Kang et al., 2002)		Chronic Effects (Gelblum & Potters, 2000)	
Grade	Percentage	Grade	Percentage
1	22%	1	9.4%
2	13%	2	6.6%
3	1.5 %	3	0.5 %
4	0%	4	0%

time (Iwamoto & Maher, 2001) while decreasing fluid intake in the evening to reduce the incidence of nocturia (Bruner et al., 1998); avoiding caffeinated products—although studies specific to patients post-radiation with prostate cancer do not exist, some evidence suggests the elimination of caffeine may assist in decreasing bothersome urinary symptoms (Albertsen, 1997; Abel et al., 1999; Gray, 2001); suggesting low-fiber/low-residue diet (Iwamoto & Maher, 2001); consider the addition of bulk agents, if loose stools are present, to absorb excess fluid (Bliss et al., 2001; Murphy, Stacey, Crook, Thompson, & Panetta, 2000).

(3) Teach patients and families about the need for nonsteroidal urinary analgesics, antispasmodics, or alpha-1 receptor blocking agents for urinary symptoms. Also, if experiencing diarrhea, teach about antidiarrheal medications. If experiencing proctitis or impotence, teach about appropriate medications.

(4) Based on the half-life of sources used for LDR and the potential for seeds to manifest themselves in the ejaculate, a condom should be worn for the first two months after the procedure (California Endocurie Therapy Cancer Center [CETMC], n.d.; UPMC, n.d.).

(5) Much controversy exists over the recommendation to patients that their exposure to children or pregnant women be minimized. Smathers et al. (1999) suggested that based on anterior skin surface exposure rates, patients with palladium or iodine implants do not need to be concerned about being a radiation risk to the general public following the procedure. Exposure information is usually dictated by institutional policy and is based on the half-life of the source used.

(6) Inform patient as to the potential for seed migration; 20% of implanted patients will develop pulmonary seed migration (Ankem et al., 2002; Dafoe-Lambie et al., 2000).

(7) Patients should be advised to notify the radiation department from where they received their implant if they discover a seed that may have been passed through their ejaculate or urine (CETMC, n.d.; UPMC, n.d.).

b) For urinary side effects
  (1) Instruct patient on expected urinary side effects and possible long-term complications of prostate brachytherapy.
  (2) Instruct patient on brachytherapy procedure and precautions as advised by the radiation oncologist.
  (3) Instruct patient to report treatment-related sequelae promptly as well any changes from baseline urinary function, including signs and symptoms of urinary infection.
  (4) Instruct patient in dietary interventions as appropriate.
  (5) Reassure patient as to the availability of medications if their symptoms become problematic. Thoroughly review side-effect profile and possible drug interactions with patient.
  (6) Inform patient that a referral to urology for other alternative treatments for urinary dysfunction is an available option.

c) For lower GI side effects
  (1) Inform patient of lower GI–related side effects and possible complications associated with prostate brachytherapy.
  (2) Encourage patient to report any side effects or changes from baseline bowel function promptly.
  (3) Instruct patient in dietary interventions as appropriate.
  (4) Teach patient sign/symptoms of dehydration.
  (5) Instruct patient to monitor frequency, consistency, and presence of blood from bowel movements.

(6) Instruct patient in appropriate hygiene techniques.

(7) Instruct patient in appropriate use of sitz baths.

(8) Inform patient and family members of medications available to alleviate treatment-related side effects. Thoroughly review side-effect profile and possible drug interactions. Instruct in appropriate use of any suppositories, foams, ointments, or enemas if prescribed.

d) For erectile dysfunction

(1) Instruct patient about the importance of communication between both partners regarding concerns and issues of sexual dysfunction.

(2) Explain side effects as they relate to sexual dysfunction resulting from RT.

(3) Instruct patient and significant other about medical and surgical interventions that may be available.

(4) Inform patient of the availability of medication use to treat some forms of sexual dysfunction. Thoroughly review side-effect profile and drug interactions of prescribed medications.

(5) Inform patient and significant other that a referral for professional counseling regarding the physical and psychological effects of sexual dysfunction is available.

References

Abel, L.J., Blatt, H.J., Stipetich, R.L., Fuscardo, J.A., Zeroski, D., Miller, S.E., et al. (1999). Nursing management of patients receiving brachytherapy for early-stage prostate cancer. *Clinical Journal of Oncology Nursing, 3,* 7–15.

Abel, L., Dafoe-Lambie, J., Butler, W.M., & Merrick, G.S. (2003). Treatment outcomes and quality of life issues for patients treated with prostate brachytherapy. *Clinical Journal of Oncology Nursing, 7,* 48–54.

Albertsen, P.C. (1997). Urologic nuisances: How to work up and relieve men's symptoms. *Geriatrics, 52,* 46–50.

Ankem, M.K., DeCarvalho, V.S., Harangozo, A.M., Hartanto, V.H., Perrotti, M., Han, K.R., et al. (2002). Implications of radioactive seed migration to the lungs after prostate brachytherapy. *Urology, 59,* 555–559.

Barsevick, A.M., Much, J., & Sweeney, C. (2000). Psychosocial responses to cancer. In C.H. Yarbro, M.H. Frogge, M. Goodman, & S.L. Groenwald (Eds.), *Cancer nursing: Principles and practice* (5th ed., pp. 1529–1549). Sudbury, MA: Jones and Bartlett.

Bliss, D.Z., Jung, H.J., Savik, K., Lowry, A., Lemoine, M., Jensen, L., et al. (2001). Supplementation with dietary fiber improves fecal incontinence. *Nursing Research, 50,* 203–213.

Bruner, D.W., Bucholtz, J.D., Iwamoto, R., & Strohl, R. (Eds.). (1998). *Manual for radiation oncology nursing practice and education.* Pittsburgh: Oncology Nursing Society.

California Endocurie Therapy Cancer Center. (n.d.). *HDR procedure for prostate cancer.* Retrieved July 28, 2003, from http://www.cetmc.com/prostate.html

Cancer Treatment Centers of America. (n.d.). *Prostate HDR brachytherapy technique.* Retrieved July 22, 2003, from http://www.brachytherapy.com/prostate-technique.html

Dafoe-Lambie, J.C., Abel, L.J., Blatt, H.J., Fuscardo, J.H., Stipetich, R.L., Lief, J.H., et al. (2000). Radioactive seed embolization to the lung following prostate brachytherapy. *West Virginia Medical Journal, 96,* 357–360.

Deglin, J.H., & Vallerand, A.H. (2003). *Davis's drug handbook for nurses* (8th ed.). Philadelphia: F.A. Davis.

Gaudin, P.B., Zelefsky, M.J., Leibel, S.A., Fuks, Z., & Reuter, V.E. (1999). Histopathologic effects of three dimensional conformal external beam radiation therapy on benign and malignant prostate tissues. *American Journal of Surgical Pathology, 23,* 1021–1041.

Gelblum, D.Y., & Potters, L. (2000). Rectal complications associated with transperineal interstitial brachytherapy for prostate cancer. *International Journal of Radiation Oncology, Biology, Physics, 48,* 119–124.

Gelblum, D.A., Potters, L., Ashley, R., Waldbaum, R., Wang, X.H., & Leibel, S. (1999). Urinary morbidity following ultrasound-guided transperineal prostate seed implantation. *International Journal of Radiation Oncology, Biology, Physics, 45,* 59–67.

Gray, M. (2001). Caffeine and urinary continence. *Journal of Wound, Ostomy, and Continence, 28,* 66–69.

Han, B.H., Demel, K.C., Wallner, K., Ellis, W., Young, L., & Russell, K. (2001). Patient-reported complications after prostate brachytherapy. *Journal of Urology, 166,* 953–957.

Held-Warmkessel, J. (2001). *Pocket guide to prostate cancer.* Sudbury, MA: Jones and Bartlett.

Howard, A., Wallner, K., Han, B., Dominitz, J., Schneider, B., Sutlief, S., et al. (2004). Clinical course and dosimetry of rectal fistulas after prostate brachytherapy. *Journal of Brachytherapy, 17,* 37–42.

Iwamoto, R.R., & Maher, K.E. (2001). Radiation therapy for prostate cancer. *Seminars in Oncology Nursing, 17,* 90–100.

Kang, S.K., Chou, R.H., Dodge, R.K., Clough, R.W., Kang, H.L., Bowen, M.G., et al. (2001). Acute urinary toxicity following transperineal prostate brachytherapy using a modified Quimby loading method. *International Journal of Radiation Oncology, Biology, Physics, 15,* 937–945.

Kang, S.K., Chou, R.H., Dodge, R.K., Clough, R.W., Kang, H.L., Hahn, C.A., et al. (2002). Gastrointestinal toxicity of transperineal interstitial prostate brachytherapy. *International Journal of Radiation Oncology, Biology, Physics, 53,* 99–103.

Kaplan, I. (2000). Minimizing rectal and urinary complications in prostate brachytherapy. *Journal of Endourology, 14,* 381–383.

Kaplan, S.A. (2002). Terazosin for treating symptomatic benign prostatic obstruction: A systematic review of efficacy and adverse effects. *Journal of Urology, 168,* 1657–1658.

Maher, K.E. (1997). Male genitourinary cancers. In K.H. Dow, J.D. Bucholtz, R. Iwamoto, V.K. Fieler, & L.J. Hilderley (Eds.), *Nursing care in radiation oncology* (2nd ed., pp. 184–219). Philadelphia: Saunders.

Marks, L.B., Carroll, P.R., Dugan, T.C., & Anscher, M.S. (1995). The response of the urinary bladder, urethra, and ureter to radiation and chemotherapy, *International Journal of Radiation Oncology, Biology, Physics, 31,* 1257–1280.

Martinez A.A., Kestin, L.L., Stromberg, J.S., Gonzalez, J.A., Wallace, M., Gustafson, G.S., et al. (2000). Interim report of image guided conformal high dose rate brachytherapy for patients with unfavorable prostate cancer: The William Beaumont phase II dose escalation trial. *International Journal of Radiation Oncology, Biology, Physics, 47,* 342–352.

Martinez, A.A., Pataki, I., Edmunson, G., Sebastian, E., Brabbins, D., & Gustafson, G. (2001). Phase II prospective study of the use of conformal high dose rate brachytherapy as monotherapy for the treatment of favorable stage prostate cancer: A feasibility study. *International Journal of Radiation Oncology, Biology, Physics, 49,* 61–69.

Merrick, G.S., Butler, W.M., Farthing, W.H., Dorsey, A.T., & Adamovich, E. (1998). The impact of Gleason score accuracy as a criterion for prostate brachytherapy patient selection. *Journal of Brachytherapy International, 14,* 113–121.

Merrick, G.S., Butler, W.M., Galbreath, R.W., Stipetich, R.L., Abel, L.J., Lief, J.H., et al. (2002). Erectile function after permanent prostate brachytherapy. *International Journal of Radiation Oncology, Biology, Physics, 15,* 893–902.

Merrick, G.S., Butler, W.M., Lief, J.H., & Galbreath, R.W. (2001). Permanent prostate brachytherapy: Acute and late toxicity. *Journal of Brachytherapy International, 17,* 229–236.

Mulcahy, J.J. (2000). Erectile function after radical prostatectomy. *Seminars in Urologic Oncology, 18,* 71–75.

Murphy, J., Stacey, D., Crook, J., Thompson, B., & Panetta, D. (2000). Testing control of radiation-induced diarrhea with a psyllium bulking agent: A pilot study. *Canadian Journal of Oncology Nursing, 10,* 96–100.

Pellizon, A.C., Nadalin, W., Salvajoli, J.V., Fogaroli, R.C., Novaes, P.E., Maia, M.A., et al. (2003). Results of high dose rate afterloading brachytherapy boost to conventional external beam radiation therapy for initial and locally advanced prostate cancer. *Radiotherapy and Oncology, 66,* 167–172.

Perez, C.A., Zwickler, R., & Williamson, J. (2004). Clinical applications of brachytherapy LDR & PDR. In C.A. Perez, L.W. Brady, E.C. Halperin, & R.K. Schmidt-Ullrich (Eds.), *Principles and practice of radiation oncology* (4th ed., pp. 538–603). Philadelphia: Lippincott.

Radiation Therapy Oncology Group. (2004a). *Acute radiation morbidity scoring criteria.* Retrieved June 28, 2004, from http://www.rtog.org/members/toxicity/acute.html

Radiation Therapy Oncology Group. (2004b). *RTOG/EORTC late radiation morbidity scoring schema.* Retrieved June 28, 2004, from http://www.rtog.org/members/toxicity/late.html

Ragde, H., Blasko, J.C., Grimm, P.D., Kenny, G.M., Sylvester, J.E., Hoak, D.C., et al. (1997). Interstitial iodine-125 radiation without adjuvant therapy in the treatment of clinically localized prostate carcinoma. *Cancer, 80,* 442–453.

Ragde, H., Grado, G.L., & Nadir, B.S. (2001). Brachytherapy for clinically localized prostate cancer: Thirteen-year disease-free survival of 769 consecutive prostate cancer patients treated with permanent implants alone. *Archivos Espanoles de Urologia, 54,* 739–747.

Saclarides, T.J. (1997). Radiation injuries of the gastrointestinal tract. *Surgical Clinics of North America, 77,* 261–268.

Smathers, S., Wallner, K., Korssjoen, T., Bergsagel, C., Hudson, R.H., Sutlief, S., et al. (1999). Radiation safety parameters following prostate brachytherapy. *International Journal of Radiation Oncology, Biology, Physics, 45,* 397–399.

Smathers, S., Wallner, K., Simpson, C., & Roof, J. (2000). Patient perception of local anesthesia for prostate brachytherapy. *Seminars in Urologic Oncology, 18,* 142–146.

Teloken, C. (2001). Management of erectile dysfunction secondary to treatment for localized prostate cancer. *Cancer Control, 8,* 540–545.

University of Pittsburgh Medical Center. (2003). *Prostate seed implantation.* Retrieved June 28, 2004, from http://patienteducation.upmc.com/pdf/implantprostateseed.pdf

University of Pittsburgh Medical Center. (n.d.). *Safety precautions for patients receiving prostate seed implants.* Retrieved July 28, 2003, from http://patienteducation.upmc.com/C.htm#CancerRadiation

Wallner, K., Merrick, G., True, L., Cavanagh, W., Simpson, C., & Butler, W. (2002). I-125 versus Pd-103 for low risk prostate cancer: Morbidity outcomes from a prospective randomized multi-center trial. *Cancer Journal, 8,* 67–73.

Zelefsky, M.J., Cowen, D., Fuks, Z., Shike, M., Burman, C., Jackson, A., et al. (1999). Long term tolerance of high dose three-dimensional conformal radiotherapy in patients with localized prostate carcinoma. *Cancer, 85,* 2460–2468.

Zelefsky, M.J., Wallner, K.E., Ling, C.C., Raben, A., Hollister, T., Wolfe, T., et al. (1999). Comparison of the five-year outcome and morbidity of three-dimensional conformal radiotherapy versus transperineal permanent iodine-125 implantation for early stage prostatic cancer. *Journal of Clinical Oncology, 17,* 517–522.

D. Accelerated partial breast irradiation
1. Procedure description
    a) Partial breast irradiation is a method of treating early breast cancer with definitive radiotherapy to the breast tumor bed following excision. This procedure reduces the time, inconvenience, and toxicity associated with traditional whole breast radiotherapy.
    b) Brachytherapy as a sole modality is considered investigational and should be performed in the context of a controlled clinical trial (Arthur, Vicini, Kuske, Wazer, & Nag, 2002).
2. Indications
    a) Nag, Kuske, Vicini, Arthur, and Zwicker (2001) selection criteria
        (1) All patients should be appropriate candidates for standard breast conservation therapy.
        (2) ≥ 45 years old
        (3) Unifocal, invasive ductal carcinoma
        (4) ≤ 3 cm in size
        (5) Negative microscopic surgical margins of excision
        (6) Axillary node negative by level I/II axillary dissection or sentinel node evaluation
    b) American Society of Breast Surgeons (2003) selection criteria
        (1) > 50 years old
        (2) Invasive ductal carcinoma or ductal carcinoma in situ (DCIS)
        (3) Total tumor size (invasive and DCIS) ≤ 2 cm in size
        (4) Negative microscopic surgical margins of at least 2 mm in all directions

(5) Axillary lymph node/sentinel lymph node negative

3. Treatment: A variety of treatment approaches are available to provide partial breast irradiation.

a) External beam: The treatment is given via one of three external beam treatment modalities, usually four to six weeks after surgery. The fields are designed to cover the tumor bed and a small rim of tissue surrounding it (El-Ghamry et al., 2003).

(1) 3-D conformal radiotherapy

(2) IMRT

(3) Proton beam radiation

b) Brachytherapy: The treatment is given either at the time of surgery or at a later time through a special set of catheters in the tumor bed.

(1) LDR interstitial implant: Uses standard catheters that are placed either at the time of surgery or at a later time. The catheters are placed through the skin and lie under the tumor bed. They are loaded at a later time with iridium-192 sources and remain in place for the prescribed length of treatment (hours).

(2) HDR brachytherapy: Uses standard catheters that are placed either at the time of surgery or at a later time. The catheters are placed through the skin and lie under the tumor bed. They are loaded at a later time for the prescribed dose, usually once or twice a day for five days, after which the catheters are removed.

(3) MammoSite® RTS (Texas MammoSite, San Antonio, TX): Catheter placement is performed either during the surgical procedure under general anesthesia or in an outpatient procedure room under local anesthesia. The MammoSite catheter is inserted into the surgical cavity through a separate pathway created by a trocar, or via the lumpectomy scar. The MammoSite catheter is inflated with saline and contrast agent to allow the surrounding tissue to conform to the balloon, the exit site is dressed, and the patient is sent home. Once the patient has sufficiently recovered from surgery, radiation therapy is provided on an outpatient basis. During therapy, an iridium-192 seed (attached to a HDR remote afterloader) is inserted into the inflated balloon for a short duration (typically less than 10 minutes). When radiation therapy is concluded, the balloon is deflated, and the MammoSite catheter is removed (Vaidya et al., 2002).

(4) The Intrabeam® System (Zeiss, Oberkochen, Germany): The radiation dose is administrated to the tumor bed in the operating room following lumpectomy. This system uses the miniature x-ray source, a highly stable support stand, and a full range of applicator options. The surgeon removes the tumor and then directly places the applicator into the tumor bed. By administering the prescribed dose to that site, the highest dose is concentrated within the tissue adjacent to the applicator surface. Following the treatment delivery, the applicator and miniature x-ray source are removed, the surgical site is closed, and the procedure is complete (Zeiss, 2003).

4. Collaborative management

a) Acute effects

(1) Pain at the wound and catheter site (Baglan et al., 2003)

(2) Mild erythema of the skin and hyperpigmentation (Baglan et al., 2003)

(3) Drainage around wound (Keish et al., 2003)

(4) Ecchymosis (Keish et al., 2003)

(5) Cellulitis

(6) Abscess development in the wound (Lawenda et al., 2003)

(7) Hematoma in the wound (Lawenda et al., 2003)

(8) Bleeding after catheter removal (Lawenda et al., 2003)

(9) Nonhealing sinus tract requiring surgical excision (Lawenda et al., 2003)

b) Late effects (Lawenda et al., 2003)

(1) Moderate to severe scarring and thickening of the skin and breast

(2) Abnormal-appearing post-treatment mammograms, including seromas, calcifications, fat necrosis, and architectural distortion

5. Patient and family education (Hogle, Quinn, & Heron, 2003)

  a) Teach patient and family about the treatment procedure and the time required for the treatment.

  b) Teach patient and family about wound care procedures to manage catheters after discharge from hospital (if going home with catheters in place).

  c) Teach patient and family about signs and symptoms of infection to report, including increased pain, erythema, wound/catheter discharge, and temperature over 101°F.

  d) Teach patient and family how to care for wound and breast after catheter removal.

  e) Teach patient and family about possible delayed wound healing, which can be attributed to radionecrosis of the wound edge (Vaidya et al., 2001, 2002).

6. Follow-up

  a) Follow-up examinations are performed at three month intervals during the initial one to two years or per protocol if the patient is enrolled by the surgeon and radiation oncologist.

  b) Ipsilateral mammograms usually are performed within 3–6 months after procedure and then every 6–12 months until stable, then once a year. If patient is on study protocol, the mammogram frequency may be different.

References

American Society of Breast Surgeons. (2003). *Consensus statement for accelerated partial breast surgeons.* Columbia, MD: Author.

Arthur, D., Vicini, A., Kuske, R., Wazer, D., & Nag, S. (2002). Accelerated partial breast irradiation: An updated report from the American Brachytherapy Society. *Brachytherapy, 1,* 184–190.

Baglan, K.I., Sharpe, M.B., Jafffray, D., Frazier, R.C., Fayed, J., Kestin, L.L., et al. (2003). Accelerated partial breast irradiation using 3D-conformal radiation therapy (3D-CRT) [Abstract]. *International Journal of Radiology Oncology, Biology, Physics, 54*(Suppl. 2), 160.

El-Ghamry, M.N., Doppke, K., Gierga, D., Aboubaker, F., Adams, J., Taghian, A., et al. (2003). Partial breast irradiation using external beams: A comparison of 3-D conformal, IMRT and proton therapy treatment planning using dose-volume histogram analysis [Abstract]. *International Journal of Radiology Oncology, Biology, Physics, 54*(Suppl. 2), 163.

Hogle, W., Quinn, A., & Heron D. (2003). Advances in brachytherapy: New approaches to target breast cancer. *Clinical Journal of Oncology Nursing, 7,* 324–328.

Keish, M., Vicini, F., Kuske, R.R., Hebert, M., White, J., Quiet, C., et al. (2003). Initial clinical experience with the MammoSite breast brachytherapy applicator in women with early stage breast cancer treated with breast-conserving therapy. *International Journal of Radiology Oncology, Biology, Physics, 44,* 289–293.

Lawenda, B.D., Taghian, A.G., Kachnic, L.A., Smith, B.L., Gadd, M.A., Mauceri, T., et al. (2003). A dose-volume analysis of radiation therapy for T1N0 invasive breast cancer treated by local excision and partial breast irradiation by low-dose-rate interstitial implant [Abstract]. *International Journal of Radiology Oncology, Biology, Physics, 54*(Suppl. 2), 162.

Nag, S., Kuske, R.R., Vicini, F.A., Arthur, D.W., & Zwicker, R.D. (2001). Brachytherapy in the treatment of breast cancer. *Oncology, 15*(2), 195–205.

Vaidya, J., Baum, M., Tobias, J., D'Souza, D., Naidu, S., Morgan, S., et al. (2001). Targeted intra-operative radiotherapy: An innovative method of treatment for early breast cancer. *Annals of Oncology, 12,* 1075–1080.

Vaidya, J., Tobias, J., Baum, M., Houghton, J., Keshtgar, M., Thompson, E., et al. (2002). *Patient information sheet.* North Billerica, MA: Photoelectron Proxima Therapeutics. Retrieved August 29, 2003, from http://www. proximatherapeutics.com

Zeiss. (2003). *Intrabeam System.* Retrieved August 29, 2003, from http://www.zeiss.com

E. Intravascular brachytherapy

  1. Procedure description

    a) Intravascular brachytherapy (IVBT or IVB) is the application of radiation directly to the site of vessel narrowing (Hansrani, Overbeck, Smout, & Stansby, 2003). IVBT is known to inhibit the processes that lead to restenosis (narrowing) of vessels after interventional treatments. Gamma or beta irradiation limits the overgrowth of normal tissue as the healing process occurs. Other terminology referring to the same procedure is coronary artery radiation therapy, vascular brachytherapy, or coronary brachytherapy.

    b) IVBT is an option to patients with coronary artery disease who are not candidates for open heart surgery and who have failed percutaneous transluminal coronary angioplasty (PTCA) (a small inflatable balloon to open an obstruction or narrowing of a coronary artery) and a coronary stent (small, slotted metal tube that expands the inner wall of the coronary artery) that developed in-stent restenosis (re-narrowing of scar tissue formation inside the stent) (SoRelle, 2000).

  2. Indications

    a) Approximately 30%–40% of stented cardiovascular patients develop re-narrowing within the stented vessel and require IVBT (Sims, Rothman, Warner, & Powell, 2002).

b) Inclusion criteria from clinical trials (START, INHIBIT, SCRIPPS, and WRIST) include (Leon et al., 2001; Teirstein et al., 1997, 2000; Waksman et al., 2000)
  (1) Patients with objective evidence of ischemic heart disease
  (2) Planned balloon angioplasty treatment (PTCA) or provisional stent placement of a single lesion in a coronary artery
  (3) Lesion located in vessels with a reference diameter between 2.5–5.0 mm
  (4) Target lesion stenosis is > 50% and < 100% by visual estimate.
  (5) PTCA criteria of >30% residual stenosis. Evidence of thrombus or dissection at the completion of the angioplasty
  (6) Patient is able to withstand the required catheter dwell time.
c) Exclusion criteria
  (1) Unprotected left main artery disease
  (2) Contraindications to antiplatelet therapy
  (3) A previous myocardial infarction less than or within 72 hours
  (4) De novo lesions, thrombotic lesions, or diffuse proliferative responses that extend beyond the limits of the stent
  (5) Left ventricular ejection fraction (pumping ability) of < 20%–30%
  (6) Totally occluded vessels
  (7) Saphenous vein bypass graft
  (8) Pregnancy
  (9) Age < 18 years
3. Treatment
  a) IVBT, used in conjunction with PTCA, temporarily implants radioactive material, either gamma or beta irradiation. The type of radiation selected will determine the amount of radiation and dwell time (Hanefeld et al., 2002).

b) IVBT is performed in the cardiac catheterization laboratory. The multidisciplinary responsibilities include the following.
  (1) Interventional cardiologist—Initially inserts the coronary catheter, determines the injury length and reference vessel diameter, and inserts the IVBT catheter. Essentially oversees the overall medical safety of the patient.
  (2) Radiation oncologist—Ensures the accurate delivery of the RT to the target area, making decisions related to dose delivery, prescription point, source delivery, and recovery, as well as safe completion of the removal of radioactive sources. Oversees the radiation safety of the procedure.
  (3) Medical physicist—Ensures radiation safety storage, disposes of radiation sources, monitors radiation exposure to personnel, and measures patient dosimetry (calculations of treatment times, dose distributions, and advising on maximum tissue doses).
  (4) Catheterization personnel (cath lab technicians and nurses)—Assist in the overall cardiac catheterization procedure and obtain any extra special equipment for IVBT.
4. Radiation safety issues
  a) Source inventory (gamma or beta)
  b) Storage between patient cases
  c) Certification for potential uses
  d) Calibration of treatment delivery device
  e) Shielding, handling, and disposal of radioisotopes
  f) Safety with catheterization laboratory (film and ring badges to monitor exposure)
  g) Emergency bailout procedures for lost sources, liquid radionuclide spills, failure of delivery, and retraction of sources for manually afterloaded and remote afterloaded machines
5. Collaborative management
  a) Acute effects—Complications can occur from the heart catheterization and/or the brachytherapy.
    (1) Major complications from heart catheterizations
      (a) Severe hypotension
      (b) Anaphylactic shock
      (c) Dissection of the coronary or femoral arteries
      (d) Femoral occlusion from the catheterization
      (e) Stroke
      (f) Arrythmias

(2) Major complications from brachytherapy
    (a) Late thrombosis
    (b) Late restenosis
    (c) "Edge effect"—closing at the ends of the treatment areas
b) Late effects—Original patient cohorts from first clinical trials are being followed for long-term risks associated with the use of radiation to the coronary arteries (Nguyen-Ho, Kaluza, Zymek, & Raizner, 2002). In animal and human studies, aneurysm, fibrosis, and restenosis at the edge or within the vessel have been reported (Fox, 2002; Waksman, 1999).

6. Patient and family education: Typically, radiation oncology nurses are not directly involved in the care of patients on IVBT; rather, patient teaching is the focus.
  a) Knowledge about IVBT to support the patient's decision process and informed consent
  b) Discussion of the roles and responsibilities of the multidisciplinary team
  c) Cardiology nurses are available to explain heart catheterization and answer questions pertaining to interventional procedure.
  d) Patients are not radioactive after the procedure; the only exposure is during the cardiac catheterization.
  e) Patients will have antiplatelet therapy after the procedure (duration is determined by cardiologist).
  f) Long-term follow-up is predominantly with the cardiologist.

References

Fox, R. (2002). Intravascular brachytherapy of the coronary arteries. *Physician Medical Biology, 47*(4), R1–R30.

Hanefeld, C., Amirie, S., Borchardt, D., Grewe, P., Muller, K., Kissler, M., et al. (2002). Dosimetric measurements in isolated human coronary arteries: Comparison of commercially available iridium with strontium/Yttrium emitters. *Circulation, 105,* 2493–2496.

Hansrani, M., Overbeck, K., Smout, J., & Stansby, G. (2003). *Intravascular brachytherapy for peripheral vascular disease* (Cochrane Review). New York: John Wiley and Sons.

Leon, M., Teirstein, P., Moses, J., Tripuraneni, P., Lansky, A.J., Jani, S., et. al. (2001). Localized intracoronary gamma radiation therapy to inhibit the recurrence of restenosis after stenting. *New England Journal of Medicine, 344,* 250–256.

Nguyen-Ho, P., Kaluza, G., Zymek, P., & Raizner, A. (2002). Intravascular brachytherapy. *Catheter Cardiovascular Intervention, 56,* 281–288.

Sims, E., Rothman, M., Warner, T., & Powell, E. (2002). Coronary artery brachytherapy. *Clinical Oncology, 4,* 313–326.

SoRelle, R. (2000). Two intravascular brachytherapy systems approved by FDA. *Circulation, 102,* 9041–9043.

Teirstein, P., Massullo, V., Jani, S., Popma, J.J., Mintz, G.S., Russo, R.J., et al. (1997). Catheter-based radiotherarpy to inhibit restensosis after coronary stenting. *New England Journal of Medicine, 336,* 1697–1703.

Teirstein, P., Massulo, V., Jani, S., Popma, J.J., Russo, R.J., Schatz, R.A., et al. (2000). Three year clinical and angiographic followup after intracoronary radiation. Results of a randomized clinical trial. *Circulation, 101,* 360–365.

Waksman, R. (1999). *Vascular brachytherapy.* Amonk, NY: Futura Publishing.

Waksman, R., White, R., Chan, R., Bass, B.G., Geirlach, L., Mintz, G.S., et al. (2000). Intracoronary gamma radiation therapy after angioplasty inhibits recurrence in patients with in-stent restenosis. *Circulation, 101,* 2165–2171.

F. Intraoperative radiation therapy (IORT)
1. Procedure description: IORT is a single, large fraction of radiation that is given to an exposed tumor or resected tumor bed during a surgical procedure.
2. Indications
  a) IORT is most commonly used in the treatment of GI, gynecologic, and genitourinary (GU) cancers, as well as in the treatment of STSs. Its use also has been reported in the treatment of head and neck, brain, and breast cancer.
  b) Patients who are candidates for IORT may receive it before or after EBRT and/or a combined modality treatment.
  c) In the pediatric setting, it represents an attractive method to increase dose to the tumor bed while minimizing the long-term risks of radiation exposure to normal tissue, such as growth retardation and secondary malignances (Hu, Enker, & Harrison, 2002).
3. Treatment
  a) The use of IORT was first reported in the early 1900s, and the technique has continued to develop over the past century (Wojtas & Smith, 1997).
  b) Wolkov (1998) identified the following advantages with the use of IORT.
    (1) Ability to treat large volumes
    (2) Homogeneous dose distribution
    (3) Potential to limit tumor seeding
    (4) Avoidance of trauma to normal tissues associated with interstitial implantation
    (5) Limited to no dose to surrounding normal structures because of mobilization and direct shielding
  c) IORT can be delivered with high-energy electrons (IOERT), an orthovoltage unit, or an HDR gamma-emitting isotope (HDR-

IORT). The first two methods require a portable electron unit and/or a linear accelerator, whereas the third requires a portable HDR remote afterloader. Each of these treatment units has specially designed applicators that come in different sizes that are attached to the unit. Cones that are used for other types of radiation treatment may be used on the linear accelerator and/or on the mobile electron linear accelerator. The Harrison-Anderson-Mick (HAM) applicator was developed at Memorial Sloan-Kettering Cancer Center and is a 1 cm thick pad made of flexible material ("super flab"), with source guide tubes running through the center and a cap at the end that secures the source guide tubes, which then attach to the remote afterloader (Harrison, Enker, & Anderson, 1995a).

d) Two challenges exist with a linear accelerator-based program (Harrison et al., 1995a).

(1) Transferring of the patient from the operating room (OR) to the radiation department and the various risks associated with this.

(2) Having a dedicated accelerator in an OR is often considered cost prohibitive based upon patient treatment volumes.

e) If IORT is going to be given in the OR, then the OR needs to be shielded and another set of monitoring equipment needs to be outside of the room to be used during IORT.

f) Preoperative care

(1) In an effort to determine tumor size, location, and extent of disease preoperatively, the patient may need to undergo numerous invasive and/or noninvasive procedures.

(2) Patients also will undergo all required preoperative studies, including chest x-ray, EKG, and other laboratory studies as deemed necessary.

(3) Informed consent for the procedure should be ascertained from the patient by the multidisciplinary team prior to the day of surgery.

(4) Patients will have necessary catheters, tubes, and IVs started prior to surgery.

g) Intraoperative care

(1) The surgical team (e.g., physician, nurse) provides status updates to the radiation oncologist about the patient and what time he or she will be ready for the radiation oncologist and medical dosimetrist in the OR.

(2) During an operation, the normal organs are physically moved out of the pathway of the radiation beam (Harrison et al., 1995a), whenever possible.

(3) If the patient is to be transported to the radiation oncology department to receive radiation, the following needs to occur.

(a) Incisions are temporarily closed with a running continuous suture or clamps, and the wound is covered with a sterile adhesive dressing.

(b) Patient is placed on a stretcher and transported to the department with portable anesthesia.

(c) Patient then is transferred to the treatment couch and reprepared and redraped.

(d) After involved personnel are regowned and regloved, the surgeon reopens the incision, and the treatment applicator is placed (Wolkov, 1998).

(4) When the radiation oncologist and medical physicist arrive, they will scrub into the case and examine the area that is to be treated. The resected specimen often is reviewed with the pathologist, and the margins are analyzed by frozen section. The desired treatment applicator is selected and secured in place, and appropriate shielding will be placed to protect the normal tissue.

(5) The radiation oncologist prescribes the treatment dosage, and the medical physicist performs the dose calculations. If using the HAM applicator, source guide tubes will need to be connected to the applicator from the HDR unit.

(6) When the treatment is delivered, the team leaves the room and monitors

the patient on another set of equipment outside of the OR.

(7) Depending on the total dose to be delivered and the activity of the source, treatment time will vary (Harrison, Enker, & Anderson, 1995b). For HDR, it is approximately 25 minutes.

(8) Although not done frequently, the patient may receive more than one fraction during the procedure because of the size of the area that needs to be treated.

(9) Generally, clips are later placed around the irradiated site volume so that it can be visualized radiographically later, at the time of a subsequent external beam treatment simulation (Wolkov, 1998).

(10) Once treatment is completed, the treatment applicator and lead shields (if HDR) are removed. The surgeon closes the incision, and the nurses complete the closing sharps, sponge, and instrument counts (Domanovic, Ouzidane, Ellis, Kinsella, & Beddar, 2003).

(11) Prior to transferring the patient, report is called to the RN in the post-anesthesia care unit (PACU).

   h) Postoperative care

(1) Depending upon the patient, once he or she is in the PACU and stabilized, he or she will be transferred to an intermediate care unit or an intensive care unit.

(2) The nurse caring for the patient who received IORT needs to be knowledgeable about the surgical procedure performed, the typical complications that arise from that type of surgery, as well as issues related to the surgical resection and any anastomoses performed.

4. Collaborative management
  a) Acute effects

(1) Complications that could occur in any patient receiving a major surgical procedure include infection, abscess, fistula, bleeding, or obstruction (Wojtas & Smith, 1997).

(2) Patients may experience pain, altered bowel patterns, and nutritional issues related to the surgical procedure.

  b) Late effects

(1) Patients may have sexuality issues related to the surgical intervention and IORT, the use of pre- or postoperative radiation, and/or chemotherapy.

(2) Azinovic, Calvo, Pueblo, Aristu, and Martinez-Monge (2001) found the incidence of severe toxicity was lower in gynecologic, head and neck, and GU, whereas higher toxicity was noted in bone sarcomas and STSs.

(3) Peripheral nerve injury was the dominant event in long-term survivors (Azinovic et al., 2001). This event appeared most frequently in those locations in which a peripheral nerve is commonly found in the surgical bed (Azinovic et al.).

(4) The development of IORT-induced neuropathy appears related to

  (a) Recurrent disease treated with prior surgery and/or EBRT

  (b) Overlap of matching IORT fields

  (c) Total IORT dose to the nerve

  (d) Volume irradiated (Wolkov, 1998).

(5) Other side effects that may arise depending upon the treatment area include ureteral and bile duct stenosis and fibrosis, hydronephrosis, pelvic fibrosis, limb edema, and cystitis (Azinovic et al., 2001; Wolkov, 1998).

5. Patient and family education
  a) Teach patient and family about the required studies prior to surgery and the length of time required for the studies.

  b) Teach patient and family about the surgical procedure and the radiation treatment. Review with them NPO status, GI prep if ordered, and where and when to arrive for surgery if the patient is not to be admitted the evening before.

  c) Teach patient and family about discharge care that may include wound care, dietary needs, and ostomy care and who to contact if issues should arise.

  d) Provide patient and family, if applicable, with counseling on sexuality as well as resources, such as ACS's (2001a, 2001b) *Sexuality and Cancer* booklets.

  e) Provide appropriate referrals to services that may include social work, vocational counseling, and pastoral support.

  f) Teach patient about treatment planning, EBRT, skin care, and acute and late side effects, if he or she is to receive postoperative radiation.

  g) Teach patient and family the signs and symptoms of peripheral neuropathy and how to manage this side effect.

  h) Teach patient and family the importance of follow-up care to assess for acute and late effects.

6. Follow-up

  a) Patients may be seen frequently over the first few months post-treatment for assessments and to determine their response to treatment.

  b) The surgical oncologist in conjunction with the radiation oncologist may follow patients.

References

American Cancer Society. (2001a). *Sexuality and cancer for the man who has cancer and his partner* [Pub. No. 4657-HCP]. Atlanta, GA: Author.

American Cancer Society. (2001b). *Sexuality and cancer for the woman who has cancer and her partner* [Pub. No. 4658-HCP]. Atlanta, GA: Author.

Azinovic, I., Calvo, F., Pueblo, F., Aristu, J., & Martinez-Monge, R. (2001). Long-term normal tissue effects of intraoperative electron radiation therapy (IOERT): Late sequelae, tumor recurrence, and second malignancies. *International Journal of Radiation Oncology, Biology, Physics, 49,* 597–604.

Domanovic, M., Ouzidane, M., Ellis, R., Kinsella, T., & Beddar, A. (2003). Using intraoperative radiation therapy—A case study. *AORN Journal, 77,* 412, 414–417.

Harrison, L., Enker, W., & Anderson, L. (1995a). High-dose-rate intraoperative radiation therapy for colorectal cancer, Part 1. *Oncology, 9,* 679–683.

Harrison, L., Enker, W., & Anderson, L. (1995b). High-dose-rate intraoperative radiation therapy for colorectal cancer, Part 2. *Oncology, 9,* 737–741.

Hu, K., Enker, W., & Harrison, L. (2002). High-dose-rate intraoperative irradiation: Current status and future directions. *Seminars in Radiation Oncology, 12*(1), 62–80.

Wojtas, F., & Smith, R. (1997). Hyperthermia and intraoperative radiation therapy. In K.H. Dow, J.D. Bucholtz, R. Iwamoto, V.K. Fieler, & L.J. Hilderley (Eds.), *Nursing care in radiation oncology* (2nd ed., pp. 36–46). Philadelphia: Saunders.

Wolkov, H. (1998). Intraoperative radiation therapy. In S. Leibel & T. Phillips (Eds.), *Textbook of radiation oncology* (pp. 276–290). Philadelphia: Saunders.

G. Stereotactic radiosurgery/radiotherapy

1. Stereotactic radiosurgery (SRS)

  a) Procedure description

    (1) Lars Leksell, MD, PhD, a Swedish neurosurgeon, was the first to describe SRS as a technique for the destruction of intracranial targets without opening the skull, using single, high doses of ionizing radiation in stereotactically directed narrow beams (Leksell, 1951).

    (2) SRS uses convergent beam irradiation (CBI) techniques to deliver highly conformal radiation to small (usually less than 4 cm), well-circumscribed lesions within the brain (Phillips, Stelzer, Griffin, Mayberg, & Winn, 1994).

    (3) SRS is a by-product of sterotaxy developed by neurosurgeons.

    (4) Radiation is delivered by using multiple beam directions and a high degree of collimation or other beam characteristics for precise tumor or vascular abnormality coverage, with rapid falloff of the dose to adjacent normal tissues (Verhey & Smith, 1995).

    (5) Single, high-dose radiation delivered to the tumor or vascular abnormality results in either vascular effects (thrombosis) or antiproliferative effects (reproductive cell death) (Larson, Flickinger, & Loeffler, 1993).

  b) Indications

    (1) SRS is indicated for patients with small tumors (i.e., generally < 3 cm in diameter) that are well circumscribed, easily seen on CT/MRI, and a high Karnofsky Performance Status.

    (2) Arteriovenous malformations (AVM) when surgical resection is not possible or the risk of embolization is too great (Flickinger, Loeffler, & Larson, 1994)

    (3) Benign tumors (i.e., acoustic/nonacoustic schwannomas, meningiomas, hemangioblastomas, trigeminal neuralgia, and pituitary adenomas)

    (4) Malignant tumors (as a boost to gliomas after conventional fractionation or for small recurrence)

    (5) Metastases (alone and as a boost to fractionated radiotherapy or for small recurrence)

    (6) The use of SRS techniques to treat extracranial sites is currently under investigation in a number of institutions. Typical targets for extracranial

stereotactic treatment are small tumors or recurrences of tumors of the lung (T1-2), lung metastases, liver metastases, abdominal tumors, pelvic recurrences of rectal or cervical cancer, and bone metastases of relatively radioresistant primaries. Usually these targets are close to radiosensitive organs at risk as mediastinal structures: the stomach and duodenum, small or large bowel, rectum, urinary bladder, nerves, or spinal cord (Wulf, Hadinger, Oppitz, Olshusen, & Flentje, 2000).

c) Treatment
  (1) Technology
    (a) Positively charged particles (protons) (Kirn, 1988)
    (b) Gamma radiation (Gamma Knife emitted from a fixed array of 201 small cobalt-60 sources) (see Figure 20) (Flickinger, Lundsford, & Kondziolka, 1994; Lundsford, Alexander, & Loeffler, 1993)
    (c) LINAC-based stereotactic techniques using circular collimators or micro-multileaf collimators
    (d) CyberKnife® (Accuray Inc., Sunnyvale, CA) uses the skeletal structure of the body as a reference frame for localizing the target instead of a rigid body or head frame that is commonly used. A small linear accelerator is mounted on a robot, and the computer controlling the radiation beam makes constant tiny corrections for the slightest movements.
  (2) Immobilization
    (a) Uses stereotactic apparatus (head frame) that securely attaches with screws to the patient's skull

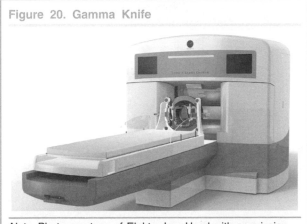

Figure 20. Gamma Knife

Note. Photo courtesy of Elekta, Inc. Used with permission.

    (b) A body frame may be used for extracranial lesions.
    (c) Provides a reference frame with coordinate system for target determination and precise patient positioning
  (3) Planning: CT scan, MRI, angiography, or a combination of the three may be used to define the coordinates of the volume of interest within the brain. In addition to radiation therapy personnel, a neurosurgeon is involved in SRS.
  (4) Steps
    (a) Preparation: No shaving or special hygiene is required the day before. Laboratory studies may include creatinine levels (CT dye) and phenytoin levels.
    (b) IV access day of procedure: Depends on institution's policy
    (c) Head immobilization application/attachment
    (d) CT imaging: Used to calculate radiation dose
    (e) Treatment planning: MRI/CT images are merged together showing lesion configuration and its location near or distant from critical neurologic tissue. Planning involves selecting the number of arcs, width of arcs, and angles of the arcs.
    (f) Dose selection: Expressed in Gy
    (g) Radiosurgery treatment delivery: The number of arcs to administer will determine how long patient is in room.

d) Collaborative management
  (1) The risk of complications following single-fraction SRS is low (3%–15%) in most reported series (Gelblum et al., 1998).
  (2) Depends on the location, size, dose, histology, and modality
  (3) Acute side effects (Flickinger et al., 1994; Krause, Lamb, Ham, Larson, & Gutin, 1991; Shaw, Coffey, & Dinapoli, 1995)
    (a) Discomfort from the invasive, fixated head frame
    (b) Bleeding/infection at the head frame pin sites
    (c) Vertigo
    (d) Nausea/vomiting
    (e) Headache
    (f) Seizures

(g) Fatigue

(h) Cerebral edema

(i) Hemiparesis

(4) Late effects

(a) Persistent headaches

(b) Asymptomatic and/or symptomatic cerebral edema

(c) Cerebral radionecrosis

(d) Cranial nerve deficits (cranial nerves 3–7)

(e) Hemorrhage (AVM)

(f) Cyst formation

(g) Changes in cognitive function

(h) Hormonal deficiency

(i) Alopecia

(5) No universal grading system specific to time course or grading of neurotoxicity for SRS currently exists (Shaw et al., 1995).

e) Patient and family education: Review procedures with the patient and family.

(1) Head frame placement usually is done early on the morning of treatment in the radiation or neuroradiology department by a neurosurgeon using local anesthesia (lidocaine hydrochloride). Premedication with lorazepam or diazepam may be used.

(2) The patient is taken to the radiology department for CT, MRI, or angiography and then returns to the radiation department or designated area to wait for the treatment planning to be finished.

(3) The treatment time depends on the number of isocenters and the machine delivering the radiosurgery.

(4) Pain medication may be used for post screw site pain or headache.

(5) Antiseizure medication should be administered as scheduled, and a blood level should be obtained prior to treatment. Some patients who are not already taking antiseizure medication may require a loading dose.

(6) Side effects will depend on size, location, and disease type. The patient may require premedication of an antiemetic and/or steroid prior to treatment.

(7) Inform patient and family that the head frame will be removed upon completion of therapy.

(8) Instruct patient and family in pin site care to prevent infection.

f) Follow-up

(1) AVM patients should have follow-up clinical examinations along with MRI/MRA scans at 12-month intervals until the AVM resolves.

(2) Patients with malignant tumors, including metastases and gliomas, require more frequent follow-up with both clinical and radiographic examinations.

2. Stereotactic radiotherapy (SRT)

a) Procedure description

(1) SRT uses convergent beam irradiation (from SRS) and applies the biologic advantages of fractionation (Phillips et al., 1994). Fractionated SRT combines radiosurgery and daily fractionation.

(2) Fractionated SRT is similar in concept to 3-D conformal radiation used in other sites.

b) Indications

(1) SRT provides the focal dose distribution (sparing normal tissue) of SRS with the biologic advantage of daily fractionation (Phillips et al, 1994).

(2) SRT allows a wider variation of fraction size; therefore, spherical tumor volumes > 3 cm in diameter can be treated. However, lesions need to be < 5 mm away from critical CNS structures (retina, cranial nerves, brain stem, motor cortex, and speech areas).

(3) Current uses (some indications are still investigational)

(a) Characteristics of tumors

i) Inoperable lesions because of location or involvement of sensitive tissues

ii) Small-volume and well-defined lesions

iii) Lesions previously treated with radiation

iv) Tumors with histologies known to respond well to radiotherapy

(b) Types of tumors
  i) Low-grade gliomas
  ii) Meningioma
  iii) Pituitary adenoma
  iv) Acoustic neuroma
  v) Craniopharyngioma
  vi) Brain metastasis

c) Treatment
  (1) Modalities (Winston & Lutz, 1988)
    (a) Modified linear accelerator
    (b) Proton beam
  (2) Immobilization: Uses a relocatable, custom-fitted head frame that accomplishes precise head immobilization without fixed screws into the skull. One example is a bite plate.
  (3) Planning usually is performed using MRI image fusion technology.

d) Collaborative management: Depends on the size, dose, and histology of tumor
  (1) Acute effects
    (a) Fatigue
    (b) Temporary alopecia
    (c) Worsening of neurologic symptoms
    (d) Seizures
    (e) Cerebral hemorrhage
    (f) Cerebral edema
  (2) Late effects
    (a) Fatigue
    (b) Hormonal imbalance secondary to pituitary/hypothalamic dysfunction
    (c) Permanent alopecia
    (d) Blindness (lesion near optic nerve/chiasm)
    (e) Stroke
    (f) Cerebral hemorrhage
    (g) Cranial nerve damage
    (h) Cerebral radionecrosis

e) Patient and family education
  (1) Prepare patient for specified head immobilization device.
  (2) Inform patient and family that verification measurements, port films, and stereotactic CT require more time than standard RT planning.
  (3) Review the same teaching as SRS.

References

Flickinger, J.C., Loeffler, J.S., & Larson, D.A. (1994). Stereotactic radiosurgery for intracranial malignancies. *Oncology, 8,* 81–84.

Flickinger, J.C., Lundsford, L.D., & Kondziolka, D. (1994). Radiosurgery. In P.M. Mauch & J.S. Loeffler (Eds.), *Radiation oncology: Technology and biology* (pp. 198–215). Philadelphia: Saunders.

Gelblum, D.Y., Lee, H., Bilsky, M., Pinola, C., Longford, S., & Wallner, K. (1998). Radiographic findings and morbidity in patients treated with stereotactic radiosurgery. *International Journal of Radiology Oncology, Biology, Physics, 42,* 391–395.

Kirn, T.F. (1988). Proton radiotherapy: Some perspectives. *JAMA, 259,* 787–788.

Krause, E.A., Lamb, S., Ham, B., Larson, D.A., & Gutin, P.H. (1991). Radiosurgery: A nursing perspective. *Journal of Neuroscience Nursing, 23,* 24–28.

Larson, D.A., Flickinger, J.C., & Loeffler, J.S. (1993). The radiobiology of radiosurgery [Editorial]. *International Journal of Radiology Oncology, Biology, Physics, 25,* 557–561.

Leksell, L. (1951). The stereotactic method and radiosurgery of the brain. *Acta Chirurgica Scandinavica, 102,* 316–319.

Lundsford, L.D., Alexander, E.A., & Loeffler, J.S. (1993). General introduction: History of radiosurgery. In E. Alexander, III, J.S. Loeffler, & L.D. Lundsford (Eds.), *Stereotactic radiosurgery* (pp. 1–4). New York: McGraw-Hill.

Phillips, M.H., Stelzer, K.J., Griffin, T.W., Mayberg, M.R., & Winn, H.R. (1994). Stereotactic radiosurgery: A review and comparison of methods. *Journal of Clinical Oncology, 12,* 1085–1099.

Shaw, E.G., Coffey, R.J., & Dinapoli, R. P. (1995). Neurotoxicity of radiosurgery. *Seminars in Radiation Oncology, 5,* 235–245.

Shrieve, D.C., Kooy, H.M., Tarbell, N.J., & Loeffler, J.S. (1996). Fractionated stereotactic radiotherapy. In V.T. DeVita, S. Hellman, & S.A. Rosenberg (Eds.), *Important advances in oncology* (pp. 205–224). Philadelphia: Lippincott-Raven.

Verhey, L.J., & Smith, V. (1995). The physics of radiosurgery. *Seminars in Radiation Oncology, 5,* 175–191.

Winston, K.R., & Lutz, W. (1988). Linear accelerator as a neurosurgical tool for stereotactic radiosurgery. *Neurosurgery, 2,* 454–464.

Wulf, J., Hadinger, U., Oppitz, U., Olshusen, B., & Flentje, M. (2000). Stereotactic radiotherapy of extracranial targets: CT-simulation and accuracy of treatment in the stereotactic body frame. *Radiotherapy Oncology, 57,* 225–236.

H. Total body irradiation (TBI)
  1. Procedure description: TBI is a technique of radiation therapy that delivers a uniform dose to the entire body while allowing for selected organ shielding. It is combined with high-dose chemotherapy for myeloablation in preparation for bone marrow transplant (BMT) or peripheral stem cell transplant (PSCT). The preferred terminology to encompass all transplants types is hematopoietic stem cell transplantation (HSCT) (Whedon & Roach, 2000).
    a) Goals of TBI
      (1) Destroy any residual malignant cells (tumor eradication).
      (2) Ablate the marrow to make room for engraftment.
      (3) Suppress the host's immune system to decrease the risk of graft rejection in allogeneic transplants (immunosuppression is not needed in autologous

transplants) (Leiper, 1995; Wujcik & Price, 2000).

b) Advantages of TBI
  (1) No "sanctuary sites" of disease (e.g., skin, testes, CNS)
  (2) Even distribution of the dosage
  (3) Dose can be adjusted for the patient's specific needs (i.e., boosted or shielded) (Wujcik & Price, 2000).

c) Types of HSCT (Alcoser & Burchett, 1999; Whedon & Roach, 2000)
  (1) Autologous—Self-donor: Malignant cells are purged with chemotherapy or biologic response modifiers and returned to patient.
    (a) Perfect human leukocyte antigen (HLA) match, avoids complications with graft versus host disease (GVHD)
    (b) A higher relapse rate but lower treatment-associated mortality
  (2) Syngeneic—Donor is identical twin of recipient (Whedon & Roach, 2000).
    (a) Share identical genes
    (b) Perfect HLA match, avoids complications with GVHD
  (3) Allogeneic—Donor may be related or unrelated.
    (a) A related donor is preferred because the HLA system (major and minor components) has a greater chance of matching.
    (b) The closer the HLA match, the less chance there is for complications (Alcoser & Burchett, 1999; Whedon & Roach, 2000).

d) Cell source for HSCT (Whedon & Roach, 2000; Wujcik & Price, 2000)
  (1) Bone marrow
  (2) Peripheral stem cell
  (3) Umbilical cord blood

2. Indications: TBI is most commonly administered to patients with hematologic malignancies and select immunologic disorders that have not already received significant doses of radiation during a prior treatment course.

a) Acute myelogenous leukemia—HSCT is the only known potentially curative treatment for patients who fail induction therapy (Whedon & Roach, 2000).

b) Acute lymphocytic leukemia—Most common childhood leukemia, with peak incidence at age five to six years. In adults, peak incidence is highest over the age of 60 years. HSCT is indicated in second remission and in first remission for children with poor prognostic features (Abramovitz & Senner, 1995; Whedon & Roach, 2000).

c) Chronic myelogenous leukemia—HSCT is the only known cure. Best outcome is observed if patient is transplanted in early chronic phase or within one year of diagnosis (Whedon & Roach, 2000).

d) Chronic lymphocytic leukemia—Use of HSCT is relatively new. Conservative treatment has been standard because of the older age of patients at diagnosis, with a median age at presentation between 50–60 years (Whedon & Roach, 2000).

e) Hodgkin's lymphoma—HSCT indicated for relapse (Whedon & Roach, 2000).

f) Non-Hodgkin's lymphoma—HSCT indicated for relapsed or refractory intermediate-grade lymphoma (Whedon & Roach, 2000).

g) Aplastic anemia—HSCT is treatment of choice (Whedon & Roach, 2000).

h) Myelodysplastic syndrome—HSCT is the only curative therapy available but is reserved for patients younger than 55 with excessive blasts or complex cytogenic complexes (O'Connell, 2000; Whedon & Roach, 2000).

i) Multiple myeloma—Incurable with standard chemotherapy; HSCT (allogeneic) is potentially curative (Whedon & Roach, 2000).

j) Selected solid tumors (e.g., breast, ovarian, neuroblastoma, small cell lung cancer, malignant melanoma) in clinical trials (Whedon & Roach, 2000)

k) Other nonmalignant and/or congenital diseases (e.g., hematologic disorders, immunodeficiency disorders, mucopolysaccharidoses, lipidoses) (Abramovitz & Senner, 1995)

3. Treatment: Initially, TBI was given as a single fraction of 8–10 Gy. Advancements in research during the last 25 years have shown that fractionated radiation allows higher doses to

be given safely, as well as improve long-term survival (Gopal et al., 2001; Leiper, 1995; Thomas et al., 2001). Total doses and fractionation schedules of TBI vary among institutions and depend on the protocol and type of HSCT the patient will receive.

a) Dose: Patients undergoing TBI receive a total dose of 12–15 Gy over the course of three to six days at 1.5–2.0 Gy per dose (Lawton, 2003; Wujcik & Price, 2000).

b) Frequency: Patients will be treated once, twice, or three times daily, depending on the treatment protocol (Bruner, Bucholtz, Iwamoto, & Strohl, 1998). The minimum time between fractions each day is five to six hours, and the maximum time is eight hours (Bruner et al., 1998).

c) Position: TBI treatment is administered while the patient is standing on a special platform, lying on a treatment table or couch, or sitting on a bicycle. Radiation is given either anteroposterior-posteroanterior (AP/PA) or by parallel opposed lateral techniques (Bruner et al., 1998; Lawton, 2003).

d) Time: Treatment times range from 20–30 minutes per treatment depending on the dose rate of the machine. The most common dose rates in use today are 0.05–0.2 Gy/min. (Lawton, 2003).

e) Pediatric consideration: Given the treatment time involved, small children may require sedation or anesthesia during the treatment (Bruner et al., 1998). If anesthesia is not used, provide for safety with appropriate immobilization devices.

f) Shielding: Selective organ shielding using thin lead shields is used to reduce the incidence of long-term toxic effects after TBI, especially of the lungs. Selective shielding of the liver and kidneys also is done at some institutions. In lateral technique, the patient's arms are used to shield the lungs (Lawton, 2003).

4. Collaborative management
   a) Acute effects (up to 90 days after HSCT) caused solely by TBI are difficult to isolate, as TBI is given in tandem with conditioning chemotherapy and the actual transplant procedure. Most of the side effects have multiple causes (Ford & Ballard, 1988; Lawton, 2003; Wujcik & Price, 2000).
      (1) During TBI treatment
         (a) Fever
            i) Onset: Immediate
            ii) Duration: 24 hours
            iii) Treatment: Acetaminophen
         (b) Nausea and vomiting
            i) Onset: Immediate
            ii) Duration: Three to five days
            iii) Treatment: Antiemetics such as ondansetron, administered before treatment with/without dexamethasone (Decadron®) (Merck, West Point, PA) have proved to be effective (Abramovitz & Senner, 1995).
         (c) Parotitis—Pain in the post-auricular region that affects the jaw. The cause of the discomfort is swelling in the parotid glands (Bruner et al., 1998; Ford & Ballard, 1988; Lawton, 2003; Wujcik & Price, 2000).
            i) Incidence: 50% of all patients experience discomfort (Bruner et al., 1998).
            ii) Onset: 12–48 hours after the initial dose of TBI
            iii) Duration: 24–72 hours
            iv) Treatment: Steroids and mild analgesics
         (d) Headache—Global headache during TBI treatment
            i) Incidence: Approximately 33% (Bruner et al., 1998)
            ii) Onset: Variable
            iii) Duration: Variable
            iv) Treatment: Mild analgesic medications, although some patients may require narcotics to relieve the pain. Narcotics must be administered with care if the protocol calls for the patient to be treated while standing (Bruner et al., 1998).

(e) Xerostomia—Dryness of the mouth
  i) Incidence: Almost 100% (Bruner et al., 1998)
  ii) Onset: Two to three days
  iii) Duration: Variable, may persist long after treatment is completed
  iv) Treatment: Establish an oral hygiene program during the transplant period using oral moisturizers, and reinforce the importance of following the program (Yeager, Webster, Crain, Kasow, & McGuire, 2000).
  v) Prophylaxis: Dental consult prior to the start of TBI and ongoing dental care, including fluoride treatments (Ford & Ballard, 1988; Sitton, 1997)

(f) Diarrhea
  i) Incidence: 33%–50% of all patients experience some degree of diarrhea (Bruner et al., 1998).
  ii) Onset: Three to five days; may develop as late as two weeks after TBI is completed (Ford & Ballard, 1988).
  iii) Duration: Usually three to five days
  iv) Treatment: Antispasmodics or antidiarrheals are effective but cannot be initiated until infectious causes of diarrhea (e.g., *C. difficile*) have been ruled out (Bruner et al., 1998).

(g) Fatigue—Decrease in energy level and inability to concentrate
  i) Onset: Three to four days
  ii) Duration: Variable

  iii) Treatment: Energy-conserving strategies

(h) Skin reaction—Generalized erythema
  i) Onset: Immediate
  ii) Duration: Three to four days
  iii) Treatment: Prescribed cream should be applied to the entire body only at night during the TBI treatment days. Examples of creams used for radiation skin reactions:
    • Aquaphor®
    • Biafine®
    • Eucerin®
    • Jeans Cream® (Jeans Cream, Peabody, MA)
    • RadiaPlex Rx™ Gel (MPM Medical, Irving, TX)

(2) During transplant course (Bruner et al., 1998)
  (a) Skin reaction—Tanning/hyperpigmentation of the entire skin. Some patients will experience severe skin changes associated with acute GVHD.
    i) Onset: 4–10 days
    ii) Duration: Variable—Begins to resolve within two weeks after TBI is complete, unless secondary to GVHD.
    iii) Treatment: Prescribed cream should be applied to the entire body twice a day after TBI is completed.

  (b) Oral mucositis
    i) Onset: 4–10 days
    ii) Duration: 21–28 days—Worsens during days 10–14 after TBI (O'Connell, 2000). Resolution often is associated with the recovery of the absolute neutrophil count (ANC) (Wujcik & Price, 2000).
    iii) Treatment
      • Meticulous oral hygiene program during the transplant period. Many studies have examined various agents in addressing the incidence of stomatitis, but as of yet, no agent has shown a statistically significant advantage over another in the treatment of stomatitis. Armstrong (1994) reviewed several

studies (Beck, 1992; DeWalt, 1975; DeWalt & Haines, 1969; Ginsberg, 1961), which agree that the frequency of oral hygiene should be based on the severity of symptoms. Beck (1990) recommended oral hygiene every four hours for prevention, every two hours for mild stomatitis, and every one to two hours for severe mucositis. Reinforce the importance of following the program to patient and family (Armstrong, 1994; Yeager et al., 2000).

- GM-CSF mouth rinses: Bez et al. (1999) tested the efficacy of a GM–CSF mouth rinse in reducing the duration of severe oral mucositis in a prospective open trial. No statistical difference was noted in mucositis scores between study and control groups, but the duration of severe mucositis was reduced. Sixty percent of the GM-CSF mouth rinse group had severe mucositis for less than nine days versus 28% in the control group. In addition, only 10% of the GM-CSF mouth rinse group experienced severe mucositis lasting 20+ days, whereas 34% of the control group had severe mucositis lasting 20+ days. Bez et al. (1999) suggested that GM-CSF mouth rinses may reduce the duration of severe mucositis, but a controlled, double-blind clinical trial is now required.

iv) Prophylaxis: Helium-neon laser applications—Cowen et al. (1997) did a double-blind randomized trial looking at prophylactic use of helium-neon laser applications performed on day –5 to –1 on five anatomic sites of the oral mucosa, with oral examina-tion performed daily from day 0 to +20. They showed a statistically significant improvement in the daily mucositis index (p < 0.05) from day +2 to +7, and the cumulative oral mucositis score was significantly reduced (p = 0.04) in patients receiving laser treatment. Occurrence and duration of grade III mucositis was reduced (p = 0.01). Oral pain assessed by the patient was reduced as evidenced by decreased need for morphine (p = 0.05). Xerostomia (p = 0.005) and ability to swallow (p = 0.01) were improved. They concluded the laser treatment was well tolerated, was feasible, and reduced oral mucositis in all cases.

(c) Alopecia—Hair loss is usually complete (Reeves, 2000).
   i) Onset: 7–14 days after TBI
   ii) Duration: 3–6 months after end of treatment
   iii) Treatment: Scarves, hats, wigs as indicated by patient preference
   iv) Education/symptom management

(d) Acute GVHD syndrome—Mainly associated with allogeneic transplants. Immunologically competent cells in the graft target antigens in the host, stimulating an immune reaction (Alcoser & Burchett, 1999). Overall incidence is 25%–70% despite GVHD prophylaxis (O'Connell, 2000).

i) Skin (Alcoser & Burchett, 1999; Bruner et al., 1998)
- Maculopapular rash (pruritic or painful) starts on palms and soles and progresses to cheeks, neck, and trunk.
- Generalized erythroderma
- Desquamation and bullae

ii) GI tract (O'Connell, 2000)
- Anorexia (early)
- Nausea and vomiting (early)
- Profuse diarrhea (several liters/day)
- GI bleeding
- Crampy abdominal pain

iii) Ileus (Alcoser & Burchett, 1999; Chou et al., 1996)

iv) Liver
- Elevated liver enzymes
- Liver tenderness
- Hepatomegaly
- Jaundice

v) Risk factors of acute GVHD (Alcoser & Burchett, 1999; O'Connell, 2000)
- Degree of major histocompatibility
- Older age of recipient
- Prior donor transfusions
- Disease stage
- Sex mismatching of donor and recipient

vi) Onset of acute GVHD: Day 7—Median is day 17 posttransplant (O'Connell, 2000)

vii) Duration: Variable up to 100 days (O'Connell, 2000)

viii) Treatment
- Cyclosporine (Alcoser & Burchett, 1999)

- Tacrolimus (Alcoser & Burchett, 1999)
- Methotrexate (Alcoser & Burchett, 1999)
- Antithymocyte globulin (Alcoser & Burchett, 1999)
- Corticosteroids (Alcoser & Burchett, 1999)
- Gut rest/hyperalimentation
- Fluid and electrolyte management
- Pain control
- Skin care for patient comfort and prevention of infection
- Prevention and treatment of infections (e.g., perineal care, handwashing, isolations)
- Octreotide acetate to decrease secretory diarrhea

ix) Prophylaxis (O'Connell, 2000)
- Cyclosporine
- Procarbazine
- Tacrolimus
- Methotrexate
- Corticosteroids
- T cell depletion of donor stem cells—Lessens the ability of donor T cells to recognize the host tissues as foreign (Alcoser & Burchett, 1999).

(e) Neutropenia—Potential for infection. Common sites for infection are the oral cavity, GI tract, skin, and catheter sites.

i) Onset: 7–10 days after chemotherapy initiated

ii) Duration: 2–4 weeks (Alcoser & Burchett, 1999)

iii) Prophylaxis
- HEPA filter or laminar flow rooms
- Neutropenic precautions

iv) Treatment
- Management of infections based on causative factor
  – Antibiotics
  – Antivirals
  – Antifungals
- Colony-stimulating factors (CSFs) to shorten the period of myelosuppression (Whedon & Roach, 2000)
  –Granulocyte–colony–

timulating factor (G-CSF)

—Filgrastim–GM-CSF—Sargramostim

(f) Veno-occlusive disease (VOD) is a life-threatening complication of the conditioning regimen in the transplant setting, where there is luminal narrowing or occlusion in hepatic venules or small sublobular veins causing liver damage. The overall risk of development is 10%–60%. It is fatal in approximately 33% of patients affected (Lawton, 2003).

  i) Signs and symptoms (Bruner et al., 1998)
- Right upper quadrant pain
- Hepatomegaly
- Liver tenderness
- Rapid development of ascites
- Weight gain/fluid retention
- Jaundice
- Coagulation abnormalities
- Elevated liver enzymes

  ii) Onset: One to four weeks after treatment (Bruner et al., 1998)

  iii) Duration: Variable

  iv) Treatment
- Maintain fluid and electrolyte balance.
- Low molecular weight heparin therapy (100 units/kg/day) with prostaglandin E1 (dose range: 0.075–0.5 microgram/kg/h) by continuous IV infusion (Schlegal et al., 1998)
- Manage symptoms supportively.

  v) Prophylaxis
- Fractionated radiation doses
- Partial organ shielding of liver at doses greater than 12 Gy in 6 fractions (Lawton, 2003)
- Low molecular weight heparin by continuous infusion therapy (Rosenthal et al., 1996)

  vi) Education/symptom management: Ascites (Walczak & Heckman, 2000)

(g) Renal toxicity (Ford & Ballard, 1988; O'Connell, 2000)

  i) Risk factors
- Chemotherapy
- Radiation
- Antibiotics
- Cyclosporine

  ii) Onset: Within 30 days

  iii) Duration: Variable

  iv) Treatment is dependent on etiology
- Diuretics
- Volume replacement
- Correct electrolyte imbalances
- Reduce nephrotoxins
- Hemodialysis

  v) Prophylaxis: Selective renal shielding during TBI (Lawton, 2003)

(h) Lung toxicity—Occurs in 40%–60% of patients after HSCT (Lawton, 2003; O'Connell, 2000)

  i) Types
- Pulmonary edema—Associated with fluid overload
- Pulmonary hemorrhage—Associated with infection and thrombocytopenia
- Pneumothorax—Associated with high-dose steroids, TBI, and poor nutrition with recent weight loss
- Interstitial pneumonitis—Considered the dose-limiting toxicity for TBI
  – Idiopathic
  – Bacterial
  – Viral—Cytomegalovirus or herpes
  – Fungal—*Aspergillus, Candida,* or *Cryptococcus*

– Opportunistic—*Pneumocystis carinii* pneumonia

ii) Risk factors (Lawton, 2003; O'Connell, 2000)
- Development of GVHD
- Pretransplant mediastinal radiation

iii) Onset: 30 days–2 months

iv) Duration: Up to 100 days

v) Treatment: Based on causative factor
- Antibiotics
- Antifungals
- Antivirals
- Steroids
- Supportive respiratory care

vi) Prophylaxis (Lawton, 2003)
- Lung shielding during TBI
- Radiation fractionation during TBI
- Trimethoprim-sulfamethoxazole (Morgan et al., 1996)

(i) Acute leukoencephalopathy—The white matter of the brain is damaged in the posterior cerebral hemispheres, characterized by cerebral edema. Incidence is unknown, but it is being increasingly reported in the literature (Moore, 2003).

i) Risk factors (Moore, 2003)
- High-dose chemotherapy
- Cranial irradiation

ii) Signs and symptoms
- Lethargy
- Somnolence
- Personality changes with possible progression to dementia and coma (Bruner et al., 1998)

iii) Onset: Variable

iv) Treatment

- Ventriculoperitoneal shunt, if indicated
- Supportive care
  - Control elevated blood pressure.
  - Control fluid retention.
  - Manage infection (Moore, 2003).

b) Late effects (generally occur 100 days after HSCT)

(1) Gonadal dysfunction

(a) Females

i) Risk factor: Radiation

ii) Incidence: 95%–100% of women over the age of 18 who undergo TBI will experience early menopause and primary ovarian failure, resulting in sterility (Abramovitz & Senner, 1995; Bruner et al., 1998; Nims & Strom, 1988). The potential for recovery of ovarian function is age dependent. Eighty percent of premenarchal females at the time of transplant ultimately achieve menarche. Postmenarchal females younger than 18 years of age at time of transplant are likely to recover sufficient ovarian function to resume menstruation (Lawton, 2003; O'Connell, 2000).

iii) Treatment: Cyclic oral or transdermal hormonal replacement is used to reduce symptoms of premature menopause and prevent long-term disorders, such as osteoporosis and vaginal atrophic changes. (This is contraindicated in hormone-sensitive tumors.) (Bruner et al., 1998)

iv) Education/symptom management
- Managing symptoms of menopause (Goodman, 2000a)
- Osteoporosis—Maximizing bone health (Goodman 2000b).
- Vaginal dryness (Bruner & Iwamoto, 2000a)
- Vaginal stenosis (Bruner & Iwamoto, 2000b)

(b) Males

    i) Risk factor: Radiation

    ii) Incidence: Most men who undergo TBI will maintain production of testosterone and luteinizing hormone, but 95%–100% will become azoospermatic, resulting in sterility (Abramovitz & Senner, 1995; Bruner et al., 1998; Nims & Strom, 1988).

    iii) Treatment—None

    iv) Management—Discuss option of sperm banking prior to HSCT if prior therapy has not altered sperm production.

(2) Thyroid dysfunction—30%–60% of patients treated with TBI experience thyroid dysfunction.

  (a) Types

    i) Subclinical compensated hypothyroidism is noted by elevated TSH in the presence of normal thyroxine levels.

    ii) Clinical noncompensated hypothyroidism (O'Connell, 2000)

  (b) Onset: Three months to two years after transplant (Bruner et al., 1998)

  (c) Management: Baseline blood levels should be obtained prior to TBI. Thyroid levels then should be monitored on an ongoing basis.

  (d) Treatment (Lawton, 2003; O'Connell, 2000)

    i) Asymptomatic patients may not require treatment.

    ii) Symptomatic patients require thyroid replacement.

(3) Growth and development impairments in children

  (a) Risk factors—Related to age when child is exposed (Abramovitz & Senner, 1995)

    i) Cranial/craniospinal irradiation prior to TBI

    ii) Radiation doses given during TBI

    iii) Chemotherapeutic agents used in conditioning

  (b) Symptoms

    i) Diminished growth (skeletal bones and lower third of face)

    ii) Dental abnormalities (arrested root development and enamel dysplasia) in children treated before the age of six (Bruner et al., 1998; Leiper, 1995; Moore & Hobbie, 2000; Sanders, 1990)

    iii) Delayed or arrested puberty (60% male/65% female) (O'Connell, 2000)

    iv) Abnormal gonadotropin levels

    v) Minor abnormalities in intelligence quotient noted at one-year post-HSCT with recovery noted within three years (Chou et al., 1996; O'Connell, 2000).

    vi) Decreased measurement of academic achievement has been noted in 7% of children who have had prior whole-brain radiation (Sanders, 1990).

  (c) Treatment (Sander, 1990)

    i) Growth hormone replacement

    ii) Sex hormone replacement

  (d) Management

    i) Physical evaluation at regular intervals using growth charts to evaluate growth development in pediatric patients

    ii) Neuropsychological evaluations at regular intervals to evaluate the cognitive effects of children who have undergone TBI (Bruner et al., 1998)

(4) Cataracts

  (a) Risk factors

    i) Pretransplant cranial irradiation

    ii) High instantaneous dose rate of radiation given during TBI

    iii) Steroids used in treating GVHD (Belkacemi et al.,

1996; Benyunes et al., 1995) in multivariate analysis and retrospective studies

(b) Onset: 6 months–11 years post-TBI (Benyunes et al., 1995)

(c) Treatment: If vision is significantly impaired, then extracapsular cataract extraction with or without intraocular lens implantation

(d) Prophylaxis
   i) Fractionated radiation doses during TBI (Benyunes et al., 1995). Incidence drops to 10% with fractionated radiation (Thomas et al., 2001).
   ii) Heparin (prophylactic treatment for VOD) offers protection from cataract genesis in both uni- and multivariate analyses in a retrospective study (Belkacemi et al., 1996).

(e) Teaching: Instruct patients that their eyes will not be shielded during TBI because the eye is a potential site of relapse.

(5) Dry eye syndrome (Sicca syndrome)
(a) Onset: Variable
(b) Treatment
   i) Artificial tears to alleviate discomfort
   ii) Protective eye ointment at night
   iii) Surgery to ligate canaliculi that normally drain the lacrimal fluid (O'Connell, 2000)

(6) Avascular necrosis (bone softening) (O'Connell, 2000)
(a) Risk factor: Steroids used in treating GVHD
(b) Onset: 2 months–10 years after HSCT
(c) Treatment
   i) Joint replacement

   ii) Physical therapy

(7) Chronic pulmonary complications: Late interstitial pneumonitis (O'Connell, 2000)
(a) Risk factor: Chronic GVHD
(b) Onset: Three months to two years post-transplant
(c) Signs and symptoms
   i) Coughing
   ii) Wheezing
   iii) Dyspnea resulting in decreased ability to perform activities of daily living
(d) Treatment
   i) Bronchodilators
   ii) Immunosuppressive therapy
   iii) Energy conservation techniques
(e) Prophylaxis: Trimethoprim-sulfamethoxazole

(8) Restrictive pulmonary disease evidenced by decreased pulmonary function tests (Bruner et al., 1998)
(a) Onset: Six months to two years post-transplant
(b) Treatment
   i) Asymptomatic—Follow with pulmonary function tests at regular intervals
   ii) Symptomatic: Bronchodilators

(9) Obstructive pulmonary disease (O'Connell, 2000)
(a) Onset: 3–12 months
(b) Risk factor: Chronic GVHD
(c) Treatment
   i) Glucosteroids alone or with cyclosporine
   ii) Does not respond to bronchodilators

(10) Neurologic complications (O'Connell, 2000)
(a) Risk factors
   i) Intrathecal chemotherapy
   ii) Cranial irradiation
   iii) Infections
   iv) Systemic chemotherapy
   v) Chronic GVHD
(b) Leukoencephalopathy—Incidence is 7% in patients treated with TBI (Bruner et al., 1998).
(c) Chronic neurologic changes in cognitive function (Bruner et al., 1998)
   i) Impaired short-term memory
   ii) Shortened attention span
   iii) Impaired verbal skills months to years after transplant

iv) Difficulty learning new skills
(d) Management
   i) Supportive care
   ii) Prevention and treatment of infections
   iii) Referral for neurologic evaluation
(11) Secondary malignancies (O'Connell, 2000)
  (a) Post-transplantation lymphoproliferative disorders, such as non-Hodgkin's lymphoma
   i) Incidence is 0.6% (Lawton, 2003).
   ii) Onset—Within months
   iii) Risk factors
- T cell depleted marrow
- HLA mismatch donor
- Underlying diagnosis of primary immunodeficiency
   iv) Treatment
- Interferon alpha
- Intravenous immunoglobulin
- Monoclonal antibodies
  (b) Solid tumors
   i) Onset: 2–15 years post-HSCT
   ii) Common diseases
- Head and neck (O'Connell, 2000)
- Breast (Bruner et al., 1998)
- Lung (Bruner et al., 1998)
- Squamous cell carcinomas (O'Connell, 2000)
- Melanomas (O'Connell, 2000)
   iii) Treatment: Appropriate chemotherapy or radiation
  (c) Hematopoietic disorders
   i) Types
- Myelodysplastic syndrome
- Leukemia (incidence is low) (Lawton, 2003)
   ii) Treatment: chemotherapy and allogeneic HSCT
(12) Graft rejection (O'Connell, 2000)
  (a) Types
   i) Primary rejection: Absence of signs of engraftment
   ii) Late rejection: Graft loss after initial signs of engraftment
  (b) Treatment

   i) Administer hematopoietic growth factors.
   ii) Second transplant
(13) Relapse—Disease still present in host cells (O'Connell, 2000). Treatment consistent of
  (a) Second transplant
  (b) Standard or low-dose chemotherapy and radiation
  (c) Clinical trials
5. Patient and family education
  a) Teach patient and family about the specific disease, indications for a transplant, risks and benefits, the TBI treatment plan, and the type of transplant the patient will undergo. Evaluate patient's understanding of teaching. Document per ONS *Radiation Therapy Patient Care Record* (Catlin-Huth, Haas, & Pollock, 2002).
  b) Review the method of TBI administration. Include number of treatments, frequency of treatment, duration of each treatment, and patient positioning during treatment.
  c) Educate patient and family about the acute and long-term side effects from TBI, their risk of development, and their expected onset. Use symptom management patient self-care guides when appropriate.
  d) Explain that the side effects from chemotherapy and TBI used in the conditioning regimen often occur simultaneously and are synergistic.
  e) Educate patient and family of the importance of following a meticulous oral hygiene program during the transplant period (Yeager et al., 2000).
  f) Educate patient and family on the need for close monitoring and follow-up visits, cancer prevention strategies, and routine cancer screening in the future.
  g) Educate patient and family on the need to repeat childhood immunizations after the

immune system recovers (Alcoser & Burchett, 1999).

h) Web sites for patients
  (1) Leukemia Research Foundation—www.leukemia-research.org
  (2) International Bone Marrow Transplant Registry—www.ibmtr.org
  (3) National Marrow Donor Program—www.marrow.org
  (4) Cancer Guide: Bone Marrow Transplant Resources—www.cancerguide.org/bone_marrow.html
  (5) BMT InfoNet Homepage—www.bmtinfonet.org
  (6) Bone Marrow Transplant and Stem Cell Support Group—www.bmtsupport.ie/
  (7) Blood and Marrow Transplant Newsletter—www.bmtnews .org
  (8) National BMT Link—http://comnet.org/nbmtlink
  (9) FertileHOPE (fertility resources for patients with cancer)—www.fertilehope.org

6. Follow-up
  a) Autologous and syngeneic (Wujcik & Price, 2000)
    (1) After discharge post-transplant, patients are seen in the home or bone marrow clinic twice daily for the first four to six weeks, with support from home health nurses, and readmission for management of complications, as indicated.
    (2) Visits are tapered to monthly as patients improve. They are followed for minimum of 90 days, or longer depending on the continuation of transplant side effects.
    (3) Follow-up visits are scheduled quarterly for the first two years, alternating between hematology oncologist and primary care physician. The majority

of patients do not have continued follow-up with the radiation oncologist.
    (4) After the first two years, follow-up visits are extended to every six months for the next three years, then yearly.
  b) Allogeneic (Wujcik & Price, 2000)
    (1) After discharge post-transplant, patients are seen in the bone marrow clinic one to two times daily, tapering to two to three times weekly for the first four weeks, with frequent support from home health nurses. Visits are adjusted based on the length of time post-transplant and the stability of the patient (Wujcik & Price, 2000).
    (2) Visits are tapered to weekly for several weeks, then every other week for several weeks. Patients extend to monthly visits, depending on their immunosuppressive therapy taper schedule and GVHD issues. They are followed for a minimum of six months, or longer depending on the continuation of transplant side effects.
    (3) Follow-up visits are quarterly for the first two years, alternating between hematology oncologist and primary care physician. The majority of patients do not have continued follow-up with the radiation oncologist.
    (4) After the first two years, follow-up visits are extended to every six months for the next three years, then yearly.

References

Abramovitz, L.Z., & Senner, A.M. (1995). Pediatric bone marrow transplantation update. *Oncology Nursing Forum, 22,* 107–115.

Alcoser, P., & Burchett, S. (1999). Bone marrow transplantation: Immune system suppression and reconstitution. *American Journal of Nursing, 99,* 26–32.

Armstrong, T.S. (1994). Stomatitis in the bone marrow transplant patient: An overview and proposed oral care protocol. *Cancer Nursing, 17,* 403–410.

Beck, S.L. (1990). Prevention and management of oral complications in the cancer patient. In S.M. Hubbard, P.E. Greene, & M.T. Knobf (Eds.), *Current Issues in Cancer Nursing Practice* (pp. 27–38). Philadelphia: Lippincott.

Belkacemi, Y., Ozsahin, M., Pene, F., Rio, B., Laporte, J.P., Leblond, V., et al. (1996). Cataractogenesis after total body irradiation. *International Journal of Radiation Oncology, Biology, Physics, 35,* 53–60.

Benyunes, M.C., Sullivan, K.M., Deeg, H.J., Mori, M., Meyer, W., Fisher, L., et al. (1995). Cataracts after bone marrow transplantation: Long-term follow-up of adults treated with fractionated total body irradiation. *International Journal of Radiation Oncology, Biology, Physics, 32,* 661–670.

Bez, C., Demarosi, F., Sardella, A., Lodi, G., Bertolli, V.G., Annaloro, C., et al. (1999). GM-CSF mouth rinses in the treatment of severe oral mucositis: A pilot study. *Oral Surgery, Oral Medication, Oral Pathology, 88,* 311–315.

Bruner, D.W., Bucholtz, J.D., Iwamoto, R., & Strohl, R. (Eds.). (1998). *Manual for radiation oncology nursing practice and education.* Pittsburgh, PA: Oncology Nursing Society.

Bruner, D.W., & Iwamoto, R. (2000a). Vaginal dryness. In C.H. Yarbro, M.H. Frogge, & M. Goodman (Eds.), *Cancer symptom management* (2nd ed., pp. 210–226). Sudbury, MA: Jones and Bartlett.

Bruner, D.W., & Iwamoto, R. (2000b). Vaginal stenosis. In C.H. Yarbro, M.H. Frogge, & M. Goodman (Eds.), *Cancer symptom management* (2nd ed., pp. 210–226). Sudbury, MA: Jones and Bartlett.

Catlin-Huth, C., Haas, M., & Pollock, V. (2002). *Radiation therapy patient care record: A tool for documenting nursing care.* Pittsburgh, PA: Oncology Nursing Society.

Chou, R.H., Wong, G.B., Kramer, J.H., Wara, D.W., Matthay, K.K., Crittenden, M.R., et al. (1996). Toxicities of total-body irradiation for pediatric bone marrow transplantation. *International Journal of Radiation Oncology, Biology, Physics, 34,* 843–851.

Cowen, D., Tardieu, C., Schubert, M., Peterson, D., Resbeut, M., Faucher, C., et al. (1997). Low energy Helium-Neon laser in the prevention of oral mucositis in patients undergoing bone marrow transplant: Results of a double blind randomized trial. *International Journal of Radiation Oncology, Biology, Physics, 38,* 697–703.

DeWalt, E. (1975). Effect of timed hygienic measures on oral mucosa in a group of elderly subjects. *Nursing Research, 24,* 104–108.

DeWalt, E., & Haines, A. (1969). The effects of oral stressors on healthy oral mucosa. *Nursing Research, 18,* 22–27.

Ford, R., & Ballard, F. (1988). Acute complications after bone marrow transplantation. *Seminars in Oncology Nursing, 4,* 15–24.

Ginsberg, M. (1961). A study of oral hygiene nursing care. *American Journal of Nursing, 61,* 67–69.

Goodman, M. (2000a). Managing the symptoms of menopause. In C.H. Yarbro, M.H. Frogge, & M. Goodman (Eds.), *Cancer symptom management* (2nd ed., pp. 29–36). Sudbury, MA: Jones and Bartlett.

Goodman, M. (2000b). Ostcoporosis: Maximizing the health of your bones. In C.H. Yarbro, M.H. Frogge, & M. Goodman (Eds.), *Cancer symptom management* (2nd ed., pp. 29–36). Sudbury, MA: Jones and Bartlett.

Gopal, R., Ha, C.S., Tuck, S.L., Khouri, I.F., Giralt, S.A., Gajewski, J.L., et al. (2001). Comparison of two total body irradiation fractionation regimens with respect to acute and late pulmonary toxicity. *Cancer, 92,* 1949–1958.

Lawton, C. (2003). Radiation therapy for bone marrow or stem cell transplantation. In J.D Cox & K.K. Ang (Eds.), *Radiation oncology: Rationale, technique, results* (8th ed., pp. 939–953). St. Louis, MO: Mosby.

Leiper, A.D. (1995). Late effects of total body irradiation. *Archives of Disease in Childhood, 72,* 382–385.

Moore, D. (2003). Toxic leukoencephalopathy: A review and report of two chemotherapy-related cases. *Clinical Journal of Oncology Nursing, 7,* 413–417.

Moore, I.M., & Hobbie, W. (2000). Late effects of cancer treatment. In C.H. Yarbro, M.H. Frogge, M. Goodman, & S.L. Groenwald (Eds.), *Cancer nursing: Principles and practice* (5th ed., pp. 597–615). Sudbury, MA: Jones and Bartlett.

Morgan, T.L., Falk, P.M., Kogut, N., Shah, K.H., Tome, M., & Kagan, A.R. (1996). A comparison of single-dose and fractionated total-body irradiation on the development of pneumonitis following bone marrow transplantation. *International Journal of Radiation Oncology, Biology, Physics, 36,* 61–66.

Nims, J.W., & Strom, S. (1988). Late complications of bone marrow transplant recipients: Nursing care issues. *Seminars in Oncology Nursing, 4,* 47–54.

O'Connell, S. (2000). Complications of hematopoietic cell transplantation. In C.H. Yarbro, M.H. Frogge, M. Goodman, & S.L. Groenwald (Eds.), *Cancer nursing: Principles and practice* (5th ed., pp. 523–542). Sudbury, MA: Jones and Bartlett.

Reeves, D.M. (2000). Alopecia. In C.H. Yarbro, M.H. Frogge, & M. Goodman (Eds.), *Cancer symptom management* (2nd ed., pp. 98–100). Sudbury, MA: Jones and Bartlett.

Rosenthal, J., Sender, L., Secola, R., Killen, R., Millerick, M., Murphy, L., et al. (1996). Phase II trial of heparin prophylaxis for veno-occlusive disease of the liver in children undergoing bone marrow transplantation. *Bone Marrow Transplantation, 18,* 185–191.

Sanders, J.E. (1990). Late effects in children receiving total body irradiation for bone marrow transplant. *Radiotherapy and Oncology, 18*(Suppl. 1), 82–87.

Schlegal, P.G., Haber, H.P., Beck, J., Krumpelmann, S., Handgretinger, R., Bader, P., et al. (1998). Hepatic veno-occlusive disease in pediatric stem cell recipients: Successful treatment with continuous infusion of prostaglandin E1 and low-dose heparin. *Annals of Hematology, 76,* 37–41.

Sitton, E. (1997). Hodgkin's disease and non-Hodgkin's lymphoma. In K.H. Dow, J.D. Bucholtz, R. Iwamoto, V.K. Fieler, & L.J. Hilderley (Eds.), *Nursing care in radiation oncology* (2nd ed., pp. 261–292). Philadelphia: Saunders.

Thomas, O., Mahe, M.A., Campion, L., Bourdin, S., Milpied, N., Brunet, G., et al. (2001). Long-term complications of total body irradiation in adults. *International Journal of Radiation Oncology, Biology, Physics, 49,* 125–131.

Walczak, J.R., & Heckman, C.S. (2000). Ascites. In C.H. Yarbro, M.H. Frogge, & M. Goodman (Eds.), *Cancer symptom management* (2nd ed., pp. 140–146). Sudbury, MA: Jones and Bartlett.

Whedon, M.B., & Roach, M. (2000). Principles of bone marrow and hematopoietic cell transplantation. In C.H. Yarbro, M.H. Frogge, M. Goodman, & S.L. Groenwald (Eds.), *Cancer nursing: Principles and practice* (5th ed., pp. 487–507). Sudbury, MA: Jones and Bartlett.

Wujcik, D., & Price, K. (2000). Techniques of hematopoietic cell transplantation. In C.H. Yarbro, M.H. Frogge, M. Goodman, & S.L. Groenwald (Eds.), *Cancer nursing: Principles and practice* (5th ed., pp. 508–522). Sudbury, MA: Jones and Bartlett.

Yeager, K.A., Webster, J., Crain, M., Kasow, J., & McGuire, D.B. (2000). Implementation of an oral care standard for leukemia and transplantation patients. *Cancer Nursing, 23,* 40–47.

I. Total nodal irradiation (TNI)
   1. Procedure description: TNI is a technique that delivers radiation to all the major lymph node regions above and below the diaphragm, including the spleen and thymus (Bruner, Bucholtz, Iwamoto, & Strohl, 1998). TNI consists of two radiation portals (Mauch & Canellos, 2003; Sitton, 1997).
      a) Mantle field includes all the supradiaphragmatic lymph nodes: bilateral cervical, supraclavicular, infraclavicular, axillary, and mediastinal and hilar lymphatics. Areas typically blocked are the lower two-thirds

of lungs, the mouth, posterior occipital, posterior spinal cord, anterior larynx, and anterior/posterior humeral heads (Sitton, 1997). The left ventricle of the heart is shielded throughout treatment unless this shielding would compromise treatment (Cox, Ha, & Wilder, 2003); otherwise, a portion of the pericardium and heart are shielded after 15 Gy (Sitton, 1997).

b) Inverted Y field is a combination of the para-aortic field (including the spleen) and pelvic field (iliac and inguinal). It extends from the diaphragm to the inguinal area, using a midline block in the pelvic field to help protect the ovaries after oophoropexy or by using testicular shielding.

2. Indications
  a) Transplant setting
    (1) In the transplant setting, TNI is used primarily in relapsed or chemotherapy-resistant Hodgkin's disease for salvage therapy in patients who have not already received significant doses of radiation.
    (2) TNI is used in a combined modality approach with autologous HSCT that limits radiation to commonly involved nodal sites and to sites of residual/bulky disease (Bruner et al., 1998; Cox et al., 2003; Yahalom et al., 1993).
  b) Conventional setting
    (1) TNI has been used to consolidate the response of patients with advanced-stage (stage IIB, III, or IV) Hodgkin's disease after combined chemotherapy, but only if the disease is more centrally located in para-aortic or iliac nodes (Cox et al., 2003).
    (2) Usually chemotherapy, consisting of doxorubicin, bleomycin, vinblastine, and dacarbazine, is the primary treatment. Radiation is used only in selected situations (Bruner et al., 1998;

Cox et al., 2003; Mauch & Canellos, 2003). Using TNI for stage III follicular non-Hodgkin's lymphoma is controversial (Sitton, 1997).

3. Treatment
  a) Transplant setting
    (1) Dose: Patients receive a total dose of 15–20 Gy over the course of four to five days, using hyperfractionated or accelerated hyperfractionated doses to increase cell kill and decrease late toxicity by shortening the period of myelosuppression. Patients are treated twice per day; the minimum time between fractions is six hours (Yahalom et al., 1993).
    (2) If there is bulky residual disease, an alternate method of treatment is to deliver a total dose of 30 Gy to the involved field, including 15 Gy to the TNI field, over the course of two weeks. Patients are treated twice per day. The minimum time between fractions is six hours. In the morning, they receive 1.5 Gy to TNI fields. In the evening, they receive 1.5 Gy to the involved field (clinically involved or enlarged lymph nodes present before chemotherapy with additional margins that include lymph nodes within the same region) (Cox et al., 2003). This is based on patterns of treatment failure that indicated nodal sites initially involved with disease are at high risk for relapse, and radiation can reduce the incidence (Yahalom, 2000).
    (3) Position: Treatment is administered anteroposterior-posteroanterior (AP/PA), with each treatment taking approximately 15–20 minutes to administer. Patient is supine, usually with arms akimbo (Cox et al., 2003).
  b) Conventional setting (used in selected situations only)
    (1) Dose: Each field (mantle, para-aortic with spleen, inverted Y) is treated separately to a total dose ranging from 24–36 Gy. Conventional fractionation is used, and patients receive 1.5–1.8 Gy per day. Approximately four weeks are needed to deliver the treatment to each field; patients generally are given a two- to four-week break between each field (Bruner et al., 1998).
    (2) Position: Treatment is administered AP/PA, with each treatment taking approximately 10 minutes to administer.

4. Collaborative management
   a) Acute side effects during TNI treatment
      (1) Fatigue—Most patients report a decrease in energy level after TNI (Bruner et al., 1998).
         (a) Onset: During first week
         (b) Duration: 6–18 months after TNI is completed (Sitton, 1997)
         (c) Treatment: Energy-conserving strategies
            i) Encourage activities at time of day when patient has the least fatigue.
            ii) Prioritize, delegate, and pace activities.
            iii) Encourage short rest periods after major activities.
            iv) Increase amount of sleep at night.
            v) Encourage moderate exercise.
      (2) Skin reaction—Patients experience mild to moderate erythema, possibly with tanning (hyperpigmentation) of the skin. Skin reaction will be most severe in the axilla and inguinal area (Sitton, 1997).
         (a) Onset: Two weeks
         (b) Duration: Begins to resolve within two weeks after TNI is completed
         (c) Treatment: Prescribed cream should be applied to the treated area twice a day.
         (d) Instruct patient to avoid applying cream during the four hours immediately prior to radiation. Some examples of creams used for radiation skin reactions:
            i) Biafine®
            ii) Aquaphor®
            iii) Radiaplex Rx™ Gel
            iv) Eucerin®
            v) Jeans Cream®
      (3) Myelosuppression
         (a) Risk factors
            i) Radiation given to the lymph system decreases the number of circulating T lymphocytes (Bruner et al., 1998).
            ii) Myelosuppression also is the result of treating bone marrow in the sternum, spine, and pelvis.
         (b) Onset: Variable
         (c) Duration: May last for more than one year (Sitton, 1997)
         (d) Treatment: G-CSF administered during subdiaphragmatic irradiation after mantle irradiation significantly increases the white blood count and ANC (Sitton, 1997).
      (4) Xerostomia—Most patients will experience some dryness of the mouth with altered taste sensation during TNI. The degree depends on the total dose of radiation and the volume of salivary glands included in the treatment field (Bruner et al., 1998; Sitton, 1997).
         (a) Onset: First week
         (b) Duration: Variable, may persist long after treatment is completed
         (c) Treatment: Establish an oral hygiene program during the transplant/mantle radiation period using oral moisturizers, and reinforce the importance of following the program (Yeager, Webster, Crain, Kasow, & McGuire, 2000).
         (d) Prophylaxis: Dental consult prior to the start of TNI and ongoing dental care, including fluoride treatments (Bruner et al., 1998; Ford & Ballard, 1988; Sitton, 1997)
      (5) Nausea and vomiting—Approximately 90% of patients treated with TNI will experience some degree of nausea and vomiting (Sitton, 1997).
         (a) Onset: May be immediate
         (b) Duration: Variable
         (c) Treatment: Antiemetics, such as ondansetron, administered before treatment with/without dexamethasone have proved to be effective (Abramovitz & Senner, 1995).
      (6) Occipital alopecia
         (a) Risk factor: Mantle radiation field that extends to mandible (Sitton, 1997)

(b) Onset: Two to three weeks after beginning mantle field

(c) Duration: Three to six months

(d) Education: Educate patient that hair loss is inevitable but is temporary the majority of the time. If patient's hair is short, he or she may wish to grow hair longer in back to cover area of alopecia.

(7) Esophagitis/mild dysphagia (Sitton, 1997)

(a) Risk factor: Radiation to mantle field

(b) Onset: Two weeks

(c) Duration: Begins to resolve within two weeks after mantle field irradiation is completed

(d) Treatment: Administer analgesics/ narcotics based on severity of discomfort.

b) If TNI is given in transplant setting

(1) Stomatoxicity—Mucositis tends to worsen during the first two weeks after TNI and resolve completely within three to four weeks (Bruner et al., 1998).

(a) Onset: First two weeks

(b) Duration: Three to four weeks

(c) Treatment: Establish an oral hygiene program during the transplant period. Multiple studies have examined the use of various agents in addressing the incidence of stomatitis, but as of yet, no agent has shown a statistically significant advantage over another in the treatment of stomatitis. The studies all agree that the frequency of oral hygiene should be based on the severity of symptoms (Armstrong, 1994; Yeager et al., 2000). Beck (1990) recommended every four hours for prevention, every two hours for mild stomatitis, and ev-

ery one to two hours for severe mucositis. Reinforce the importance of following the program to patient and family.

(2) Lung toxicity

(a) Noninfectious idiopathic pneumonitis

i) Incidence: 11%–26% of patients receiving TNI will experience pneumonitis within the first month (Bruner et al., 1998).

ii) Risk factors

• Prior chemotherapy with lung toxicities (e.g., bleomycin, nitrogen mustard, doxorubicin) (Bruner et al., 1998)

• Bulky mediastinal disease (volume of lung in the field) (Bruner et al., 1998)

• Boost irradiation to the mediastinum (total dose of radiation and fractionation) (Bruner et al., 1998; Sitton, 1997)

iii) Prophylaxes

• Hyperfractionated radiation doses decrease risk of pulmonary toxicity (Yahalom et al., 1993).

• Smoking cessation

iv) Treatment

• High-dose corticosteroids

• Administration of growth factors to decrease engraftment time (Yahalom et al., 1993)

(b) Pulmonary hemorrhage

i) Risk factors: Patients with bulky mediastinal disease are at higher risk for developing spontaneous bleeding into the lung due to increased capillary permeability and alveolar leakage (Bruner et al., 1998; Sitton, 1997).

ii) Prophylaxis: Hyperfractionated radiation doses decrease risk of pulmonary toxicity (Yahalom et al., 1993).

iii) Treatment

• High-dose corticosteroids

• Administration of growth factors to decrease engraftment time (Yahalom et al., 1993)

c) Late effects

    (1) Sepsis (Sitton, 1997)

      (a) Risk factors

          i) Splenectomy or splenic irradiation

          ii) Modified production of specific antibodies

          iii) Modified immunologic responses

      (b) Prophylaxes

          i) Pneumococcal pneumonia vaccination prior to start of treatment

          ii) *Haemophilus influenzae* vaccination prior to start of treatment

          iii) Prophylactic antibiotics prior to invasive procedures

    (2) Herpes zoster (shingles)

      (a) Incidence: 15%–20% of patients treated for Hodgkin's disease (Gomez, 1995; Sitton, 1997)

      (b) Onset: Within one to two years after treatment

      (c) Treatment: Acyclovir

    (3) Radiation pneumonitis develops in approximately 10% of patients treated with TNI (Bruner et al., 1998).

      (a) Risk factors

          i) Prior chemotherapy with lung toxicities

            • Bleomycin

            • Nitrogen mustard

            • Doxorubicin

          ii) Bulky mediastinal disease (volume of lung in the field)

          iii) Boost irradiation to the mediastinum.

          iv) Total dose of radiation

          v) Fractionation dose used (Sitton, 1997)

      (b) Onset: Three months to two years post-transplant (Bruner et al., 1998)

      (c) Signs and symptoms (Sitton, 1997)

          i) Fever

          ii) Rapid pulse rate at rest

          iii) Mild cough

          iv) Wheezing

          v) Pleuritic chest pain

          vi) Dyspnea resulting in decreased ability to perform activities of daily living (Bruner et al., 1998; Harwood, 2000)

      (d) Treatment: Symptoms can be treated with high-dose steroids (Yahalom et al., 1993).

    (4) Cardiotoxicity: Pericarditis

      (a) Incidence: Occurs in less than 5% of patients (Bruner et al., 1998; Mauch & Hoppe, 2003; Sitton, 1997)

      (b) Risk factors

          i) Mantle field radiation causes dose-dependent risk.

          ii) Age younger than 20 years at time of radiation

          iii) Minimal prophylactic cardiac blocking

          iv) Administration of cardiotoxic chemotherapy (e.g., doxorubicin) (Sitton, 1997)

      (c) Onset: Usually 4–12 months post-irradiation, may be delayed

      (d) Symptoms

          i) Fever

          ii) Friction rub

          iii) Pleuritic chest pain

      (e) Treatment: Analgesics and NSAIDs

      (f) Acute myocardial infarction—Radiation doses greater than 30 Gy to proximal coronary arteries can increase the relative risk (Cox et al., 2003).

    (5) Gonadal dysfunction: Female

      (a) Risk factors

          i) Radiation to pelvis: Prior to TNI, premenopausal women may be offered oophoropexy, where their ovaries are moved centrally in the abdomen and then shielded (Bruner et al., 1998; Sitton, 1997). Menopausal symptoms after pelvic irradiation may occur in women older than 30 years due to scatter radiation, even after oophoropexy (Bruner & Iwamoto, 2000; Sitton, 1997).

ii) The combination of chemotherapy, especially alkylating agents, with pelvic irradiation can cause impaired menstrual function and infertility in women younger than 30 (Sitton, 1997).

iii) Management: Cyclic oral or transdermal hormonal replacement is used to reduce symptoms of premature menopause and prevent long-term disorders such as osteoporosis and vaginal atrophic changes.

(6) Gonadal dysfunction: Male

(a) Risk factors

i) Radiation to pelvis

ii) Most men who undergo TNI will maintain testosterone and luteinizing hormone production, but some of them will become sterile (Bruner et al., 1998). Shielding of the testes reduces azoospermia and allows some recovery of sperm count; however, direct or scatter radiation to the gonads can result in sterility (Sitton, 1997). Sperm banking prior to treatment is an option.

iii) Cyclophosphamide doses can affect sperm counts. High doses may cause permanent sterility (Sitton, 1997).

(b) Management: Discuss option of sperm banking prior to TNI if previous therapy has not altered sperm production.

(7) Thyroid dysfunction

(a) Risk factor: Boost irradiation administered to the mediastinum before TNI (Yahalom et al., 1993)

(b) Incidence: Approximately 60% of patients receiving TNI (Bruner et al., 1998)

(c) Types

i) Subclinical compensated hypothyroidism is noted by elevated thyroid-stimulating hormone in the presence of normal thyroxine levels.

ii) Clinical noncompensated hypothyroidism (O'Connell, 2000)

(d) Onset: Three months to two years post-treatment (Bruner et al., 1998)

(e) Management: Baseline blood levels should be obtained prior to TNI. Thyroid levels will be monitored on an ongoing basis. Instruct the patient that thyroid function tests should be monitored as part of follow-up care.

(f) Treatment

i) Asymptomatic—May not require treatment

ii) Symptomatic—Requires thyroid replacement

(8) Lhermitte's sign may be caused by transient demyelinization of the spinal cord (Sitton, 1997).

(a) Signs and symptoms: "Electric shock-like" sensations extending into the arms and legs with neck flexion

(b) Incidence: 10%–15% of patients receiving TNI (Gomez, 1995)

(c) Onset: One-and-a-half to three months after mantle radiation

(d) Duration: Two to six months

(e) Treatment: Usually resolves without treatment (Sitton, 1997)

(9) Second malignancies: Risk is approximately 13% at 15 years after treatment of Hodgkin's disease (Mauch & Hoppe, 2003).

(a) Leukemia: Occurrence after treatment is rare if radiation is given alone. If a combination of radiation and alkylating chemotherapy is given, risk increases, with peak incidence four to nine years post-treatment (Sitton, 1997).

(b) Non-Hodgkin's lymphoma: Risk is 1% at 10 years post-treatment, increasing to 4% at 20 years post-treatment (Cox et al., 2003).

(c) Solid tumors: Account for 75% of second malignancies (Mauch &

Hoppe, 2003). Most common are breast and lung cancers, with a risk period up to 20 years post-treatment.

5. Patient and family education

    a) Teach patient and family about Hodgkin's disease, indications for TNI, risks and benefits, and the TNI treatment plan. Evaluate patient's understanding of teaching. Document per ONS *Radiation Therapy Patient Care Record* (Catlin-Huth, Haas, & Pollock, 2002).

    b) Review the TNI administration. Include the number of treatments, duration of each treatment, and patient positioning during treatment.

    c) Educate patient and family about the acute and long-term side effects from TNI, their risk of development, and their expected onset. Use symptom management patient self-care guides when appropriate (see individual references listed under side effects).

    d) Explain that the side effects from chemotherapy and TNI used in the transplant setting often occur simultaneously and can be synergistic.

    e) Explain to patient and family the importance of a meticulous oral hygiene program during the transplant or mantle field period (Yeager et al., 2000).

    f) Educate patient and family on the need for close monitoring/follow-up visits, cancer prevention strategies, and routine cancer screening in the future.

6. Follow-up

    a) First follow-up visit is two weeks to one month after the completion of radiation or the last cycle of chemotherapy. A PET scan should be done to evaluate all known sites of disease to check for residual disease.

    b) Follow-up visits then taper to every three months during first two years if no evidence of disease. PET scans should be done on an ongoing basis to check for recurrence.

    c) During the next three years, patients are seen every six months.

    d) Five years after complete remission, the interval between follow-up visits is extended to once a year.

    e) Yearly breast exam and screening mammograms in younger women (less than 30 years of age at time of mantle field radiation) should begin within 10 years after treatment (Sitton, 1997).

    f) Thyroid levels need to be checked on an ongoing basis (Sitton, 1997).

References

Abramovitz, L.Z., & Senner, A.M. (1995). Pediatric bone marrow transplantation update. *Oncology Nursing Forum, 22,* 107–115.

Armstrong, T.S. (1994). Stomatitis in the bone marrow transplant patient: An overview and proposed oral care protocol. *Cancer Nursing, 17,* 403–410.

Beck, S.L. (1990). Prevention and management of oral complications in the cancer patient. In S.M. Hubbard, P.E. Greene, & M.T. Knobf (Eds.), *Current issues in cancer nursing practice* (pp. 27–38). Philadelphia: Lippincott.

Bruner, D.W., Bucholtz, J.D., Iwamoto, R., & Strohl, R. (Eds.). (1998). *Manual for radiation oncology nursing practice and education.* Pittsburgh, PA: Oncology Nursing Society.

Bruner, D.W., & Iwamoto, R. (1999). Vaginal dryness. In C.H. Yarbro, M.H. Frogge, & M. Goodman (Eds.), *Cancer symptom management* (2nd ed., pp. 549–580). Sudbury, MA: Jones and Bartlett.

Catlin-Huth, C., Haas, M., & Pollock, V. (2002). *Radiation therapy patient care record: A tool for documenting nursing care.* Pittsburgh, PA: Oncology Nursing Society.

Cox, J.D., Ha, C.S., & Wilder, R.B. (2003). Leukemias and lymphomas. In J.D. Cox & K.K. Ang (Eds.), *Radiation oncology: Rationale, technique, and results* (8th ed., pp. 821–855). St. Louis, MO: Mosby.

Ford, R., & Ballard, F. (1988). Acute complications after bone marrow transplantation. *Seminars in Oncology Nursing, 4,* 15–24.

Gomez, E. (1995). A teaching booklet for patients receiving mantle field irradiation. *Oncology Nursing Forum, 22,* 121–126.

Harwood, K.V. (1999). Dyspnea. In C.H. Yarbro, M.H. Frogge, & M. Goodman (Eds.), *Cancer symptom management* (2nd ed., pp. 45–58). Sudbury, MA: Jones and Bartlett.

Mauch, P.M., & Canellos, G.P. (2003). *Staging and selection of treatment modality in patients with Hodgkin's disease* (version 11.2). Retrieved April 23, 2003, from http://www.uptodateonline.com

Mauch, P.M., & Hoppe, R.T. (2003). *Treatment of favorable prognosis stage I & II Hodgkin's disease* (version 11.2). Retrieved April 23, 2003, from http://www.uptodateonline.com

Moore, G.J., & Hayes, C. (2001). Maintenance of comfort (fatigue and pain). In D.W. Bruner, G. Moore-Higgs, & M. Haas (Eds.), *Outcomes in radiation therapy: Multidisciplinary management* (pp. 459–492). Sudbury, MA: Jones and Bartlett.

O'Connell, S. (2000). Complications of hematopoietic cell transplantation. In C.H. Yarbro, M.H. Frogge, M. Goodman, & S.L. Groenwald (Eds.), *Cancer nursing: Principles and practice* (5th ed., pp. 523–542). Sudbury, MA: Jones and Bartlett.

Sitton, E. (1997). Hodgkin's disease and non-Hodgkin's lymphoma. In K.H. Dow, J.D. Bucholtz, R. Iwamoto, V.K. Fieler, & L.J. Hilderley (Eds.), *Nursing care in radiation oncology* (2nd ed., pp. 261–292). Philadelphia: Saunders.

Yahalom, J. (2000). Bone marrow transplantation for hematologic malignancies. In L.L. Gunderson & J.E. Tepper (Eds.), *Clinical radiation oncology* (pp. 1203–1223). Philadelphia: Churchill Livingstone.

Yahalom, J., Gulati, S.C., Toia, M., Maslak, P., McCarron, E.G., O'Brien, J.P., et al. (1993). Accelerated hyperfractionated total-lymphoid irradiation, high-dose chemotherapy, and autologous bone marrow transplantation for refractory and relapsing patients with Hodgkin's disease. *Journal of Clinical Oncology, 11,* 1062–1070.

Yeager, K.A., Webster, J., Crain, M., Kasow, J., & McGuire, D.B. (2000). Implementation of an oral care standard for leukemia and transplantation patients. *Cancer Nursing, 23,* 40–47.

J. Total skin irradiation (TSI)
1. Procedure description: TSI is a type of RT that is delivered to the entire skin surface with electrons and also is referred to as total skin electron beam therapy.
2. Indications (Micaily & Vonderheid, 1997)
   a) TSI is most commonly used in the treatment of cutaneous T cell lymphoma (CTCL), which incorporates two major subgroups.
      (1) Mycosis fungoides (MF)
      (2) Sézary syndrome
   b) TSI may be a localized treatment in patients with unilateral or localized MF, lymphoma cutis, and Kaposi's sarcoma.
3. Treatment
   a) There are a variety of treatments for MF that can be used alone or in combination with chemotherapy, biotherapy, RT, or photochemotherapy.
   b) The role of TSI was first described in 1953 and historically is considered the single most effective method in treating CTCL (Becker, Hoppe, & Knox, 1995).
   c) Procedure
      (1) Treatment is typically delivered via a 6 MeV electron beam, and the patient is placed in a standing position in front of the beam.
      (2) A six-field treatment approach is used that encompasses the following fields: straight anterior, right posterior oblique, and the left posterior oblique.
      (3) The following day, the patient receives treatment to the straight posterior, right anterior oblique, and left anterior oblique.
         (a) Patient positioning is important so folds in the skin are minimized. Typically this includes the breast, perineum, and the panniculus of obese patients.
         (b) Patients may have their hands and feet shielded during the six-field

approach and then receive supplemental therapy to these sites and additionally to the scalp if warranted.
      (4) External or internal eye shields may be used to protect the cornea and lens.
      (5) Treatment typically is delivered four days a week for 30–45 minutes over the course of six to eight weeks for a total dose of 36–40 Gy to the skin and 18–20 Gy to the hands and feet.
4. Collaborative management
   a) Acute effects
      (1) Patients will experience epithelial reactions, including pruritus, erythema, dry desquamation, and moist desquamation (see section IV, C—Skin Reactions).
      (2) Superficial atrophy with wrinkling, telangiectasia, xerosis, and uneven pigmentation are the most common changes (Chao, Perez, & Brady, 1999).
      (3) Patients may experience pain related to skin changes.
      (4) Patients will experience alopecia, which is reversible in four to six months (Maingon et al., 2002).
      (5) Patients will experience nail loss.
      (6) At higher does (> 25 Gy), some patients may develop transient swelling of the hands, edema of the ankles, and occasionally large blisters, necessitating local shielding or temporary discontinuation of therapy (Chao et al., 1999) (see section IV, C—Skin Reactions).
      (7) Patients may report an inability to sweat properly for the first 6–12 months following therapy (Kim & Hoppe, 1999).
      (8) Gynecomastia also may develop; the mechanism for this is unknown (Micaily & Vonderheid, 1997).
   b) Late effects
      (1) Superficial atrophy with wrinkling, telangiectasis, xerosis, and uneven pigmentation are the most common changes (Chao et al., 1999).
      (2) Although rare, higher doses may cause permanent alopecia, frank poikiloderma (mottled skin appearance), skin fragility, and subcutaneous fibrosis.
5. Patient and family education
   a) Teach patient and family about the treatment procedure and the time required for the treatment each day, as well as positioning used for the treatment.

b) Teach patient and family that the majority of the treatment area will be exposed during the treatment, and measures will be implemented to protect the patient's privacy.

c) Teach male patients about the potential risk of infertility due to the dose received to the testes and options such as sperm banking (Jones et al., 2002).

d) Teach patient about eye rinses to minimize irritation from eye shields.

e) Teach patient and family about the use of skin products to minimize dry pruritus and dry desquamation.

f) Teach patient and family about skin care if blisters and/or moist desquamation should arise.

g) Teach patient and family to elevate extremity if swelling/edema should arise.

h) Teach patient and family about doing skin checks and to report any new lesions or changes in lesions.

i) Teach patient and family the importance of follow-up care to assess for late effects.

6. Follow-up

a) Patients may be seen frequently over the first few months post-treatment for skin assessments and to determine their response to treatment.

b) Patients may be followed by the dermatologist in conjunction with the radiation oncologist.

References

Becker, M., Hoppe, R., & Knox, S. (1995). Multiple courses of high-dose total skin electron beam therapy in the management of mycosis fungoides. *International Journal of Radiation Oncology, Biology, Physics, 32,* 1445–1449.

Chao, K., Perez, C., & Brady, L. (1999). *Radiation oncology: Management decisions*. Philadelphia: Lippincott Williams & Wilkins.

Jones, G., Kacinski, B., Wilson, L., Willemze, R., Spittle, M., Hohenberg, G., et al. (2002). Total skin electron radiation in the management of mycosis fungoides: Consensus of the European Organization for Research and Treatment of Cancer (EORTC) cutaneous lymphoma project group. *Journal of the American Academy of Dermatology, 47,* 364–370.

Kim, Y., & Hoppe, R. (1999). Mycosis fungoides and the Sézary syndrome. *Seminars in Oncology, 26,* 276–289.

Maingon, P., Truc, G., Dalac, S., Barillot, I., Lambert, D., Petrella, T., et al. (2002). Radiotherapy of advanced mycosis fungoides: Indications and results of total skin electron beam and photon beam irradiation. *Radiotherapy and Oncology, 54,* 73–78.

Micaily, B., & Vonderheid, E. (1997). Cutaneous T cell lymphoma. In C. Perez & L. Brady (Eds.), *Principles and practice of radiation oncology* (3rd ed., pp. 763–776). Philadelphia: Lippincott Williams & Wilkins.

K. Hyperthermia

1. Procedure description: Hyperthermia generally is defined as a modest elevation of temperature to a range of 40°–43°C (approximately 106°F) (Jones, Samulski, Vujaskovic, Prosnitz, & Dewhirst, 2004; Wojtas & Smith, 1997). When tumor cells are heated, a number of events occur that have significant biologic consequences for cancer therapy. Hyperthermia causes direct cytotoxicicty and also acts as a radiosensitizer. Hyperthermia also can kill cells in its own right, but more importantly, it can sensitize tumor cells to other forms of therapy, including radiotherapy and chemotherapy.

2. Indications

a) The physiologic consequences of hyperthermia have implications for radiotherapy, such as thermally induced reoxygenation. Mechanisms of action appear complimentary to radiation effects with regard to inhibition of potential lethal damage, sublethal damage repair, cell cycle sensitivity, and effects of hypoxia and nutrient deprivation.

b) Hyperthermia has effects on blood flow and tumor physiology, which may be of interest with regard to tumor oxygenation and combination therapy with liposomal agents.

c) Thermotolerance is the adaptive response to hyperthermia and may augment host immune responses against tumor cells.

d) Hyperthermia may play a role in the field of gene therapy as a strategy for targeted, localized induction of gene therapy using the HSP-70 promoter to induce heat shock and cell death (Jones et al., 2004).

3. Implementation of hyperthermia (Jones et al., 2004)

a) Hyperthermia techniques include superficial, regional, and interstitial heating.

b) Hyperthermia is a treatment that generally uses microwave or radiofrequency energy and ultrasound applicators to heat the area of the tumor.

c) Several approaches have been taken and applicator devices developed to deliver hyperthermia treatments. It remains a challenge to heat tumor tissue volumes uniformly and with precision using superficial, regional, and interstitial heating devices.

4. Treatment

a) Microwaves and ultrasound pass through water before entering the body. De-ionized water-filled pillows or other devices are placed around the tumor area being treated.

b) Hyperthermia treatments generally take about 60–90 minutes and are given once or twice weekly. When hyperthermia is combined with other treatments, such as chemotherapy or RT, additional time and scheduling are required.

c) Prior to the treatments, a small, plastic catheter is inserted into the tumor under local anesthesia. Instruments for determining the tumor temperature are placed inside the catheters to provide critical information during the treatment. The amount of heat then can be applied to obtain the desired tumor temperature based on this information.

d) Conscious sedation may be given for patient tolerance; however, patients usually are awake enough to provide critical feedback during the treatments.

5. Contraindications

a) Patients with widely metastatic cancer are not eligible for regional hyperthermia treatments.

b) Because of the microwave and ultrasound equipment used, patients with cardiac pacemakers, orthopedic metal rods, plates, or prostheses are not eligible.

c) Unstable cardiac disease, severe neuropathy, skin grafts/flaps, surgical implants or implanted devices, or pregnancy

d) Inadequate blood counts

6. Collaborative management

a) Acute effects

(1) Burns—The most significant side effect is a thermal injury. These may be first-, second-, or third-degree burns. Typically involves a small area of redness, usually about an inch or less in diameter, and occurs in approximately 5% of all hyperthermia treatment sessions (Jones et al., 2004)

(2) Pain—Power during treatments may occur from the amount of heat directed to the treatment area. Narcotics are given during treatments, and pain usually resolves after power is turned off (see section IV, D—Pain).

(3) Bleeding and infection—May occur from the insertion of the sterile catheters into tumor to monitor temperatures during treatment

(4) Dehydration—May occur from a combination of chemotherapy, RT, and hyperthermia or may be induced by the hyperthermia treatment alone. During the treatment, patients usually will become diaphoretic, flushed, and thirsty.

(5) Nausea and vomiting—May occur from a combination of chemotherapy, RT, and hyperthermia or may be induced by the hyperthermia treatment alone. Nausea and vomiting associated with this large amount of heat given in a short period of time usually will be short-term and resolve after the power is turned off and the treatment has stopped.

(6) Fatigue—May occur from a combination of chemotherapy, RT, and hyperthermia or may be induced by the hyperthermia treatment alone. The patient usually will feel "washed out" after the hyperthermia treatment and require a short nap or resting period afterward. Usually within 24 hours the patient is back to his or her baseline activities (see section IV, B—Fatigue).

b) Late effects

(1) Fat necrosis—Area of subcutaneous tissue burned during treatment; may become firm and sore. Because of firmness, patient may be mistakenly alarmed of tumor recurrence. Routinely feels like a bruise. Takes weeks to months to resolve. No treatment necessary to expedite healing process.

(2) Thermal injury—Skin surface burn, third-degree burn requiring a skin graft

7. Patient and family education

a) Teach patient and family about treatments, including procedure and time required to receive treatments. Discuss treatment scheduling, including total time involved for hyperthermia, radiotherapy, and/or chemotherapy treatments.

b) Teach patient and family about side effects directly from the hyperthermia treatments and the increased sensitivity heat adds to radiotherapy and chemotherapy.

c) Teach patient and family how to recognize degree of skin burn.

d) Teach patient and family to assess skin area and to report any new skin breakdown.

e) Teach patient and family about the use of skin care products to minimize discomfort if burn arises.

f) Teach patient and family to report fever, chills, redness, swelling, pain, bleeding, and drainage from skin breakdown.

g) Teach patient and family to monitor blood counts frequently, as adding hyperthermia to existing treatment therapies may increase hematologic toxicities.

h) Teach patient and family to take medications needed prior to hyperthermia treatments. These medications include medications for pain, nausea, and anxiety.

i) Teach patient and family relaxation and distraction techniques to help patient tolerate anticipated treatment sessions.

j) Teach patient and family to eat small, bland meals prior to treatment and drink plenty of liquids, including water, juices, decaffeinated beverages, and/or sports drinks with electrolytes.

k) Teach patient and family to decrease fatigue by saving energy for more important activities; alternate activity with rest periods; use relaxation techniques; and exercise regularly.

l) Teach patient and family the importance of follow-up care for assessment and management of side effects of treatment.

8. Follow-up

a) Patients are to be seen frequently over the first year post-treatment by surgical, medical, and radiation oncology specialties for assessment and evaluation to determine their response to treatment.

b) Patients who have skin grafts associated with a third-degree burn will be followed by radiation oncologists and plastic reconstructive surgery specialists.

References

Jones, E., Samulski, T., Vujaskovic, Z., Prosnitz, L., & Dewhirst, M. (2004). Hyperthermia. In C. Perez, L. Brady, E. Halperin, & R. Schmidt-Ullrich (Eds.), *Principles and practice of radiation oncology* (4th ed., pp. 699–735). Philadelphia: Lippincott Williams & Wilkins.

Wojtas, F., & Smith, R. (1997). Hyperthermia and intraoperative radiation therapy. In K.H. Dow, J.D. Bucholtz, R. Iwamoto, V.K. Fieler, & L.J. Hilderley (Eds.), *Nursing care in radiation oncology* (2nd ed., pp. 36–40). Philadelphia: Saunders.

L. Photodynamic therapy (PDT)

1. Procedure description: PDT is a cancer treatment modality that uses a combination of a photoactive drug and nonthermal laser light to treat certain types of cancers. It works specifically to target and destroy cancer cells while limiting the damage to surrounding healthy tissues. The appeal of PDT in oncology is that the photosensitizer tends to be retained in tumor tissues for a longer period of time as compared with normal tissues, resulting in a large therapeutic index (Hsi, Rosenthal, & Glatstein, 1999). The tumor is illuminated through a fiberoptic scope with a visible light in a wavelength that matches the absorption characteristics of the photosensitizer. Light interacting with the photosensitizer triggers the release of free radicals that attack and destroy tumor cells. This chemical reaction causes a decrease in the size of the tumor, as well as cutting off the blood supply. The dead cells begin sloughing and aid in debulking the tumor. The main advantage of PDT is that it can be repeated multiple times without producing immunosuppression or myelosuppression and can be used despite prior surgery, chemotherapy, or RT (Goddell & Muller, 2001).

2. Indications

a) PDT has achieved the status of a standard treatment modality for centrally located, early-stage lung cancer in some countries; however, it is not the standard of care in the United States (Okunaka & Kato, 2002).

b) To be considered for PDT, patients must be ineligible for Nd:YAG laser therapy, surgery, or RT (Durkin, 1999).

c) Can be a potentially curative therapy for certain types of early-stage micro-invasive lung cancer when patients are not eligible for surgery or radiotherapy (Ahmad & Mukhtar, 2000)

d) May be used for palliation of symptoms associated with obstructing tumors of the lung or esophagus

e) PDT is not indicated if tumor is eroding into major blood vessels or the tracheal or bronchial trees. No tracheolesophageal or bronchoesophageal fistulas can be present. The patient must not have an allergy to porfimer sodium (Photofrin®, Sanofi Pharmaceuticals, New York) or porphyrins. The patient must not have any coagulopathy.

f) PDT also is being used to treat head and neck cancer, mesothelioma, bladder cancer, and some cutaneous malignancies (Shackley et al., 2000).

g) Use in age-related macular degeneration, dermatology, and precancerous conditions, such as Barrett's esophagus, is under investigation (Ackroyd et al., 2000).

3. Treatment: The sequence for a single PDT treatment covers a minimum of five days and is conducted in several stages (Sanofi Pharmaceuticals, 1997, 1999).

   a) Day 1 involves the IV administration of Photofrin, a photosensitizing agent. The drug can be given in the outpatient setting or administered while the patient is in the hospital. The patient can eat and drink normally on the day of injection. Photosensitivity to the skin and eyes can begin within five minutes of the injection. The patient is instructed on the clothing and special precautions that must be taken during this period of photosensitivity that lasts for four to six weeks.

   b) The standard dose of Photofrin is 2 mg/kg (Sanofi Pharmaceuticals, 1996). When reconstituted, Photofrin is stable for two to four hours and must be protected from light. Photofrin is given via slow IV push over three to five minutes. Photofrin is classified as an antineoplastic agent. Although it is not a vesicant, caution should be used to prevent extravasation of the drug. The person preparing the Photofrin should wear gloves and protective eyewear to avoid contact with skin and eyes (Bruce, 2001).

   c) On day 3, the patient is ready for the light activation step of the PDT process. The patient is NPO for eight hours prior to the laser light treatment. The application of the light is performed in the OR, and the patient may receive a sedative, local anesthetic, or conscious sedation to provide comfort during the procedure. Some institutions may use general anesthesia and intubate the patient. The patient and staff are given protective eye goggles to wear during the procedure. The laser light is directed to the cancer cells through a fiberoptic guide that is passed through a scope. The instrument is positioned close to or into the tumor, and the precise amount of light is delivered. The light application takes 12½ minutes, and the entire procedure takes approximately 30 minutes to complete. Recovery is brief unless the patient had general anesthesia and intubation, when the patient will go to the surgical intensive care unit or a step-down unit for close observation of the airway.

   d) On day 5, another endoscopy or bronchoscopy is performed for the purpose of removing necrotic tissue and exudates that could cause obstruction of the airway or esophagus. This is also an opportunity to evaluate the response to the PDT. This second look procedure does not require another injection of Photofrin.

4. Collaborative management

   a) Acute effects

      (1) Photosensitivity is the main side effect that occurs immediately after administration of Photofrin and lasts for a minimum of 30 days. Side effects range from mild skin erythema to severe, debilitating burns (Durkin, 1999). Other side effects directly related to the administration of Photofrin include nausea, constipation, and fever (Sanofi Pharmaceuticals, 1997).

      (2) Symptoms experienced post-PDT include localized swelling and inflammation to the treated area, which may cause local discomfort (Bruce, 2001).

      (3) Other common symptoms include mucositis, pharyngitis, nausea/vomiting, constipation, bleeding at the site, fever, infection (pneumonia or bronchitis), dyspnea, chest pain, and dysphasia.

      (4) Symptoms usually are transient and self-limiting. Most symptoms respond to conventional symptom management strategies.

   b) Late effects: There are essentially no chronic side effects from the administration of Photofrin or the PDT process (Sanofi Pharmaceuticals, 1996).

5. Patient and family education (Lightdale & Mang, 1997)

   a) Teach patient and family about Photofrin injection, side effects, photosensitivity, use of protective clothing, and strategies to protect against photosensitivity.

(1) Photosensitivity begins immediately after injection of Photofrin and lasts for approximately four to six weeks.

(2) Photofrin-induced photosensitivity reaction is characterized by swelling, redness, or blistering (Bruce, 2001).

(3) Protective clothing includes tightly woven, light-colored long-sleeve shirt and long pants, wide-brimmed hat, scarf, gloves, and dark sunglasses.

(4) Sunscreen of any SPF factor offers no protective value against the photosensitivity.

(5) Avoid direct sunlight from skylights or undraped windows; patient should remain at least six feet from windows.

(6) Limit outdoor activities to after the sun has gone down.

(7) Avoid helmet-type hair dryers to prevent burns on scalp.

(8) Do not stay in a totally darkened room, as low levels of indoor light are necessary to help break down the Photofrin retained in the skin (photo bleaching reaction).

(9) Patients requiring emergency or elective abdominal surgery need to tell their surgeon that they have had PDT so that special draping and OR light filters can be used (Bruce, 2001).

(10) Women of childbearing age should practice effective methods of birth control during use of Photofrin and photodynamic therapy.

(11) Fever, nausea, and constipation related to the Photofrin responds to conventional use of antipyretics, antinausea medication, and a good bowel regimen.

b) Teach patient and family about the PDT procedure and recovery phase.

(1) Close monitoring: EKG, pulse oximetry, suction, oxygen, and IV access

(2) Warn patients that a burning chest pain may occur during the procedure and that analgesics will be administered to reduce the discomfort.

c) Teach patient and family how to test for photosensitivity on day 31.

(1) Have patient place his or her hand in a paper bag with a two-inch hole in it.

(2) Expose it to direct sunlight for 10 minutes.

(3) If a reaction occurs within 24 hours, continue with photosensitivity precautions for an additional two weeks, then repeat the test.

(4) If no reaction occurs within 24 hours, the patient may gradually increase his or her exposure to sunlight, while continuing to watch for skin reactions.

d) Signs and symptoms to report to the healthcare team

(1) Red or blistered skin at any point following treatment

(2) Unrelieved nausea, fever, or constipation

(3) Mucositis, pharyngitis, and dysphasia

(4) Infection

(5) Difficulty breathing and/or chest pain

(6) Bleeding

6. Follow-up

a) After discharge from the hospital, the patient will return initially for follow-up endoscopy or bronchoscopy one week after treatment, then monthly for three months.

b) The patient then has endoscopies or bronchoscopies at 6, 12, and 18 months after treatment (Kitzrow, 1992).

References

Ackroyd, R., Brown, N., Davis, M., Stephenson, T., Marcus, S., Stoddard, C., et al. (2000). Photodynamic therapy for dysplastic Barrett's esophagus: A prospective, double bind, randomized, placebo-controlled trial. *Gut, 47,* 612–617.

Ahmad, N, & Mukhtar, H. (2000). Mechanisms of photodynamic therapy-induced cell death. *Methods in Enzymology, 319,* 342–358.

Bruce, S. (2001). Photodynamic therapy: Another option in cancer treatment. *Clinical Journal of Oncology Nursing, 5,* 95–99.

Durkin, S. (1999). Photodynamic therapy: A cancer treatment for the 21st century. *Gastroenterology Nursing, 22*(3), 115–120.

Goddell, T., & Muller, P. (2001). Photodynamic therapy: A novel treatment for primary brain malignancy. *Journal of Neuroscience Nursing, 33,* 296–300.

Hsi, R., Rosenthal, D., & Glatstein, E. (1999). Photodynamic therapy in the treatment of cancer: Current state of the art. *Drugs, 57,* 725–734.

Kitzrow, C. (1992). Photodynamic therapy in bronchial and esophageal tumors: Perioperative implications. *American Operating Room Nurse, 35,* 1483–1492.

Lightdale, C., & Mang, T. (1997). *Photodynamic therapy with Photofrin; A new modality.* New York: Sanofi Pharmaceuticals.

Okunaka, T., & Kato, H. (2002). Photodynamic therapy for lung cancer: State of the art and expanded indications. Nippon Geka Gakkai Zasshi. *Journal of Japan Surgical Society, 103*(2), 258–262.

Sanofi Pharmaceuticals. (1996). Photofrin [Package insert]. New York: Author.

Sanofi Pharmaceuticals. (1997). *A picture guide to Photofrin for injection.* New York: Author.

Sanofi Pharmaceuticals. (1999). *Answers to questions patients commonly have about photodynamic therapy with Photofrin.* New York: Author.

Shackley, D., Whitehurst, C., Moore, J., George, N., Betts, C., & Clarke, N. (2000). Light penetration in bladder tissue: Implications for intravesical photodynamic therapy of bladder tumours. *British Journal of Urology International, 86,* 638–643.

VIII.   Special populations: Pediatric radiation oncology

A. Pediatric radiation oncology
  1. Pediatric cancers (Ruble & Kelly, 1999)
     a) Childhood cancers account for only 1%–2% of all cancers diagnosed in the United States.
     b) Childhood cancer is the leading cause of death by disease in children younger than 15 years, second only to accidents and trauma. See Figure 21 for percentages of pediatric cancers.
  2. Specific differences between pediatric and adult cancers (Ruble & Kelly, 1999)
     a) Childhood cancers differ from cancers that occur in adults. The majority of childhood cancers arise from the mesodermal germ layer, giving rise to cancers such as leukemia, lymphoma, sarcoma, or cancers of the primitive embryonal tissue. The majority of adult cancers arise from tissue of epithelial origin, giving rise to carcinomas.
     b) The majority of childhood cancers have distant metastasis at diagnosis because the cancers arise from very deep-seated tissue.
  3. Issues associated with treating children with radiation
     a) Developmental issues—Every child is a unique person with an individual temper, learning style, family background, and pattern and timing of growth.
        (1) Universal predictable sequences of growth and change occur at various ages of a child's life. Learning these various developmental stages and assessing if the child is at the appropriate age is important for the radiation oncology nurse (Ruble & Kelly, 1999).
        (2) Developmental considerations in treating children with cancer (see Table 21)
     b) Psychosocial issues—There is an enormous need for psychosocial care for the child with cancer and his or her family.
        (1) 20%–40% of the physically healthy population shows moderate to severe psychosocial stress or mental disorder (Kusch, Labouvie, Ladisch, Fleischhack, & Bode, 2000).
        (2) Certain factors may place families at risk for stresses in coping with the disease. The principal familial risk and protective factors include the following (Kusch et al., 2000).
           (a) Social support
           (b) Self-confidence
           (c) Social competence
           (d) Coherence of the family
           (e) Socio-economic factors
           (f) Psychiatric disorders
        (3) Enlisting the expertise of social workers, behavioral medicine, and psychology will benefit the child and family with coping skills during the course of treatment. Standardized protocols defining principles, programs, and quality psychosocial care for children with cancer and their families are called for by many researches (Kusch et al., 2000).
        (4) The *Manual of Psycho-Social Care in Pediatric Oncology* (Kush, 1994) illustrates a program of standardized basic psychosocial care provided to patients and families.
     c) Nutritional issues—Malnutrition in the pediatric oncology population has been reported to occur in 8%–32% of patients (Hanigan & Walter, 1992; Han-Markey, 2000).
        (1) Compared to adults, children's nutritional needs must include energy requirements for growth and development, in addition to needs required to support them during treatment of their disease. Because of their particular body composition (higher water content and decreased fat), children have decreased caloric reserves, making

Figure 21. Types of Childhood Cancer

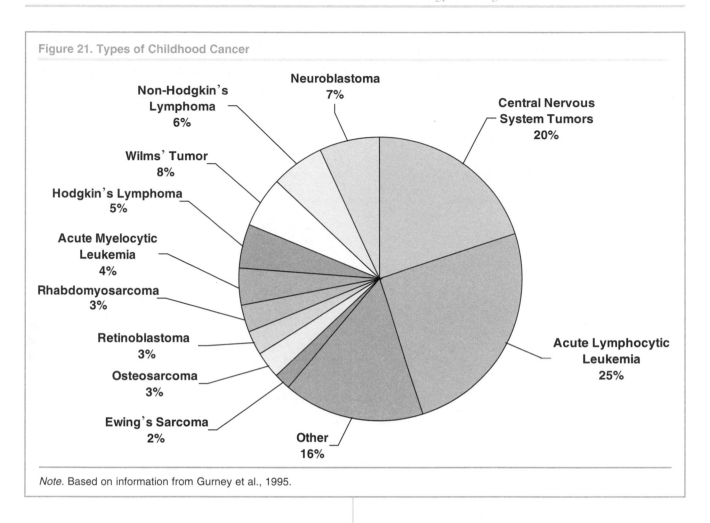

Note. Based on information from Gurney et al., 1995.

them susceptible to malnutrition sooner than adults.

(2) Children are dependent individuals, and often they are not responsible for preparing their own food and require the nutrition support and counseling of members of the family or caregivers. Input from a registered dietitian using established pediatric treatment in assessing, planning, and implementing a nutritional plan of care is preferable to assist in ensuring that the nutritional needs of this specialized population are met.

(3) A history of weight loss, weight for age, weight for height percentiles, along with simple subjective questions concerning appetite, number of meals consumed per day, or modified diet or supplement use can be asked by the radiation oncology nurse.

d) Immobilization/sedation issues—One of the most challenging factors in treating children with radiation is maintaining the child in a fixed and reproducible position on a daily basis where the tumor can be

targeted and normal tissue is spared (Bucholtz, 1992, 1994; Scott, Langton, & O'Donoghue, 2002).

(1) Generally, children older than three years may be capable of lying still on the radiation therapy table.

(2) Younger children (< three years), developmentally disabled children, and occasionally older, anxious children may require sedation for planning and/or treatment. This challenges the physician, nurses, and technologists in choosing the correct method(s) of immobilization and sedation to be used, along with use of monitoring the child daily, and timing the actual treatment sessions.

(3) It is important to allot time during the initial consultation for assessing the need for sedation. This requires the early involvement of anesthesia staff familiar with pediatric anesthesia and RT treatment. Data regarding the child's age, developmental assessment, diagnosis, present physical status, past experiences during other

Table 21. Developmental Considerations in Treating Children With Cancer

Stage	Infants (Birth to 1 yr.)	Toddler (1–3 yr.)	Preschool (4–6 yr.)
Psychosocial stage	Trust versus mistrust Develop a basic sense of trust.	Autonomy versus shame and doubt Independence and self-mastery	Initiative versus guilt Increase autonomy and initiative through mastery of new skills.
Cognitive development	Sensorimotor Reflex actions to symbolic activities Object permanence	Preoperational thought (preconceptual phase) Concrete thinking Prelogical thinking Egocentric	Preoperational thought (intuitive phase) Differentiate self from others and fantasy from reality.
Concept of illness	Incomprehension	Incomprehension Phenomenistic	Phenomenistic Contagion Contamination
Risks to child	Separation from parents Side effects of therapy affect sensorimotor experiences and alter development.	Temperamental/poor impulse control Separation from parents Fear of strangers Interfere with exploration of environment Limited verbal skills to express self Unable to understand what is happening Lack of predictable routines	Separation Isolation leads to decrease in development of social skills. Magical thinking leads to increased fears. Decreased play leads to decreased sense of accomplishment. Limitation to both parents may affect sexual identity.
Suggested intervention	Encourage trust. Parental presence Comforting touch/voice Allow to suck. Soothing music Will require general anesthesia for radiation therapy	Establish treatment routines. Consistent caregivers Therapeutic play Participate in care as able. Encourage mobility/play activities. Set limits. Will require general anesthesia or sedation for radiation therapy	Continue routines as possible in hospital. Encourage mastery in self-care and promote independence. Provide play experiences. Provide brief simple explanations; focus on sights, sounds, tactile experiences. Remember inability to understand time. Maintain safe places, such as bed/playroom. May be able to elicit cooperation with help of child life therapy. Use behavioral techniques to reward cooperation. Will need to schedule extra time to allow child to explore and become comfortable with environment.

Note. Based on information from Bibace & Walsh, 1980; Hooke, 1998; Madsen, 1998.
From "Radiation Therapy in Childhood Cancer," by K. Ruble and K.P. Kelly, 1999, *Seminars in Oncology Nursing, 15,* p. 297. Copyright 1999 by Elsevier. Reprinted with permission.

procedures with lying still, and type of radiation treatment will be required. The expertise of a child life specialist is very helpful with the use of play and role playing to decrease anxiety experienced by children and may prevent the need for sedation (Lew, 1997).

(4) Special considerations and interventions are needed dependent upon the age of the child (Lew, 1997) (see Table 22).

(5) The use of sedation agents such as chloral hydrate, meperidine, chlorpromazine, or promethazine intramuscularly is practiced at some centers as an alternative to general anesthesia. Some limitations of the agents include variability in absorption and onset of action, sub-optimal sedative effects, prolonged somnolence, and increased potential for serious adverse reactions, such as

Table 22. Developmental Issues in the Preparation of Children Receiving Radiation Therapy

Considerations	Interventions
Preparation of Infants Receiving Radiation Therapy	
Trust versus mistrust	Provide consistency in caregivers, and be attentive to comfort, nurturance, and security needs.
Object permanence/ separation anxiety	Assess parents' ability to be involved in their child's care during procedures and examinations. Parental participation should be encouraged if it provides a source of comfort and reassurance for the child.
Sensorimotor	Provide toys that are soft, cuddly, and colorful and that provide visual and auditory stimulation.
Comfort	Provide a quiet environment for waking after anesthesia. Foster a sense of security by providing touch, soothing voices, and warmth.
Nurturance	Carefully monitor for nutritional disturbances, such as anorexia, dehydration, altered gastrointestinal function, and hypoglycemia. During recovery, assess degree of alertness, cough, and gag reflexes. Introduce clear liquids slowly. Instruct parents to introduce soft solid foods and fluids at home.
Parent teaching	Assess the level of understanding of disease and treatment, and identify learning needs. Incorporate parent teaching in child's plan of care. Review treatment plan with parents, and instruct them in guidelines for children receiving daily anesthesia and skin care. Identify treatment-related side effects and instruct parents in their management.
Preparation of Toddlers Receiving Radiation Therapy	
Trust	Provide consistency in caregivers and approach to child. Establish a daily routine.
Separation object permanence	Parents should accompany child for procedure. Talking or reading to a child via intercom provides reassurance that parents are nearby.
Security	Use transitional objects, such as a favorite toy or blanket, to accompany child.
Limited reasoning	Inform child of procedure just before it happens, and explain what he or she will see, feel, and hear. Provide simple explanations and commands.
Control mastery	Orient child to treatment rooms. Assist child to explore environment to see and touch objects in room. Praise good behavior; provide simple rewards. Set up rules and guidelines.
Imitative	Role-playing—Child may feel more comfortable if he or she can watch the parent or another child go through a similar procedure.
Body integrity	Protect privacy as much as possible. Allow child to wear his or her own clothes and uncover only those areas that need to be exposed. Maintain child's sense of integrity by protecting dressings, bandages, and intravenous catheters.
Preparation of Preschoolers Receiving Radiation Therapy	
Initiative versus guilt	Use parents' knowledge of child and previous response to procedures to develop approach to child. Identify coping mechanisms. Assess the child's concept of illness, fears, and understanding of radiation therapy. Encourage child's autonomy by permitting him or her to explore the environment and ask questions. Set reasonable limits on behavior. Offer praise for good behavior and accomplishment of tasks.
Fear of unknown, limited comprehension	Determine readiness to learn. Provide simple explanations about what is going to happen, what child will see, feel, and is expected to do. Use a picture to illustrate points. Practice the position that will be required for the procedure. Provide opportunity for role-playing using miniature XRT machine. Start with inanimate object, such as toy or stuffed animal, then advance to doll.
Imitative security	Have the child observe another child receiving the same treatment. Encourage parents to accompany child to treatment room, and inform child that he or she will be waiting close by. Parents may talk to child via intercom to offer encouragement. Encourage child to bring a favorite toy, stuffed animal, or security object to hold during treatment.
Body integrity	Talk to child during procedure. Explain things as they are about to occur (e.g., dimming lights, repositioning, placing markings on skin). Protect privacy as much as possible by limiting the amount of clothing that needs to be removed.

(Continued on next page)

Table 22. Developmental Issues in the Preparation of Children Receiving Radiation Therapy *(Continued)*	
Considerations	**Interventions**
Hero worship/fantasy	Explore the child's sense of imagination. Use fantasy as a distraction technique while treatment is being given (e.g., astronaut buckling up for space shuttle, superhero becoming energized with special powers). Use storytelling to prepare child for treatment.
Preparation of School-Age Children Receiving Radiation Therapy	
Industry versus inferiority (reasoning, mastery, sense of accomplishment)	Assess level of understanding of illness and treatment. Provide descriptions of behaviors required during procedure, sequence of events, and length of time. Illustrate explanations with photographs, bodygram, or demonstration with miniature XRT machine. Provide opportunity to rehearse procedure or role-play event with miniature XRT machine. Orient to treatment room. Provide simple explanation of how machine works and equipment that will be used. Talk to child during treatment setup. Reinforce behavioral expectations. Provide encouragement and empathetic support. Acknowledge child's participation in procedure: Reinforce sense of accomplishment.
Body image	Discuss with the child/parents the temporary side effects of treatment and what measures can be taken to minimize them. Explore child's feelings about changes in body image and offer suggestions about how to cope with changes in appearance, physical limitations, and peer/family reactions. Respect child's need for privacy by limiting exposure of body.
Independence	Encourage self-care activities. Promote participation in school/social activities. Encourage family to establish daily routine and to maintain normal limit setting and behavioral expectations. Provide some flexibility in choices (e.g., schedule of daily treatment, route of blood drawing).
Security/trust	Provide consistency in caregivers and approach to treatment. Establish daily routine. Provide opportunities for child to verbalize concerns, frustrations, and fears. Assist child to work through feelings with play and art. Refer for additional counseling as needed.
Preparation of Adolescents Receiving Radiation Therapy	
Identity/independence	Determine perceptions of illness and treatment. Clarify misconceptions. Explain rationale for treatment, procedures, behavioral expectations, and potential side effects. Encourage participation in decision-making by providing opportunities for the individual to express feelings and opinions. Encourage individual to take responsibility for self-care (e.g., skin care, medications, fluoride treatments, nutrition, physical activity). Promote continued participation in school and physical and social activities. Arrange treatment schedule to accommodate these needs.
Body image	Provide supportive relationship that allows for open communication.
Self-concept	Reassure individual of staff's availability to him or her. Provide opportunities to discuss feelings about changes in body image, sexuality, and physical limitations. Provide empathy and reassurance. Acknowledge concerns. Assist individual to establish effective coping skills and to adjust to alterations in body image and role. Encourage independence and participation in peer activities. Protect confidentiality and need for privacy during treatments and physical examinations.

Note. From "Pediatric Cancers—The Special Needs of Children Receiving Radiation Therapy" (pp. 338–339, 343, 345, 347) by C.C. Lew in K.H. Dow, J.D. Bucholtz, R. Iwamoto, V.K. Fieler, and L.J. Hilderley (Eds.), *Nursing Care in Radiation Oncology* (2nd ed.), 1997, Philadelphia: Saunders. Copyright 1997 by Saunders. Reprinted with permission.

respiratory or cardiac depression when multiple drugs or high doses of medications are used. Therefore anesthesia is the better choice in treating very young children.

(6) The approach to sedation and anesthesia varies with the available institutional resources. The expertise of pediatric anesthesiologists is desirable because of their knowledge and familiarity of the agents that are appropriate for children and their abil-

ity to intervene when complications occur.

(7) Arrangements for early morning treatments are recommended and should be coordinated with the anesthesia department and radiation therapists.

(8) Separate consents for anesthesia should be obtained by the anesthesiologist along with daily evaluation of the child's health status.

(9) Parents should be instructed to withhold solid food and milk products

from the child for six to eight hours prior to anesthesia and liquids two hours prior to anesthesia, depending on the anesthesiologist's recommendations.

(10) An RN with experience in CPR, recovery room experience, and proficiency in airway management should be available to assist the anesthesiologist.

(11) An identified policy/procedure for obtaining assistance in emergencies should be in place. The use of closed-circuit television to focus directly on the child and display the monitoring device, EKG, pulse oximeter, blood pressure, and carbon dioxide analyzers are essential. All emergency equipment, including oxygen source, suction equipment, an anesthesia machine and monitoring equipment, a pediatric code cart that contains airways and endotracheal tubes of appropriate size, Ambu bags, code drugs, and IV equipment, should be checked daily prior to initiation of treatment.

(12) Continual monitoring during the recovery period is performed until the child is fully awake and vital signs are stable (Lew, 1997).

e) Late effects—Success in the treatment of childhood cancers has led to an increase in the number of long-term survivors. Unfortunately, late side effects caused from radiation treatment continue to be seen (see Table 23).

Table 23. Late Effects of Radiation Therapy

System	Late Effect	Dose
Central nervous system	Neurocognitive deficit	> 18 Gy
	Leukoencephalopathy	> 18 Gy
Peripheral nervous system	Peripheral neuropathy	60 Gy
Neuroendocrine	Growth hormone deficiency	> 18 Gy hypopituitary axis
	ACTH deficiency	> 40 Gy hypopituitary axis
	Thyroid hormone deficiency	> 40 Gy hypopituitary axis
	Precocious puberty	> 20 Gy hypopituitary axis
	Gonadotrophin deficiency	> 40 Gy hypopituitary axis
	Hyperprolactinemia	> 40 Gy hypopituitary axis
Ophthalmic	Cataract	> 8 Gy single dose/>10–15 Gy fractionated
	Retinal/lacrimal/conjunctiva/scleral/corneal/lens/iris/retinal damage	> 45–50 Gy
Head and neck	Xerostomia	> 40 Gy or >25 Gy to 50% of gland
	Abnormal craniofacial growth	> 30 Gy
	Abnormal teeth and roots	= 1 Gy
	Chronic otitis	= 40–50 Gy
	Sensorineural hearing loss	= 40–50 Gy
	Thyroid dysfunction	> 20 Gy local or > 7.5 Gy total body irradiation
Cardiac	Cardiomyopathy	> 35 Gy or > 25 Gy with anthracyclines
	Valvular damage	> 40 Gy
	Pericardial damage	> 35 Gy
	Coronary artery disease	> 30 Gy
Pulmonary	Fibrosis	> 10 Gy
Gastrointestinal	Enteritis/fibrosis	> 40–50 Gy
	Hepatic dysfunction	> 30 Gy

(Continued on next page)

Table 23. Late Effects of Radiation Therapy *(Continued)*

System	Late Effect	Dose
Gonads	Ovarian failure	4–12 Gy (increasing age decreases tolerance)
	Oligospermia/azoospermia	1–6 Gy
	Leydig cell damage (testosterone deficiency)	> 24 Gy
Genitourinary	Hypoplastic kidney	20–30 Gy (10–15 Gy with chemotherapy)
	Nephrotic syndrome	20–30 Gy
	Bladder dysfunction	> 30 Gy prepubertal > 50 Gy postpubertal
	Prostate dysfunction	40–60 Gy
	Vaginal fibrosis	> 40 Gy
	Uterine fibrosis	> 20 Gy prepubertal > 40–60 Gy postpubertal
	Ureter/urethral dysfunction	> 50–60 Gy
Musculoskeletal	Hypoplasia	> 20 Gy growing child
	Spinal abnormalities	10–20 Gy
	Length discrepancy	> 20 Gy
	Pathological fractures	> 40 Gy
Integumentary	Alopecia (permanent)	> 40 Gy
	Hyperpigmentation	> 30 Gy
	Increased melanocytic nevi	Any dose
	Hypoplasia of soft tissue	> 20 Gy growing child
	Telangiectasia	> 40 Gy
Breast	Hypoplasia	> 10 Gy (pubertal breast most sensitive)

Note. Based on information from Schwartz et al., 1994.

From "Radiation Therapy in Childhood Cancer," by K. Ruble and K.P. Kelly, 1999, *Seminars in Oncology Nursing, 15,* p. 300. Copyright 1999 by Elsevier. Reprinted with permission.

(1) It is important to educate the family of these effects and to inform them that there is still research under investigation.

(2) Follow-up care and counseling to the potential side effects should be discussed; information regarding prevention and early detection is essential. The objective is to provide patients with the knowledge to lead a healthy life as adults after they have survived cancer.

References

Bibace, R., & Walsh, M.E. (1980). Development of children's concept of illness. *Journal of Pediatrics, 66,* 912–917.

Bucholtz, J. (1992). Issues concerning the sedation of children for radiation therapy. *Oncology Nursing Forum, 19,* 649–655.

Bucholtz, J. (1994). Comforting children during radiotherapy. *Oncology Nursing Forum, 21,* 987–994.

Gurney, J.G., Severson, R.K., Davis, S., & Robison, L.L. (1995). Incidence of cancer in children in the United States. Sex, race, and one year age specific rates by histologic type. *Cancer, 75,* 2186–2195.

Hanigan, M., & Walter, G. (1992). Nutritional support of the child with cancer. *Journal of Pediatric Oncology Nursing, 9*(3), 110–118.

Han-Markey, T. (2000). Nutritional considerations in pediatric oncology. *Seminars in Oncology Nursing, 16,* 146–151.

Hooke, C. (1998). Development of infants (birth–1 year), toddlers (1–3 years), preschoolers (4–6 years). In M. Hockenberry-Eaton (Ed.), *Essentials of pediatric oncology nursing: A core curriculum* (pp. 182–185). Glenview, IL: Association of Pediatric Oncology Nurses.

Kusch, M. (1994). *Manual of psycho-social care in pediatric oncology.* Bonn, Germany: Department of Pediatric Hematology/Oncology of the University of Bonn.

Kusch, M., Labouvie, H., Ladisch, V., Fleischhack, G., & Bode, U. (2000). Structuring psychosocial care in pediatric oncology. *Patient Education and Counseling, 40,* 231–245.

Lew, C.C. (1997). Pediatric cancers—The special needs of children receiving radiation therapy. In K.H. Dow, J.D. Bucholtz, R. Iwamoto, V.K. Fieler, & L.J. Hilderley (Eds.), *Nursing care in radiation oncology* (2nd ed., pp. 314–354). Philadelphia: Saunders.

Madsen, L. (1998). Development of school-age children (7–12 years), adolescents (13–18 years). In M. Hockenberry-Eaton (Ed.), *Essentials of pediatric oncology nursing: A core curriculum.* Glenview, IL: Association of Pediatric Oncology Nurses.

Ruble, K., & Kelly, K.P. (1999). Radiation therapy in childhood cancer. *Seminars in Oncology Nursing, 15,* 292–302.

Schwartz, C.L., Hobbie, W.L., Constine, L.S., & Ruccionne, K. (1994). *Survivors of childhood cancer: Assessment and management.* St. Louis, MO: Mosby.

Scott, L., Langton, F., & O'Donoghue, J. (2002). Minimizing the use of sedation/anesthesia in young children receiving radiotherapy through an effective play preparation programme. *European Journal of Oncology Nursing, 6*(1), 15–22.

IX. Chemical modifiers of cancer treatment

A. Radiosensitizers (see also section II, B—Radiobiology)

1. Definition: Radiosensitizers are chemical or pharmacologic agents that increase radiation damage to sensitive cells when given concurrently with radiation (Wilkes, Ingwersen, & Barton-Burke, 2003).

2. Rationale: To enhance damage to tumor cells while minimizing normal tissue toxicity (Bryer, 2001)

3. Types

a) Hypoxic cell sensitizers (nitroimidazoles: misonidazole, etanidazole, and nimorazole) increase oxygenation of tumor cells, which contributes to DNA damage from radiation. Neurotoxicity limits the use of effective doses (Hall & Cox, 2003). Currently it is only used in clinical trials.

b) Non-hypoxic (aerobic) cell sensitizers (halogenated pyrimidines: bromo-deoxyuridine and iododeoxyuridine) are incorporated into the DNA of rapidly dividing tumor cells, increasing sensitivity to radiation (Bryer, 2001; Wilkes et al., 2003). They are highly toxic to normal tissues as well, and side effects at effective dose levels limit use with extended RT courses (Hall & Cox, 2003). Currently they are used in clinical trials.

c) Hypoxic cell cytotoxic agents selectively kill hypoxic cells. Examples include tirapazamine, currently used in multiple clinical trials, and mitomycin-C, used in clinical practice (Stevens, 2003).

d) Chemotherapy sensitizers are in widespread use in clinical practice, singly or in combinations. The most commonly used are

(1) Fluoropyrimidines: 5-FU

(2) Taxanes (docetaxel, paclitaxel), platinum compounds (carboplatin, cisplatin), etoposide (VP-16), gemcitabine hydrochloride, and bleomycin sulfate

(3) Topoisomerase inhibitors: irinotecan hydrochloride, topotecan hydrochloride

References

Bryer, M. (2001). Combined modality therapy. In M. Perry (Ed.), *The cancer sourcebook* (3rd ed., pp. 73–81). Philadelphia: Lippincott Williams & Wilkins.

Hall, E.J., & Cox, J.D. (2003). Physical and biological basis of radiation therapy. In J. Cox & S.K. Ang (Eds.), *Radiation oncology: Rationale, technique, results* (8th ed., pp. 3–62). St. Louis, MO: Mosby.

Stevens, C.W. (2003). Clinical applications of new modalities. In J. Cox & S.K. Ang (Eds.), *Radiation oncology: Rationale, technique, results* (8th ed., pp. 987–1002). St. Louis, MO: Mosby.

Wilkes, G., Ingwersen, K., & Barton-Burke, M. (2003). *Oncology nursing drug handbook.* Sudbury, MA: Jones and Bartlett.

B. Radioprotectors

1. Definition: Radioprotectors are defined as chemical modifiers designed to minimize normal tissue damage resulting from RT without compromising local tumor control (Capizzi, 1999; Kemp et al., 1996).

2. Cytoprotectants are defined as chemical modifiers designed to minimize normal tissue damage resulting from chemotherapy administration without compromising tumor control (Capizzi, 1999; Kemp et al., 1996).

3. Radioprotective agent with FDA approval: Amifostine

4. Radioprotective or cytoprotective agents being investigated include the following.

a) Gene therapy: Intratumor injection of manganese superoxide dismutase-plasmid/liposome (SOD2-PL)

b) Transforming growth factor-beta

c) Keratinocyte growth factor (KGF)

d) Glutamine

e) IL-15

f) Melatonin

g) Omega-3 fatty acids (Jatoi & Thomas, 2002).

5. The update of recommendations for the use of cytoprotectants and radioprotectants and Clinical Practice Guidelines of the American Society of Clinical Oncology (2002) include mesna, dexrazoxane, and amifostine.

a) Mesna—Chemoprotectant used to decrease the incidence of ifosfamide-associated bladder/urethral toxicity.

b) Dexrazoxane—Chemoprotectant used to reduce the incidence of cardiotoxicity that may be suggested but not routinely used for patients with metastatic breast cancer who received more than 300 mg/m^2 of doxorubicin in the metastatic setting and who may benefit from continued doxorubicin-containing therapy. Increased nausea and vomiting are noted with use of this therapy.

c) Amifostine

(1) FDA approved as a chemoprotectant to reduce the cumulative renal toxicity associated with repeated administration of cisplatin with advanced ovarian cancer or non-small cell lung cancer (NSCLC) (Kemp et al., 1996; Schiller et al., 1996).

(2) FDA approved as a radioprotectant to reduce the incidence of moderate to severe xerostomia in patients under-

going postoperative RT for head and neck cancer, where the radiation field includes a substantial portion of the parotid gland (Brizel et al., 2000).

(3) Numerous clinical trials have examined the safety and efficacy of amifostine in the prevention of mucositis in radiation and combined modality therapy induced mucositis in three major areas: head and neck cancer, NSCLC, and pelvic cancer (Antonadou et al., 2001; Buntzel, Kuttner, Frohlich, & Glatzel, 1998; Koukourakis et al., 2000).

(4) Based on extensive data available, additions were made to the amifostine USP-DI monograph for off-label use: Mucosal RT or RT combined with chemotherapy (USP, 2002).

6. Head and neck cancer (see section V, B—Head and Neck)

a) Significant toxicities arise from head and neck radiation.

(1) Acute mucositis

(2) Acute and chronic xerostomia

(3) Acute esophagitis

(4) Candidiasis

(5) Skin reactions

b) Results of significant toxicities caused by radiation to the head/neck region

(1) Weight loss

(2) Taste alterations

(3) Oral complications and pain

(4) Extreme fatigue

(5) Dehydration

(6) Dental complications

(7) Treatment interruptions

(8) Dose limitations

(9) Discontinuation of treatment

(10) Hospitalizations

(11) Ultimately poor outcomes

c) Combined modality treatment with chemotherapy and RT increases the toxicities

of xerostomia, mucositis, and esophagitis.

d) Amifostine as a radioprotector in head and neck cancer

(1) Amifostine is a pro-drug that is dephosphorylated by alkaline phosphatase in tissues to pharmacologically active free thiol metabolite.

(2) The active free thiol metabolite is believed to be responsible for the reduction of the toxic effects of radiation on normal tissue (Capizzi, 1999).

(3) Clinical trials have suggested that amifostine protects against radiation-induced toxicity in both patients receiving radiotherapy alone and those receiving radiochemotherapy (Anne & Curran, 2002; Brizel et al., 2000; Buntzel et al., 1998).

(4) In a phase III randomized trial with amifostine as a radioprotector in squamous cell cancer of the head and neck, amifostine reduced acute and chronic xerostomia while preserving antitumor efficacy and reducing the overall incidence of grade 2 or higher xerostomia from 78% to 51% (p < 0.0001) (Brizel et al., 2000). The median time to onset of grade ≥ 2 acute xerostomia was longer in the amifostine + RT group (45 days) compared to the control group (30 days, p = 0.0001). In addition, patients pretreated with amifostine were able to tolerate larger doses of RT (60 Gy) compared to the RT alone group (42 Gy, p = 0.0001). The radiation dose necessary to cause grade 2 or higher acute xerostomia was 40% higher in the amifostine + RT group (Brizel et al., 2000).

(5) Clinical benefit was measured by the use of an eight-item validated Patient Benefit Questionnaire (PBQ) during and up to 11 months after RT. Amifostine-treated patients consistently reported better PBQ scores beginning at week 4 of radiation (p < 0.05), which was indicative of improved oral toxicity–related outcomes and improved clinical benefit (Wasserman et al., 2000).

(6) Additionally, 18- and 24-month follow-up data recently obtained from a pivotal phase III study further established the selective cytoprotection and lack of tumor protection with the use of amifostine. At 18 and 24 months, there was no statistically significant

difference in locoregional control (p = 0.610; p = 0.535, respectively), progression free survival (p = 0.958; p = 0.982, respectively), and overall survival rate (p = 0.184; p = 0.184, respectively) between patients receiving amifostine and those in the control group, confirming that amifostine did not compromise antitumor efficacy of radiotherapy (Brizel et al., 2000).

7. NSCLC
   a) Toxicities from NSCLC radiation (Antonadou et al., 2000; Gopal et al., 2003; Komaki et al., 2002)
      (1) Dysphagia
      (2) Esophagitis
      (3) Dyspnea
      (4) Cough
      (5) Pneumonitis
      (6) Fibrosis
   b) Amifostine has shown a reduction in the incidence of both radiation-induced toxicities, such as esophagitis and pneumonitis, as well as chemotherapy-related toxicities, including nephrotoxicity, hematologic toxicity, and possibly neurotoxicity (Antonadou et al., 2000, 2001; Antonadou, Marizenia, Synodinou, Puglisi, & Throuvalas, 2002; Komaki et al., 2002; Leong et al., 2001; Movsas et al., 2003; Werner-Wasik et al., 2001).
   c) Multiple trials have demonstrated a reduction in acute and late lung toxicity without affecting antitumor efficacy of radiation treatment in advanced lung cancer. In one study, the incidence of esophagitis grade $\geq$ 2 during week four of treatment with daily fraction of 2 Gy/five days/week was 42% (31/73) in the radiation alone group compared to 4% (3/73) in the group that also received amifostine (p < 0.001). Amifostine was administered daily at 340 mg/m². Two months post-therapy, 97 patients were evaluated for the incidence of pneumonitis. Forty-three percent (23/53) of patients in the radiation arm and 9% (4/44) in the amifostine plus radiation arm demonstrated changes representative of grade $\geq$ 2 lung damage (p < 0.001). Fibrosis was present in 53% (19/36) of patients receiving RT alone versus 28% (9/32) receiving radiation plus amifostine (Antonadou et al., 2001).
   d) In a study of 26 patients treated with thoracic irradiation for lung cancer, 11 patients received concurrent hyperfractionated radiation with chemotherapy (cisplatin, etoposide) with amifostine (Gopal et al., 2003). The cytoprotective benefit of amifostine in this report is illustrated with the increase in the threshold for DL_{CO} loss from 13 to 36 Gy. As noted above, amifostine also has been previously found to reduce the decrease in DL_{CO} from 42% to 24% in patients with NSCLC treated with chemoradiation. The authors emphasize the importance of evaluating the relationship between local radiation dose and the loss of local diffusion capacity in the lung. The utilization of this information in combination with a DVH allows for the prediction of the expected loss of whole-lung diffusion capacity associated with a treatment plan. Clinically, this is relevant because the DL_{CO} should not decrease much more than 50% than predicted if patients are to maintain a reasonable quality of life.
   e) Data from preclinical studies support the hypothesis that cytoprotection in the clinical setting appears to be time and dose dependent (Bachy, Fazenbaker, Kifle, & Cassatt, 2003; Cassatt, Fazenbaker, Kifle, & Bachy, 2002; Fazenbaker, Bachy, Kifle, & Cassatt, 2003).
   f) Several large clinical trials have demonstrated significant cytoprotection with the use of amifostine as a single injection prior to each standard fraction of radiation treatment five days each week for six to seven weeks (Antonadou et al., 2000, 2001, 2002; Brizel et al., 2000).

8. Dosing and administration of amifostine
   a) The recommended dose of amifostine in patients with head and neck cancer is 200 mg/m² administered once daily as a three-minute IV push starting 15–30 minutes prior to RT (package insert) for xerostomia protection.

b) Several clinical trials have provided evidence that amifostine at 300–340 mg/m^2 can provide mucosal protection and reduction of mucositis associated with radiation or radiochemotherapy (Antonadou et al., 2001, 2002; Buntzel et al., 1998).

c) Although not approved by the FDA, research has shown rapid IV push as a 10-second push may reduce the occurrence of nausea, vomiting, and hypotension associated with amifostine versus a slower IV push, while still maintaining the effectiveness and the antitumor efficacy of radiation or chemotherapy (Boccia, 2002; Wagner, Radmard, & Schonekaes, 1999).

d) Other research and preliminary data suggest subcutaneous administration at a 500 mg flat dose mixed in 2.5 ml of normal saline, given in one to two injections daily, 20–60 minutes prior to daily radiation, demonstrates a reduction in xerostomia and mucositis (Anne & Curran, 2002; Koukourakis et al., 2000). Future clinical studies are using 2.9 ml of normal saline given in two injections to minimize temperature and volume variations in solubility.

e) Adverse effects of amifostine as a radioprotector
  (1) Nausea/vomiting
  (2) Hypotension
  (3) Cutaneous reactions
  (4) Fever, chills
  (5) Asthenia (Anne & Curran, 2002; Boccia, 2002; Koukourakis et al., 2000).

9. Patient and family education
  a) Premedicate with an oral antiemetic 90–120 minutes before amifostine daily
    (1) Compazine 10 mg oral may be effective for most patients.
    (2) Assess patient's nausea profile and recommend a 5HT3 antagonist if patient has risk factors for increased nausea and vomiting. Keep in mind the patient's full treatment regimen when assessing need for antiemetics.
  b) Hydration is necessary
    (1) Encourage patient to drink two to three 8 oz. glasses of water or sports drink prior to amifostine.
    (2) If patient has a g-tube or peg tube, have patient give himself or herself 250 ml of fluid (water or sports drink) prior to amifostine.
    (3) Encourage patient to drink an additional liter throughout the day.
    (4) Assess for symptoms of dehydration daily before giving amifostine.
      (a) Dizziness
      (b) Light-headedness
      (c) Hypotension
      (d) Tachycardia
      (e) Concentrated urine
    (5) Hold if dehydrated or hypotensive.
    (6) Give IV hydration if needed.
    (7) Monitor blood pressure daily with a baseline and every 5–15 minutes or until stable or as clinically indicated (Daly, Holloway, & Ameen, 2003; Wagner et al., 1999).
  c) Cutaneous reaction with or without a fever
    (1) Local cutaneous reaction at the injection site can be treated with injection site rotation, local steroidal cream, and an oral antihistamine one hour before daily amifostine (Daly et al., 2003; Wang, Kagan, & Tome, 2003).
    (2) If a systemic rash occurs, which is defined as a rash outside the RT portal or local injection site, amifostine should be discontinued. Rash can be treated with comfort measures.
    (3) Discontinue if a fever occurs, and rule out other possible etiologies before continuing use (Boccia et al., 2003).

References

American Society of Clinical Oncology. (2002). 2002 Update of recommendation for the use of chemotherapy and radiotherapy protectants: Clinical practice guidelines of the American Society of Clinical Oncology. *Journal of Clinical Oncology, 20,* 2895–2903.

Anne, P.R., & Curran, W.J. (2002). A phase II trial of subcutaneous amifostine and radiation therapy in patients with head and neck cancer. *Seminars in Radiation Oncology, 12*(1), 18–19.

Antonadou, D., Coliarakis, N., Synodinou, M., Athanassiou, H., Kouveli, A., Verigos, C., et al. (2001). Randomized phase III trial of radiation treatment + amifostine in patients with advanced stage lung cancer. *International Journal of Radiation Oncology, Biology, Physics, 51,* 915–922.

Antonadou, D., Marizenia, P., Synodinou, M., Puglisi, M., & Throuvalas, N. (2002). Prophylactic use of amifostine to prevent radiochemotherapy-induced mucositis and xerostomia in head and neck cancer. *International Journal of Radiation Oncology, Biology, Physics, 52,* 739–747.

Antonadou, D., Synodinou, M., Boufi, M., Sagriotis, A., Paloudis, S., & Throuvalas, N. (2000). Amifostine reduces acute toxicity during radiochemotherapy in patients with localized advanced stage non small cell lung cancer [Abstract]. *Proceedings of the 36th Annual Meeting of the American Society of Clinical Oncology, 19,* 1960.

Bachy, C.M., Fazenbaker, C.A., Kifle, G., & Cassatt, D.R. (2003). Daily dosing with amifostine is necessary for full protection against oral mucositis caused by fractionated radiation in rats: Protection and pharmacokinetics [Abstract]. *Proceedings of the 39th Annual Meeting of the American Society of Clinical Oncology, 22,* 2081.

Boccia, R.V. (2002). Improved tolerability of amifostine with rapid infusion and optimal patient preparation. *Seminars in Oncology, 29*(Suppl. 19), 9–13.

Boccia, R.V., Bourhis, D., Brizel, D., Daly, C., Holloway, N., Hymes, S., et al. (2003). Management of cutaneous reactions associated with Ethyol®: Summary findings of an independent panel [Abstract]. *Proceedings of the 39th Annual Meeting of the American Society of Clinical Oncology, 22,* 3175.

Brizel, D.M., Wasserman, T.H., Henke, M., Strnad, V., Rudat, V., Monnier, A., et al. (2000). Phase III randomized trial of amifostine as a radioprotector in head and neck cancer. *Journal of Clinical Oncology, 18,* 3339–3345.

Buntzel, J., Kuttner, K., Frohlich, D., & Glatzel, M. (1998). Selective cytoprotection with amifostine in concurrent radiochemotherapy for head and neck cancer. *Annals of Oncology, 9,* 505–509.

Capizzi, R.L. (1999). The preclinical basis for broad-spectrum selective cytoprotection of normal tissues from cytotoxic therapies by amifostine. *Seminars in Oncology, 26*(Suppl. 7), 3–21.

Cassatt, D.R., Fazenbaker, C.A., Kifle, G., & Bachy, C.M. (2002). Preclinical studies on the radioprotective efficacy and pharmacokinetics of subcutaneously administered amifostine. *Seminars in Oncology, 29*(Suppl. 19), 2–8.

Daly, C., Holloway, D., & Ameen, D. (2003). Subcutaneous administration of amifostine during radiotherapy: A clinical perspective [Abstract]. *Proceedings of the 39th Annual Meeting of the American Society of Clinical Oncology, 22,* 3154.

Fazenbaker, C.A., Bachy, C.M., Kifle, G., & Cassatt, D.R. (2003). Dose and schedule dependency of amifostine protection against hyperfractionated radiotherapy in a rat model [Abstract]. *Proceedings of the 39th Annual Meeting of the American Society of Clinical Oncology, 22,* 2083.

Gopal, R., Tucker, S.L., Komaki, R., Liao, Z., Forster, K.M., Stevens, C., et al. (2003). The relationship between local dose and loss of function for irradiated lung. *International Journal of Radiation Oncology, Biology, Physics, 56,* 106–113.

Jatoi, A., & Thomas, C.R. (2002). Esophageal cancer and the esophagus: Challenges and potential strategies for selective cytoprotection of the tumor-bearing organ during cancer treatment. *Seminars in Oncology, 12*(Suppl. 1), 62–67.

Kemp, G., Rose, P., Lurain, J., Berman, M., Manetta, A., Roullet, B., et al. (1996). Amifostine pretreatment for protection against cyclophosphamide induced and cisplatin induced toxicities: Results of a randomized control trial in patients with advanced ovarian cancer. *Journal of Clinical Oncology, 14,* 2101–2112.

Komaki, R., Lee, J.S., Kaplan, B., Allen, P., Kelly, J.F., Liao, Z., et al. (2002). Randomized Phase III study of chemoradiation with or without amifostine for patients with favorable performance status inoperable stage II–III non-small cell lung cancer: Preliminary results. *Seminars in Oncology, 12*(Suppl. 1), 46–49.

Koukourakis, M.I., Kyrias, G., Kakolyris, S., Kouroussis, C., Frangiadaki, C., Giatromanolaki, A., et al. (2000). Subcutaneous administration of amifostine during fractionated radiotherapy: A randomized phase II study. *Journal of Clinical Oncology, 18,* 2226–2233.

Leong, S.S., Tan, E.H., Fong, K.W., Ong, Y.K., Ang, P.T., Wilder-Smith, E., et al. (2001). Randomized double blind study of combined modality treatment with or without amifostine in unresectable stage III non-small cell lung cancer (NSCLC) [Abstract]. *Proceedings of the 37th Annual Meeting of the American Society of Clinical Oncology, 20,* 1310.

Movsas, B., Scott, C., Langer, C., Werner-Wasik, M., Nicolaou, N., Komaki, R., et al. (2003). Phase III study of amifostine in patients with locally advanced non-small cell lung cancer (NSCLC) receiving intensive chemo/hyperfractionated radiation. Radiation Therapy Oncology Group (RTOG) 98-01 [Abstract]. *Proceedings of the 39th Annual Meeting of the American Society of Clinical Oncology, 22,* 2559.

Schiller, J.H., Storer, B., Berlin, J., Wittenkeller, J., Larson, M., Pharo, L., et al. (1996). Amifostine, cisplatin and vinblastine in metastatic non-small-cell lung cancer: A report of high response rates and prolonged survival. *Journal of Clinical Oncology, 14,* 1913–1921.

United States Pharmacopeia. (2002). *Amifostine, finalized drug information.* Rockville, MD: Author.

Wagner, W., Radmard, A., & Schonekaes, K.G. (1999). A new administration schedule for amifostine as a radioprotector in cancer therapy. *Anticancer Research, 19*(3B), 2281–2283.

Wang, R., Kagan, R.A., & Tome, M.A. (2003). Subcutaneous (SC) amifostine (A) is safe and effective in the treatment of head and neck cancers [Abstract]. *Proceedings of the 39th Annual Meeting of the American Society of Clinical Oncology, 22,* 2065.

Wasserman, T., Mackowiak, J.I., Brizel, D.M., Oster, W., Zhang, J., Peeples, P., et al. (2000). Effect of amifostine on patient assessed clinical benefit in irradiated head and neck cancer. *International Journal of Radiation Oncology, Biology, Physics, 48,* 1035–1039.

Werner-Wasik, M., Axelrod, R.S., Friedland, D.P., Hauck, W., Rose, L.J., Chapman, A.E., et al. (2001). Preliminary report on reduction of esophagitis by amifostine in patients with non-small-cell lung cancer treated with chemoradiotherapy. *Clinical Lung Cancer, 2,* 284–289.

C. Concurrent chemotherapy
1. Definition: Chemotherapy given at the same time as RT, which provides more activity on tumor cells than either agent alone, with acceptable toxicity (Eisbruch, 2003). Has provided better clinical results than induction or adjuvant chemotherapy and RT (Milas & Cox, 2003).
2. Rationale: To take advantage of the radiosensitizing effects of chemotherapy agents (Schantz, Harrison, & Forastiere, 2001). May increase overall and disease-free survival by

reducing the risk of local recurrence and distant metastases (Adelstein et al., 2003; Eisbruch, 2003; Gerard et al., 2003; Kleinberg et al., 2003).

3. Generally used for locally advanced and/or unresectable solid tumors and preoperatively (neoadjuvant) to reduce tumor size. The most commonly treated cancers include (Eisbruch, 2003; Gerard et al., 2003; Kleinberg et al., 2003)

   a) Head and neck
   b) Lung (non-small cell)
   c) GI (esophagus, gastric, colorectal).

4. Numerous treatment regimens are used; the most common ones include (Eisbruch, 2003; Gerard et al., 2003; Kleinberg et al., 2003)

   a) RT + weekly IV low-dose carboplatin and taxanes for lung cancer
   b) RT + Monday–Friday fluorouracil by continuous infusion pump for GI and head and neck cancers
   c) RT + fluorouracil combined with other agents.

5. Many pharmacologic and biologic agents currently are being tested in clinical trials, in combination with RT or chemotherapy and RT. Some promising agents are

   a) Anti-angiogenesis inhibitors, which prevent formation of new blood vessels necessary to tumor growth and metastasis (Coutinho & Lima, 2003; Wilkes, Ingwersen, & Barton-Burke, 2003). Agents in this group generally have low toxicity (Stevens, 2003).
      (1) Thalidomide
      (2) Tyrosine kinase inhibitors, such as gefitinib
      (3) NSAIDs, which may suppress prostaglandin secretion by tumors, inhibiting tumor development (Eisbruch, 2003)
   b) Immunotherapy agents enhance the ability of the immune system to kill tumor cells (Stevens, 2003).

      (1) Antitumor monoclonal antibodies such as C225 (cetuximab), which block epidermal growth factor receptor function
      (2) Vaccines made from tumor cells, which may be able to improve the ability of the immune system to target and destroy similar tumor cells

6. Nursing considerations: RT nurses face increasing challenges in caring for patients receiving concurrent therapies.

   a) Incorporating new information into clinical practice related to new radiation techniques, new agents, and genetic and molecular therapies
   b) Serving as a resource for RT staff regarding concurrent therapies, schedules, and patient assessment
   c) Collaborating with medical oncology, nuclear medicine, and other departments or offices regarding treatment schedules, lab work, side-effect management, and follow-up to ensure that patients receive comprehensive care
   d) Monitoring patients receiving concurrent therapy: Although most chemotherapy agents are given in lower doses than if given alone, concomitant side effects can be severe and necessitate treatment interruptions (Schantz et al., 2001).
      (1) Bone marrow suppression: Almost all chemotherapy agents, especially taxanes, gemcitabine, carboplatin, and mitomycin
      (2) GI (nausea, vomiting, diarrhea, anorexia): Taxanes, platinum compounds
      (3) Stomatitis: Taxanes, fluorouracil
      (4) Peripheral neuropathies: Platinum compounds, taxanes
      (5) Esophagitis: Cisplatin + etoposide + RT (Milas & Cox, 2003)
      (6) Patients should be provided with the same information and cautions as those receiving chemotherapy or radiation alone.

References

Adelstein, D., Li, Y., Adams, G., Wagner, Jr., H., Kish, J., Ensley, J., et al. (2003). An intergroup phase III comparison of standard radiation therapy and two schedules of concurrent chemoradiotherapy in patients with unresectable squamous cell head and neck cancer. *Journal of Clinical Oncology, 21,* 92–98.

Coutinho, A., & Lima, C. (2003). Metastatic colorectal cancer: Systemic treatment in the new millennium. *Cancer Control, 10,* 224–238.

Eisbruch, A. (2003). *Advances in radiation therapy 2003: Highlights from the Radiation Therapy Oncology Group winter meeting.* Retrieved July 30, 2003, from http://www.medscape.com/viewarticle/450746

Gerard, J., Chapet, O., Nemoz, C., Romestaing, P., Mornex, F., Coquard, R., et al. (2003). Preoperative concurrent chemoradiotherapy in locally advanced rectal cancer with high-dose radiation and oxaliplatin-containing regimen: The Lyon R0-04 phase II trial. *Journal of Clinical Oncology, 21,* 1119–1124.

Kleinberg, L., Knisely, J., Heitmiller, R., Zahurak, M., Salem, R., Burtness, B., et al. (2003). Mature survival results with preoperative cisplatin, protracted infusion 5-fluorouracil, and 44-Gy radiotherapy for esophageal cancer. *International Journal of Radiation Oncology, Biology, Physics, 56,* 328–334.

Milas, L., & Cox, J.D. (2003). Principles of combining radiation therapy and chemotherapy. In J. Cox & S.K. Ang (Eds.), *Radiation oncology: Rationale, technique, results* (8th ed., pp. 108–124). St. Louis, MO: Mosby.

Schantz, S., Harrison, L., & Forastiere, A. (2001). Tumors of the nasal cavity and paranasal sinuses, nasopharynx, oral cavity, and oropharynx. In V.T. DeVita, S. Hellman, & S.A. Rosenberg (Eds.), *Cancer: Principles and practice of oncology* (6th ed., pp. 797–860). Philadelphia: Lippincott Williams & Wilkins.

Stevens, C.W. (2003). Clinical applications of new modalities. In J. Cox & S.K. Ang (Eds.), *Radiation oncology: Rationale, technique, results* (8th ed., pp. 987–1002). St. Louis, MO: Mosby.

Wilkes, G., Ingwersen, K., & Barton-Burke, M. (2003). *Oncology nursing drug handbook.* Sudbury, MA: Jones and Bartlett.

D. Radioimmunotherapy and radionuclide therapy
1. Radioimmunotherapy (radioimmunoconjugate treatment)
   a) Definition: Radioimmunotherapy is the administration of radionuclides chemically conjugated to antibodies. The antibodies can recognize and bind to antigens on tumor cells and serve as carriers (Weiner, Adams, & von Mehren, 2001).
   b) Rationale
      (1) Monoclonal antibodies are produced in laboratories and combined with a radioisotope to provide targeted specificity to the cytotoxic process and allows for a targeted dose of radiation. Murine monoclonal antibodies are produced from mice. Chimeric monoclonal antibodies are derived from both mice and humans (Witzig, 2000).
      (2) The monoclonal antibody is bound to a radioactive isotope by a strong linking agent to deliver therapeutic radioisotopes to produce tumor kill by a single cell mechanism. The radiation from the isotope destroys the tumor cell through the nuclear structure (Witzig, 2000).

      (3) Hematologic neoplasms are more responsive than solid tumors (Witzig, 2000).
      (4) Radioimmunotherapy can systemically deliver targeted radiation to areas of disease with relative sparing of tissues (Witzig, 2000).
      (5) Radioimmunotherapy often is used in combination with chemotherapy to enhance targeting and cell kill (Gopal et al., 2002; Yanik et al., 2002).
   c) Types: Two radionuclides used for radioimmunotherapy regimens are iodine-131 and yttrium-90 (Hendrix, deLeon, & Dillman, 2002).
      (1) Yttrium-90 has a long path length, high-energy beta emissions, lack of volatility, and ease and safety of its conjugation to antibodies and patient administration (Weiner et al., 2001).
         (a) Ibritumomab tiuxetan (Zevalin™, Biogen IDEC, Gaithersburg, MD) is composed of a murine monoclonal antibody, ibritumomab
         (b) Ibritumomab is bound to tiuxetan, which chelates the radioactive isotope (yttrium-90) (Clayton, 2003).
      (2) Iodine-131, a beta- and gamma-emitting radionuclide, has a relatively short average path length and enables both patient dose optimization and tumor cell kill with a single agent (Wade, Elliott, Fleck, Hon, & Knox, 2001).
         (a) Iodine-131 tositumomab (Bexxar®, GlaxoSmithKline) is composed of a murine monoclonal antibody, tositumomab
         (b) Tositumomab is bound to a radiolabeled monoclonal antibody, iodine-131.
      (3) Both antibodies target the CD-20 antigen on the surface of mature B cells

and B cell tumors (Meredith et al., 2001).

d) Indications: To date, phase I, II, and III trials and an open-label study are completed. Results show that ibritumomab tiuxetan and iodine-131 tositumomab regimens are effective for refractory low-grade follicular or transformed B cell NHL, including patients with rituximab refractory follicular NHL (Baker, 2002; Witzig et al., 2002; Zelenetz, 2003).

e) Contraindications
   (1) Patients should not receive the regimens if they have more than a 25% lymphoma marrow involvement or impaired bone marrow reserve because of the increased potential for hematologic toxicities.
   (2) Type I sensitivity, production of human anti-mouse antibodies (HAMA), to murine proteins (mouse antibodies). The number of patients who develop HAMA seems to be directly proportional to the amount of prior chemotherapy the patient has received and his or her degree of immunosuppression (Vose, 1999).

f) Pretreatment tests
   (1) Bilateral bone marrow biopsy and aspiration to determine extent of lymphoma bone marrow
   (2) HAMA test: If the test is positive, there is an increased risk of allergic reaction.

g) Treatment regimen for radioimmunotherapy: Dosing guidelines are based on the weight and platelet count.
   (1) Dosing for Zevalin
      (a) Single infusion of rituximab followed by In-III ibritumomab tiuxetan to assess biodistribution using whole-body gamma camera images
      (b) Second infusion of rituximab followed by Y-90 ibritumomab tiuxetan
   (2) Dosing for Bexxar
      (a) I-131 tositumomab requires thyroid blockage to prevent uptake of radioactive iodine for at least two weeks following the therapeutic dose.
      (b) Dosimetric dose of unlabeled tositumomab improves biodistribution of the radiolabeled antibody prior to labeled infusion (Hohenstein, Augustine, Rutar, & Vose, 2003).
      (c) Three whole-body gamma scans are performed.

h) Administration
   (1) Zevalin (Biogen IDEC, 2002)
      (a) Premedicate with acetaminophen and diphenhydramine.
      (b) Rituximab 250 mg/m^2 at 50 mg/hour
      (c) Increase 50 mg/hour at 30-minute intervals. **Never administer by IV push or bolus.**
      (d) In-III ibritumomab tiuxetan (5 mCi/1.6 mg antibody) calibrated and prepared by nuclear medicine/radiation physicist for injection
      (e) First whole-body camera image taken 2–24 hours after first dose is given.
      (f) Second whole-body camera image taken 48–72 hours later.
      (g) Zevalin regimen is initiated seven to nine days after rituximab is administered.
      (h) Premedicate with acetaminophen and diphenhydramine.
      (i) Rituximab 250 mg/m^2 infused at 100 mg/hour at 30-minute intervals to maximum rate of 400 mg/hour.
      (j) Within four hours of the completion, the patient receives Y-90 ibritumomab tiuxetan intravenously by a physician.
      (k) Acrylic shielding blocks beta emissions; absorbent pads are placed under infusion sites (Hendrix et al., 2002).
   (2) Bexxar (GlaxoSmithKline, 2003; Hohenstein et al., 2003)
      (a) Oral iodine supplements are administered beginning day 1 for 14 days.

(b) Patients are pretreated with acetaminophen and diphenhydramine.

(c) 450 mg of tositumomab (unlabeled) is given on day 0 over 60 minutes.

(d) A 5-mCi dosimetric dose of I-131 is administered over 20 minutes.

(e) The whole-body gamma scan is done on day 0.

(f) The patient usually returns for two subsequent whole-body scans on days 2–4 and 6–7.

(g) The patient's therapeutic dose is calculated.

(h) Between days 7–14, the patient will repeat steps (b) through (e).

i) Toxicities: When absorbed doses to tumors are large, the absorbed dose to adjacent tissues also can be large, potentially causing unexpected toxicities in surrounding tissues and organs (Sparks, Crowe, Wong, Toohey, & Siegel, 2002).

(1) Hematologic (Biogen IDEC, 2002; GlaxoSmithKline, 2003).

(a) Bone marrow suppression
   i) Thrombocytopenia
   ii) Neutropenia
   iii) Anemia
   iv) Asthenia

(b) Hematologic support allowed with G-CSF and epoetin.

(c) Hematologic toxicity is the most common acute side effect. The median time to nadir is seven to nine weeks (Witzig et al., 2002).

(d) The risk of hematologic toxicities increases with bone marrow involvement.

(2) Non-hematologic (Biogen IDEC, 2002; GlaxoSmithKline, 2003)

(a) Rash
(b) Fever
(c) Chills
(d) Myalgia
(e) Diaphoresis
(f) Pruritus
(g) Nausea and vomiting
(h) Diarrhea
(i) Nasal congestion
(j) Hypotension

(3) Other toxicities
(a) Rigors
(b) Bronchospasm
(c) Laryngeal edema

j) Documentation (Catlin-Huth, Haas, & Pollock, 2002)

(1) Monitoring: Injury potential, bleeding, infection

(2) CBC with differential weekly until levels recover

k) Nursing care

(1) Treatment with radioimmunotherapy involves the coordinated efforts of hematologists/oncologists, nurses, pharmacists, nuclear medicine personnel, physics staff, and radiation oncologists.

(2) Nurses must adhere to strict guidelines for radiation safety and protection (see section III of this manual).

(3) All personnel involved in the administration of tositumomab and iodine-131 should follow the precautions for standard radioactive iodine.

(4) Guidelines for outpatient care for patients treated with radioimmunotherapy for NHL have been suggested in the literature (Hendrix et al., 2002; Hohenstein et al., 2003).

(5) Early patient education to facilitate early recognition of symptoms of infusion side effects (Kostis & Callaghan, 2000)

(6) Review with patient the importance of premedications, such as acetaminophen and diphenhydramine, steroids, antihistamines, oxygen, and pain medications (Kostis & Callaghan, 2000).

l) Patient and family education

(1) Zevalin
(a) Low-dose radiation exposure: No limits on activity.
(b) May have family contact
(c) Avoid exposure to patient's body fluids (saliva, urine, and stool) for one week.
(d) A condom must be used during sexual relations.

(e) Patient may experience flu-like symptoms (Biogen IDEC, 2002).

(2) Bexxar

(a) Isolation of patient with restriction to persons entering the room during infusion

(b) The release of patients after administration must be carried out with specific guidelines. By following patient-specific instructions, radiation exposure of family members and caregivers who are close to the patient is maintained as low as reasonably achievable and within the Nuclear Regulatory Commission (NRC) limits (Hohenstein et al., 2003).

(c) The patient must sleep in a separate bed with at least six feet of separation from the next person (Hohenstein et al., 2003).

(d) Patient should not take long trips (in car, bus, plane, or train) sitting near others (Hohenstein et al., 2003).

(e) Patient should wash hands frequently (Hohenstein et al., 2003).

(f) Encourage patient to drink fluids to assist in clearing the drug from the system (Hohenstein et al., 2003).

(g) Hold clothing and linen in a separate bag for one week before laundering (Hohenstein et al., 2003).

(h) Limit contact with individuals, as well as time and distance (Hohenstein et al., 2003).

(i) Avoid contact with pregnant women and children (Hohenstein et al., 2003).

m) Related Web sites

(1) Lymphoma Research Foundation—www.lymphoma.org

(2) Partners Against Lymphoma—www.lymphomation.org—A nationwide one-to-one support program where patients with lymphoma and their caregivers can share their experiences and find emotional support.

2. Radionuclide therapy (Bruner, Bucholtz, Iwamoto, & Strohl, 1998)

a) Definition: Systemic radionuclide is brachytherapy that is administered using unsealed radioactive sources in a liquid, capsule, or colloidal suspension that is ingested, injected, or instilled directly into the body.

b) Rationale: Radionuclide therapy is very effective in treating specific tumors and has relatively few side effects (Bruner et al., 1998).

c) Types and uses in specific cancers

(1) Iodine-131 (also referred to as MIBG): Used mainly for thyroid cancer and other neuroendocrine tumors; localizes within well-differentiated thyroid cancer cells (Fraker, Skarulis, & Livolsi, 2001).

(a) Administration: Given by mouth, either capsules or liquid

(b) Nursing care

i) Less than 33 mCi: Treated as outpatient

ii) Greater than 33 mCi: Hospitalization required

iii) Radiation precautions (see section III of this manual)

iv) Encourage oral intake of fluids to facilitate disbursement/absorption of iodine-131.

v) Body fluid precautions (blood, saliva, urine, stool, and perspiration)

vi) Use plastic covering on pillows, mattresses, and anything the patient touches while in the hospital (e.g., phone, television, sink handles, bedside table).

vii) Use disposable eating utensils.

(c) Patient and family education

i) Educate regarding all of the above.

ii) Offer emotional support: Experience can be very distressing to patient (Stajduhar et al., 2000).

iii) Offer suggestions for passing time and reducing anxiety (reading, television, music, telephone, crossword puzzles).

(d) Inpatient staff education
  i) Provide in-service regarding brachytherapy/iodine-131/radiation safety.
  ii) Provide written instructions/protocols/references.
  iii) Be available for consultation or questions in person or on the telephone.

(2) Strontium-89: Used mainly for bone metastasis. Localizes in the mineral of the bone by combining with calcium (Brown & Healy, 2001).

(a) Administration
  i) Outpatient procedure
  ii) Administered by radiation oncologist or nuclear medicine physician (Dunne-Daly, 1997)
  iii) IV administration

(b) Nursing care
  i) Establish IV access.
  ii) Provide education regarding rationale and side effects.
  iii) Obtain baseline blood count (platelets can be affected).
  iv) Check order for and results of repeat blood count every two weeks (for 12 weeks) (Dunne-Daly, 1997).

(c) Patient and family education: For first week
  i) Wipe up spills and flush after each use.
  ii) Wash hands after each use of the toilet.
  iii) Wash linens separately when they are exposed to body fluids.

(d) Other education
  i) Educate about pain flare up to 72 hours after administration; treat with analgesics (acetaminophen or stronger). Flare may last up to one week (Dunne-Daly, 1997). The use of glucocorticoids has been beneficial.
  ii) Instruct per lab appointments, importance of follow-up, and thrombocytopenia precautions, if necessary.

(3) Samarium Sm-153 (Quadramet® [Berlex Laboratories, Richmond, CA]): Is neutron irradiation of isotopically enriched Samarium Sm-152 oxide. It emits both medium-energy beta particles and a gamma photon (Berlex, 2001). Quadramet is indicated for use in patients with ostcoblastic mctastatic bone lesions (Serafini et al., 1998).

(a) Administration (Berlex, 2001)
  i) Outpatient procedure
  ii) Given IV over one minute followed by IV flush
  iii) Dosage: 1 mCi/kg of patient's body weight
  iv) Administered by radiation oncologist or nuclear medicine physician

(b) Nursing care
  i) Obtain baseline CBC, platelet count, and creatinine.
  ii) Establish IV access.
  iii) No fasting is necessary.
  iv) Infuse 500 cc NSS or have the patient drink two quarts of water before arriving.
  v) Provide a shielded syringe for physician.
  vi) Monitor for 20 minutes after injection.

(c) Patient and family education
  i) Educate patient that mild and transient flare of pain may occur within 72 hours of injection (Serafini et al., 1998)
  ii) Instruct patient to follow up with repeat blood counts weekly for eight weeks. The most common adverse events are reversible hematologic events (Sartor, Quick, Reid, Hostin, & Duschene, 1997).

iii) Urinary precautions need to be taken 12 hours after administration (Berlex, 2001).

iv) Flush toilet several times after each use.

v) Spilled urine should be cleaned up completely.

vi) Wash hands thoroughly with soap and water.

vii) Drink extra fluids to speed the elimination of radiation.

viii) Do not have sexual contact with your partner for 12 hours after receiving Quadramet.

(4) Phosphorus-32: A pure beta emitter radionuclide. Used for the treatment of chronic myeloproliferative disorder, primary proliferative polycythemia (PPP), and malignant ascites usually associated with ovarian cancer.

(a) PPP: An unnatural proliferation of one or more elements of the hemopoietic system (Balan & Critchley, 1997)

i) The radionuclide targets the nucleic acids of rapidly proliferating cells.

ii) Without therapy, complications of panmyelosis, splenomegaly, and a predisposition to venous or arterial thrombosis, myelofibrosis, and acute leukemia have been reported (Streiff, Smith, & Spivak, 2002).

iii) The rationale for its use is to reduce the patient's hematocrit level, maintain a normal platelet count, and prevent complications of cerebral thrombosis, thrombophlebi-

tis, or myocardial infarction (Balan & Critchley, 1997).

iv) Administration: Given by a radiation oncologist or nuclear medicine physician by IV injection. Phosphorus-32 is mixed in an isotonic solution of sodium orthophosphate and calibrated by a radiation oncology physicist (Balan & Critchley, 1997).

v) Patients with polycythemia vera are at risk for the following side effects after use of phosphorus-32: 5.5% risk of myelofibrosis, 7.6% risk of acute leukemia, and 8% risk of developing other cancers (Balan & Critchley, 1997; Parmentier, 2003).

(b) Nursing care

i) Baseline clinical laboratory evaluation for measurement of red cell volume to establish diagnosis of PPP

ii) Outpatient/clinic setting

iii) Establish IV access.

iv) Acrylic shielding blocks beta emissions; absorbent pads are placed under infusion sites.

v) Body fluid precautions

(c) Patient and family education

i) Instruct patient to increase fluid intake.

ii) Flush toilet twice with lid closed.

iii) Wash hands after using toilet.

iv) Wash linens separately.

v) Stress importance of follow-up.

(d) The use of intraperitoneal phosphorus-32 in the treatment of epithelial ovarian cancer continues to be controversial; however, its use is revisited on a fairly regular basis (Saul et al., 1996). It is still sometimes used for management of malignant ascites.

i) Because of the high rate of late bowel complications, including chronic abdominal cramping and small bowel obstruction, it has been recommended that cisplatin be used as standard adjuvant treatment for ovarian cancer rather than phosphorus-32 (Condra, Mendenhall, Morgan, & Marcus, 1997; Vergote et al., 1992).

ii) Phosphorus-32 also has been shown to lack efficacy in one of its traditional uses, in stage III ovarian cancer after a negative second-look laparotomy (Varia et al., 2003).

iii) Administered through an intraperitoneal catheter by a radiation oncologist or nuclear medicine physician.

iv) Often instilled as an outpatient procedure

v) Nursing care—Wound dressing should be observed for drainage and discarded in a doubled plastic bag.

vi) Patient and family education—Once instilled into the patient, special precautions are required; the patient's body is enough to shield others from radiation.

(5) Related Web sites

(a) *What You Need to Know About™ Thyroid Cancer*—www.cancer.gov

(b) *Cancer Pain Release* (World Health Organization)—www.whocancerpain.wisc.edu/eng/15_4/online.html

(c) World Nuclear Association—www.world-nuclear.org/info/inf55.htm

(d) State Government of Victoria, Australia, Department of Human Services, Radiation Safety Program—www.health.vic.gov.au/environment/downloads/guidelines_strontium.pdf

References

Baker, D. (2002). Zevalin (ibritumomab tiuxetan): A promising new regimen for treatment of NHL. *Druglink in Oncology Times, 9,* 1–8.

Balan, K.K., & Critchley, M. (1997). Outcome of 259 patients with primary proliferative polycythemia (PPP) and idiopathic thrombocythemia (IT) treated in a regional nuclear medicine department with phosphorus-32—A 15-year review. *British Journal of Radiology, 70,* 1169–1173.

Berlex. (2001). Quadramet [Package insert]. Richmond, CA: Author.

Biogen IDEC. (2002). Zevalin (ibritumomab tiuxetan) [Package insert]. Gaithersburg, MD: Author.

Brown, H.K., & Healy, J.K. (2001). Metastatic cancer to the bone. In V.T. DeVita, S. Hellman, & S.A. Rosenberg (Eds.), *Cancer:*

Principles and practice of oncology (6th ed., pp. 2713–2720). Philadelphia: Lippincott Williams & Wilkins.

Bruner, D.W., Bucholtz, J.D., Iwamoto, R., & Strohl, R. (Eds.). (1998). *Manual for radiation oncology nursing practice and education.* Pittsburgh, PA: Oncology Nursing Society.

Catlin-Huth, C., Haas, M., & Pollock, V. (2002). *Radiation therapy patient care record: A tool for documenting nursing care.* Pittsburgh, PA: Oncology Nursing Society.

Clayton, J. (2003). Nursing a patient during and after 90Y- ibritumomab tiuxetan (Zevalin) therapy. *Leukemia and Lymphoma, 44*(Suppl. 4), 549–555.

Condra, K.S., Mendenhall, W.M., Morgan, L.S., & Marcus, R.B. (1997). Adjuvant 32P in the treatment of ovarian carcinoma. *Radiation Oncology Investigations, 5,* 300–304.

Dunne-Daly, C. (1997). Principles of brachytherapy. In K.H. Dow, J.D. Bucholtz, R. Iwamoto, V.K. Fieler, & L.J. Hilderley (Eds.), *Nursing care in radiation oncology* (2nd ed., pp. 29–31). Philadelphia: Saunders.

Fraker, D.L., Skarulis, M., & Livolsi, V. (2001). Thyroid tumors. In V.T. DeVita, S. Hellman, & S.A. Rosenberg (Eds.), *Cancer: Principles and practice of oncology* (6th ed., pp. 1740–1763). Philadelphia: Lippincott Williams & Wilkins.

GlaxoSmithKline. (2003). Bexxar [Package insert]. Cambridge, MA: Author.

Gopal, A.K., Rajendran, J.G., Petersdorf, S.H., Maloney, D.G., Eary, J.F., Wood, B.L., et al. (2002). High-dose chemo-radioimmunotherapy with autologous stem cell support for relapsed mantle cell lymphoma. *Blood, 99,* 3158–3162.

Hendrix, C.S., deLeon, C., & Dillman, R.O. (2002). Radioimmunotherapy for non-Hodgkin's lymphoma with yttrium 90 ibritumomab tiuxetan. *Clinical Journal of Oncology Nursing, 6,* 144–148.

Hohenstein, M.A., Augustine, S.C., Rutar, F., & Vose, J.M. (2003). Establishing an institutional model for the administration of tositumomab and iodine 131 tositumomab. *Seminars in Oncology, 30*(Suppl. 4), 39–49.

Kostis, C., & Callaghan, M. (2000). Rituximab: A new monoclonal antibody therapy for non-Hodgkin's lymphoma. *Oncology Nursing Forum, 27,* 51–59.

Meredith, R.F., Leigh, B.R., Wiseman, G.A., Kornmehl, E.M., Raubitschek, A.A., Welsh, I.S., et al. (2001). Zevalin radioimmunotherapy is effective for patients with bulky non-Hodgkin's lymphoma. *International Journal of Radiation Oncology, Biology, Physics, 51*(Suppl. 1), 69–70.

Parmentier, C. (2003). Use and risks of phosphorus-32 in the treatment of polycythemia vera. *European Journal of Nuclear Medicine and Molecular Imaging, 30,* 1413–1417.

Sartor, O., Quick, D., Reid, R., Hostin, P., & Duschene, G. (1997). A double blind placebo controlled study of 153-samarium-EDTMP for palliation of bone pain in patients with hormone-refractory prostate cancer [Abstract]. *Journal of Urology, 157,* 321.

Saul, H.M., Sedlacek, T.V., Heller, P.B., Glassburn, J.R., Riva, J., Bertoli, R., et al. (1996). Intracavitary use of radioactive colloidal phosphorus 32 in the treatment of epithelial ovarian cancer. *Journal of the American Osteopathic Association, 96,* 727–732.

Serafini, A.N., Houston, S.J., Resche, I., Quick, D.P., Grund, F.M., Ell, P.J., et al. (1998). Palliation of pain associated with metastatic bone cancer using samarium-153 lexidronam: A double-blind placebo-controlled clinical trial. *Journal of Clinical Oncology, 16,* 1574–1581.

Sparks, R.B., Crowe, E.A., Wong, F.C., Toohey, R.E., & Siegel, J.A. (2002). Radiation dose distributions in normal tissue adjacent to tumors containing (131)I or (90)Y: The potential for toxicity. *Journal of Nuclear Medicine, 43,* 1110–1114.

Stajduhar, K.I., Neithercut, J., Chu, E., Pham, P., Rohde, J., Sicotte, A., et al. (2000). Thyroid cancer: Patients' experiences of receiving iodine-131 therapy. *Oncology Nursing Forum, 27,* 1213–1218.

Streiff, M.B., Smith, B., & Spivak, J.L. (2002). The diagnosis and management of polycythemia vera in the era since the polycythemia vera study: A survey of American Society of Hematology members' practice patterns. *Blood, 99,* 1144–1149.

Varia, M.A., Stehman, F.B., Bundy, B.N., Benda, J.A., Clarke-Pearson, D.L., Alvarez, R.D., et al. (2003). Intraperitoneal radioactive phosphorus (32P) versus observation after negative second-look laparotomy for stage III ovarian carcinoma: A randomized trial of the Gynecologic Oncology Group. *Journal of Clinical Oncology, 21,* 2849–2855.

Vergote, I.B., Vergote-De Vos, L.N., Abeler, V.M., Aas, M., Lindegaard, M.W., Kjorstad, K.E., et al. (1992). Randomized trial comparing cisplatin with radioactive phosphorus or whole-abdomen irradiation as adjuvant treatment of ovarian cancer. *Cancer, 69,* 741–749.

Vose, J.M. (1999). Antibody therapy for non-Hodgkin's lymphoma. *Updates in Clinical Oncology, 2*(4), 1–11.

Wade, J.L., Elliot, E.C., Fleck, R., Hon, J., & Knox, S. (2001). Efficacy and safety of Bexxar™ in a large multicentered expanded access study. *International Journal of Radiation Oncology, Biology, Physics, 51,* 359–360.

Weiner, L.M., Adams, G.P., & von Mehren, M. (2001) Pharmacology of cancer biotherapeutics. In V.T. DeVita, S. Hellman, & S.A. Rosenberg (Eds.), *Cancer: Principles and practice of oncology* (6th ed., pp. 495–508) Philadelphia: Lippincott Williams & Wilkins.

Witzig, T.E., (2000). The use of ibritumomab tiuxetan radioimmunotherapy for patients with relapsed B-cell non-Hodgkin's lymphoma. *Seminars in Oncology, 27,* 74–78.

Witzig, T.E., Flinn, I.W., Gordon, L.I., Emmanouilides, C., Czuczman, M.A., Saleh, M.N., et al. (2002). Treatment with ibritumomab tiuxetan radioimmunotherapy in patients with rituximab-refractory follicular non-Hodgkin's lymphoma. *Journal of Clinical Oncology, 20,* 3262–3269.

Yanik, G.A., Levine, J.E., Matthay, K.K., Sisson, J.C., Shulkin, B.L., Shapiro, B., et al. (2002). Pilot study of iodine-131-metaiodobenzylguanidine in combination with myeloablative chemotherapy and autologous stem-cell support for the treatment of neuroblastoma. *Journal of Clinical Oncology, 20,* 2142–2149.

Zelenetz, A.D. (2003). A clinical and scientific overview of tositumomab and iodine 131 tositumomab. *Seminars in Oncology, 30*(Suppl. 2), 22–30.

X.   General radiation oncology issues

A. Palliative care and end-of-life issues

1. Radiotherapy and palliative care

   a) In radiation oncology, an estimated 40%–50% of therapy undertaken is for palliation (Chow et al., 2000; Janjan, 1998; Kirkbride & Barton, 1999).

   b) Unlike local control of a variety of malignancies treated with radiation, palliation of symptoms often does not have a clear dose-response relationship.

   c) It is important that palliation be achieved with as efficient a fractionation schedule as possible in patients with limited life expectancy and with as few side effects as possible (Anderson & Coia, 2000).

   d) However, palliative care in radiation oncology is not limited to the appropriate fraction schedule, and issues such as symptom management and quality of life are relevant not only for patients and families at the end of their illness but for all dealing with advanced cancer.

2. Definition of palliative care: An approach that improves the quality of life of patients and their families facing the problems associated with life-threatening illness, through the prevention and relief of suffering by means of early identification and impeccable assessment and treatment of pain and other problems, physical, psychosocial, and spiritual. Palliative care (WHO, 2003)

   a) Provides relief from pain and other distressing symptoms

   b) Affirms life and regards dying as a normal process

   c) Intends neither to hasten nor postpone death

   d) Integrates the psychological and spiritual aspects of patient care

   e) Offers a support system to help patients live as actively as possible until death

   f) Offers a support system to help the family cope during the patient's illness and in their own bereavement

   g) Uses a team approach to address the needs of patient's and their families, including bereavement counseling, if indicated

   h) Will enhance quality of life, and also may positively influence the course of illness

   i) Is applicable early in the course of illness, in conjunction with other therapies that are intended to prolong life, such as chemotherapy or radiation therapy, and includes those investigations needed to better understand and manage distressing clinical complications.

3. Indications for the use of RT in palliative care

   a) Use of palliative RT had been declining, perhaps inappropriately, because of several possible misconceptions among healthcare professionals.

      (1) Perception that RT is not paid for by insurance while patient is in hospice. Coverage for this varies by insurer.

      (2) Perception that patient would have to travel to the department of radiotherapy

numerous times at a point when he or she is very ill and in pain. However, numerous studies show that as little as one fraction of 6–8 Gy (delivered on a single visit) can have a major positive impact on pain control (Hartsell et al., 2003; Madsen, 1983; Price et al., 1986; Tong, Gillick, & Hendrickson, 1982). Palliative radiation is given for pain relief, particularly in cases of bone metastases.

    (a) A recent study (Hartsell et al., 2003) was conducted to determine whether 8 Gy in a single fraction provides equivalent complete pain relief compared to 30 Gy in 10 fractions for patients with painful bone metastases from breast or prostate cancers. It found fractionation schemes equivalent in terms of pain control and a decreasing need for narcotics.

    (b) Pain relief was evaluated at three months using the patient self-assessed Brief Pain Inventory. For the entire group, complete response was seen in 17% and partial response in 49%, for an overall response rate of 66%; only 10% of patients had progression of pain (Hartsell et al., 2003).

    (c) At three months, 33% of patients no longer required narcotic medications (Hartsell et al., 2003).

    (d) Pain response was similar whether or not the patient was on bisphosphonates (Hartsell et al., 2003).

(3) Perception that RT is toxic and that all patients will have side effects. However, a recent study (Hartsell et al., 2003) showed that the acute toxicity rate for 8 Gy in one fraction was very low; 9% of patients had grade 2–3 acute toxicity and < 1% had grade 4 toxicity.

(4) Indications for RT

    (a) Oncologic emergencies (Ciezki, Komurcu, & Macklis, 2000; Kirkbride & Barton, 1999)

      i) Spinal cord compression

      ii) Vena cava obstruction

      iii) Bronchial obstruction

      iv) Ocular nerve compression

    (b) Skeletal metastasis (Ciezki et al., 1999)

    (c) Brain metastasis

    (d) Control of bleeding-hemoptysis and vaginal and rectal bleeding

    (e) Control of fungation or ulceration

    (f) Metastatic skin lesions

4. End-of-life issues: Americans are afraid to die in the current healthcare system because of the fear of a painful, protracted death along with financial repercussions (American Health Decisions, 1997; Covinsky, Desbiens, & Lynn, 1994; Singer, Martin, & Kelner, 1999).

    a) Studies have shown shortcomings in end-of-life care for patients and families (Miller & Walsh, 1991; Support Principal Investigators, 1995). Other studies, however, have been more positive.

      (1) Higginson et al. (2002) looked at whether palliative care teams within hospitals improved care at the end of life for patients and families. The evidence reviewed indicated a small but positive effect of the hospital-based palliative care teams.

      (2) In 2003, Higginson et al. undertook a systematic review and meta-analysis related to the impact of palliative care teams on the experience of patients and caregivers at the end of life. Although the evidence was limited, it did support the positive effects of teams delivering palliative care.

    b) Definitions

      (1) Hospice—"A program of care that supports the patient and family through the dying process and the surviving family members through bereavement" (Ferrell & Coyle, 2002, p. 164). Hospice care may be provided in a variety of settings but primarily is given in homes and nursing homes.

      (2) Family—"Being unique and whomever the person defines as being family. Family members can include, but are

not limited to, parents, children, sib-
lings, neighbors and significant people
in the community" (Registered Nurses
Association of Ontario, 2002, p. 16).

5. Philosophy of palliative care
   a) Palliative care assessment
      (1) Comprehensive holistic assessment is
          undertaken at the initial visit.
      (2) General criteria for acceptance into a
          palliative care program: Diagnosis of
          an illness that is life-threatening and
          noncurative (Billings, 1998; Super,
          2001)
      (3) General criteria for acceptance into a
          hospice program
          (a) "Prognosis of six months or less"
              (Billings, 1998, p. 76)
          (b) Willingness to consent to forgo
              treatments with a curative intent
              and only accept care from hospice
              (Billings, 1998; Lynn, 2001)
          (c) Requires health insurance that will
              cover care given by hospice (Bill-
              ings, 1998; Lynn, 2001)
      (4) Nursing assessment is ongoing during
          and after treatment. Patients should be
          followed one to two weeks post-treat-
          ment.
      (5) Using Ferrell's (1995) quality-of-life
          framework, the assessment focuses on
          (a) Physical well-being
          (b) Psychological well-being
          (c) Social well-being
          (d) Spiritual well-being (Ferrell, 1995;
              Glass, Cluxton, & Rancour, 2001)
   b) Plan of care: Develop a plan of care and
      evaluate and adjust it as required on an
      ongoing basis, with patient and family set-
      ting mutual goals (Cherny, Coyle, & Foley,
      1996; Scanlon, 2001).
      (1) Assist patients in their understanding
          of diagnosis and prognosis, and pro-
          mote informed choice.

      (2) Respect patients' values, goals, and
          priorities.
      (3) Honor preferences of patient and fam-
          ily.
      (4) Respect patients' cultural and spiri-
          tual perspective.
      (5) Attempt to meet patients' preferences
          related to living situations, care set-
          tings, and services.
      (6) Encourage patients and families to
          address planning of advanced care
          and directives (i.e., living will, do not
          resuscitate [DNR] order, preference re-
          garding end-of-life care, such as hos-
          pice involvement).
      (7) Identify potential areas of conflict be-
          tween patient, family, financial institu-
          tions, and care providers, and develop
          a plan to bring about a resolution.
   c) Acknowledge and address caregiver needs
      (Cherny et al., 1996; Covinsky et al., 1994;
      Miller & Walsh, 1991; Scanlon, 2001;
      Weitzner, McMillan, & Jacobsen, 1999).
      (1) Appreciate the considerable demands
          and responsibilities that caregivers face
          (emotional, financial, and physical),
          while caring for the person at home and
          attempting to meet their own needs.
      (2) Ensure supportive services are avail-
          able to caregivers (e.g., telephone sup-
          port, respite care, help with personal
          care for patient, counseling following
          bereavement).
      (3) Recognize that certain caregivers are
          at high risk for fatigue and physical
          and emotional illnesses/distress. Ad-
          dress these needs when implementing
          services.
      (4) Recognize and address possible fi-
          nancial concerns that caregivers may
          face (e.g., loss of income) while look-
          ing after a person at home.
   d) Pain and symptom management (see sec-
      tion IV, D—Pain)
      (1) Providing relief of pain and other symp-
          toms experienced by patients with
          cancer can contribute significantly to
          their quality of life.
      (2) Support Principal Investigators (1995)
          found that seriously ill patients expe-
          rienced moderate to severe pain in the
          last days of life even though pain is
          recognized as an important issue to
          deal with. Pain and symptom manage-
          ment issues are still a large concern of
          the American public (American Health
          Decisions, 1997).

(3) Pain and symptom management strategies should be the first priority of care and implemented, assessed, and adjusted accordingly during and after treatment (Abrahm, 1998; Cleary, 2000; Miller & Walsh, 1991; Perron & Schonwetter, 2001).

   e) Interdisciplinary approach to care: Use an interdisciplinary approach (i.e., nurses, physicians, social workers, dietitians, pastoral caregivers, pharmacists, psychologists, family, and volunteers) to deal with the multifaceted needs of care (Bascom & Tolle, 1995; Scanlon, 2001).

(1) Ensure that smooth communication and continuity of care among members of the interdisciplinary team within healthcare settings/institutions is facilitated, particularly as illness progresses (Scanlon, 2001).

(2) Ensure that there is open, ongoing, and consistent communication between patient and family members (Bascom & Tolle, 1995).

   f) Perform ongoing documentation of symptoms, assessment, plan of care, and evaluation (as per site-specific sections).

6. Related Web sites

   a) American Academy of Hospice and Palliative Medicine—www.aahpm.org

   b) Open Society Institute—www.soros.org/death

   c) National Hospice and Palliative Care Organization—www.nhpco.org

   d) Hospice Foundation of America—www.hospicefoundation.org

   e) Palliative Care—www.palliativecarenursing.net

   f) Palliative.net—www.albertapalliative.net

   g) Canadian Hospice Palliative Care Association—www.chpca.net

   h) Institute of Palliative Care—www.pallcare.org

   i) Edmonton Regional Palliative Care Program—www.palliative.org

References

Abrahm, J.L. (1998). Promoting symptom control in palliative care. *Seminars in Oncology Nursing, 14,* 95–109.

American Health Decisions. (1997). The quest to die with dignity: An analysis of Americans' values, opinions and attitudes concerning end-of-life care. Retrieved April 1, 2003, from http://www.ahd.org/ahd/library/statements/quest.html

Anderson, P.R., & Coia, L.R. (2000). Fractionation and outcomes with palliative radiation therapy. *Seminars in Radiation Oncology, 10,* 191–199.

Bascom, P.B., & Tolle, S.W. (1995). Care of the family when the patient is dying. *Western Journal of Medicine, 163,* 292–296.

Billings, J.A. (1998). What is palliative care? *Journal of Palliative Medicine, 1*(1), 73–81.

Cherny, N.I., Coyle, N., & Foley, K.M. (1996). Guidelines in the care of the dying cancer patient. *Hematology/Oncology Clinics of North America, 10,* 261–287.

Ciezki, J.P., Komurcu, S., & Macklis, R.M. (2000). Palliative radiotherapy. *Seminars in Oncology, 27,* 90–93.

Chow, E., Danjoux, C., Wong, R., Szumacher, E., Franssen, E., Fung, K., et al. (2000). Palliation of bone metastases: A survey of patterns of practice among Canadian radiation oncologists. *Radiotherapy in Oncology, 56,* 305–314.

Cleary, J.F. (2000). Cancer pain management. *Cancer Control, 7*(2), 120–131.

Covinsky, K.E., Desbiens, N., & Lynn, J. (1994). The impact of serious illness on patients' families. *JAMA, 272,* 1839–1844.

Ferrell, B.R. (1995). The impact of pain on quality of life: A decade of research. *Nursing Clinics of North America, 30,* 609–624.

Ferrell, B.R., & Coyle, N. (2002). An overview of palliative nursing care. *Lippincott's Case Management, 74*(4), 163–168.

Glass, E., Cluxton, D., & Rancour, P. (2001). Principles of patient and family assessment. In B.R. Ferrell & N. Coyle (Eds.), *Textbook of palliative nursing* (pp. 37–50). New York: Oxford University Press.

Hartsell, W.F., Scott, C., Bruner, D.W., Scarantino, C.W., Ivker, R., Roach, M., et al. (2003). Phase III randomized trial of 8 Gy in 1 fraction vs. 30 Gy in 10 fractions for palliation of painful bone metastases: Preliminary results of RTOG 97-14. Plenary abstract presentation at the 45th American Society of Therapeutic Radiologists and Oncologists (ASTRO), Salt Lake City, UT, October 19–23. *International Journal of Radiation Oncology, Biology, Physics, 57*(Suppl. 2), 124.

Higginson, I.J., Finlay, I.G., Goodwin, D.M., Cook, A., Hood, K., Edwards, A.G.K., et al. (2002). Do hospital-based palliative teams improve care for patients or families at the end of life? *Journal of Pain and Symptom Management, 23*(2), 96–106.

Higginson, I.J., Finlay, I.G., Goodwin, D.M., Hood, K., Edwards, A.G.K., Cook, A., et al. (2003). Is there evidence that palliative care teams alter end-of-life experiences of patients and their caregivers? *Journal of Pain and Symptom Management, 25*(2), 150–168.

Janjan, N.A. (1998). An emerging respect for palliative care in radiation oncology. *Journal of Palliative Medicine, 1*(1), 83–88.

Kirkbride, K., & Barton, R. (1999). Palliative radiation therapy. *Journal of Palliative Medicine, 2*(1), 87–97.

Lynn, J. (2001). Serving patients who may die soon and their families. *JAMA, 285,* 925–932.

Madsen, E.L. (1983). Painful bone metastasis: Efficacy of radiotherapy assessed by the patients: A randomized trial comparing 4 Gy x 6 versus 10 Gy x 2. *International Journal of Radiation Oncology, Biology, Physics, 9,* 1775–1779.

Miller, R.D., & Walsh, T.D. (1991). Psychosocial aspects of palliative care in advanced cancer. *Journal of Pain and Symptom Management, 6*(1), 24–29.

Perron, V., & Schonwetter, R.S. (2001). Assessment and management of pain in palliative care patients. *Cancer Control, 8*(1), 15–24.

Price, P., Hoskin, P.J., Easton, D., Austin, D., Palmer, S.G., & Yarnold, J.R. (1986). Prospective randomized trial of single and multifraction radiotherapy schedules in the treatment of painful bony metastases. *Radiotherapy Oncology, 6,* 247–255.

Registered Nurses Association of Ontario. (2002). *Supporting and strengthening families through expected and unexpected life events.* Toronto, Canada: Author.

Scanlon, C. (2001). Public policy and end-of-life care: The nurse's role. In B.R. Ferrell & N. Coyle (Eds.), *Textbook of palliative nursing* (pp. 682–689). New York: Oxford University Press.

Singer, P.A., Martin, D.K., & Kelner, M. (1999). Quality end-of-life care: Patients' perspectives. *JAMA, 281,* 163–168.

Super, A. (2001). The context of palliative care in progressive illness. In B.R. Ferrell & N. Coyle (Eds.), *Textbook of palliative nursing* (pp. 27–36). New York: Oxford University Press.

Support Principal Investigators. (1995). A controlled trial to improve care for the seriously ill hospitalized patients. The study to understand the prognoses and preferences for outcomes and risks of treatment (SUPPORT). *JAMA, 274,* 1591–1598.

Tong, D., Gillick, L., & Hendrickson, F.R. (1982). The palliation of symptomatic osseous metastases. Final results of the study by the Radiation Therapy Oncology Group. *Cancer, 50,* 893–899.

Weitzner, M.A., McMillan, S.C., & Jacobsen, P.B. (1999). Family caregiver quality of life: Differences between curative and palliative cancer treatment settings. *Journal of Pain and Symptom Management, 17,* 418–428.

World Health Organization. (2003). *WHO definition of palliative care.* Retrieved June 30, 2004, from http://www.who.int/cancer/palliative/definition/en/

B. Nuclear/radiologic bioterrorism
1. Medical effects of catastrophic radiation exposure
   a) Catastrophic radiation scenarios are becoming more likely in the modern world.
   b) Wartime/terrorism-related events (American College of Radiology [ACR], 2002; Hall, 1994; Military Medical Operations Office, 1999)
      (1) Nuclear detonation ("atomic bomb")
      (2) Attack on an existing nuclear reactor
      (3) Use of radiation dispersal explosive ("dirty bomb")
      (4) Nonexplosive, purposeful dispersal of radiation sources
   c) Potential accidental scenarios (ACR, 2002)
      (1) Nuclear reactor accident (e.g., Chernobyl, Three Mile Island)
      (2) Industrial or military accidents (e.g., accidental radiation exposure following nuclear tests)
      (3) Medical radiation accidents (e.g., radiation brachytherapy misadministrations)
      (4) Inadvertent radiation dispersal (e.g., accidental fallout from nuclear tests affecting Marshall Islanders)
2. Historical sources of information about medical radiation effects (Mettler & Voelz, 2002)
   a) Immediate data and long-term follow-up research on WWII atomic bomb survivors from Hiroshima and Nagasaki
   b) Medical records from Chernobyl nuclear reactor accident
   c) Historical data from Marshall Islanders inadvertently exposed to radioactive fallout from U.S. nuclear tests
   d) Medical data from individuals exposed to very high radiation in work- or research-related reactor accidents—Ionizing radiation exposure (ACR, 2002; Military Medical Operations Office, 1999)
      (1) External exposure—Relates to dose received from a radioactive source, which may be distant or in close proximity to the victim.
         (a) Whole body exposure—Homogenous doses to entire body produce more toxicity at lower doses.
         (b) Partial body exposure—Doses to limited parts of anatomy result in higher dose tolerances in general.
      (2) Contamination relates to dose received from radioactive material directly on or in the body.
         (a) External contamination—Refers to coating of external surfaces with dusts, liquids, or particles
         (b) Internal contamination—Refers to ingestion, inhalation, or internalization of radiation sources
   e) Progression of medical events following catastrophic exposure (Mettler & Voelz, 2002; Military Medical Operations Office, 1999)
      (1) Quantification of radiation exposure
         (a) Dose is expressed in Gray, centigray, or RAD (1 Gy = 100 cGy = 100 RAD)
         (b) Equivalent dose is expressed in Sievert or rem (1 Sv = 100 rem) and accounts for varying degrees of biologic damage caused by differing types of radiation (e.g., neutrons cause 10 times the biologic damage as gamma rays).
         (c) $LD_{50/60}$ refers to the TBI dose that kills 50% of individuals at 60 days.
            i) In humans, this dose is around 3–4 Gy without medical treatment.
            ii) With appropriate medical treatment, $LD_{50/60}$ increases to 6–8 Gy.
            iii) Total body doses of < 2 Gy are rarely fatal in humans.
            iv) There are no reports of any human surviving doses of > 10 Gy.
      (2) Effects
         (a) Prodromal syndrome—Precedes later lethal syndromes

i) This phase immediately follows whole body exposure (< 30 min.) and lasts hours to days.

ii) Severity of syndrome is directly proportional to dose received, whereas its length is indirectly proportional to this dose.

iii) Symptoms include nausea, vomiting, headache, listlessness, fatigue, and hypotension.

iv) Treatment (e.g., antiemetics, IV fluids, narcotics) is symptomatic.

(b) Latent phase—This is a variable time period lasting hours to weeks, between the prodromal and lethal syndromes, during which the victim may have few or no symptoms.

i) Lethal or potentially lethal syndromes

ii) Acute syndromes occur over hours to weeks.

(c) Cerebrovascular syndrome

i) Occurs with received doses of > 20 Gy

ii) Uniformly fatal within 24–48 hours

iii) Etiology is radiation-induced cerebral edema with symptoms including disorientation, headache, seizures, anuria, respiratory distress, and coma.

iv) Treatment (oxygen, anticonvulsants, narcotics, sedatives, IV fluids, **no** role for steroids) is palliative only.

(d) GI syndrome

i) Occurs with received doses of > 5 Gy

ii) Death, if it occurs, is in 3–10 days (not uniformly fatal).

iii) Etiology is radiation-induced depletion of GI tract epithelium with symptoms including nausea, vomiting, bloody diarrhea, weight loss, dehydration, and infection.

iv) Treatment (antiemetics, antidiarrheals) is directed toward symptoms, nutritional and fluid support (IV fluids and parenteral hyperalimentation), and prevention of infection (antibiotics).

(e) Hematopoietic syndrome

i) Occurs with received doses of > 1 Gy

ii) Death, if it occurs, is in three to eight weeks (not uniformly fatal).

iii) Etiology is radiation-induced depletion of bone marrow stem cells resulting in neutropenia with fevers and infection and thrombocytopenia with petechiae and hemorrhage.

iv) Treatment (transfusions and growth factors) is directed toward support and prevention of infection (antibiotics and isolation); role of bone marrow transplantation remains questionable.

(f) Late syndromes occur over years to decades.

i) Carcinogenesis

• Stochastic effect—No minimum dose requirement but increasing dose increases the probability of development (but not severity) of the effect.

• Onset of the effect is variable but typically is 5–7 years for leukemias and 15–30 years for solid tumors.

• Etiology is radiation-induced damage to normal cellular DNA, resulting in development of cancers and leukemias, including acute myeloid leukemia and lung, breast, thyroid, colon, and bladder cancers.

- Treatment for and prognosis of these induced cancers are identical to that of similar randomly occurring cancers.

    ii) Noncancerous late effects—Japanese survivor data point to a possible evolving risk of excess deaths due to heart disease and stroke at 40–50 years.

3. Collaborative management of catastrophic radiation causalities (ACR, 2002; Mettler & Voelz, 2002; Military Medical Operations Office, 1999)

    a) Treat and stabilize life-threatening injuries (shock, trauma, hemorrhage, burns) without regard to radiation received or possible contamination.

    b) Prevent or minimize further whole body exposure or contamination through evacuation and wound dressing.

    c) Assess for external and/or internal contamination.

    d) Check for history concerning nature of accident or incident and exposure to, ingestion of, or inhalation of dusts or gases.

    e) Examine patient for dusts, wounds, and liquids.

    f) Use radiation measurements of body surfaces and excreta (stool, emesis, urine).

    g) Contain any contamination to triage or treatment area using controlled access to well-demarcated areas with controlled disposal of contaminated clothes and fluids and use of extensive radiation monitoring.

    h) Decontaminate external contamination using clothing removal, showers, scrubs, and soaps—conceptually similar to cleaning a patient who has fallen into raw sewage.

    i) Decontaminate internal contamination through enhanced elimination (e.g., gastric lavage, emesis, induction, cathartics, urine alkalization), blockage of absorption (e.g., chelation, antacids), or displacement (e.g., potassium iodide).

    j) Minimize radiation exposure to medical personnel via external decontamination, containment of contamination, controlled disposal of contaminants, and controlled radiation monitoring; patients who have been exposed to external radiation but are not contaminated pose no radiation risk to medical personnel.

    k) Assess and treat non–life-threatening burns and injuries.

    l) Assess and treat whole body radiation exposures.

    m) Estimate dose received. May use the following.

        (1) Objective measurements by trained personnel at site of accident or incident

        (2) Severity of prodromal syndrome

        (3) Onset of potential lethal syndromes

        (4) Quantification of chromosomal effects on circulating lymphocytes

        (5) Serial measurement of WBC counts

    n) Treat radiation syndromes based on dose received.

        (1) No treatment is necessary if < 1 Gy.

        (2) Doses of 1–9 Gy requires symptomatic treatment of prodromal syndrome and GI syndrome and expectant management of hematopoietic syndrome.

        (3) Doses of > 9 Gy are nearly uniformly fatal because of cerebrovascular or GI syndrome, so treatment is symptomatic and palliative.

    o) Counsel victims on acute and late radiation effects, including hematopoietic syndrome and carcinogenesis risks.

References

American College of Radiology. (2002). *Disaster preparedness for radiology professionals: Response to radiological terrorism* (Version 2.1). Washington, DC: Author.

Hall, J. (1994). *Radiobiology for the radiologist.* Philadelphia: Lippincott Williams & Wilkins.

Mettler, F., & Voelz, G. (2002). Major radiation exposure—What to expect and how to respond. *New England Journal of Medicine, 346,* 1554–1561.

Military Medical Operations Office. (1999). *Medical management of radiological casualties.* Bethesda, MD: Armed Forces Radiobiology Research Institute.

C. Cancer clinical trials
 1. Definition: Translating scientific discovery and technical advancement into procedures and products to offer a prospect of a better life (Koski, 2000)
 2. Purpose
    a) Evaluating safety and efficacy of novel treatments
    b) Mechanism for developing better methods for detecting, treating, and preventing cancer
    c) Potential for improving outcomes—Meta-analysis of clinical trial participation associated with higher survival (Lara et al., 2001)
 3. Phases (NCI, 2002)
    a) Phase I—Determines the safety and appropriate dosage of new treatment
    b) Phase II—Evaluates the effectiveness of the new treatment and its side effects
    c) Phase III—Evaluates the effectiveness of new treatment compared to standard treatment
 4. Types of trials (NCI, 2002)
    a) Treatment—Evaluates the effectiveness of a new treatment
    b) Prevention—Evaluates the effectiveness and safety of various treatments for people at risk for developing cancer
    c) Screening—Evaluates the effectiveness of new methods for detecting cancer at earlier stages
    d) Supportive care—Evaluates interventions to improve quality of life
    e) Diagnostic trials—Evaluates use of equipment for improving diagnostic procedures and abilities
    f) Genetics trials—Evaluates targeted treatments based on the genetics of a tumor
 5. Nurse's role
    a) Recruitment and accrual of participants
       (1) Have knowledge of current clinical trials and resources for obtaining information for current trial availability. RT—Specific clinical trials can be found on the RTOG's Web site, www.rtog.org, and the American College of Radiology Imaging Network's Web site, www.acrin.org. Additional sites that offer professional and consumer information on clinical trials
           (a) NCI—http://cancer.gov
           (b) NIH clinical trials site—www.clinicaltrials.gov
           (c) Food and Drug Administration's Cancer Clinical Trials Directory—www.fda.gov/oashi/cancer/trials.html#table
           (d) Pharmaceutical Research and Manufacturers of America—www.phrma.org
           (e) Ongoing trials at NCI's Clinical Center—http://ccr.nci.nih.gov
       (2) Understanding barriers to accrual
           (a) Only 2%–4% of all adult patients newly diagnosed with cancer participate in NCI clinical trials annually (Lara et al., 2001).
           (b) Health provider barriers
               i) "Physician bottleneck"—Lack of time, limited staff, burden of paperwork, and costs of data management (NCI, 2001)
               ii) Lack of awareness and willingness to refer patients (Lara et al., 2001)
           (c) Patient-related barriers (Barrett, 2002)
               i) Lack of awareness
               ii) Misconceptions
               iii) Practical considerations (e.g., burden on caregivers, inconvenience, expense of additional care, transportation restraints)
               iv) Quality-of-life issues (e.g., fear of potential side effects)
               v) Lack of health insurance coverage—Medicare only will cover routine patient care that would be covered regardless of trial. Patient care costs for clinical trial participation are similar to standard therapy (Wagner et al., 1999).
    b) Education
       (1) Explain complex and highly technical protocol in terms that patients can understand derived from assessment

of patient's educational, emotional, and psychological status.

(2) Provide patients with additional educational resources.

(3) Outline progression of protocol and what participants can expect at each stage.

(4) Offer ways to minimize or manage side effects.

(5) Provide contact numbers, and encourage patients when and what to report regarding changes in health status.

(6) Explain patient's rights as a research participant (Joshi & Ehrenberger, 2001; NCI, 2002).

c) Patient advocate (Ocker & Plank, 2000)

(1) Participate in informed consent process.

(2) Assess informed consent for appropriate reading level, language, and font size.

(3) Guide patient in verifying healthcare coverage.

(4) Assist patient in recognizing his or her personal expectations or reasons for participating.

(5) Support patient in making decisions based on his or her values.

(6) Act as a liaison between the patient and physician.

(7) Assess ability of patient to adhere to protocol requirements (e.g., completion of diaries, keeping treatment schedule, afford out-of-pocket expenses).

(8) Ensure that informed consent for clinical trial addresses the Health Information Portability and Accountability Act of 1996 (HIPAA) privacy rule; a covered entity may neither use nor disclose protected health information for research unless the patient provides authorization in advance (Holt,

2003). There are six essential elements for authorization.

(a) A description of the information to be disclosed

(b) Notice of patient's right to revoke the authorization

(c) To whom it will be disclosed

(d) The purpose for which it will be disclosed

(e) The expiration date for transferring protected health information

(f) A patient's dated signature

d) Study coordinator (Ocker & Plank, 2000)

(1) Familiarize self with protocol (i.e., purpose, objectives, procedures, eligibility, potential adverse effects).

(2) Validate eligibility criteria.

(3) Facilitate informed consent process (i.e., assess patient level of understanding, ability to provide informed consent).

(4) Coordinate protocol-related tests and appointments.

(5) Perform timely identification, documentation, and communication of serious or unexpected side effects.

(6) Ensure protocol guidelines are followed.

(7) Incorporate study instruction in discharge planning.

References

Barrett, R. (2002). A nurse's primer on recruiting participants for clinical trials. *Oncology Nursing Forum, 29,* 1091–1095.

Holt, E. (2003). The HIPAA privacy rule, research and IRBs. *Applied Clinical Trials, 12*(6), 48–66.

Joshi, T.G., & Ehrenberger, H.E. (2001). Cancer clinical trials in the new millennium: Novel challenges and opportunities for oncology nursing. *Clinical Journal of Oncology Nursing, 5,* 148.

Koski, G. (2000). Risks, benefits and conflicts of interest in human research: Ethical evolution in the changing world of science. *Journal of Law, Medicine, and Ethics, 28,* 330–331.

Lara, P.N., Higdon, R., Lim, N., Kowan, K., Tanka, M., Lau, D., et al. (2001). Prospective evaluation of cancer clinical trial accrual patterns: Identifying potential barriers to enrollment. *Journal of Clinical Oncology, 19,* 1728–1733.

National Cancer Institute. (2002). *Cancer clinical trials: The indepth program.* Retrieved February 18, 2003, from www.cancer.gov/clinicaltrials/resources/in-depth-program

Ocker, B.M., & Plank, D.M. (2000). The research nurse role in a clinic-based oncology research setting. *Cancer Nursing, 23,* 286–292.

Wagner, J.L., Alberts, S.R., Sloan, J.A., Cha, S., Killian, J., O'Connell, M.J., et al. (1999). Incremental costs of enrolling cancer patients in clinical trials: A population-based study. *Journal of the National Cancer Institute, 91,* 847–853.

D. Informed consent
1. Definition: A continuous process (Milton, 2000) involving the patient's right to autonomous self-determination founded on the healthcare professional's duty to provide information of sufficient quality, scope, and choice, enabling the patient to make an informed decision (Booth, 2002; Usher & Arthur, 1998).
2. Legal components—The following are essential components of the informed consent process.
   a) Right to self-determination (*Canterbury v. Spence,* 1972): Standard of disclosure—Places greater duty of reasonable disclosure on practitioners (Hartgerink, McMullen, McDonough, & McCarthy, 1998).
   b) Fiduciary relationship between patient and practitioners (*Nathanson v. Kline,* 1960)
   c) Sufficient information: "As much information as reasonably needed for consent to be legitimate" (Booth, 2002, p. 44)
   d) Voluntary: Able to exercise choice without duress or undue influence (Booth, 2002)
   e) Competency: Having the qualities and abilities necessary to make an autonomous decision (Welie & Welie, 2001)
      (1) Patient can comprehend, absorb, and retain information.
      (2) Patient can manipulate and critically analyze knowledge.
      (3) Patient has freedom of will.
      (4) Patient can communicate and account for decision.
   f) Validity (Booth, 2002)
      (1) Voluntary
      (2) Competent adult
      (3) Specific to proposed treatment
      (4) Assessment of patient's decision-making competence must be specific to the situation.
      (5) Information of sufficient quality, scope, and choice
   g) HIPAA—This privacy rule governs the use and disclosure of protected health information that is transmitted or maintained in any form (Holt, 2003). Web resource for further details
      (1) American Medical Association—www.ama-assn.org
      (2) U.S. Department of Health and Human Services—www.os.dhhs.gov/ocr/hipaa
3. Nurse's role
   a) Patient advocate
      (1) Goal: Providing patient or his or her legal designate with quality information at his or her level of understanding, with sufficient scope and choice to make autonomous decisions to accept or reject a proposed course of treatment or care.
      (2) Ensure content of consent is complete and includes
         (a) Purpose of treatment
         (b) Alternate therapies, including clinical trials
         (c) Risks versus benefits
         (d) Potential side effects
         (e) Treatment planning experience
         (f) Treatment experience
         (g) Recommended follow-up.
      (3) Ensure content of informed consent for research clinical trials includes the information above and the following six essential elements to comply with HIPAA privacy rule (Holt, 2003).
         (a) A description of information to be disclosed
         (b) Notice of patient's right to revoke the authorization
         (c) To whom it will be disclosed
         (d) The purpose for which it will be disclosed
         (e) The expiration date for transferring protected health information
         (f) A patient's dated signature
      (4) Assess patient's and family's decision-making capacity.
         (a) Age—Predicts poor comprehension of information (Sugarman, McCrory, & Hubal, 1998), and poor comprehension in elderly is related to all elements of the consent (Stanley, Guido, & Stanley, 1984).
         (b) Education—Educational level was the most significant predictor

of the inability to provide a completely accurate definition of terms routinely used in consent forms (Lawson & Adamson, 1995).

(c) Illness—Severity of illness has an impact on the patient's ability to retain information and his or her understanding of the purpose of a clinical trial in which he or she has consented to participate (Schaffer, Krantz, & Wichman, 1996).

(d) Physician/patient relationship—Fear of upsetting relationship on which they depend may make consent only "partially voluntary" (Hewlett, 1996).

(e) Timing of discussion—Avoid information overload and maintain sensitivity for patient's state.

b) Educator

(1) Assess patient's and family's understanding of information presented.

(2) Clarify and expand on information given by physicians.

(3) Provide and assist patients in gathering additional relevant sources of information.

(4) Provide sufficient time for patient to read, ask questions, and digest meaning of decision.

(5) Verify understanding of content by summarizing and asking open-ended questions. There is a positive correlation when patients are asked to recall specific relevant information (White, Mason, Feehan, & Templeton, 1995).

(6) Assess for unspoken reluctance and uncertainty about procedure or treatment.

c) Participate in the informed consent process.

(1) Assess informed consent for appropriate reading level (Coyne et al.,

2003), language (Roberts, 2001), and font size (for elderly).

(2) Provide sufficient time for decision-making.

(3) Provide multiple opportunities for interaction.

(4) Respond to individual patients' informational needs. Patient satisfaction with health interactions is directly linked to expectations that information has been fulfilled (Degner & Russell, 1988).

(5) Verify that patients' goals and expectations are realistic and congruent with their values and proposed procedural outcome. Discrepancies in what patients think they understand may lead to unrealistic expectations and ability to make an informed choice (Schutta & Burnett, 2000; Yoder, O'Rourke, Etnyre, Spears, & Brown, 1997).

References

Booth, S. (2002). A philosophical analysis of informed consent. *Nursing Standard, 16,* 43–46.

Canterbury v. Spence. (1972). 464 F.2d 772, 784. Washington, DC: U.S. Circuit Court of Appeals.

Coyne, C.A., Xu, R., Rauch, P., Plomer, K., Dignan, M., Wenzel, L.B., et al. (2003). Eastern Cooperative Group randomized, controlled trial of an easy-to-read informed consent statement for clinical trial participation. *Journal of Clinical Oncology, 21,* 836–842.

Degner, L., & Russell, C.A. (1988). Preferences for treatment control among adults with cancer. *Research in Nursing and Health, 11,* 367–374.

Hartgerink, B., McMullen, P., McDonough, J., & McCarthy, J. (1998). A guide to understanding informed consent. *CRNA: The Clinical Forum for Nurse Anesthetists, 9*(4), 128–134.

Hewlett, S. (1996). Consent to clinical research—Adequately voluntary or substantially influenced? *Journal of Medical Ethics, 22,* 232–237.

Holt, E. (2003). The HIPAA privacy rule, research and IRBs. *Applied Clinical Trials, 12*(6), 48–66.

Lawson, S.L., & Adamson, H.M. (1995). Informed consent readability: Subject understanding of 15 common consent form phrases. *IRB, 17*(5–6), 16–19.

Milton, C. (2000). Informed consent: Process or outcome? *Nursing Science Quarterly, 3,* 291–292.

Nathanson v. Kline. (1960). 350 F.2d 1093. Washington, DC: U.S. Circuit Court of Appeals.

Roberts, D.M. (2001). Meeting the needs of patients with limited English proficiency. *Journal of Medical Practice Management, 17*(2), 71–75.

Schaffer, M.H., Krantz, D.S., & Wichman, A. (1996). The impact of disease severity on the informed consent process in clinical research. *American Journal of Medicine, 100,* 261–268.

Schutta, K.M., & Burnett, C.B. (2000). Factors that influence a patient's decision to participate in a phase I cancer clinical trial. *Oncology Nursing Forum, 27,* 1435–1438.

Stanley, B., Guido, J., & Stanley, M. (1984). Informed consent and eligibility: Empirical data. *JAMA, 252,* 1302–1306.

Sugarman, J., McCrory, D.C., & Hubal, R.C. (1998). Getting meaningful informed consent from older adults: A structured literature review of empirical research. *Journal of the American Geriatric Society, 46,* 517–524.

Usher, K., & Arthur, D. (1998). Process consent: A model for enhancing informed consent in mental health nursing. *Journal of Advanced Nursing, 27,* 692–697.

Welie, J., & Welie, S. (2001). Patient decision-making competence: Outlines of a conceptual analysis. *Medicine, Health Care, and Philosophy, 4*(2), 127–138.

White, C.S., Mason, A.C., Feehan, M., & Templeton, P.A. (1995). Informed consent for percutaneous lung biopsy: Comparison of two consent protocols based on patient recall after the procedure. *American Journal of Roentgenology, 165,* 1139–1142.

Yoder, L.H., O'Rourke, T.J., Etnyre, A., Spears, D.T., & Brown, T.D. (1997). Expectations and experiences of patients with cancer participating in phase I clinical trials. *Oncology Nursing Forum, 24,* 891–896.

E. Nursing management in radiation oncology
   1. Definition: Nursing management is "the coordination and integration of nursing resources through planning, organizing, coordinating, directing, and controlling in order to accomplish specific institutional goals and objectives" (Huber, 1996, p. 5).
      a) Managing staff
         (1) Staffing
            (a) Evaluate the needs of the practice.
               i) Setting (e.g., academic, private practice)
               ii) Patient population (e.g., most common diagnoses, percentage of curative and palliative patients, patient volume, acuity, percentage of healthy follow-ups, percentage of pediatrics, elderly patients, socioeconomic status)
               iii) Treatments (e.g., EBRT, brachytherapy, SRS, investigational therapies)
               iv) Physician expectations
               v) Hours of operation (e.g., consideration of flexible scheduling, four-day workweek)
               vi) Reimbursement practices (based on third party payor policies, contracts, and state regulations)
            (b) Determine the types of nursing personnel needed.
               i) RN: Expertise in assessment, education, symptom management, support, and counseling (Bruner, 1993; Moore-Higgs et al., 2003a; Shepard & Kelvin, 1999)
               ii) Clinical nurse specialist: Masters' prepared with advanced clinical knowledge and skills as well as proficiency in education, clinical leadership, consultation, and research (Hilderley, 1991).
               iii) Nurse practitioner: Can perform a history and physical, order and interpret diagnostic tests, diagnose and treat symptoms of disease and side effects of treatment, prescribe medication, and/or perform designated procedures (Kelvin et al., 1999; Kelvin & Moore-Higgs, 1999; Moore, 1996).
            (c) Determine the number of nursing personnel needed.
               i) The American College of Radiology (ACR, 1991) recommended one full-time nurse to provide direct patient care per 300 patients treated annually, with staffing increased if the nurse is providing other non-nursing services to the practice or department.
               ii) Acuity models for outpatient staffing exist, but these have not been tailored to radiation oncology. However, they may have components helpful to those seeking to develop similar systems (Karr & Fisher, 1997; Medvec, 1994; Prescott & Soeken, 1996).

(d) Establish the model of practice.

   i) Clinic model/team: Nurse supports all patients; assignment is task-oriented and based on the patient care needs of the day.

   ii) Collaborative model/primary nursing: Nurse works with one or two physicians and shares responsibility for caring for all patients within their caseloads; works in clinic with the physician, so the assignment is based on the physician's schedule; role ensures continuity from consultation through treatment and follow-up.

(e) Write the job descriptions.

   i) List responsibilities and performance standards (observable behaviors that define acceptable performance for the job) (see Appendix C).

   ii) The American Academy of Ambulatory Care Nursing (AAACN, 2000) has developed a conceptual framework for ambulatory care nursing practice that may be helpful in developing a job description. Moore-Higgs et al. (2003b) applied this framework to radiation oncology nursing practice.

   iii) Identify essential functions: Physical demands (e.g., strength, mobility); environmental demands (e.g., workspace, noise levels); mental abilities (e.g., stress, demands of patients) (Cascio, 1998).

   iv) Based on the Americans with Disabilities Act (1990), if essential functions can be performed, employer has to make reasonable accommodations (e.g., modifying work schedule, reassigning nonessential functions, modifying equipment).

   v) Identify required personal characteristics (knowledge, skills, and abilities).

(2) Hiring

(a) Recruit eligible candidates (e.g., advertisements, word of mouth, job fairs).

(b) Screen applicants.

   i) Review curriculum vitae/resume for education, previous clinical experience, skills, and specific accomplishments.

   ii) Identify areas or issues that require clarification (e.g., involvement in projects/changes, gaps in employment, frequent job changes, contradictions).

(c) Interview applicants (Sachs, 1994).

   i) Prepare questions to obtain information needed to decide if candidate is suitable.

    • Categorize questions to evaluate ability, motivation, and attitude about work, professional accomplishments, compatibility with your management style, and fit with your department/practice.

    • Formulate open-ended questions.

    • Structure questions to evaluate past performance as a predictor of future performance.

   ii) Schedule the interview to allow for privacy, without interruptions.

   iii) Conduct the interview.

    • Open with a short welcome and brief description of the role.

    • Clarify information on resume as needed.

    • Ask planned questions. Lead the interview; ensure applicant does most of the speaking; actively listen; and probe for details.

- Take notes during or immediately after the interview.
- Avoid discriminatory questions (e.g., national origin, religion, marital status, parental status, age).
- Describe job responsibilities, hours, and working conditions.
- State requirements and essential functions and ask if applicant is able to meet them.
- For specific disabilities, decide if reasonable accommodations can be made.

iv) Allow applicant to ask questions.

v) Explain next steps.

(d) Check references. Although former employers are only obligated to verify the applicant's employment, you may want to ask if the applicant is timely and efficient with his or her work, reliable, a team player, supportive of management, and if they would rehire the applicant.

(e) Select the best candidate while promoting gender, ethnic, and cultural diversity in hiring when possible and appropriate.

(3) Staff development

(a) Incorporate Malcolm Knowles' assumptions regarding adult learning (Abruzzese, 1996): Adults are self-directed and need to know the reason they should learn something. They are ready to learn when they perceive the need to learn and when the information is immediately applicable.

(b) Plan and implement educational programs.

i) Assess learning needs. Identify knowledge, skills, and attitudes required.

- Orientation at time of initial employment
- In-services on new equipment, supplies, procedures, and regulatory requirements

- Continuing education to maintain or enhance professional practice

ii) Establish learning objectives that are observable and measurable (begin with action verbs).

iii) Develop outline of content needed to ensure achievement of objectives.

iv) Determine method of presenting content. Use various methodologies (e.g., readings, didactic presentations, audiovisuals, interactive media, clinical rotations with preceptors). Consider strategies to make educational programs meaningful to the learner (Lankard, 1995; Stein, 1998).

v) Develop tool to evaluate if objectives were met.

- Post-test for didactic information
- Competency checklist for skills

(4) Performance appraisals: Key points as outlined by Huber (1996) include

(a) Performance appraisal is the systematic evaluation of the quality of the employee's performance based on defined standards. It provides

i) An opportunity to reinforce positive behaviors and to identify and discuss behaviors needing improvement.

ii) A basis for deciding on rewards.

iii) A basis for improving performance.

(b) Use evaluation tools listing desired observable, measurable behaviors (e.g., performance standards from the job description) with Likert-type scales rating performance on a continuum (e.g., 1 = fails to meet expectations; 2 = inconsistently meets expectations; 3 = consistently meets expectations; 4 = consistently exceeds expectations; 5 = performance results in substantial impact to the organization).

(c) For problem areas, differentiate between lack of ability (knowledge or skill) and lack of motivation (attitude).

(d) Have employee participate in the process, performing a self-evaluation. Consider peer evaluation and physician input.

(e) Follow-up with a developmental plan. Set mutually agreed-upon goals, and identify strategies for achieving these and improving performance.

(5) Coaching

(a) Coaching is a strategy for "equipping people with the tools, knowledge, and opportunities they need to develop themselves" (Gebelein et al., 2000, p. 374).

(b) Key points as outlined by Gebelein et al. (2000) include

　i) Forge a partnership: Build trust (be consistent and predictable); listen to gain an understanding of what is important to them; demonstrate that you care about them and their development.

　ii) Inspire commitment: Identify the person's priorities and match them with the organization's goals; create a development plan.

　iii) Grow skills: Promote experimentation and give permission to make mistakes as long as the person learns from them; consider different methods for learning (e.g., work one-on-one; provide relevant opportunities on the job; link staff with mentors; recommend appropriate conferences and readings; encourage self-reliance).

　iv) Promote persistence: Provide regular nonjudgmental feedback to enhance insight; describe the potential impact of behaviors on others and the likely consequences; help them apply what they have learned; celebrate success.

(6) Team building

(a) Key points as outlined by Gebelein et al. (2000) include

　i) Divide workload as evenly as possible, and recognize everyone's contributions.

　ii) Establish mutually agreed-upon behaviors to guide how staff are expected to interact.

　iii) Communicate needed information.

　iv) Plan meetings with a clear agenda and enough time for discussion. Encourage open communication among staff. Record minutes so those not present are aware of the issues discussed.

　v) Identify projects staff can work on together. Praise their accomplishments.

　vi) Provide staff with authority to make decisions when appropriate. Staff involvement in decision making is more likely to result in them feeling ownership of the decision and feeling responsible for the outcome.

　vii) Clarify the boundaries of their authority when they are not empowered to make the decision but only to offer their opinion.

(b) Model conflict management behavior (Gebelein, 2000).

b) Managing operations

(1) Collaboration
  (a) Definition: Collaboration is "working together with mutual respect for the contributions and accountabilities of each profession to the shared goal of quality patient care" (Aroskar, 1998, p. 313).
  (b) The manager must be a role model for staff in collaboration when interacting with colleagues in leadership roles. This will build relationships and ensure the manager participates in administrative and clinical decision making. In addition, it will enhance team building within the department and the larger organization.
  (c) Promote collaboration in all spheres.
    i) Intradepartmental
      • Physicians, therapists, treatment planning, physics, radiation safety, and administration
      • Openly discuss radiation team roles and responsibilities to avoid confusion and duplication of services (Bruner & Movsas, 2001)
    ii) Interdepartmental: Division of nursing, inpatient, OR, medical oncology, and surgical oncology
  (d) Use a variety of strategies to promote collaboration (Aroskar, 1998; Corser, 1998; Hanson & Spross, 1996).
    i) Personal strategies
      • Demonstrate interest and commitment.
      • Maintain clinical knowledge and competence.
      • Recognize social realities.
      • Recognize conflicting values.
    ii) Interpersonal strategies
      • Clarify roles and expectations.
      • Establish elements of sphere.
      • Recognize each other's strengths and contributions.
      • Communicate effectively.
      • Identify common goals.
      • Make joint decisions.
      • Share control, balancing being assertive with being cooperative.
      • Resolve conflict.
(2) Information technology (IT)
  (a) Be aware of the IT used in your department/practice.
  (b) Develop your skills to ensure proficiency in using IT (e.g., word processing, spreadsheets, e-mail, electronic calendars, patient scheduling, patient records, staff scheduling, an intranet, the Internet).
  (c) Provide staff with needed resources and training to ensure their proficiency.
(3) Finances: Key points as outlined by Finkler (2001) include
  (a) Budgeting is a process that involves planning and control.
  (b) Planning: Anticipate patient activity and forecast future needs.
    i) Salary budget projects cost of staff (e.g., salary, benefits, differentials) required based on predicted activity or workload.
    ii) Nonsalary budget projects all other expenses (e.g., supplies, equipment, books, conferences).
  (c) Control: Monitor variations and take corrective actions.
    i) Variance analysis involves comparing results (actual) with plan (budget).
    ii) Develop skills in creating, analyzing, and interpreting reports based on data generated from the practice/department (e.g., staffing records, patient activity, usage of supplies) to identify causes of variance.

c) Managing quality patient care
  (1) Policies, procedures, and standards
    (a) Policies define who can do what under what circumstances.
    (b) Procedures outline steps of doing a particular psychomotor task.
    (c) Standards define the level of care by which quality can be evaluated. Donabedian's framework of structure, process, and outcome standards are useful in monitoring and improving care (1992).
      i) Structure standards: Characteristics of the organization and staff (describe environment, staffing plan, and physical resources)
      ii) Process standards: Expected nursing activities (e.g., assessments, patient education, interventions)
      iii) Outcome standards: Expected results of nursing care (e.g., health status, functioning, knowledge, behavior)
    (d) Use best current evidence to develop policies, procedures, and standards. Many Internet resources are available for searching for evidence, although at some sites, full-text articles are available only to members or subscribers. Useful Internet sites include
      i) Searching within a specific database
        • MEDLINE®: National Library of Medicine, PubMed—www.ncbi.nlm.nih.gov/entrez/query.fcgi
        • CINAHL®: Members-only search—www.cinahl.com

      ii) Searching for systematic reviews from multiple resources/sites
        • SumSearch—http://sumsearch.uthscsa.edu/searchform45.htm
        • TRIP database—www.tripdatabase.com
      iii) Searching for systematic reviews within particular sites (nursing)
        • Evidence-Based Nursing: Select "collections" to browse or "search" to look for a specific topic— www.evidencebasednursing.com
        • National Institute of Nursing Research—http://ninr.nih.gov/ninr/news-info/publications.htm
        • Online Journal of Knowledge Synthesis for Nursing—www.stti.iupui.edu/library/ojksn/
        • Joanna Briggs Institute for Evidence-Based Nursing and Midwifery—www.joannabriggs.edu.au
      iv) Searching for systematic reviews within particular sites (general)
        • Agency for Healthcare Research and Quality— www.ahrq.gov/clinic/epcix.htm
        • Bandolier: Summarizes systematic reviews, includes focus on pain— www.jr2.ox.ac.uk/bandolier/index.html
        • Cochrane Library—www.cochrane.org
        • Clinical Evidence—http://clinicalevidence.org
        • EBM Online—http://ebm.bmjjournals.com
        • National Health Service Centre for Reviews and Dissemination—www.york.ac.uk/inst/crd/welcome.htm
      v) Searching for practice guidelines
        • Agency for Healthcare Research and Quality: National Guideline Clearinghouse—www.ngc.gov/index.asp

- ONS—www.ons.org
- Society of Gynecologic Nurse Oncologists—www.sgno.org
- Association of Pediatric Oncology Nurses—www.apon.org
- American Nurses Association—www.nursingworld.org
- American Association of Critical-Care Nurses—www.aacn.org
- American Society of Peri-Anesthesia Nurses—www.aspan.org
- Society of Gastroenterology Nurses and Associates—www.sgna.org
- Dermatology Nurses' Association—www.dna.inurse.com
- American Medical Association—www.ama-assn.org
- American Hospital Association—www.aha.org

(2) Documentation
  (a) Define documentation expectations.
  (b) Ensure appropriate forms are available (e.g., multidisciplinary, nursing-specific). A resource is *Radiation Therapy Patient Care Record: A Tool for Documenting Nursing Care* (Catlin-Huth, Haas, & Pollock, 2002).

2. Patient education
  a) Identify existing resources that can be obtained and kept on hand.
    (1) NCI—www.cancer.gov
    (2) ACS—www.cancer.org
    (3) National Comprehensive Cancer Network—www.nccn.org
    (4) Cancer Information Network—www.thecancer.info
    (5) OncoLink—www.oncolink.com
    (6) ONS's CancerSymptoms.org—www.cancersymptoms.org/
  b) Develop departmental/practice-specific information.

3. Research
  a) Encourage reading and critique of relevant nursing research articles and application of research findings to practice.
  b) Develop nursing studies (e.g., symptom management, quality of life).

  c) Participate in the development of medical protocols that have nursing involvement (Klimaszewski et al., 2000).

4. Leadership
  a) Leadership competencies will enhance the manager's effectiveness.
  b) Bennis and Nanus (1985) described four leadership strategies.
    (1) Attention through vision: Create a mental image of what is possible and desirable for the future.
    (2) Meaning through communication: Articulate this idea in a way that makes it clear and meaningful to those who need to implement it.
    (3) Trust through positioning: Be constant and reliable to engender trust.
    (4) Deployment of self through positive self-regard: Know your strengths; develop your strengths; find a fit between your strengths and the needs of the organization; create an atmosphere of excellence.
  c) Coleman (1997) described competencies of emotional intelligence needed for effective leadership.
    (1) Self-awareness: Recognize your own emotions and their effects; know your strengths and limits; maintain self-confidence.
    (2) Self-regulation: Control disruptive emotions; be trustworthy, conscientious, adaptable, and innovative.
    (3) Motivation: Drive to achieve; be committed; have initiative; and be optimistic.
    (4) Empathy: Understand others; develop others; service orientation; leverage diversity; be politically aware.
    (5) Social skills: Provide influence and leadership; promote communication,

conflict management, collaboration, and cooperation; be a catalyst for change; build bonds; build team capabilities.

5. The American Nurses Association (2004) has developed a document for nurse administrators that is a useful resource for the nurse manager.

References

Abruzzese, R.S. (1996). *Nursing staff development: Strategies for success* (2nd ed.). St. Louis, MO: Mosby.

American Academy of Ambulatory Care Nursing. (2000). *Ambulatory care nursing administration and practice standards.* Pitman, NJ: Author.

American College of Radiology. (1991). *Report of the inter-society council for radiation oncology: Radiation oncology in integrated cancer management.* Reston, VA: Author.

American Nurses Association. (2004). *Scope and standards for nurse administrators* (2nd ed.). Washington, DC: Author.

Americans with Disabilities Act. (1990). Public law 101-336. Retrieved June 24, 2004, from http://www.ada.gov/pubs/ada.txt

Aroskar, M.A. (1998). Ethical working relationships in patient care: Challenges and possibilities. *Nursing Clinics of North America, 33,* 313–324.

Bennis, W., & Nanus, B. (1985). *Leaders: The strategies for taking charge.* New York: HarperPerennial.

Bruner, D.W. (1993). Radiation oncology nurses: Staffing patterns and role development. *Oncology Nursing Forum, 20,* 651–659.

Bruner, D.W., & Movsas, B. (2001). Role of the multidisciplinary team in radiation therapy. In D.W. Bruner, G. Moore-Higgs, & M. Haas, (Eds.), *Outcomes in radiation therapy: Multidisciplinary management.* Sudbury, MA: Jones and Bartlett.

Cascio, W.F. (1998). *Managing human resources: Productivity, quality of work life, profits* (5th ed.). Boston, MA: Irwin/McGraw-Hill.

Catlin-Huth, C., Haas, M., & Pollock, V. (2002). *Radiation therapy patient care record: A tool for documenting nursing care.* Pittsburgh, PA: Oncology Nursing Society.

Coleman, D. (1997). *Emotional intelligence.* New York: Bantam Books.

Corser, W.D. (1998). A conceptual model of collaborative nurse-physician interactions: The management of traditional influencer and personal tendencies. *Scholarly Inquiry for Nursing Practice: An International Journal, 12,* 325–341.

Donabedian, A. (1992). The role of outcomes in quality assessment and assurance. *Quality Review Bulletin, 18,* 356–360.

Finkler, S.A. (2001). *Budgeting concepts for nurse managers* (3rd ed.). Philadelphia: Saunders.

Gebelein, S.H., Stevens, L.A., Skube, C.J., Lee, D.G., Davis, B.L., & Hellervik, L.W. (2000). *Successful manager's handbook: Development suggestions for today's managers.* Atlanta, GA: Personnel Decisions International.

Hanson, C.M., & Spross, J.A. (1996). Collaboration. In A.B. Hamric, J.A. Spross, & C.M. Hanson (Eds.), *Advanced nursing practice: An integrative approach* (pp. 229–248). Philadelphia: Saunders.

Hilderley, L.J. (1991). Nurse-physician collaborative practice: The clinical nurse specialist in a radiation oncology private practice. *Oncology Nursing Forum, 18,* 585–591.

Huber, D. (1996). *Leadership and nursing care management.* Philadelphia: Saunders.

Karr, J., & Fisher, R. (1997). A patient classification system for ambulatory care. *Nursing Management, 28,* 27–28.

Kelvin, J.F., Moore-Higgs, G.J., Maher, K.E., Dubey, A.K., Austin-Seymour, M.M., Daly, N.R., et al. (1999). Non-physician practitioners in radiation oncology: Advanced practice nurses and physician assistants. *International Journal of Radiation Oncology, Biology, Physics, 45,* 255–263.

Kelvin, J.F., & Moore-Higgs, G.J. (1999). Description of the role of non-physician practitioners in radiation oncology. *International Journal of Radiation Oncology, Biology, Physics, 45,* 163–169.

Klimaszewski, A., Aikin, J., Bacon, M., DiStasio, S., Ehrenberger, H., & Ford, B. (Eds.). (2000). *Manual for clinical trials nursing.* Pittsburgh, PA: Oncology Nursing Society.

Lankard, B.A. (1995). *New ways of learning in the workplace.* Columbus, OH: ERIC Clearinghouse.

Medvec, B.R. (1994). Productivity and workload measurement in ambulatory oncology. *Seminars in Oncology Nursing, 10,* 288–295.

Moore, G.J. (1996). Collaborative role of a nurse practitioner in a university radiation oncology department. *Cancer Practice, 4,* 285–287.

Moore-Higgs, G.J., Bruner, D.W., Balmer, L., Johnson-Doneski, J., Komarny, P., Mautner, B., et al. (2003a). The role of licensed nursing personnel in radiation oncology part A: Results of a descriptive study. *Oncology Nursing Forum, 30,* 51–58.

Moore-Higgs, G.J., Bruner, D.W., Balmer, L., Johnson-Doneski, J., Komarny, P., Mautner, B., et al. (2003b). The role of licensed nursing personnel in radiation oncology part B: Integrating the ambulatory care nursing conceptual framework. *Oncology Nursing Forum, 30,* 59–64.

Prescott, P.A., & Soeken, K.L. (1996). Measuring nursing intensity in ambulatory care. Part I: Approaches to and uses of patient classification systems. *Nursing Economics, 14*(1), 14–21, 33.

Sachs, R.T. (1994). *How to become a skillful interviewer.* New York: American Management Association.

Shepard, N., & Kelvin, J.F. (1999). The nursing role in radiation oncology. *Seminars in Oncology Nursing, 15,* 237–249.

Stein, D. (1998). *Situated learning in adult education.* Columbus, OH: ERIC Clearinghouse.

XI. Accreditation/quality improvement

A. Joint Commission on Accreditation of Healthcare Organizations (JCAHO)

1. Purpose/goals of JCAHO (JCAHO, 2003a)

   a) Independent, not-for-profit organization

   b) Dedicated to continuously improving safety and quality of care in organized healthcare settings

   c) Develops and updates state-of-the-art professionally based standards and evaluates compliance of healthcare organizations against these benchmarks

   d) Major functions (JCAHO, 2003a; JCAHO & Joint Commission Resources, 2003)

   (1) Developing accreditation standards

   (2) Awarding accreditation decisions

(3) Providing education and consultation to healthcare organizations
(4) Supporting performance improvement in healthcare organizations

2. Types of accreditation/standards applicable to RT centers
   a) Hospital
      (1) Standards apply to hospital-based facilities.
      (2) Accreditation standards and requirements delineated in *2003 Comprehensive Accreditation Manual for Hospitals: The Official Handbook* (JCAHO & Joint Commission Resources, 2003)
   b) Ambulatory care
      (1) Standards apply to freestanding facilities.
      (2) Accreditation standards and requirements delineated in *2002–2003 Comprehensive Accreditation Manual for Ambulatory Care* (JCAHO & Joint Commission Resources, 2002)
   c) Additional standards/manuals exist for accreditation of other types of healthcare organizations: Long-term care, clinical laboratories, and healthcare networks.

3. Manual organization
   a) The accreditation manual is organized by functions critical to patient care, not by disciplines or departments.
   b) Organization of hospital and ambulatory manuals are similar except for additional structures with functions in the hospital manual (see Figure 22).
   c) Content in each is adapted to the appropriate healthcare setting.
   d) A new medication management standard was added in 2004 and includes some requirements from the 2003 Care of Patients (TX) Standards (JCAHO, 2004a).

4. Dimensions of performance (JCAHO & Joint Commission Resources, 2003)
   a) Nine definable, measurable, and improvable attributes of organizational performance related to "doing the right things right" and "doing things well"
   b) Strongly influenced by the organization's design and operation of important functions, as described in the JCAHO manuals
   c) Performance of functions is reflected in the organization's patient outcomes and cost of services.
   d) Dimensions related to "doing the right thing"
      (1) **Efficacy** of procedure or treatment for a patient's condition to accomplish the desired outcome

Figure 22. Comparison of Functions Included in Hospital and Ambulatory Care JCAHO Manuals

	Hospital (CAM/H)	Ambulatory (CAM/AC)
Section 1: Patient-focused functions		
• Patient rights and organization ethics	X	X
• Assessment of patients	X	X
• Care of patients	X	X
• Education	X	
• Education of patients and family		X
• Continuum of care	X	X
Section 2: Organization-focused functions		
• Improving organization performance	X	X
• Leadership	X	X
• Management of the environment of care	X	X
• Management of human resources	X	X
• Management of information	X	X
• Surveillance, prevention, and control of infection	X	X
Section 3: Structures with functions		
• Governance	X	
• Management	X	
• Medical staff	X	
• Nursing	X	

Note. Based on information from JCAHO & Joint Commission Resources, 2002, 2003.

(2) **Appropriateness** of care and services provided to meet the patient's clinical needs, given the current state of knowledge
   e) Dimensions related to "doing the right thing well"
      (1) **Availability** of appropriate care and services to meet the patient's needs
      (2) **Timeliness** of care and services provided is most beneficial for the patient.
      (3) **Effectiveness** of care and services provided in the correct manner, to achieve the desired or projected outcome for the patient
      (4) **Continuity** of services provided to the patient as demonstrated by coordination among disciplines, organizations, and over time
      (5) **Safety** by reducing risks of interventions and in the care environment for

patients and others, including healthcare providers

   (6) **Efficiency** with which care and services are provided, in relationship to the outcomes and resources used in delivering that care

   (7) **Respect and caring** as services are provided with sensitivity and respect for the patient's needs, expectations, and individual differences; degree to which patient or a designee is involved in own care and service decisions

5. Shared visions—New pathways (Joint Commission Resources, 2003, January)

   a) Implemented in January 2004

   b) Dramatically redesigns and improves the value of the accreditation process

   c) Focuses evaluation to a greater extent on

      (1) Actual delivery of clinical care

      (2) Increase in value and satisfaction with accreditation

      (3) Decrease in accreditation-related costs

      (4) Shift in focus from survey preparation to continuous operational improvement in support of safe, high-quality care

      (5) Enhancement in educative purpose of the survey

      (6) Make accreditation process more continuous.

      (7) Increase public's confidence that healthcare organizations continuously comply with standards that emphasize patient safety and healthcare quality.

   d) Survey focus will be organization specific, critical patient care processes and systems most relevant to safety and quality of healthcare. Components include (Joint Commission Resources, 2003, May)

      (1) Self-assessment process

      (2) Priority focus process

      (3) Tracer methodology: Focuses surveyors' site visits on organization-spe-

cific critical care processes and systems. After analyzing data from multiple sources, surveyors will trace a path for organized facility tours to glean areas of possible vulnerability within the organization's patient care or operations.

6. National Patient Safety Goals (JCAHO, 2004b)

   a) Purpose is to standardize evidence-based risk-reduction strategies that hospitals use to reduce patient injury and enable evaluation of their effectiveness (Kirkpatrick, 2003).

   b) Hospitals are required to comply with six patient safety goals as of January 1, 2003.

   c) Yearly, the existing goals and associated recommendations will be evaluated; some may continue, others may be replaced with newer priorities.

   d) New goals and recommendations are announced in July and become effective the following January 1 (JCAHO, 2004b).

   e) Six patient safety goals for 2003 (Not all goals will be applicable to every clinical area.) (Kirkpatrick, 2003)

      (1) Accurate patient identification

      (2) Effective communication among caregivers

      (3) Safe use of high-alert medications

      (4) Elimination of wrong-site, wrong-patient, wrong-procedure surgery

      (5) Safe use of infusion pumps

      (6) Safe use of clinical alarm systems

   f) New goal added for 2004: Reduce the risk of healthcare-acquired infections (JCAHO, 2004b)

7. Performance improvement requirements mandated by JCAHO

   a) Commitment to performance improvement is part of JCAHO's mission.

   b) JCAHO's standards function on an organization's ability to

      (1) Provide safe, high-quality care.

      (2) Evaluate an organization's actual performance.

   c) ORYX® (launched February 1997)

      (1) Goal: To create a more continuous, data-driven, comprehensive, and valuable accreditation process that evaluates both methods of compliance with standards and outcomes of these methods (JCAHO, 2003c).

      (2) Integrates outcomes and performance measurement data into the accreditation process

      (3) Performance measurements provide a more targeted basis for the regular accreditation process.

(4) Mandates continuous monitoring of actual performance

(5) Stimulates continuous improvement activities

(6) Measurement system must generate

    (a) Internal comparisons on performance over time

    (b) External comparisons among participating organizations (JCAHO, 2003b)

8. Related Web sites

    a) JCAHO's official Web site—www.jcaho.org

    b) Joint Commission Resources, for *Perspectives* and other newsletters—http://jcrinc.com

    c) JCAHO, ORYX initiative (facts, measures, process, definitions)—www.jcaho.org/accredited+organizations/hospitals/oryx/oryx+facts.htm

References

JCAHO & Joint Commission Resources. (2002). *2002–2003 comprehensive accreditation manual for ambulatory care.* Oakbrook Terrace, IL: Author.

JCAHO & Joint Commission Resources. (2003). *2003 comprehensive accreditation manual for hospitals: The official handbook.* Oakbrook Terrace, IL: Author.

Joint Commission on Accreditation of Healthcare Organizations. (2003a). *Facts about the Joint Commission on Accreditation of Healthcare Organizations.* Retrieved July 20, 2003, from http://www.jcaho.org/about+us/index.htm

Joint Commission on Accreditation of Healthcare Organizations. (2003b). *Facts about ORYX: The next evolution of accreditation.* Retrieved July 20, 2003, from http://www.jcaho.org/accredited+organizations/hospitals/oryx/the++next+evolution.htm

Joint Commission on Accreditation of Healthcare Organizations. (2003c). *Facts about the review of performance measurement systems.* Retrieved July 20, 2003, from http://www.jcaho.org/accredited+organizations/hospitals/oryx/review+of+systems.htm

Joint Commission on Accreditation of Healthcare Organizations. (2004a). *Crosswalk of 2003 standards for hospitals to 2004 medication management standards for hospitals.* Retrieved June 23, 2004, from http://www.jcaho.org/accredited+organizations/hospitals/standards/new+standards/mm_xwalk_hap.pdf

Joint Commission on Accreditation of Healthcare Organizations. (2004b). *2004 national patient safety goals.* Retrieved June 23, 2004, from http://www.jcaho.org/accredited+organizations/patient+safety/04+npsg/index.htm

Joint Commission Resources. (2003, January). The countdown to SVNP: What's up for measurement? *Joint Commission Benchmark, 5*(1) 1, 7.

Joint Commission Resources. (2003, May). The EC accreditation process using tracer methodology: Looking ahead to Shared Visions-New Pathways in EC. *Environment of Care News, 6*(5), 5–6.

Kirkpatrick, C. (2003, March 24). Safety first: JCAHO introduces new patient safety goals. *Nurseweek* (California edition), *16*(7), 20–21.

B. Principles of improving organizational performance (IOP)

1. IOP contrasted with quality assurance (Bruner, Bucholtz, Iwamoto, & Strohl, 1998)

    a) In IOP, performance and patient outcomes can be objectively measured.

    b) In IOP, performance and outcomes can be improved.

    c) IOP recognizes that organizational systems, not particular individuals, disciplines, or departments, are responsible for poor performance.

    d) IOP is participatory and undertaken by employees at all levels of the organization.

2. IOP requires incorporation of continuous quality improvement or total quality management concepts (Bruner et al., 1998).

    a) Customer judgment is crucial; customers may be external (e.g., patients, families, vendors, the community) or internal (e.g. staff, other departments).

    b) Poor performance usually is not the result of an individual's inability but a problem with the system and/or process in place.

    c) Collaboration is essential to improve performance; multidisciplinary teamwork across departments is required for success.

    d) Improvement activities require commitment from top leadership within the organization. Leadership must set priorities and provide resources to enable all employees to participate.

3. Performance improvement methods: Steps to improve organizational performance focus on a process or outcome related to a particular function. A systematic method to guide members through data analysis and actions that attain the desired results is required. The cycle is continuous and can be entered at any step. There are multiple methods available with IOP.

    a) Plan-Do-Check-Act cycle, also known as the Shewart Cycle (JCAHO, 2000)

        (1) Plan: Requires an understanding of the process, the proposing of an improvement, and how data will be collected and tested.

        (2) Do: Means to perform the test by implementing the action on a small scale

        (3) Check: Involves analyzing the effect of the action being tested

(4) Act: Means to fully implement the action or reassess the improvement action and perhaps choose another action (see Figure 23).

b) JCAHO's (2000) cycle for improving performance consists of four key activities: design, measurement, assessment, and improvement.

(1) Design phase involves identifying the objectives for a process and then creating a design that meets those objectives.

(a) Must consider how the process affects patients, staff, and other groups.

(b) Use expertise and experience within the organization.

(c) Identify data necessary to design the process and how it will be collected and analyzed.

(d) Identify resources needed (e.g., funds, staff time, equipment).

(2) Measurement phase collects valid, reliable data that are used to assess how well a process is working and where improvement may be needed.

(a) Ongoing measurement contains information about performance, outcomes, satisfaction, cost, and judgments about quality and value.

(b) Indicators usually are related to dimensions of performance (e.g., efficacy, availability, continuity, safety, efficiency).

(3) Assessment phase translates data collected into information that can be used to draw conclusions about performance and to improve processes.

(a) Compare current performance with historical patterns of performance.

(b) Benchmarking compares performance to that of other organizations that routinely perform key

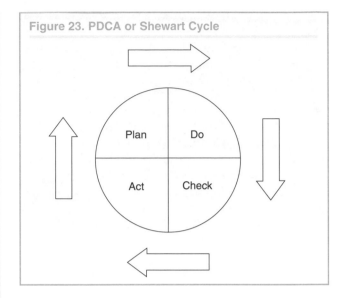

Figure 23. PDCA or Shewart Cycle

processes and achieve good outcomes.

(4) Improvement phase actions are based on the results of measurement and assessment. Identifies the causes of variation and opportunities for improvement.

(a) An improvement action is selected and often results in a redesign of a process.

(b) Determine who will implement and how an action will be implemented.

(c) Implement the action on a small scale or in limited time.

(d) Assess effectiveness of the action and implement if results warrant it (see Figure 24).

c) Outcomes management (Bruner & Hanks, 2001)

(1) Method of measuring, evaluating, and improving patient care

(2) Broader based than continuous quality improvement

(3) Leads to evidence-based practice

(4) Types of outcomes

(a) Clinical outcomes (e.g., recurrence rate in stage I breast cancer)

(b) Humanistic outcomes (e.g., QOL, patient satisfaction)

(c) Economic outcomes (e.g., days lost from work, cost of daily radiation treatments)

d) Performance improvement tools/techniques

(1) Effective tools are available for planning, teams, data collection, data analysis, and understanding root causes.

Many tools work in more than one category (e.g., tools for planning also may be used in data collection and analysis).

(2) Using performance improvement tools

    (a) Clinical pathways may be used for planning, data collection, and data analysis. Steps to development (JCAHO, 1997; Macario, 2000)

        i) Identify target population.

        ii) Gather a team to collect data.

        iii) Create a pathway based on identified needs of patient population (see Table 24).

        iv) Educate caregivers.

        v) Implement and revise pathway.

        vi) Document results and analyze variances (see Figure 25).

    (b) Check sheets show how often an event occurs. They are used at the beginning of data collection and provide a foundation for more complex analysis (JCAHO, 1997) (see Figure 26).

    (c) Surveys

        i) Patient satisfaction is a measure of quality care and is a requirement for accreditation.

        ii) Reports of patient satisfaction with the quality of care and services are as important as many clinical health measures (Bolus & Pitts, 1999) and are associated with improved patient outcomes (Bruner et al., 2001; Gesell, 2003). Consider the following in the survey process (Bolus & Pitts).

        • Identify which instrument to use.

        • How to distribute

        • Frequency of the survey

        • Number of patients to be surveyed

        • How to analyze the data

        • The report format to be used (see Figure 27 for an example)

    (d) Cause and effect diagrams present picture of many causal relationships between outcomes and factors in those outcomes (JCAHO, 1997). Steps to follow include

        i) Identify the problem statement or outcome.

        ii) Identify general categories of all causes.

        iii) Under general categories, list all causes or sub-causes.

        iv) Analyze the diagram (see Figure 28 for an example).

    (e) Indicators are quantitative measures (expressed in units of measurement) of a process or outcome (JCAHO, 2000).

        i) Chosen for their frequency of occurrence, prone to problems or importance to the institution

        ii) Divided into two categories: Aggregate data and sentinel events

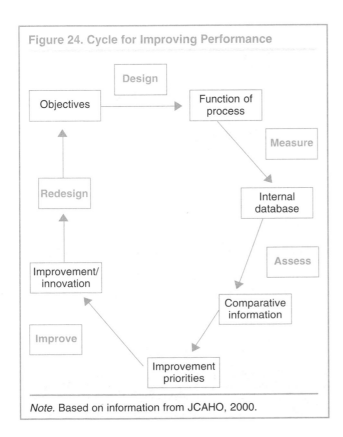

Figure 24. Cycle for Improving Performance

Note. Based on information from JCAHO, 2000.

Table 24. Clinical Pathway: Stereotactic Radiosurgery

Category	Prior to Surgery Date: _____	Day Prior to Surgery Date: _____	DOS Date: _____	POD 1 Date: _____
Physician	Radiation/oncology consult Neurosurgery consult Obtain informed consent.		Radiation oncology neuro-surgeon Place head frame at 7 am. Perform SRS.	
Diagnostic studies	CT scan, MRI Dilantin level prn		Treatment planning—CT at 7:30 am	
Nursing	Nursing assessment Obtain IV contrast consent.	Pre-procedure phone call	Baseline vital signs then q 4 hr Pain assessment q 4 hr Check neuro status and pin sites.	Follow-up phone call Query for headache, pin site drainage, increased temperature
Patient education	Pre-op teaching Patient education video	Review prep, time of arrival, NPO status. Wash hair the night before surgery.	Review procedure. Discharge instructions Instruct to keep pin sites dry 24 hours.	
Medications	Review current meds. Prescriptions for Valium/Percocet	Patient should bring current meds to SRS.	Patient to take 5 mg Valium po at 6:30 am Patient to take current meds prn.	Continue current meds.
Diet	As trial of labor (TOL)	NPO after midnight	NPO prior to frame placement As TOL	As TOL
Scheduler	Schedule fusion MRI, SRS, and CT. Notify physics/treatment machine/nursing/MD		Schedule six-week follow-up with MRI.	
Physics		Pre-plan SRS	Attend treatment planning CT, complete plan Capture charges.	
Treatment machine		Reschedule patients prn for SRS.	Prepare machine and perform SRS late pm. Capture charges	
Activity		As TOL	Bathroom privileges only	As TOL
Social Work	Referral prn			
Outcome	Patient verbalizes understanding of SRS	Patient completes SRS prep.	Patient completes SRS without incident. Patient pain rating < 3	Patient remains free from infection
Signatures	_____	_____	_____	_____

Note. Courtesy of Maine Medical Center, Portland, ME. Based on information from JCAHO, 1997, 2000.

Figure 25. Stereotactic Radiosurgery Variances

Variance	Date	Reason	Initials

Figure 26. Indicator: Patients on Radiation, Precautions for Gynecologic Implants

Radiation Precautions Checklist	Yes	No
Bedrest orders		
Visitors limited to 20 minutes		
Visitors' line in room		
Radiation sign on door		
Radiation label on chart, door, and bed		
Radiation wrist band		
Linen/trash screen prior to removal		
Two bins trash/linen		
Additional bin for disposable trays		
Shielded pig with forceps		
Lead shield in room		
Personal dosimeter for all personnel		
Private room		

Name: _____

Date: _____

Figure 27. Satisfaction Survey for Patients With Cancer Receiving Radiation Therapy

Please rate the following:　　　　　　　　　　　　　　　　**Poor (1)—Excellent (5)**

1. Access to parking　　　　　　　　　　　　　　　　1　2　3　4　5

2. Directions to the facility　　　　　　　　　　　　　　1　2　3　4　5

3. Department clearly marked with signs　　　　　　　　1　2　3　4　5

4. Wheelchairs accessible (if appropriate)　　　　　　　1　2　3　4　5

5. Information given on nutrition　　　　　　　　　　　1　2　3　4　5

6. Educational materials　　　　　　　　　　　　　　1　2　3　4　5

7. Waiting room comfort　　　　　　　　　　　　　　1　2　3　4　5

8. Social work services available (if appropriate)　　　　1　2　3　4　5

Please rate the staff in the following areas:

9. Showed care and compassion　　　　　　　　　　　1　2　3　4　5

10. Explained schedule delays　　　　　　　　　　　　1　2　3　4　5

11. Respected your privacy　　　　　　　　　　　　　1　2　3　4　5

12. Answered questions to your satisfaction　　　　　　1　2　3　4　5

13. Knowledgeable and organized about your care　　　　1　2　3　4　5

14. Explained and managed side effects　　　　　　　　1　2　3　4　5

Other

15. Rate your opinion of the doctor(s) involved in your care.　　1　2　3　4　5

16. Rate your opinion of the therapist(s) involved in your care.　1　2　3　4　5

17. Rate your opinion of the nurse(s) involved in your care.　　1　2　3　4　5

18. Rate your overall experience in radiation therapy.　　　　1　2　3　4　5

Comments: Is there anything else you would like to tell us?

Note. Courtesy of Maine Medical Center, Portland, ME.

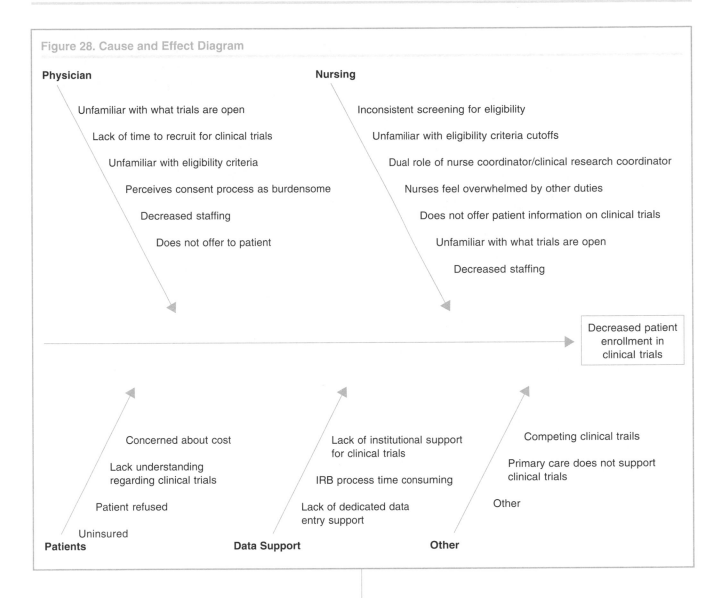

Figure 28. Cause and Effect Diagram

Physician

Unfamiliar with what trials are open

Lack of time to recruit for clinical trials

Unfamiliar with eligibility criteria

Perceives consent process as burdensome

Decreased staffing

Does not offer to patient

Nursing

Inconsistent screening for eligibility

Unfamiliar with eligibility criteria cutoffs

Dual role of nurse coordinator/clinical research coordinator

Nurses feel overwhelmed by other duties

Does not offer patient information on clinical trials

Unfamiliar with what trials are open

Decreased staffing

Decreased patient enrollment in clinical trials

Concerned about cost

Lack understanding regarding clinical trials

Patient refused

Uninsured

Patients

Lack of institutional support for clinical trials

IRB process time consuming

Lack of dedicated data entry support

Data Support

Competing clinical trails

Primary care does not support clinical trials

Other

Other

- Aggregate data measure many events. They may be continuous, such as elapsed days of treatment for stage I breast cancer, or rate-based indicators, which reflect the frequency of the event shown as a proportion or ratio.
- Sentinel events usually are undesirable and trigger further investigation each time they occur (see Figure 29).

(f) Competency measurement

   i) Competency is actual performance in the real work situation and only can be assessed by observing job performance (Johnson,

Figure 29. Examples of Indicators

Sentinel event indicator
- Patient's death is related to a misadministration of radiation.
- The wrong patient was transported from inpatient unit and treated with radiation.

Continuous variable indicator
- Radiation consult date to treatment start date
- Number of elapsed treatment days for lung cancer

Rate-based indicator
- Number of patients on treatment breaks
- Total number of patients
- Incidence of cystitis in patients with prostate seed implant
- Incidence of cystitis in patients with external beam prostate treatment

Opfer, VanCura, & Williams, 2000).

ii) Competency assessment is outcome-oriented, with the goal of evaluating performance for the effective application of knowledge and skill in the practice setting (Redman, Lenburg, & Walker, 1999).

iii) JCAHO requires clinical competence be assessed for all nursing staff. The institution must ensure competency is assessed, maintained, demonstrated, and continually improved (Redman et al., 1999).

iv) Steps to evaluate competency (Johnson et al., 2000)
- Develop competency statements.
- Establish performance criteria.
- Identify learning options.
- Identify assessment methods.
- Identify evaluation formats.
- Identify resources (see Figure 30).

(g) Resources on the Internet
i) JCAHO official Web site— www.jcaho.org
ii) JCAHO publications—www .jcrinc.com
iii) SkyMark Corporation— www.skymark.com/ resources/methods/process _improvement.asp

References

Bolus, R., & Pitts, J. (1999). Patient satisfaction: The indispensable outcome. *Managed Care Magazine, 8*(4), 24–28.

Bruner, D.W., Bucholtz, J., Iwamoto, R., & Strohl, R. (Eds.). (1998). *Manual for radiation oncology nursing practice and education.* Pittsburgh, PA: Oncology Nursing Society.

Bruner, D.W., & Hanks, G.E. (2001). An outcome-based management model of patient care. In D.W. Bruner, G. Moore-Higgs, & M. Haas (Eds.), *Outcomes in radiation therapy: Multidisciplinary management* (pp. 1–24). Sudbury, MA: Jones and Bartlett.

Dow, K.H., Bucholtz, J.D., Iwamoto, R., Fieler, V.K., & Hilderley, L. (Eds.). (1997). *Nursing care in radiation oncology* (2nd ed.). New York: Saunders.

Gesell, S. (2003). Listening to your patients: Assessing service quality in cancer care. *Oncology Issues, 18*(1), 25–28.

Johnson, T., Opfer, K., VanCura, B., & Williams, L. (2000). A comprehensive interactive competency program Part 1: Development and framework. *Medsurg Nursing, 9,* 265–268.

Joint Commission on Accreditation of Healthcare Organizations. (1997). *Nursing practice and outcomes measurement.* Oakbrook Terrace, IL: Author.

Joint Commission on Accreditation of Healthcare Organizations. (2000). *Using performance improvement tools in health care settings.* Oakbrook Terrace, IL: Author.

Macario, A. (2000, November). How to develop clinical pathways. *Outpatient Surgery Magazine,* 1–2. Retrieved June 10, 2004, from http://www.outpatientsurgery.net

Redman, R.W., Lenburg, C.B., & Walker, P.H. (1999, September 30). Competency assessment: Methods for development and implementation in nursing education. *Online Journal of Issues in Nursing.* Retrieved September 23, 2003, from http://www.nursingworld.org/ojin/topic10/tpc10_3.htm

---

Figure 30. Nursing Competency: Care of Patient Receiving External Beam Radiation Therapy

The nurse will develop knowledge in radiation therapy, treatment processes, site-specific side effects, and symptom management.

Initial competency of this skill is validated by:	Date Completed
1. Reading the *Manual for Radiation Oncology Nursing Practice and Education*	
2. Preceptor chooses articles from the *Clinical Journal of Oncology Nursing* and *Oncology Nursing Forum* that are pertinent to radiation practice with supplements from other textbooks.	
3. Successful completion of competency-based orientation	
4. Review of patient care standards	
5. Successful completion of post-test, with a score of 85% or more	
To maintain competency in this skill, the nurse must: 1. Maintain annually 12 oncology-related CEUs verified by CEU certificate. This is attained by attending conferences, self-study, online courses.	
2. Demonstrate proper documentation: Evaluated by review of the patient care record (chart and IMPAC) annually. a. Nursing assessment b. ONS documentation tool c. Patient teaching documentation	

XII. Radiation oncology resources

A. ONS Web site—The official Web site of the Oncology Nursing Society—www.ons.org
  1. Authorship
    a) Group, ONS
      (1) Privacy issues: Present and easy to find
      (2) Financial disclosure issues
        (a) Multiple sponsors
        (b) Mostly large pharmaceutical companies
        (c) Transparent to the user
  2. Radiation content highlights
    a) RT SIG Virtual Community
      (1) This is a Web page for RT nurses. To register, select "New User" from the top left (allows you to create log-in credentials). Type required information into the test fields, as prompted, and click "finish" when done.
      (2) Registration on the site notifies RT nurses of information and announcements and provides a means of contact to other RT nurses who have registered for the virtual community's Radiation SIG discussion forum.
    b) RT resource areas
      (1) RT discussion forum: This area affords the opportunity for exchange of information between members and nonmembers on topics specific to RT.
      (2) *Oncology Nursing Forum*: An official journal of ONS that features general oncology articles, including those on radiation-related topics.
      (3) *Clinical Journal of Oncology Nursing*: An official journal of ONS in which numerous clinically related articles about RT can be found.
      (4) RT books: *Radiation Therapy Patient Care Record: A Tool for Documenting Nursing Care* provides tools for the RT staff nurse to use in clinical practice.
      (5) Practice standards: The scope and standards for the RT nurse was written by the Radiation SIG group and is published in this document.
      (6) RT awards and scholarships offered by ONS—www.ons.org/awards/index.shtml
        (a) Susan Baird Oncology Excellence in Writing Award in Clinical Practice, Supported by SuperGen, Inc.: $1,250 award and a plaque—www.ons.org/awards/onsawards/bairdCp.shtml
        (b) Excellence in Radiation Therapy Nursing Award (EC06) Supported by Varian Medical Systems: $1,000 award and a plaque—www.ons.org/awards/onsawards/radiation.shtml
      (7) RT conference highlights
        (a) Virtual Congress
        (b) Institutes of Learning sessions

B. American College of Radiology (ACR)
  1. Purpose: To make imaging safe, effective, and accessible to those who need it
  2. Goals: To provide accreditation programs, research, guidelines for quality imaging, education, and advocacy
  3. Membership
    a) Radiologists
    b) Radiation oncologists
    c) Medical physicists
  4. Benefits to nurses
    a) Practice guidelines and technical standards on a variety of topics (e.g., use of IV contrast, LDR and HDR brachytherapy, stereotactic radiosurgery).
    b) The Radiological Society of North America and ACR developed a Web site (www.radiologyinfo.org) that provides patient information on diagnostic radiology, interventional radiology, and RT.
    c) Site provides a list of ACR-accredited facilities by modality and ZIP code.
  5. The Web site of ACR (www.acr.org) provides information in the following areas.
    a) ACR News
    b) Healthcare headlines
    c) ACR Web casts and meetings
    d) Clinical research
    e) Departments (e.g., practice guidelines, government regulations, economics)
    f) Publications/products
    g) Patient information

C. Personal digital assistant (PDA) devices and applications
  1. PDA content delivery
    a) Benefits
      (1) Portable
      (2) Immediate access
      (3) Easy to update
    b) Disadvantages
      (1) Data entry awkward
      (2) Easy to lose

(3) Privacy
    (a) New HIPAA regulations
    (b) Storage of patient data
c) Platforms
  (1) Palm® OS
  (2) Pocket PC®

2. Selected PDA programs
  a) The Washington Manual™ of Oncology—
    www.lww.com
    (1) Platforms available
      (a) PalmOS
      (b) Pocket PC
    (2) Radiation content highlights
      (a) Tumor type
      (b) Presentation
      (c) Workup
      (d) Staging
      (e) Therapy by stage
      (f) Side effects of treatment and disease
  b) ACR Appropriateness Criteria™—
    www.acr.org
    (1) Platforms available
      (a) Palm OS
      (b) Pocket PC
    (2) Radiation content highlights
      (a) Two applications
        i) Diagnostic/interventional
        ii) Radiation oncology
      (b) Customization
        i) Incorporate personal notes
        ii) Summary of literature
        iii) ICD-9 + CPT-4 coding
  c) PEPID RN-Clinical Nurse Companion—
    www.pepid.com
    (1) Platforms available
      (a) Palm OS
      (b) Pocket PC
    (2) RT content highlights
      (a) Clinical oncology content database
      (b) Weight-based dosing
      (c) Wide selection of calculators

      (d) Patient teaching guides
      (e) Complete drug database
      (f) Oncology nursing module (PEPID RN + ONS)

D. American Society for Therapeutic Radiology and Oncology (ASTRO)—Nursing resources
  1. Purpose
    a) ASTRO's goals
      (1) Advance the practice of radiation oncology by promoting excellence in patient care.
      (2) Provide opportunities for educational and professional development.
      (3) Promote research and disseminate research results.
      (4) Represent radiation oncology in the socioeconomic healthcare environment.
    b) ASTRO nursing committee's goals
      (1) Promote excellence in patient care and advance the practice of radiation oncology.
      (2) Provide educational opportunities by presenting the nursing program at ASTRO's annual meeting.
      (3) Integrate nursing within the annual meeting through refresher courses, panels, and scientific sessions.
      (4) Maintain liaison with ONS and other professional organizations.
      (5) Advocate radiation oncology nursing through a Web site, networking, and supporting the role of the radiation oncology nurse.
  2. Nursing committee
    a) Strategic plan/goal
      (1) Promote excellence in patient care through education.
      (2) Advocate for radiation oncology nursing.
    b) Structure—The nursing committee is under the education council of the ASTRO Board of Directors.
    c) Committee membership
      (1) There are eight nurses, one physician, one ASTRO board liaison, and an ASTRO staff liaison. The terms of board members are one year, renewable up to six times.
      (2) Committee members are employed at different treatment facilities, from all regions of the country, and hold a wide variety of job responsibilities.
      (3) Members sit on other committees within the ASTRO organization, such

as the workforce, publications, and refresher course groups.

    (4) The committee is directed by a chair and the vice-chair.

    (5) New members are nominated by the departing member of the committee.

        (a) They suggest a new member who will maintain the geographic and level of practice balance to the committee.

        (b) The recommendations are forwarded to the president of ASTRO who decides on the final naming of the members.

3. ASTRO nurse membership/benefits

  a) Opportunity to network with nurses and other professionals in radiation oncology

  b) Online updates and notification of educational opportunities related to radiation oncology

  c) Low annual fees

  d) Discounts on registration at the annual meeting (CEUs provided)

  e) Substantial discount on a subscription for the *International Journal of Radiation Oncology, Biology, Physics* ("The Red Journal")

  f) ASTRO membership directory

4. Web page—www.astro.org

  a) Provides specific information on the annual nursing program, nursing committee strategic plan, and links to oncology Web sites of interest

  b) Provides other professional links to patient advocacy groups, online journal, free MEDLINE search engines, clinical trial information, patient screening, treatment, supportive care, physician treatment information, and other professional organizations.

E. National Comprehensive Cancer Network (NCCN)—www.nccn.org

1. Authorship

  a) Group

  b) Most major cancer centers in the United States

2. Privacy issues: Present and easy to find

3. Financial disclosure issues

  a) Nonprofit

  b) No external financial support

4. Radiation content highlights

  a) Practice guidelines in oncology

  b) Standard reference for appropriate practice

    (1) By site

    (2) By symptom

  c) Outcomes database

    (1) Measures adherence of practice to NCCN guidelines

    (2) Clinical outcomes

  d) Information services

    (1) Where to find resources among centers

    (2) Treatment guidelines

F. National Cancer Institute or Cancer.gov—www.nci.nih.gov or www.cancer.gov

1. Authorship

  a) Group

  b) Multiple review boards

2. Privacy issues: Present and easy to find

3. Financial disclosure issues

  a) Government site

  b) No external financial support

4. Radiation content highlights

  a) RT clinical information

    (1) By treatment

    (2) By disease

    (3) By symptom

  b) RT clinical trials

    (1) Primer

    (2) Search engine

  c) Recent developments in RT

    (1) Cancer statistics

        (a) By treatment

        (b) By disease

        (c) By symptom

    (2) New types of treatment

        (a) Brachytherapy

        (b) XMRT

  d) Radiation Oncology Sciences Program—www.dcs.nci.nih.gov/branches/rob/index.html

    (1) Umbrella organization

        (a) Radiation oncology branch

        (b) Radiation biology branch

        (c) Radiation research program

    (2) Disseminates research in RT

        (a) Clinical trials

        (b) Treatment guidelines

Appendix A. Fatigue Scale

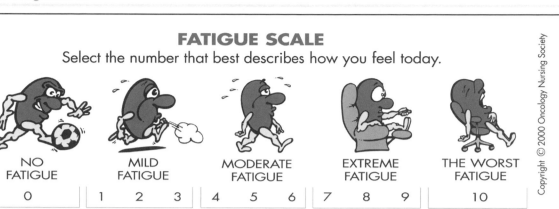

FATIGUE SCALE
Select the number that best describes how you feel today.

NO FATIGUE	MILD FATIGUE	MODERATE FATIGUE	EXTREME FATIGUE	THE WORST FATIGUE
0	1 2 3	4 5 6	7 8 9	10

Copyright © 2000 Oncology Nursing Society

ESCALA DE LA FATIGA
Seleccione el número que mejor describa cómo se siente hoy.

NADA DE FATIGA	FATIGA LEVE	FATIGA MODERADA	FATIGA EXTREMA	LA PEOR FATIGA
0	1 2 3	4 5 6	7 8 9	10

Copyright © 2000 Oncology Nursing Society

Note. Copyright 2000 by the Oncology Nursing Society.

Appendix B. Scored Patient-Generated Subjective Global Assessment (PG-SGA)

Scored Patient-Generated Subjective Global Assessment (PG-SGA)

Patient ID Information

History

1. Weight *(See Table 1 Worksheet)*

In summary of my current and recent weight:

I currently weigh about _____ pounds
I am about _____ feet _____ tall

One month ago I weighed about _____ pounds
Six months ago I weighed about _____ pounds

During the past two weeks my weight has:

☐ decreased (1) ☐ not changed (0) ☐ increased (0)

2. Food Intake: As compared to my normal, I would rate my food intake during the past month as:

☐ unchanged (0)
☐ more than usual
☐ less than usual (1)
    I am now taki*ng*:
      ☐ *normal food* but less than normal (1)
      ☐ little solid food (2)
      ☐ only liquids (3)
      ☐ only nutritonal supplements (3)
      ☐ very little of anything (4)
      ☐ only tube feedings or only nutrition by vein (0)

3. Symptoms: I have had the following problems that have kept me from eating enough during the past two weeks (check all that apply):

☐ no problems eating (0)

☐ no appetite, just did not feel like eating (3)

☐ nausea (1) ☐ vomiting (3)
☐ constipation (1) ☐ diarrhea (3)
☐ mouth sores (2) ☐ dry mouth (1)
☐ things taste funny or have no taste (1) ☐ smells bother me (1)
☐ problems swallowing (2) ☐ feel full quickly (1)

☐ pain; where? (3) _____

☐ other** (1) _____

    ** Examples: depression, money, or dental problems

4. Activities and Function: Over the past month, I would generally rate my activity as:

☐ normal with no limitations (0)

☐ not my normal self, but able to be up and about with fairly normal activities (1)

☐ not feeling up to most things, but in bed or chair less than half the day (2)

☐ able to do little activity and spend most of the day in bed or chair (3)

☐ pretty much bedridden, rarely out of bed (3)

Additive Score of the Boxes 1-4 ☐ **A**

The remainder of this form will be completed by your doctor, nurse, or therapist. Thank you.

5. Disease and its relation to nutritional requirements *(See Table 2)*

All relevant diagnoses (specify) _____

Primary disease stage (circle if known or appropriate)   I   II   III   IV   Other _____

Age _____

Numerical score from Table 2 ☐ **B**

6. Metabolic Demand *(See Table 3 Worksheet)*

☐ no stress   ☐ low stress   ☐ moderate stress   ☐ high stress

Numerical score from Table 3 ☐ **C**

7. Physical *(See Table 4 Worksheet)*

Numerical score from Table 4 ☐ **D**

Global Assessment *(See Table 5 Worksheet)*
    ☐ Well-nourished or anabolic (SGA-A)
    ☐ Moderate or suspected malnutrition (SGA-B)
    ☐ Severely malnourished (SGA-C)

Total numerical score of boxes A+B+C+D ☐
(See triage recommendations below)

Clinician Signature _____ RD RN PA MD DO Other ___   Date _____

Nutritional Triage Recommendations: Additive score is used to define specific nutritional interventions including patient & family education, symptom management including pharmacologic intervention, and appropriate nutrient intervention (food, nutritional supplements, enteral, or parenteral triage). First line nutrition intervention includes optimal symptom ɪ   gement.

0-1   No intervention required at this time. Re-assessment on routine and regular basis during treatment.

2-3   Patient & family education by dietitian, nurse, or other clinician with pharmacologic intervention as indicated by symptom survey (Box 3) and laboratory values as appropriate.

4-8   Requires intervention by dietitian, in conjunction with nurse or physician as indicated by symptoms survey (Box 3).

≥ 9   Indicates a critical need for improved symptom management and/or nutrient intervention options.

© FD Ottery, 2000   fottery@noat.org   Grateful acknowledgement is given to the Society for Nutritional Oncology Adjuvant Therapy (NOAT) & the Oncology Nutrition Dietetic Practice Group of the American Dietetic Association.

(Continued on next page)

Tables & Worksheets for PG-SGA Scoring   © FD Ottery, 2000

The PG-SGA numerical score is derived by totaling the scores from boxes A-D of the PG-SGA on the reverse side. Box(
designed to be completed by the patient. The points assigned to items in boxes 1-4 are noted parenthetically after each ite   The
following worksheets are offered as aids for calcuating scores of sections that are not so marked.

Table 1 - Scoring Weight (wt) Loss

Determined by adding points for subacute and acute wt change. **Subacute**: If information is available about weight loss during past 1 month, add the point score to the points for acute wt change. Only include the wt loss over 6 months if the wt from 1 month is unavailable. **Acute**: refers to wt change during past two weeks: add 1 point to subacute score if patient lost wt, add no points if patient gained or maintained wt during the past two weeks.

Wt loss in 1 month	Points	Wt loss in 6 months
10% or greater	4	20% or greater
5-9.9%	3	10 -19.9%
3-4.9%	2	6 - 9.9%
2-2.9%	1	2 - 5.9%
0-1.9%	0	0 - 1.9%

Points for Box 1 = Subacute + Acute = ☐

Table 2 - Scoring criteria for disease &/or condition

Score is derived by adding 1 point for each of the conditions listed below that pertain to the patient.

Category	Points
Cancer	1
AIDS	1
Pulmonary or cardiac cachexia	1
Presence of decubitus, open wound, or fistula	1
Presence of trauma	1
Age greater than 65 years	1

Points for Box 2 = ☐ B

Table 3 Worksheet - Scoring Metabolic Stress

Score for metabolic stress is determined by a number of variables known to increase protein & calorie needs. The score is additive so that a patient who has a fever of > 102 degrees (3 points) and is on 10 mg of prednisone chronically (2 points) would have an additive score for this section of 5 points.

Stress	none (0)	low (1)	moderate (2)	high (3)
Fever	no fever	>99 and <101	$\geq$101 and <102	$\geq$102
Fever duration	no fever	<72 hrs	72 hrs	> 72 hrs
Steroids	no steroids	low dose (<10mg prednisone equivalents/day)	moderate dose ($\geq$10 and <30mg prednisone equivalents/day)	high dose steroids ($\geq$30mg prednisone equivalents/day)

Points for Table 3 = ☐ C

Table 4 Worksheet - Physical Examination

Physical exam includes a subjective evaluation of 3 aspects of body composition: fat, muscle, & fluid status. Since this is subjective, each aspect of the exam is rated for degree of deficit. Muscle deficit impacts point score more than fat deficit. Definition of categories: 0 = no deficit, 1+ = mild deficit, 2+ = moderate deficit, 3+ = severe deficit. Rating of deficit in these categories are *not* additive but are used to clinically assess the degree of deficit (or presence of excess fluid).

Fat Stores:

orbital fat pads	0	1+	2+	3+
triceps skin fold	0	1+	2+	3+
fat overlying lower ribs	0	1+	2+	3+
Global fat deficit rating	**0**	**1+**	**2+**	**3+**

Fluid Status:

ankle edema	0	1+	2+	3+
sacral edema	0	1+	2+	3+
ascites	0	1+	2+	3+
Global fluid status rating	**0**	**1+**	**2+**	**3+**

Muscle Status:

temples (temporalis muscle)	0	1+	2+	3+
clavicles (pectoralis & deltoids)	0	1+	2+	3+
shoulders (deltoids)	0	1+	2+	3+
interosseous muscles	0	1+	2+	3+
scapula (latissimus dorsi, trapezius, deltoids)	0	1+	2+	3+
thigh (quadriceps)	0	1+	2+	3+
calf (gastrocnemius)	0	1+	2+	3+
Global muscle status rating	**0**	**1+**	**2+**	**3+**

Point score for the physical exam is determined by the overall subjective rating of total body deficit; again muscle deficit takes precedence over fat loss or fluid excess.

No deficit	score = 0 points
Mild deficit	score = 1 point
Moderate deficit	score = 2 points
Severe deficit	score = 3 points

Points for Worksheet 4 = ☐ D

Table 5 Worksheet - PG-SGA Global Assessment Categories

Category	**Stage A** Well-nourished	**Stage B** Moderately malnourished or suspected malnutrition	**Stage C** Severely malnourished
Weight	No wt loss **or** Recent non-fluid wt gain	~5% wt loss within 1 month (or 10% in 6 months) No wt stabilization or wt gain (i.e., continued wt loss)	a. > 5% loss in 1 month (or >10% loss in 6 months) b. No wt stabilization or wt gain (i.e., continued wt loss)
Nutrient Intake	No deficit **or** Significant recent improvement	Definite decrease in intake	Severe deficit in intake
Nutrition Impact Symptoms	None **or** Significant recent improvement allowing adequate intake	Presence of nutrition impact symptoms (Box 3 of PG-SGA)	Presence of nutrition impact symptoms (Box 3 of PG-SGA)
Functioning	No deficit **or** Significant recent improvement	Moderate functional deficit **or** Recent deterioration	Severe functional deficit **or** recent significant deterioration
Physical Exam	No deficit **or** Chronic deficit but with recent clinical improvement	Evidence of mild to moderate loss of SQ fat &/or muscle mass &/or muscle tone on palpation	Obvious signs of malnutrition (e.g., severe loss of SQ tissues, possible edema)

Global PG-SGA rating (A, B, or C) = ☐

Note. Acknowledgment is given to the Society for Nutritional Oncology Adjuvant Therapy and the Oncology Nutrition Dietetic Practice Group of the American Dietetic Association. Reprinted with permission.

Appendix C. Radiation Oncology Nurse Job Description

Responsibility	Performance Standard
Assessment	• Obtain patient history at consultation by reviewing medical information and interviewing patient and family. • Assess baseline status (e.g., physical, function, social, emotional). • Assess symptoms at weekly treatment/status check visits. • Assess problems that arise in between status check visits, either in the department or over the phone. • Assess for long-term effects at follow-up visits. • Integrate findings of assessment to correctly identify actual and potential problems.
Patient education	• Educate patients and families regarding the disease, diagnostic procedures needed, and goals of treatment with radiation therapy. • Educate patients and families regarding simulation, the administration of radiation therapy, the schedule of treatment, and potential side effects. • Educate patients and families on the management of symptoms and side effects (e.g., use of medications, dietary changes, activity changes, skin care, oral care).
Support and counseling	• Assess psychosocial issues (e.g., home situation, availability of support, past coping mechanisms, financial concerns, work status). • Actively and supportively listen to patient and family concerns. • Clarify information to assist patients and families in making treatment decisions. • Counsel on specific issues of concern (e.g., sexuality, end-of-life issues). • Refer as needed for social work, psychiatry.
Physical care	• Assist with procedures (e.g., physical exams, simulation, brachytherapy). • Collect blood and urine specimens. • Provide skin care (e.g., sprays/irrigations, application of specific skin care products, dressing changes). • Assess oral cavity and sprays/irrigates as needed. • Assist with tube feedings. • Administer hydration as ordered. • Administer medication (e.g., pain medication, IV contrast) as ordered. • Monitor patients receiving treatment (e.g., conscious sedation, pediatric anesthesia, systemic treatments [TBI, TLI, TSEB], brachytherapy, stereotactic radiosurgery). • Manage urgent problems (e.g., allergic reactions to IV contrast, seizures, loss of consciousness).
Continuity of care	• Coordinate care for patients receiving multimodality treatment (e.g., provides patient calendars with dates of surgery, radiation, chemotherapy; communicates and collaborates with physicians and nurses in surgical and medical oncology regarding timing of treatments and management of patient problems). • Refer as needed for nutrition, enterostomal therapy, speech therapy, and physical therapy. • Coordinate care with primary care physician, skilled nursing facility, rehabilitation, home care, and hospice as needed. • Coordinate transfers to emergency room or to inpatient units. • Make hospital rounds to assess, educate, and support patients and to collaborate with inpatient staff in the planning of patient care.
Research	• Assist with the implementation of medical protocols. • Explain the protocol as needed for informed consent. • Schedule baseline and ongoing diagnostic studies. • Provide patient calendars to ensure compliance with protocol regimen. • Coordinate care to ensure protocol requirements are met. • Administer medications (e.g., radiation sensitizers or protectors). • Collect data (e.g., results of laboratory and other diagnostic studies, toxicity assessment). • Contribute to publications and presentations. • Maintain knowledge of relevant research findings. • Apply evidence in practice. • Develop and implement research protocols as a principal investigator.
Clinical leadership	• Educate nurses related to the care of patients receiving radiation therapy. • Develop policies, procedures, and standards of care. • Develop patient education materials. • Lead patient education and support groups.
Administrative leadership	• Participate in performance improvement activities. • Provide consultation to administrators and physicians in the implementation of new clinical programs. • Participate in scheduling of staff. • Participate in managing supplies and equipment.

Note. Based on information from Shepard, N., & Kelvin, J.F. (1999). The nursing role in radiation oncology. *Seminars in Oncology Nursing, 15,* 237–249.

Index

The letter *t* after a page number indicates relevant content appears in a table; the letter *f*, in a figure.